MONETARY THEORY

Economics Handbook Series

Anderson: *National Income Theory and Its Price Theoretic Foundations*
Atkinson and Stiglitz: *Lectures on Public Economics*
Carlson: *Economic Security in the United States*
Chacholiades: *International Monetary Theory and Policy*
Chacholiades: *International Trade Theory and Policy*
Hansen: *A Survey of General Equilibrium Systems*
Hansen: *The American Economy*
Harris: *The Economics of Harvard*
Harris: *Monetary Theory*
Harrod: *The British Economy*
Henderson and Quandt: *Microeconomic Theory: A Mathematical Approach*
Hirsch: *The Economics of State and Local Government*
Hirsch: *Urban Economic Analysis*
Jones: *An Introduction to Modern Theories of Economic Growth*
Kindleberger and Herrick: *Economic Development*
Maddala: *Econometrics*
Nourse: *Regional Economics*
Ott, Ott, and Yoo: *Macroeconomic Theory*
Quirk and Saposnik: *Introduction to General Equilibrium Theory and Welfare Economics*
Taylor: *A History of Economic Thought*
Taylor: *Macro Models for Developing Countries*
Theil, Boot, and Kloek: *Operations Research and Quantitative Economics*
Walton and McKersie: *A Behavioral Theory of Labor Negotiations*

MONETARY THEORY

Laurence Harris

Faculty of Social Science
The Open University
Milton Keynes, U.K.

McGraw-Hill Book Company

New York St. Louis San Francisco Auckland Bogotá Hamburg
Johannesburg London Madrid Mexico Montreal New Delhi
Panama Paris São Paulo Singapore Sydney Tokyo Toronto

To Richard S. Sayers

This book was set in Times Roman.
The editors were Bonnie E. Lieberman and Elisa Adams;
the production supervisor was John Mancia.
The drawings were done by ECL Art Associates, Inc.
Fairfield Graphics was printer and binder.

MONETARY THEORY

1234567890 FGFG 89876543210

Library of Congress Cataloging in Publication Data

Harris, Laurence.
Monetary theory.

(Economics handbook series)
Bibliography: p.
Includes index.
1. Money. I. Title. II. Series: Economics handbook series (New York).
HG221.H3 332.4 80-13243
ISBN 0-07-026840-1

CONTENTS

PREFACE

The literature on monetary theory is voluminous and has grown apace since the appearance of Harry Johnson's well-known survey article "Monetary Theory and Policy" (1962), but it exists only in journal articles and in a few classic books such as Patinkin's *Money, Interest and Prices* (1965). So, despite its impact on teaching, the literature has not been synthesized and presented in a comprehensive textbook. This book aims to remedy the situation. It is designed to benefit graduate students following four types of courses:

Monetary theory
Money and banking
Macroeconomic theory
History of economic thought

Because the text is unique in being related to such a wide range of courses, an overview is in order.

Monetary theory is presented here in terms of its historical development, and in the main, its development since the 1930s. In this way, particular issues and the works of particular authors can be understood in terms of their relationships to one another. (It is this that makes the book relevant to courses in the history of economic thought.) The form of organization is not arbitrary; it reflects the fact that monetary theory cannot be fairly presented as a unified body of accepted theory since there are many controversial issues. These controversies make the subject exciting and a source of fascination for all economists, and they can be understood only in terms of their recent historical development.

Moreover, monetary theory essentially concerns the question of the role of money in macroeconomic models (although an understanding of this role frequently requires the study of the micro foundations of such models). Since this book has as a central concern debates over how to build macroeconomic models that are appropriate to a monetary economy, it is fundamentally related to graduate macro courses.

In regard to money and banking courses, the material included here relates to money, with no attention given to the theory of banking or to the institutions and implementation of monetary policy. This structure reflects the attempt to treat monetary theory as such as comprehensively as possible and to relate it to macro theory and to its own history. The theory of the balance of payments and international monetary relations is excluded, since it, like banking, warrants a textbook of its own.

The reader is required to have a sound understanding of undergraduate economic theory (both macro and micro), but nothing more. A high level of mathematical ability is not necessary, for the material is presented primarily in terms of words and diagrams. Although equations and algebraic notation are used, the reader does not have to follow through any mathematical derivation of results.

The material is organized so that Chapters 4 through 7 are concerned with the Quantity Theory tradition. The first two of these chapters are concerned with modern debates about the pre-Keynesian Quantity Theory, and they illuminate the problems of general equilibrium macro models applicable to monetary economics. Chapter 6 examines the writings of the Quantity Theorists and considers the relationship between simple versions of the theory and what the theory was really about. Chapter 7 looks at some elements of the modern Quantity Theory tradition developed at Chicago. The modern Quantity Theory, however, has many aspects and ramifications, and not all these are considered in Chapter 7. Some of the most interesting aspects are not discussed until Chapter 19 (where we consider inflation), Chapter 20 (on empirical studies), and Chapter 21. That final chapter summarizes the debate between monetarists and nonmonetarists particularly as it concerns policy issues, for it is in the formulation of the theory of policy—"crowding out" and the application of the rational expectations hypothesis—that monetarism has found its best-developed theoretical basis.

Chapters 8 through 14 are concerned with the development of monetary theory within the Keynesian tradition. They include developments in the theory of the demand for money within the framework of the portfolio approach, together with a discussion of the validity of that approach (Chapters 9 through 11), the Neoclassical/Keynesian synthesis approach to macro theory (Chapters 8 and 12), and the new Keynesianism developed since the late 1960s from a critique of that synthesis (Chapters 13 and 14).

In the other chapters, we consider the theory of interest (Chapters 15 through 17), and dynamic monetary models concerned with growth (Chapter 18) and inflation (Chapter 19).

Nearly every chapter makes use of theories and concepts developed in earlier chapters, and cross-references are given. Nevertheless, the reader need not read straight through from page 1 to the end. Different reading patterns can be followed according to the reader's main interest or the structure of the lecture course. A reader interested primarily in monetarism, for example, can proceed from Chapters 7 and 8 to 19, 20, and 21. One interested in the theory of the demand for money should start with Chapter 6 and read Chapters 7, 9, 10, 11, and 20. Readers interested in some of the main developments in the history of thought will concentrate on Chapters 4, 6, 12, 13, 15, 16, and 21. In following any of these patterns or an alternative devised for other needs, readers will find that they are not hindered by having missed intervening material.

There are two things about this book that, I think, make it uniquely valuable for students. First, it brings together theories and discussions many of which are otherwise accessible only in their original forms. Second, while emphasizing the historical development of theories, the book examines the latest theoretical developments (such as the new Keynesianism prompted by Clower and Leijonhufvud and the application of the rational expectations hypothesis). This structure results from my experience in teaching monetary theory at the London School of Economics, Birkbeck College, London University, and at the University of California, Berkeley. In consequence, my greatest debt for assistance in writing this book is owed to the students who have participated in my courses; I am grateful to them both in a general sense and for the specific comments they have offered on the various drafts that have existed over the years.

In fact, there are many people whom I thank most sincerely for assistance while in no way implicating them. David Currie and David Winter very generously read the final typescript at a time when they had many things to do, and they made careful and invaluable suggestions. Stanley Fischer read a portion of a very early draft and made comments that greatly assisted the preparation of the final draft. Viv Brown and Jerry Coakley took on the laborious task of compiling the bibliography, and while many people have given secretarial assistance at various times, the greatest burden of typing the final manuscript has fallen on Gill Robinson and BB Walker. All those mentioned already know that I am grateful to them, but here I offer both my thanks and my apologies. And I also record my thanks and apologies to Marjy, Clyde, and Scarlet, the apologies for having neglected my role as a father in order to write this book.

Teaching monetary economics has always stimulated my interest in the subject, and I hope that the reader discovers an equal interest. In my case, the experience of teaching monetary theory with my late colleague Carol Nussey from 1973 to 1975 was a particularly valuable experience. Her death in 1975 was a loss not only to her friends at Birkbeck but also to everyone who would have learned from the contributions to economics that such an enthusiastic and intelligent economist was due to make.

Laurence Harris

PART ONE

PRELIMINARY PROBLEMS AND CONCEPTS

CHAPTER

ONE

APPROACHES TO THE THEORY OF MONEY

There are two fundamental questions that constantly recur in the theory of money and that, in fact, lie behind many advanced developments in monetary theory. What is money? and, Why is money used? These two problems are, of course, closely related, and in what follows we shall treat them as one. They are problems that have received the attention not only of economists, but also of historians, philosophers, and social anthropologists.

1.1 MONEY IS A SOCIAL PHENOMENON

Economics textbooks provide a traditional answer to the question, "What is money?" Money is defined as any commodity that acts as a Medium of Exchange, a Unit of Account, and a Store of Value. At this stage let us briefly examine the meaning of this definition, and to do so, let us consider whether a dollar bill satisfies it. A dollar acts as a Medium of Exchange in the sense that if you wish to sell a commodity (say, an automobile) and buy another commodity (say, a television set), you are not likely to exchange your automobile directly for a television set but will, instead, exchange it for dollar bills and then exchange some of the dollar bills for the set. The dollars in this example are used as a *Medium of Exchange* in the sense that you have exchanged an automobile for a television; this exchange has not come about *directly* by your giving an automobile to the television dealer, but *indirectly* by your selling the automobile to one individual and buying the television set from another, and you have done this by using dollars as an intermediary. In this transaction the dollars also act as a *Unit of Account* because the prices of the automobile and the television will each have been expressed in terms of dollars. That is, instead of saying that the automobile is worth five television sets, or that the price of the automobile in relation to that of the television is 5:1, the price of the automobile is expressed as $1,000 and that of the television as $200. Finally, in this transaction the dollars also act as a *Store of Value*, for if you sell the automobile one day and buy the television set the next, the dollars you hold will have retained the value of the automobile for use the next day in purchasing the television.

This is a simple example and scarcely needs spelling out, but we shall return several times to the concepts of Medium of Exchange, Unit of Account, and Store of Value and shall encounter some complex issues in connection with them. This example, however, enables us to illustrate the most fundamental characteristic of money: the fact that *money is a social phenomenon*. That is, not only does money exist because humans are social beings and all their activities (including economic activity) take place within a social framework, but, more important, it exists only within *particular* social and economic frameworks. And different types of money exist in different social and economic structures. Social and economic structures differ from one country to another and even between regions of a single country; moreover, within one country or region the social and economic structure changes over time in patterns of historical development. As we examine different structures of society (either between societies or over time), we find different monetary systems. In some societies, money does not exist; in others, money takes varying forms (gold in one society, cattle in another, dollar bills and bank accounts in another). In other comparisons, we find that money is used for varying purposes (in a capitalist society, money is used for the payment of rents, whereas, in feudal society, rents had a different nature and were paid in goods or service).

Systems of Exchange

Consider our example of an exchange of an automobile for a television set. Money is used only because an exchange takes place, and an exchange occurs only because the social and economic structure in the United States is what it is. There are laws, institutions, and attitudes that permit and encourage the exchange of commodities; in fact, the social arrangements of the United States would not exist in their present form if society were not based on the production and exchange of commodities. These arrangements are so much a fact of life that it is difficult to think of the alternative, but imagine the social arrangements of the Pilgrim Fathers in the few months after disembarking from the *Mayflower*. Their immediate need was to conquer nature and provide themselves with food, clothing, and shelter, and there were at least three social arrangements they could have decided on to achieve this victory (although it is an exercise in mythology to assume that they enjoyed a complete freedom of choice). They could have all worked communally as a team, sharing by mutual consent the food they grew and the housing they built (a form of primitive communism); in this case, there would have been no exchange of one commodity for another, say corn for timber, among families because all commodities would be owned by the whole community and shared out on an equitable basis by a decision of the community. Alternatively, each family could have claimed a different plot of land and different sources of raw material (for example, different timber forests) as its own private property, and each could then have cultivated just those crops which were required to satisfy its own needs (as happens in several primitive peasant communities today). Here, too, there would be no exchange, for all the family's needs would be satisfied from its own production. Finally, each family could have had its own private property but each could have specialized in the production of particular items; the family with a comparative advantage in corn production would produce only corn, and the family with a comparative advantage in woodland would produce only timber. In this last case where there is a social division of labor, there would be a need for exchange to take place, for the timber-producing family would need corn to eat and the corn-producing family would need timber for housing and fuel.

In this third type of society that the Pilgrims might have chosen, they might have effected the exchange of commodities through the medium of money, but our description assumes such a small, simple society that money would not really have been necessary. Exchange could take place in the form of *barter.* That is, the corn producer could make a deal with the timber producer to give a certain amount of corn in return for an amount of timber. Thus, money exists only in societies where exchange occurs—where, for example, the form of production is based on the division of labor and where the legal and ethical system permits private property. But it does not necessarily exist in all societies where exchange takes place, since exchange in simple societies can in principle be achieved by barter (although it may be questioned whether an economy based on generalized barter has ever existed).

Why Money—Not Barter?

In advanced capitalist society, however, barter is impossible and money exists as a necessary basis of exchange. One reason for this is that many different commodities are available for exchange and, indeed, this large and complex market is essential for modern industrial production. Where there is such a complexity of goods and individuals involved in exchange, barter is very difficult and inefficient. Suppose, again, that you wish to sell an automobile and buy a television set. But the television seller may wish to sell a television and buy a boat, and therefore is not willing to take your automobile in exchange for the television. You could conclude a barter transaction by finding someone who wanted to buy an automobile and sell a boat, carrying out the exchange, and then offering the boat to the television seller in exchange for the set you want. This procedure is obviously difficult and inefficient, and it is clearly easier to use money as a Medium of Exchange. A related reason for the necessity of money in advanced capitalist society is that capitalism's mode of production is based on the sale of labor-power. The producing individuals do not cultivate their own plots of land with their own tools and decide what to produce and sell. They each sell one commodity, their ability to work. In return they could, of course, receive the different commodities they need and desire, but this would involve an enormously intricate operation. Such a complex operation is avoided by payment in money, which can then be used to purchase the desired commodities.

It is possible to treat with some degree of rigor the theory that a society based on monetary exchanges involves lower social costs than one conducting exchange through barter arrangements. Following Clower (1967, 1969a), we may define a barter economy as one where any good is directly exchangeable for any other good. By contrast, a monetary economy is one where a particular commodity, money, is exchangeable for any good and any good is exchangeable for money, but goods (nonmoney commodities) are not exchangeable for one another. This definition can be represented by a simple matrix. Suppose that there are three commodities in the economy: C_A, C_B, and C_C. We can construct a matrix to represent the exchanges that are permitted in the economy by denoting the relevant element as X if an exchange is permitted and as O if it is not permitted. Thus, in Table 1.1, each commodity can be exchanged for itself (the diagonal consists of X's) and, in addition, any commodity can be directly exchanged for any other (C_A for C_B, C_B for C_A, C_A for C_C, and so on). Such a matrix represents Clower's definition of a barter economy. Table 1.2, however, represents a monetary economy where commodity C_A is defined as money and C_B and C_C as goods. It illustrates the idea that the C_B and C_C cannot be exchanged for each other since O is entered in the relevant elements, but that money (C_A) can be exchanged for itself and for the two goods C_B and C_C, and that each of the goods can be exchanged for money (and, in addition, for itself). More generally, for a barter economy, all the elements of the matrix have an X entry; for a monetary economy, all the elements of the diagonal and all the elements of the column and the row

Table 1.1

	C_A	C_B	C_C
C_A	X	X	X
C_B	X	X	X
C_C	X	X	X

Table 1.2

	C_A	C_B	C_C
C_A	X	X	X
C_B	X	X	O
C_C	X	O	X

corresponding to the commodity used as money have an X while all other elements have an O.

Now, to illustrate the reduction in costs that arises from using money rather than barter, imagine that in the monetary economy, several dealing posts or stores exist for trading in goods—buying and selling goods for money. There is one such store for each good (that is, for each nonmoney commodity). If there are n commodities including the money commodity, only $(n-1)$ such stores need exist. For the economy illustrated in Table 1.2, there need be only two such stores: we ignore the X's on the diagonal since they do not represent exchanges of goods for money and there are two X's above the diagonal (representing, say, selling of C_B and C_C for money, C_A) and two below the diagonal (representing, say, buying of C_B and C_C with C_A). Thus, only two stores need be established to ensure that such trades can occur.

Now imagine that a similar structure of stores is established for the barter economy. Since goods exchange for one another rather than for money, it is necessary to have one store for each exchange pair: one store for exchanges from C_A to C_B and the same store for exchanges from C_B to C_A, one for exchanges from C_A to C_C and C_C to C_A, and so on, but no store for exchanges from C_A, C_B, and C_C into themselves. The number of stores that would be required for an n commodity economy would be $1/2\,n(n-1)$. Inspection of Table 1.1 indicates that in the three-commodity example, three such stores would be required, the X's above or below the diagonal.

It follows, therefore, that fewer stores or trading posts are required to effect exchanges in an economy with one commodity designated as money than in a barter economy. The transactions costs involved in operating the exchange system are reduced by the existence of money and, in that sense, a monetary economy is more efficient. Two points should be noted about this example. The first is that the higher transactions costs of the barter economy do not result directly from the type of difficulty that has been discussed earlier in this chapter. They do not arise directly from the fact that the seller has to search for a willing buyer who wants to buy what the seller has and sell what the seller wants. The existence of trading posts overcomes those search costs, but the operation of the trading posts themselves is assumed to involve costs. The second point is that this type of example makes no pretence of explaining how a monetary economy emerges historically. It illustrates in a simplified manner how a monetary economy reduces the social costs of transactions, but it cannot deal with the question of how the interests of individuals, groups, and classes (which are not the same thing as the social interest) impel them to develop monetary systems. Consideration of these dynamic historic factors would illustrate in greater detail that money is a social phenomenon just as is any other economic category. Its existence and the form it takes reflect the social and economic structure within which it is used.

Another way of making the same point is to consider the forms that money takes. A dollar bill is, in itself, a useless thing—a valueless piece of paper; it acquires value only because society, through its laws and customs, has invested it with the power to act as a Medium of Exchange, Unit of Account, and Store of Value. Similarly, seashells, which have been used as money in some societies, would have no value if the social structure in which they were used did not have a need for a form of money and give seashells this role.

Three Major Functions of Money

Having established the social nature of money, we must now examine more closely its functions as Medium of Exchange, Unit of Account, and Store of Value in advanced capitalist society. There are two methods of approach. The first, which is examined in the following section, involves the analysis of the role of money in different models of society—models that, to varying degrees, may be thought to approximate historical phases of real society. The second, which is examined thereafter, involves the analysis of the role of money in modern capitalist economies.

1.2 MONEY IS A STORE OF VALUE

We have established that money acts as a Medium of Exchange and a Store of Value in many types of society, and particularly in capitalist society. It also acts as a Unit of Account insofar as the values of commodities are commonly measured in units of money. It is clear that a dollar bill fulfills these functions and is money, but there are several things that cannot easily be defined as money or nonmoney. Is a checking account at a bank money? a time-deposit account? a credit card? The definition of money is a matter of controversy that will arise at several points in this book. A primary question behind the controversy is that of which of money's functions is the most important, or whether the functions are indissolubly linked.

Hicks (1967) argues that money could fulfil its function as a Medium of Exchange without being a Store of Value. He develops the argument by examining a simplified model of the exchange of commodities—a model that he claims can be visualized as what actually happened historically at mediaeval fairs, or in the weekly or monthly markets that still exist. The market opens at the beginning of the day with numerous individuals ($\alpha, \beta, \lambda, \ldots, \phi$) bringing goods. They each plan to exchange their own goods for others owned by other individuals; they plan to do so in such a way as to obtain that mixture of goods which maximizes their utility at the particular exchange prices that are established during the market. The market closes at the end of the day with all these utility-maximizing transactions having been completed, and with no one having bought more than he or she has sold and vice versa.

Money comes into the picture once we consider how these exchanges are carried out. There could be a system of direct barter (man α exchanging good A, which he does not want, with woman β's good B, which he does want). But such systems are cumbersome, time-consuming, and, hence, costly, thus reducing the utility that can be gained from the exchanges. A less costly system that may emerge is for some merchants to act as agents; they will buy goods from α in return for a good, say seashells, which α, although not wanting them for their own sake, will accept in return for the merchants' selling him goods he wants.

At this point, note that we appear to have reached the realm of reality. Various commodities have been, and still are, used as money in some societies. Seashells actually have been used in precapitalist societies; gold, silver, and other scarce natural commodities have been widely used in many societies; cigarettes were an exchange medium in Germany when bank notes were depreciated by the interwar inflation. Bank notes (dollar bills, for example) themselves are similar to such commodity money in that they are used as a Medium of Exchange because they are known to be generally acceptable in exchange for commodities. The factors that affect whether such instruments are generally acceptable vary from society to society: from the influence of the priests bestowing religious properties on, say, seashells in a society dominated by religion and a belief in magic, to the influence of the state in secular capitalist society denominating dollar bills as "legal tender."

A Simple Banking System

Hicks goes further and extends his model to include a type of banking system. Individual α comes to the market to sell good A, but he has no bank account. He wants to acquire good B, but instead of bartering directly with β for good B, he sells good A to another individual, γ, who wants good A. He does not buy anything from individual γ but, instead, receives a credit balance at the bank for the value of good A sold to γ (and γ receives a debit balance—a loan from the bank—to an equivalent amount). Individual α can then use this credit balance to buy good B from individual β (thereby reducing his credit balance by a corresponding amount and increasing β's credit balance). The actual transactions that would take place would be more complex than these—involving more exchanges and more debits and credits at the bank, between more individuals and more goods—but, however intricate the trading, there is one implication that follows from Hicks's initial assumptions. This is that when the market closes at the end of the day, no individual is left with any credit or debit balance at the bank. It rises from the assumption that over the day no individuals have sold more than they have bought, and vice versa.

This model is a simplified picture of commodity exchange, but it can be extended to approximate more closely the real-life, day-to-day continuous exchanges that actually occur. There is no need to be concerned with its reality at this stage, but there is some question about the conclusions Hicks draws: first, that the credit balances at the bank that individuals build up during the day are a form of money; and second, that this money is a "partial" money that is only a Medium of Exchange and not a Store of Value. There is no doubt that the credit balances at the bank *are* a form of money (a form which, in Chapter 3, we refer to as *inside* money) and that they do at least act as a Medium of Exchange. It is easy to see why they should develop (and why similar forms have developed historically), for it is cheaper for society to use bank accounts, rather than commodities, as a medium of exchange. If society were to use as money a commodity that is useful in its own right as a consumer good (like cigarettes in Germany), it would be a costly process in that a quantity of that commodity would be withdrawn from consumption and would thereby reduce the total utility that consumers could achieve. If society were to use a good that has no use-value as a consumption good (such as seashells), there would be costs involved owing to (1) the awkwardness of transferring such physical items from one owner to the other, (2) the necessity of grading and standardizing the qualities of the materials (such as seashells, gold, or silver), and (3) the high social costs of actually producing the good (such as mining gold). By using bank money, society avoids these costs, and although the operation of the banking system involves costs, they may be lower than those of commodity money. However, although bank accounts in Hicks's model do act as a Medium of Exchange, it is not correct to conclude that they act only as a Medium of Exchange. They also serve as a Store of Value and, in fact, they could not act as a Medium of Exchange if they did not act as a Store of Value.

One of the fundamental principles of monetary theory is:

> Money is a Store of Value. There are other categories of things that act as Stores of Value yet are not money, but there are no forms of money that are not Stores of Value.

Hicks concludes that in the model we have been examining, bank accounts are a form of money because they act as a Medium of Exchange, but they do not act as a Store of Value. They are thought not to be a Store of Value because at the end of the day all bank accounts are reduced to zero and none can be carried over to the next market day. In this Hicks is mistaken because, although bank balances in this model cannot be carried forward to the next day, they *do* act as a Store of Value *during* the market day. If one man, say α, sells good A in return for a bank balance and then uses the bank balance later to purchase good B, the bank balance has acted as a store of α's wealth between the two transactions. Instead of α's holding his wealth in the form of good A, or in the form of good C obtained by exchanging good A, he holds it in the form of a bank balance which he subsequently offers in exchange for good B. That is, α uses his bank balance as a Medium of Exchange (an intermediary between disposing of A and obtaining B) *because* the bank balance is a Store of Value over time. As Friedman (1956a) has it, money is a temporary abode of purchasing power.

The Element of Nonsynchronization

This conclusion enables us to view once again the difference between a barter economy and an economy where exchanges take place through the medium of money. The crucial difference is that in a monetary economy exchanges are *nonsynchronized.* In a barter economy individuals exchange goods for goods; a sale of a good by an individual is simultaneously the same individual's purchase of another good. In a monetary economy, an individual can sell a good and *subsequently* use the money proceeds to purchase another good. This can be illustrated by the real situation of most people under capitalism. The workers sell to the capitalists the commodity they own—labor-power—and they do so in order to obtain the means of existence—food, clothing, and other essentials. But, because the capitalists do not own the full range of means of existence, they cannot offer to pay the workers directly in these necessities. Instead, they pay the workers in money which the workers subsequently use to buy these goods. That is, the workers sell one good, labor-power, without simultaneously receiving the goods they want in exchange, but they receive, instead, money that enables them to buy such goods at a different time from different capitalists.

It can be seen, then, that money's role as a Medium of Exchange implies that money is a Store of Value; that money is used in a nonbarter system because, outside of barter, sales and purchases are nonsynchronized; that the concept of *time*, therefore, is crucial to the analysis of money (as made clear by Gilbert [1953]); and that money as a Store of Value is a means, in capitalist society, by which individuals record how much they have contributed to society in the form of labor-power or other commodities that they have sold and how much they are entitled to receive from society in the form of commodities to be purchased (see Kuenne [1963, Chapter 5]).

The fact that money is necessarily a Store of Value, however, must not be allowed to obscure the fact that it is a Medium of Exchange. It is this that distinguishes money from other Stores of Value and, as we saw above, it is this that distinguishes a monetary economy from a barter economy. For this reason Clower (1967, 1969a) emphasizes the primacy of the Medium of Exchange function of money and thereby corrects a tendency that has been noticeable in monetary economics since the time of Keynes—the tendency to concentrate on money's role as a Store of Value, an asset among other assets, and to analyze the problems of money as problems concerning choices among essentially similar assets. The strength of this tendency will be seen from the theorems discussed in the remainder of this book.

1.3 THE ROLE OF TIME IN VARIOUS MONETARY MODELS

Monetary theory employs various simplified models to explore the role of money in the economy. Each of these models makes particular assumptions concerning the manner in which activities take place over time. In this section these differences are briefly illustrated.

In Hicks's model, money is required because of the nonsynchronization of sales and purchases, and the assumption of nonsynchronization is a necessary minimum if a model is to be realistic. However, in economic theory there exist other models that are highly important for the development of particular theorems but are so simplified as to be unrealistic. Among them is the broadly Walrasian modeling of equilibrium. In this model, individuals come to the market with goods to exchange; throughout the market day, they make deals with one another to buy and sell at stated prices, but they do not actually hand over their sales or receive their purchases until the end of the market day. The deals they make at particular prices during the day are recorded by contracts to hand over or receive the goods at the end of the day; but these are conditional contracts that must be honored at the end of the day only if the prices at which they are reached are those at which all individuals are able to sell all of each commodity they wish to sell and purchase all they wish to purchase. In other words, the contracts are to be honored only if the prices at which they are reached turn out to be equilibrium prices. Since the actual physical exchange of goods does not take place until the end of the day when equilibrium is established, exchange in this model is synchronized and there is no role for money. (However, there is some question of whether the conditional contracts may be seen as a form of money; see Harris [1969].)

Although it would appear that the Walrasian model excludes any role for money, Patinkin (1965) uses the Walrasian model for the analysis of monetary phenomena. In order to do so, he has to extend the model to introduce an element of time and nonsynchronization of exchange. This is achieved by assuming that although conditional contracts are made during the market day and become firm at the close of the day when equilibrium (market-clearing) prices are established, the purchases and sales of goods are not immediately exchanged. Instead, the goods sold and bought are to be delivered and collected at random times during the ensuing week before the next market day. Thus, although the individuals may know that they have bought goods of the same value as they have sold, they are not sure whether they will deliver their sales at the same moment as they receive their purchases. They each need to use money to store their wealth during any interval that may arise between their random deliveries of sales and their random collection of purchases (or, from the other point of view, they need to have money to pay for any purchases that they may collect before they have delivered the goods sold). Patinkin, therefore, is able to analyze money within a Walrasian model by introducing an assumption of nonsynchronization of exchange, but introducing it by different assumptions from those used by Hicks.

The Factor of Uncertainty

Patinkin's model is examined in greater detail in Chapters 4 and 5, where we will see that he has developed theorems that play a central role in modern monetary economics. Before proceeding further, it is worth noting that he has introduced another element into the analysis of money: the factor of *uncertainty*. Uncertainty enters Patinkin's model because the deliveries and collections of goods are timed according to a random process. Individuals know at the end of the market day what commodities they have bought and sold, but they are uncertain as to when they each will be allowed to deliver and collect. Here uncertainty affects their need for money, because they cannot predict whether they will need to receive their purchases (and pay for them) before they deliver their sales. Their requirement for money is affected by their desire to avoid the possibility of being embarrassed (or forced into bankruptcy) by being unable to pay for their purchases.

Now, uncertainty, like time, plays a major part in the analysis of money, especially when we come to consider the relationship between money and other Stores of Value (in Section 1.4). Indeed, when Hicks (1967) extends his model to consider the role of money as a Store of Value, he concludes that the distinguishing features of money as compared with other Stores of Value are related to the existence of uncertainty in the economy. However, in the simple models considered so far where money is the only Store of Value, the crucial factor that necessitates the existence of money is *time*, the nonsynchronization of exchange, rather than uncertainty. In Patinkin's model, he could have assumed complete certainty, with all individuals knowing precisely when they each will have to deliver their sales and collect their purchases, but they would still need money as long as these deliveries and collections were not synchronized.

1.4 ELEMENTS OF THE PORTFOLIO APPROACH

We have seen that money is a Medium of Exchange and a Store of Value and, most important, that it cannot be the former without being the latter. Thus, we can say that money is an *asset*, something that is held over time, unlike true consumer goods, such as food or entertainment, that are bought for consumption and that can in principle be treated as though they are to be consumed instantaneously. Money is measured as a stock rather than a flow, a concept that is explained in Section 2.2. It is held as a form of wealth over several periods.

This view of money lies behind a particular approach to monetary theory: the *portfolio approach*. This is the basis for all modern monetary theory and forms the basis of the exposition in this book. People in capitalist society have the opportunity to hold their wealth in various forms, of which money is only one form. A person may hold money, government bonds of different types, equities in private companies, savings and loan association shares, and physical capital such as a house. Or, according to one school of thought, a person may even invest in human capital (buying an education). The portfolio approach envisages the individual at a point of time, owning a certain amount of wealth, and deciding on the type of asset in which to hold that wealth over a given period. In particular, the person is concerned with such questions as how much of that wealth should be held in the form of money.

The approach has been developed along lines first explicitly suggested by Hicks (1935). The individual has to allocate personal wealth, $\bar{W}$, among a range of assets. Each model used by a particular writer includes a particular, arbitrary range of assets; at this stage we shall arbitrarily limit ourselves to two assets, money (M) and government bonds (B). In choosing the amount of each asset to be held over the period, the individual is limited by the wealth constraint:

$$\bar{W}_t = M_t + B_t$$

(where subscript t denotes the moment of time when the decision is made). It is assumed that the objective is to maximize the return on this wealth over the period for which the decision is being made (although, as will be seen later, other factors, such as the desire to minimize risk, must enter the objective function once we introduce the assumption that the individual's knowledge of rates of return is subject to uncertainty). People choose the proportions of their wealth to be held in the form of money and bonds respectively by weighing the relative returns on each. But what are these returns? Bonds offer at least two types of return: the interest that is paid to the bond owner and the capital gain that can be obtained if the bond's price rises during the period it is held. Similarly, other assets offer particular types of return. But what is the return on money? That is a somewhat more elusive problem with which we deal in later chapters. For the moment, let us assume that money offers a return, r^M, just as bonds offer a return, r^B. The individual's decision will be to hold those amounts of money and of bonds at which the marginal rates of return on each are equal. As long as this general condition is satisfied, the person will be maximizing the total returns on his or her wealth.

As Turvey (1960) points out, the principles of portfolio analysis are analagous to those of consumer theory. In the latter, the consumer has a flow of income to allocate to the consumption of alternative goods sought so as to maximize the utility derived from the consumption of this income. The individual does so by consuming that amount of each good at which the marginal utility per dollar of each good is equal to that of each other good. In the case of portfolio analysis, the individual is allocating wealth (rather than income) among a portfolio of assets (rather than a bundle of consumer goods), but does so on the same principles.

We shall leave our discussion of portfolio analysis here at this level of generality. It is necessary to proceed to Chapter 2 for a discussion of some of the basic concepts crucial to monetary theory that will recur throughout the book in our use of the portfolio approach.

CHAPTER

TWO

BASIC CONCEPTS

Monetary theory is not something to be considered as separate from the rest of economic theory. It has close connections with all the specialist areas of economics, including the theory of consumer behavior, the theory of the firm, and general equilibrium theory. It uses the basic assumptions that are central to all orthodox economic theory, asks the same type of question, uses the same concepts and methods of analysis. Advances in one branch of economic theory affect monetary theory and vice versa. Yet, monetary theory does have a specificity of its own: In its historical development, it has concentrated on certain specific questions, and several concepts have had a greater importance in monetary theory than elsewhere. In Chapter 3 we will outline some of these central questions; in the present chapter we explain some of the concepts that are especially important in answering these questions.

2.1 MODELS

Economic theory employs simplified models of the world. The economic relationships and behavior of the many individuals in a society are so complex that their essential features can be analyzed only by building simplified models of the economy that enable us to pinpoint the central systematic relationships and chains of causality within the economy. This goal always raises, of course, the question of the degree to which these models enable us to answer questions about the real-world economy; we shall consider this question to some extent in later chapters. In the present section, we are concerned only to outline the various types of models that are employed in monetary theory.

The simplest type of model is that of the single individual where we analyze the principles on which his or her wealth is allocated over a portfolio of alternative assets. The range of assets varies according to the particular problem in hand, and different writers concentrate on different aspects of the problem. The equilibrium point in the model is reached where the composition of the portfolio maximizes the utility (or, in a simple model, the returns) to the individual. Such a model is generally employed to analyze the demand for money and, in more recent times, the supply of money: to construct demand and supply curves, or, in other words, to investigate the question of which variables determine the demand for and supply of money. These models give rise to single-equation functions such as:

$$M^D(\alpha) = f_\alpha[r^M, r^A, r^B, \bar{W}(\alpha)] \tag{2.1}$$

They describe individual α's demand for money (M^D) as a function of the rates of return on money (r^M), on asset A, (r^A), and asset B, (r^B), and of the level of α's wealth, ($\bar{W}$). Such an equation is derived from an underlying theoretical analysis that demonstrates *why* these particular variables are thought to influence the demand for money. These analyses show how, when there is a change in one of the independent variables, such as r^A (the return on asset A), the individual desires to move to a new utility-maximizing composition of the asset portfolio with a different amount of money balances in it. Our demand function Equation 2.1 merely summarizes such conclusions, and it can therefore be seen that this type of model is derived from the individual's utility-maximizing behavior. Such models and the demand functions derived from them are examined in Chapters 9, 10, and 11.

The predictions of such models can be represented algebraically, as in Equation 2.1; in words ("the demand for money depends upon the level of the rate of return on asset A, etc."); or alternatively, in diagrams. Figure 2.1, for example, summarizes the information given by Equation 2.1. The demand

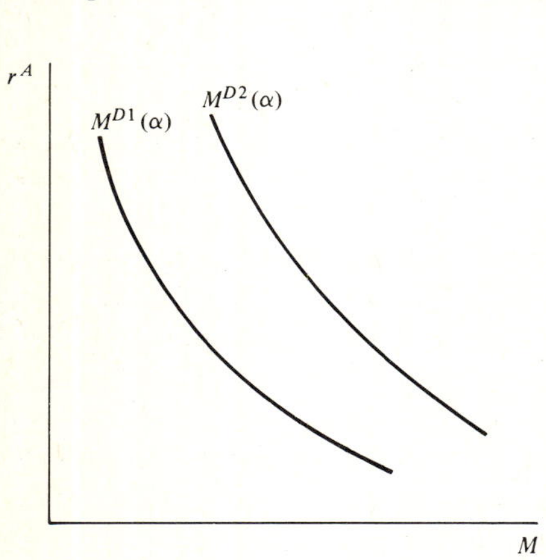

Figure 2-1

curve $M^{D1}(\alpha)$ shows α's demand for money as a function of the rate of return on asset A (M^D is higher, the lower is r^A) when the other independent variables are at particular levels, r^{M1}, r^{B1}, $\bar{W}^1(\alpha)$. If the independent variables were to change—if, for example, α's wealth were to rise to $\bar{W}^2(\alpha)$—the demand curve would shift to, say, $M^{D2}(\alpha)$, thereby demonstrating that α's demand for money is also a function of her or his wealth (as in Eq. 2.1).

Models such as these are particularly important in analyzing the individual's behavior with regard to money. They can be extended to the analysis of market behavior—the analysis, say, of the demand for money in the whole economy—merely by adding individuals' demand curves horizontally to derive an aggregate demand curve. There are some problems about such aggregation (see, for example, Green [1964]) but they are highly specialized problems and in the main will not concern us in this book.

Problems connected with the behavior of individuals are central to monetary economics, but their ultimate rationale is to enable us to analyze the role of money in the economy as a whole and the effects that changes in monetary policy have upon variables such as national income. In order to analyze this latter type of problem, we have to consider models that consist of systems of several interconnected equations (or figures). The simplest are those that are concerned to explain what determines the amount of money in the economy. For the most elementary of such models, we need only consider a demand equation and a supply equation connected by an equilibrium equation, such as:

$$M^D = f(r^A, \bar{W}) \tag{2.2}$$

$$M^S = f(r^A, \bar{R}) \tag{2.3}$$

$$M^D = M^S \tag{2.4}$$

where M^D and M^S represent the aggregate demand for and supply of money, $\bar{W}$ represents aggregate wealth, and $\bar{R}$, the reserves of the banking system. Equation 2.4 is the condition for equilibrium, and the three equations together enable us to determine the equilibrium amount of money, M^*, and the equilibrium rate of return on asset A, r^{A*}. This can be seen diagrammatically from Figure 2.2 where, with particular levels of W and R, we have demand curve M^{D1} representing Equation 2.2 and supply curve M^{S1} representing Equation 2.3. The equilibrium amount of money is M^* and the equilibrium rate of return is r^{A*}; that is, with the variables at these levels, Equation 2.4 is satisfied: the demand for money by individuals and the supply of money by the banking system are equal. Note that this particular model treats as a dependent variable not only the amount of money but also the rate of return on asset A; the latter is here a variable determined within the model, whereas, in our model of the individual (Eq. 2.1), it was treated as an independent variable since, to the individual in an atomistic model, it was a *given* that could not be affected by the individual, whereas it *can* be affected by the market as a whole. The only independent variables in this model are $\bar{W}$

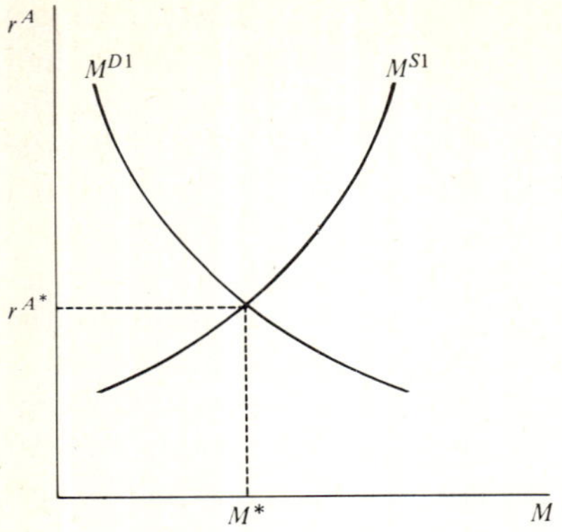

Figure 2-2

(wealth determined by past savings) and $\bar{R}$ (the banking system's reserves assumed to be determined by government policy).

Monetary Variables and the Real Economy

We can proceed from here to consider the effects of monetary policy upon other economic variables. The models used for such purposes are basically similar to the last model inasmuch as they consist of systems of equations, but they contain more equations with more complex interconnections. Consider a simple version of such a model, one that is concerned with explaining *I*, the level of planned investment in physical capital. We may postulate that investment depends on the level of the rate of return on financial asset *A* (this is particularly plausible if asset *A* takes the form of company stocks):

$$I = f(r^A) \tag{2.5}$$

If we consider this together with the previous equations, we have a model, consisting of Equations 2.2 to 2.5, that determines the equilibrium amount of money in the economy, the equilibrium rate of return on asset *A*, and the planned level of investment in physical capital. We can investigate how a change in *R*, the reserves provided to the banking system by the government, may change *I*, the level of planned investment. Such a model is represented diagrammatically by Figure 2.3 simply by juxtaposing the investment function with the money demand and supply functions. In this figure, an increase in *R*, bank reserves, causes the supply curve for money to shift rightward. With this new curve, the rate of return that now equilibrates the money market is r^{A2} (rather than r^{A1}), and at this rate of return the level of investment I^2, rather than I^1, is planned. In algebraic terms, Equations 2.2, 2.3, and 2.4 determine the rate of return that equilibrates the money market when $\bar{R}$ (and $\bar{W}$) are at particular levels, and Equation 2.5 indicates the level of investment that will be planned when the rate of return is at this level.

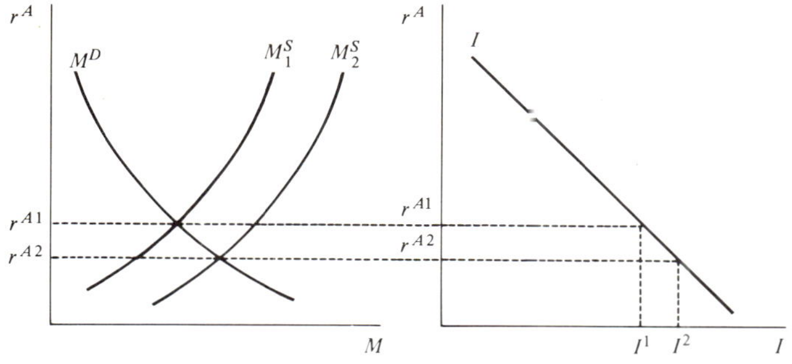

Figure 2-3

Although this is a particularly simple model, it contains a feature that is central to monetary economics: a relationship between the demand for and supply of money on the one hand, and "real" variables (physical investment) on the other hand. It illustrates the economist's assumption that theories concerned with the demand and supply functions of money are not purely academic exercises, for, if the model used here were to be a true model of the economy, the shape and position of the demand and supply curves for money would have a crucial effect on the level of investment in plant, machinery, and inventories. Suppose, for example, that monetary theory concluded that the demand curve for money were horizontal instead of being like M^{D1} in Figure 2.3. In that case, a rise in bank reserves would shift the supply curve from M^{S1} to M^{S2}, but this would not lead to a fall in the equilibrium rate of return on asset A and, hence, would not cause any change in physical investment.

Despite the simplicity of this model, we shall, in fact, build on it and extend it to arrive at what has become established as the dominant model of a monetary economy, the Keynesian model. We do this in Part 3 of the book. Technically, the most significant difference between our present model and the full Keynesian model is that in the latter, there is not a one-way relationship between equilibrium in the money market and the level of physical investment, but there is, instead, a multidirectional relationship. In other words, there is a relationship of general equilibrium between the money market and the markets for goods, labor, and nonmoney assets, with *mutual* interrelationships between the money market and the other markets. *General equilibrium models* of two types are employed in monetary economics. One is typified by the Keynesian model of Part 3, where the variables are defined in a concrete manner that can be identified empirically: They lend themselves to empirical measurement and testing, and much emphasis is placed on the theoretical and empirical characteristics of the behavioral functions (such as the shape, position, and stability of the demand curve for money). The other type is represented by models such as Patinkin's (1965), which we explore in Chapter 4; it is a highly abstract model and the emphasis is on its logical properties and its internal consistency.

Finally, we must consider another type of model, one that highlights the relationships between monetary variables and the rest of the economy. Such models, *reduced form models*, are simplified versions of models such as that represented by Equations 2.2, 2.3, 2.4, and 2.5 (or Figure 2.3). We have seen that in that model, $\bar{r}^A$, M, and I are determined within the model and are therefore endogenous variables. The only variables determined outside the model (by, for example, government policy) are $\bar{R}$, bank reserves, and $\bar{W}$, wealth, the exogenous variables. We saw from our exercise with Figure 2.3 that a change in $\bar{R}$ would, in this model, indirectly cause a change in I. If, from the point of view of monetary policy, we are most interested in how a change in government policy can, through changing bank reserves, change the level of investment, we could reduce the model to the following equation:

$$I = f(\bar{R}, \bar{W}) \tag{2.6}$$

Equation 2.6 can be derived from the whole system of Equations 2.2 to 2.5, and, assuming $\bar{W}$ to be fixed, the functional relationship between I and $\bar{R}$ which it represents is determined by the demand function for money, the supply function, and the investment function (that is, the shapes and positions of the curves in Figure 2.3.).

We shall consider such reduced form models in Chapter 20, where we look at their empirical significance. They are, however, severely limited from a theoretical point of view because, although they pinpoint the relationship between important variables, they obscure the detailed behavioral relationships that underlie the overall relationship. The demand function for money, the money supply function, and the determinants of investment are all "contained within" the function shown in Equation 2.6 and cannot be separated out and examined in detail unless we consider the whole system of equations rather than their reduced form equation.

2.2 STOCKS AND FLOWS

In economic models, we designate real quantities by categories that fall under the generic name of variables. There is a fundamental distinction that can be made between two classes of variables: those that are stocks and those that are flows. The distinction applies throughout economic theory, in consumption theory and labor market theory as well as monetary theory, but it is particularly significant in monetary theory. Monetary economics contains several examples of debates where inaccurate understanding of the distinction has led to serious confusion.

The distinction between a stock and a flow relates to the variable's measurement in terms of time:

> A stock variable is one that can be measured only at a point of time; its quantification has no time dimension.

> A flow variable is one that can be measured only as a rate over a period of time (although the period may be infinitesimally small); its quantification has a time dimension.

To illustrate these definitions, consider a certain man's ownership of government bonds—a loan to the government of a certain amount of money on which the government pays a certain rate of interest. The man's holdings of government bonds are a *stock* variable: at the moment t he owns B_t, at time $(t+1)$ he owns B_{t+1}. It would make no sense to say that he owns B bonds per year (or per minute); one can say only that he owns B bonds at a particular point in time. On the other hand, the interest received on these bonds is a *flow* variable and can be expressed only as so much per year (or per minute, week, or other time *period*): the rate of interest on the bonds, r^B, is expressed as a rate of interest, r^B percent *per year.*

Confusion can arise because time *periods* can legitimately creep into our consideration of stocks, and *points* of time can legitimately come into our consideration of flows.

When considering stocks, for example, we could say that the individual owns B bonds *over a period of a year*. But this does not mean that the period in question affects our measurement of the individual's bond holdings; it means that the individual holds B bonds at each point of time during that year. The bond holding would still be the same even if we restricted our view to half that year. When considering flows, it is a different matter. If the rate of interest is r^B percent *per year,* the rate of interest per half-year would be only $(\frac{1}{2})r^B$ percent. If the government pays \$10 per year interest on a \$100 bond, the rate of interest is 10 percent per year, but it is only 5 percent per half-year, since the bond holder receives only \$5 per \$100 bond each half-year. Thus, the crucial difference between a stock and a flow is that the latter cannot be measured without defining the relevant time period, whereas the former can.

A further confusion could arise from the fact that, although a flow variable can be measured only with reference to a period of time, we can refer to the level of a flow variable as being its level at a particular point in time. We could say, for example, that at time t_1—the point of time t_1—the rate of interest on bonds is r^{B1} percent per annum. At time t_2, it may be r^{B2} percent per annum. By saying this, we do not take the rate of interest out of the category of flows and into the category of stocks; even though we can talk about the level of the rate of interest at a particular point, we can conceive of it only as a rate per period and it can be measured only by defining the relevant time period for measurement (a year, in this case).

It should also be noted that, although a stock can be measured only at a point of time, the *change* in a stock is a flow and can be measured only over a period of time. If the stock of bonds at time t_1 is B^1 and at time t_2 it is B^2, the change in the stock is $B^2 - B^1$ and it has taken place over the period $T_1(=t_2-t_1)$. If, say, the period T_1 is equal to one year, the *rate of change* of the stock of bonds is $B^2 - B^1$ per year. Thus, a *change* in a stock must be measured and conceptualized as a flow, although the *level* of a stock cannot be thought of in the same terms.

2.3 A DIGRESSION ON BOND VALUES

Having pinpointed some possible sources of confusion between stocks and flows and thereby having more rigorously defined the categories, we can now proceed to the proposition that:

> A stock may, in many cases, be conceptualized as a capitalized flow.

That is, we must now turn our attention to the idea of capitalizing a flow. A government bond, for example, bears a rate of interest and thereby yields a flow of income. If $\hat{r}^B$ is the coupon rate of interest per annum on a bond, and $\hat{B}$ is the face value of the bond held, then the (flow) amount of income per year, Y, obtained by the bond owner until the repayment (redemption) of the bond is:

$$\hat{r}^B\hat{B} = Y \tag{2.7}$$

We can go further than this. We can show that the market value of bonds held is determined by capitalizing (or *discounting*) the value of future income from the bond. To do this, we must first clarify several concepts. When a borrower, say the government, borrows money, it issues a bond promising to repay the lender after n years. This bond may represent \$100 borrowed, and the face value (or *par value*) of the bond is therefore \$100. We shall denote this par value by $\hat{B}$. The government promises to pay interest of a certain amount each year, which can be expressed as a percentage of the bond's par value—as $\hat{r}^B$ percent per annum. We call this the *coupon rate* of interest. But the bond can be bought and sold on Wall Street and its price may be different from its par value; we shall call this price the bond's value and denote it by B. If the price is different from the par value, the *yield*, which is the income received by the bond owner *expressed as a percentage of this market value*, rather than as a percentage of par value, is different from the coupon rate. Let us denote this yield by r^B. If the coupon rate $\hat{r}^B$ is 5 percent per annum on a bond of \$100 par value, the bond holder receives \$5 per annum; if the price of the bond drops to $B = \$50$, the bond holder's \$5 per annum represents a yield of $r^B = 10$ percent on the market value of the bond. Note that, in the main, in this book we shall be considering the yield and market value of assets rather than the coupon rate and par value.

Now, we have put forward the proposition (Eq. 2.7) that the income from a bond is the product of its coupon rate and its par value. It is also equal to the product of its yield and its market value:

$$r^B B = Y \tag{2.8}$$

(if we define yield, Y, so as to exclude the money received upon redemption of the bond, a procedure that is legitimate in certain cases). The proposition to be considered is that the market value, B, of the bond can be derived from the future income yielded by the bond; a stock variable can be derived from a flow variable. The reasoning is as follows.

If an individual, say a woman, buys a bond of value B, she is buying a title to a future stream of income equal to Y (or $r^B B$) per year. The price, B, she is willing to pay must, if she is a utility maximizer, equal the value she places upon this stream of future income. We assume that this woman has a rate of *time preference.* She places a higher value upon income Y received this year than upon the same amount received next year; she places a higher value upon income received next year than upon income to be received the year after. We assume she prefers early income to later income even in the absence of uncertainty; that is, even though she is as certain of the prospect of the later income and her future circumstances as she is of the earlier income and circumstances. This time preference can be expressed as a rate that we denote by ρ. To express this idea algebraically, we can write:

$$PV_t = \frac{Y_{T+1}}{(1+\rho)} \qquad 0<\rho<1 \tag{2.9}$$

or, in words, the *present value* at time t of income to be received in period $T+1$ ("next year") is that income reduced by a factor $[1/(1+\rho)]$ where ρ is the annual rate of time preference. The logic of this is that if the individual were given a choice between Y this year (Y_T) and Y next year (Y_{T+1}), she would prefer Y this year. She would be indifferent toward the two alternatives only if the income offered for next year were larger than the income offered this year; she would consider the two alternatives equal if:

$$Y_{T+1} = Y_T + Y_T\rho$$

or

$$Y_{T+1} = Y_T(1-\rho) \qquad 0<\rho<1 \tag{2.10}$$

To put the matter in a different way, she would consider an income next year of Y_{T+1} equivalent to a present income, Y_T, that is smaller than Y_{T+1}, if:

$$\frac{Y_{T+1}}{1+\rho} = Y_T \qquad 0<\rho<1$$

This equation is the same as our present value Equation 2.9. We can also consider the relationship between present income and income two years hence. The relationship between income next year and income the year after must be, following Equation 2.10:

$$Y_{T+2} = Y_{T+1}(1+\rho) \tag{2.11}$$

But from Equation 2.10 we can substitute for Y_{T+1} in Equation 2.11 to obtain:

$$Y_{T+2} = Y_T(1+\rho)(1+\rho) = Y_T(1+\rho)^2 \tag{2.12}$$

or, dividing:

$$\frac{Y_{T+2}}{(1+\rho)^2} = Y_T$$

Thus, we can express the present value of Y_{T+2} as $Y_{T+2}/(1+\rho)^2$ and the present value of Y_{T+1} as $Y_{T+1}/1+\rho$. A bond is a title to a stream of such payments:

$$Y_T,\ Y_{T+1},\ Y_{T+2},\ Y_{T+3}, \ldots,\ Y_{T+n}$$

We can express the present value of this stream as:

$$PV_B = Y_T + \frac{Y_{T+1}}{1+\rho} + \frac{Y_{T+2}}{(1+\rho)^2} + \frac{Y_{T+3}}{(1+\rho)^3} + \cdots + \frac{Y_{T+n}}{(1+\rho)^n} \tag{2.13}$$

This present value is the same thing as the amount of money that, if received now, the individual would consider to be equal, at time preference rate ρ, to a future stream of income, $Y_T, Y_{T+1}, \ldots, Y_{T+n}$. It is, therefore, the amount of money a person would be just willing to pay to obtain a title to that stream of income. In other words, it is the price the individual would be willing to pay for the bond, B.

It can be seen, therefore, that the value of a bond, B, a stock variable, is determined by the capitalized value of a stream of future income, a flow variable.[1]

Bear in mind that although we have illustrated in terms of bonds the idea that a stock is a capitalized flow, the proposition also applies to other assets. The value of a machine, for example, is the capitalized value of the future returns from that machine.

Before leaving the subject of bonds, however, there is a further proposition we must establish, for it often is a source of confusion:

The market price B of a bond is inversely related to its yield.

[1]In this analysis of a bond there is one element of future income that we have neglected to take into account. That is the sum of money received upon redemption of the bond, the par value of the bond, B. Although this can complicate matters, it can easily be incorporated so that the value of the bond becomes:

$$B = PV_B = Y_T + \frac{Y_{T+1}}{1+\rho} + \frac{Y_{T+2}}{(1+\rho)^2} + \cdots + \frac{Y_{T+n}}{(1+\rho)^n} + \frac{\hat{B}_{t+n}}{(1+\rho)^n} \tag{2.14}$$

For the sake of simplicity, this is omitted in many areas of monetary theory by assuming that the bond is an irredeemable one. That is, it represents a loan on which the borrower has not fixed any date for repayment, and it is therefore assumed that the period before repayment will be infinity. As a result, the number n in Eq. 2.14 equals infinity, and as n approaches infinity, the ratio $\hat{B}_{t+n}/(1+\rho)^n$ approaches zero and can be neglected.

The reasoning behind this is straightforward. For simplicity, ignore the compounding of interest (the operation of reinvesting interest receipts so that they themselves earn interest) and the redemption value of the bond. Consider a bond with par value $\hat{B}$ of \$100 and a coupon rate of 5 percent (that is, \$5 interest per year). If on comparable assets one could obtain \$5 per year for every \$100 invested, asset holders would be willing to pay \$100 for this bond; its market value, B, would be \$100 and its yield, r^B, would be 5 percent. If, however, the yield obtainable on comparable assets were 10 percent, individuals would be willing to hold these bonds only if their value, B, were \$50. With a price of \$50 and interest at \$5 per year, their yield, r^B, would be 10 percent. Thus, when we refer to a rise (or fall) in the yield of a fixed-interest (fixed coupon rate) bond, we are also implying a fall (or rise) in its price. As presented here, the yield is not only an inverse function of the price, but it also takes the special form of the reciprocal of the price (multiplied by the value of the coupon). This is the case only because we have defined the yield in such a way that it ignores the compounding of interest and the fact that an additional item of income is, eventually, the redemption value of the bond. However, even taking account of the redemption value, the yield on an *irredeemable* bond is given by this reciprocal. These matters are elaborated in Chapter 17 where we make a distinction between what we have called here the yield (or interest yield) on a bond and what may be called the bond's maturity yield.

2.4 ASSETS AND LIABILITIES: INDIVIDUAL BALANCE SHEETS

In our introduction to portfolio analysis, we have referred to individuals faced with the problem of choosing how much of their wealth they should hold in the form of money and how much they should hold in the form of other assets. It is important to realize that individuals also hold "negative assets" or liabilities. Their assets comprise such stock variables as money, government bonds, corporation stocks, and physical assets such as houses and automobiles. Their liabilities include stock variables such as bank loans or mortgages. These assets and liabilities are comparable: whereas their holdings of government bonds represent money loaned to the government on which they receive interest and (except in the case of an irredeemable bond) a promise of future repayment, their bank loans or mortgages represent money loaned to them on which they pay interest and which they promise to repay to the bank or savings and loan society.

In principle, we consider all the individual's assets and liabilities as being part of that person's portfolio. Thus, we can draw up an individual balance sheet along the following lines:

	Assets			Liabilities
	Money	M	L	Bank loan
	Government bonds	B		
	Corporation stocks	C		
	Physical capital K	K	Q	Mortgage
			Z	Hire-purchase contract
	Gross assets			Gross liabilities
minus	Gross liabilities			
	Net worth			

The individual's net worth (or net wealth) consists of assets less liabilities:

$$NW = M + B + C + K - L - Q - Z \tag{2.15}$$

The portfolio problem is, in the light of this, more complicated than it was when we considered it simply in terms of allocating the person's wealth among different assets.

First, there is the question of whether the individual's problem is to act as before and merely consider the returns on alternative assets, or whether the individual should also consider the costs (or "negative returns") on liabilities. In monetary theory we assume that the portfolio allocation problem is to allocate this net worth among different assets *and* liabilities so as to maximize the total return on the portfolio. That is, we do not assume that the person has a certain gross value of assets that are allocated among money, bonds, and other items. The individual can now increase the amount of these assets by simultaneously increasing the liabilities. For example, a bank loan can be incurred by borrowing money, in which event one of the liabilities (L) increases and the immediate effect is that one of the assets (M) increases by the same amount.

This implies that, unlike people who have no liabilities and simply have to compare returns from alternative assets, this individual now has three distinct types of comparisons to make: a comparison of returns on alternative assets; a comparison of "negative" returns on alternative liabilities; and a comparison between the returns on particular assets and the "negative" returns on particular liabilities. As an example of the first, the individual has to choose between holding wealth in the form of government bonds or corporation stocks on the basis of the returns on these alternatives. As an example of the second, the person has to choose between borrowing money by means of either a bank loan or hire-purchase finance, a choice that is affected by the relative costs—the "negative" returns—on the two liabilities. As an example of the third, the individual has to consider whether to increase or decrease the liabilities. Whatever the decision, the assets will move in the same direction as the liabilities and by the same amount so that the net worth remains unchanged. If the individual borrows, the assets will go up, and if the loan is repaid, the assets will go down. The person will choose to change the gross value of liabilities and assets only if the change increases the net returns; the person will, say, increase the assets by borrowing money if the marginal cost of a bank loan is lower than the marginal return on the assets in which the borrowed money would be invested.

Second, there is the question of the individual's budget constraint in any portfolio allocation decisions. If there are no liabilities, the person is constrained by the gross assets. But where there are liabilities, is the person constrained by gross assets or net worth? In fact, the gross assets are not a constraint in this case, since they can be increased by borrowing (increasing liabilities); the only fixed constraint is the net worth, and it is this that is considered to be the constraint within which the portfolio is allocated between alternative assets and liabilities.

Here we have introduced, from the point of view of the *individual*, the concept of the balance sheet of assets and liabilities. This balance sheet is important in the portfolio analysis of the individual's demand for money and other assets and liabilities (Chapters 9 to 11). We shall see there that portfolio choices have regard not only to marginal returns but also to risk and other factors. In Chapter 3 we consider the *aggregate* balance sheet of the economy and its subsectors. This is significant for the controversial questions of whether particular items (for example, particular types of money) are assets of the private sector or not.

2.5 PRICES, REAL AND NOMINAL VARIABLES

A characteristic of exchange economies is that goods exchange at definite ratios. This is particularly characteristic of capitalist monetary economies, but some economic models also assume it to be a feature of barter economies. These exchange ratios are the relative prices of the goods. If there are n goods, $1, 2, 3, \ldots, n$, there are $(n-1)$ *relative* prices $p_1/p_2, p_1/p_3, \ldots, p_1/p_n$ (or, equivalently, $p_2/p_1, p_2/p_3, \ldots, p_2/p_n$, and so on).

Moreover, in a monetary economy each good has a price in terms of money: If there are n goods, there are n such *money* prices of goods $p_1, p_2, p_3, \ldots, p_n$. To complicate matters, one could consider money as the $(n+1)$st commodity and consider the money prices of these $(n+1)$ commodities as relative prices $p_1/p_{n+1}, p_2/p_{n+1}, \ldots, p_n/p_{n+1}$. It is convenient, however, to define money as the *numeraire* or unit of account so that its price is unity ($p_{n+1} \equiv 1$) and money prices are defined simply as $p_1, p_2, p_3, \ldots, p_n$.

Monetary theory is not in general concerned with the relative prices of goods or even the money prices of individual goods (except in some special cases, such as the relative price of future goods in terms of present goods, the rate of interest). It is, however, concerned with the money price of goods as a whole, for this ratio is crucial to the relationship between the money market and the goods market. This ratio is represented by the symbol p and we denote it by the *absolute price level.* There is a problem in defining the absolute price level more precisely. It is generally defined as a weighted average of the money prices of the individual goods:

$$p \equiv \sum_{i=1}^{n} \theta_i p_i \qquad (i = 1 \ldots n)$$

but it is only under specific assumptions that the weights can be defined so as to yield a useful definition of the absolute price level.

We may use the concept of the absolute price level to give us an alternative definition of relative prices—one that is applicable to a monetary economy. Instead of defining the set of relative prices of the n goods as the $(n-1)$ ratios:

$$\frac{p_1}{p_2} \ldots \frac{p_1}{p_n}$$

we may define it as the n ratios of the goods' money prices to the absolute price level:

$$\frac{p_1}{p}, \frac{p_2}{p}, \ldots, \frac{p_n}{p}$$

The existence of money prices makes it desirable to distinguish *real* from *nominal* variables. The nominal value of a bundle of goods $(x_1, x_2, \ldots, x_n)$ is the sum of these physical quantities weighted by their money prices:

$$\sum_{i=1}^{n} p_i x_i$$

However, in economics we distinguish between a change in a nominal value (which can arise through a change either in quantity or in money prices) and a change in quantity alone. The latter is called a change in real value. To give the concept of real values operational content, we must overcome the problem that the physical quantities of heterogeneous commodities are incommensurable; 10 meters of cloth and 4 pounds of oranges cannot be added together and compared with 15 meters of cloth plus 31 pounds of oranges. The problem is solved by defining real values as nominal values divided by money prices, or the absolute price level. Thus, if we write the nominal value of national income or output as Y, we can define real national income (output) as $y = (Y/p)$.

There are two particular real variables that frequently recur in monetary theory. The first is the concept of real, as opposed to nominal, money balances. Using M to denote nominal money balances (or, for example, M^D to denote the demand for nominal balances), we are referring to the face value of money balances, \$100 in a bank deposit, for example. If we divide nominal balances by the absolute price level, we have a measure of their real value M/p; we call this variable real money balances. It is a measure of the quantity of goods for which the nominal balances can be exchanged. Clearly, nominal balances can change without any change in real balances. If the stock of nominal balances and the absolute price level each double simultaneously, M/p, real balances, remain unchanged: the higher stock of cash and bank balances cannot buy a higher quantity of goods than the initial stock. Similarly, real balances can change while nominal money balances remain unchanged. A rise in the absolute price level with an unchanged stock of nominal balances implies a fall in M/p, real balances: the given stock of nominal balances is worth less than before the price change.

The second real variable that is especially important in monetary theory is the real rate of interest. If one owns a bond whose financial yield is r^B percent per annum, r^B is its nominal yield or interest rate. Its real yield or interest rate may be higher or lower. Suppose one lends (buys a bond at) $100 and the nominal yield is 5 percent per annum and at the same time the absolute price level is rising at 5 percent per annum: then the lender is not receiving any real return. The person's power to purchase goods is not increased by the receipt of interest. The reason is that the price inflation of 5 percent is reducing the real value of the asset, the $100 bond by 5 percent per annum. The receipt of nominal interest at 5 percent per annum is merely sufficient to maintain the real value of the asset, and it is therefore not a real return in the sense of net income. We can approximately define the real rate of interest ρ as the nominal rate minus the rate of change of the price level:

$$\rho = r - \dot{p}$$

(where $\dot{p}$ is the rate of change of the price level). If there is inflation, $\dot{p}$ is positive and the real rate of interest is lower than the nominal rate. If deflation exists, $\dot{p}$ is negative and the nominal rate is lower than the real rate. In this book we shall, except where explicitly stated otherwise, assume that inflation and deflation are absent and that the nominal rate, r, equals the real rate of interest. The latter may be conceived as the marginal product of capital in a neoclassical model.

CHAPTER
THREE

PRELIMINARY QUESTIONS CONCERNING MONEY IN THE ECONOMY

As pointed out in the previous chapters, money has a fascination for economists and others not for its own sake, but because money affects "real" variables in the economy, such as national income and employment. As such, monetary theory is mainly concerned with the behavior of aggregates; although considerable attention is paid to models of *individuals'* behavior, the ultimate purpose of these models is to enable economists to analyze the behavior of *groups* of individuals. For this purpose, the aggregate aspects of monetary theory use models where the economy is divided into broad sectors. The simplest such sectoral model is one where the economy is assumed to have no international transactions (that is, it is a closed economy) and is divided into a public (government) sector and a private sector. From there, one can increase the complexity of the sectoral structure stage by stage until one approaches closer to the situation where, as in reality, a large number of sectors can be distinguished by their function, behavior, and the types of assets and liabilities they hold. In Sections 3.1 to 3.3 we use such sectoral models to analyze the question: *Can money be considered as an asset in portfolios*? Although in Section 2.4 we did consider money as a balance sheet asset, this assumption is the subject of some controversy.

3.1 INSIDE MONEY AND OUTSIDE MONEY

The first major attempt by modern theorists to come to grips with the question of whether money is an asset was made by Gurley and Shaw (1960). They drew a distinction between *inside money*, which, for the private sector as a whole, could not be counted as an asset (or as a part of the private sector's aggregate net worth) and *outside money*, which could.

Their reasoning can best be explained by assuming that the economy is divided into three sectors: the private sector (firms and individuals), the banking sector, and the public sector. Let us consider each in turn.

First, the private sector. In the simplified world we are considering, individuals (α) would have balance sheets like the following one:

Individuals

Assets		Liabilities	
Cash	$M_C(\alpha)$		
Bank deposits	$M_B(\alpha)$	$L(\alpha)$	Bank loans
Government bonds	$B(\alpha)$		
Corporation stocks	$C(\alpha)$		
Physical capital	$K(\alpha)$		
Gross assets		Gross liabilities	

Firms (β) would have balance sheets of the following type:

Firms

Assets		Liabilities	
Cash	$M_C(\beta)$		
Bank deposits	$M_B(\beta)$	$L(\beta)$	Bank loans
Government bonds	$B(\beta)$		
Physical capital	$K(\beta)$	$C(\beta)$	Corporation stocks
Gross assets		Gross liabilities	

Now, for simplicity, assume that all the corporation stocks issued by firms are held by individuals, so that $C(\beta)$ on the liability side of the firms' balance sheets equals the value of $C(\alpha)$ on the asset side of the individuals' balance sheets.

The balance sheet of the private sector as a whole is made up by aggregating or adding together the balance sheets of individuals and firms. Doing this with the above balance sheets produces a private sector balance sheet:

Private sector

Assets		Liabilities	
Cash	$M_C(\alpha)+M_C(\beta)$	$L(\alpha)+L(\beta)$	Bank loans
Bank deposits	$M_B(\alpha)+M_B(\beta)$		
Government bonds	$B(\alpha)+B(\beta)$		
Corporation stocks	$C(\alpha)$	$C(\beta)$	Corporation stocks
Physical capital	$K(\alpha)+K(\beta)$		
Private sector gross assets		Private sector gross liabilities	

With this illustration we can highlight an important property of aggregation which, as will be seen shortly, is fundamental to an understanding of the nature of inside money and outside money. That is:

> An item that affects the net worth of an individual unit (individual or firm) may not necessarily affect the net worth of the sector comprising those individual units.

In the illustration we have developed so far, this property is exhibited by the item of corporation stocks, C. Corporation stocks are an asset, $C(\alpha)$, to households, and an increase in $C(\alpha)$ involves an increase in households' gross assets and net worth (*ceteris paribus*). They are a liability, $C(\beta)$, to firms, and an increase involves an increase in the gross liabilities and a decrease in the net worth of firms. Corporation stocks, therefore, do affect the net worth of both individuals and firms. But, when we consolidate the balance sheets of individuals and firms into the private sector's balance sheet, corporation stocks cancel out and have no effect on the net worth of the private sector. $C(\alpha)$ appears on the asset side and $C(\beta)$ on the liabilities side, and since we have assumed that $C(\alpha)$ equals $C(\beta)$—all corporation stocks issued by firms are held by individuals—these items have no effect on the private sector's net worth (gross assets less gross liabilities).

Now consider the balance sheet of the banking sector (γ). Banks' assets consist of their loans to the private sector, $L(\gamma)$ [$=L(\alpha)+L(\beta)$], and their loans to the public sector by way of their holdings of government bonds, $B(\gamma)$. These, together with the banks' holdings of cash, $M_C(\gamma)$, are the banks' assets. Their liabilities are the bank deposits that are owned by firms and individuals $M_B(\gamma)$ [$=M_B(\alpha)+M_B(\beta)$]. The balance sheet of the banking sector is, therefore, as shown in the table on page 33, top.

Gurley and Shaw assume that the banking sector's net worth is zero; its liabilities equal its assets. This assumption obviously ignores the fact that in the real world, banks own physical assets (such as real estate) and other

Banking sector

Assets		Liabilities	
Cash	$M_C(\gamma)$		
Bank loans	$L(\gamma)$		
Government bonds	$B(\gamma)$	$M_B(\gamma)$	Bank deposits
Gross assets		Gross liabilities	

assets that give them a positive net worth. As discussed in Section 3.3, this omission has been a source of a major dispute over Gurley and Shaw's work.

We can now move directly to consider the nature of inside money. The private sector's balance sheet, shown above, lists money as an asset, one part of which consists of bank deposits $[M_B(\alpha)+M_B(\beta)]$. It also shows bank loans $[L(\alpha)+L(\beta)]$ as a liability. The banking sector's balance sheet, however, shows these bank loans as an asset and these bank deposits as a liability. We can say, therefore, that a part of the private sector's bank deposits [a part equal to $L(\gamma)$ or $L(\alpha)+L(\beta)$] is backed, or offset, by bank loans to the private sector. *This part of the private sector's bank deposits is inside money.*

Gurley and Shaw argued that this inside money is not part of the private sector's net worth; this portion of the private sector's bank deposits cancels out with the private sector's bank loans in the same way that, as we showed, corporation stocks as assets and liabilities cancel out in the private sector's balance sheet. Corporation stocks cancel out because they represent a debt from one part of the private sector to another; the inside money part of bank deposits and bank loans cancel out because they, too, represent a debt from the private sector to itself (although in this case the debt is an indirect debt, routed through the intermediary of the banking sector).

To clarify the fact that inside money is not part of the private sector's net worth, consider the following example. Suppose that the private sector's and banking sector's balance sheets had the following values:

Private sector

Assets		Liabilities	
Cash	\$ 50	\$100	Bank loans
Bank deposits	\$250		
Gov't bonds	\$100		
Corporation stocks	\$150	\$150	Corp. stocks
Physical capital	\$250		
Gross assets	\$800	\$250	Gross liabilities
—Gross liabilities	\$250		
Net worth	\$550		

Banking sector

Assets		Liabilities	
Cash	\$ 20		
Bank loans	\$100		
Gov't bonds	\$130	\$250	Bank deposits
Gross assets	\$250	\$250	Gross liabilities
– Gross liabilities	\$250		
Net worth	0		

Now suppose that the banking sector increases its loans to the private sector by \$50 and that it does this by increasing the private sector's bank deposits by \$50. These additional bank deposits are entirely inside money. Bank deposits increase to \$300 and bank loans to \$150 in the balance sheets of the private sector (and the banking sector); therefore, the private sector's net worth remains unchanged by this injection of money.

In contrast, *outside money* does affect the private sector's net worth. *Outside money is an asset of the private sector that is not offset by a liability (direct or indirect) of the private sector.* We can for the moment think of it as the counterpart of public sector liabilities. We introduce now the public sector (government) balance sheet of our simple model.

Public sector

Assets	Liabilities	
	$M_C(\epsilon)$	Cash
	$B(\epsilon)$	Government bonds

or, to match the values in the private and banking sectors' balance sheets:

Public sector

Assets		Liabilities	
		\$ 70	Cash
		\$230	Government bonds
Gross assets	0	\$300	Gross liabilities
—Gross liabilities	\$300		
Net worth	− \$300		

Now consider the extent to which cash and bank deposits held by the private sector are *outside money.* If the government issues more cash to the private sector, an increase of \$20, say, then the private sector's gross assets *and* net worth increase by \$20 (and so do the public sector's liabilities). Therefore the private sector's holding of \$50 cash in the above balance sheet is outside money. In addition, \$150 of bank deposits owned by the private sector is outside money, for, in the banking sector's balance sheet, this value is backed by government bonds and cash, not by private sector liabilities. Suppose that the government were to borrow money by issuing an additional \$50 of government bonds to the banking sector, that the banks paid for this by creating an additional \$50 of bank deposits, and that the government used these borrowed deposits to pay subsidies to oil firms so that this \$50 of bank deposits finished up in the hands of the private sector. As a result, the private sector's bank deposits would be increased by $50 and thus its net worth would be increased accordingly, since private sector liabilities would not have increased. These deposits are, therefore, outside money. In the banking sector's balance sheet, bank deposits and government bonds will both have been increased by $50, and in the public sector's balance sheet, liabilities will have risen by an increase of $50 in government bonds.

Gurley and Shaw's distinction between inside money and outside money is therefore clear-cut: Inside money consists of the private sector's holdings of monetary items that do not contribute to its net worth; outside money consists of those monetary items that, when held by the private sector, do contribute to its net worth.

As will be seen in the remaining chapters of this book, net worth is assumed to be an important variable in determining the private sector's behavior. Gurley and Shaw's distinction between inside and outside money is, therefore, significant, and it enabled them to reach some important conclusions in monetary theory. However, since the distinction was first proposed, it has come under serious attack, and we now turn to consider these attacks.

3.2 IS OUTSIDE MONEY REALLY OUTSIDE MONEY?

We have assumed that bank deposits held by the private sector and offset in banks' balance sheets by government bonds fall within the outside money category. This is because the bank deposits are an asset of the private sector, whereas the government bonds are not a liability of that sector.

If this were the case, it would imply that any effect on private sector behavior caused by a rise in this outside money would be due to a distribution effect. That is, an increase in outside money represents a redistribution of wealth to the private sector (whose net worth is increased) from the public sector (whose net worth falls); this redistribution is assumed to affect the behavior of the private sector but not the behavior of the public sector.

But the question is whether such a distribution effect is, in fact, caused by that portion of money that is backed by government bonds. Is such money really outside money? This boils down to the question of whether the government bonds backing this money are outside bonds. Are government bonds held by the private sector net assets to that sector?

We showed in Section 2.3 that a bond (or other asset) is the capitalized value of the stream of future income that it yields. Similarly, a liability is the capitalized value of the stream of future costs (negative yield) to which it commits the holder. Government bonds are assets to their private sector owners because of the future yield they promise in the form of interest (and redemption payments). But, if the private sector's behavior is affected by its holding of these bonds as assets, it is strange to assume that the public sector's behavior should not be affected by its having these bonds as liabilities. The accepted explanation for this assumption is that the public sector has a unique power—the power of taxation. The government is able to pay interest on its bonds out of the taxes that it raises and, because it has this unique power, its attitude to its liabilities is different from what it would be if it were a private concern with liabilities.

These taxes themselves, however, raise a problem. Since we generally make an all-embracing assumption of perfect knowledge, we must assume that the private sector anticipates that interest received on its (or the banking sector's) holdings of government bonds is matched by future tax payments to the government. If this tax liability were capitalized at the same discount rate as the expected yield of government bonds, there would be a liability on the right-hand side of the private sector's balance sheet equal to the value of the private sector's holdings of government bonds plus its holdings of bank deposits that have been issued by the banks against their holdings of government bonds.

In such a case, therefore, government bonds and outside money held by the private sector would not contribute to private sector net worth and cannot meaningfully be considered as outside assets.

Even in such an instance, though, it should not be assumed that there is no outside money in the model. The cash issued by the government, and that portion of bank deposits backed by the banking sector's holdings of cash, are outside money. Moreover, in a modern economy, not all the interest on government bonds is paid from taxation. Part is paid from the returns on the government's holdings of physical assets (such as nationalized industries), which would appear on the asset side of the public sector's balance sheet, and part is paid from the government's returns on assets, which are the liabilities of foreign countries—the fourth sector, the foreign sector. Finally, one may question the assumption that the private sector capitalizes future taxes at the same discount rate as is used to capitalize interest receipts. The question arises in part because the private sector is not composed of homogeneous units, although monetary general equilibrium models invariably assume that it is. Firms have behavior functions and operate in markets entirely different from those of individuals. Even among individuals, wealthy subgroups have different functions and circumstances from those of poor subgroups, and the old differ from the young. Such subgroups may therefore be assumed to have different rates of time preference, different discount rates, and if taxes and interest payments are differently distributed within the private sector, they will be discounted at different rates.

3.3 IS INSIDE MONEY REALLY INSIDE MONEY?

Having severely qualified the view that outside money as defined by Gurley and Shaw really does contribute to the private sector's net worth, we now turn to the argument that, contrary to Gurley and Shaw's view, inside money *is* part of the private sector's net worth.

The main contestants against Gurley and Shaw's view that inside money is not a net asset of the private sector are Pesek and Saving (1967) and Johnson (1969). In fact, these writers not only argue that inside money is a net asset of the private sector; they also reject the critical view of outside money that was presented in Section 3.2 and reaffirm the view that outside money is a net asset.

Although the views of Gurley and Shaw had great influence on monetary theory for a decade, Pesek and Saving and Johnson have attacked their view from its base. The base of the Gurley and Shaw view is that all money, while being an asset to its owner, is a debt for someone else in the economy. Inside money is, directly or indirectly, a debt of some part of the private sector while being an asset of another part. Outside money is a debt of the public sector to the private sector. The difference between the two, according to Gurley and Shaw, arises because the public sector ignores its debts, and therefore outside money is a net asset to the private sector. In such an analysis, all money is a debt of someone, but some money, outside money, is a net asset to the private sector because (as noted in Section 3.1) a distribution effect is assumed to exist: a distribution effect whose foundations were shown to be weak in Section 3.2. Johnson (1962) notes dissatisfaction with this approach. Upon reflection, it seems to carry the implication that without arbitrary assumptions about the behavior of the public sector (or other sectors), money would not be a part of net wealth and its effects on the economy would be severely limited.

Pesek and Saving take a diametrically opposed view: that *all money is a net asset.* They argue that the distinction between inside money and outside money is irrelevant. All money is an asset to the community (not merely the private sector) and, although some things that serve as money also serve a function as debts, their essential function as money has nothing to do with being an asset to one sector and a debt of another sector.

To understand this emphasis of Pesek and Saving on the view that money is a net asset, reconsider the arguments in Sections 2.2 to 2.4 describing the nature of an asset (and a liability). There it was explained that an asset is a stock variable whose value is measured as the capitalized value of a stream of future income receipts (and a liability is the capitalized value of a stream of future payments). We usually think of these future income receipts as being receipts of money (as, for example, when we are concerned with the money value of a government bond or with that of a machine that is the capitalized value of the future profits from the machine), but we could equally well think in terms of a stream of future goods. From the point of view of society, for example, the value of a machine (say, a power station) is the capitalized social value of the goods it produces over its expected life rather than of the money revenue it produces. We can even go further and consider returns less tangible than goods. This is the view applied by Pesek and Saving to the case of money. It is argued that money as an asset is the capitalized value of the returns it yields in the form of services.

In examining the services yielded by money, Pesek and Saving emphasize the service it yields as a Medium of Exchange. All assets yield services of some type, but money's distinction is that it uniquely offers the service of being a Medium of Exchange. This unique property of money is important in Pesek and Saving's argument that all money is an asset. We shall return to it shortly.

The basis of the argument that money is an asset, however, is simple. Money is an asset to its owner because it provides a stream of returns, a yield of services as a Medium of Exchange. Money is not a liability to its issuer (bank, government, or other institution) because it does not involve a negative return to the issuer.

Suppose the government prints money and gives it away. The recipient of the money clearly acquires an asset—a unit of money that yields a return of utility because it provides the unique service of acting as a Medium of Exchange. The issuer of the money—the government—does not, by creating the money and giving it away, incur a liability; there is no negative yield to the government arising from this act.

Now imagine a more realistic case. The government prints money and, instead of giving it away, it uses the money to buy physical assets (for example, a building) from the private sector. Society (the government and the private sector) as a whole has gained an asset. The private sector has exchanged one asset (a building) for another asset (money), thereby neither gaining nor losing in terms of monetary values of assets. But the government has gained an asset (a building), so there is a net increase in society's assets to exactly the same extent as money has been created. This creation of money is, therefore, the creation of an asset.

Even the followers of Gurley and Shaw would agree that a creation of money in such a way involves the creation of an asset. A more difficult case is that of bank money. Consider a bank that issues demand deposits on which no interest is paid. It creates these deposits by purchasing assets from the private sector: that is, it creates deposits by making loans to the private sector. In Gurley and Shaw's analysis, these deposits, although money, are not net wealth to the community (or private sector): for the private sector, these deposits are assets but are offset by the corresponding loan liability, while for the banks, these deposits are liabilities precisely offset by the assets acquired in the form of loans to the private sector. For Gurley and Shaw, therefore, the creation of inside money does not add to the net wealth of any sector.

Pesek and Saving, however, argue that such inside money is net wealth to society. The creation of demand deposits involves the creation of an asset for the private sector that owns them, since these demand deposits give a stream of utility as a Medium of Exchange and their value as an asset is the capitalized value of this stream. It does *not*, however, involve the creation of

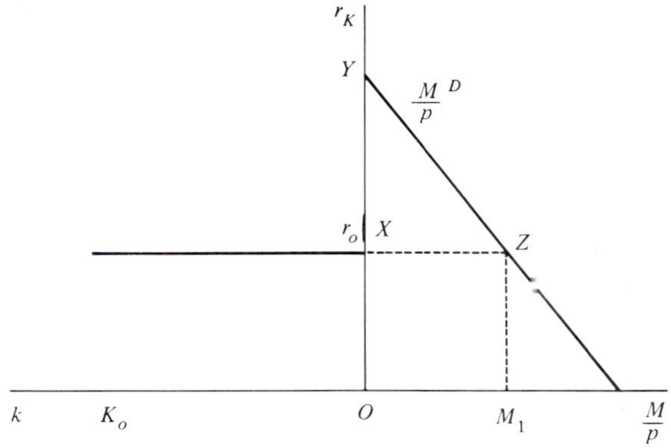

Figure 3-1

an offsetting genuine liability for the banking sector (although for bookkeeping purposes the deposits are presented as being liabilities). By creating deposits, the bank does not lose any stream of utility-yielding services, and neither does it incur a monetary liability by the creation of demand deposits, since the bank is assumed to pay no interest on demand deposits. In Pesek and Saving's analysis, therefore, the creation of demand deposits by the bank giving loans to the private sector *does* create net wealth. The private sector gains an asset (money) while the banking sector does not increase its liabilities except in a bookkeeping sense, since demand deposits on which no interest is paid are not a genuine liability to the banking sector. In the process, the private sector has also incurred a liability (loans from the banking sector) and the banking sector has, in these loans, acquired an asset. But, since these are identical in value, they offset each other in the analysis of the change in the community's wealth.

Johnson (1969a, 1969b) carries Pesek and Saving's analysis further and illustrates the points with a simple diagram. Consider Figure 3.1, which is drawn on the basis of simplifying assumptions.[1] The curve in the right-hand sector of the figure is the demand curve for money (real balances): it is based on the proposition that the marginal utility of the services of real balances diminishes as the quantity of real balances (M/p) increases and, in equilibrium, the demand for real balances is such that the marginal utility of their services is equated to the marginal rate of return on other assets. We assume that the only alternative asset is physical capital whose rate of return is r_k. On the left-hand side, we measure the stock of physical capital, k, (on the horizontal axis) and its (constant) rate of return, r_k, on the vertical axis.

With Figure 3.1 we can examine the effect on net wealth of the creation of

[1]The major assumption is that the introduction of money into a nonmonetary economy (or an increase in the quantity of money) does not affect either the marginal productivity of capital and labor or the marginal utility of other commodities, and that the demand for money does not depend on the value of national income. Figure 3.1 is similar to, but not identical with, Johnson's.

bank deposits. We can do this by assuming that we initially have an economy without money into which money is then introduced. In the nonmonetary barter economy, the stock of physical capital is OK_o and the stock of real balances is zero. If, now, the banking sector creates non-interest-bearing demand deposits by making loans to the private sector, the community's stock of physical capital remains unchanged and an additional asset, real balances in the form of demand deposits, is created to the extent that they are demanded by the private sector. In Figure 3.1, real balances will be demanded and created to the extent Om_1, and the real income imputed to the services of these balances is $OXZm_1(=r_{ko}m_1)$. The addition to society's net wealth caused by the creation of inside money appears, therefore, as the capitalized value of $OXZm_1$.

This illustration of the argument that even inside money is net wealth highlights two issues in the debate. The first is Johnson's argument that the measurement of wealth should include the capitalized value of intramarginal utility. In Figure 3.1, the "true" or "welfare" measure of the value of wealth, created by the creation of Om_1 real balances, should take account of the consumer surplus measured by the area of triangle XYZ. This represents the utility of the services of real balances over and above the utility measured by the rectangle $OXZm_1$, and its capitalized value should be included in the "welfare" measure of society's wealth.

The second issue is the problem of the ownership of the wealth created by the creation of inside money. Gurley and Shaw were primarily concerned with the relationship between money and private sector net wealth, whereas, in this section, we have focused on the community's net wealth. We have seen that on the arguments of Pesek and Saving and Johnson, inside money is part of the community's net wealth. But is it part of the private sector's net wealth? By selling liabilities to the banking sector (obtaining loans) in return for money (demand deposits), the private sector increases both its liabilities and its assets. It would appear, therefore, that, as in Gurley and Shaw's analysis, inside money is not net wealth to the private sector.[2] But the creation of inside money has clearly increased the wealth of the banking sector. By issuing deposits on which it pays no interest and, on the other side of its balance sheet, acquiring assets from which it receives interest, the banking sector makes a profit and the capitalized value of this profit stream is part of the banking sector's wealth. The important point is that the banking sector in capitalist societies is owned by the private sector, and therefore the increase in banking sector wealth caused by the creation of inside money is, according to Johnson, an increase in private sector wealth.

Thus, a crucial aspect of this section's analysis of inside money and net wealth is the assumption that demand deposits yield no interest (or, if interest is paid, it is lower than the interest yielded by the banking sector's assets). If

[2]If we take account of the consumers' surplus yielded by the services of money, however, the two may not be equal.

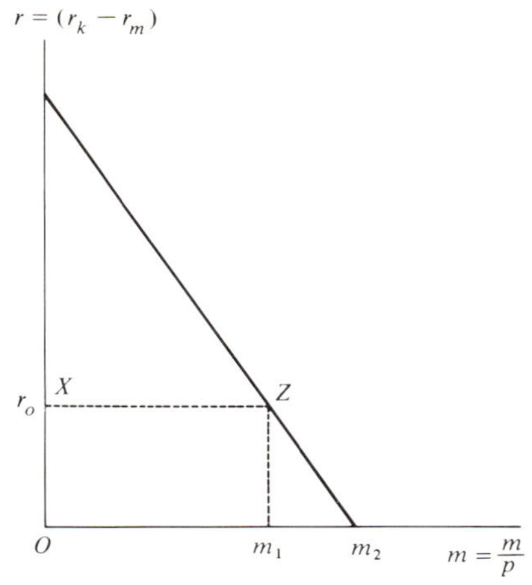

Figure 3-2

interest were paid by banks on demand deposits at the same rate as interest is earned on bank's assets, the creation of inside money by banks would involve a self-canceling increase in banking sector assets and liabilities.

To illustrate such a case, modify Figure 3.1 to Figure 3.2 so that the vertical axis explicitly measures the difference (r) between the rate of return on physical assets and the financial rate of return on money, the interest banks pay on deposits ($r \equiv r_k - r_m$). Assume that returns on all assets and liabilities are equated at the margin, that physical capital and bank loans bear only financial returns, r_k and r_L, whereas bank deposits yield to their owners both a financial return in the form of interest, r_m, and a return in the form of services as the Medium of Exchange. Then, if the rate of interest paid by banks is below the return on physical capital, r is at a point such as r_0 and the banks make a profit of $OXZm_1$. If the two rates were equated, their difference, r, would be zero, the amount of real balances held would be at the satiety level, m_2, and the banks would make no profit. In the latter case, the net asset value of banks would be zero and money would not be an asset in the portfolio of the private sector (which owns the banks).

Patinkin (1969) emphasizes that bank deposits are a liability of the banks in the sense that they equal the capitalized value of a stream of costs even if banks do not pay interest on deposits. For banks do provide services to owners of bank deposits and these are not costless. They include the operation of the payments mechanism (clearing checks, providing statements of account, and so on), and to the extent that holders of bank deposits receive these services free or at less than their full cost, banks incur their costs. These costs, capitalized, must be counted as a liability of banks; Patinkin demonstrates that under certain conditions (including perfect competition and the absence of interest payments on deposits), it equals the amount of bank deposits outstanding. In such a case, bank deposits are equivalent to a liability that, in a bank's balance sheets, offsets the loans to the private sector, which enter as an asset. This is equivalent to the situation discussed in the last paragraph, where, in the assumed absence of operating costs, the interest differential is zero. The rationale for each case is similar, too: the absence of monopolistic elements forces banks to compete for deposits (by paying interest or incurring operating costs) until monopoly profits are eliminated. In the more realistic situation where banks do have some monopoly power because the government restricts the issue of "licenses" to banks, the capitalized value of net monopoly profits is an item in the net worth of the nonbank private sector, as both Patinkin (1969) and Johnson (1969a) argue.

The significance of this debate is its implication that the distinction between inside and outside money is not the most relevant for the question of whether money is net wealth. The important distinction is between interest and non-interest-bearing bank deposits (Johnson) or money whose cost of production is less than, or equal to, the returns available on assets that can be bought with money (Patinkin). And from either of these points of view, the crucial question is the extent to which the money supply is produced under monopolistic, rather than competitive, conditions.

3.4 THE NEUTRALITY OF MONEY

As will be seen in Chapter 12, the question of whether money is a net asset of the private sector has been, since the work of Metzler (1951) and Gurley and Shaw (1960), fundamental to the question of whether money is neutral. The neutrality question itself is, however, as old as monetary economics and is a theoretical problem that is implicitly or explicitly central to all analyses of the role of money in the economy.

What is the nature of this problem? What is meant by the neutrality of money? The question of whether money is neutral is sometimes framed as the question of whether money is merely a veil, and that terminology gives a clue to the nature of the problem. In the writings of the classical monetary theorists, it is the problem of whether a monetary economy is in any important respects different from a nonmonetary barter economy: Is a monetary economy the same as a barter economy with the sole exception that money acts as a veil over the "real" workings of the economy, or, to put it another way, does money act merely as a lubricant for the economic mechanism without altering its mode of operation? That is the general question here, but the analysis of it has become formalized within the framework of general equilibrium models (see Chapter 12), thus enabling us to define the question of the neutrality of money more formally.

Since there are conceptual difficulties in comparing a nonmonetary general equilibrium model with a model that includes money, the debate over the neutrality of money is conducted within the framework of *monetary* general equilibrium models alone. It involves a comparison between the model's initial equilibrium and its equilibrium after a change in the supply of nominal money, rather than a comparison between a barter and a monetary model. This method is sometimes thought to allow us to approach a comparison between a monetary and a barter economy if we conceive of a barter economy, not as one where there are zero nominal money balances, but as a monetary economy where nominal balances are an infinitely small positive amount. That is, we can in principle consider the effect of decreasing the money supply toward zero in the limit without actually reaching zero. Within the framework of monetary general equilibrium models, neutrality can be defined as follows:

> Money is neutral if, following a disturbance to initial equilibrium caused by a change in the nominal money supply, a new equilibrium is reached in which all real variables have the same values as before the change in money supply. Money is nonneutral when the model does not satisfy these conditions.

If money is neutral by this definition, then it can be said that money is merely a veil, since a change in the nominal money stock will not change the equilibrium real values of investment, consumption, wealth, or income, nor will it change the equilibrium value of real money balances.

The most common criterion for judging whether money is neutral in a particular model is the determination of whether a change in the nominal money supply leads to a change in equilibrium relative prices and interest rates or, on the other hand, merely to a proportional change in the absolute price level. This criterion follows from our definition of neutrality, since a change in relative prices or interest rates would involve a change in consumption or investment patterns (and hence money would not be neutral), whereas, if a change in nominal money balances merely caused a proportional change in the absolute price level, all real variables, including the real value of money balances, would be unchanged. If, say, a doubling of the nominal money supply led only to a doubling of the absolute price level, money would be neutral.

Note, however, that this method of discussing neutrality rather changes the question from the one posed at the beginning of this section, the question of the difference between a barter and a monetary economy. This method examines merely quantitative changes within a monetary economy, whereas the most significant aspect of the money/barter distinction is the qualitative distinction between the two types of economy. The question of the qualitative distinction has in modern times been revived in terms of the problem of explaining the existence of money. Theories in these terms are reviewed in Chapter 14.

As will be seen in the following chapters, concern with the neutrality of money frequently caused confusion, at least indirectly, in classical monetary theory. In modern times, it has led to an examination of the conditions that must hold if money is to be neutral. Finally, it should be noted that the concept of neutrality discussed here is only one interpretation of the idea. Another, described in Chapter 18 and sometimes called *superneutrality*, concerns the equilibrium growth path of the economy rather than its comparative static equilibria. Yet another, discussed in Chapter 21, focuses on the neutrality of stabilization policy: the question of whether not only changes in money supply but any stabilization policy can, in a world where expectations are formed in a particular manner, affect real variables.

PART TWO

QUANTITY THEORY TRADITION

CHAPTER
FOUR

THE QUANTITY THEORY AND GENERAL EQUILIBRIUM ANALYSIS

For centuries the major propositions concerning the manner in which money affected the economy constituted the body of thought known as the Quantity Theory of Money. In Chapter 6 we shall show that this body of thought was highly complex and meant different things to different writers, but students since the days of Keynes have come to think of the Quantity Theory as the simple proposition that:

> An exogenous change in the supply of money causes a proportionate change in the absolute price level.

This was, indeed, an oft-repeated refrain in the writings of many Quantity Theorists. In this chapter, we shall consider this proposition, known as the Crude Quantity Theory, to be *the* Quantity Theory.

If the money supply affects the absolute price level, the money prices of goods, there must be some connection between the money supply and the markets for goods. In this chapter we consider one of the problems of building a theoretical model that contains some connection between money and the goods markets. This problem, pointed up by Patinkin (1965), relates to the difficulty of integrating the Quantity Theory with Walrasian general equilibrium theory. As we shall see here and in Chapter 5, Patinkin's work offers us a solution for the problem that remains within the Walrasian framework. In Chapter 14 we shall see that recent work argues that a more fundamental solution to the problem of modeling a monetary economy requires us to abandon the Walrasian framework.

In this chapter we begin by outlining the Quantity Theory and Walrasian general equilibrium theory separately (Sections 4.1 and 4.2); in Section 4.3 we show that in their unmodified forms there is an inconsistency between them, and in Section 4.4 we demonstrate that if they are modified by the inclusion of the *real balance effect*, the inconsistency is removed.

4.1 A SIMPLE VERSION OF THE QUANTITY THEORY

The Quantity Theory of Money was the dominant macroeconomic theory before the widespread adoption of Keynesian ideas in the 1930s and 1940s. But it is inaccurate to describe it as one theory. Quantity Theorists dealt with questions such as the determinants of the absolute price level, the determinants of interest rates, the theory of the supply of money, and the theory of the demand for money. And the fact that Quantity Theorists themselves were in dispute on all these matters further indicates that we should not think of *the* Quantity Theory but, instead, of a Quantity Theory paradigm, framework, or school of thought within which different writers dealt with various questions and frequently came to different conclusions.

As noted earlier, however, it is frequently thought that the Quantity Theory consists of the single proposition that the absolute price level is determined by the supply of nominal money balances. This proposition, called the Crude Quantity Theory, is the only version with which we are concerned in this chapter. Two alternative equations are commonly used to express this theory. The first, the *Cambridge Equation*, is written as:

$$\bar{M}^S = kpy$$

whereas the second, the *Fisher Equation*, is written as:

$$\bar{M}^S V = py$$

Without worrying about the meaning of all the variables, we can immediately see how these equations express the idea of the Crude Quantity Theory. In the Cambridge Equation, if k and y are constants, then a change in the nominal money supply, $\bar{M}^S$, must lead to a proportionate change in the absolute price level, p. A doubling of one leads to a doubling of the other if the equality is to hold. The same principle holds in the Fisher Equation. If V and y are constant, a change in $\bar{M}^S$ must involve an equiproportionate change in p. The Crude Quantity Theory is a theory of the absolute price level.

Now consider the Cambridge Equation in more detail. It is, in fact, a reduced form equation derived from a system of three equations. The first is a demand function for nominal money balances:

$$M^D = kpy$$

The second is a supply function:

$$M^S = \bar{M}^S$$

The third is the equilibrium condition stating that the planned demand for money must equal the planned supply in equilibrium:

$$M^S = M^D$$

The Cambridge Equation is derived by substituting the demand function into the right-hand side and the supply function into the left-hand side of the equilibrium condition. The Crude Quantity Theory is, therefore, a theory of the *equilibrium* absolute price level.

The interesting points about the Cambridge Equation concern the demand and supply functions. The latter represents the idea that the supply of money is exogenously determined—it is fixed by the government, for example—and it is not determined by the activities of the private sector. (But it should be borne in mind that this assumption was by no means generally adopted by Quantity Theorists.) The demand function for money represents the idea that the private sector plans to hold a given proportion, k, of its nominal income (real income, y, multiplied by the absolute price level, p) in the form of nominal money balances. If aggregate real income is 100, if the price level is 2, and if individuals and firms plan to hold an average 0.5 of their nominal income in the form of money balances, then the demand for money is 100.

The two specific features of the demand function are that y, real income, and k, the proportionate relation between nominal income and desired money balances, are both assumed constant. The assumption of y's constancy is frequently attributed to the idea that real national output was assumed to be at its full-employment level, its maximum attainable level. Since national income equals national output by definition (as we explain in Chapter 8), this assumption would imply that real national income was at its full-employment level, and in a stationary economy with no technical progress or population growth, this would imply that real national income was constant. The assumption of k's constancy stems from the assumption that the pattern of transactions in the economy is constant. The significance of this assumption will be explored when we consider Keynes's demand function for money (Chapters 9 and 10), but its relevance can be understood now by considering an individual's money holdings.

Suppose a certain man receives a nominal salary of \$200 per month in the form of a cash receipt at the beginning of the month, and he spends it by spending an equal amount at each moment of the month until his cash balances are zero at the end of the month. His average cash balances over the month will be \$100, and the relationship between cash balances and nominal income, M^D/py, or k, will be 100/200, or 0.5. Now suppose that instead of receiving a monthly salary of \$200, he receives two wage payments per month of \$100 each so that he still receives \$200 per month. His expenditure, we assume, is the same as in the previous example, but it must now take the form of running down his cash balances from $100 to zero in the first half of the month and from $100 to zero in the second half of the month (after receiving his second wage payment, that is). His average cash balance at any moment of time will be $50, but his monthly nominal income is, as before, $200. In consequence, the ratio M^D/py, or k, is now 50/200, or 0.25. From this reasoning, therefore, it can be seen that k depends upon the pattern of income receipts and expenditure; for the economy as a whole, k will increase if there is, for example, a general move away from weekly wage payments to monthly salary payments. The constancy of k, therefore, stems from an assumption that the transactions pattern is constant, and that it alone determines the desired level of k.

The Fisher Equation is identical in form to the Cambridge Equation. The variable V is the velocity of money, or the speed with which a unit of nominal money balances circulates. It is defined as the reciprocal of k, and therefore the constancy of V can be justified on the same grounds as the constancy of k. The fact that velocity is the reciprocal of the proportion k can be seen by dividing both sides of the Fisher Equation by V and comparing the resulting equation with the Cambridge Equation. On a less formal level, it can be appreciated from the following reasoning. We saw above that k declines if, with a given income per period, the pattern of income payments changes in such a way that smaller lump sums of cash are handled as wage payments. Instead of $200 of cash being necessary to finance income payments, only $100 of cash is required. Therefore a smaller stock of cash supports the same value of transactions per month, but each unit of cash—each $1 note— has to do more work or, in other words, has to circulate faster. The velocity of money is therefore inversely related to the proportion of nominal income held as cash balances: as k falls, V rises.

4.2 WALRASIAN GENERAL EQUILIBRIUM MODELS

Although in Chapter 1 we briefly discussed some aspects of Walrasian general equilibrium models, we must now consider them more explicitly. In this section, we examine the main features of such a model as applied to an exchange economy, one where there is no production.

We shall assume that time can be divided into distinct market days and that we confine ourselves to examining one such day. At the beginning of the day, all individuals are in possession of their own bundle of goods, their endowment. They are then able to enter the market and trade goods with other individuals in an attempt to maximize their own utility. The market is conducted in such a manner that no trades actually occur unless they are negotiated at a set of relative prices that equilibrates the market. An equilibrium set of relative prices is one at which the individuals are willing to trade so that the total of such trades causes no excess demand or supply for any good. Before proceeding, it is necessary to be clear, first, on how this process occurs and, second, on precisely what is meant by excess demand and supply.

The Walrasian process by which the equilibrium relative price set is reached is known as *tâtonnement* (often translated as "groping"). The idea is that the market is overseen by an auctioneer whose task is to call out a set of relative prices for the *n* goods. Individuals then indicate how much of each good they wish to buy and sell at these relative prices. These desired deals are made by the individual participants in such a way as to maximize their utility at the given set of prices. They can be considered as contracts but only as conditional contracts that will be torn up if the auctioneer finds that at the set of prices called, there is in aggregate an excess supply of some goods and an excess demand for others.

A situation like that can easily arise. Suppose that the total number of apples with which individuals are endowed at the start of the day is similar to society's total endowment of oranges, but that the auctioneer calls out a set of prices in which the price of apples relative to other goods is considerably lower than that of oranges. It is easy to imagine that there will be such a high demand for apples that the demand will exceed the supply and such a low demand for oranges that there will be an excess supply. Observing a pattern of excess demands and supplies of that nature, the auctioneer is supposed to call out a new set of relative prices, following the rule that in the new set, the prices of goods for which there was formerly excess demand are raised and the prices of those which were in excess supply are lowered. This new set of relative prices may again result in excess demands and supplies for some goods (although the pattern will be different from that obtained under the first set of prices), and again the individuals will have to cancel their contracts and a new set of prices will be called. It can be shown that under certain assumptions this process will eventually lead to a set of relative prices at which the aggregate excess demand and supply for each good is zero. That set is the equilibrium set of prices; contracts agreed to on the basis of it are honored and trades occur.

Walras' Law

Now let us be more precise about the meanings of excess demand and excess supply. For individual α, for example, the excess demand for a good x_1 is the difference between her planned demand for the good and the supply of the good she already owns (which, in this model, she received in her endowment at the beginning of the day):

$$x_{i\alpha}^{XD} = x_{i\alpha}^{D} - \bar{x}_{i\alpha}^{S} \tag{4.1}$$

If her planned demand, $x_{i\alpha}^{D}$, is lower than the given supply in her hands, $\bar{x}_{i\alpha}^{S}$, then her excess demand, $x_{i\alpha}^{XD}$, is negative and we say that she has an excess supply. Excess supply therefore is defined as being excess demand when the latter takes a negative value. If this individual has an excess demand, she tries to buy good x_i; if she has an excess supply, she tries to sell it. Aggregate excess demand or supply for good x_i is defined simply by summing the excess demands and supplies of all individuals, so that if the number of individuals is Ω, we have aggregate excess demand for good x_i, expressed as:

$$\sum_{\alpha=1}^{\Omega} x_{i\alpha}^{XD} = \sum_{\alpha=1}^{\Omega} x_{i\alpha}^{D} - \sum_{\alpha=1}^{\Omega} \bar{x}_{i\alpha}^{S}$$

To simplify notation we shall write these aggregate variables as

$$x_i^{XD} = x_i^D - \bar{x}_i^S \tag{4.2}$$

Thus, if society's total endowment of good x_i at the beginning of the market day is $\bar{x}_i^S$ and if the total amount that individuals wish to own or consume, x_i^D, is greater than $\bar{x}_i^S$ at the particular set of relative prices called by the auctioneer, there will be an aggregate excess demand for good x_i at that set of prices.

Having defined the excess demand and supply for commodities, we can immediately state one principle that is central to Walrasian general equilibrium models, the principle known as *Walras' Law*. There are competing interpretations of this principle, but for the present we shall state:

> Walras' Law is the proposition that the sum of the excess demands and supplies over *all* markets must identically equal zero.

In other words, if, at a particular set of relative prices, there is an aggregate excess demand in some markets, there must be an excess supply in at least one other market of a magnitude such that the sum of excess supplies equals the sum of excess demands. Using money prices to value excess demands and supplies, and assuming that there are $(n + 1)$ markets, Walras' Law can be stated formally as the identity:

$$\sum_{i=1}^{n+1} p_i x_i^{XD} \equiv 0 \tag{4.3}$$

It can also be expressed in an equivalent but more illuminating form. If the sum of excess demands in n markets (for example, the n goods markets) is positive, then there is an excess supply in the $(n + 1)$st market (for example, the money market) equal in value to the sum of excess demands in the first n markets:

$$p_{n+1} x_{n+1}^{XD} = (-1) \sum_{i=1}^{n} p_i x_i^{XD} \tag{4.4}$$

or, since the money price of money, p_{n+1}, is unity, this becomes:

$$x_{n+1}^{XD} = (-1) \sum_{i=1}^{n} p_i x_i^{XD} \tag{4.5}$$

if the $(n + 1)$st market is the money market. Thus, the excess demand for money is, according to Walras' Law, equal to the sum of the nominal excess supplies in all other markets.

Walras' Law plays a significant role in monetary economics, and we shall encounter it again in Chapters 12 and 16. For the moment, it is important to note that it is not a postulate that is arbitrarily inserted into general equilibrium models as a convenient way to link the money and goods markets. Instead, it follows from the fact that individuals are subject to a budget constraint in their market transactions.[1] An individual α enters the market with an endowment of n goods and money. In nominal terms, this endowment is $\sum_{i=1}^{n} p_i \bar{x}_{i\alpha}^s + \bar{x}_{(n+1)\alpha}^s$ [where $\bar{x}_{(n+1)\alpha}^s$ is the stock of nominal money balances with which the individual enters the market]. The budget constraint is simply a statement that the individual cannot, through market trading, obtain a greater value of goods and money than the initial endowment. Assuming that individuals cannot hold goods into the next period, this means that although they each may consume less goods and hold more money (or vice versa) at the end of the market, the value of the total of the two must equal the value of the initial endowment. Assuming that rational individuals know that they cannot avoid this equality between initial endowments and their consumption of goods and final holdings of money balances, they will ensure that their own demand for goods and money does not exceed their own initial endowment. Their demand is $\sum_{i=1}^{n} p_i x_{i\alpha}^D + x_{(n+1)\alpha}^D$, and the implied equality is:

$$\sum_{i=1}^{n} p_i \bar{x}_{i\alpha}^D + x_{(n+1)\alpha}^D = \sum_{i=1}^{n} p_i \bar{x}_{i\alpha}^s + \bar{x}_{(n+1)\alpha}^s$$

If we sum this individual budget constraint over all individuals, we may write it in the same form but without the α subscript. If we then subtract $\bar{x}_{(n+1)}^s$ and $\sum_{i=1}^{n} p_i \bar{x}_i^s$ from both sides and remember that $x_i^{XD} = x_i^D - \bar{x}_i^s$, we obtain Equation 4.3 (or its derivatives, Eqs. 4.4 and 4.5). Thus, Walras' Law is derived from the individuals' budget constraint.[2]

[1]That Walras' Law can be derived from the individual's budget constraints is generally true, but under some highly special assumptions, the derivation will not be possible. This exception is demonstrated in the context of Cassell's work by Patinkin (1965, Note H).

[2]The budget constraint and the expression for Walras' Law considered here are in a simple form appropriate to an economy where the individual trades only in goods and money. But suppose that individuals can borrow (and lend) so that they may have debts outstanding at the end of the market. It would no longer be the case that their demands are constrained by their initial endowments. Nevertheless, if we alter the budget constraint to take account of this borrowing, the constraint would still hold and Walras' Law would remain valid. The point is that the act of borrowing involves the supply of a bond in exchange for money (and lending involves the purchase of a bond). We should therefore amend the budget constraint and Walras' Law to cover $(n+2)$ markets—the markets for goods, money, and bonds. In such a case, Walras' Law would state that the value of the excess demand in any one market equals the value of the sum of the excess supplies in the remaining $(n+1)$ markets. If, for example, all the markets for goods are in equilibrium, any excess demand for money must be matched by an excess supply of bonds.

The Homogeneity Postulate

In addition to Walras' Law, a principle that is frequently employed in general equilibrium models is one known as the *Homogeneity Postulate.* This is simply stated as the proposition that:

> The demands and excess demands in the n goods markets will not change in response to a change in the absolute price level alone.

This principle can best be understood if we write out the demand and excess demand functions for goods explicitly.

Consider the aggregate demand for good x_i. Applying utility theory to a barter model—one where money's only function is as a Unit of Account since it does not act as Medium of Exchange or Store of Value—we obtain particular demand functions for goods. The special feature of these demand functions is that the only variables upon which demand depends are the relative prices of goods and the real value of income. We can write the set of relative prices for the n goods as $(p_1/p, p_2/p, \ldots, p_i/p, \ldots, p_n/p)$ where p is the absolute price level ($p = \Sigma\, \theta_i p_i$). We can write the real value of an individual's income in this model of a single day's exchange economy as the nominal value of the individual's initial endowment of goods divided by the absolute price level. For the aggregate of individuals, we can in general simply sum their incomes and write $\Sigma_{i=1}^{n} (p_i/p)\bar{x}_i^s$. We can therefore write the aggregate *demand function* for good x_i as:

$$x_i^D = f_i\left(\frac{p_1}{p}, \frac{p_2}{p}, \ldots, \frac{p_i}{p}, \ldots, \frac{p_n}{p}, \sum_{i=1}^{n} \frac{p_i}{p}\bar{x}_i^s\right) \tag{4.6}$$

We can also write the aggregate *excess demand function* for good x_i as the aggregate demand for it less the aggregate of each individual's initial endowment of good x_i:

$$x_i^{XD} = f_i\left(\frac{p_1}{p}, \frac{p_2}{p}, \ldots, \frac{p_i}{p}, \ldots, \frac{p_n}{p}, \sum_{i=1}^{n} \frac{p_i}{p}\bar{x}_i^s\right) - \bar{x}_i^s \tag{4.7}$$

These demand and excess demand functions incorporate the principle of the Homogeneity Postulate. A change in the absolute price level alone will, according to Equations 4.6 and 4.7, cause no change in the quantity demanded or the excess demand for good x_i. This follows because the meaning of the phrase "a change in the absolute price level alone" specifically implies that relative prices remain unchanged. In other words, each of the money prices $(p_1, \ldots, p_i, \ldots, p_n)$ must change in the same proportion as the absolute price level. Thus, $(p_1/p, p_2/p, \ldots, p_i/p, \ldots, p_n/p)$ remains unchanged and $\Sigma_{i=1}^{n} (p_i/p)\bar{x}_i^S$, the real value of initial endowments, remains unchanged. Since nothing on the right-hand side of the equations changes as a result of a change in the absolute price level alone, the demand and excess demand variables on the left-hand side remain unchanged.

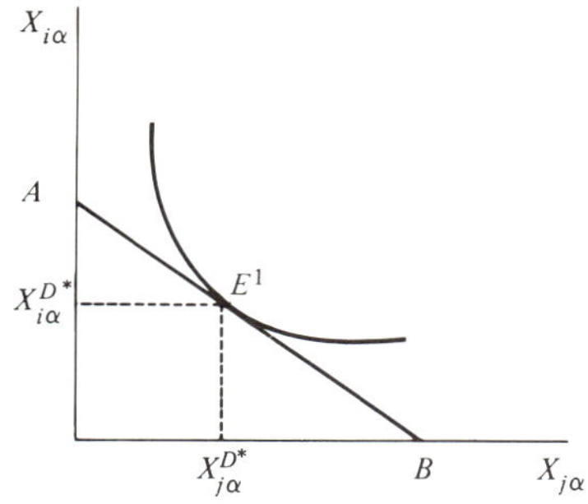

Figure 4-1

There are two points that should be clarified concerning the Homogeneity Postulate. The first is that it is not an unusual principle; it is a commonplace result in the utility analysis encountered in microeconomics courses. Consider individual α's choice, in a two-good economy, between the two goods, x_i and x_j. Figure 4.1 illustrates the indifference map, which represents the individual's utility function, and the budget line AB, which represents a given budget constraint. The point of tangency, E^1, between this budget line and an indifference curve determines the utility-maximizing demand for x_i and x_j at $x^{D*}_{i\alpha}$ and $x^{D*}_{j\alpha}$. If the slope or intercept of the budget line changes, the demand for x_i and x_j changes. The slope depends only on the relative price of the goods, (p_i/p_j), and its intercept depends only on the real value of the individual's income or endowment, $((p_i/p)\bar{x}^S_{i\alpha} + (p_j/p)\bar{x}^S_{j\alpha})$. Therefore, only the relative prices and the real value of the individual's endowment determine his or her demands for goods in this model.

The second point concerns the derivation of the term Homogeneity Postulate. It is derived from the mathematical concept of a homogeneous function, which we will find useful later in this chapter. A function such as $x = f(y, z)$ is said to be homogeneous of degree q with respect to, say, variable y when, and only when, it has the property that when y is multiplied by some number λ, the dependent variable x changes by the factor λ^q. In other words, the function is homogeneous of degree q with respect to the independent variable y if we can write the function as $\lambda^q x_0 = f(\lambda y_0, z_0)$, where x_0, y_0, and z_0 represent particular levels of the variables. If the function were homogeneous of the first degree in y, then a change in y would cause a proportionate change in x; a doubling of y, for example, would cause x to double. Since $\lambda^1 = \lambda$, such a case can be written as $\lambda x_0 = f(\lambda y_0, z_0)$; such a function has the convenient property that $x = f(y, z)$ can also be written as $x = yf(1, z)$. If the function is homogeneous of degree zero in y, it implies that a change in y causes *no change* in x or, in other words, $x_0 = f(\lambda y_0, z_0)$. This follows from the mathematical fact that λ raised to the power zero is equal to unity, $\lambda^0 = 1$.

From this we can see why we can express as the Homogeneity Postulate the idea that the demand and excess demand in the n goods markets are not functions of money prices and the absolute price level but are functions of relative prices. The full name of the Homogeneity Postulate should be the "postulate that the demand and excess demand functions for goods are homogeneous of degree zero in money prices and the absolute price level." A doubling of all money prices (and therefore of the absolute price level)—a multiplication of $(p_1, \ldots, p_i, \ldots, p_n)$ and p by $\lambda = 2$—would cause no change in x_i^D or x_i^{XD}, as can be seen from Equations 4.6 and 4.7.

Indeterminacy of the Price Level

Walras' Law, together with the excess demand equations for goods which, like Equation 4.7, have the Homogeneity Postulate as a property, gives us the basic elements of simple Walrasian general equilibrium models. If, in addition, we note that equilibrium in any market requires the excess demand in that market to be zero, we are able to proceed to consider the model in full. In doing so, we wish to demonstrate a particular point:

> The n goods markets by themselves cannot determine the absolute price level, p, or the money prices $(p_1, \ldots, p_i, \ldots, p_n)$, but can determine only the n relative prices $(p_1/p, \ldots, p_i/p, \ldots, p_n/p)$.

In order to demonstrate this point, we shall apply the Walrasian general equilibrium model to a world where there is no money market. Money is used only as a Unit of Account, so the relative prices $(p_1/p, \ldots, p_n/p)$ are the ratios of the goods' individual money prices to the absolute price level, but since there is no money commodity or credit money no individual can own money balances. In the absence of money balances, the model consists of the n goods markets without any money market. This assumption is equivalent to assuming the existence of barter.

The equilibrium conditions for the n goods markets are that excess demand in each of the n markets must be zero:

$$\left.\begin{aligned} x_1^{XD} &= f_1\left(\frac{p_1}{p}, \ldots, \frac{p_i}{p}, \ldots, \frac{p_n}{p}, \sum_{i=1}^{n} \frac{p_i}{p} \bar{x}_i^S\right) - \bar{x}_1^S = 0 \\ x_i^{XD} &= f_i\left(\frac{p_1}{p}, \ldots, \frac{p_i}{p}, \ldots, \frac{p_n}{p}, \sum_{i=1}^{n} \frac{p_i}{p} \bar{x}_i^S\right) - \bar{x}_i^S = 0 \\ x_n^{XD} &= f_n\left(\frac{p_1}{p}, \ldots, \frac{p_i}{p}, \ldots, \frac{p_n}{p}, \sum_{i=1}^{n} \frac{p_i}{p} \bar{x}_i^S\right) - \bar{x}_i^S = 0 \end{aligned}\right\} \tag{4.8}$$

These equations, plus the equation defining p, the absolute price level, completely specify the Walrasian general equilibrium model for the n goods barter economy. The equation defining p is, as we saw in Chapter 2,

$$\sum_{i=1}^{n} \theta_i \frac{p_i}{p} = 1 \tag{4.9}$$

Equations 4.8 and 4.9 give us $(n+1)$ equations to determine the n dependent variables, the relative prices $(p_1/p, \ldots, p_i/p, \ldots, p_n/p)$.

The question now is whether this number of equations does enable us to determine these relative prices and, if so, whether it also enables us to determine other variables. To answer this, it must be borne in mind that as a general rule (the exceptions to which need not concern us), we require exactly n linearly independent equations to determine n variables. In the light of this rule, it appears at first sight as though we have too many equations $(n+1)$ to determine the n dependent variables. However, the application of Walras' Law enables us to reduce the number of independent equations by one, so that we are left with n independent equations. This can be seen if we rewrite Equation 4.4, the expression for Walras' Law, in a form appropriate to this n good barter economy:

$$p_n x_n^{XD} = (-1) \sum_{i=1}^{n-1} p_i x_i^{XD} \tag{4.10}$$

It is evident from this equation that the excess demand in the nth market (or, indeed, for any individual market that we may have chosen to enter on the left-hand side) is completely determined as a linear function (the sum multiplied by -1) of the excess demands in the other $(n-1)$ markets. Thus, given the validity of Walras' Law, only $(n-1)$ of the n equations in Equation 4.8 are linearly independent equations. We therefore have n independent equations [Eq. 4.9 plus $(n-1)$ from Eq. 4.8] to determine the n endogenous variables, the n relative prices $(p_1/p, \ldots, p_i/p, \ldots, p_n/p)$.

In this model, therefore, we can determine relative prices. We cannot, however, determine the n money prices and the absolute price level $(p_1, \ldots, p_i, \ldots, p_n, p)$ for, as a result of Walras' Law, we have only n independent equations, which are insufficient to determine these $(n+1)$ variables. The absolute price level is therefore indeterminate. If the set of relative prices, $(p_1^1/p^1, \ldots, p_i^1/p^1, \ldots, p_n^1/p^1)$, is an equilibrium set, a doubling of all money prices and the absolute price level, *ceteris paribus*, yields the set of relative prices $(p_1^2/p^2, \ldots, p_i^2/p^2, \ldots, p_n^2/p^2)$. Since both the denominator and the numerator of each equation have doubled, this set is the same as the initial set of relative prices and is therefore also an equilibrium set. Any level of money prices, and therefore any absolute price level, is consistent with equilibrium.

The commonsense interpretation of this conclusion is straightforward. The excess demand functions in the markets of this model (Eq. 4.8) are based on the Homogeneity Postulate. They state that the excess demand for each good is a function of relative prices and the endowment of goods alone. If there is initially equilibrium in these goods markets at a given set of money prices and absolute price level, a proportionate change in all these money prices will not disturb equilibrium, since it will not affect the relative prices upon which the excess demands depend. Therefore, given equilibrium relative prices, any set of money prices (any absolute price level) is consistent with equilibrium. The Homogeneity Postulate, although it is commonplace and appears quite innocent, yields this strong implication. We shall see in the next section that the Homogeneity Postulate, together with Walras' Law, has another strong implication: Its inclusion makes it impossible to extend the Walrasian general equilibrium model from a barter economy to a monetary economy.

4.3 THE PROBLEM OF CONSISTENCY AND THE INVALID DICHOTOMY

In the preceding two sections we have examined respectively the Quantity Theory (in its crude form) and a simple Walrasian general equilibrium model of a barter economy. Each by itself is unsatisfactory as a model of a monetary economy. The Quantity Theory gives us determination of the absolute price level but says nothing of relative prices; the Walrasian general equilibrium model gives us determination of relative prices but says nothing of the absolute price level. The question we must now face is whether we can have an integrated model of relative prices and the absolute price level. Is it possible to integrate microeconomic price theory with monetary theory? The question was indicated by Lange (1942) but has been pursued by other writers and has received its most complete treatment from Patinkin (1965).

An obvious, deceptively simple solution to the problem would be to build a model consisting of the Walrasian general equilibrium model of a barter economy with the Quantity Theory added to it as an equation for the money market. In such a model, it might appear that we can dichotomize the pricing process so that relative prices are determined in the goods markets by the principles of general equilibrium analysis, while the absolute price level is determined in the money market by the Quantity Theory. After all, we saw in Section 4.2 that in a model without a money market, we have sufficient equations to determine relative prices. If we add a money market equation, we will surely then have sufficient equations to determine an extra variable, the absolute price level. This is indeed true, but unfortunately such a model would involve an internal inconsistency, or, in other words, such a dichotomization would be an invalid dichotomy. Patinkin's proof of this follows.

Inconsistency and Invalid Dichotomy

The inconsistency in such a model can be seen by isolating its essential features. It has a set of n goods market equilibrium equations modeled according to the Homogeneity Postulate:

$$x_i^{XD} = f_i\left(\frac{p_1}{p}, \ldots, \frac{p_i}{p}, \ldots, \frac{p_n}{p}, \sum_{i=1}^{n} \frac{p_i}{p} \bar{x}_i^s\right) - \bar{x}_i^s = 0 \qquad (i = 1 \ldots n) \qquad (4.11)$$

plus an equation to define the absolute price level:

$$\sum_{i=1}^{n} \theta_i \frac{p_i}{p} = 1 \tag{4.12}$$

These equations are the same as those that made up the barter model of the previous section. In addition, the present model has a money market demand function modeled according to the Quantity Theory:

$$M^D = kpy \tag{4.13}$$

By subtracting M^S from both sides, this equation can be written as an equilibrium condition in terms of the excess demand for nominal money balances:

$$M^{XD} = kpy - M^S = 0 \tag{4.14}$$

Finally, the element that links the money and the goods markets is Walras' Law. As we saw in the last section, Walras' Law can yield an excess demand function for money as a function of the excess demands for goods:

$$M^{XD} = (-1) \sum_{i=1}^{n} p_i x_i^{XD} \tag{4.15}$$

A model incorporating the Quantity Theory and Walras' Law therefore yields two excess demand functions for money, Equations 4.14 and 4.15. But, *because of the inclusion of the Homogeneity Postulate, these equations are mutually inconsistent.*

The inconsistency arises because each equation has different properties. In Equation 4.15, the excess demand function for money is homogeneous of degree one in the absolute price level. If all money prices were to double, for example, the excess demands for commodities would remain unchanged as a result of the Homogeneity Postulate having been incorporated in Equation 4.11. Therefore the x_i^{XD} terms on the right-hand side of Equation 4.15 would not alter, but the money prices, p_i, would all double, and the excess demand for nominal money balances, M^{XD}, would double as a result. However, the excess demand function for money yielded as Equation 4.14 by the Quantity Theory is nonhomogeneous in the absolute price level. A change in p will cause a change in M^{XD}, but it will not, according to the Quantity Theory equation, cause a proportionate change in M^{XD}, since it affects only the demand for money (kpy) and not the supply (M^S). The Quantity Theory excess demand equation is therefore not homogeneous of degree zero or of degree one; in fact, it is not homogeneous to any degree. It is therefore inconsistent with the excess demand function for money which, via Walras' Law, is implied by the Homogeneity Postulate in the goods market equations.

The inconsistency can equally well be expressed without referring to the mathematical properties of the equations. Suppose that the goods markets and the money market are in equilibrium. Now imagine that the absolute price level doubles and no exogenous variable (such as the money supply) changes. Because the excess demands for goods depend only on relative prices (the Homogeneity Postulate) the goods markets remain in equilibrium with zero excess demands. Walras' Law indicates that since the goods markets have zero excess demand, the remaining market, the money market, also has zero excess demand. The Quantity Theory, however, indicates that this increase in the absolute price level *does* cause a positive excess demand for money; while the supply of money remains unchanged, the demand for money increases because the Quantity Theory proposes that it depends on the absolute price level. The Quantity Theory analysis of the money market is therefore inconsistent with the existence of the Homogeneity Postulate in the goods markets and the existence of Walras' Law, which links together all the markets.

It is impossible to refute Patinkin's demonstration that an internal inconsistency exists in any model containing the Quantity Theory, Walras' Law, and the Homogeneity Postulate. Nevertheless, his argument generated considerable controversy, and several writers, including Valavanis-Vail (1955), have attempted to dispute it. One of the arguments attacking Patinkin has been the idea that there is no inconsistency in the model if we examine the economy at a point of equilibrium. This is, in a sense, true. It comes down to saying that the $(n+2)$ equations of the model (the n goods market equations, the price level definition, and the Quantity Theory) include $(n+1)$ independent equations as a result of applying Walras' Law, and these are sufficient to determine $(n+1)$ variables (the n relative prices and the absolute price level) when all excess demands are zero.

The point of Patinkin's argument, however, is that the inconsistency is revealed as soon as we explore the possibility of disequilibrium and non-zero excess demands; such disequilibrium analysis has to be undertaken if we are to consider the determinateness of the absolute price level in a meaningful way. Disequilibrium analysis must be undertaken in order to determine the stability of equilibrium. At an equilibrium point, the inconsistency between the two excess demand functions for money, Equations 4.14 and 4.15, need not greatly concern us, although it continues to be present. It is of little interest because both of them take the value zero in equilibrium. However, as soon as we consider a change in equilibrium or the disequilibrium forces that bring about equilibrium, their inconsistency prevents analysis even though the number of independent equations matches the number of endogenous variables. Suppose, for example, that we analyze whether the absolute price level is determinate by imagining that it diverges from its initial equilibrium level and examining what happens to the model. We would find that Equation 4.14 tells us that there will be an excess demand for money, whereas Equation 4.15 tells us that there will not.

Say's Identity

We have seen, therefore, that a model containing the Quantity Theory, Walras' Law, and the Homogeneity Postulate is not an internally consistent model of the determination of relative prices and the absolute price level. We could equally well show that the inconsistency exists if we ignore the role of the Homogeneity Postulate and include the principle of Say's Identity in the model.

Say's Identity is a proposition that, like the Homogeneity Postulate, is commonly found at least implicitly in microeconomic theory. It states that:

> The demand for goods as a whole always equals the supply of goods; the two are identically equal.

Equivalently, it can be read as stating that the excess demand in the goods markets as a whole is identically equal to zero. There may be a positive excess demand for some goods, but this is always balanced by excess supplies of other goods. Thus, for an economy with n goods markets, Say's Identity can be written in symbols as:

$$\sum_{i=1}^{n} p_i x_i^{XD} \equiv 0 \tag{4.16}$$

This expression appears to be very similar to Walras' Law, as can be seen by comparing Equation 4.16 with Equation 4.3. The important distinction between the two is that Walras' Law refers to the sum of excess demands aggregated over all markets—both the goods and money markets—whereas Say's Identity refers to the sum of excess demands in the goods markets alone. It has the strong implication that there can never be gluts of goods, or oversupply, whereas Walras' Law merely implies that if there is a glut of goods, it is accompanied by an excess demand for money.

If we were to build a model containing the Quantity Theory, Walras' Law, and Say's Identity, it would be internally inconsistent, just as a model including the Homogeneity Postulate is. This can be seen from the following reasoning: Suppose we are initially at equilibrium and the absolute price level were to double while all exogenous variables remain unchanged. The existence of Say's Identity would ensure that this change in p prevents there being an excess demand or supply for the goods markets as a whole. The sum of excess demands in the n goods markets is, according to Say's Identity, identically equal to zero (Eq. 4.16). In consequence, Walras' Law implies that the excess demand in the $(n + 1)$st market is also identically zero. But the Quantity Theory tells us that the excess demand for money becomes positive as a result of the rise in p. There is, therefore, again an inconsistency between the excess demand function for money derived from the goods markets via Walras' Law and the excess demand function derived from the Quantity Theory.

The inconsistency in Walrasian general equilibrium models that have the Quantity Theory added can therefore be demonstrated either by specifying the Walrasian model to include the Homogeneity Postulate or as including Say's Identity.

Patinkin was concerned, not only to demonstrate the existence of inconsistency in models of the type we have discussed, but also to argue that inconsistent models such as these are found in the published work of many economists who wrote within the Quantity Theory tradition before the 1930s. Thus, a part of his work is an exercise in the history of economic thought; if his interpretation of the Quantity Theorists' work is correct, then the existence of an inconsistency in such models is a serious flaw in the quantity theory tradition. There is, however, room for doubt as to whether the Quantity Theorists' work contains the Quantity Theory, Walras' Law, and Say's Identity (or the Homogeneity Postulate). This is a question to which we return in Chapter 6 where we consider in some detail the development of the Quantity Theory.

4.4 THE REAL BALANCE EFFECT

Patinkin's work demonstrates, as seen earlier, that it is impossible to reconcile the established theory of relative price determination (based on the Homogeneity Postulate or Say's Identity) with the Quantity Theory explanation of the absolute price level. We are therefore left with the question posed at the beginning of the last section: How can we build a model of a monetary economy where relative prices and the absolute price level are both determinate?

One apparent solution would be to drop the Quantity Theory. Then we would have a model consisting of the n goods market equations (Eq. 4.8), the equation for the $(n + 1)$st market, the money market, and the equation for the absolute price level (Eq. 4.9). Walras' Law, the Homogeneity Postulate, and Say's Identity would still be present. Walras' Law would determine the relationship between the n goods markets and the money market, the $(n + 1)$st, and there would be no Quantity Theory equation to contradict the money market equation derived via Walras' Law. Walras' Law also enables us to eliminate the money market equation as being not an independent equation. We are left with $(n + 1)$ equations, the n goods market equations, and the definitional equation for the absolute price level. Say's Identity, however, implies that we must eliminate yet one more equation, for it states that one of the n goods market equations is dependent on the remaining $(n - 1)$. If the sum of excess demands in $(n - 1)$ of the n goods markets is positive, then there must be an equivalent excess supply in the nth market, for otherwise Say's Identity would not be satisfied. Thus, through the application of both Walras' Law and Say's Identity, we have eliminated as dependent equations two of the $(n + 2)$ original equations. We are left with just n independent equations, and these are sufficient only to determine the n relative prices of goods. There are not sufficient equations to determine the absolute price level. Therefore, it is impossible to avoid the inconsistency between the Quantity Theory, Walras' Law and Say's Identity (or the Homogeneity Postulate) by dropping the Quantity Theory. That procedure would lead to the absolute price level's being indeterminate.

The Real Balance Effect

An alternative procedure is to amend the model presented in Section 4.3 so that the Homogeneity Postulate and Say's Identity are abandoned. This procedure is the one proposed by Patinkin. He demonstrates that a consistent monetary model of relative prices and the absolute price level can be built, and that it can comprise both the Quantity Theory and Walras' Law. It cannot, however, comprise the Homogeneity Postulate or Say's Identity; instead, the excess demand functions for goods and money must incorporate the *real balance effect*. The real balance effect can be defined as the proposition that:

> The demands for goods (and for real money balances) are not only functions of relative prices and the endowment of goods; they are also functions of the real value of money balances.

Thus, the excess demand functions for the n goods markets must be written as:

$$x_i^{XD} = f_i\left(\frac{p_1}{p}, \ldots, \frac{p_i}{p}, \ldots, \frac{p_n}{p}, \sum_{i=1}^{n} \frac{p_i}{p} \bar{x}_i^S + \frac{\bar{M}^S}{p}\right) - \bar{x}_i^S \qquad i = (1, \ldots, n) \tag{4.17}$$

The difference between these excess demand functions and those we have considered previously (Eq. 4.8) is that here the demand and excess demands for goods depend on the real value of money balances. In particular, it is assumed that the relationship is positive ($\partial x^{XD}/\partial(M^S/p) > 0$). We can therefore interpret Equation 4.17 as saying that if relative prices and the endowment of goods remain unchanged, an increase (or decrease) in the real value of money balances causes an increase (or decrease) in the demand and excess demand for goods.

With the goods market equations written in this form so that they include the real balance effect, the demands and excess demands for goods depend on the absolute price level. If the stock of nominal money balances, $\bar{M}^S$, is unchanged, an increase in the absolute price level will reduce the value of real balances, $\bar{M}^S/p$—the real value of \$100 in notes declines if the absolute price level increases. This decline in real balances causes a fall in the demand for goods and also, if the goods markets were initially in equilibrium, an excess supply of goods. Thus, the inclusion of the real balance effect ensures that a change in the absolute price level alone *does* affect the demand for goods, thereby ensuring that the Homogeneity Postulate does not hold in the goods market. The inclusion of the real balance effect also ensures that Say's Identity does not hold, for a change in the absolute price level affects the excess demands for all goods, all in the same direction: If the goods markets are initially all in equilibrium, a rise in the absolute price level, causing a fall in real balances, produces excess supply in all goods markets, a position that is inconsistent with Say's Identity.

Thus, the existence of the real balance effect in a model implies the nonexistence of the Homogeneity Postulate or Say's Identity. On the basis of it, we can build a Walrasian model of a monetary economy without encountering an inconsistency, and the problem discussed in the last section can be resolved. Such a model would consist of the Quantity Theory as the equation of the money market, Walras' Law (Eq. 4.15) linking the money market and all the goods markets, the n excess demand equations of Equation 4.17 (set to zero to express the goods market equilibrium conditions) to represent the n goods markets, and the equation defining the price level (Eq. 4.9). It is important to note, however, that to treat the real balance effect rigorously and to ensure the internal consistency of the model, we can no longer represent the Quantity Theory by Equation 4.14. For, if the demand for goods depends upon real balances, so does the demand for real balances itself, as will be demonstrated in Chapter 5. Thus we can write the demand for nominal balances as:

$$M^D = pf_{n+1}\left(y, \frac{\bar{M}^s}{p}\right)$$

and the excess demand as:

$$M^{XD} = pf_{n+1}\left(y, \frac{\bar{M}^s}{p}\right) - \bar{M}^s$$

These can be considered as the Quantity Theory equations of the money market when amended to take specific account of the real balance effect.

Consistency and Determinateness

First we must examine the model to check that the number of independent equations is sufficient to determine the endogenous variables. There are $(n+2)$ equations of which, by applying Walras' Law, $(n+1)$ are independent. These are exactly sufficient to determine the n relative prices *plus* the absolute price level, or, what is the same thing, the n money prices $(p_1, \ldots, p_i, \ldots, p_n)$ and p, the absolute price level. This, however, is of relatively little interest, since we saw in the last section that the internal consistency of the model is separate from the question of the equality between independent equations and endogenous variables.

Our second task, then, is to consider the internal consistency of the model. Again imagine that the model is initially in equilibrium in all markets and that all money prices and the absolute price level double with no other exogenous change. Once again, this will induce an excess demand for nominal money balances in the money market, as described by the Quantity Theory. For internal consistency, this must be accompanied by equivalent excess supply in the n goods markets, for otherwise Walras' Law would not be satisfied. The real balance effect ensures that this excess supply of goods does occur. For the increase in p reduces the real value of money balances,

$(\bar{M}^S/p)$, and, as suggested by Equation 4.17, this reduction causes the demand for each of the n goods to decline and a negative excess demand (an excess supply) to develop in the goods markets. The rise in the absolute price level in this monetary model, then, throws each market into disequilibrium in such a way that the excess supply in the goods markets and excess demand in the money market are consistent with the relationship between the markets postulated by Walras' Law. It can immediately be seen that Say's Identity is abandoned in this model, for the increase in prices has brought about excess supply of goods as a whole.

We have found, therefore, that the Walrasian monetary model with the real balance effect is internally consistent and does have sufficient equations to determine money prices and the absolute price level. This does not quite complete the analysis, however, since a full discussion of the determinateness of p should consider what forces occur in disequilibrium to bring the economy to a new equilibrium. In the preceding paragraph, the economy has been left dangling in the air, with disequilibrium in all markets having resulted from the increase in money prices and p. This situation is easily resolved if we make an assumption that is common in economics. Assume that when there is excess demand in a market, the price in that market rises, and that it falls when there is excess supply. This, it will be recalled, is the rule that the auctioneer of Walrasian models is assumed to follow. Now, as a result of p and the n money prices being higher than in the initial equilibrium, there is excess supply in all goods markets and excess demand in the money market. Our assumption ensures that the price of each good in terms of money $(p_1, \ldots, p_i, \ldots, p_n)$ falls, and, what comes to the same thing, the price of nominal money balances in terms of goods ($1/p$, or the inverse of the absolute price level) rises. Thus, the disequilibrium brought about by the increase in money prices and p causes a fall in money prices and p until equilibrium is restored. It must be the case that equilibrium is restored only when the money prices and p have fallen to their original level, for at that level there was equilibrium with the given exogenous variables, and since the exogenous variables have not changed, the initial levels of $(p_1, \ldots, p_i, \ldots, p_n)$ and p will again be the equilibrium levels. Thus, the money prices and absolute price level are determinate in this model. Given the exogenous variables, an arbitrary rise in $(p_1, \ldots, p_i, \ldots, p_n)$ and p sets up forces that restore their initial equilibrium levels. The real balance effect, in particular, ensures this result. An arbitrary rise in prices reduces the value of real balances, since the money supply $\bar{M}^S$ is unchanged. This brings about disequilibrium, which is overcome only when prices, and therefore real balances, are restored to their initial levels.

We have demonstrated the internal consistency of this model (and the determinateness of all prices) and pointed out that this is achieved by abandoning Say's Identity. We could equally well note that consistency is achieved by abandoning the Homogeneity Postulate. Since the goods market excess demand equations (Eq. 4.17) contain real balances, $\bar{M}^S/p$, on the right-hand side, excess demands do now depend on the absolute price level. Here p enters as a price variable on its own, whereas, in the model examined in the last section (Eq. 4.8), p enters only in ratios of prices. In the present model, therefore, the excess demand functions for goods are not homogeneous of degree zero in p. In fact, they are not restricted to being homogeneous of any degree in p. Therefore, the money market equation that is derivable from the goods market equations via Walras' Law is not restricted to being homogeneous in p and is the same as the nonhomogeneous excess demand function for money derived from the Quantity Theory.

Neutrality

Finally, it should be noted that in this Walrasian monetary model, which includes the real balance effect, *money is neutral* in the sense explained in Chapter 3. In the experiments we have considered so far, we have held all exogenous variables constant. Now let us construct a different experiment.

Imagine that the model is initially at equilibrium and that the nominal money supply, $\bar{M}^S$, doubles as a result of government policy. This will cause excess demand in each of the n goods markets because it causes real balances, $(\bar{M}^S/p)$, to increase. It will cause excess supply in the money market because the supply of nominal balances has increased, and demand, although raised by this rise in real balances, rises less than $\bar{M}^s$. The forces activated in this disequilibrium will therefore cause a rise in the n money prices of goods and in the absolute price level. The rise will continue until these prices have doubled, for only then will equilibrium be restored. Only when prices have doubled in response to the doubling of the nominal money supply will the real value of money balances, $(\bar{M}^S/p)$, be restored to its initial level, thereby eliminating excess demand in the goods markets. And only then will the demand for nominal balances have increased sufficiently to match the doubling of the supply of nominal balances, thereby eliminating excess supply in the money market. Thus, the doubling of the money supply leads to a new equilibrium level of money prices and the absolute price level where these too have doubled. In consequence, if we compare the new equilibrium with the old, no real variables are changed. Real balances, $(\bar{M}^S/p)$, are unchanged, and relative prices, the ratios of money prices to the absolute price, $(p_1/p, \ldots, p_i/p, \ldots, p_n/p)$, are unchanged, as are the exogenous endowments of goods. Since the demand for each of the n goods (and, in a model more fully specified than the one presented here, the demand for real balances) depends only on these variables, these real demands are unchanged. Therefore, the change in the nominal money supply affects no real variables. Money is neutral in this model.

CHAPTER

FIVE

FURTHER ANALYSIS OF THE REAL BALANCE EFFECT, ITS THEORETICAL BASIS, AND ITS SIGNIFICANCE

In Chapter 4 we saw that Patinkin has shown that a Walrasian monetary model without the real balance effect is internally inconsistent, whereas the inclusion of the real balance effect permits the construction of a consistent Walrasian model of a monetary economy [although it leaves open the question of why money exists (see Chapter 14)]. Patinkin, in fact, goes so far as to argue that the real balance effect is the sine qua non of monetary theory for an exchange economy: without it, monetary theory cannot exist. And, indeed, the real balance effect has, since Patinkin and others began to develop the concept, become an integral part of the dominant macroeconomic models of a monetary economy, as we shall see in Chapter 12, where we consider the Neoclassical-Keynesian synthesis.

In view of its apparent theoretical significance, we have so far devoted insufficient attention to analyzing the real balance effect. In the last chapter we defined the real balance effect simply as the theory that the demands for goods and real balances are positive functions of the real value of money balances. In this chapter we examine in detail the theoretical basis of this proposition. In Sections 5.1 and 5.2 we study its basis in utility theory and discuss the robustness of the theory. In Section 5.3 we investigate the distinction between short-run analysis and long-run analysis of the real balance effect. On the basis of the discussion presented in these sections, we consider, in Section 5.4, whether Patinkin is justified in claiming that the real balance effect is essential for monetary theory.

5.1 UTILITY ANALYSIS AND THE REAL BALANCE EFFECT

We shall conduct our analysis in terms of the Walrasian market model employed by Patinkin and outlined in Chapter 4. The individual begins the week on Monday morning with real balances which have been carried over from the previous week and an endowment of goods which have arrived like manna from heaven. These together constitute the wealth[1] and determine the budget constraint of the individual. The market occurs on Monday, and during it the individual enters into contracts so as to attain desired levels of consumption over the remainder of the week. Any goods bought or sold during the Monday market are delivered during the rest of the week. Goods that are bought and goods that are in the individual's initial endowment and are not sold are consumed in the period from Tuesday through Sunday, so that no goods are carried into the next week. During those six days, discrepancies between goods delivered and goods received are financed by running down or building up the stock of real balances inherited from the previous week. If, at the end of the week, real balances are greater or less than they were on Monday morning, the reason is that in the utility-maximizing trades that occurred during Monday, the individual decided to have greater or less real balances at the end of this week (for use, that is, from Tuesday through Sunday of the following week) than were chosen last week to have at the beginning of this week.

To examine the basis of the real balance effect in the individual's utility-maximizing decisions taken on the Monday, we shall assume that the individual obtains utility from real balances. As we shall see in Section 5.4, this assumption is not strictly necessary. Nevertheless, its rationale in the present model can easily be intuitively understood. The utility of real balances can be thought of as stemming from the desire to avoid bankruptcy in the process of delivering and receiving goods in the next week.

The implication of assuming that the individual derives utility from real balances is that the utility function contains as variables goods to be consumed during the week and real balances to be held at the end of the week:

$$U_\alpha = f_\alpha\left(x_{1\alpha}, \ldots, x_{i\alpha}, \ldots, x_{n\alpha}, \frac{M_\alpha}{p}\right) \tag{5.1}$$

The individual's budget constraint requires that the real values of goods consumed during the week and of real balances held at the end of the week—both chosen in decisions made on Monday—equal the endowment of

[1]More commonly, we would consider the endowment of goods as real income measured as so much per period—per week, in this case. Since, however, in this model we regard the endowment as being a stock at the first moment of the week, and the week is here a purely abstract concept whose length is assumed fixed, the distinction is immaterial in this particular case. The question of whether models in terms of flows are equivalent to those in terms of stocks is discussed more fully in Chap. 16, Secs. 16.1 and 16.3.

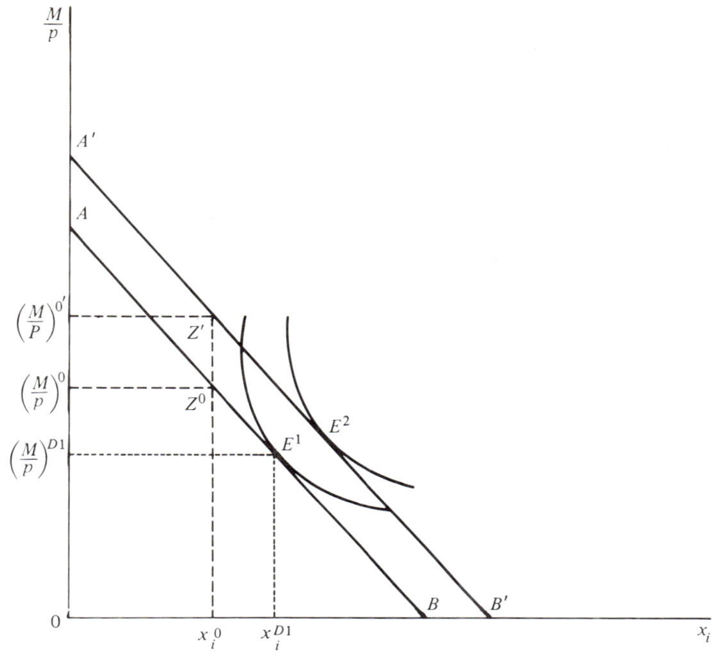

Figure 5-1

goods and the stock of real balances that the individual holds when waking on Monday:

$$\sum_{i=1}^{n} \frac{p_i}{p} \bar{x}_{i\alpha}^{s} + \frac{\bar{M}_{\alpha}^{s}}{p} = \sum_{i=1}^{n} \frac{p_i}{p} x_{i\alpha}^{D} + \frac{M_{\alpha}^{D}}{p} \tag{5.2}$$

We shall analyze diagrammatically the process of maximizing the utility function subject to the budget constraint.[2]

Wealth and Substitution Effects

Consider Figure 5.1. It isolates the problem of choice between two items that enter the utility function, real balances on the vertical axis and good x_i on the horizontal axis; we shall for the moment ignore the other goods in the economy although they remain present. Suppose that the initial endowment is

[2]As seen in Sec. 4.2, this budget constraint can be considered as the basis of Walras' Law in a monetary economy (Eq. 4.10). If we consider Eq. 5.2 as an aggregate of individuals' budget constraints (we write it, that is, without the subscript), rearrange terms, and multiply both sides by p, we obtain an equation with the excess demand for nominal balances on one side and the sum of the excess demands for goods (multiplied by minus unity) on the other side, as in Eq. 4.15.

represented by the point Z^0—an endowment of x_i^0 of the good and a stock $(M/p)^0$ of real balances carried over from the previous week. The budget line AB must, as illustrated, go through point Z^0. The slope of the budget line is the rate at which the individual can exchange *good* x_i for real balances. Two factors determine this: first, the money price p_i of *good* x_i, since this is the rate of exchange between x_i and nominal money balances; second, the absolute price level p, since this determines the rate of transformation between nominal and real balances. Thus, the slope of the budget line $0A/0B$ is determined by the ratio of the money price of x_i and the absolute price level, p_i/p. Utility is maximized at E^1 where the consumption demand for the good is x_i^{D1} and the demand for real balances to hold at the end of the week is $(M/p)^{D1}$. The excess demand for the good is $x_i^{XD1} = x_i^{D1} - x_i^0$, that for real balances is $(M/p)^{XD1} = (M/p)^{D1} - (M/p)^0$.[3]

Clearly the individual's demand and excess demand for good x_i is a function of the initial endowment of goods and stock of real balances, $(M/p)^0$, and of the relative price of x_i in terms of real balances, p_i/p. These determine the slope and intercept of the budget line.[4] Thus, the absolute price level is a variable in the excess demand function, for it affects both the slope and the intercept of the budget line. Suppose the money price of good x_i (and those of all other goods) and the absolute price level were to fall *ceteris paribus*. The budget line would shift rightward to $A'B'$ because the initial stock of real balances would be higher at $(M/p)^{0'}$, and with the given endowment of goods, the budget line must go through Z'. The individual would then be in equilibrium at E^2, with a higher demand and excess demand for good x_i (and a higher demand for real balances). Thus, there is a real balance effect in the demand for good x_i; a change in the real value of initial money balances affects the demand for the goods x_i.

This example is a pure wealth effect: the change in real balances causes a parallel shift in the budget line. It is analogous to the income effect in the customary microeconomic models of demand theory. We could also use Figure 5.1 to imagine a substitution effect. If the money price of good x_i fell while the money prices of all other goods remained unchanged, the absolute price level would fall but by a smaller proportion than p_i. In consequence, the ratio p_i/p would fall, and in the figure the budget line would become less steep, leading to a higher demand for x_i.

Generalizing to explicitly introduce other goods and aggregating over all individuals, this analysis implies excess demand functions for goods of the form:

$$x_i^{XD} = f_i\left(\frac{p_1}{p}, \ldots, \frac{p_i}{p}, \ldots, \frac{p_n}{p}, \sum_{i=1}^{n} \frac{p_i}{p}\bar{x}_i^s + \frac{\bar{M}^s}{p}\right) - \bar{x}_i^s$$

$$(i = 1, \ldots, n) \qquad (5.3)$$

[3]In this example, $(M/p)^{XD1}$ is negative—there is an excess supply of real balances.

[4]In addition, if our diagram could represent the remaining $(n-1)$ goods, we would see that the demand for x_i also depends on the ratios of *their* money prices to the absolute price level.

These are the same as the excess demand functions employed in Chapter 4 (Eq. 4.17) and include the real balance effect.

Pure Wealth Effect

In Chapter 4 we considered only the pure wealth effect aspect of the real balance effect. The experiments we discussed all assumed an equiproportionate change in all money prices and the absolute price level. This, strictly speaking, is appropriate to the definition of the real balance effect. Since we are concerned, therefore, with fixed relative prices of goods, we can analyze the real balance effect most conveniently using Figure 5.2. Here, instead of representing just one good on the horizontal axis, we represent G, goods as a whole. G is strictly defined as a "composite commodity," and Hicks (1946) and Patinkin (1965) have demonstrated what assumptions are necessary for us to be able to treat the set of goods as one "composite commodity" (one possible justification being that their relative prices are fixed). It should be noted that in Figure 5.2, in contrast with Figure 5.1, the absolute price level determines only the intercept of the budget line, not its slope. The slope is invariant because one unit of real balances is by definition equal to one unit of the "composite commodity": it is a measure of the quantity of goods that a

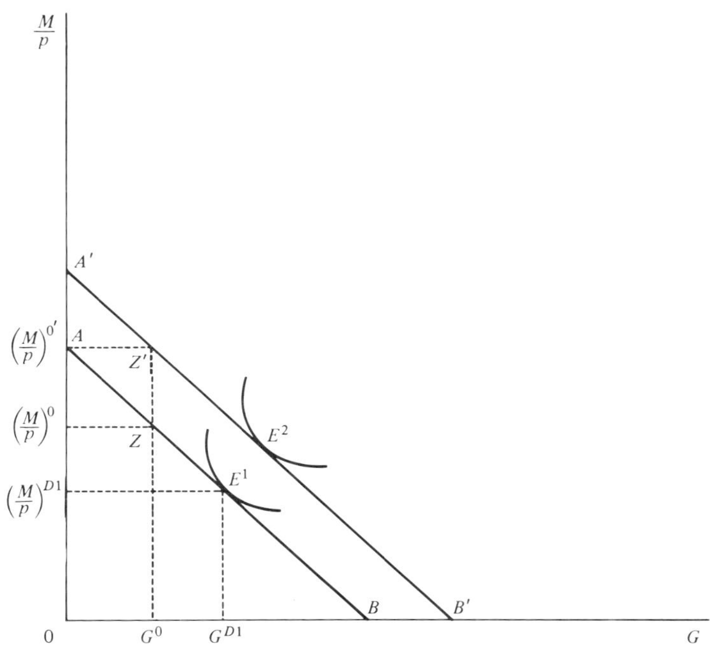

Figure 5-2

unit of nominal balances can buy. If p rises, a unit of *nominal* balances will buy less of G, but a unit of *real* balances will buy the same amount. Thus, the slope of the budget line $0A/0B$ in Figure 5.2 is always (minus) 1. The budget constraint represented by budget line AB is Figure 5.2 is

$$(M/p)_0 + G_0 = (M/p)^D + G^D \quad \text{or} \quad (M/p)^{XD} + G^{XD} = 0$$

This can be written as

$$(M/p)^{XD} = (-1)G^{XD} \quad \text{or} \quad (M/p)^{XD} \div G^{XD} = -1$$

This follows from the fact that the rate of exchange between real balances and the composite commodity is unity.

Figure 5.2 can be used to illustrate the real balance effect in the strict sense of a pure wealth effect. It cannot illustrate the substitution effect because it is based on the assumption that relative prices are fixed, so that goods are treated as one composite good with a 1 : 1 rate of exchange with real balances, and this assumption implies that the budget line always has a slope of -1. Suppose that the individual has an initial endowment of goods of G^0 and a stock of real balances of $(M/p)^0$. The budget line is then AB going through Z^0. Equilibrium will be reached at E^1, with $(M/p)^{D1}$ and G^{D1} being the amounts of real balances and goods demanded. If all money prices and the absolute price level were to fall, *ceteris paribus*, the budget line would shift to $A'B'$ going through Z', since the stock of real balances would be higher while the endowment of goods is unchanged. Equilibrium would then be established at E^2, with a higher demand (and excess demand) for goods and a higher demand for real balances.

This analysis therefore provides a basis for the real balance effect, the proposition that a change in real balances induces a change in the demand for goods. The change in real balances may be caused, for example, by a change in the absolute price level, although it could equally well be caused by a change in the stock of nominal balances. Although we have constructed Figure 5.2 by reference to the individual, it may be assumed that there are no difficulties in aggregating the resulting demand functions over individuals to obtain the aggregate demand function for goods as a whole (the "composite commodity"):

$$G^D = f\left(\sum_{i=1}^{n} \frac{p_i}{p}\,\bar{x}_i^s + \frac{\bar{M}^s}{p}\right) \tag{5.4}$$

We shall see in Chapter 12 that this aggregate demand function for goods that includes the real balance effect is also known as a consumption function based on the *Pigou Effect*.

Although the utility analysis discussed here appears simple and unexceptionable, it has given rise to several controversies. These are examined in the remaining sections of this chapter.

5.2 ASSUMPTIONS CONCERNING EXPECTATIONS AND WEALTH

Two assumptions that are implicit in Section 5.1's analysis of the real balance effect are open to question.

The first concerns the nature of money balances as wealth. As we saw in Chapter 3, money balances are a component of net wealth for an individual. In fact, we are considering it as the only asset, the only thing that can be held from one week to the next. But we also saw in that chapter that if it is inside money, then, on one interpretation, it cannot be considered as net wealth to the private sector as a whole. If we follow that interpretation and if all money is inside money, we cannot sum the individuals' demand functions or excess demand functions for goods to obtain aggregate demand functions based on the real balance effect. One individual's money balances are another's liability; a fall in prices increases the real value of the former's assets and increases the latter's liabilities. So the net effect is that the real value of the private sector's net wealth remains unchanged at zero. For the real balance effect to be significant, it must therefore be the case that not all money is inside money or that, as Pesek and Saving (1967) argue, even inside money is, in fact, a component of the private sector's net wealth. An alternative assumption that would justify summing individuals' demand functions to obtain an aggregate demand function in an inside money economy would be the notion that there is a *distribution effect* within the private sector. That is, those whose real liabilities increase (meaning that their real net wealth decreases) reduce their demand for goods by less than the increase in the demand of those whose real wealth rises, even though the change in real value of the former's liabilities equals that of the latter's assets. Such distribution effects, however, are generally assumed to be absent in modern monetary theory.

The second assumption implicit in Section 5.1's analysis concerns the individual's expectations. Recall that the individual's optimum real balances are intended for use in the next week. But, suppose that next week's absolute price level is found to be unexpectedly different from this week's. If it is higher, the individual will then find that the real balances available for financing transactions in the next week are lower than the real balances which, in this week's plan, were to be carried into next week. Equally, this may, however, not come as a complete surprise, for the individual may have expected a fall in prices next week, but the basic model we have considered does not explicitly recognize the role of such expectations. In our model, the individual must be interpreted as having a one-week horizon, never thinking further than the endowment and price level of the present week. This is obviously rather paradoxical since the individual's behavior this week—his or her demand for real balances and therefore demand for goods—is based on the desire for real balances to be used in the next week.

Ambiguity of Effects of Expectations

We can easily overcome this paradox by assuming that the individual expects next week's absolute price level to be the same as this week's. But such an assumption would be arbitrary and would make it difficult to apply the theory of the real balance effect to reality. Alternatively, we can explore the effect on the model of expectations that next week's price level will differ from this week's. Figure 5.2 is ill-suited to such an exercise, since the variables represented there all refer to the present week. The only way in which we could consider expectations in that figure would be by assuming that the indifference curves shift if expectations change. Let us say that the indifference curves drawn in Figure 5.2 are those that exist when the individual expects next week's absolute price level will be the same as this week's. If, instead, the individual were to expect that next week's absolute price level will be lower (or higher), we might imagine the indifference curves shifting so that a greater or smaller demand for real balances occurs. It is impossible to know, however, in which direction the indifference curves will shift: Will the expectation of lower prices cause a shift in the curves in such a way that greater or lesser amounts of goods are demanded this week?

The problem and the impossibility of answering this question are best examined by using a two-period figure. Figure 5.3 represents goods available

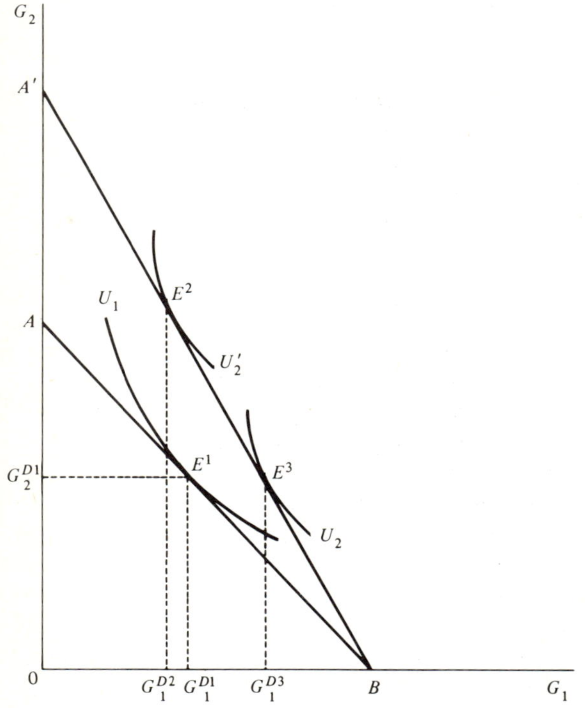

Figure 5-3

for consumption this week, G_1, on the horizontal axis and next week's goods, G_2, on the vertical axis. We can interpret G_2 as being equivalent to the real value next week of money balances chosen and carried forward from this week if we assume that the individual receives no goods in next Monday's endowment and that goods cannot be held from this week to the next (this assumption is made for simplicity in considering expectations and is relaxed in Section 5.3). The indifference curves indicate that the individual has a set of preferences between present and future consumption. In fact, the slope of an indifference curve at a particular point reflects the individual's rate of time preference, the concept discussed in Chapter 2: the steeper is the tangent to an indifference curve at a particular point, the higher is the rate of time preference—or the marginal rate of substitution between future and present consumption—at that point. The horizontal intercept of the budget line AB is determined by this period's endowment of goods and initial stock of real balances, for these determine the maximum possible amount of this week's consumption, $0B$. Its slope, $0A/0B$, could be determined by the ratio of this week's absolute price level, p_1, to next week's p_2. But since next week's actual price level is not known this week, the slope $0A/0B$ must be conceived as the ratio of p_1 to the expected level of next week's prices, $p^e_{1.2}$.

The budget line AB is drawn with a slope of (-1), which implies that the individual expects next week's absolute price level to be the same as this week's: $(p_1/p^e_{1.2}) = 1$. The individual will then be in equilibrium at E^1, demanding goods this week equal to G_1^{D1} and choosing real balances this week equal to G_2^{D1}, for these real balances would permit consumption of G_2^{D1} next week. Now assume that next week's prices are expected to be lower than this week's, so that $(p_1/p^e_{1.2}) > 1$. We will then have the new budget line $A'B$, which is steeper than AB because the individual, if consuming nothing this week and carrying $0B$ of real balances (valued at p_1) into next week, can obtain more goods next week if next week's prices are lower than this week's (the individual could obtain A' instead of A).

This brings us to the nub of the problem. With expectations of a fall in the price level, would the individual reach equilibrium at E^2 or E^3? Utility theory provides no answer to this question. The outcome is ambiguous, for the indifference curve map may take the form represented by either U_2 or U'_2. The problem arises because the substitution effect of a decline in $p^e_{1.2}$, the expected price of G_2, unambiguously leads to a decline in the demand for the current week's goods, G_1^D, whereas the wealth effect, as we saw above, is assumed to increase the demand for G_1 (and the current demand for real balances).[5] The relative strengths of these opposing forces cannot be known a priori, and therefore the net outcome may be E^2, E^3, or another position.

This ambiguity has serious consequences for the real balance effect. It

[5]Note that here the substitution and wealth effects are those resulting from a change in expected future prices, whereas, in Sec. 5.1, we were concerned with the effect of a change in present prices, assuming that expected future prices equal present prices.

implies that we cannot unambiguously predict the effect of changes in expectations upon this week's demand for real balances and goods. If next week's price level is expected to be the same as this week's, the demand for goods this week will be measured by $0G_1^{D1}$ and this week's demand for real balances will be $(0B - 0G_1^{D1})$. If an expected fall in prices causes equilibrium to be reached at E^2 instead of E^1, this week's demand for goods will be lower at $0G_1^{D2}$, and the demand for real balances valued at this week's prices will be correspondingly higher at $(0B - 0G_1^{D2})$. But it may equally well cause equilibrium to be reached at E^3. In that case, this week's demand for goods will be higher at $0G_1^{D3}$ and demand for real balances lower.

Most significant for the real balance effect is the fact that expectations concerning next week's prices and their relationship to this week's prices may be determined by what happens to this week's prices. Suppose that the absolute price level this week is initially p_1^1 and that next week's price level is expected to be the same, $p_{1.2}^{e1} = p_1^1$. Then the budget line will be AB, as illustrated in Figure 5.4, equilibrium will be at E^1, by assumption, and this

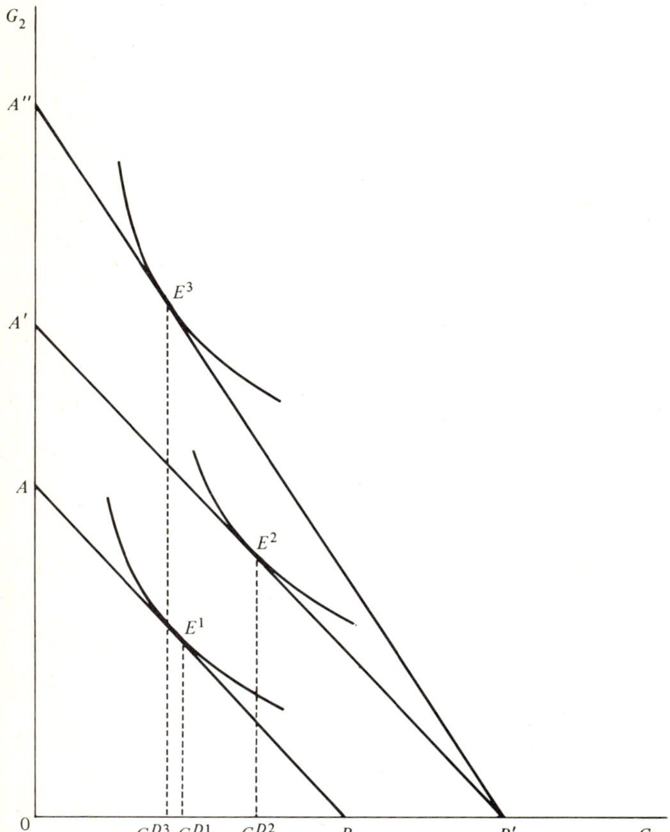

Figure 5-4

week's demand for goods will be G_1^{D1}. Now suppose that within the current week, the absolute price level falls from p_1^1 to p_1^2 and that next week's price level is now expected to be the same as the new current price level, $p_{1.2}^{e2} = p_1^2$. The budget line will then shift to $A'B'$ (parallel to AB). Bearing in mind that the theory of the real balance effect assumes that the wealth effect on the demand for current goods and real balances is positive, we see that this may lead to a shift of equilibrium from E^1 to E^2, and that the demand for goods in this period will increase to G_1^{D2} as a result of the real balance effect. Now assume that the fall in the absolute price level during this week leads to expectations that the absolute price level will fall yet further in the next week, so that $p_{1.2}^{e2} < p_1^2$. Then the new budget line will be $A''B'$ and equilibrium may be established at E^3. At such a point, the demand for goods in the current period, G_1^{D3}, is lower than the demand for goods, G_1^{D1}, that existed before the current absolute price level fell from p_1^1 to p_1^2. The increase in real balances caused by a drop in the absolute price level would in this case, therefore, lead to a *fall* in this week's demand for goods instead of an increase, as predicted in the basic theory of the real balance effect.[6]

Thus, the existence of what one could consider to be a realistic process of expectations formation—the idea that a change leads to expectations of further changes in the same direction—may cause the real balance effect to work in the opposite direction from that assumed by Patinkin. The intuitive rationale for this result is as follows: What we have called the substitution effect in the discussion of Figures 5.3 and 5.4 reflects the idea that if one expects next week's prices to be lower than this week's, one will choose to postpone consumption and therefore consume less this week. In other words, one would choose to hold large money balances at the end of this week so that one will benefit from the increase in their real value that arises from the expected fall in prices.

We can see from the argument in this section that at the theoretical level, the existence of the real balance effect is not a foregone conclusion. At the aggregate level, it rests on an assumption concerning the nature of money as net wealth. At the individual level, once we introduce price expectations, we cannot preclude the possibility that a rise in real wealth (induced by a fall in the absolute price level) causes a decline in the demand for goods.

5.3 LONG-RUN AND SHORT-RUN ANALYSIS

Hitherto, we have essentially been concerned with analyzing the real balance effect by examining behavior within one week. Even though, in Section 5.2 when considering expectations, we did introduce the relationship between this

[6]In the Walrasian model employed by Patinkin, it is difficult to conceive of a fall in p during a week. To be more rigorous, we should think of p_1^2 being less than p_1^1 without conceiving of a change taking place. We are then thinking merely of two separate regimes for the model.

week and next, we focused primarily on how expectations concerning next week influence this week's behavior. We must now abandon this restricted analysis and consider the individual's behavior over a sequence of weeks. By doing precisely this, Archibald and Lipsey (1958) produced a significant critique of Patinkin's theory as he had presented it in the first edition of his book (1956).

Goods and Money

Employing the same assumptions as Patinkin—especially, ignoring expectations—and examining the individual's behavior over a sequence of weeks, Archibald and Lipsey demonstrate that there is a unique equilibrium point to which the individual will move over a succession of weeks. In particular, if the endowment of goods received each Monday morning is constant, the eventual result of a fall in the absolute price level disturbing the initial equilibrium will be that individuals return to their initial equilibrium where their demand for goods (and real balances) is the same as in the initial equilibrium. Thus, in the eventual equilibrium position, the demand for goods is unaffected by the increase in the real value of money balances in the first week.

To understand the argument, we should distinguish between the concepts of temporary equilibrium and full equilibrium for the individual. We shall define full equilibrium as a utility-maximizing demand for goods and real balances in any one week such that there is no tendency for the following week's demands to be different unless there is a change in some exogenous variable, such as the absolute price level or the endowment, that is not under the individual's control. By contrast, temporary equilibrium is defined by the utility-maximizing demand for goods and real balances in any one week irrespective of whether those demands can, without a change in exogenous variables, be maintained in subsequent weeks.

Figure 5.5 can be used to elucidate the meanings of temporary and full equilibrium and to demonstrate Archibald and Lipsey's conclusion. It is an extension of Figure 5.2 to allow consideration of a sequence of weeks, and, similarly, it ignores the role of price expectations by assuming $p^e_{1.2} = p_1$. Suppose that the individual has in week 1 the budget line AB and that equilibrium is established at E^0 with a demand for goods of G^{D0} and for real balances of $(M/p)^{D0}$. For simplicity, we shall also assume that the person's endowment of goods $\bar{G}^s$ and initial stock of real balances are equal to G^{D0} and $(M/p)^{D0}$ respectively. Imagine that in the first week the absolute price level falls so that the budget line shifts rightward to A^1B^1. Now, instead of reaching equilibrium at E^0, the individual's equilibrium will be at E^1, with demands for goods and real balances that, at G^{D1} and $(M/p)^{D1}$, will be higher than they were before the fall in prices. This result is the real balance effect analyzed within the context of a single week. It is the same as the result we obtained in Section 15.1's analysis of the real balance effect. Now, however,

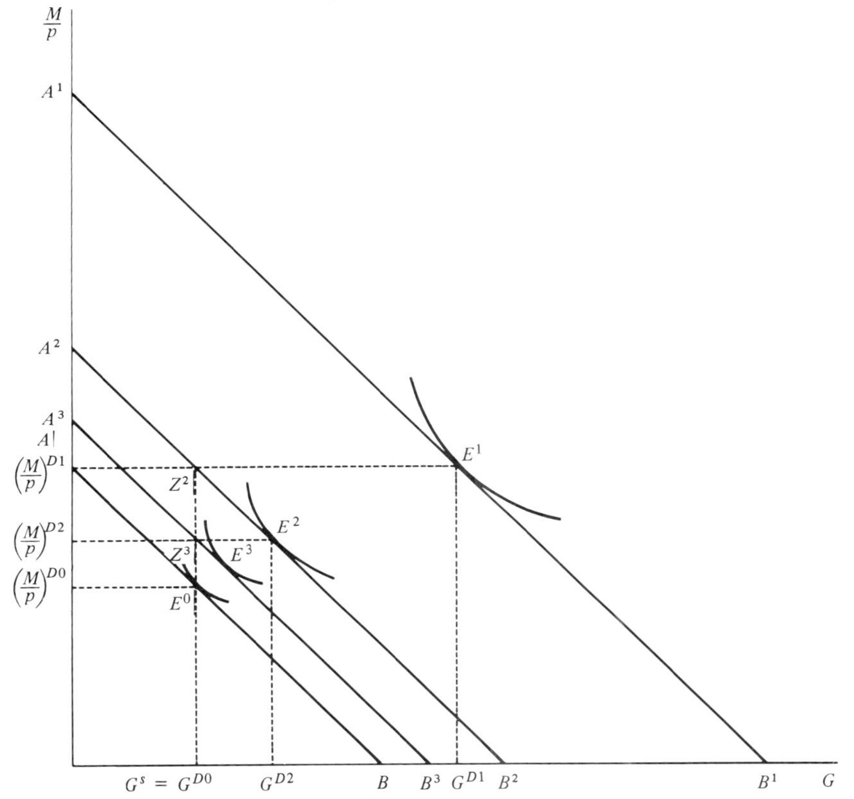

Figure 5-5

we can see that E^1 is only a point of temporary equilibrium. Next week's equilibrium will not be at the same point. The real balances with which the individual chooses to end week 1 are $(M/p)^{D1}$. Thus, $(M/p)^{D1}$ represents the real balances at the beginning of week 2. These, together with the unchanging endowment of goods, $\bar{G}^s$, ensure that the budget line for week 2 goes through Z^2 and is, therefore, A^2B^2. With this budget line, the individual will reach equilibrium in week 2 at E^2 where the demand for real balances is $(M/p)^{D2}$. This level of real balances is what is carried into week 3, and since it is lower than the real balances that were carried into week 2, $(M/p)^{D1}$, the budget line in week 3 must be further to the left. Week 3's budget line is A^3B^3 through Z^3 and the individual reaches equilibrium at E^3. By similar reasoning, $(M/p)^{D3}$ ensures that week 4's budget line will be to the left of week 3's. Clearly, this process will repeat itself until the budget line AB is reached. But this budget line is the same as the one that applied in week 1 before the fall in prices. Therefore, when budget line AB is reached, the individual's equilibrium will be at E^0 and the demand for goods and real balances will be the same as in the initial equilibrium, G^{D0} and $(M/p)^{D0}$. The change in real balances that resulted from week 1's fall in prices leads eventually to an equilibrium position where the demand for goods and real balances are the same as they were before the price fall.

Moreover, this equilibrium point is full equilibrium. Once at E^0, there is nothing to cause next week's equilibrium to differ from it unless there is a change in an exogenous variable (such as another fall in the price level). $(M/p)^{D0}$ real balances will be demanded and therefore carried into the next week, and next week's endowment of goods will again be G^{D0} $(=\bar{G}^s)$, so that next week's budget line will again be AB and equilibrium will be established at E^0. It is clear from this that the definition of full equilibrium requires the weekly endowment of goods to be fully consumed at that point. If that were not the case, the individual would build up real balances (or run them down by consuming more than the endowment), next week's budget line would therefore be different from this week's, and a different equilibrium position would be reached.

Archibald and Lipsey's conclusion that a change in real balances leads to no long-run or permanent change in the demand for goods appears at first sight to be completely destructive of the real balance effect. We shall see in Section 5.4, however, that this is not so and that the real balance effect survives this attack unscathed. In the rest of the present section, we consider a question different from that of whether Archibald and Lipsey's invariance result negates the real balance effect. We discuss whether this invariance is achieved only on the basis of special assumptions or whether it can be generalized. In particular, does the invariance result necessarily hold if the model is extended to allow for the existence of bonds or other assets that can be held from one period to the next and yield income to their owner? Contrary to the assertion of Clower and Burstein (1960) that Archibald and Lipsey's result does hold in such a model, Liviatin (1965) has demonstrated that in general it does not.

Goods, Money, and Bonds

In order to be clear on the nature of Liviatin's argument, we must begin by isolating the essential structure of Archibald and Lipsey's model. The lines illustrated in Figure 5.6 enable us to do this. The line LL' is the locus of points of full (or long-run) equilibrium. It must be a vertical line above the given endowment of goods, $\bar{G}^s$, since we have seen that only if the endowment is exactly consumed can full equilibrium exist. The line SS' is the locus of temporary equilibria and consists of points such as E^0, E^1, E^2, and E^3 in Figure 5.5, points of tangency between the budget line and an indifference curve as the budget line changes its intercept. The line SS' slopes upward because of the fundamental assumption of the real balance effect—that real balances and goods are not inferior commodities with respect to real wealth. The lines LL' and SS' are the skeletons of Archibald and Lipsey's analysis in

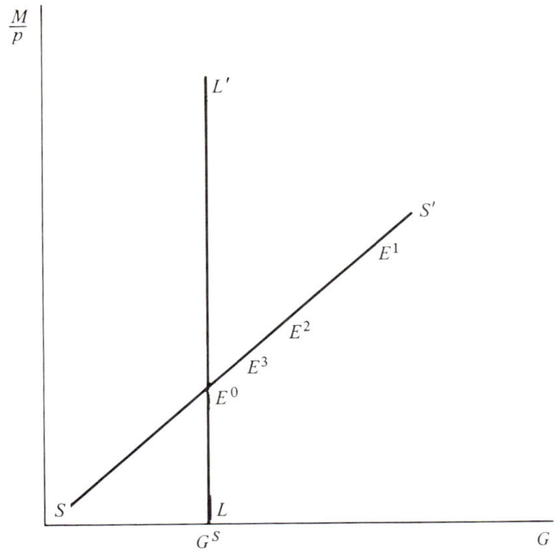

Figure 5-6

Figure 5.5. Points on SS' are attainable in any one week, but only one such point is simultaneously a point of full equilibrium. This is the point of intersection between LL' and SS', that is, E^0. This point of full equilibrium is both unique (since it is the only intersection of SS' and LL') and stable. It is stable because, as we have seen, since SS' slopes upward to the right and LL' is vertical, a move from E_0 to any other point on SS' would cause an adjustment over several weeks until E_0 is regained.

Now, by introducing bonds into the model, such a unique, stable, full equilibrium position may never be reached. This is so because the inclusion of bonds changes the slope of LL', the locus of full equilibrium points. The SS' locus of temporary equilibria has the same properties as in Archibald and Lipsey's money-only model, but LL' now slopes upward to the right instead of being vertical. These features are illustrated in Figures 5.7, 5.8, and 5.9, but to explain them and the conclusions that follow, it is first necessary to note that the axes of these figures represent variables different from those of the money-only model of Figure 5.6. The vertical axis measures end-of-week assets, assets held at the beginning of the following week, but these now consist of the real value of money balances plus the real value of bonds rather than the former alone. The vertical axis, therefore, measures $A/p = M/p + B/p$ where B is the nominal value of bonds. The horizontal axis again measures consumption of goods and, in this instance, services. In Liviatin's model, it is measured by z, which consists not only of consumption goods, but also the liquidity services of real money balances.

These changes in the definitions of the variables on the axes do not by themselves change the conclusions of the model. The essential difference between this model and the money-only model stems from the altered

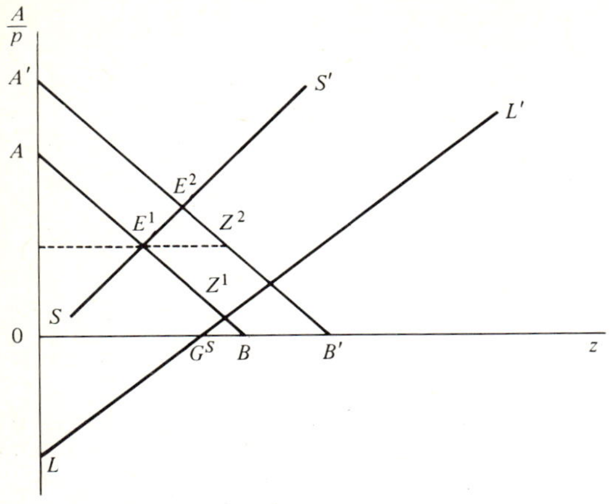

Figure 5-7

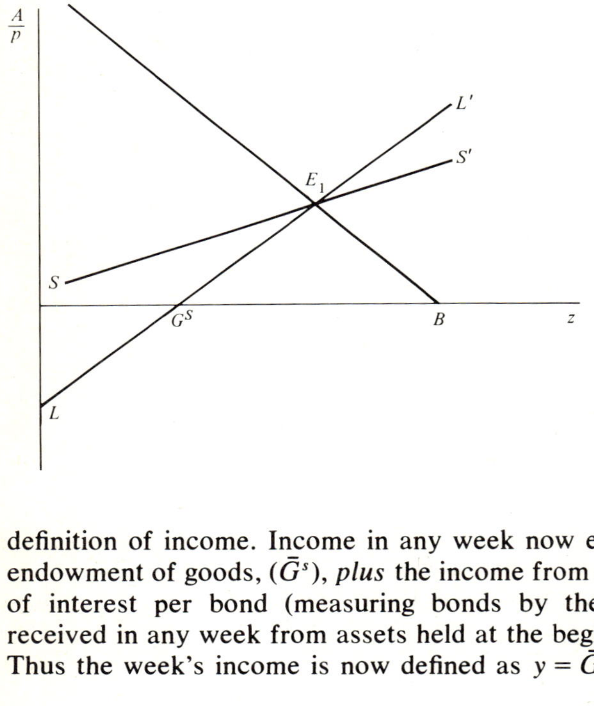

Figure 5-8

definition of income. Income in any week now equals the (constant) weekly endowment of goods, ($\bar{G}^s$), *plus* the income from asset holding. If r is the rate of interest per bond (measuring bonds by their real value), the income received in any week from assets held at the beginning of that week is rA/p.[7] Thus the week's income is now defined as $y = \bar{G}^s + r(A/p)$. This redefinition

[7]We use r, the bond interest rate, to represent the rate of interest on all assets (bonds *and* money) even though the explicit rate of interest on money is zero. We do this because we assume that money balances give an implicit yield in the form of liquidity and security from bankruptcy, and that this implicit yield equals the bond rate of interest at the margin. Bearing in mind the arguments of Chap. 3, we must define bonds as being of the truly outside variety (for example, government bonds backed by state-owned industrial assets) if r is to represent net income.

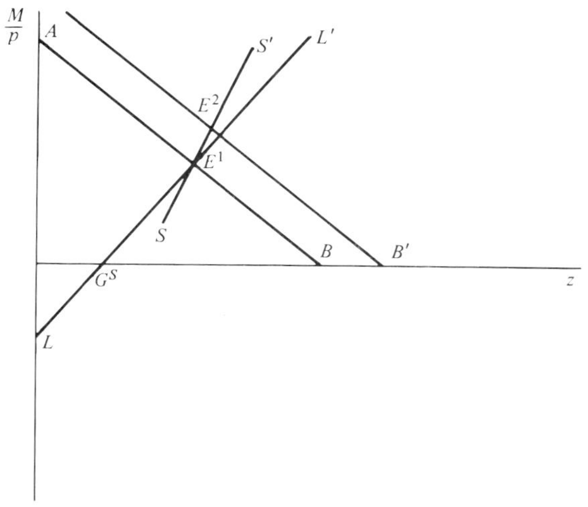

Figure 5-9

of income ensures that the LL' curve slopes upward to the right instead of being vertical. Recall that LL' represents points where all the week's income is consumed ($y = z$), so that no saving or dissaving occurs. Now, the higher are the week's initial assets A/p, measured on the vertical axis, the higher is income y. For full equilibrium, therefore, the higher are initial assets, the higher must be z, measured on the horizontal axis. Thus, the LL' curve slopes upward to indicate this relationship. The horizontal intercept of LL' is $\bar{G}^s$ (indicating that when initial assets are zero, the only form of income is the endowment of goods), and its slope is determined by r, the interest rate.

An upward-sloping LL' line may give rise to any of the three relationships between LL' and SS', illustrated in Figures 5.7, 5.8, and 5.9. Consider Figure 5.7. If the loci take the positions indicated there, the individual may never reach a point of full equilibrium since there is no point at which SS' intersects LL'. Suppose the budget line is initially AB, so that the individual's temporary equilibrium in the first week is E^1. This is not a point of full equilibrium since it is not on LL'; in fact, at E^1 the individual is a net saver since, being to the left of LL' at that week's asset level, the individual fails to consume all the week's income. As a result of this saving, next week's budget line is further to the right at $A'B'$. It goes through Z^2 because the next week begins with the assets chosen at E^1 in week 1 and income that is higher than in week 1 because of the income earned on the additional assets accumulated in week 1. With the budget line $A'B'$ in week 2, the individual reaches temporary equilibrium at E^2. Again, this position involves net saving and the budget line in week 3 is further to the right. It can be seen that full equilibrium will never be reached, and in each week the individual's consumption z and real assets A/p will be higher than in the preceding week.

This conclusion is clearly different from Archibald and Lipsey's. Figure 5.8, however, indicates that the relative slopes of SS' and LL' may be such that, as in Archibald and Lipsey's model, there is a unique, stable, full equilibrium. There, the individual, if at any temporary equilibrium other than E^1, will be accumulating assets (if to the left of E^1) or running them down (if to the right), so that, over successive weeks, the budget line moves toward AB where the temporary equilibrium is also full equilibrium. Although this result is similar to Archibald and Lipsey's, it differs inasmuch as E^1 is determined not only by the commodity endowment, $\bar{G}^s$, but also by the bond rate of interest that determines the slope of LL'.

Lastly, Figure 5.9 illustrates the possibility that a nonvertical LL' line may permit the existence of a unique full equilibrium E^1, but one that is not stable. Because the SS' curve is steeper than the LL' curve, any divergence from full equilibrium will lead to an explosive movement further away from equilibrium. Suppose, for example, that a fall in the absolute price level causes the budget line to shift to $A'B'$. Temporary equilibrium will then be established at E^2, and at that point, since it is to the left of the LL' line, the individual is saving. In consequence, next week's budget line will be further to the right. This process will continue ad infinitum as long as E^1 is the only point where SS' intersects LL'.

We have seen, therefore, that Archibald and Lipsey's conclusion cannot unambiguously be assumed to exist in a model where both money and bonds (or other interest-bearing assets) are available.

5.4 ASSESSMENT OF THE SIGNIFICANCE OF THE REAL BALANCE EFFECT

As we saw in Chapter 4, Patinkin has proposed that the real balance effect is a necessary postulate for Walrasian monetary models. It is the sine qua non of such monetary theory since it provides the necessary link between the money market and the goods market. But this proposition has been criticized.

One criticism is based on Archibald and Lipsey's work, for they claim to have shown that on examining positions of full equilibrium, no real balance effect exists. In full equilibrium, the demand for goods and real balances is unaffected by disturbances in initial real balances; therefore, they would argue, no real balance effect exists in full equilibrium. This interpretation of Archibald and Lipsey's invariance result is, however, mistaken. The real balance effect is the theory that the demand and excess demand *functions* for goods (and real balances) contain real balances as variables. The functions implicit in Archibald and Lipsey's model do have this property even at points of full equilibrium, and so the real balance effect does exist there. The model shows, not that the demand functions are independent of real balances, but that the individual's full equilibrium position is independent of an initial change in real balances. This is true because the real balances that enter the demand functions return over time to their initial level.

Moreover, Archibald and Lipsey's result is a trivial one from the point of view of building aggregate models of the economy. This is so not only because it cannot unambiguously be generalized to an individual in a world where both money and bonds exist, but also because it applies to an individual rather than to the economy as a whole. If we consider the effect on aggregate behavior of an initial fall in the absolute price level so that all individuals' budget lines shift rightward, the immediate effect will be excess demand in the goods market. As we saw in Chapter 4, this will induce a rise in the absolute price level so that it returns to its initial value. Each individual's budget line returns to its initial position in the same week, so the analysis of each individual's behavior in successive weeks is irrelevant.

Real or Nominal Balances?

A more substantial criticism of the importance of the real balance effect is that of Lloyd (1962), although it too is ill-founded, as we shall see. Lloyd argues that a unique and stable price level can be shown to exist even if real balances are not a variable in the utility function. In his model, by contrast with Patinkin's, utility is a function of goods and *nominal*, rather than real, balances:

$$U_\alpha = f_\alpha(x_{1\alpha}, \ldots, x_{i\alpha}, \ldots, x_{n\alpha}, M_\alpha) \tag{5.5}$$

He attempts to demonstrate that these nominal balances provide the link between the goods and money markets that ensures the determinateness of the absolute price level.

To examine the uniqueness and stability of the price level in this model, let us conduct the same experiment as in Section 4.4. Assume that the economy is initially in equilibrium at the prevailing set of absolute and relative prices; at those prices there is no excess supply or demand for goods in aggregate. Now suppose that, with everything else unchanged, there is an equiproportionate change in the money prices of all commodities—they all double, for example. As a result, the real value of the individual's resources falls, for the real value of the endowment of goods is unchanged but the real value of the money balances falls. Now, even though the individual's utility is affected, not by the real value of the money held at the end of the period, but only by its nominal value, this change in the real value of the initial balances must affect the individual's behavior: with the higher price level, the money will not go so far as it would at the lower level. If the individual wishes to finish the period with the same amount of nominal balances as would have existed at the lower price level, less goods must be consumed; the individual who wishes to consume the same amount of goods must finish the week with a lower amount of nominal balances.

We may assume that at this higher price level, the individual desires to consume less goods and hold more nominal balances than would otherwise have been held. That is because the rise in the price level is, in effect, a change in the relative price of goods and money: goods having become dearer in terms of nominal money balances (although, as seen in Section 5.1, the relative price of goods and real balances is unchanged). From this, there is a substitution effect in the direction of increasing desired holdings of nominal balances and decreasing consumption. There is also a wealth effect that may offset the substitution effect, but it is assumed not to. As a result of the doubling of prices, then, there is a fall in all individuals' demands for goods. This creates an excess supply of goods and a fall in their money prices. Prices will continue to fall until they have reattained their initial level, for only then will excess supply again be zero. Thus, even in this model where the individual's utility is a function of nominal rather than real balances, there is a unique equilibrium price level that is stable in the sense that, at any other price level, forces would exist that would cause the price level to move toward this equilibrium.

This analysis is illustrated in Figure 5.10, which has nominal rather than real balances on the vertical axis. The individual's initial budget line is AB, for the endowment of commodities is $\bar{G}^s$, the initial nominal money balances are M^0, and the price level is such that one unit of commodities can be exchanged for $0A/0B$ money balances. With this budget line the individual's equilibrium is at E^1: the equilibrium demand for goods is G^{D1} and the desired holding of nominal balances is M^{D1}. We assume that, aggregating over all individuals, the economy is in equilibrium because this individual's excess demand for goods is balanced by other individuals' excess supplies (and similarly for the first individual's excess supply of nominal balances). Now suppose that the price level is higher. The slope of the budget line will change, so that the new budget line $A'B'$ exists. This will involve a new equilibrium, say E^2, where the individual's demand for goods, G^{D2}, is less than it was previously and the desired holdings of nominal balances are greater. That is, due to the rise in the price level, the individual's excess demand for commodities falls

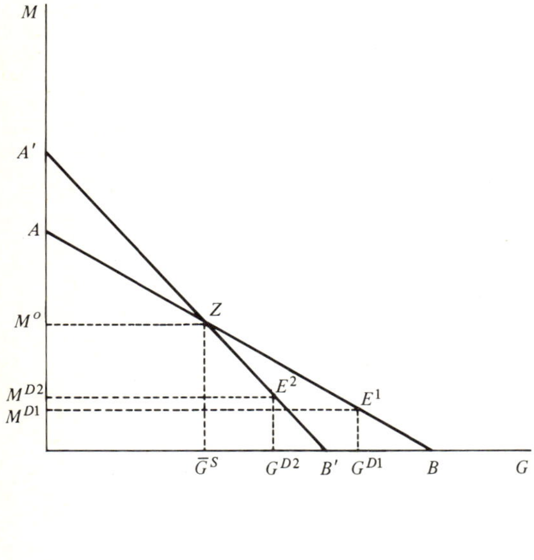

Figure 5-10

from $(G^{D1} - \bar{G}^s)$ to $(G^{D2} - \bar{G}^s)$. Similarly, the other individuals' demands for goods will fall and, in aggregate, there will be an excess supply of commodities. This will cause prices to fall until the individual's budget line has returned to *AB*.

Thus, it is possible to achieve the fundamental proposition that the absolute price level is determinate by postulating that the individual desires to end the period with a certain holding of nominal balances rather than real balances. This seems to be a strong rebuttal of the importance of the real balance effect. Meinich (1964) has shown, however, that this analysis does not do away with the real balance effect. Indeed, the effect is an integral part of it, for the real balance effect does not require real balances to be in the utility function. Patinkin's real balance effect is defined as "the influence on demand of a change in the real value of the initial money holdings." In Lloyd's model, analyzed here, the absolute price level is stable because of two factors: A change in the price level (with the endowment of goods and the stock of nominal money balances constant) causes a change in both the real value of initial money balances *and* the relative price of nominal balances vis-à-vis goods. The change in demand resulting from the price change comes from both these factors: the change in real balances and the change in the relative price of nominal balances. So, in Lloyd's model, there is an "influence on demand of a change in the real value of the initial money holdings," and the real balance effect therefore exists.

This conclusion is not really very surprising, for the real balance effect in any model is derived from the budget equation rather than the utility function. This fact can be seen from the equations of Section 5.1. They show the demand for goods as a function of prices, the *endowment* of goods and *initial* real balances—variables which don't enter the utility function (although the consumption of goods and end-of-period real balances do)—but come into the demand functions because they are in the budget equation. Similarly, in Lloyd's model the effect of a change in the real value of initial money holdings comes from the budget constraint. A fall in the price level means that if all the individual's endowment and nominal balances are to be used up for desired consumption or money holdings (that is, if the budget constraint is to be satisfied), the individual's demand either for goods or for nominal balances must be increased.

We can conclude, therefore, that rather than show that the real balance effect need not exist in a monetary economy, Lloyd has constructed a model showing that the real balance effect may exist even though the individual desired no particular level of real balances, but only nominal balances.

It is nevertheless important to note that, although there is a real balance effect in Lloyd's model, money affects the model in a manner different from the mechanism in Patinkin's model. A striking difference can be seen by considering a rise in nominal balances *accompanied* by an equiproportionate rise in the absolute price level. In Patinkin's model, since this change involves no change in real balances, endowment of goods, or relative prices (including the rate of exchange between real balances and goods, which is unity by definition), it has no effect upon the equilibrium demand for goods. In Lloyd's model, however, such a change does affect equilibrium since the change in the price level is a change in the rate of exchange between nominal balances and goods (a change in the slope of the budget line), and the new equilibrium is reached with a higher demand for goods. The difference is illustrated by Figures 5.11 and 5.12. Figure 5.11 represents Patinkin's model and has real balances on the vertical axis because they enter the utility function. Start with the budget line *AB* and imagine that the individual's nominal money balances then are increased as if by a gift from heaven while the absolute price level is increased in the same proportion. The budget line remains unchanged by these changed circumstances since initial real balances are unaltered thereby

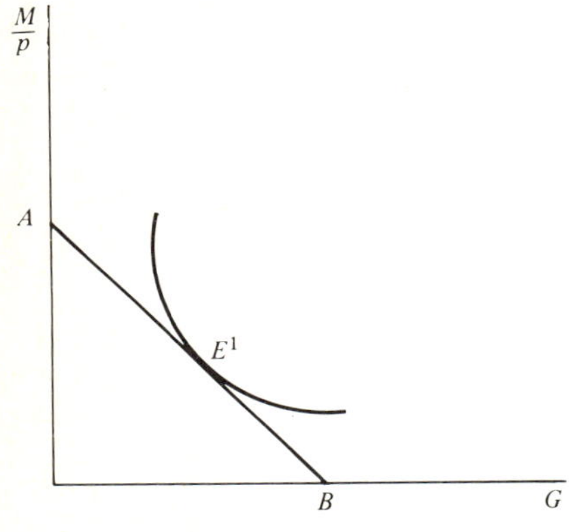

Figure 5-11

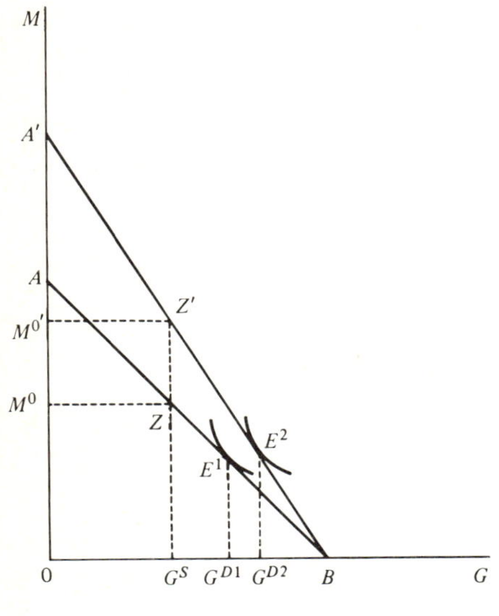

Figure 5-12

and the endowment of goods is unaffected. In consequence, equilibrium remains at E^1 and the demand for goods is unchanged. However, in Lloyd's model, represented by Figure 5.12 (with nominal balances on the vertical axis), this change of circumstances does alter the budget line from AB to $A'B$. This occurs because the real value of the individual's money balances is unaffected. Consequently, a person who consumed the whole budget could continue to consume $0B$ goods, but goods could now be sold at higher money prices; so, if all the budget was used to acquire nominal balances, the person could obtain $0A'$ instead of $0A$ nominal balances. (To look at it another way, the stock of nominal balances in the budget has increased from M^0 to $M^{0'}$, so the budget line must go through Z' rather than Z and must have a slope reflecting the altered rate of exchange between goods and nominal balances.) In consequence, the individual's equilibrium may shift from E^1 to E^2, at which point the demand for goods is higher than it was before the change.

From this it can be seen that in Lloyd's model the individual's behavior reflects *money illusion*. Behavior with respect to a real variable, the demand for goods, is affected by a change in a nominal variable (initial nominal money balances) even when that nominal variable's change is unaccompanied by any change in initial real variables (such as initial real balances). Patinkin's model, on the other hand, assumes the absence of money illusion. The consequence is that money is not neutral in Lloyd's model. A change in the nominal money supply alone could not give rise to an equiproportionate change in the absolute price level (thereby leaving the real variable, M/p, unchanged in the new equilibrium) without affecting a real variable, the equilibrium demands for goods.

Determinateness without a Wealth Effect

A final criticism of the idea that the real balance effect is the sine qua non of all monetary theory arises from the fact that the analysis considered in Chapter 4 and the present chapter for the most part concerns an exchange economy where there are no production and no bonds. Therefore, no demand for investment goods exists. It is possible to show that if we introduce investment goods and a bond market, the absolute price level will be determinate and the model will be internally consistent. This is so *even if* all money is inside money and there are no distribution effects, so that real balances do not enter the aggregate demand functions for goods. We shall postpone a full consideration of this model until Chapter 12, but the general outline of its workings can be indicated here.

The existence of bonds that can be carried into future weeks and investment goods that also have this property, together with money balances, ensures that there is one variable that acts in all markets in such a way as to affect each market's excess demand. That variable is the interest rate on bonds. The interest rate can be interpreted as the relative price of future goods in relation to present goods (even assuming that the level of money prices is expected to remain unchanged) and the relative price of money in relation to bonds. These aspects ensure that the utility-maximizing demands for both investment and consumption goods depend on the interest rate. The demand for investment goods will decline if the interest rate rises, because the marginal return on investment goods will fall in relation to the return on the alternative form of wealth, bonds. (Or, assuming that investors finance their purchases of investment goods by issuing bonds as liabilities, the cost of financing these purchases has risen relative to the return obtained by using the goods for future production.) The demand for consumption goods will decline if the rate of interest on bonds rises, since, by holding bonds, one can postpone consumption, and the attractiveness of doing so will increase as the profitability of holding bonds rises. (In terms of the two-period consumption figure, Figure 5.3, the budget line becomes steeper and, in general, is assumed to stimulate a greater demand for future goods and a lower demand for present goods.) Thus, the aggregate demand in all goods markets is an inverse function of the bond rate of interest. Moreover, since this interest rate determines the relative price of money in terms of bonds, the demand for bonds will increase and the demand for money will decrease in response to a rise in the interest rate.

Thus, the rate of interest on bonds affects the excess demands in the goods markets, money market, and bond market in this model. It therefore ensures that Say's Identity does not hold in the goods markets, since a change in the interest rate can cause excess demand or supply in those markets accompanied by excess demands or supplies in the money and bond markets (in such a way as to satisfy Walras' Law). The model therefore contains no internal inconsistency. Moreover, the absolute price level is determinate in this model, as will be demonstrated in Chapter 12, for a divergence in the absolute price level from its initial equilibrium, *ceteris paribus*, causes changes in the rate of interest. These changes create excess demands or supplies in the goods (and other) markets and therefore create forces to restore the price level to its initial equilibrium. This occurs even though, as a result of all money being inside money, aggregate real balances are identically zero. To state this fact more strongly, it occurs even when both money and bonds are of the inside variety, with bonds being issued only by firms and held directly or indirectly by households, so that their effect on the households' assets is offset by their effect on firms' liabilities. In that case, the model's properties result even though the real value of aggregate financial wealth (money and bonds) is identically zero and hence invariant. A model of this kind was first given prominence by Gurley and Shaw (1960), and its property of consistency and determinateness led Johnson (1962) to question the significance of the real balance effect (or wealth effect) for aggregate, macroeconomic models.

CHAPTER

SIX

THE PRE-KEYNESIAN QUANTITY THEORY TRADITION

The crude version of the Quantity Theory employed in Chapter 4 is nowadays often accepted as *the* Quantity Theory as it existed before Keynes. This is regrettable since the Crude Quantity Theory is a complete misrepresentation of the work of the Classical and Neoclassical economists. So total a misrepresentation is it that we can even state that no Quantity Theorist ever put forward the unqualified Crude Quantity Theory. At most, in the rare cases where it was used, it was presented as an abstraction that summarized the simplified relation between money and prices when important complications are left in the background. The real meat of the Quantity Theory tradition lay precisely in the consideration that the Quantity Theorists gave to these complications. Moreover, the problem that Patinkin has formalized—the inconsistency between Say's Identity and the Crude Quantity Theory—cannot be said to have existed in general within the Classical Quantity Theory tradition. The Classical Quantity Theorists not only did not put forward the Crude Quantity Theory; they also did not generally advance the proposition that we have called Say's Identity (although some Neoclassical writers did suffer from confusion, in particular in their use of the Homogeneity Postulate).

To understand the Quantity Theory tradition, we must go back to the sources and examine the literature of Classical and Neoclassical economics. The difficulty of this exercise and the possibility of misinterpretation arise because of the imprecise and frequently self-contradictory manner in which the writers expressed their arguments. In consequence, an understanding of any particular quotation extracted from these writings requires careful consideration of the context from which the quotation is drawn. In this chapter we shall follow this procedure to examine whether any of the particular components of the Crude Quantity Theory—the hypotheses concerning M^S, k, and y—do have a basis in the Quantity Theory tradition. In this way, we shall gain an overall picture of the nature of this tradition.

In Section 6.1 we shall examine the idea that real income and output, y, are always at their full-employment level. Did the Quantity Theorists support the proposal that the aggregate demand for goods ensures that goods supplied with full employment of resources could always be sold? Did they support Say's Identity, in other words? In Section 6.2 we shall consider whether the Quantity Theorists did maintain that k, the relationship between nominal income and the demand for nominal money balances, is constant. In Section 6.3 we shall discuss whether M^S, the money supply, was regarded as being determined exogenously. Finally, in Section 6.4 we bring together the conclusions of the preceding sections and consider the work of Wicksell, the most sophisticated of Quantity Theorists. Before embarking on this survey, it should be remembered that, whereas in Chapters 4 and 5 we were concerned with an exchange economy where the goods in the model arrive from heaven, the Quantity Theorists were, in general, concerned with the real world where goods have to be produced.

6.1 SAY'S IDENTITY AND SAY'S LAW

There is no doubt that the Classical economists with few exceptions adopted the law that is generally ascribed to Jean-Baptiste Say. His work was published at the beginning of the nineteenth century (although, as Sowell [1974] points out, versions of the law can be found in the works of earlier writers). The question we have to consider is: Precisely what was meant by Say's Law, for it was interpreted in different ways by different Quantity Theory writers? Specifically, we are concerned with whether *Say's Law* is to be interpreted as *Say's Identity*, the proposition employed in the preceding chapters.

Recall that Say's Identity can be expressed algebraically as:

$$\sum_{i=1}^{n} x_i^{XD} \equiv 0 \tag{6.1}$$

But what exactly does this expression imply? We can interpret it as a general statement saying that "the demand for goods equals the supply of goods," but such a statement is too general. It is the kind of statement that Quantity Theorists frequently made, and its generality and vagueness have given rise to controversy over precisely what they meant. The interpretation of Say's Identity (Eq. 6.1) is more specific than that statement. First, because it is an identity, it says that the demand for goods *always* equals the supply of goods.

Therefore the quantity of goods produced and supplied, when there is full employment of labor and the means of production, *always* equals the demand for goods. Second, Say's Identity says that it is the *planned*, or *ex ante*, demand for goods that equals the *planned* supply:[1] the excess of planned demand over planned supply for goods as a whole is zero. In other words, if the supply of goods planned by producers is such that its production will fully employ all resources, buyers will choose to buy precisely that output. Thus there is no reason why national production and the national income derived from it, y, should diverge from the full-employment level. These two propositions of Say's Identity combine, therefore, to assert that real national income is *always* at the full-employment level, since the corresponding supply of goods is always matched by demand.

That is Say's Identity. Is that how the Quantity Theorists interpreted Say's Law? In order to consider this question, one must first appreciate that Say's Identity has several corollaries and that a Quantity Theorist's statement of any of these corollaries could potentially be interpreted as a statement of Say's Identity. One such is the idea that no one holds money even for an instant. That this is a corollary of Say's Identity can be seen by considering its opposite, or what actually happens in capitalist, monetary economies. The real-life process of exchange of goods in such economies takes the form of:

$$pG^S - M - pG^D$$

An individual exchanges (sells) goods for money and *then*, in a *separate* transaction, exchanges money for (buys) goods. We can interpret the sale as planned supply and the purchase as planned demand, and for our purposes the most important aspect of this process is that the two transactions are separated in time. Thus, the individual necessarily holds money for some period of time; money is a temporary abode of purchasing power. In consequence, the individual's planned supply of goods does not *always* equal the individual's planned demand. At the instant of the first transaction, for example, the person has a planned supply of goods that is positive and a demand that is zero. But what about *aggregate* planned demand and supply? Surely, if the individual at the first instant plans to supply goods, other individuals must plan to buy them? This is not true. At that first instant, the other individuals may in their transactions be at the point, M, where they are holding money, rather than at the point where they choose to buy goods. This possibility arises from the very fact that in a monetary economy, each individual's purchases and sales are separated in time and each holds money for the intervening period. The length of time for which a person holds money is the subject of personal choice: one may, for example, choose to sell goods

[1]In the exchange economy considered in the preceding chapters, the concept of planned supply is meaningless—there are no producers, hence no supply plans. Therefore, in the formulation of those chapters, the supply term in the excess demand equation and the Say's Identity equation referred to actual supply.

and build up a hoard of money over a substantial period, rather than use the proceeds to buy goods. It follows that in a monetary economy, the existence of money holdings for a period of time (however short) ensures that there is no guarantee that aggregate planned demand always, at every instant, equals planned supply. For the two to be always equal, as Say's Identity states, money must never be held even for an instant. Therefore, a corollary or statement of Say's Identity could take the form: "Money is never chosen to be held for an instant."

Another corollary of Say's Identity would be the statement: "There is never a general glut of unsold goods." Goods willingly produced, desired supply, are always willingly bought, since they equal planned demand. Underlying this idea there may be an idea of the direction of causation. Common to many interpretations of Say's Identity is the idea that causality runs from supply to demand: planned supply instantly *creates* an exactly equal planned demand—indeed, Say himself saw causality in this way. This, then, implies a strong statement of the neutrality of money: "Since planned demand for goods always equals and is determined by planned supply, an exogenous change in the supply of money cannot affect for an instant the real demands and supplies of goods."[2]

Now, having established these versions, implications, and corollaries of Say's Identity, we can consider whether the Classical and Neoclassical Quantity Theorists included it as a component of their theories.

Statements of Say's Identity

Jean-Baptiste Say himself certainly appears to have done so. As well as being an original thinker in his own right, he was a popularizer of Adam Smith's general propositions. In combining these two functions, he also saw his task as systematizing the ideas advanced by Smith, setting out the basic propositions that must lie at their foundation, and criticizing what he considered to be errors in Smith's work. Like Smith, Say was an apologist for the new economic system, capitalism, which was in its infancy at the time, although, again like Smith, he had a social conscience and was a critic of some of the social conditions that accompanied the development of capitalism. As an apologist, Say was concerned to demonstrate that capitalism had limitless possibilities of expansion if only the barriers to trade were eliminated. In the process, he wrote his *Treatise of Political Economy*, first published in 1803, which became a best-seller and went through many

[2]Note that such a statement implies an assumption that the supply of money cannot directly affect the supply of goods. It can affect supply only if it is able first to affect demand (and this is precluded by Say's Identity). This assumption that money does not directly affect supply is common in the Quantity Theory tradition (which, as we shall see, is not based on Say's Identity as expressed here). It is also common in modern Keynesian and monetary theory.

editions.[3] The book contained a proposition that has been translated as the "law of markets" and made it especially clear in its second and subsequent editions. This is now known as Say's Law and sometimes interpreted as Say's Identity.

If we examine an English translation,[4] we find a clear statement of Say's Identity:

> A product is no sooner created, than it, *from that instant* [emphasis in original translation], affords a market for other products to the full extent of its own value. When the producer has put the finishing hand to his product, he is most anxious to sell it immediately, lest its value should diminish in his hands. Nor is he less anxious to dispose of the money he may get for it; for the value of money is also perishable. But the only way of getting rid of money is in the purchase of some product or other. Thus the mere circumstance of the creation of one product *immediately* [emphasis added] opens a vent for other products.

We must, however, ask whether Say was stating this as a strict theoretical proposition or merely as a polemical point. Was it put forward only to drive home, in his role as an apologist, the idea that the opportunities for capitalism are limitless, since the expansion of production that capitalism entails cannot be halted in the long run by an oversupply of goods? The answer must be in the affirmative, for the passage quoted here is (as Patinkin notes) immediately preceded by the much weaker statement that "even when money is obtained with a view to hoard or bury it, the *ultimate* object is always to employ it in a purchase of some kind" (emphasis added). Clearly, therefore, Say understood that in a monetary economy there is a break in time between sale and purchase, and the emphasis on the *immediate* link between purchase and sale in the previous quotation is merely polemical.

Since we can find no other quotations from the Quantity Theorists that emphasize the immediacy of the disbursement of money received from sales, we must conclude that the interpretation of Say's Identity, presented in the second paragraph of this section, is too extreme to be attributed to any Quantity Theorist. They clearly recognized, at least implicitly, that (as explained in Chapter 1) time is of the essence for the existence of money; money allows a real separation in time of purchases and sales.

An explicit statement of this was made by John Stuart Mill (1844):

> Although he who sells, really sells only to buy, he need not buy at the same moment when he sells: and he does not therefore necessarily add to the *immediate* demand for one commodity when he adds to the supply of another. The buying and selling being now separated, it may very well occur, that there may be at some given time, a very general inclination to sell with as little delay as possible, accompanied with an equally general inclination to defer all purchases as long as possible.

[3]Say also wrote a *Complete Course of Practical Political Economy* (1828–1829).

[4]J.-B. Say, *A Treatise on Political Economy* (trans. from 4th French ed. by C. R. Prinsep), Philadelphia, 1834. Longman's, London, 1821.

But we can modify the concept of time that we have employed so far to arrive at a version of Say's Identity that is formally unchanged. That is, we can arbitrarily divide time into discrete periods, a *short run*, and a *long run* which is a succession of such short runs. We can then state Say's Identity as the proposition that the planned supply of goods over the short-run period (a flow concept) is identically equal to the planned demand over that period. Money is held between the transactions occurring within the period but not from one short-run period to the next;[5] individuals are eager to spend money balances within some such period, and they want to do it as quickly as possible, so the period is as short as possible. This seems to be Patinkin's interpretation of Say's Identity, since he quotes as examples of it passages that make no mention of immediate disbursement of money or synchronization of planned purchases and sales at every instant.

Quotations from Classical economists that appear to support Say's Identity in this modified form are legion. For example, they are to be found in the writings of James Mill. In his *Commerce Defended* (1808), he provided a more explicit statement of the law than Say had offered at that time, and in his *Elements of Political Economy* (1821), we find:

> When a man produces a greater quantity of any commodity than he desires for himself, it can only be on one account; namely that he desires some other commodity.

And:

> No man wants money but in order to lay it out, either in articles of productive or articles of unproductive consumption.

We can also find in Ricardo's writings statements of Say's Law in the form of an identity—or, as Ricardo called it, "Mr. Mill's theory." They are found not so much in Ricardo's great *Principles of Political Economy and Taxation* (1817), where the main reference is a laudatory remark in the preface, but in his correspondence with, and comments on, Malthus. For example, Ricardo writes:

> Whoever is possessed of a commodity is necessarily a demander, either he wishes to consume the commodity himself, and then no purchaser is wanted; or he wishes to sell it, and purchase some other thing with the money.

Similarly, McCulloch, a rather crude defender of Ricardo's system of thought, argued (1844):

> It is . . . the acquisition of [other goods] . . . and not of money, that is the end which every man has in view who carries anything to market.

[5]This concept of time is clearly analogous to the market day in Hicks's (1967) monetary model, discussed in Chapter 1.

Finally, we have the well-known statement of John Stuart Mill in his *Principles of Political Economy* (1848):

> All sellers are inevitably . . . buyers. Could we suddenly double the productive powers of the country, we should double the supply of commodities in every market; but we should, by the same stroke, double the purchasing power. Everybody would bring a double demand as well as supply; everybody would be able to buy twice as much, because everyone would have twice as much to offer in exchange.

Say and Ricardo in Context

Although we can find these, and more, statements by Classical economists that *appear* to support Say's Identity, reading them in their context indicates that these writers most certainly did not support the proposition. One aspect of the context is the intellectual climate at the time that the Classical writers wrote. They were engaged in a fierce battle with those writers, the precursors of Keynes in a sense, who argued that a general glut was possible. Malthus, Chalmers, Sismondi, and others emphasized that supply does not create its own demand, that a general overproduction of goods is possible because of inadequate aggregate demand for goods as a whole, and that such a situation will depress production. One way to clarify the debate is to say that Ricardo and the followers of Say's Law emphasized that the conditions of supply determine aggregate output, whereas Malthus and the "general glut" theorists emphasized demand as the determining factor. *Neither* side, it should be noted, argued that crises, slumps, and unemployment are impossible. In general, however, followers of Say's Law argued that they stem from a misallocation of resources—too few being used in sectors where there is high demand and too many being used in sectors with low demand—whereas the general glut theorists argued that crises reflect an inadequacy of demand in general.

It would be untrue to say, however, that in the course of this debate, the followers of Say's Law denied the existence of general gluts. Consider in turn each of the writers we have quoted. As Sowell (1974) demonstrates, even Say himself admitted the possibility of general gluts. In his correspondence with the general glut theorists, Say eventually revealed that he had made a "concession" to their views in preparing the fifth edition of his *Treatise*; in that edition, we find him arguing that there are limits to production in the short run and that recognition of this is necessary when "we are studying practical political economy" rather than "abstract quantities."

Ricardo, too, recognizes the possibility of general gluts in the short run. His difference with the general glut theorists appears to stem partly from the fact that he worked at a level of abstraction where he fixed his eyes firmly on the long-run potential for capitalist accumulation and growth. He appears to have believed that in the short run, supply may be limited by demand, but in the long run, the limits to production are determined by the rate of profit, which depends on the distribution of national income among workers' wages, landlords' rent, and capitalists' profits. As he said in a letter (1966, Vol. 7) to his adversary Malthus:

> It appears to me that one great cause of our difference in opinion, on the subjects which we have so often discussed, is that you always have in your mind the immediate and temporary effects of particular changes—whereas I put these immediate and temporary effects quite aside, and fix my whole attention on the permanent state of things which will result from them.[6]

Similarly, in Ricardo's notes to James Mill, dated December 18, 1821 (1966, Vol. 9), there is a clear distinction between the possibility of a general glut in the short run and its impossibility in the long run:

> If every man was intent on saving, more food and necessaries . . . would be produced than could be consumed. The supply above the demand would produce such a glut, that with the increased quantity you could command no more labour than before [that is, prices of goods would fall].

So a fall in the absolute price level comes through a short-run excess supply in the goods markets (as is the case with Patinkin's real balance effect). But matters are different in Ricardo's long run. For the fall in the prices of goods involves an increase in real wages, a redistribution to workers, as a result of which "all motive to save would cease," the excess supply would be eradicated, and, moreover, it would not have permanently hindered accumulation because the rise in real wages evokes an increased labor supply, which lowers real wages to their initial level.

Ricardo, like most Classical writers, is not always consistent. We can, therefore, find places where he denies the possibility of a general glut in the short run, but even there he does not support the Say's Identity proposition that supply creates its own demand. Instead, in such places he argues that in the short run, supply is determined by demand and a fall in demand can push supply below the full-employment level. But he contends that supply falls instantaneously in response to this decrease in demand, so that excess supply is immediately eradicated. For example, in a letter to Malthus dated July 9, 1821 (1966, Vol. 9), Ricardo wrote:

> If you had said "after arriving at a certain limit there will in the actual circumstances be no use to try to produce more—the end cannot be accomplished, and if it could, instead of more, less would belong to the class which provided the capital," I should have agreed with you.

[6]But it is clear that a difference between concentrating on the short run and on the long run is not the sole source of the difference between Ricardo and Malthus, since Malthus wrote, in his *Definitions in Political Economy*: "The question of a glut is exclusively whether it may be general, as well as particular, and not whether it may be permanent as well as temporary." Malthus, unlike Ricardo, clearly considered that long-run stagnation, with excess supply of goods arising from inadequate demand, was possible. The important point that the passage suggests, however, is that Ricardo thought excess supply, a general glut, to be possible in the short run.

Ricardo followed this with an emphasis on the impossibility of a general glut because a limit on demand immediately ensures that supply, too, is limited so that demand and supply remain in balance:

> I acknowledge there may not be adequate motives for production, and therefore things will not be produced, but I cannot allow . . . that with these inadequate motives commodities will be produced.[7]

Finally, and in the same vein, we find in Ricardo's "Essay on the Influence of a Low Price of Corn on the Profits of Stock" (1966, Vol. 4) a consideration of the effects of a government's restricting exports. This, again, shows that Ricardo recognized that a fall in demand causes a fall in supply when he wrote: "No interruption could be given to the export trade [in corn] . . . without the most extensively ruinous commercial distress." He added that the fall in supply is preceded by a short-run excess supply or glut:

> The immense capital which would be employed on the land could not be withdrawn suddenly, and under such circumstances without immense loss; besides which the glut of corn in their markets, which would affect their whole supply, and lower its value beyond calculation . . . would occasion a scene of wide spreading ruin.

From our consideration of Say and Ricardo, then, it can be seen that it is quite wrong to suppose that they believed in Say's Identity except as a long-run proposition that enabled them to isolate those factors, such as distribution, prices, and values, that determine long-run growth. Say's Identity as a short-run proposition cannot be pinned on them. It is therefore inaccurate for Keynes, who was primarily (but not wholly) concerned with short-run analysis, to write (1936): "From the time of Say and Ricardo the classical economists have taught that supply creates its own demand."

McCulloch, Mill, and Marshall

Moreover, it is not only Say and Ricardo whose expressions of Say's Law are qualified so as to make them read like Say's Identity only when torn out of context. We have quoted McCulloch as giving an apparent statement of Say's Identity, but that statement is immediately followed by one where he makes clear that he is thinking of the long run and that short-run general gluts *are* possible:

[7]Although Sowell (1974) interprets this letter to Malthus as indicating acceptance of the idea that demand influences supply, its interpretation is, in fact, less clear-cut. Ricardo was writing of the motives for production as determining supply. In general, in his work he considered this motive to be profit and showed how the profit rate changes even if supply were to create its own demand. In this letter, however, he can be read as implying that the motive is influenced by demand, since the level of demand can influence the profit rate in the short run. This is the way in which Sowell reads it and in which we have interpreted it in the text.

> These changes [in the quantity of money] may, as already stated, exert a powerful influence; and have frequently, indeed, occasioned the most extensive derangement in the ordinary channels of commercial intercourse . . . any sudden diminution of the quantity, and consequent rise in the value of money [fall in the absolute price level] . . . may be such as materially to abridge the power of society to make their accustomed purchases, and thus to occasion a glut of the market.

This, surely, is as clear a statement as one could want of the invalidity of Say's Identity in the short run and the operation of the real balance effect.[8]

Last, John Stuart Mill. His statement (1848), quoted above, was interpreted by Keynes as a statement of Say's Identity. It appears to be such, but a more careful reading indicates that it is not. Mill talks of an increase in supply causing an increase in "purchasing power" so that everybody would "be able" to buy more. It says nothing of whether people would actually choose to buy more and thus use the increased purchasing power. Indeed, as Patinkin (1965) has noted, Mill subsequently makes absolutely clear that the distinction is important:

> When these writers speak of the supply of commodities as outrunning the demand, it is not clear which of the two elements of demand they have in view—the desire to possess, or the means of purchase; whether their meaning is that there are, in such cases, more consumable products in existence than the public desires to consume, or merely more than it is able to pay for. In this uncertainty it is necessary to examine both suppositions.

Moreover, using a concept similar to Walras' Law, Mill makes a clear statement of the short-run invalidity of Say's Identity:

> I have already described the state of the markets for commodities which accompanies what is termed a commercial crisis. At such times there is really an excess of all commodities above the money demand: in other words, there is an under-supply of money.

We should not end with John Stuart Mill, however, for, if we were to do so, we would have considered only the Classical economists. There remains the question of whether the Neoclassical economists, those writing at the end of the nineteenth century and adopting the ideas of marginal analysis, accepted Say's Identity. Keynes thought that they had done so, for he lumped them with the Classical economists on precisely these grounds and named them, too, Classical economists. We shall not devote much attention to the Neoclassical economists here, but it is worthwhile at least to examine the

[8]It reflects the operation of the real balance effect because it says that a fall in M, by reducing the real value of money balances, leads to an excess supply of goods. As such, it is marred by bringing in the fall in prices ("rise in the value of money") too early in the exposition. This makes the argument inconsistent, since, if a fall in p accompanies the fall in M, real balances will not fall. The drop in prices should be stated at the end of the passage; it should be a consequence of the excess supply of goods.

writings of Marshall, for his position is similar to that of John Stuart Mill. Despite advocating Say's Identity in statements such as, "The whole of a man's income is expended in the purchase of services and of commodities," and, in his *Principles of Economics*, giving support to Mill's apparent statement of the Identity, Marshall stated in his *Economics of Industry* (1879) and elsewhere in his *Principles* (1890) that, "though men have the power to purchase, they may not use it."

He also made clear (1879) that when he denied the possibility of overproduction, a general glut, he was referring only to its long-term possibility:[9]

> After a commercial crisis the warehouses are overstocked with goods in almost every important trade; scarcely any trade can continue undiminished production.... And it is thought that this state of things is one of general over-production. We shall, however, find that it really is nothing but a state of commercial disorganisation; and that the remedy for it is a revival of confidence.

What Keynes complains of about Marshall is not really his belief in Say's Identity (Marshall did not believe in it as a short-run proposition), but the fact that Marshall focused his attention on the long run and minimized the significance of short-run gluts. It is as such a criticism that we can appreciate Keynes's dictum that in the long run we are all dead. In justice, Keynes should equally have recognized that the Classical writers, such as Say, Ricardo, McCulloch, and Mill, also did not subscribe to Say's Identity as a short-run proposition, but instead, they minimized the significance of the short run and concentrated on the long run. This, in Keynesian eyes, could be considered their real sin, for it could be argued that the long run is merely a succession of short runs.

Appraisal

We are now at a point where we can summarize the debate over whether the pre-Keynesian Quantity Theorists held to Say's Identity. Any conclusion turns on how one interprets Say's Identity. We have seen that if one interprets it as the proposition that money is never held, no Classical writers supported this idea. If it is interpreted as the proposition that in the short run, however defined, supply creates its own demand, those writers who *appear* to have suggested this generally qualified their views so as to make clear that they were really referring to the long run.

Becker and Baumol (1952) and Patinkin (1965) are more or less agreed that the Classical writers were indeed referring to the long run. Much of the

[9]This demonstration of Marshall's nonsupport for the short-run Say's Identity does not deny Patinkin's contention (1965) that many Neoclassical economists did build models with an internal inconsistency that arose from the use of the Homogeneity Postulate or, at best, a failure to examine disequilibrium forces.

Classical debate over Say's Identity was an argument over whether long-run stagnation could arise as a result of inadequate demand. On this interpretation, it was a debate concerning long-run equilibrium with Ricardians emphasizing that in the long run but not in the short run Say's Identity holds, and Malthus arguing that even (or especially) in the long run there may be a general glut.[10] Sowell (1974), however, argues that the distinction to be made is not between those who concentrated on the short and long runs, such as Malthus, and those, like Ricardo, who concentrated on the long run. Instead, it was between those, like Ricardo, who employed a comparative static method of analysis—comparing two points of equilibrium and neglecting the processes by which society moves from one equilibrium to another—and those, like Malthus, who were concerned with the continuous dynamic of the economy. Sowell notes Malthus's denial that the issue is over the question of whether long-term gluts are possible.[11]

Another way in which one can interpret the debate over Say's Identity is to say that for some writers it is a nondebate. Patinkin suggests that several writers who appear to state Say's Identity are in fact merely stating that actual supply always equals actual demand (and actual income). This differs from Say's Identity, for the latter refers to identity between *planned* demand and supply. Equality of actual demand, actual supply, and actual income is a truism. It follows from the fact that every sale (actual supply) always involves a purchase (actual demand) and gives rise to revenue for the seller (actual income). This truism is at the basis of National Income Accounting, as we shall see in Chapter 8.

Finally, it could be argued that some of the writers who apparently put forward Say's Identity were in fact describing Say's Equality. Say's Identity, as expressed in Equation 6.1, implies that demand always equals supply, or, in the context of a short-run period of definite non-zero duration, that demand equals supply in the short run. This may be stated in a strong form to say that there may be excess supply at some instants within the short-run period if demand falls, but that *somehow or other* demand rises again so that short-run equality is reestablished. In such a version, the mechanism by which demand

[10]Two points are worthy of note. First, Ricardo did not deny the possibility of long-run stagnation but attributed it to a distribution of national income, which minimized the profit rate and thereby depressed growth, rather than to inadequate demand. Second, Malthus's specter of long-run stagnation resulting from inadequate demand was taken up and developed in the present century by the Keynesian stagnation theorists.

[11]See p. 98*n* for this denial. For this reason, Sowell's interpretation is plausible, but there are two qualifications we should make. First, Malthus may have misunderstood the nature of the debate in which he was engaged. Second, we should not neglect the fact that Ricardo did analyze the short-run processes by which the economy moved from one equilibrium to another, but he frequently (though not always) analyzed them in terms of changes in distribution rather than of an excess supply of, or demand for, goods.

rises again is not specified and not thought to be caused by the disequilibrium forces of excess supply.[12] Alternatively, Say's Identity may take the weaker form, maintaining that when excess supply exists at some instants within the short run, it sets up specific forces that eradicate it. Then Say's Identity, the proposition that in the short run excess demand or supply does not exist although it may at some instants within the short run, would take the form of a short-run equilibrium condition and should be expressed as *Say's Equality* rather than an identity. Say's Equality would imply that goods market equilibrium within the short run requires:

$$\sum_{i=1}^{n} x_i^{XD} = 0 \tag{6.2}$$

This is an equilibrium equation rather than an identity, and it may be thought that some Classical writers did hold to Say's Equality.[13] For example, we have seen (on page 98) that Ricardo employed Say's Identity when concerned with the possibility of long-run excess supply in his debate with Malthus. In other places, however, he was concerned with the possibility of short-run excess demand for goods. In his 1810 pamphlet *The High Price of Bullion* (1966, Vol. 3) and related writings, Ricardo frequently considered this question. He made absolutely clear that equilibrium could be disturbed in the short run by a change in the money supply. A rise in the money supply would give rise to an excess demand for goods. This would lead to a rise in the absolute price level and, thereby, to eradication of excess demand and restoration of equilibrium within the short run. This is a clear statement of the real balance effect and implies only Say's Equality (Eq. 6.2), a short-run equilibrium condition that is much weaker than Say's Identity (Eq. 6.1) and does not give rise to an internal inconsistency in general equilibrium models.

[12]A quotation from Say, cited by Becker and Baumol (1952), is a version of such a strong statement of Say's Identity: "Should the increase in traffic require more money to facilitate it, the want is easily supplied. . . . In such cases, merchants know well enough how to find substitutes for the product serving as the medium of exchange or money (by bills at sight, or after date, bank-notes, running credits, write-offs, etc., as at London and Amsterdam) and money itself soon pours in." Thus, the idea is that the supply of money and credit can in principle limit demand for goods (prevent an "increase in traffic"), but that if an excess supply of goods were to appear, it would be eradicated within the short run by the fact that the supply of money and credit increases for some unspecified reason.

[13]The term *Say's Equality* was used by Becker and Baumol (1952) to distinguish an equilibrium equation from Say's Identity. Their use is different from ours and rather confusing, for they consider Say's Equality as a long-run equilibrium condition. The questions of whether Say's Law refers to the long run and of whether it is an equilibrium condition (in either the short run or the long run), rather than an identity, are two separate questions. In the text we have maintained the distinction, but Becker and Baumol tend to confuse the two questions.

6.2 THE CONSTANCY OF VELOCITY

In Chapter 4's representation of the Crude Quantity Theory, we set out the Fisher Equation[14]

$$M^S V = py \tag{6.3}$$

and emphasized its equivalence with the Cambridge Equation

$$M^S = kpy \tag{6.4}$$

This equivalence stems from the fact that V, velocity, is defined as the inverse of k, the demand for money expressed as a proportion of nominal income. In each equation an assumption of constancy was made: constancy of V in the first, or constancy of k in the second. The question concerning us in this section is whether the Quantity Theorists did in fact assume k (or V) to be constant.

In the light of modern Keynesian theory, it is thought that the Quantity Theorists made a serious error if they did assume constancy. For, in an economy where there is nonsynchronization of purchases and sales, an individual need not hold money in the intervening interval (as assumed in Section 6.1), but could hold bonds. The difference between the two is that a bond pays interest to its holder, whereas money does not. Thus, given the level of national income and the pattern of transactions, a Keynesian would argue that we cannot immediately determine the amount of money held at any moment.

To determine how much money is held, we need to know what proportion of their financial assets individuals choose to hold in the form of money rather than bonds. This, it is argued, will depend on the reward obtained from holding bonds: the bond rate of interest. With any given nominal income and transactions pattern, the amount of money held would, in Keynesian analysis, depend on the rate of interest. Therefore, k would not be constant but would be a function of the rate of interest. When the interest rate is high, k would be low (V would be high) and vice versa.

Now, some Quantity Theorists saw matters in precisely this way. The earliest major example of such writers was Henry Thornton, whose book ***Paper Credit***, published at the very beginning of the nineteenth century, contains a clear statement of the relationship between the demand for money and the rate of interest.[15] Thornton concentrated on the idea that people choose to hold money balances in order to protect themselves against the

[14]The Fisher Equation is more usually written as $MV = pT$, the important difference from Eq. 6.3 being that T (the quantity of transactions) replaces y, the real value of output and income. The difference need not affect our analysis, for we may assume that there is a strict proportional relationship between the level of income and the volume of transactions: if society's income and output doubles, we shall assume that the quantity of transactions involved doubles.

[15]Indeed, Hicks (1967, Chap. 10) contends that Thornton's arguments in *Paper Credit* were Keynesian in other important respects, too.

contingency of having to repay their debts. Therefore, the demand for money depends upon their state of confidence as to the smoothness of trade, since if business is good, debts are easily met. But given a state of sound confidence, the amount of money they choose to hold depends upon the opportunity cost of holding money—the interest forgone by not holding bonds or the interest they have to pay for borrowing the money they hold (that is, for "having issued" a bond). In Thornton's (1802) words:

> Now a high state of confidence contributes to make men provide less amply against contingencies. At such a time, they trust, that if the demand upon them for a payment, which is now doubtful and contingent, should actually be made, they shall be able to provide for it at the moment; and they are loath to be at the expense of . . . getting a bill discounted [borrowing money], in order to make provision much before the period at which it shall be wanted. When, on the contrary, a season of distrust arises, prudence suggests that the loss of interest arising from a detention of notes for a few additional days should not be regarded.

Thus, Thornton clearly related the demand for money balances, or hoarding, as it was commonly called, to the rate of interest. But it should be noted that the stability of that relationship depends on the stability of the state of confidence, and Thornton emphasized fluctuations in confidence. We can say, then, that Thornton considered k as anything but a constant. It would vary as the rate of interest changed, but, more important, it would vary sharply with sharp fluctuations in confidence.

Similarly, Fullarton (1844) writes that "the amount of the hoards is not governed by the state of prices, but by the market rate of interest." Clearly, the idea that the demand for money, the rate of interest, and confidence were interrelated had become commonplace by the mid-nineteenth century.

Marshall and Cambridge

The most significant development in the theory of the determinants of k came with the writings of the Cambridge economists at the end of the nineteenth and beginning of the twentieth century. These economists owed the origin of their work to Marshall, for, although he avoided algebraic expressions of the Quantity Theory, he gave detailed consideration to the determinants of the proportion of nominal income (or the more general concept of resources) that individuals choose to hold in money balances. His work lay behind the Cambridge Equation as represented in Equation 6.4 and the more complicated variants developed by the later Cambridge writers. Marshall considered more than the choice between money and bonds out of a given level of financial assets; he also considered the choice between money and goods. In his *Money, Credit and Commerce* (1923) he wrote:

> But currency held in hand yields no income: therefore everyone balances (more or less automatically and instinctively) the benefits which he would get by enlarging his stock of

> currency in the hand, against those which he would get by investing some of it either in a commodity—say a coat or a piano—from which he would derive a direct benefit; or in some business plant or stock exchange security, which would yield him a money income.

Moreover, Marshall thought, the choice between money and commodities ("a coat or a piano") does not depend only upon the direct benefit, the utility, of the commodity. It also depends on expectations of changes in the price of commodities. If the price of commodities is expected to rise, then money can be spent "to buy when markets are depressed, and therefore things can be bought at low prices" in order to "sell when markets turn the other way and prices are high." From this consideration of expectations of price changes, Marshall (1926) formulated his "law of hoarding":

> The demand for a metal for the purposes of hoarding is increased by a continued rise in its value [continued fall in the absolute price level] and diminished by a continued fall, because those people who hoard believe that what has been rising in value is likely to go on rising and vice versa.

Thus, Marshall, who initiated the modern development of the concept of k, explicitly considered the influence on it of the bond interest rate and the expected rate of change of prices. These may be considered as reflecting the relative rates of return (or relative prices) of money, goods, and bonds as assets.

But what is significant in his analysis of short-run variations in the demand for money is that, like Thornton and others, he emphasized sharp fluctuations in confidence. Whereas, in the law of hoarding, a simple theory of the systematic formation of expectations is presented, elsewhere Marshall emphasized that business expectations and therefore expectations of price changes may fluctuate violently. Such fluctuations are caused by "wars and rumours of wars, by good and bad harvests, and by the alternate opening out of promising new enterprises, and the collapse of many of the hopes founded on them" (Marshall [1925]).

The development of the Quantity Theory at Cambridge was pursued by Marshall's pupils and especially by Pigou, Lavington, Robertson, and Keynes. In all their work, explicit consideration was given to the determinants of the demand for money, and in this respect, Keynes was, as we shall see in Chapter 9, one of the truest followers of Marshall. However, Keynes, in his *General Theory*, emphasized the stability of the relationship between the demand for money (and therefore the Cambridge k) and the rate of interest, and he underemphasized (although he did not ignore) the effect of price expectations and violent changes in confidence on the demand for money.

Robertson, on the other hand, continued to emphasize the role of expectations and changes in confidence in determining the demand for money. It is also worth noting that one characteristic of all the Cambridge writers' work is the idea that not all individuals are alike. To understand the determinants of the private sector's demand for money, we must examine separately the influences on the demands of different groups—businesses and consumers being a common classification. This idea is also to be found in the work of earlier writers, such as Adam Smith and Tooke, but it is one that, as we shall see in later chapters, is largely ignored in modern, post-Keynesian monetary theory. Indeed, Eshag (1963) judges that the overdevelopment of the distinctions between different subsectors' demands for money was partially responsible for the downfall of the Cambridge Quantity Theory (and, hence, we may suppose the neglect of these distinctions is the strength of modern monetary theory).

Fisher and Simons

If the Cambridge Quantity Theorists did not assume k to be constant, did their approximate contemporaries in America—Fisher and the Chicago Quantity Theorists—assume V to be constant? Although k and V are formally equivalent concepts since one is the reciprocal of the other, it is generally thought that concentration on desired money balances as a proportion of income (k) enabled the Cambridge economists to explore the determinants of the demand for money, whereas concentration on velocity (V) encouraged the view that V, and therefore the demand for money, is mechanically determined by the payments pattern (or transactions pattern) of society. There is some truth in this view, but it certainly does not imply that V was seen as being constant.

One factor, of course, is that the payments pattern itself may change, and this change may even be fairly rapid at times. If people, instead of relying on money to facilitate exchanges, increasingly exchange goods on the basis of credit, the velocity of money—the value of transactions that can be made with a given stock of money in society—will increase accordingly. The idea that such changes may be rapid and unpredictable has been given prominence in modern times by the Radcliffe Committee (1959). It also has very early antecedents. We saw in Section 6.1 that Say thought a shortage of money would be offset by a rapid development of credit. Similarly, in *The High Price of Bullion*, Ricardo, considering the rapid increase in velocity that accompanied the development of the banking system's credit mechanism, wrote:

> The daily improvements which we are making in economising the use of the circulating medium, by improved methods of banking, would render the same amount of notes excessive now, which were necessary for the same state of commerce at a former period (1966, Vol. 3).

And of course, in Fisher's major statement of his Quantity Theory in *The Purchasing Power of Money* (1911), he explicitly discussed the effect on velocity of changes in the payments pattern of society. Moreover, Simons, a leading Chicago Quantity Theorist, emphasized that changes in the credit system may be very rapid and involve sharp fluctuations in velocity. Simons

(1936) brings Ricardo's idea up to date thus:

> The fixing of the quantity of circulation media might merely serve to increase the perverse variability in the amounts of "near moneys" [credit instruments] and in the degree of their acceptability, just as the restrictions on the issue of bank notes presumably served to hasten the development of deposit banking.

Fisher, however, gave much less attention to the second type of factor, such as the interest rate and price expectations that, with a given transactions pattern, determine the demand for money as an asset compared with bonds and goods. As Patinkin (1969) points out, Fisher, in his *Rate of Interest* (1907), did write of the convenience of money holdings that makes an individual willing to forgo the interest that could be earned. And in Fisher's *Purchasing Power of Money*, the influence of interest on velocity is briefly mentioned. But these references do not constitute a detailed consideration of the influence of the interest rate on the demand for money. Similarly, Fisher mentioned the influence of price changes on the demand for money: When money "is depreciating [the absolute price level rising], holders will get rid of it as fast as possible." But this is nothing like Marshall's more precise statement that the demand for money changes in such circumstances, rather than, as implied by Fisher, reduces to zero.

The survey by Patinkin (1969) of the writings, lectures, and theses of the Chicago writers demonstrates that they did not explore in detail the effect of the rate of interest on velocity or the demand for money. Attention was indeed given to the role of price changes and expectations of price changes on velocity but, as in the case of Marshall and others, we must note that the effect of price expectations was thought to be sharp fluctuations or "extreme alternations" in velocity. This emphasis on instability is in contrast with the view of Friedman (1956a, 1968) that the Chicago Quantity Theory tradition included the view that the demand for money and velocity is a stable function of interest rates and the expected rate of change of prices.

Appraisal

We may conclude that the pre-Keynesian Quantity Theory tradition is not accurately represented by the assumption of the Crude Quantity Theory that k or V is constant. Not only was it thought that k and V depend upon the rate of interest, price expectations, and the development of the credit system. It was also believed that the last two factors at least, and expectations or confidence in particular, can give rise to sharp fluctuations in velocity. Indeed, this idea was in many cases the basis of theories of short-run fluctuations in business activity and prices: p and y can change, there can even be an economic crisis, even if the money supply remains unchanged.

Since the Quantity Theorists generally did consider changes in V or k, how are we to rationalize their statements that appear to correspond to the

Crude Quantity Theory? Such statements are easily found. Even Marshall, who, as we have seen, was a sophisticated theorist of the determinants of the demand for money, comes close to the Crude Quantity Theory in stating that:

> Whatever the state of society, there is a certain volume of their resources which people of different classes, taken one with another, care to keep in the form of currency; and, if everything else remains the same, then there is this direct relation between the volume of currency and the level of prices, that, if one is increased by 10 percent, the other will also be increased by 10 percent.

In this context Marshall considered only gradual changes in the methods of business (transactions pattern and credit system) and in "the amounts of commodities" (that is, $\bar{y}$) within the phrase "everything else." Thus, he did not consider the role of the interest rate or price changes and expectations in determining k. The fact that such a relatively crude statement of the Quantity Theory coexists in Marshall's writings with sophisticated analyses of the determinants of k is explicable in terms of a distinction between long-run and short-run analysis. Consideration of the fluctuations in velocity that result from changes in expectations was thought to be highly relevant for analysis of the business cycle and crises, but such matters could be safely neglected when considering long-run movements, when comparing one decade with another.

We are drawn to the same conclusion as the one we reached when discussing Say's Identity. Say's Identity was often (although not wholly) presented as a long-run proposition, rather than as the idea that in the short run or at every instant within that period, planned demand equals planned supply. Similarly, the Crude Quantity Theory's constancy of k or V was generally stated as a long-run proposition, and an emphasis on this constancy would obscure the fact that the Quantity Theorists explored in detail the determinants of k and thought that changes in them were significant in the short run. In particular, they forcefully emphasized the possibility of sharp fluctuations in k and the associated possibility of financial crises.

6.3 DETERMINANTS OF THE MONEY SUPPLY

In the Crude Quantity Theory, it is usually assumed that the money supply is exogenously determined, so that causation goes in one direction only. With k and y constant, it is assumed that a rise in money supply causes a rise in prices, rather than vice versa.[16] Again, however, we find that with some exceptions, this proposition was not an integral part of the Quantity Theory tradition. In general, it was argued that there is a two-way relationship

[16]See, for example, the lecture notes that Patinkin took as a student of the Chicago Quantity Theorists (Patinkin, 1969). From Mints he learned that "P is the dependent variable (in the long run) of the equation $MV = PT$."

between prices and the money supply: an increase in prices during booms affects the money supply, and these changes in the money supply then react upon prices. A dynamic process was assumed to be at work and this was particularly important for the analysis of short-term fluctuations, the business cycle, rather than long-term price movements.[17]

The manner in which the price level was thought to affect the money supply varied among different writers. In general, we can say that with the Classical writers of the eighteenth and early nineteenth centuries, the main mechanism was through the effect of prices on *foreign exchange reserves* and the effect of foreign exchange reserves on the supply of money. With the Neoclassical writers of the Cambridge and American schools, the main concern was with the effect of changes in prices and nominal income on the behavior of the banking system. This change in emphasis is understandable and reflects the changes in society during the periods in which the writers lived. For the Classical writers, a major preoccupation was the necessity to develop international trade in order to encourage the development of capitalism at home (and abroad). At that time, the modern banking system was in its early infancy (although it was neither insignificant nor ignored by the Classical writers). For the Neoclassical writers, their world was one that contained a well-developed modern banking system and one of their most urgent tasks was to analyze how it worked and how it might be controlled (or whether it was necessary to control it).

Classical Writers

The clearest statement of the Classical writers' understanding of how prices affected the money supply is that of Hume. In his "Of the Balance of Trade," published in 1752, Hume started by imagining an exogenous change in the money supply, examined its effects on prices in terms of the Quantity Theory, and then examined the effects of these price changes upon the money supply:

> Suppose four-fifths of all the money in Great Britain to be annihilated in one night, and the nation reduced to the same condition, with regard to specie [gold or commodity money], as in the reigns of the Harrys and Edwards, what would be the consequence? Must not the price of all labour and commodities sink in proportion, and everything be sold as cheap as they were in those ages? What nation could then dispute with us in any foreign market, or pretend to navigate or to sell manufactures at the same price, which to us would afford sufficient profit? In how little time, therefore, must this bring back the money which we had lost, and raise us to the level of all the neighbouring nations? Where after we have arrived, we immediately lose the advantage of the cheapness of labour and commodities; and the farther flowing in of money is stopped by our fulness and repletion.

[17]To quote again from Patinkin (1969), Mints's statement concerning the long-run dependency of prices is followed by: "But in the short run all the variables tend to move together."

This is the classic statement of the theory of the balance of payments under a pure gold standard—one where all domestic and international money is gold or "specie." How this process was affected by the introduction of paper money such as bank notes was also of concern to Hume. What interested him in this case, however, was not the determinants of the supply of paper money, but the effect of this supply on the balance of trade and the stock of gold.

This was generally true of Ricardo and his Classical successors and, like Hume, they based their thinking on the principle that a change in prices causes an inflow or outflow of gold. A detailed analysis of Hume's proposition with particular attention to the consequences of paper money existing alongside gold was the subject of Ricardo's *The High Price of Bullion* (1966, Vol. 3). Ricardo's analysis was accepted by John Stuart Mill (1848), and among Ricardo's predecessors, Thornton (1802) gave a clear statement of propositions similar to Hume's, while, as the words "Paper Credit" in his title indicate, concentrating attention on the relationship between the *banking system*, prices, and foreign exchange reserves. In his *Principles* (1817), Ricardo presented a proposition similar to Hume's but of greater interest because of its different focus. Instead of starting with an imaginary exogenous change in the money supply, Ricardo examined an impetus which is much closer to the phenomena of reality. He assumed that technical progress in a country's manufacturing industry allows it to produce manufactures more cheaply and thereby to improve its balance of trade. He then examined the effect on the money supply and the consequences for the prices of other goods (such as corn and manufactured goods):

> When any particular country excels in manufactures, so as to occasion an influx of money towards it, the value of money will be lower, and the prices of corn and labour will be relatively higher in that country, than in any other (Ricardo [1966, Vol. 1]).

This focus of Ricardo's emphasizes that the Classical writers were not merely concerned with abstract theoretical experiments, but with examining the consequences of the progress of capitalist development with its increases in productivity.

Neoclassical Writers

Whereas the Classical writers emphasized the effects of prices on the money supply through foreign trade, the Neoclassical writers were notable for their analysis of the effect on the banking system's creation of money. Marshall did not generally define money as including bank deposits, although his successors at Cambridge did. Nevertheless, Marshall did develop the theory of the creation of deposits under a banking system or, as it is now known, the bank-deposit multiplier:

> Thus I should get a geometrical progression; the effect being that if each bank could lend two-thirds of its deposits, the total amount of loaning power got by the banks would amount to three times what it would otherwise be. If it could lend four-fifths, then it will be five

times; and so on. The question how large a part of its deposits a bank can lend depends in a great measure on the extent to which the different banks directly or indirectly pool their resources" (Marshall [1926]).

The proportion of its deposits that a bank could lend was determined by its desired ratio of cash reserves (gold, for example) to its total deposits, for cash reserves plus loans equal total deposits. Therefore, an expansion in total bank deposits (an expansion of their "loaning power") could be effected by an expansion in their cash reserves and would, in fact, be a multiple of the expansion in reserves.

Marshall was well aware of the argument of his contemporary, Giffen, that the amount of the banks' cash reserves and therefore of bank deposits was affected by the level of nominal income (py). The causal chain proposed by Giffen was as follows: An increase in nominal income, a boom, causes a drain of cash reserves. Because, for example, wages rise in a boom, more cash is needed by the private sector for transactions such as the payment of wages that cannot be paid by checks. In consequence, it was argued, both the cash reserves of the banks and the volume of bank deposits will decline. When Marshall's successors changed the definition of money so that it included bank deposits, such a mechanism clearly implied that the absolute price level and real income have an effect on the supply of money. For example, in Pigou's (1917) statement of the Quantity Theory,[18] the supply of money is given full consideration and the flavor of his view is expressed by the statement: "In the real world we cannot always hope to meet only with causes that act either on demand alone or on supply alone. The same cause may easily act upon both."

Similarly, the Neoclassical Quantity Theorists of the Chicago school recognized the influence on the money supply of a change in nominal income or fluctuations in business activity. Among other factors, the mechanism which was assumed was one where a rise in business activity causes banks to be willing to hold a lower proportion of cash reserves to total deposits. This may occur either because an increase in business activity raises bankers' confidence, or, as modern monetary theory would have it, because it leads to a rise in interest rates, so that banks are induced to hold greater interest-bearing loans as assets and less (non-interest-bearing) cash reserves. The details of the mechanism were not always made explicit by the Chicago Quantity Theorists, but they clearly took the view that business expansion would cause an expansion of bank lending and bank deposits and a contraction would have the opposite effect. This relationship between economic activity and the money supply meant that the banking system would cause economic fluctuations to be magnified. An expansion would cause an

[18]Pigou appears to work with a Quantity Theory where money is defined as cash and excludes bank deposits. In fact, however, his equations are modified versions of the Cambridge Equation and the modifications are equivalent to defining money in the Cambridge equation as cash plus bank deposits (or, as he called it: "titles to legal tender").

expansion of money supply which, as the Fisher Equation suggests, would react back on business activity, encouraging its further expansion.[19] It was these destabilizing possibilities that led Simons to his polemical proposals for monetary (and other) reforms in his "Rules versus Authorities in Monetary Policy" (1936). There he makes the position clear: "In the very nature of the system, banks will flood the economy with money . . . during booms and precipitate futile efforts at general liquidation afterward."[20] Because he considered such a possibility so real and so dangerous to the stability of capitalism, Simons formulated a radical, in fact a utopian, proposal for reform of the monetary system.

6.4 ASSESSMENT OF THE QUANTITY THEORY TRADITION IN THE LIGHT OF WICKSELL'S WORK

We have seen in this chapter that the pre-Keynesian Quantity Theory tradition was a rich one with many sophisticated insights. If we take care to understand it correctly, we find that real income is not assumed to be always at full employment, velocity is not assumed to be constant, and the money supply is not assumed to be exogenous. Thus, it is incorrect to define the Quantity Theory as the simple proposition that an exogenous change in the money supply causes a proportionate change in the absolute price level. Even merely dropping the assumption that real income is every instant at its full-employment level makes the Quantity Theory more sophisticated and emphasizes the effects on real income and employment of a change in the money supply. As early as Hume's essay "Of Money" (first published in 1750), this was well recognized:

> It is certain that since the discovery of the mines in America, industry has increased in all the nations of Europe . . . ; and this may justly be ascribed, among other reasons, to the increase of gold and silver. Accordingly, we find that in every kingdom, into which money begins to flow in greater abundance than formerly, everything takes on a new face; labour and industry gain life; the merchant becomes more enterprising, and even the farmer follows his plough with greater alacrity and attention . . . .

The impact of a change on money supply was explained in a way that tends to imply a real balance effect theory:

> To account, then, for this phenomenon, we must consider, that though the high price of commodities be a necessary consequence of the increase of gold and silver, yet it follows not immediately upon that increase; but some time is required before the money circulates

[19]This explosive tendency was, in addition, thought to be magnified by changes in velocity. As we saw in Sec. 6.2, a rise in prices was believed to create expectations of future price rises and thereby reduce the demand for money and increase velocity.

[20]The term "money substitutes," rather than "money," appeared in the original, but it is clear from Simons's preceding paragraph that he identified these as being the same as money.

> through the whole state, and makes its effect be felt on all ranks of people. At first, no alteration is perceived; by degrees the price rises, first of one commodity, then of another; till the whole at last reaches a just proportion with the new quantity of specie which is in the kingdom (Hume, [1875]).

The mechanism that Hume appears to have had in mind (in this particular statement) to explain the effect of the increase in money supply on the demand for goods is some direct mechanism, some mechanism analogous to the real balance effect. Other early Quantity Theorists, in recognizing the relationship between the demand for money (or velocity) and interest rates, seem to have perceived some indirect mechanism for explaining the effect of money supply on the economy. The indirect mechanism is similar to the ideas developed by Keynes in his *General Theory* insofar as it proposes that an increase in the money supply *first* has an effect of lowering interest rates, and this result *then* increases demand for goods and causes prices to rise. Such an indirect mechanism can be found explicitly in other statements by Hume and also in the writings of Ricardo and John Stuart Mill. Perhaps the clearest Classical statement of the indirect mechanism is that of Joplin (1823):

> Money, being more abundant, creates itself employment, either by the increased facilities with which it is lent out, *or by the reduced interest which is charged for it*; by which means traders are induced to increase their merchant stocks [investment demand for goods], and people in general to enter into undertakings in which the employment of labour is involved; but which, with a greater scarcity of money, they would not have attempted.

This type of analysis is a precursor of Keynes's approach. In addition, like the Neoclassical writers, Joplin developed a theory of time preference to explain the effect of the interest rate on the demand for consumption goods (or its opposite, saving). A fall in the interest rate has this effect:

> The man of landed or fixed income is less tempted to save than he was before. Saving is made by a sacrifice of present enjoyment, for a future good, in the shape of an increase of annual income. But as the annual income to be derived from saving diminishes, the temptation to save is reduced (Joplin [1832]).

Thus, in Joplin's work we have the elements of a theory that indicate that a rise in the money supply causes a fall in the interest rate. This increases the demands for investment goods and consumption goods, thereby increasing business activity, real income and employment, and eventually raising prices.

An earlier work which concentrated on the effect of the interest rate on investment was that of Thornton (1802). But what was remarkable about Thornton's work was that he analyzed not only how a fall in the interest rate on loans would increase the demand for investment goods, but also how, in an economy with a system of bank credit and paper money, it would involve an expansion in the supply of credit and paper money. Thus, Thornton analyzed what we would now call the effect of the rate of interest on the money supply (but what in those days was called its effect on the velocity of money, since money was defined to include only gold or its equivalent). This aspect of Thornton's work was appreciated by later writers, such as Ricardo and Mill. Moreover, Ricardo gave particularly strong support to Thornton's analysis of how changes in the money supply cause excess demand for goods by temporarily influencing interest rates. In *The High Price of Bullion* (1966, Vol. 3), he wrote that if the supply of money (notes) were increased:

> [These notes] would be sent into every market, and would everywhere raise the prices of commodities, till they were absorbed in the general circulation. It is only during the interval of the issue, and their effect on prices, that we should be sensible of an abundance of money; interest would, during that interval be under its natural level; but as soon as the additional sum of notes or of money became absorbed in the general circulation, the rate of interest would be as high.

As Schumpeter (1954) argues, however, Thornton's work should really be seen as an early form of Wicksell's. For Wicksell, working nearly a century later, independently developed his own similar ideas on the subject and, in particular, on the relationship between the interest rate and the supply of bank deposits.

Wicksell's Direct and Indirect Mechanisms

It is time to summarize the pre-Keynesian Quantity Theory by turning to Wicksell. Not only is it to Wicksell that we owe the terms *direct* and *indirect mechanism*. More important is it that his writings at the end of the nineteenth century present the Quantity Theory in its most sophisticated pre-Keynesian form. It takes account of the existence of unemployment and excess supplies of goods in transition periods (that is, the invalidity of Say's Identity), and it is built around the effect of the rate of interest on the demands for money (or credit) and goods and on the supply of money by the banking system. Wicksell's analysis of the role of the interest rate is summarized in his well-known theory of "the cumulative process." We shall examine it on the assumption that the economy is at full employment, but before doing so, it must be made clear that Wicksell explicitly repudiated Say's Identity and understood that the mechanism behind the Quantity Theory can be based on the real balance effect and disequilibrium in the goods markets. The following quotation from *Interest and Prices* (1898) shows this:

> Now let us suppose that for some reason or other commodity prices rise while the stock of money remains unchanged, or that the stock of money is diminished while prices remain temporarily unchanged. The cash balances will gradually appear to be *too small in relation to the new level of prices*. . . . I therefore seek to enlarge my balance. This can only be done—neglecting for the present the possibility of borrowing, etc.—through a *reduction* in my *demand* for goods and services, or through an *increase* in the *supply* of my own commodity . . . or through both together. The same is true of all other owners and consumers of commodities . . . the universal reduction in demand and increase in supply of commodities will necessarily bring about a continuous fall in all prices. This can only cease when prices

> have fallen to the level at which the cash balances are regarded as *adequate.* (In the first case prices will now have fallen to their original level) (Wicksell [1936].)

In this passage Wicksell was assuming a constant stock of money and ignoring the banking system. The real interest of his work lies, however, in his analysis of the operation of an economy with a banking system. In his examination of the cumulative process that results from the operation of such a system, he was working (as were Thornton and other Classical writers) with a definition of money as gold but not bank deposits. Therefore, a change in bank deposits is considered as a change in the velocity of gold money.

Assume that gold is discovered in a foreign country. That country will, because of its increased money stock, import more goods from the home country. That is, there will be an excess demand for goods and this will push home prices in an upward direction. This is Wicksell's *direct mechanism.* It is first to be found in his *Lectures on Political Economy* (1906; 1935, Vol. 2), and there he emphasizes its practical importance and the relative unimportance of the *indirect mechanism.* The latter, however, was the only mechanism Wicksell discussed in his *Interest and Prices* (1898; 1936) and it is at the center of the cumulative mechanism.

The indirect mechanism concerns the effect of an increase in money supply on interest rates, supply of bank deposits (or loans), and demand for goods. Suppose that the individuals who receive gold from foreign purchasers as a result of the direct mechanism then deposit this gold in banks. The level of the banks' cash reserves will thereby be increased, and in consequence, they will wish to expand their supply of loans and bank deposits. They will be able to do so only by lowering their rate of interest charged on loans. At the lower rate of interest, capitalists find it more profitable than previously to borrow in order to buy investment goods: the banks' rate of interest is lower than what Wicksell termed the "natural rate," the marginal rate of return on the stock of physical capital. This demand for investment goods creates excess demand in the goods market (and, Wicksell argued, this is reinforced by a multiplier effect on consumption). The consequence is that prices rise. Thus, the increase in money supply has, through the indirect mechanism (accompanied by the direct mechanism), caused an increase in prices.

Moreover, the indirect mechanism's cumulative process is not explosive. It does not carry on forever through self-magnifying feedbacks. As Patinkin (1952, 1965) shows, Wicksell assumed that there is a stabilizing factor within the process. The rise in prices causes a return of the banks' planned supply of loans to its initial level. This is so because it induces a greater demand for cash (gold) for use by the private sector to make wage and other payments. Thus, there is a drain on the banks' cash reserves, and as their level falls, so does the banks' desire to supply loans. The consequence is that the banks return their interest rate to its initial level in order to protect their reserves. It then again equals the "natural rate," so the excess demand for investment and other goods is eradicated and the price rise is halted. The cumulative process would be explosive only in the special case (which Wicksell considered an extreme one) where the economy is a pure credit or *inside money* economy. Here, all money takes the form of bank deposits and the banks hold no gold or other form of cash as reserves. In such a case, the banks could permanently keep their rate of interest below the "natural rate" and would not be constrained by any loss of reserves.

Wicksell's cumulative process is similar to that analyzed by the Classical and Neoclassical writers considered in preceding paragraphs. It is closest to that of Giffen, for both emphasize that the factor that causes the process to be determinate and the interest rate to return to its initial level is the drain of reserves that affects the *supply* of bank loans and deposits. The indirect mechanism suggested by Thornton and Ricardo, on the other hand, works through the effect of price increases on the *demand* for bank credit, since the rise in the price of investment goods increases the demand for credit at any given interest rate. But the important point is that Wicksell's work is the summation of a long Quantity Theory tradition—and Wicksell made clear that he saw his work as an elaboration and defense of the Quantity Theory. This tradition is not far removed from the propositions developed by Keynesians.

CHAPTER

SEVEN

THE MODERN QUANTITY THEORY

The Quantity Theory tradition reviewed in Chapter 6 was all but totally eclipsed between the 1930s and 1950s by the acceptance, in academic circles at least, of Keynesian ideas. There were important exceptions to this eclipse. From the Cambridge school, D. H. Robertson (1940, 1966) continued to attack his fellow Cambridge economist, Keynes, for many years after World War II. His textbook *Money* continued to be used for teaching even though its first edition was published in 1922, and even in its revised editions its basis was the Quantity Theory, however sophisticated. At Chicago, the Quantity Theory continued to be taught by adherents such as Mints. But they were probably exceptions, and even in their teaching, the old Quantity Theory tradition had to take account of Keynes's work.

In the 1960s, however, there began a substantial renewal of interest in the Quantity Theory. But it concerned a modern version of the Quantity Theory, the first major developments of which are found in two articles by Friedman (1956a, 1959), written in the 1950s. We shall see in this chapter that this modern Quantity Theory is to some extent different from the tradition of the Old Quantity Theory as it was taught at Chicago, even though Friedman claims that it does represent the Chicago, "oral tradition." In certain respects, however, it continues some of the ideas that were developed at Cambridge and it is parallel to some of the work of Keynesians. This is particularly true of the modern Quantity Theory's analysis of the demand for money. More generally, we shall note that many of its conclusions parallel those reached by the old Quantity Theorists.

In this chapter we concentrate on the theory of the demand for money developed by Chicago's new Quantity Theorists (Sections 7.1 and 7.2). But the modern Quantity Theory is not only a theoretical system derived from a priori principles; it is a body of thought having as a major component systematic empirical relationships that are claimed to have been found in historical data but for which, in many cases, no well-developed theoretical explanation has been offered. Therefore, we consider here some of these empirical relationships, although a full, detailed consideration of empirical studies is left until Chapter 20. In the present chapter, we look in particular at early empirical studies upon which the modern Quantity Theorists drew to support their theory of the demand for money and the idea that the money supply is exogenously determined (Sections 7.2 and 7.3). There are two other matters that are not explicitly considered until later chapters since an appreciation of them requires an understanding of Keynesian analysis and econometric findings. The first is the underlying theoretical framework of the new Quantity Theory; the second is the question of whether the new Quantity Theory represents a body of thought, *monetarism*, that is significantly different from, and better than, Keynesianism. This is one of the most hotly pursued debates in modern monetary theory and we devote a special chapter, Chapter 21, to it.

7.1 FRIEDMAN'S PURE THEORY OF THE DEMAND FOR MONEY

The pure theory of the demand for money put forward by Friedman (1956a), the leading writer among the new Quantity Theorists, is in his essay "The Quantity Theory of Money: A Restatement." Friedman considered the question of the demand for money to be a highly significant aspect of the new Quantity Theory, or as itself being the Quantity Theory:

> The Quantity Theory is in the first instance a theory of the *demand* for money. It is not a theory of output, or of money income, or of the price level. Any statement about these variables requires combining the quantity theory with some specifications about the conditions of supply of money and perhaps about other variables as well (Friedman [1956a]).

The theory is developed along lines that would be recognizable to an old Quantity Theorist from Cambridge. It is based on the principle that an individual's demand for money is constrained by her or his "resources" (to use a Cambridge term) and is determined by equating at the margin the returns on money holdings with the returns on alternative assets. The return on money derives from its intangible services in facilitating exchanges and providing security against bankruptcy; the returns on other assets are, in general, measurable in nominal or real terms. Although the general principles of the analysis would have been recognizable to many pre-Keynesian Quantity Theorists, Friedman's analysis is considerably more formal, sophisticated, and complete than those that went before. Specifically, much of his "Restatement" essay is concerned with a sophisticated elaboration of the nature of the returns on assets that are alternatives to money and with the nature of the resources (or budget) constraint. Having completed this task, Friedman makes several simplifying assumptions to arrive at a demand function for nominal money balances of the following form (expressed in symbols that are ours rather than Friedman's):

$$M^D = pf(r^B, r^E, \dot{p}, h, y, u) \tag{7.1}$$

The variables have the following meaning and rationale: M^D is planned demand for nominal money balances and p is the absolute price level. By dividing through with p, therefore, Equation 7.1 could be expressed as a demand function for real balances, M^D/p, with the same variables within the brackets. The variables r^B, r^E, and $\dot{p}$ reflect the nominal yields on assets that could be held as alternatives to money (per $1 of nominal value held). The variable r^B is the rate of interest on bonds; r^E is the market yield of equities. The variable $\dot{p}$ is the percentage rate of change of the price level. It therefore reflects the nominal rate of return on holdings of goods as assets. These goods may include automobiles, houses, or (in the case of firms) machinery: that is, any goods that are not consumed soon after purchase but are held for the services they yield over time.

Returns on Assets

We have not yet considered all the variables in Friedman's demand function, but we can summarize the meaning of what has so far been discussed. The existence of the first three variables within parentheses arises because it is assumed that for households, the alternative forms in which wealth can be held are money, bonds, equities, and goods. The demand for nominal money balances is determined by equating the returns on each at the margin. If, starting from a position of utility-maximizing equilibrium, the rates of return on bonds, equities, and goods were to rise, the demand for nominal balances would fall to the point at which their marginal return would equal the new (marginal) returns on these three alternative assets. A reduction in nominal balances is presumed to increase their marginal return because, with a smaller amount of money, each increment would provide more services than if there were a larger initial amount: each unit of money balances would have to work harder to facilitate exchange, provide security, and do the other undefined but "good" things that money does.

The existence of p on the right-hand side of Equation 7.1 requires some elaboration. As it stands, the equation expresses the idea that (dividing through by p) the demand for *real* balances is a function of *nominal* returns per nominal dollar of alternative assets and *real* income (which, as we shall see, indirectly represents the budget constraint). This differs from the more satisfactory idea that the demand for an asset in real terms is a function of the *real* returns on alternative real assets and a budget constraint in real terms. In fact, however, Equation 7.1 is the same as a function expressed solely in real terms. Consider, for example, the nominal rate of return on a \$1 bond, r^B, representing receipts of $\$(1/100)r^B$ per annum. If the price level is initially unity and then doubles in the first period, the real value of the bond halves to \$0.5, as does the real value of interest receipts [to $0.5\$(1/100)r^B$ per annum]. Therefore the nominal interest yield on an asset whose value is measured in nominal terms r^B, for example, is the same as the yield on the asset valued in real terms. Equation 7.1 can therefore be regarded as the demand for real balances as a function of the relative real returns on alternative real assets. This reasoning assumes that the price level in the first period obtains in future periods. If inflation or deflation is expected for future periods, the real rate will be the nominal rate minus $\dot{p}^e$ where $\dot{p}^e$ is the expected rate of inflation. This last term may, on simplifying assumptions, be treated as $\dot{p}$, the current rate of inflation, which is another way of rationalizing the existence of $\dot{p}$ in Equation 7.1.

Income and Wealth Constraints

The fact that money balances are considered as an asset comparable with other assets makes clear that Friedman's theory is framed in terms of *stocks* rather than *flows*. This approach enables us to proceed with examining the equation by jumping one variable (h) and considering the role of y, real income. This variable is relevant as the budget constraint. Comparing the returns on alternative assets, as in the last paragraph, only enables the individual to decide on the *proportion* of total wealth to be held in the form of money. It does not determine the *level* of desired money balances. Introduction of the total size of wealth (together with the relative returns) does permit this. Real income, y, enters as a representative of this wealth constraint.

This, however, appears puzzling, since real income is a *flow* variable and the constraint on the choice between assets should be a *stock* variable. The explanation is that Friedman considers y to be a *proxy* for the stock variable, total real wealth, $\bar{w}$. The argument for this is interesting and is fundamental to much of Friedman's work (including that on the consumption function [1957]). In general terms, income can be thought of as a return on wealth:

$$y = r\bar{w} \tag{7.2}$$

where r is a measure of yield. Therefore, wealth can be defined as:

$$\bar{w} = \frac{y}{r} \tag{7.3}$$

We could, therefore, have y/r on the right-hand side of Equation 7.1 to represent the wealth constraint. However, by making the simplifying assumption that such returns are functionally related to one another, we need not include the denominator, r, explicitly, for it is a weighted average of the returns on all forms of wealth, and, as we have seen, some of these returns are already included in the function. Friedman therefore approximates the total real value of wealth by y, real income.

Two points about this procedure are immediately worthy of note. First, the rationale for the inclusion of y means that its inclusion does not violate the status of the demand function as a theory framed in terms of stocks. This is in contrast to the pre-Keynesian Cambridge Quantity Theorists, who were considerably less rigorous in specifying the concept of time in their model. Most frequently, it appears that their model was one where the demand for a *stock* of nominal money balances was determined by the *flow* of nominal income.[1] Second, a moment's reflection indicates that an individual's income does not only consist of the yield on financial and physical assets. For the vast majority of persons, income is derived from work. Within Friedman's framework, this objection is easily overcome, for $\bar{w}$, wealth, consists not only of financial and physical assets, but also comprises *human wealth*. Similarly, r in Equations 7.2 and 7.3 is not only an average of the yields on financial and physical assets, but it also reflects the yield on human wealth, r^H. This yield, r^H, can be thought of as the wages and other payments earned through work. Therefore human wealth can be regarded as the capitalized (or discounted) value of future earnings from work; in this way it is analogous to the wealth or asset value of a bond or machine which, as we saw in Chapter 2, can be considered as the capitalized value of the future receipts produced by that asset. One can invest in human wealth by, for example, buying an education, since this presumably raises one's future earnings and therefore raises the capitalized value of future earnings.

It can be seen, therefore, that y represents a wealth constraint so comprehensive as to include human wealth. This enables us to return to a consideration of the variable h in Equation 7.1. If human wealth is one of the assets in the wealth constraint, it must be considered as an asset alternative to money. Consequently, the return on human wealth, r^H, should enter the demand function for money just as do the returns on other alternative assets. Friedman, however, argues that the possibilities of substituting between human wealth and other assets (including money) are severely restricted, at least in the short run: one cannot decide one day to sell oneself as a slave, thereby drastically reducing one's ownership of human wealth and substantially increasing the amount of money held. Therefore, the return on human wealth is not a relative return that is relevant to the decision at any instant on how much money one should hold. Instead, the variable h is introduced as a measure of the ratio between human wealth and all other forms of wealth, a ratio that is fixed and not, at any instant, the subject of a choice relevant to money holdings.

[1]Some, like Pigou (1917), were more circumspect in writing R, resources, instead of y, on the right-hand side and saying that it could be thought of as income *or* wealth. Others argued that both income *and* wealth were included in resources.

Finally, the variable u is a portmanteau variable. It reflects changes in tastes and preferences, and these, to some extent, may be linked to objective circumstances, such as uncertainty (or, in the words of the old Quantity Theorists, confidence) and geographic mobility. Its vagueness reflects the level of abstraction at which Friedman's theory is developed—a level permitting many simplifying assumptions to be made in arriving at Equation 7.1.

Friedman's theory of the individual's demand for money is, therefore, constructed on the principles of utility maximization that are fundamental to Neoclassical economics. Given tastes (a particular level of u), individuals maximize utility subject to their budget constraints. The budget constraints are determined by their total wealth (approximated by y) and the relative returns on feasible assets (these relative returns being conceptually equivalent to the relative prices used in consumer theory). The result is a demand function for money (Eq. 7.1) where desired money balances are a *stable* function of, among other things, interest rates and real income. This demand function can also be written in the form of a velocity equation:

$$V = \frac{py}{M^D} = g(r^B, r^E, p, h, y, u) \tag{7.4}$$

indicating that the desired velocity of money is a stable function of those same variables.

7.2 PERMANENT INCOME AND THE DEMAND FOR MONEY

Friedman's pure theory of the demand for money, outlined above, is well developed and is acceptable to a majority of monetary theorists. It is, in fact, similar to many of the demand functions for money developed by Keynesians. Keynesian demand functions, however, usually take a simplified form by assuming that the only alternative assets to money are government bonds, and such simplifications ease the problems of econometric work and of building macroeconomic models of the whole economy. Friedman and the other new Quantity Theorists also, and for similar reasons, do not work with the complicated demand and velocity functions represented by Equations 7.1 and 7.4. They adopt simplified demand functions, but their simplification is very different from that used by Keynesians. The new Quantity Theory's demand function for money is simplified by treating the demand for money as a function of *permanent income* alone (whereas Keynesians include a rate of interest as a principal variable in the demand function). The possibility of this simplification was hinted at in Friedman's "restatement" essay (1956a) but was not developed until the necessity for a link between the "Restatement" and empirical studies became pressing. It is therefore set out in Friedman's article "Theoretical and Empirical Results" (1959), and it is closely related to his consumption function theory (1957), where the demand for consumption goods is treated as a function of permanent income.

Permanent Income

The first point in an exposition of this simplified theory of the demand for money must be an explanation of the concept of permanent income. An individual's *permanent* income differs in principle (and, generally, in quantity) from current or *measured* income. We can state the following general definition.

> An individual's permanent income is a weighted average of expected future income receipts.

If the individual's planning horizon is his or her expected lifetime, we can calculate the permanent income if we know the lifetime income the person expects to receive and if we know, in addition, the discount rate used in capitalizing future income streams. This can be seen most easily if we give a more exact specification of permanent income and its relationship to the individual's wealth.

Let $\bar{w}_1$ be the individual's real wealth at time 1 and let us define this as including both human and nonhuman wealth. We have seen in Chapter 2 that wealth can be represented as the capitalized value of a future income stream. Therefore, if $y^e_{1.i}$ represents the real income the individual expects now (in period 1) to receive in the ith period from the ownership of nonhuman assets and from work (the ownership of human wealth), then the individual's human and nonhuman wealth is:

$$w_1 = \frac{y_1}{(1+r)} + \frac{y^e_{1.2}}{(1+r)^2} + \frac{y^e_{1.3}}{(1+r)^3} + \cdots \frac{y^3_{1.i}}{(1+r)^i} + \cdots \frac{y^e_{1.n}}{(1+r)^n} \tag{7.5}$$

where r is the discount rate.[2] Let us say that this discount rate also equals the rate of return per period on wealth, r. The individual's *permanent income* in the current period is then

$$y^P_1 = r\bar{w}_1 \tag{7.6}$$

It is clearly a weighted average of expected future income receipts, since the variable $\bar{w}_1$ in Equation 7.6 is a weighted (geometric) average of expected future income, as is shown by Equation 7.5. In a sense, then, this period's permanent income can be defined as the amount of income which, if it were actually received this period—if measured income in this period equaled permanent income, $\bar{y}_1 = y^P_1$—could be wholly consumed without lowering the

[2]Equation 7.5 assumes that the individual's remaining span is n periods (n years). By applying the discount factor to y_1, the current period's income, we are assuming that current period wealth w_1 is measured at the beginning of the period and that income is received in a lump sum at the end of the period. It should also be noted that Eq. 7.5 implies a particular specification of the concept of permanent income. Friedman is unwilling to commit himself to any such specification of an individual's permanent income. See Friedman (1957, Chap. 3).

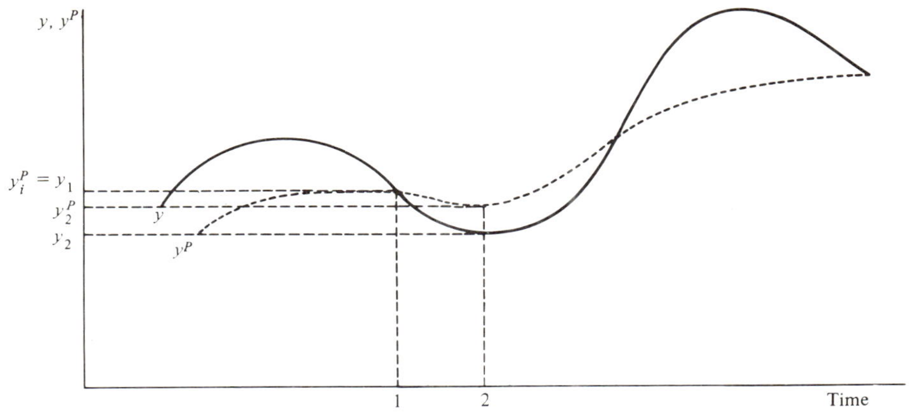

Figure 7-1

individual's wealth.[3] This follows from Equation 7.6, since it defines permanent income as the return on wealth rather than wealth itself.

The important characteristics of permanent income are that it is not the same as current measured income *and* that its time path is, in general, different from that of current income. The difference between their time paths is illustrated in Figure 7.1 for the case of an "average" individual in an economy that is growing over time but is subject to cyclical fluctuations. The time path of measured income is represented by the solid line, while that of permanent income is shown by the broken line.

It is clear from this illustration that permanent income is considerably more stable than measured income. The rationale for this can be deduced from Equations 7.5 and 7.6, and although several explanations of this relative stability are possible, we shall employ the simplest one. Equation 7.6 indicates that permanent income is a rate of return, r, multiplied by wealth, w. If we suppose that r is constant (an arbitrary assumption), then, to examine the relationship between measured income and permanent income, we must examine the relationship of both to wealth. Equation 7.5 indicates that, given r, wealth is wholly determined by present and expected future income ($\bar{y}_1, y^e_{1.2}, y^e_{1.3}, \ldots, y^e_{1.n}$). If only present income, $\bar{y}_1$, changes, then wealth changes in the same direction but to a smaller extent, since its other components ($y^e_{1.2}, y^e_{1.3}, \ldots, y^e_{1.n}$) are unchanged. Since wealth changes by less than the change in present measured income and since r is assumed constant, it follows that permanent income, $y^P = rw$, changes by less than measured income. In terms of Figure 7.1, if the individual is initially at time 1 where

[3]Or, more accurately, this income could be consumed without lowering the individual's wealth by more than it would be lowered by the passing of one period. For, given that any life is finite, the passing of time lowers the individual's wealth, *ceteris paribus*, since the number of future periods' receipts to be discounted is reduced. This effect can be offset, however, by abstention from consumption.

permanent income equals measured income, at time 2 the measured income will have fallen because the economy has moved into recession. This does not, however, cause a proportionate fall in permanent income because the individual's sudden impoverishment does not lead to a change in expectations of future income.

The example is unrealistic since it is likely that, in fact, individuals' expectations *are* affected by their current experiences. A small modification would increase the plausibility of the explanation. We may assume that the individual's expectations of future income ($y^e_{1.2}, y^e_{1.3}, \ldots, y^e_{1.n}$) are a function of present income, $\bar{y}_1$, but that expectations are sticky. In other words, a fall in present measured income does cause a fall in expected future incomes but it is less than proportionate: a 10 percent fall in one causes a fall of less than 10 percent in the others. It will then still be true that a fall in present measured income causes a smaller fall in wealth and, therefore, in permanent income.[4]

The rationale for the relative stability of permanent income can also be appreciated at a more intuitive level. If a person's current income falls, this decrease does not, in general, lead to a feeling that their lifetime income will fall proportionately. It will have some effect in that direction, but we may assume that the individual, in calculating lifetime income takes account of the fact that income has ups and downs. The person will know that cyclical fluctuations are inherent in the economy, that there are slumps in which wage and interest earnings fall below the average income and booms in which they rise above it. In other words, we can say, as Friedman does, that current measured income consists of two components, permanent income, y^P, and transitory income, y^T:

$$y_1 = y^P_1 + y^T_1 \tag{7.7}$$

Transitory income consists of receipts that are known to be temporary and therefore do not affect permanent income. Thus, transitory income includes receipts of gambling winnings, unexpected gifts (which are thought of as once-and-for-all receipts), and most of the extra earnings gained in booms (if they are expected to be offset by earnings lost in slumps).

Simplified Demand Function

Friedman (1959) argues that permanent income is the variable to which individuals respond in adjusting their planned money holdings. This is because, as Equation 7.6 shows, permanent income can be treated as a proxy

[4]An even more complex example is one where the fall in present income is accompanied by a fall in the discount rate and rate of return on wealth, r. Here, there are several influences at work on $y^P = rw$. First, the factors enumerated in the text change w, but by less than the percentage by which $\bar{y}$ changes. Second, since the discount rate falls, w may rise or, in any case, not fall by as much as it would otherwise do. Third, since r falls, the product rw with a given w falls, but, as we have seen, w is not given. The net outcome will again be that y^P falls by a smaller percentage than the fall in $\bar{y}_1$.

for wealth. In other words, permanent income is a proxy for the budget constraint or wealth constraint in the individual's choice among alternative assets. In Section 7.1 we saw that in Friedman's pure theory of the demand for money, current measured income, $\bar{y}$, is used as a proxy for the wealth constraint. Once we distinguish between the permanent and the transitory components of current income, it can be argued that permanent income is the relevant proxy, since transitory income does not have a significant relationship to wealth. That is, the more specific Equation 7.6 becomes relevant, rather than the general Equation 7.2.

Thus, if we consider Equation 7.1 again:

$$M^D = p \,.\, f(r^B, r^E, \dot{p}, h, \bar{y}, u) \tag{7.1}$$

Friedman's argument (1959) implies that current income, $\bar{y}$, should be replaced with permanent income, y^P. Moreover, he argues by analogy that the current absolute price level, p, should be replaced with a variable measuring *permanent prices*, p^P. That is, the individual's demand for money is not affected by purely temporary movements of the price level but only by those that are expected to be permanent. It follows that Equation 7.1 can be transformed to:

$$M^D = p^P \,.\, f(y^P, z) \tag{7.8}$$

where z stands for all the variables on the right-hand side of Equation 7.1 except for y and p. Specifically, z includes the rate of return (or interest rate) variables which Equation 7.1 includes as determinants of the demand for nominal balances.[5]

If, in order to simplify further we assume or find empirically that the interest rates and other variables included in z do not have a systematic effect on the demand for money, we can replace Equation 7.8 with the simpler equation:

$$M^D = p^P f(y^P) \tag{7.9}$$

This equation could also be expressed in the form of an equation determining the desired velocity of money:[6]

$$V = \frac{Y}{M^D} = \frac{Y}{Y^P}\, g(y^P) \tag{7.10}$$

[5]Permanent income itself, in Eq. 7.8, reflects permanent prices, for y^P represents permanent *real* income. Friedman argues that this should be defined as permanent nominal income divided by permanent prices. Thus, $y^P = Y^P/p^P$ or, speaking in general terms, expected real income equals expected nominal income divided by the expected absolute price level. Also note that the reference in the text to interest-rate variables includes $\dot{p}$, the nominal rate of return on goods. This practice is followed hereafter in this chapter.

[6]The transformation of the demand function for money into a desired velocity function requires the prior assumption that the demand function for money refers to aggregate demand, since velocity is usually thought of as an aggregate concept. The derivation of the velocity function Eq. 7.10 from Eq. 7.9 is as follows: Velocity is defined as $V = Y/M^D$ and, substituting from Eq. 7.9, we have $V = Y/p^P f(y^P)$. By definition, $p^P y^P = Y^P$ or $p^P = Y^P/y^P$. Therefore, $V = Y/Y^P(y^P/f(y^P))$ or $V = Y/Y^P(g(y^P))$.

Equations 7.9 and 7.10 are the forms in which Friedman (1959) expresses the new Quantity Theory's concept of the demand for money. Clearly, they can be derived from the theory expressed in his "Restatement" (1956a) only in consequence of the many simplifications enumerated in this section. One of the most important simplifications is the dropping of z (the variable that reflects interest rates) from the demand function for money. As we shall see, Friedman contends that this simplification is justified on empirical grounds; from econometric investigation of United States data he (erroneously) concludes that measurable interest rates do not, in fact, have a systematic influence on velocity or the demand for money (although he does argue that a broad spectrum of yields, which are not all measurable, do have an effect).

We contended above that there is an advantage to be gained by simplifying theories to the point where they are expressible by equations (like Eqs. 7.9 and 7.10) that capture the theory's essentials in terms of a small number of variables. The advantage is that this simplification facilitates empirical work, the testing of theories against empirical data.[7] Indeed, Friedman maintains that an equation of the same form as Equation 7.10 is supported by the data. But before considering this, we must discuss yet another modification in the manner in which the theory is formulated.

Anticipated Income

The problem with using Equation 7.10 in empirical work is that permanent income is not directly observable. No data exist on individual or aggregate permanent income. This is not surprising: consideration of Equations 7.5 and 7.6 shows that to calculate permanent income, we must either have estimates of (human and nonhuman) wealth and the average rate of return or estimates of expected future income receipts and the discount rate. These data do not exist. Friedman therefore proposes that in order to apply Equations 7.9 and 7.10 to empirical data, we must find an empirical measure that acts as a proxy for permanent income. This proxy is defined by Friedman as "expected income," but, to avoid confusion, we shall name it *anticipated income.*[8] The consequence of this and the use of a similar proxy for permanent prices is that Equations 7.9 and 7.10 are replaced by

$$M^D = p^A f(y^A) \tag{7.11}$$

$$V = \frac{Y}{Y^A} g(y^A) \tag{7.12}$$

where the superscript A indicates anticipated variables.

[7]We shall see in Chapter 20 that such simplifications also have disadvantages in this respect, and they may outweigh the advantages.

[8]The possibility of confusion arises because, at the beginning of this section, we used "expected income" in the normal sense of income that, in this period, is expected to be received in a specific future period: $y^e_{1,2}$ is the real income that in period 1 is expected to be received in period 2. Permanent income, and therefore the proxy for it which we here call anticipated income, is a weighted average of such expected incomes.

The use of anticipated income as a proxy for permanent income does not immediately solve the problem of measurability, since a direct measure of individuals' anticipations or expectations does not exist. One further step is required, therefore, before fitting the demand function and velocity equation to empirical data. It is necessary to supplement the theory of the demand for money (velocity) with a theory of what determines anticipations. The theory employed by Friedman and frequently used in econometric work is known as the error adjustment hypothesis. It is assumed that the income that, in period T, one expects to obtain in future periods, y_T^A, is equal to what in the previous period was expected to obtain in the future, y_{T-1}^A, plus some adjustment for any error made in the last period's forecast. That is, period T's anticipations of real income are:

$$y_T^A = y_{T-1}^A + \beta(\bar{y}_T - y_{T-1}^A) \tag{7.13}$$

If last period's anticipations, y_{T-1}^A, are proved correct by this period's experience, $\bar{y}_T$, then this period's anticipations, y_T^A, are the same as last period's, y_{T-1}^A. [That is, in such circumstances, $y_T^A = y_{T-1}^A$ because $\bar{y}_T - y_{T-1}^A = 0$, and therefore $\beta(\bar{y}_T - y_{T-1}^A) = 0$.] If this period's actual measured income is greater than last period's anticipations of income, $\bar{y}_T > y_{T-1}^A$, then anticipations are adjusted so that this period's anticipations are greater than last period's, $y_T^A > y_{T-1}^A$. However, they are not adjusted by the full extent of the error in last period's forecast, but only by the proportion $0 < \beta < 1$ of the error.

This hypothesis concerning the manner in which anticipations are formed has a highly convenient property. Equation 7.11 can be expanded to permit anticipated income to be expressed as a function of past periods' actual incomes:[9]

$$y_T^A = \beta[\bar{y}_T + (l - \beta)\bar{y}_{T-1} + (l - \beta)^2\bar{y}_{T-2} \cdots\cdots (l - \beta)^n\bar{y}_{T-n}] \tag{7.14}$$

In other words, if the error adjustment hypothesis of Equations 7.13 and 7.14 is valid, then current anticipations of future income are determined by past actual income receipts.[10] Since the exact form of Equation 7.14 gives y_T^A as a weighted average of past actual incomes with the weights declining geometrically, the hypothesis implies that incomes received in the recent past have a greater influence on current anticipations than do incomes received in more distant periods.[11]

[9]The derivation of Eq. 7.14 from Eq. 7.13 can be achieved through the following procedure: Eq. 7.13 implies that $y_{T-1}^A = y_{T-2}^A + \beta(\bar{y}_{T-1} - y_{T-2}^A)$ and that y_{T-2}^A and y_{T-3}^A can be defined similarly. Substitute this expression for y_{T-1}^A into Eq. 7.13 and simplify terms; substitute the similar expression for y_{T-2}^A into the resulting equation and successively repeat this procedure. It will quickly be evident that Eq. 7.14 is the approximate result.

[10]The error adjustment hypothesis is also known as the adaptive expectations hypothesis. Here we have assumed that no explicit allowance is made for growth. The equations can easily be amended to allow explicitly for the fact that individuals' anticipations are based on a general expectation of growth as well as on the levels of past income receipts. For simplicity, however, we shall not make this amendment.

[11]Since $0 < \beta < 1$, it follows that $(1 - \beta)$ is between 0 and 1. Therefore $(1 - \beta)^2$ is smaller than $(1 - \beta)$; $(1 - \beta)^3$ is smaller still, and so on. After a certain number of periods, the weights become so small that the income of those periods can be ignored.

Anticipated income, though conceptually different from permanent income, has a time path with properties similar to the time path of permanent income. Specifically, anticipated income is, like permanent income, generally more stable than measured actual income. The relationship between anticipated income, y_T^A, and measured actual income, $\bar{y}_T$, is broadly similar to the relationship between $\bar{y}_T$ and permanent income that was illustrated in Figure 7.1. It is this similarity that permits the use of anticipated income as a proxy for permanent income in empirical work. The reason for the relative stability of anticipated income is clear. Anticipated income is a weighted average of present and past actual incomes. Past incomes are unchangeable at any point in time; therefore, a fall in current measured income affects only the first term on the right-hand side of Equation 7.14. Thus, a change in measured income affects anticipated income in the same period less than proportionately.

We have now reached the final form in which Friedman's Quantity Theory demand function for money can be estimated. If we express Equation 7.12 in the shorthand form:

$$y_T^A = \beta \sum_{i=0}^{n} (1-\beta)^i \bar{y}_{T-i} \tag{7.15}$$

and, reasoning by analogy, if we develop a similar expression for the anticipated price level, p^A:

$$p_T^A = \beta \sum_{i=0}^{n} (1-\beta)^i p_{T-i} \tag{7.16}$$

we can use these variables as proxies for permanent income and permanent prices. Substituting Equations 7.15 and 7.16 into Equation 7.9, we obtain a demand function for nominal balances that can be estimated, since the variables on the right-hand side are the present and past values of actual measured variables:

$$\left.\begin{aligned} M_T^D &= p_T^A f(y_T^A) \\ \text{or} \\ M_T^D &= \left[\beta \sum_{i=0}^{n} (1-\beta)^i p_{T-i}\right]\left[\beta \sum_{i=0}^{n} (1-\beta)^i \bar{y}_{T-i}\right] \end{aligned}\right\} \tag{7.17}$$

Similarly, the velocity equation, Equation 7.10, can be written as:

$$\left.\begin{aligned} V_T &= \frac{p_T \bar{y}_T}{p_T^A y_T^A}\, g(y_T^A) = \frac{\bar{Y}_T}{Y_T^A}\, g(y_T^A) \\ \text{or} \\ V_T &= \frac{p_T \bar{y}_T}{\left[\beta \sum_{i=0}^{n} (1-\beta)^i p_{T-i}\right]\left[\beta \sum_{i=0}^{n} (1-\beta)^i \bar{y}_{T-i}\right]}\, g\left[\beta \sum_{i=1}^{n} (1-\beta)^i \bar{y}_{T-i}\right] \end{aligned}\right\} \tag{7.18}$$

Both the demand function for nominal money balances and desired velocity are expressed in terms of present and past actual price levels and income receipts.

An Empirical Estimate

Equations 7.17 and 7.18 represent a version of the new Quantity Theory's permanent income hypothesis of the demand for money. It is a version reached, as we have seen, by a series of simplifying assumptions and additional hypotheses. The most significant of these are the assumptions, first, that there is no role for measurable interest-rate variables as systematic determinants of the demand for money or velocity; and second, that anticipated income (and prices) is determined in accordance with the error adjustment theory and represents a satisfactory proxy for permanent income. The justification to which Friedman appeals in support of these assumptions is the empirical support which the data give to the resulting equations: the question of how well they fit the facts.[12] The assumption concerning the error adjustment model of anticipated income has not been directly tested against data by Friedman, and we shall see in Chapter 20 that this omission creates difficulties in appraising his empirical work. The assumption concerning the role of measured interest rates is, however, justified by Friedman on the ground that it fits the data. Friedman (1959) finds that an equation of the form of Equation 17.18, fits the data well, and that it appears to leave no room for a separate influence of measured interest rates on velocity. The data suggest to Friedman that velocity, $\bar{Y}/M^D$, is a function of two variables alone: permanent real income, y^p, and the ratio of measured to permanent nominal income, $\bar{Y}/Y^p$.

One striking empirical phenomenon that Friedman cites as support for the theory encapsulated in Equation 7.18 is the following: United States data for the period 1870–1954 suggest that over the whole period, measured real income, $\bar{Y}_T$, rises while velocity, Y/M^D, falls—there is an inverse relationship between the two if we use averages of the data so as to eliminate cyclical fluctuations. If, on the other hand, we examine any one business cycle within the same period, we find a positive relationship— as real income rises in the boom, velocity rises, and velocity falls in the slump. The secular, long-run, relationship which Friedman finds for 1870–1954 is illustrated in stylized form in Figure 7.2; the cyclical relationship is illustrated in Figure 7.3. Equations 7.17 and 7.18 can account for this apparent paradox.

Consider, first, the secular data. Using constructed data of y^A and p^A and employing averages of y^A over each cycle as the data to be fitted (thereby eliminating cyclical influences), Friedman estimates the values of the parameters of Equation 7.18. He finds that in response to a 10 percent increase in anticipated real income, the demand for nominal balances increases by 18 percent. In other words, the demand for nominal balances has an elasticity of 1.8 with respect to anticipated real income: money is, in a sense, a "luxury" commodity. This implies that velocity falls if measured on the same secular basis. For, as y^A rises, M^D and M^D/p^A rise more than proportionately, and therefore $p^A y^A/M^D$ or Y^A/M^D falls. In the long run, however,

[12]This is in accordance with Friedman's support (1953) for the methodology known as positivism.

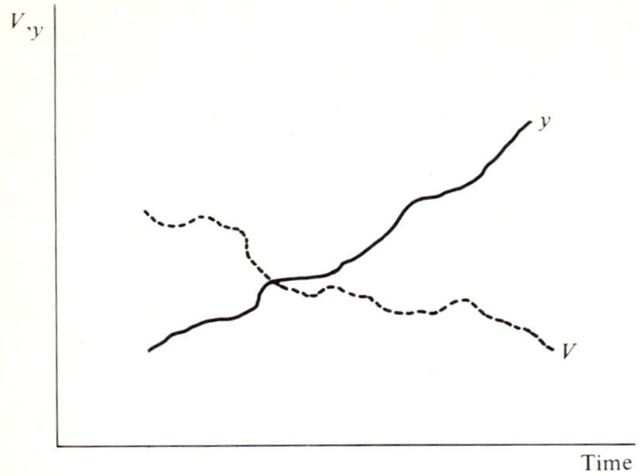

Figure 7-2

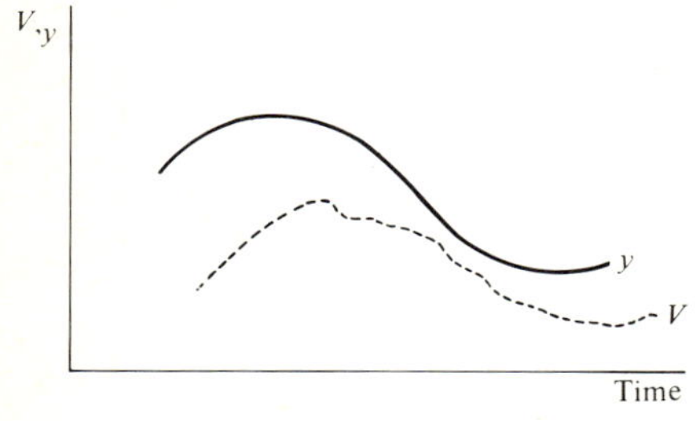

Figure 7-3

measured nominal income $\bar{Y}$ is approximately equal to Y^A, since the secular data on $\bar{Y}$ is constructed as an average for each cycle. The time path of this average is similar to the broken line in Figure 7.1 and is therefore similar to the time path of anticipated income Y^A. Therefore, since Y^A/M^D falls when measured by such secular data, so does Y/M^D— and Y/M^D is, of course, the definition of velocity.[13]

Consider now the cyclical data—behavior of the variables on an annual (rather than average) basis within each business cycle. Bear in mind that the data show that as real income rises in a boom, velocity rises, and vice versa. Equations 7.17 and 7.18 conform to this cyclical behavior, since they imply that the demand for nominal balances is a stable function of anticipated real income and anticipated prices. These are relatively stable over the cycle, and therefore the demand for nominal balances is, too. However, nominal measured income, $\bar{Y}$, is much less stable than the series of anticipated variables and therefore less stable than M^D. It rises by more than the demand for nominal balances in the boom and falls by more in the slump. Therefore

[13]The implication that velocity falls secularly can be seen more directly from Eq. 7.18. The similarity between the time path of anticipated income and the path of measured income, when measured as cycle averages, implies that the ratio $\bar{Y}/\bar{Y}^A$ on the right-hand side equals approximately 1. What remains is $\bar{Y}/M^D = V = g(Y^A)$, and Friedman's estimate of the demand function for money implies that this has a negative elasticity between 0 and (minus) 1.

the ratio $V = \bar{Y}/M^D$ rises in booms and falls in slumps.[14] The cyclical as well as the secular phenomena fit Equations 7.1 and 7.18. Friedman is therefore able to conclude that the data support the theory of the demand for money (and velocity) represented by those equations and all the hypotheses and assumptions that lie behind them.

Moreover, Friedman (1959) conducts an independent test of the underlying assumption that measured interest rates have no systematic influence on the cyclical demand for money or velocity.[15] He concludes that this assumption is supported by the data, although we shall see in Chapter 20 that this conclusion is contentious. In fact, it is based on an invalid statistical procedure, and other writers within the new Quantity Theory framework do find that, empirically, velocity is related to both anticipated income and interest rates.[16] Friedman's version of the new Quantity Theory demand function for money (or velocity function) denies the role of measurable interest rates, and we shall see the significance of this in Chapter 21. For the moment, however, we can note that this denial involves in some respects a departure from the pre-Keynesian Quantity Theory tradition examined in Chapter 6. It also entails a departure from Friedman's pure theory of the demand for money, examined in Section 7.1. There, determination of the demand for money by relative interest rates is emphasized, while the role of permanent income is only hinted. Here, permanent income (or its proxy, anticipated income) is given the completely dominant role, while the role of relatively measurable interest rates appears to be negligible.[17] It is this final version that is central to the new Quantity Theory.

7.3 DETERMINANTS OF THE MONEY SUPPLY

Friedman (1956) states three criteria that distinguish a Quantity Theorist from supporters of other macroeconomic theories. These are their views on "(1)

[14]This can also be seen directly from Eq. 7.18. Since y_T^A is relatively stable over the cycle (abstracting from the growth trend), this factor causes no significant change in V_T. But, since $\bar{Y}_T$ is less stable than Y_T^A, the ratio $\bar{Y}_T/Y_T^A$ rises in booms and falls in slumps. Therefore V_T follows the same pattern as $\bar{y}_T$ within the cycle.

[15]More specifically, Friedman finds that the residual movements in velocity (those movements remaining after the influence of the variables in Eq. 7.18 is taken into account) do not have a strong systematic relationship to interest rates within cycles. Within some types of cycle, however, there is some relationship with interest rates and especially with expectations of changes in the price level, the rate of return on goods. This is also emphasized by Friedman and Schwartz (1963b).

[16]See Meltzer (1963) and Laidler (1966) for two examples. These matters are discussed further in Chapter 20.

[17]Friedman has argued, however, that nonmeasurable components of the yield on assets may account for this finding, and therefore, in principle, his empirical results do not contradict the pure theory of his "Restatement." Moreover, the significance of the finding must be weighed in the light of the exceptions noted in footnote 16.

the stability and importance of the demand function for money; (2) the independence of the factors affecting demand and supply; and (3) the form of the demand function or related functions." In Section 7.2 we considered many of the points in (1) and (3). We have seen that Friedman proposes that the demand for money is a stable function of certain variables and that, in the permanent income hypothesis, this function implies that, given permanent income and other variables, the demand for money is inelastic with respect to interest rates. We now turn to consider item (2), the independence of demand and supply of money.

Again we must distinguish between pure theory and empirical findings. In pure theory we may conclude that changes in the supply of money may be determined by exogenous factors, such as the discovery of a new source of gold under a gold standard system or borrowing by the government to finance a war. They may also be determined by the demand for money, so that an increase in the demand for money leads the banking sector to increase its planned supply of money. Alternatively, the demand for and supply of money may both be affected by the same factors; a rise in nominal income, for example, may cause simultaneous increases in the demand for money and in the banking system's planned supply of money.

Friedman and Schwartz (1963a) and Cagan (1965) employ a formal framework that illustrates the theoretical possibility of each of these relationships, although the framework itself is not a theory of the supply of money; it is merely a system of accounting definitions. Define the money stock as consisting of currency held by the private sector and bank deposits owned by the private sector thus:

$$M(PS) \equiv C(PS) + D(PS) \tag{7.19}$$

Next, define total cash in the hands of the private and banking sectors as "high-powered money," $H(PBS)$. This equals currency held by the private sector, $C(PS)$, plus cash held as reserves by the banking system, $R(BS)$:

$$H(PBS) \equiv C(PS) + R(BS) \tag{7.20}$$

Divide both sides of Equation 7.19 by the total money stock $M(PS)$ to obtain:

$$\frac{H(PBS)}{M(PS)} \equiv \frac{C(PS)}{M(PS)} + \frac{R(BS)}{M(PS)} \tag{7.21}$$

and replace the last term, $R(BS)/M(PS)$, with the expression $R(BS)/D(PS)$ $[1 - C(PS)/M(PS)]$[18] to obtain:

[18]This substitution is possible because Eq. 7.19 implies $D = M - C$. Therefore $D = M - MC/M = M(1 - C/M)$. Dividing both sides of this equation by R, we obtain $D/R = M/R(1 - C/M)$ or, in other words, $R/M = R/D(1 - C/M)$, which is the expression we require to carry out the substitution.

$$\left.\begin{aligned} &\frac{H(PBS)}{M(PS)} \equiv \frac{C(PS)}{M(PS)} + \frac{R(BS)}{D(PS)} - \frac{C(PS)}{M(PS)}\frac{R(BS)}{D(PS)} \\ \text{or} \\ &M(PS) \equiv H(PBS) \cdot \frac{1}{\dfrac{C(PS)}{M(PS)} + \dfrac{R(BS)}{D(PS)} - \dfrac{C(PS)}{M(PS)}\dfrac{R(BS)}{D(PS)}} \end{aligned}\right\} \quad (7.22)$$

The interpretation of Equation 7.22 is straightforward. It tells us that, following from the two basic definitions, the changes in money stock in the hands of the private sector consist only of changes in:

1. $H(PBS)$, the stock of high-powered money, which in a modern system may be determined by the government (although it is not necessarily so)
2. $C(PS)/M(PS)$, the ratio that the private sector has between its holdings of cash and its total money balances, which is primarily determined by the private sector
3. $R(BS)/D(PS)$, the ratio which the banking system has between its cash reserves and its total deposits (or total assets in a simplified model)

All this is a matter of definitions. The interesting problem is to find to what extent movements in each of these three variables have historically influenced the money supply, and what determines each of these variables, for only then can we find what has historically determined changes in the money supply. If, for example, the ratios C/M and R/D have been relatively constant over time, so that all changes in the money supply can be accounted for by changes in the stock of "high-powered money," H, and if these changes in H are determined exogenously by the government, we can conclude that the money supply is exogenous. If, however, we find that changes in the money supply are attributable to changes in the banks' reserve ratio, R/D, and that these changes in R/D are systematically related to variables that influence the demand for money, we can conclude that the money supply is an endogenous variable.

The works of Friedman and Schwartz (1963a) and of Cagan (1965) are investigations of these questions. The two works complement each other. That of Friedman and Schwartz is a historical study which examines monetary factors in United States economic history for the period 1867–1960 and does so in such a way that many nonquantifiable factors are examined; the work of Cagan, on the other hand, is primarily a quantitative study of the influences on the money supply. Both studies are concerned not only with the influences that have operated on the money supply, but also with the effects of changes in the money supply.

The conclusions reached from these investigations are that in the short run—within an average business cycle—the money supply is an endogenous variable. Changes in nominal income and other endogenous variables influence the money supply. In other words, in a Quantity Theory equation, $M^s = (1/V)py$, changes in p, y, and V cause changes in M^s in the short run. But over the long run, and in the case of major business cycles, the money supply can be thought of as essentially exogenous. Changes in the money stock are the cause of changes in nominal income in the long run and at the inception of major slumps or expansions. In other words, given the stability of V, or at least the stability of the trend in V, exogenous changes in M^s cause changes in p and y if we examine long-run data. Friedman and Schwartz (1963) summarize this conclusion as follows:

> While the influence running from money to economic activity [via a stable interest inelastic demand function for money or velocity function] has been predominant, there have clearly also been influences running the other way, particularly during the shorter-run movements associated with the business cycle. The cyclical pattern of the deposit-reserve ratio is one example.... Mutual interaction, but with money rather clearly the senior partner in longer-run movements and in major cyclical movements, and more nearly an equal partner with money income and prices in shorter-run and milder movements—this is the generalization suggested by our evidence.

And Cagan (1965) reaches the similar conclusion that "Nine-tenths of the secular growth of the money stock over the whole period [1875–1960] was accounted for by the expansion of high-powered money," and "Secular changes in high-powered money can be attributed largely to the gold stock and, after 1914, in about equal measure also to Federal Reserve operations." These Federal Reserve operations may be thought of as exogenous factors, and Cagan appears to make this assumption although its validity is arguable. Short-run movements, cyclical fluctuations in the money supply, however, were found by Cagan to be largely attributable to changes in the ratio of currency to total money supply, C/M. This can be viewed as an endogenous factor, since Quantity Theorists argue that it is determined by the private sector's choice between holding money in the form either of cash or of currency. But even if C/M is an endogenous variable, Cagan is unable to isolate the variables that determine it.

7.4 THE NEW QUANTITY THEORY AND THE OLD

Friedman (1968) has claimed that the new Quantity Theory is a development of the pre-Keynesian theory at least insofar as the latter existed as an oral tradition at Chicago. Patinkin (1969) has contested this view. We may make our own assessment.

Friedman's pure theory of the demand for money, with its emphasis on the stability of the demand and velocity functions and the importance of their interest rates, is not a development of the old Quantity Theory developed at Chicago, although it does have some relationship to Fisher's work. It is best seen as a development of the work of the Quantity Theorists at Cambridge, since they emphasized the role of interest rates in determining velocity, at least in the short run.[19]

The applied theory of the demand for money, the permanent (or anticipated) income hypothesis, must also be considered, for it has a strong flavor of the old Quantity Theory in its distinction between the long run and the short run. Like many of the pre-Keynesian Quantity Theorists from Classical to Neoclassical days, Friedman emphasizes the long-run constancy of velocity in this work. Not that velocity is constant over the long run, but that it has a predictable, secular rate of change. In Friedman's work, this is explained on the ground that the demand for money is the demand for a "luxury," so velocity declines; in Marshall's work (see page 109), the development of credit institutions gives velocity a rising secular trend, but the "vision" is the same, so that secular movements in velocity are regarded as predictable long-run trends and changes in the money supply are, in the work of both Friedman and the old Quantity Theorists, seen as having a systematic effect on nominal income.[20] In the short run, however, Friedman concludes that velocity fluctuates around its trend. This, again, is similar to the views of the pre-Keynesian Quantity Theorists surveyed in Section 6.2. Friedman's explanation of this phenomenon is different from his predecessors' in that he emphasizes the influence of divergences between current measured income and permanent income. The old Quantity Theorists emphasized the role of interest rates (including price expectations) and the highly unstable role of general confidence in explaining these short-run fluctuations.

When we look at the Quantity Theorists' views on the supply of money, we again find a similarity between the old and the new. Friedman and his followers conclude that in the short run economic activity influences the supply of money, while long-run trends in the money supply are exogenously determined. This is similar to the old Quantity Theorists' analysis of the endogenous factors which in the short run influence the supply of money. Although some, like Wicksell, emphasized the role of interest rates (together with the private sector's demand for currency) in determining the supply of money in the short run, new Quantity Theorists, such as Cagan, stress the role of the private sector's demand for currency rather than the role of interest rates.

If we look at the Quantity Theory tradition as a set of propositions concerning both long-run and short-run behavior, it is clear that the new Quantity Theorists have certain similarities to the old. When, in later chapters, we consider further aspects of the new Quantity Theory, we shall find that they support the same interpretation.

[19]In fact, Friedman (1972) concedes Patinkin's point as far as the pure theory of the demand for money is concerned.

[20]Moreover, as we shall see in Chapter 21, Friedman assumes that the level of real income in the long run is the full-employment level, so that the long-run influence of money on nominal income is an influence on prices.

PART THREE

KEYNESIAN TRADITION

CHAPTER
EIGHT

A KEYNESIAN MODEL OF A MONETARY ECONOMY

Following the publication of Keynes's *General Theory* (1936), a particular interpretation of his theory became the dominant macroeconomic model in academic research, teaching, and the formulation of policy. It is important to emphasize, however, that this widely accepted Keynesian model is only one possible interpretation of Keynesian theory; therefore we shall call it the old Keynesian model rather than Keynes's own. The development of this interpretation of Keynes's work is attributable primarily to Hicks (1937) and Hansen (1953) (and is therefore often known as the Hicks-Hansen model), but other important contributions to its development have been Klein (1947), Samuelson (1948), and Modigliani (1944). The validity of this Keynesian model as the one appropriate interpretation of Keynes's work went unchallenged until the mid-1960s, when it was questioned by Clower (1965). Since then, the criticism of it and the development of an alternative interpretation of Keynes's work have been pursued by Clower (1967), Leijonhufvud (1968), Barro and Grossman (1971), and others. We shall consider this new interpretation of Keynes's work in Chapter 13.

Not only has the old Keynesian model's interpretation of Keynes's ideas been challenged by new Keynesians. From an early date it was questioned to a greater or lesser extent by Quantity Theorists beginning with Pigou (1943, 1947) and continuing into modern times as a result of Friedman's work. This challenge is understandable in view of the fact that Keynes saw his *General Theory* as an attack on the Quantity Theory tradition that had dominated thought until his day. He regarded this tradition as having a central feature from the days of Ricardo until the 1930s—belief in Say's Law, which Keynes seemed to interpret as belief in Say's Identity. We have seen in Chapter 6 that it would be wrong to assume that Say's Identity was accepted in that tradition, and Keynes did Ricardo and John Stuart Mill an injustice in singling them out for attack. But the problem that Keynes faced was that of massive unemployment—a general glut—that existed in the 1930s, and indeed, many of the orthodox analyses of this slump were based on Say's Identity. As Hancock (1960) shows, several British economists took the view that the unemployment resulted not from a general glut but from excess supplies in some markets balanced by (unsatisfied) excess demands in others. In attacking Say's Law, Keynes was attacking the way in which the contemporary representatives of the Quantity Theory tradition analyzed the major problem of the day and the policy prescriptions that they put forward.

Keynes saw his task as demonstrating that full-employment equilibrium is not the general case. The general case is equilibrium with unemployment, and full employment is merely a special case. To achieve the desirable goal of full employment, the state is obliged to undertake deliberate policies to achieve it, since automatic market forces, unaided, will not guarantee its attainment. In this chapter we examine this contention's basis in the old Keynesian model.

The Keynesian tradition, however, not only consists of an interpretation of Keynes's work. It also includes a representation of the model that is supposed to have dominated macroeconomics up to the Keynesian era—the so-called Classical model. In this chapter, therefore, we not only examine the old Keynesian model, but we also compare it with the Classical model. However, it is most important to remember that this Classical model is a serious misrepresentation of the Quantity Theory tradition. As will be seen by a comparison between this chapter and Chapter 6, the Classical model is a great oversimplification of the Quantity Theory tradition. In oversimplifying that tradition, it misrepresents it.

8.1 PRELIMINARY POINTS

The Keynesian model is framed in terms of macroeconomic aggregates. Two types of aggregation are involved. First, the model is concerned with the aggregate behavior of all individuals and firms in the private sector and of the whole public sector.[1] This is in contrast to models of individual behavior. Second, the model involves aggregation of particular types of goods and variables into composites. Thus, we are not concerned with the aggregate demand for consumption good, x_i, but with the aggregate demand for consumption goods as a whole, c. We shall see in Chapter 13 that the precise way in which goods and other variables are aggregated in Keynes's work—the

[1]Keynesian models also incorporate the foreign sector, but throughout this book we generally assume a closed economy.

precise nature of the simplifying assumptions used—is open to debate. The old Keynesian model interprets aggregation in the following way.

There is assumed to be a *market for goods* as a whole, so that investment goods are not fundamentally distinguished from consumption goods. There is some distinction between the two, but this distinction is made only on the demand side, since the demands for consumption goods and investment goods depend on different variables. This is a superficial distinction. For there to be a fundamental disaggregation of the markets for consumption and investment goods, the model must introduce the relative price of one in terms of the other as a relevant variable. Since this is not done in the old Keynesian model, the model aggregates the markets for all goods into one market. There is assumed to be a *market for money*, and this is distinguished from the *market for bonds*. The relative price of money in terms of bonds is the bond rate of interest. But the market for bonds is itself an aggregation of the markets for all types of bonds and nonmoney financial assets; we do not consider the structure of interest rates, but one interest rate alone. Moreover, the market for bonds is not explicitly regarded as distinct from the market for the stock of physical capital, since in this model the rate of return on physical capital (the stock of investment goods) is assumed to equal the rate of return on bonds in equilibrium. Finally, the fourth market in this model is the *labor market*.

Our task in this chapter is to specify the workings of each of these markets and, most important, the interconnections among them. But even at the present level of generality, we can see the channels through which monetary policy is assumed to affect output in this Keynesian model. An increase in the money supply, effected, for example, by the printing of new money and its distribution to the private sector, alters the rate of exchange between money and bonds. Since there is relatively more money now, it will be held only if the price of the alternative asset, bonds, rises or, in other words, if the rate of interest falls. If the rate of interest on bonds falls, the rate of return on physical capital must fall, since bonds and physical capital are assumed to be close substitutes. But, assuming diminishing marginal productivity, the rate of return on physical capital is lower the greater is the stock of physical capital. Therefore, the fall in its rate of return must imply a demand for a greater stock of physical capital, which can be achieved only through a demand for new investment goods. This demand for investment goods is a component of the demand for goods as a whole (since we have aggregated investment and consumption goods); it therefore affects aggregate demand for goods and, thereby, the supply of goods or national output.

What has been discussed so far concerns *ex ante*, or planned, variables—the planned demands and supplies in the various markets. However, Keynes's work also permitted the development of the modern system of National Accounting, which concerns the quantification of *ex post*, or actual, variables. The distinction between *ex ante* and *ex post*, or planned and actual variables, is familiar from microeconomic theory. Consider Figure 8.1, which represents the market for a single good, x_i. The market demand and supply curves are

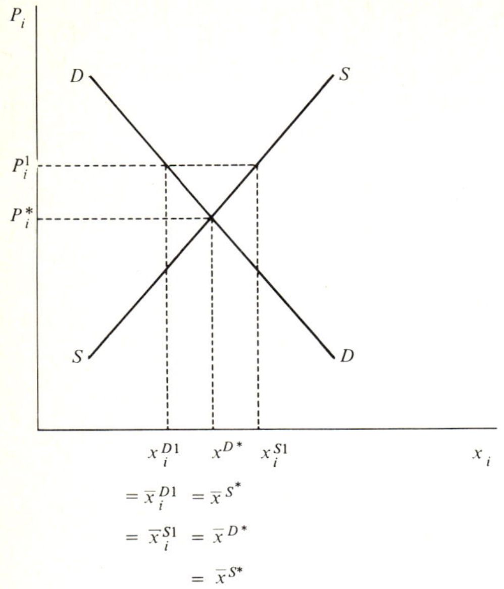

Figure 8-1

DD and *SS* respectively. They indicate the quantities of the good that the sum of individuals plans to demand and plans to supply at particular prices. If the good's price is p_i^1, then planned demand is x_i^{D1} and planned supply is x_i^{S1}. These are *ex ante* variables. They differ from the actual demand and supply, the actual amounts bought and sold. If the price is p_i^1, it is impossible for plans to buy and to sell to be satisfied simultaneously, since planned demand is less than planned supply; there is excess supply of the good. To determine actual demand and supply, we must make some assumption about which of the variables dominates. In general, we assume that the "short end" of the market dominates; if planned demand is less than planned supply, planned demand determines the actual demand and supply. In this case, therefore, when price is p_i^1, the actual amount bought (actual demand $\bar{x}_i^{D1}$) and the actual amount sold (actual supply $\bar{x}_i^{S1}$) equal the planned demand x_i^{D1} but are less than planned supply x_i^{S1}. In equilibrium, at price p_i^*, planned supply and planned demand are equal. Therefore at that point both equal actual demand and supply.

At all points, even nonequilibrium points, actual demand equals actual supply, $\bar{x}_i^D \equiv \bar{x}_i^S$, and this identity follows simply from the fact that every actual sale must simultaneously be a purchase by another individual. This identity between *ex post*, actual demand and supply is at the basis of National Income Accounting. What makes this accounting system distinctively Keynesian is that its structure reflects the Keynesian method of aggregation in the goods market.

National Income Accounting concerns the flow of newly produced goods within a given period. Since different variables are assumed to affect the demand for private consumption, private investment, and goods purchased by the public sector, the National Income Accounts disaggregate these types of goods. Aggregate national expenditure, *ex post*, on goods equals:

$$\sum p_i \bar{x}_i^D \equiv \bar{E} \equiv \bar{C}^D + \bar{I}^D + \bar{G}^D \tag{8.1}$$

where C, I, and G refer to nominal expenditure by private consumers, private investors, and government respectively. Since this expenditure is measured *ex post*, it can be thought of as actual demand and therefore is, as seen in the preceding paragraphs, equal to actual supply or the actual production, $\bar{Q}$, of new goods (in nominal terms):

$$\bar{E} \equiv \sum p_i \bar{x}_i^D \equiv \sum p_i \bar{x}_i^S \equiv \bar{Q} \tag{8.2}$$

But the actual supply of new goods is a source of income to the factors of production that produce them. If these factors are only capital and labor, then:

$$\bar{Q} \equiv \text{actual total wages} + \text{actual total profits} \tag{8.3}$$

(in nominal terms). In other words, actual output is always equal to actual National Income, which, in nominal terms, we write as $\bar{Y}$:

$$\bar{Q} \equiv \bar{Y} \tag{8.4}$$

One final definition is in order. Newly produced goods must either be consumed in the same period or saved and held into future periods. Since actual production equals actual income, we can say that actual income is identically equal to actual consumption plus actual saving:

$$\bar{Y} \equiv \bar{C}^D + \bar{S}^D \tag{8.5}$$

National Income Accounting is therefore based on the principle that, *ex post*, National Expenditure equals National Product and equals National Income:

$$\bar{E} \equiv \bar{Q} \equiv \bar{Y} \tag{8.6}$$

Each of these concepts can be subdivided. Keynesian models find particularly useful the subdivisions of $\bar{E}$ and $\bar{Y}$. Bearing in mind the equality of $\bar{E}$ and $\bar{Y}$, we can substitute from Equations 8.1 and 8.5 to express Equation 8.6 as:

$$\bar{C}^D + \bar{S}^D = \bar{C}^D + \bar{I}^D + \bar{G}^D \tag{8.7}$$

If we assume for simplicity that the actual expenditure of the public sector is zero ($\bar{G}^D = 0$), we obtain from Equation 8.7 the familiar proposition that actual investment is identically equal to actual saving. This, of course, does not imply that *planned* saving and investment are always equal. It will be seen in the following sections that the distinction is important for the Keynesian analysis of the goods market and of the model as a whole.

8.2. THE OLD KEYNESIAN MODEL AND THE CLASSICAL MODEL: THREE MARKETS CONSIDERED SEPARATELY

The Keynesian and classical models can each be considered as a model composed of three interrelated submodels. These three submodels are models of the behavior of three markets—the market for labor, the market for financial assets (bonds and money), and the market for (investment and consumption) goods. Neither Keynes nor Classical writers actually presented their models in such a way, but it is pedagogically useful to begin examining the differences between the old Keynesian and the Classical model by comparing their theories of each of these markets individually. That will be done in this section, and in Sections 8.3 to 8.5 the old Keynesian and the Classical models as wholes will be compared.

Labor Market

Consider, first, the *labor market.* The market is described by three relationships: a demand function, a supply function, and an equilibrium condition. We shall consider each relationship in turn.

In the Classical model the demand function for labor is derived from two hypotheses: (1) firms are profit maximizers and are perfectly competitive in supplying goods and hiring labor; and (2) the marginal product of labor declines as employment increases *ceteris paribus* ("the law of diminishing returns"). From hypothesis (1) it follows that a firm is in equilibrium when the amount of labor it employs is such that the marginal product of labor equals the (market-determined) real wage of labor. From hypothesis (2) it follows that (as long as the employment of other factors, for example, capital, is unchanged) for a firm to equate labor's marginal product and real wage, it will be induced by a fall in the real wage to try to increase its employment of labor up to the point where the marginal product has fallen as far as the real wage. The individual firm's demand for labor is, then, supposed to be an inverse function of the real wage.[2] Aggregating such functions over all firms, we have

[2]The proposition can be derived using differential calculus. The basic hypothesis is that firms aim to maximize profits, that is, revenue minus costs:

$$\pi = pq - Wl \qquad (i)$$

where π represents the firm's profit, p is the price of its output, and q is the volume of its output. W is the money wage rate and l is the amount of labor employed in producing output q (for simplicity it is assumed that labor is the only factor of production). In maximizing equation (i) the firm is restricted by its production function—a technological relationship between the amount of output (q) and the amount of labor (l) that must be employed to produce it:

$$q = q(l) \quad \frac{dq}{dl} > 0, \quad \frac{d^2q}{dl^2} < 0 \qquad (ii)$$

(although the assumption of a negative second derivative here has a different basis from the law of the hypothesis of the Classical model that the market demand for labor is an inverse function of the real wage.

The supply of labor in this model is also a function of the real wage. It is postulated that, as real wages rise, workers will offer a greater amount of labor services (since the higher the real wage is, the higher is the opportunity cost of leisure).

The equilibrium condition is that the real wage should be such as to equate demand for and supply of labor.

These Classical hypotheses about the labor market are represented in Figure 8.2. There, N^DN^D designates the aggregate demand function for labor and N^SN^S the supply function. In equilibrium, the real wage will be $w^* = (W/p)^*$ and the level of employment will be N^*. It is postulated that there is an automatic tendency to move toward these equilibrium levels. If, for example, the real wage is $(W/p)^1$, the excess supply of labor $(N^{S1} - N^{D1})$ is assumed to drive down real wages. It is usually postulated that this would be caused by the involuntarily unemployed workers' driving down money wages (W), and that if prices (p) fell as a result, they would fall by less than money wages. Hence, real wages w would fall to $(W/p)^*$.

---

diminishing returns, since here we assume that labor is the only factor).

Combining equations (i) and (ii), we obtain:

$$\pi = pq(l) - Wl \qquad (i')$$

The condition $d^2q/dl^2 < 0$ in equation (ii) is the hypothesis of diminishing returns.

From equation (i') we obtain the first-order condition for profit maximization.

$$p\frac{dq}{dl} - W = 0 \qquad (iii)$$

or

$$\frac{dq}{dl} = \frac{W}{p}$$

The profit-maximizing firm plans to employ labor up to the point where marginal product equals the real wage.

We are now in a position to determine the change in planned employment that results from a change in real wages while the condition for profit maximization continues to be satisfied. Differentiating the profit maximization condition, equation (iii), with respect to (W/p), we obtain:

$$\frac{d^2q}{dl^2}\;\frac{dl}{d\left(\frac{W}{p}\right)} = 1 \qquad (iv)$$

From the hypothesis of diminishing returns (see equation (ii)), we know that $d^2q/dl^2 < 0$. Hence, for equation (iv) to be satisfied, we must have:

$$\frac{dl}{d\left(\frac{W}{p}\right)} < 0$$

In other words, the demand for labor [by a profit-maximizing firm faced with a production function like that in equation (ii)] declines as the real wage rises, and vice versa. The individual firm's demand curve for labor with respect to the real wage is downward sloping; summing over all firms, we obtain a downward-sloping aggregate demand curve.

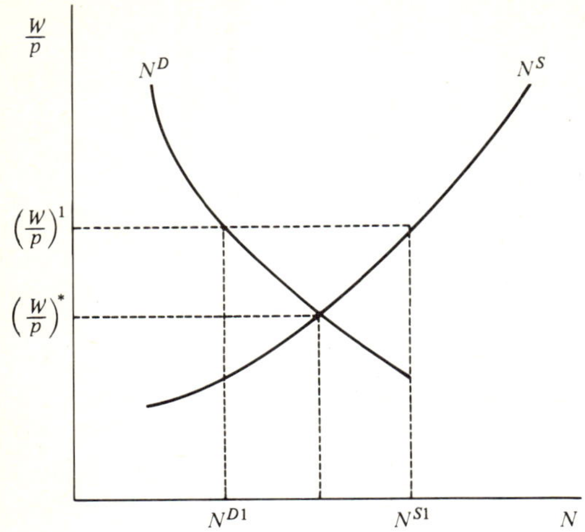

Figure 8-2

Formally, the old Keynesian labor market theory (as represented in Figure 8.3) is very similar to the Classical hypothesis. The demand for labor again depends on the real wage and the marginal product of labor; the supply of labor is again a positive function of the real wage, and the market is, again, in equilibrium at that real wage which equates demand and supply. But in two important respects Keynes's views on the labor market differed from those of the Classicists. First, although the *real* wage (w) can change in any direction, Keynes believed that there is some level below which the *money* wage cannot fall. In the old Keynesian model this rigidity is assumed to be caused by minimum wage laws or other institutional factors or by the (not necessarily irrational) unwillingness of workers to work for lower money wages (though

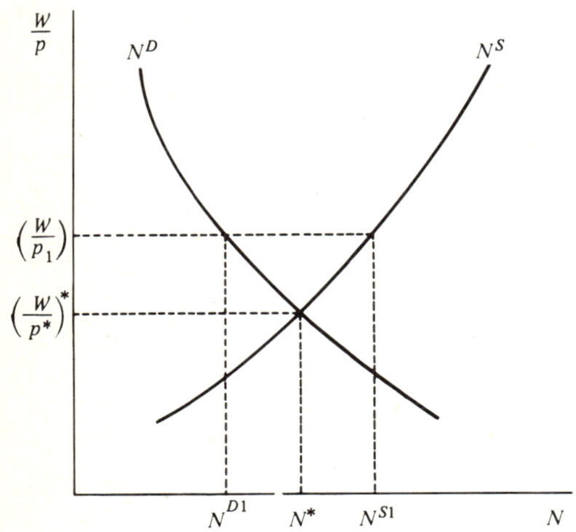

Figure 8-3

they would accept lower *real* wages). It implies that if real wages are initially at $(\bar{W}/p^1)$, since, by assumption, money wages cannot fall below $\bar{W}$, the excess supply of labor can be eliminated only by a rise in prices to p^* until the equilibrium real wage, $(\bar{W}/p^*)^*$, is reached. Secondly, the old Keynesian model implies that even if *money wages were flexible*, equilibrium in the labor market would not be achieved so easily as is predicted by the Classical model. It is postulated that a cut in money wages would lead to a proportionate fall in prices, and so real wages would not necessarily fall. A cut in money wages *could* help to equilibrate the labor market in this Keynesian model, but only indirectly via its effect on the money market.

Thus, the old Keynesian theory of the labor market differs from the Classical theory because of its two new theories about the mechanism by which the labor market adjusts to equilibrium. The significance of these two Keynesian views cannot really be appreciated by considering the labor market in isolation. They will be explained and their importance will be seen when, in Section 8.3, all the submodels of the Classical and the old Keynesian theories have been brought together. Moreover, it will be seen in Section 8.3 that this version of the labor market in the old Keynesian model is not really appropriate for the analysis of unemployment. While presenting no problem if the economy is assumed to be at full employment, the demand curve for labor in Figure 8.3 gives rise to an inconsistency in the model when there is unemployment and an excess supply of goods. We shall see there that the old Keynesian demand function for labor (and the labor market equilibrium condition) has to be radically changed to permit the analysis of unemployment.

Financial Market

Consider now the *financial market* (or money market). Again, we are concerned with a demand function, a supply function, and an equilibrium condition. The Classical and Keynesian theories of the financial market concentrate on the demand and supply for money rather than other financial assets. Underlying Keynes's theory of money, however, there is an implied theory about the market for government bonds (and other financial assets).

The Classical model's theory of the demand for money, the Crude Quantity Theory, is that the aggregate demand for money is a function of the level of money income [real income (y) times the average price level (p)]. The relationship is assumed to be proportionate—desired money balances equal the proportion k of money income. The supply of money is assumed in this model to be exogenously fixed. The market is in equilibrium when the demand for money equals the supply. We have already examined the Crude Quantity Theory and its place in the Quantity Theory tradition in Chapters 4 and 6.

This model is represented in Figure 8.4. OM^{D1} is the demand curve for nominal money and M^SM^S is the supply curve of money. Since in the diagram only p (rather than py) is represented, the slope of OM^D depends upon the

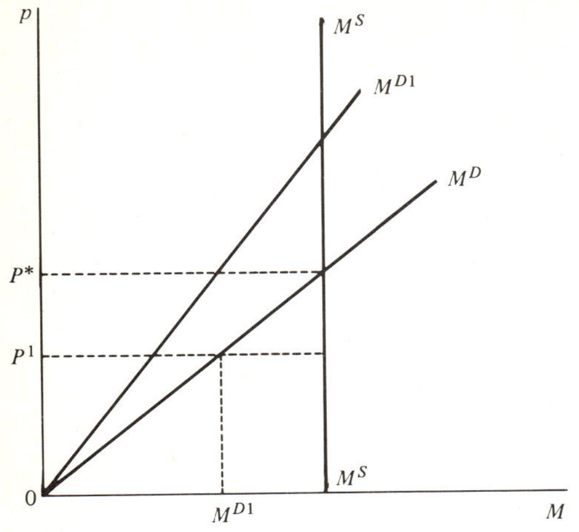

Figure 8-4

level of y. (The higher y is, the greater will be the demand for nominal money balances at any price level: OM^{D1} exists at a lower level of y than OM^D.) However, the Classical model's money market assumes that y is fixed (at the full-employment level), and so we may confine our attention to one curve, OM^D. In the figure, the market is in equilibrium when the price level is p^*. It is assumed that there is an automatic tendency toward equilibrium. If, for example, the price level were p^1 and there were an excess supply of money $\bar{M}^S - M_1^D$, it is postulated that the level of prices would rise to p^* (in some versions of the Classical model, this would occur through the operation of the real balance effect). If we did not assume that y was constant, then, clearly, equilibrium could be reached by *either* a change in p *or* a shift in OM^D caused by a change in y (or both), but the Classical model's assumption of constancy of y puts the full burden of adjustment upon p.

The Keynesian model of the financial market is rather different. The important difference arises in the treatment of the *demand* for money. According to the Keynesian model, individuals' cash balances can be viewed in two parts. First, there are "transactions" balances, held in order to effect the transactions associated with a given level of money income; second, there are "speculative" balances, held as an asset or investment and not used for any transactions except the purchase and sale of the other financial asset, bonds. The demand for transactions balances depends on money income in the same way as does the demand for money in the Crude Quantity Theory of the Classical model. The demand for speculative balances depends on the rate of interest on bonds: the greater the rate of interest, the less speculative balances are demanded. This theory of the demand for money is explained in greater detail in Chapter 9, but we already have sufficient elements to construct the Keynesian model of the money market.

Figure 8.5 illustrates how the Keynesian aggregate demand function for

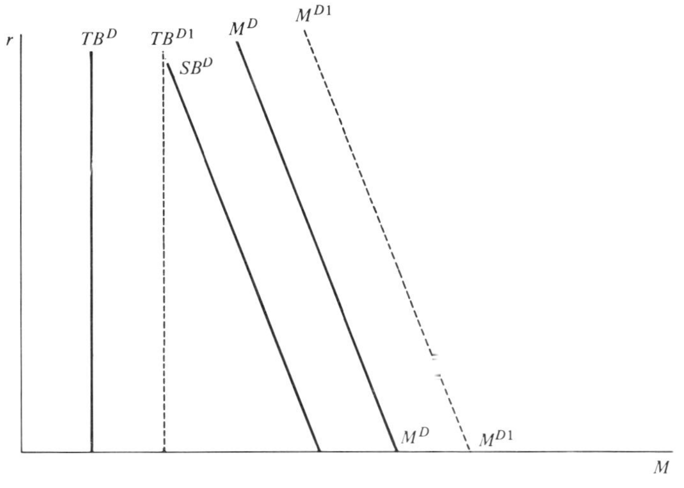

Figure 8-5

money is derived by combining the demand functions for transactions and speculative balances. The demand for speculative balances is an inverse function of the bond interest rate, r, and is represented by SB^D. The demand for transactions balances is unrelated to r and depends only on py, so it is represented by a vertical line, such as TB^D. The demand for total money balances at any interest rate is represented by M^DM^D, which is obtained by adding SB^D and TB^D. M^DM^D is the Keynesian *liquidity preference* curve. Note that the demand for transactions balances would rise to TB^{D1} if py were higher, and (by adding SB^D and TB^{D1}) the liquidity preference curve would be $M^{D1}M^{D1}$. Thus, the position of Keynes's liquidity preference curve depends upon the levels of p and y.

Figure 8.6 represents the Keynesian model of the money market. The demand curve for money, M^DM^D, is derived from Figure 8.5. The supply curve of money is M^SM^S—the supply of money being exogenously determined at $\bar{M}^S$. The market is in equilibrium when the rate of interest is r^*. Note that if p or y were higher so that the liquidity preference curve were $M^{D1}M^{D1}$ rather than M^DM^D, the market would be in equilibrium only at an interest rate higher than r^*. It is assumed that there is an automatic tendency toward equilibrium. If, for example, the rate of interest were r^1 and there were an excess demand for money, $(M_1^D - \bar{M}^S)$, the interest rate would rise to r^*. It can be seen from this adjustment process that some theory of the bond market is implicit in the Keynesian theory of the money market, for disequilibrium in the money market is assumed to have an effect on the rate of interest on bonds. The simplest way to rationalize this would be to assume that excess supply in the money market always equals excess demand in the bond market, so that when one is in equilibrium, the other is, too. On this

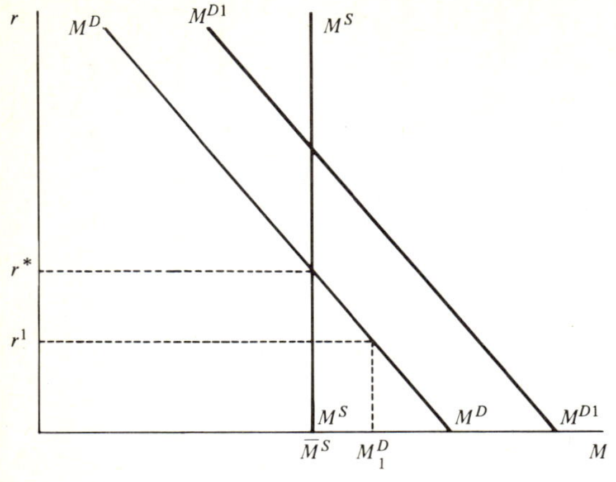

Figure 8-6

assumption we do not have to consider explicitly the bond market, since its excess demand function is not independent of the money market's. When, at r^1, there is an excess demand for money, there is, on this assumption, an excess supply of bonds which pushes their price down and raises r. But we shall see in Chapter 16 that this assumption is oversimple and not very satisfactory.

The major difference, then, between the Keynesian theory of the money market and that of the Classical model is that the demand for money in Keynesian theory is related to the demand for bonds. It is a function of the rate of interest on bonds as well as of the level of money income. The variable that *directly* equilibrates the money market in the Keynesian model is the interest rate rather than, as in the Classical model, the absolute price level. It will be seen in Section 8.3 when the models are seen as wholes, however, that the price level and the level of income do *indirectly* influence the equilibrium of the money market in the Keynesian model.

Goods Market

Finally, we examine the *goods market* in the Classical and Keynesian models. We have examined the labor market and the financial market models in terms of the demand for and supply of labor and financial assets. Similarly, it is possible to describe the goods market theories in terms of the demand and supply functions for goods[3] (although we could also do so in terms of saving and investment functions).

Consider, first the Classical model's theory of the goods market. The demand for goods (or planned expenditure) is the sum of the demands for

[3]In many of the early versions of the Keynesian model, the planned supply of goods was neglected in the analysis of the goods market. We are following Patinkin (1949, 1965) in introducing it explicitly.

consumption goods and investment goods, assuming that government expenditure is zero. The theory is that both consumption demand and investment demand are inverse functions of r, the rate of interest on bonds. The rationale for this is that in the case of consumption, the higher is r, the greater is the return on saving, and so a higher proportion of income will be saved and a smaller proportion spent on consumption goods. In the case of investment, the higher is r (the rate employed in discounting to present value the future returns from investments), the lower will be the present value of any given investment project. So some projects which, at low discount rates, have a small positive present value will have a negative present value at higher interest rates and will not be accepted by a profit-maximizing investor. Note that the demand for consumption and investment goods is *not* a function of the level of income in this model.

In the Classical model, the supply of goods is a function of the level of employment determined in the labor market. It was seen earlier that when the labor market is in equilibrium, employers are hiring labor up to the point where profits are maximized (that is, where the marginal product of labor equals the real wage). It is assumed that each firm has a production function such that for each level of employment there is a unique level of output (*ceteris paribus*). We may aggregate these production functions and, given the equilibrium aggregate level of employment, derive the aggregate level of output—the planned supply, that is, of consumption and investment goods. The goods market is in equilibrium when planned expenditure equals aggregate planned supply.

The Classical goods market is illustrated in Figure 8.7. Planned output, or *ex ante* national income, is measured by y, and e is planned expenditure. The supply of goods (the level of output) is determined (via the labor market and the aggregate production function) at the level G^S. Since it is assumed that the level of supply depends on neither y nor e, the supply function is represented by the vertical line G^SG^S. The demand for goods is determined by the rate of interest and, since in this model it depends on neither y nor e, the demand function is

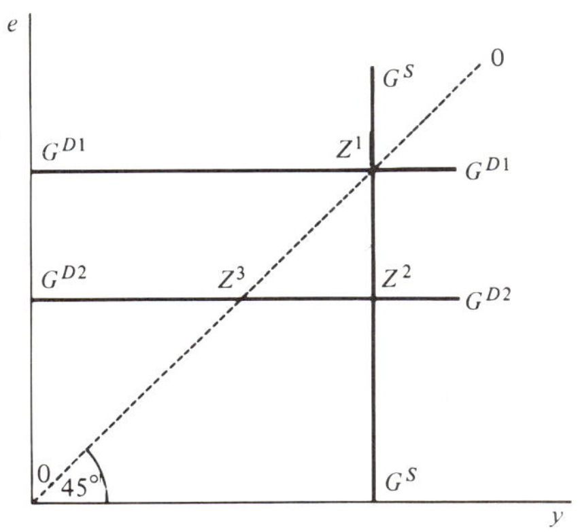

Figure 8-7

represented by a horizontal line like $G^{D1}G^{D1}$ or $G^{D2}G^{D2}$ (at relatively low rates of interest, $G^{D1}G^{D1}$ will be the demand function, while $G^{D2}G^{D2}$ will be the demand function at relatively high interest rates). If the demand function is $G^{D1}G^{D1}$, equilibrium will be reached at the point Z^1, with expenditure of G^{D1} and the output of G^S.

It is important to note, however, that equilibrium can be reached only at points (like Z^1) on the 45-degree line 00. At a point like Z^2, equilibrium does not exist, although it is the point of intersection between an aggregate demand curve, $G^{D2}G^{D2}$, and an aggregate supply curve, G^SG^S. Z^2 cannot be an equilibrium point because aggregate demand cannot equal aggregate supply at a point like Z^2. Demand and supply can be equal only along 00, for, since 00 makes a 45-degree angle with the axes, any point on 00 has a coordinate on the horizontal axis and a coordinate on the vertical axis that are equidistant from the origin. Since the horizontal axis measures planned supply and the vertical axis measures planned demand in terms of the same units of measurement, a point on 00 has coordinates that represent a certain value of planned supply and an equal value of planned demand. A point like Z^2, being to the right of 00, has a coordinate on the horizontal axis that represents a larger planned supply than the planned expenditure represented by its coordinate on the vertical axis. If the demand curve were to remain at $G^{D2}G^{D2}$, there would be excess supply of $(Z^2 - Z^3)$. However, the Classical model implies that $G^{D2}G^{D2}$ would not remain stable. For the excess supply of goods involves the undesired accumulation of goods or, to express the disequilibrium in another way, it involves unplanned investment, or an excess of planned saving over planned investment. The model postulates that saving is positively related to the interest rate, that investment is negatively related, and that an excess of planned saving over planned investment will then lead to a fall in the interest rate. This drop in the interest rate will raise planned investment and lower planned saving (thereby raising consumption). As a result of the rise in planned consumption and planned investment, the planned expenditure curve $G^{D2}G^{D2}$ would rise to $G^{D1}G^{D1}$ and equilibrium would be reached at Z^1. The conclusion of this model is that, given the level of output determined in the labor market, the demand for goods will, in equilibrium, always equal that supply because of the automatic equilibrating force of the interest rate. This automatic tendency of the Classical goods market to equilibrium is further examined in Section 8.5, but at this stage we can see that it is related to Say's Equality (discussed in Chapter 6).

The Keynesian goods market employs different hypotheses and gives an importantly different conclusion. In the Keynesian model the *ex ante* supply function of goods is, as in the Classical model, determined from the labor market. The demand for goods is again composed of a demand for consumption goods and a demand for investment goods. As in the Classical model, the demand for investment goods is an inverse function of the rate of interest. But a major innovation is that the planned demand for consumption

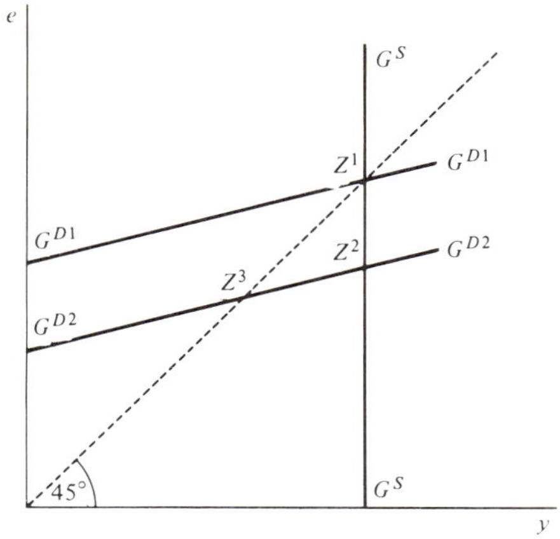

Figure 8-8

goods is postulated to be a positive function of actual national income, $\bar{y}$, and not to be a function of the rate of interest.[4]

This Keynesian goods market is illustrated in Figure 8.8. It differs from the diagram of the Classical model's goods market only in the slope of the planned expenditure function. The expenditure function is drawn as having a positive slope because of Keynes's theory that planned consumption rises as actual income rises. Since investment demand is assumed to be unaffected by income, planned expenditure (the sum of investment and consumption demand) rises as income rises. As in the Classical model, equilibrium may be reached at Z^1 if the planned expenditure function is $G^{D1}G^{D1}$. And, like the Classical model, even if $G^{D2}G^{D2}$ is the planned expenditure function, Z^2 is a point of disequilibrium because it is not on the 45-degree line.

A major difference between the Keynesian model and the Classical model can be seen when we consider the point Z^3 on $G^{D2}G^{D2}$. At that point there is an excess planned supply of goods, and so we cannot say that the goods market is cleared. That is, we cannot say that planned supply (desired sales) equals planned demand (desired purchases). However, in this model there is no reason to believe that the market will move from Z^3 to Z^1: no always-functioning mechanism is postulated by which the expenditure function automatically shifts to $G^{D1}G^{D1}$. In its most *general* form, though, an automatic shift in the expenditure function is postulated so that equilibrium is not established at Z^3; the general Keynesian model *does* lead to the conclusion that the excess supply at Z^3 will (via a fall in the price level and, hence, a downward shift in the demand function for money) lead to a fall in the rate of interest, to a rise in investment (but not directly to a rise in consumption), and, hence, to a return to $G^{D1}G^{D1}$. However, in three theoretically important cases, this mechanism breaks down and there is then no reason why the

[4]In the present analysis of the goods market, we are assuming government expenditure to be zero.

expenditure function should shift from $G^{D1}G^{D1}$ or why the market should shift from Z^3.

In order to analyze why there may be no automatic tendency for the expenditure function to shift from $G^{D2}G^{D2}$ to $G^{D1}G^{D1}$, and in order to understand the connection between planned supply, actual supply, and the labor market, the easiest way is to consider the goods market within the context of the Keynesian model as an integrated whole. Analysis of integrated Classical and Keynesian models is considered in the following sections.

8.3 THE KEYNESIAN MODEL AND THE CLASSICAL MODEL: THE COMPLETE MODELS

The crucial thing about the models is the *interaction* of the three markets, which we have so far considered *separately*. It is most easy to study these interactions when the models are set out algebraically and diagrammatically. The following algebraic presentation of the models exactly parallels the verbal presentation of the preceding section. The models are summarized as follows:

The classical model		**The Keynesian model (full employment)**	
	Labor market		
$N^S = N^S\left(\frac{W}{p}\right)$		$N^S = N^S\left(\frac{W}{p}\right)$	(8.8)
$N^D = N^D\left(\frac{W}{p}\right)$		$N^D = N^D\left(\frac{W}{p}\right)$	(8.9)
$N^S = N^D = N^*$		$N^S = N^D = N^*$	(8.10, 8.11)
	Money market		
$M^S = \bar{M}^S$		$M^S = \bar{M}^S$	(8.12)
$M^D = kp\bar{y}$		$M^D = kp\bar{y} + L_2(r)$	(8.13)
$M^S = M^D = M^*$		$M^S = M^D = M^*$	(8.14, 8.15)
	Goods market		
$y = y(N^*)$		$y = y(N^*)$	(8.16)
$e = c(r) + i(r)$		$e = c(\bar{y}) + i(r)$	(8.17)
$y = e = \bar{y}$		$y = e = \bar{y}$	(8.18, 8.19)

In view of our earlier comments on the old Keynesian labor market, the Keynesian model represented here is called the full-employment version. An unemployment version is considered later.

In both the Classical and old Keynesian (full-employment) models, each market has four equations: a supply equation, a demand equation, and two equations defining the conditions for equilibrium. In the labor market in both models, the supply of labor, N^S, is a function of the real wage, (W/p) (Eq.

8.8). The demand for labor, N^D (Eq. 8.9), is also a function of the real wage, since entrepreneurs are assumed to hire labor up to the point where its marginal product, $\partial y/\partial N$ (the first derivative of the production function employed in Eq. 8.16), equals the real wage. The equilibrium condition (Eq. 8.10), equality between planned supply and demand, determines (Eq. 8.11) the level of employment that equilibrates the labor market, N^*. In the money market, the supply of money, M^S, is assumed in both models to be exogenously fixed at $\bar{M}^S$ (Eq. 8.12). The demand for money, M^D (Eq. 8.13), in the Classical model is expressed in the form of the Crude Quantity Theory. In the Keynesian model, the demand for money is a function of actual money income and of the rate of interest, (r), on bonds, which are the only nonmonetary financial assets. Equilibrium in the money market is established by equality of the demand for, and the supply of, money (Eqs. 8.14, 8.15). In the goods market, the planned supply of goods, y, is a function of the level of employment that equilibrates the labor market (as shown by the production function, Eq. 8.16). The planned demand for goods, e, is the sum of the planned demands for consumption goods and investment goods (Eq. 8.17). In the Classical model, the demand for both types of goods is a function of the interest rate; in the Keynesian model, the demand for consumption goods is a function of the actual supply of goods (or actual real income, $\bar{y}$), while the demand for investment goods is a function of the interest rate. Equilibrium in the goods market (Eq. 8.18) requires equality between planned supply of goods, planned demand for goods, and (Eq. 8.19) actual supply of goods.

The models represented by this equation system appear to differ only in the theory of the demand for money and the demand function for goods (Eqs. 8.13, 8.17). This relative similarity arises because we have considered only the old Keynesian model at full employment. If we consider it at positions of unemployment, we find that the equation system has to be altered, and the alterations highlight the fact that in the Keynesian model the interrelations and direction of causation between markets are different from those of the Classical model. It is convenient to begin by considering the equations of the labor market and, in particular, the demand function for labor.

Unemployment and the Labor Market

Keynes's theory of the labor market is difficult to interpret. Keynes himself discussed it in Chapter 2 of his *General Theory* and clearly considered it to be of central importance in distinguishing his theory from those of his predecessors. But the old Keynesian presentation in Section 8.2 (and Eqs. 8.8 to 8.11) makes the theory seem very much like the labor market of the Classical model. In both, the demand for and supply of labor are functions of the real wage, and the main difference is that in the old Keynesian model it was assumed that money wages may be rigid. This rigidity was presented as emanating from the *supply* side of the labor market.

This model is not an unfair representation of Keynes's own views on the labor market (although it is a highly simplified version). In Chapter 2 of the *General Theory*, he goes to considerable length to discuss the supply function of labor and to argue that it is such that, while there need not be rigidity of real wages, there may be downward rigidity of money wages (real wages varying through changes in p, with W unchanged at $\bar{W}$). And there he explicitly accepts the Classical model's demand function for labor, which makes demand a function of the real wage alone. However, although Figure 8.3 may be a simplified but fair representation of Keynes's views, it is inconsistent with the theory of unemployment that Keynes was trying to reach, for it is difficult to integrate it with his model of the goods and money markets when the system is at less than full employment. The reason for this difficulty is elucidated by Patinkin (1965). It is that the demand function for labor of Figure 8.3 makes sense only when the economy is at full employment; when the economy is at less than full employment, the demand for labor should be treated as a function of the demand for goods rather than of real wages alone. This idea has far-reaching implications, which are explored in Chapter 13. For the moment, however, we are concerned only with the question of how its inclusion modifies the presentation of the old Keynesian model.

First let us see how the labor market model with Keynes's demand function for labor involves inconsistency at unemployment. Consider Figure 8.9. It indicates that if the real wage is $(W/p)^*$, the demand for labor, N^D, is equal to N^*. From the production function, Equation 8.16, we know that this amount of employment is consistent with an output of y. We call y the planned supply of goods or, defining N^* as full employment, it is the full-employment level of real output. But suppose that, for reasons we shall explore in Section 8.4, the demand for output, e, is less than full-employment output, y. In that case, Keynes argued, actual output, $\bar{y}$, will equal planned demand and therefore be less than y. This has an effect on the labor market, for, with the given production function, $\bar{y}$ can be produced with less labor than y. The implication is that firms' demand for labor will, in these circumstances, be $\bar{N}_1^D$ in Figure 8.9. The assumption that the real wage is $(W/p)^*$ does not prevent the goods market's determining output at $\bar{y}$ and employment at $\bar{N}_1^D$; in such a case, therefore, there would be one level of employment determined in the labor market, (N^*), and a different level determined in the goods and money markets, $\bar{N}_1^D$. Which one does the Keynesian theory of unemployment take to be the level of employment?

The answer is unequivocal. The whole thrust of the *General Theory* and of Keynesian theory in general is that the demand for labor is determined by effective demand for goods or, in other words, by equilibrium in the goods and money markets. In the present case, therefore, $\bar{N}_1^D$ is the demand for labor and, assuming that in these circumstances employment is determined by the demand for labor rather than by the supply, $\bar{N}_1^D$ is the level of employment. *This is the case even though, by assumption, the real wage is at* $(W/p)^*$ *and the demand curve implies that the corresponding demand for labor is* N^*. In Figure

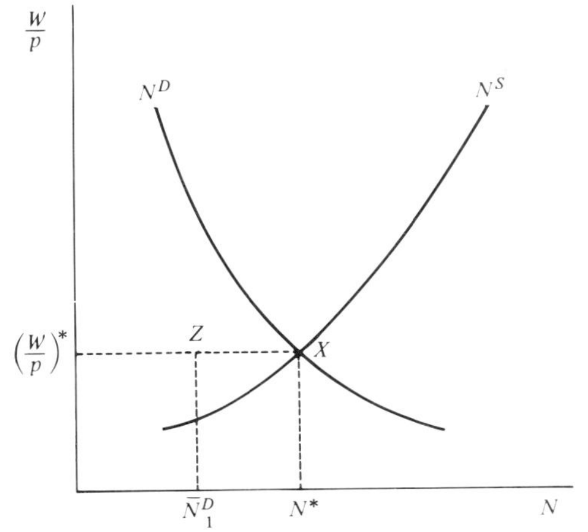

Figure 8-9

8.9 the implication is that firms are at Z or, in other words, are ***off their demand curve for labor.*** If we continue to define N^* as the full-employment amount of employment, then $N^* - \bar{N}_1^D$ measures the unemployment that occurs when the demand for goods causes actual output to be at a level, less than full employment, $\bar{y}_1$ and $(W/p)^*$ is the real wage.[5]

The idea of firms' demand for labor being represented by a point off their demand curve for labor is difficult to grasp. The puzzle arises because, as we saw in footnote 2, the demand curve for labor is derived from the assumption that firms are profit maximizers and nothing has been said in this section to indicate that they cease to be profit maximizers. This hints at the answer to the puzzle. As will be seen in Chapter 13, the idea that firms are forced off their demand curves to a point like Z stems from the contention that when the effective demand for goods is only $\bar{y}_1$ firms are prevented from fully maximizing profits, even though they try to, because they cannot sell as much as they wish to sell; therefore, the demand curve for labor that is derived from the assumption of profit maximization is no longer relevant. If the demand for goods were y, then, by assumption, firms would be able to sell all the goods they wish to sell; they would therefore be fully maximizing profits, their demand curve, N^DN^D, would be relevant, and the demand for labor would be N^*. That is, as we saw in the previous section, y is defined as the planned supply of goods, $y = y(N^*)$, and we can now see that it is the planned supply in the sense that it allows full profit maximization.

We can use the concept of firms being off the demand curve for labor in order to analyze unemployment in the old Keynesian model. We have not yet discussed why income should remain below its full employment level. This question is discussed in Section 8.4; for the present, we simply assume that

[5]This is not the only possible measure of unemployment. It is based on a definition of unemployment as the difference between the actual amount of labor demanded and the planned supply at the given real wage.

equilibrium can occur with $\bar{y} < y$. First, we must consider the extent to which the algebraic representation of the Keynesian model in Equations 8.8 to 8.19 must be modified. For those equations are appropriate only to full employment and have to be altered in order to deal with unemployment, or situations where firms are off their demand curves for labor.

Modifications to the Model

We must begin by noting that the planned supply function for goods, Equation 8.16, is a special case of the production function which says that the actual level of output is a function of the actual level of employment:

$$\bar{y} = y(\bar{N}) \tag{8.16a}$$

If we are concerned with levels of employment other than N^*, full employment, Equation 16 must be replaced by Equation 16a. Moreover, the discussion in the present section indicates that the relevant demand for labor is determined via Equation 16a's production function, by the actual level of output $\bar{y}$. Thus, the demand function, Equation 8.9, must be replaced by:

$$\bar{N}^D = N^D(\bar{y}) \tag{8.9a}$$

Finally, the market-clearing equilibrium conditions in the goods and labor markets, Equations 8.10, 8.11, 8.18, and 8.19, must be replaced by equilibrium conditions that are relevant when markets do not clear. One of Keynes's major innovations was the idea that equilibrium in the goods market can occur even if planned supply does not equal planned demand ($e \lesseqgtr y$); it is enough that *actual* supply equal planned demand ($e = \bar{y}$). This idea was discussed in Section 8.2 in the context of Figure 8.8. For the equation system, it means that Equation 8.18 is not appropriate to the Keynesian model at unemployment, and Equation 8.19 alone is the relevant equilibrium condition. Since there can be equilibrium with $\bar{y} < y$, it follows from Equation 8.9a that the labor market can be in equilibrium with $\bar{N}^D < N^*$ (and also $\bar{N}^D$ less than the planned supply of labor N^S). Equilibrium in the labor market is dependent only on equilibrium in the goods market. Thus, Equations 8.10 and 8.11 become redundant.

These alterations mean that the Keynesian model at unemployment should be represented by the following equations:

The Keynesian model (unemployment)

Labor market

$$N^S = N^S\left(\frac{W}{p}\right) \tag{8.8}$$

$$\bar{N}^D = N^D(\bar{y}) \tag{8.9a}$$

Money market

$$M^S = M^S \tag{8.12}$$

$$M^D = kp\bar{y} + L_2(r) \tag{8.13}$$

$$M^S = M^D = M^* \tag{8.14, 8.15}$$

The Keynesian model (unemployment) (*cont'd*)

Goods market	$\bar{y} = y(\bar{N})$	(8.16a)
	$e = c(\bar{y}) + i(r)$	(8.17)
	$\bar{y} = e$	(8.19)

A comparison of these equations with Equations 8.8 to 8.19 on page 156 indicates that, whereas the old Keynesian model appears to be formally very similar to the Classical model when it is at full employment, it is quite different when, as here, it is at unemployment. The demand function for labor, the equilibrium conditions in the goods and labor markets, and the presentation of the production function (so as to concern actual supply) are all radically changed.

These changes highlight two of Keynes's greatest innovations in his theory of how the markets are interconnected. One is the idea that goods market equilibrium requires equality only between planned demand and actual supply. The other is the proposal that actual demand for labor is determined by actual output and, therefore, is at an equilibrium level when the goods market is in equilibrium.[6] Put most generally, Keynes's innovation as represented in this set of equations is that equilibrium can occur, in the sense that the economy is at a state of rest, while the goods and labor markets remain uncleared.

IS/LM General Equilibrium

We now have three equation systems representing three models, the Classical, the old Keynesian (full-employment), and the old Keynesian (unemployment) models. The working of each model and the relationships between the markets within each model are not immediately obvious from the equation systems and are commonly illustrated in terms of diagrams. In the rest of this section and in the next, we shall consider the old Keynesian model in diagrammatic terms. The diagrams we use are appropriate to both the full-employment and unemployment versions and we begin with the goods and money markets. The analysis of these two markets is greatly simplified by using the *IS/LM* curves developed by Hicks (1937) and Hansen (1953). These curves represent equations that are derived from the equation systems we have considered, so we start by examining this derivation.

To understand this *IS* part of the analysis, consider the Keynesian goods market as represented in Equations 8.16a, 8.17, and 8.19 and in Figure 8.8. The goods market can reach a point of equilibrium (with or without market clearing) by movements in either $\bar{y}$ or r, or both. The *IS* curve is a locus of

[6]As indicated at the beginning of this section, however, Keynes himself began the *General Theory* with a theory of demand for labor that is consistent with this idea only when the economy is at full employment.

those combinations of r and $\bar{y}$ at which the goods market is in equilibrium (and it includes one point at which the goods market is not only in equilibrium, but is also cleared, with the planned expenditure curve intersecting the planned supply line on the 45-degree line). Algebraically, it is derived by solving Equations 8.17 and 8.19 for $\bar{y}$ in terms of r. Substituting Equation 8.17 into 8.19:

$$\bar{y} = c(\bar{y}) + i(r)$$

and if $c(\bar{y}) = a + b\bar{y}$ and $i(r) = d - fr$:

$$\bar{y} = a + b\bar{y} + d - fr$$

$$\bar{y} = \frac{a+d}{1-b} - \frac{fr}{1-b} \tag{8.20}$$

Equation 8.20 is the equation of the *IS* curve. Diagrammatically, the *IS* curve is represented in Figure 8.10. It slopes downward to the right because, by assumption, $0 < b < 1$, and $f > 0$. The derivation of the *IS* curve can be understood intuitively from Figure 8.11. Consider the initial point of equilibrium Z^1. Z^1 is reached because the planned expenditure curve is $G^{D1}G^{D1}$; that is, planned expenditure on $G^{D1}G^{D1}$ equals planned consumption plus that level of investment which is planned when the rate of interest is $r^1[i(r^1)]$. So, at Z^1, the goods market is in equilibrium, with actual income at $\bar{y}^1$ and the rate of interest at r^1. A different point of equilibrium would correspond to a different combination of $\bar{y}$ and r. The important point is that the lower is $\bar{y}$, the higher must be r in order for a point of equilibrium to be reached (as indicated by the slope of the *IS* curve). This can be seen from Figure 8.11 by assuming that $\bar{y} = \bar{y}^2$. If the rate of interest remains at r^1, the point on the expenditure function corresponding to $\bar{y}^2$ would be Z^2, which (since it is not on the 45-degree line) is not a point of equilibrium; it is not even a point of

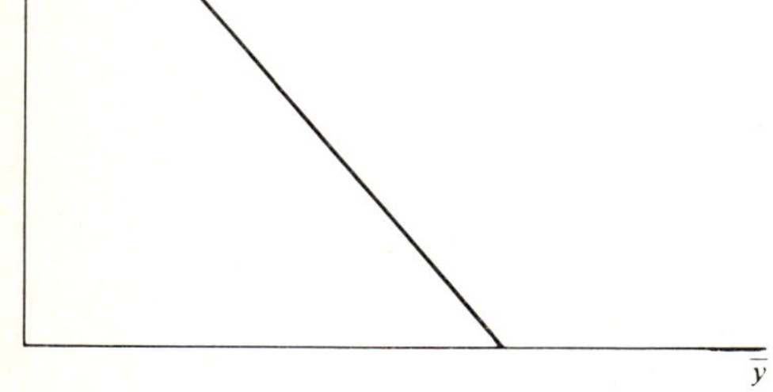

Figure 8-10

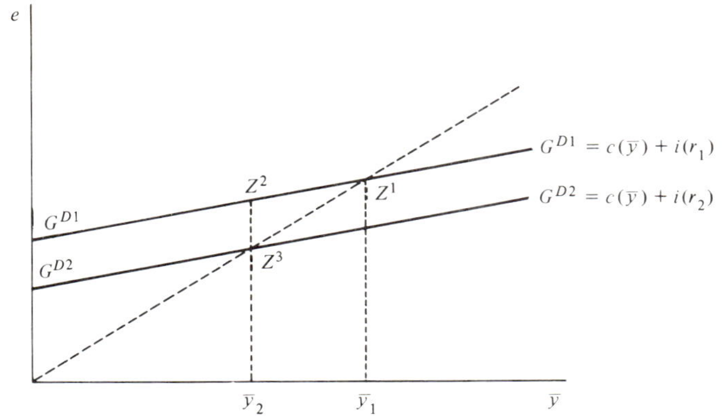

Figure 8-11

nonclearing equilibrium. But if the rate of interest rises to r^2, the planned expenditure function will shift to $G^{D2}G^{D2}$, and equilibrium can be reached at Z^3 with the combination of $\bar{y}$ and r at the levels $\bar{y}^2(>\bar{y}^1)$ and $r^2(>r^1)$.

The *LM* part of the analysis is derived from the Keynesian model of the money market as represented in Equations 8.12 to 8.14 and in Figure 8.6. Given $\bar{M}^S$ and p, the money market can reach an equilibrium as a result of movements in either $\bar{y}$ or r, or both. The *LM* curve is a locus of those combinations of r and $\bar{y}$ at which the money market is in equilibrium. Algebraically, it is derived by solving Equations 8.12 to 8.14 for r in terms of y. Substituting Equations 8.12 and 8.13 into Equation 8.14 and rearranging terms, we obtain:

$$\bar{y} = \frac{\bar{M}^S}{kp} - \frac{L_2(r)}{kp}$$

and, if $L_2(r) = h - jr$,

$$\bar{y} = \frac{\bar{M}^S - h}{kp} + \frac{jr}{kp} \tag{8.21}$$

Equation 8.21 is the equation of the *LM* curve. Geometrically, it is represented in Figure 8.12. It slopes upward to the right because, by assumption, $j < 0(\partial M^D/\partial r < 0)$. The derivation of the *LM* curve can be understood intuitively from Figure 8.13. Assume that p and $\bar{M}^S$ are constant at p^0 and $\bar{M}^{S0}$ respectively, and consider the initial point of equilibrium, Z^1. Z^1 is reached because the demand curve for money is $M^{D1}M^{D1}(p^0\bar{y}^1)$, rather than $M^{D2}M^{D2}(p^0\bar{y}^2)$, because the level of nominal income is $p^0\bar{y}^1$. Thus, equilibrium Z^1 in the money market is reached when money income is $p^0\bar{y}^1$ and the rate of interest is r^1. If the level of money income were higher at $p^0\bar{y}^2$, for example, the demand curve would be $M^{D2}M^{D2}(p^0\bar{y}^2)$ and equilibrium would be reached at Z^2. That is, equilibrium at Z^2 is reached when income is $p^0\bar{y}^2(>p^0\bar{y}^1)$ and the rate of interest is $r^2(>r^1)$. This implication is indicated by the *LM* curve of Figure 8.12; given p, the higher the level of real income $\bar{y}$ is, the higher

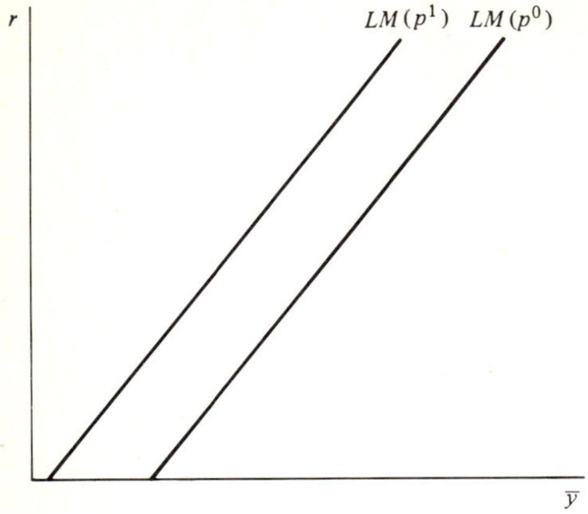

Figure 8-12

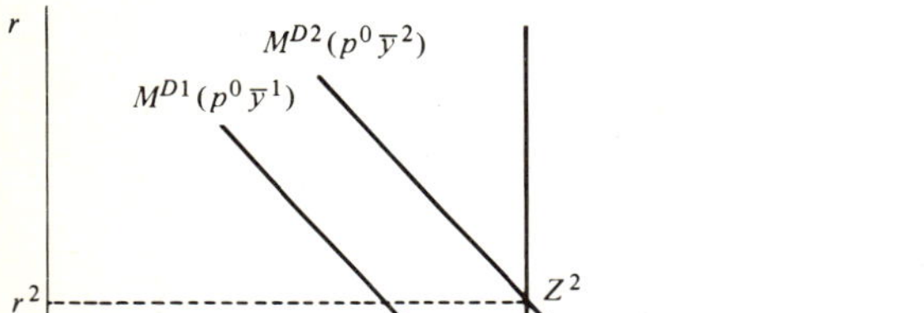

Figure 8-13

must be the rate of interest, r, if the money market is to be in equilibrium. Since in Figure 8.12 we have $\bar{y}$ (rather than $p\bar{y}$) as one coordinate of the *LM* curve, it should be noted that the position of the *LM* curve changes as the price level changes. The higher is p, the further to the left will be the *LM* curve [as indicated by $LM(p^0)$, $LM(p^1)$, and their derivation]. As can be seen from Equation 8.21, the effect of a change in money supply is similar to, but not the same as, the effect of a change in price level. A rise in the money supply will shift the *LM* curve rightward but will not change its slope. A fall in the absolute price level will shift the *LM* curve rightward and change its slope.

The *IS* curve indicates all the combinations of r and $\bar{y}$ that are consistent with equilibrium in the goods market, but it does not indicate which of these points of stability will actually be reached—it does not show at which combination of r and $\bar{y}$ the goods market will stabilize. Similarly, the *LM*

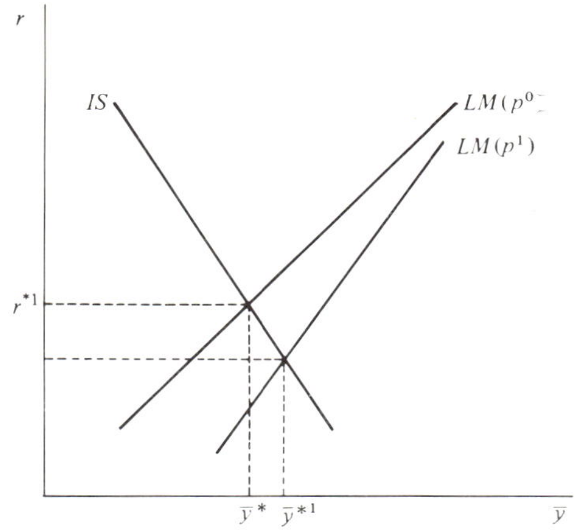

Figure 8-14

curve (for any given p and $\bar{M}^S$) does not indicate which combination of r and $\bar{y}$ will actually hold when the financial market is in equilibrium, which of the equilibrium combinations represented by the *LM* curve will indeed be reached. However, if we combine the two curves (as in Figure 8.14), we find that (given p and $\bar{M}^S$) there is only *one* combination of r and $\bar{y}$ that enables stability to be reached in *both* the financial market and the goods market (r^* and $\bar{y}^*$). These, then, are the values for r and $\bar{y}$ that must hold if stable positions are simultaneously reached in the Keynesian model's goods and money markets. Corresponding to different levels of p (and $\bar{M}^S$), there are different *LM* curves, and, hence, different combinations of r and $\bar{y}$ that stabilize the markets (for example, r^{*1} and $\bar{y}^{*1}$ when p falls from p^0 to p^1 with $\bar{M}^S$ constant). *Ceteris paribus*, the higher the price level, the further to the left is the *LM* curve and, hence, the higher is the rate of interest and the lower is the level of income at the point at which the goods and financial markets are stable.

The *IS-LM* analysis, then, enables us to consider the levels of $\bar{y}$ and r from which there is no tendency to change. And it enables us to do this in a relatively simple manner by considering interrelationships between the goods market and the financial market.

But this *IS-LM* figure does not complete the analysis of the Keynesian model's static behavior, for we have not yet considered the labor market. The important point now is the relation between the labor market and the goods and financial markets. This can best be explored by incorporating the *IS-LM* figure into a larger diagram (Figure 8.15). Figure 8.15a is the *IS-LM* diagram (taken from Figure 8.14); Figure 8.15b is the graph of the production function Equation 8.16 (and, by reinterpreting the variables, Eq. 8.16a) and indicates how, at higher levels of income, ($\bar{y}$) there must be higher levels of employment, ($\bar{N}^D$). Figure 8.15c is the diagram of the labor market (it is Figure 8.3 on its side). This combination of diagrams indicates the interrelationships among

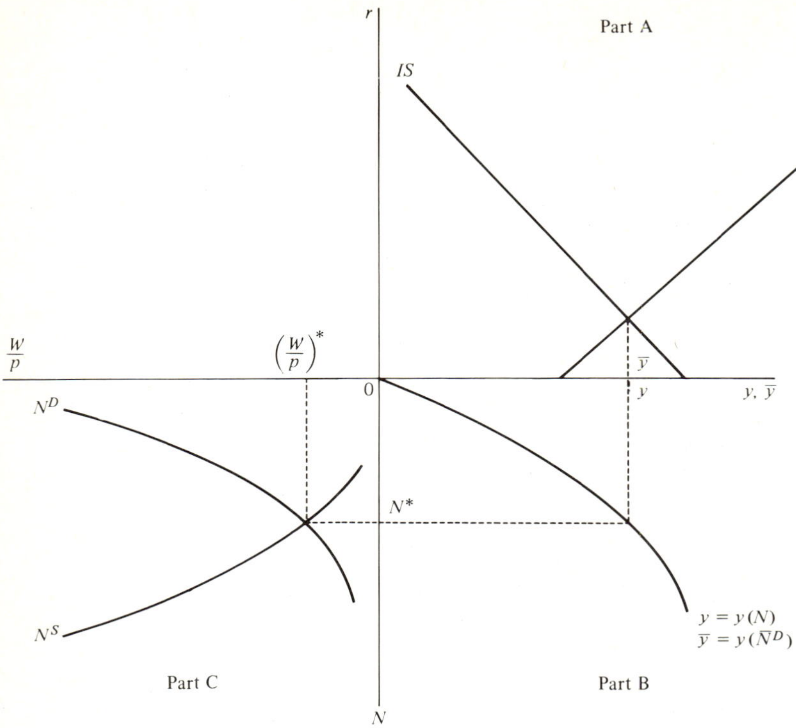

Figure 8-15

the three markets. The money and goods markets together, as represented by the *IS* and *LM* curves in Figure 8.15a, determine the equilibrium levels of $\bar{y}$ and *r*. The equilibrium level of actual income, $\bar{y}$, determines the actual demand for labor, $\bar{N}^D$, via the production function of Figure 8.15b. The direction of causation, therefore, runs from the goods and money markets to the labor market via the production function, and the labor market has a relatively unimportant role to play. If we were to start from the labor market, Figure 8.15c, we can say that if the real wage were $(W/p)^*$ and *if* firms are on their demand curve for labor, the demand for labor will be at N^*, the full-employment level. But, since we have argued that the actual demand for labor is determined by $\bar{y}$ rather than by (W/p), that firms may be off their demand curves, the only relevance of $(W/p)^*$ and N^* is as a definition of full employment rather than as a theory of what determines the demand for labor. If there were full employment, N^*, the supply of goods would be *y* (via the production function), and this full-employment output is what we define as the planned supply of goods. The planned supply curve is represented in Figure 8.15a by the vertical line above *y*.

8.4 STABILITY WITH INVOLUNTARY UNEMPLOYMENT IN THE OLD KEYNESIAN MODEL

Now that we have an apparatus for analyzing the old Keynesian model, we may use it to explore Keynes's major result. His main purpose in setting up his model was to demonstrate the possibility that the system could settle at a position of equilibrium where involuntary unemployment existed (that is, where there was an excess supply of labor) and an excess planned supply of goods (that is, where the goods market was not cleared). It can be shown that the old Keynesian model reaches this conclusion by inserting three special assumptions.

Before using the apparatus of Figure 8.15 to analyze the implications of these three assumptions, it will be useful to demonstrate that, if none of these assumptions do hold, the Keynesian model does have an automatic tendency toward full-employment equilibrium (equilibrium with market clearing), and no stable position can be reached while involuntary unemployment exists. Consider, then, Figure 8.16, where all three of these special Keynesian assumptions are excluded. In particular, money wages are completely flexible, thereby excluding the assumption that they are fixed at $\bar{W}$. In Figure 8.16, full

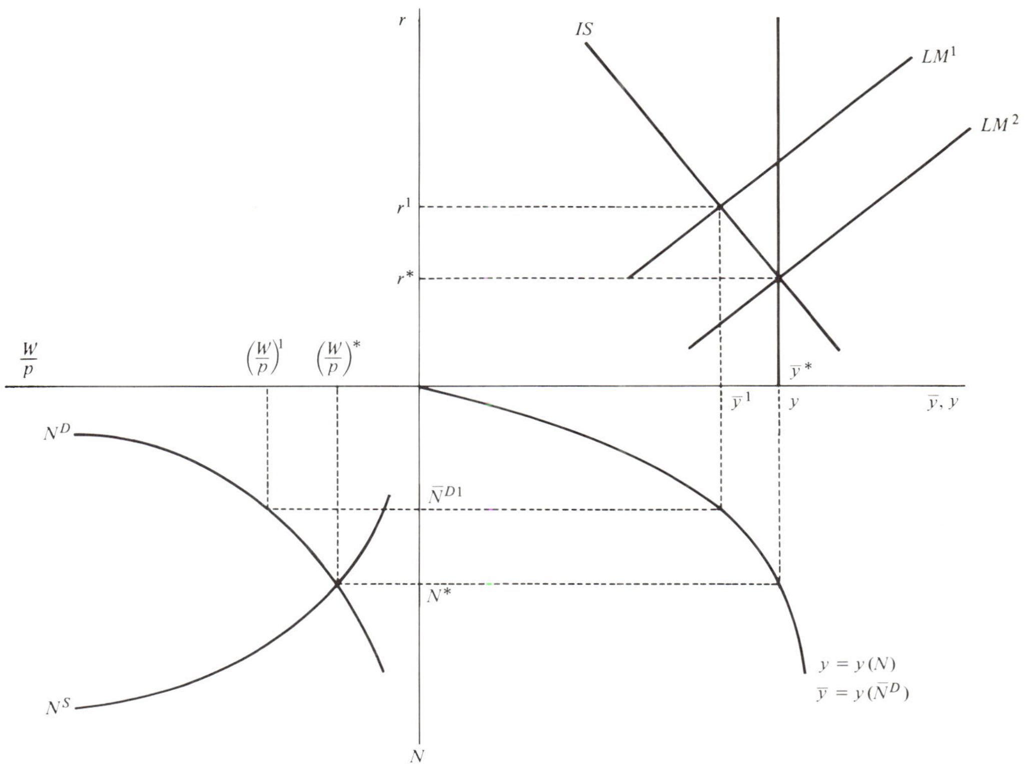

Figure 8-16

employment would be reached (by definition) at the level of employment, N^*.

That level of employment would require the other variables to take the values $(W/p)^*$, $\bar{y}^*(=y)$, and r^* if the money and goods markets were to be in equilibrium. Hence, full-employment equilibrium would require the LM curve to be at LM^2. But suppose that the LM curve were initially at LM^1, the rate of interest were at r^1, income and employment were only at $\bar{y}^1$ and $\bar{N}^{D1}$, and the real wage were at $(W/p)^*$. Would there then be any tendency for anything to happen in the model to induce a move toward equilibrium at N^*? Yes, there would, for the excess supply of labor would lead to attempts to reduce real wages. If these attempts were to take the form of cuts in money wages, (W), they would reduce costs and therefore lead to cuts in prices. W and p would both fall, therefore, and the fall in the price level would induce a shift of the LM curve rightward to LM^2. With LM^2 established, the level of income consistent with equilibrium in the financial and goods markets is the full-employment level, y; the employment is at N^* and the real wage at $(W/p)^*$. There is, then, an automatic tendency toward full employment caused by the effects of the labor market on the financial market, which, interacting with the goods market, reacts on the labor market.

This automatic tendency toward full employment disappears, however, if we adopt any of Keynes's three special assumptions. *First*, let us assume that money wages are fixed at $\bar{W}$. This situation is represented in Figure 8.17,

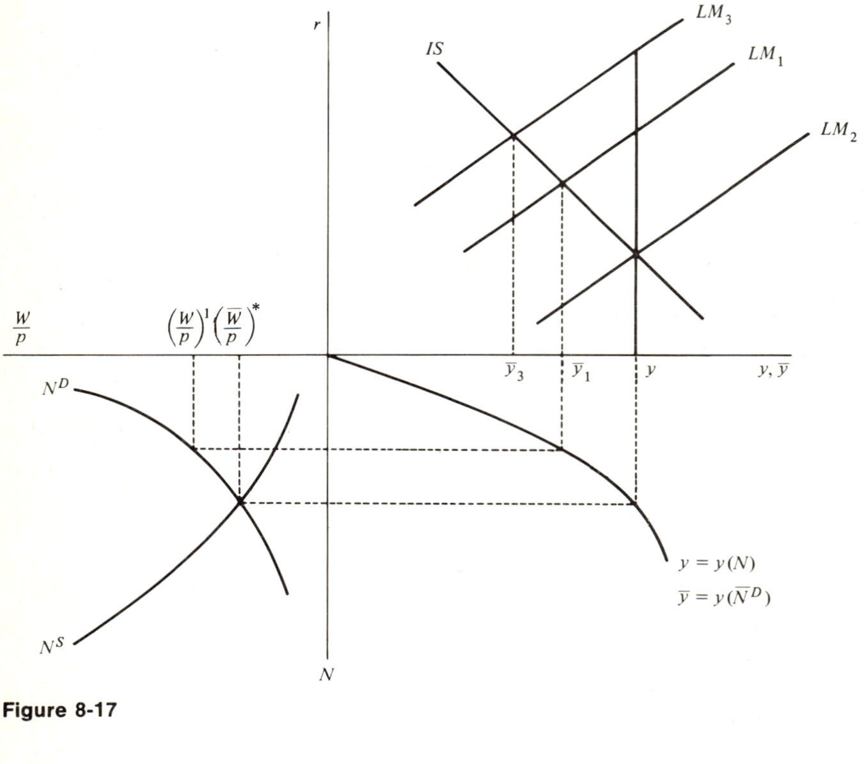

Figure 8-17

where the *LM* curve is initially LM^1. With this *LM* curve and the real wage of $(W/p)^*$, there is an excess supply of labor, and for full employment to be reached, we would require the *LM* curve to move to LM_2. But, if the price level is related to money wage rates and the latter are fixed at $\bar{W}$, the fall in *p*, which in the previous example caused the *LM* curve to shift rightward, will not occur. Moreover, even if it somehow did, the result would be that with $\bar{W}$ given, the real wage would rise above $(W/p)^*$ and would therefore not be consistent with full employment even though the *IS* and *LM* curves would be.

In this case, then, because money wages are fixed, there is no automatic tendency toward full employment. There is no guarantee that the level of prices that gives $(W/p)^*$ in the labor market is consistent with an *LM* curve that ensures equilibrium at full-employment income in the goods and financial markets.

But the Keynesian model does not rely on wage rigidity alone as a source of "underemployment equilibrium" (that is, equilibrium where the goods and labor markets are uncleared). Second, it postulates that there may be a "liquidity trap." That is, there may be some rate of interest at which the elasticity of the demand for money with respect to the rate of interest becomes infinite.[7] The liquidity preference curve would then be of the shape shown in Figure 8.18, and this would imply an *LM* curve of the shape shown in Figure 8.19a. That is, at the rate of interest r^0, the financial market will be in equilibrium at any level of income within a wide range, for, however low the income level, any amount of excess of money supply over the amount required for transactions balances will be absorbed into speculative balances without any fall in the rate of interest. However large the money supply, the

[7]But see Bronfenbrenner and Mayer (1960, 1963) and Eisner (1963) for a discussion of whether this is the meaning of the liquidity trap.

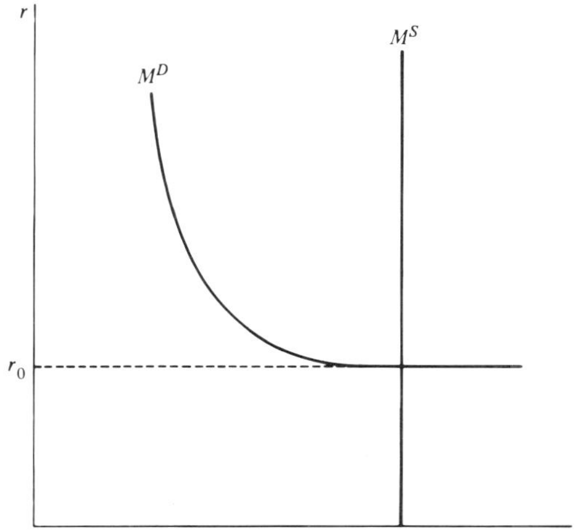

Figure 8-18

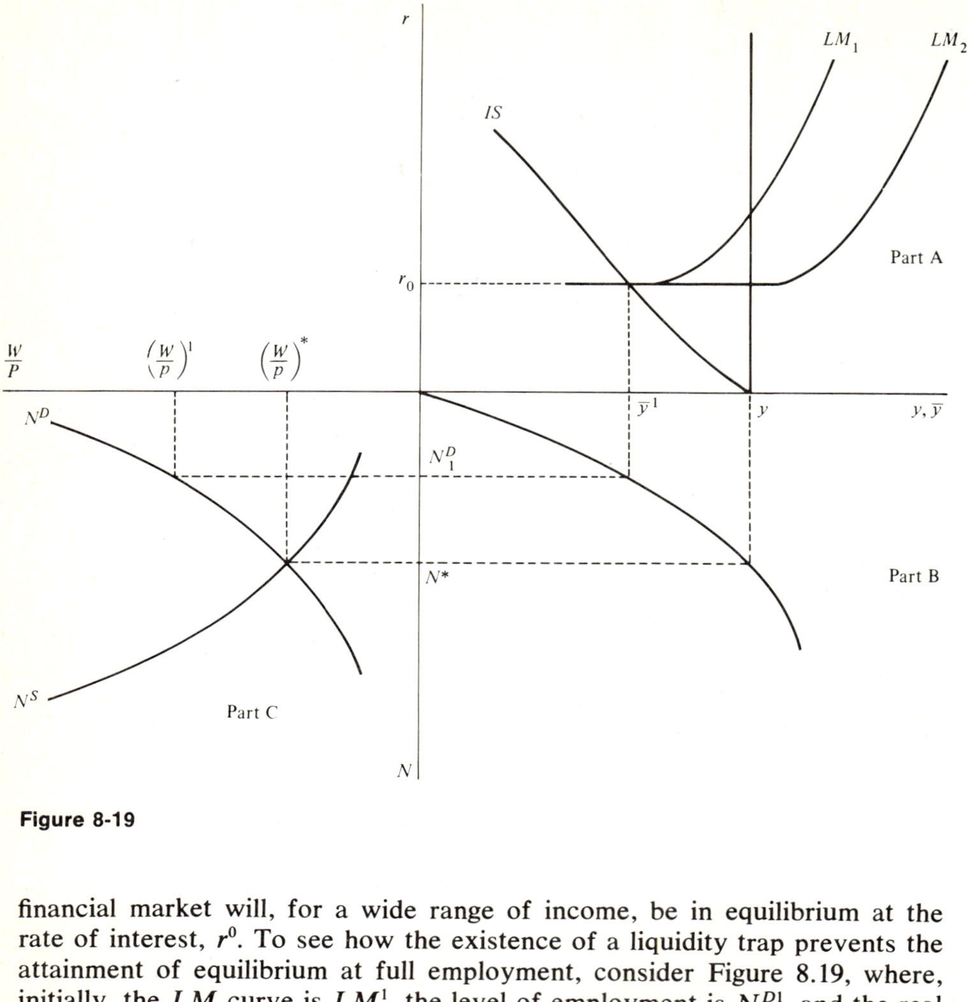

Figure 8-19

financial market will, for a wide range of income, be in equilibrium at the rate of interest, r^0. To see how the existence of a liquidity trap prevents the attainment of equilibrium at full employment, consider Figure 8.19, where, initially, the *LM* curve is LM^1, the level of employment is N^{D1}, and the real wage is $(W/p)^*$. The fall in money wages and prices resulting from this excess supply of labor and goods causes a rightward shift of the *LM* curve to a position like that of LM^2, but, of course, the infinitely elastic part of the *LM* curve does not shift. That is, the fall in the price level releases cash from transactions balances but, in the liquidity trap, this cash is absorbed into speculative balances without any fall in the rate of interest. Thus, in the liquidity trap, even though the price level falls, the financial market remains in equilibrium without any change in the rate of interest or the level of real income. The fall in the price level that is induced by the excess supply of labor and goods does not alter the rate of interest, (r^0), or the level of income, ($\bar{y}^1$), at which the goods and financial markets are in equilibrium. Thus, when the economy is initially stable in the range of the liquidity trap, there will be no automatic mechanism to eliminate the excess supply of labor. The economy will remain in equilibrium with involuntary unemployment and wasted resources (excess supplies in the goods and labor markets).

Third, even if money wages are flexible and even if the liquidity trap does not exist, the economy may not reach full-employment equilibrium, and may remain in a position of nonclearing equilibrium with unemployment. This condition may arise as a result of an interest-inelastic demand function for investment goods. More accurately it may be that, given the consumption function, the level of planned investment expenditure necessary to equate total planned expenditure with planned output (that is, to reach $e = y$) is so large that, given the demand function for investment goods, it cannot be reached unless the rate of interest is negative. If we assume that the rate of interest can never be negative, then the level of planned investment can never be sufficient to raise e to y.

This hypothesis is represented by the *IS* curve of Figure 8.20. This *IS* curve crosses the y axis at a point where $\bar{y}$ is less than y, indicating that if income were y, the goods market would be in equilibrium only at a negative rate of interest. As long as the *LM* curve nowhere crosses the y axis, there can be no intersection of the *IS* and *LM* curves (no general equilibrium of money and goods markets) at a negative rate of interest. The *IS* and *LM* curves therefore must intersect at a nonnegative rate of interest and a level of income less than y. If the *LM* curve is initially LM^1 (Figure 8.20), the excess supply of labor and goods will cause a fall in money wages and prices and the *LM* curve will therefore shift to a position like that of LM^2. But since, by assumption, the *LM* curve will never reach a position where any part of it has a negative coordinate on the vertical axis, the level of real income can never reach y and the money and goods market must reach a position of equilibrium at some $\bar{y}$ below the full-employment level, y.

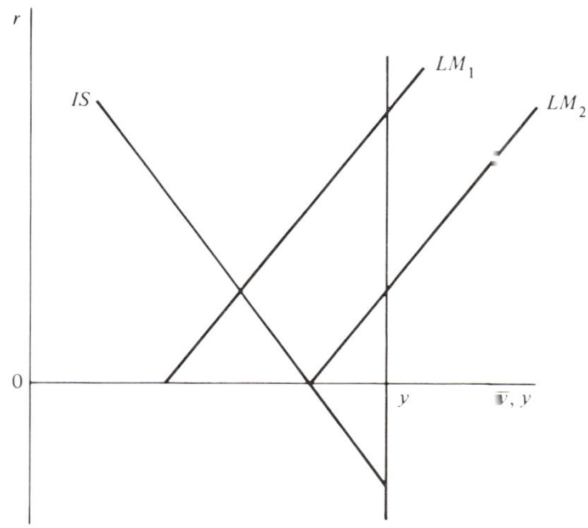

Figure 8-20

These three special assumptions of the old Keynesian model, then, give rise to the possibility that the economy may reach a position where it is in equilibrium but where planned expenditure in the goods market is less than planned supply, and, hence, where the labor market has an excess supply of labor. Without any of these assumptions about wage rigidity, the liquidity trap, or the low interest elasticity of the demand function for investment goods, the old Keynesian model would have an automatic tendency toward equilibrium at y, full-employment income. If any one of the three assumptions were valid, full-employment equilibrium might never be reached, and this model consequently would be very different from, and more realistic than, the Classical model. To conclude this chapter, therefore, the Classical model is examined and the differences between it and the Keynesian model are made clear.

8.5 THE CLASSICAL AND OLD KEYNESIAN MODELS COMPARED

As seen above, unless one of the Keynesians' three special assumptions is admitted, their model does have an automatic tendency to full-employment equilibrium. If one of these assumptions is included in the model, the model will generate a point of equilibrium with unemployment. The Classical model differs from this Keynesian model with respect to both these aspects. First, in the Classical model, equilibrium with unemployment will never exist—the model will always reach full-employment equilibrium. Second, the interrelationships between the markets in the Classical model differ from the interrelationships in the Keynesian model, so the mechanism ensuring full-employment equilibrium in the Classical model is different from that in the general Keynesian model. The Classical model cannot easily be represented in terms of *IS-LM* analysis, so, to demonstrate these points, it is best to examine the algebraic representation of the model.

Consider the labor market Equations 8.8 to 8.11. Given p, these equations are sufficient to determine the existence of equilibrium (that is, full employment) at N^*. It is assumed that p is determined outside the labor market (in the money market) and that N^* is automatically reached by adjustments in W. When there is excess supply, money wages, W, fall and so do real wages, W/p (since p is determined independently) until the excess supply is eliminated. The level of N^* determined in the labor market determines (via the production function, Eq. 8.16) the level of planned supply of goods, y. From this point two alternative paths may be taken: first, following a naïve Classical model, we could restrict further analysis to the financial market (Eqs. 8.12 to 8.15); second, following a more sophisticated model as represented by Equations 8.8 to 8.19, we could analyze the behavior of expenditure and equilibrium in the goods market. It is illuminating to consider both types of analysis, for the first is analogous to a model employing Say's Identity, whereas the latter is analogous to Say's Equality.

To describe a naïve Say's Identity model, we should replace Equations 8.18 to 8.19 with the identities:

$$y \equiv e \equiv \bar{y}$$

and we should eliminate Equation 8.17. Having determined y, as described above, from the labor market and production function Equations 8.8 to 8.11 and Equation 8.16, we may use these identities to see that the level of planned supply, y, is identically equal to the level of planned expenditure, e, and actual supply, $\bar{y}$. Thus, $\bar{y}$ is determined by the labor market and production function—actual output $\bar{y}$ is automatically at that level which involves full-employment equilibrium in the labor market. Given $\bar{M}^S$ and k, this level of $\bar{y}$ then determines, via the money market Equations 8.12 to 8.15, the equilibrium price level p, and thus the demand for money, M^D (although, as we saw in Chapter 4, this process involves an internal inconsistency).

The essence of this naïve model, then, is that full employment is ensured by equilibrating adjustments of money wages (and, hence, real wages) in the labor market. The resulting level of planned supply of goods is then *automatically* equal to planned demand for goods, and so it equals the actual supply of goods. This proposition is what has been called *Say's Identity* in previous chapters. With $\bar{y}$ thus determined, the money market merely determines p.

A more sophisticated version of the Classical model is described by the whole set of Equations 8.8 to 8.19. In this model, planned output, y, is determined in the same way as in the naïve model, but e and $\bar{y}$ equal y only in equilibrium; they are not identically equal. It is assumed that there would be an automatic tendency toward this equilibrium, for it was assumed that if ever e were (for example) greater than y, e would be reduced by a rise in the interest rate (r) (Eq. 8.17) until the equilibrium conditions of equality between y, e, and $\bar{y}$ were satisfied. With the equilibrium level of $\bar{y}$ thus determined, the financial market equations are sufficient to determine p and M^D. The difference between this model, which represents a form of Say's Equality, and the naïve model is that, instead of asserting an identical equality between y, e, and $\bar{y}$ (and thereby precluding the possibility of the model ever being in disequilibrium even temporarily), the sophisticated model proposes that y, e, and $\bar{y}$ are equal only when the model is in equilibrium and it suggests a mechanism (the interest rate) by which this equilibrium may be reached. This Say's Equality version of the Classical model nevertheless denies the possibility of unemployment equilibrium and asserts that an equilibrium will always be reached where $y = e$.

Thus we have seen that either form of the Classical model differs from the Keynesian model insofar as there is no possibility of unemployment equilibrium in the model.

There is a further difference between the Keynesian and Classical models, for it can be seen that when the Keynesian model *does* have an automatic tendency toward full-employment equilibrium, it does so through a mechanism different from the mechanism of the Classical models. In regard to Say's Identity and Say's Equality, the money market's only role in the Classical model is the determination of p and M^D—the stock of money plays no part in determining output or employment. The mechanism is different in the Keynesian model, however, for there the money market is crucial to the determination of equilibrium in the goods and labor markets. Suppose that, in the Keynesian model, we start from a position of excess supply in the labor market and the goods market. It is assumed that W and p will fall. The fall in p is assumed in the Keynesian model, *ceteris paribus*, to decrease the demand for money and to lead to a fall in r to equilibrate the financial market. This fall in r was assumed to cause a rise in e until Equations 8.18 and 8.19 are satisfied and output is equal—that level of output which is produced by a fully employed labor force, N^*. This crucial role of the money market in the Keynesian system is not paralleled in the Classical model.

There is another significant difference in the mechanism of the models, and it has been particularly important in the application of Keynesian theory to policy decisions and to forecasting the behavior of the economy. Assume that policy is concerned with changing $\bar{y}$, affecting actual National Income in real terms. The question then arises: In order to reach an equilibrium where $y = e = \bar{y}$, should we influence y and let the economy adjust until e and $\bar{y}$ have caught up, or should we influence e and wait for the other variables to adjust? That is, should we persuade firms to change their planned supply of goods, or should we persuade households and firms to change their planned demand? This question cannot be answered unless we are willing to discuss what happens when the economy is out of equilibrium, for the answer can be arrived at only by seeing how the economy responds when y and e are artificially changed. The Classical model so certainly ensures that the economy will be in equilibrium that it pays relatively little attention to disequilibrium behavior. Keynes's book, however, was so concerned with positions of nonclearing equilibrium (equilibrium with excess supply) and policies to cure them that he had to provide an answer to our question. His policy recommendations for changing $\bar{y}$ involved changing aggregate expenditure, e, rather than influencing y via the labor market or production function.

This is the basis of all modern short-run macroeconomic policy (but for influencing the long-term growth of countries, policymakers pay much more attention to the factors influencing y, the planned supply of goods). A comparison of Keynes's approach with Chapter 6's survey of Classical writers indicates that, whereas the latter generally saw supply conditions as determining national income in the long run, the Keynesian model emphasizes demand conditions in the short run.

CHAPTER

NINE

THEORY OF THE DEMAND FOR MONEY IN THE KEYNESIAN MODEL

It can be seen from Chapter 8 that the *financial market* plays a crucial role in the Keynesian model. If there is an automatic tendency toward full employment in that model, it operates via shifts in the *LM* curve, and if equilibrium is reached at less than full employment, it will do so because the effects of shifts in the *LM* curve are thwarted. For this reason, it is important to fully understand the Keynesian model's analysis of the financial market—to understand its theory of the demand for money.

The demand for money is sometimes thought to be a difficult concept to grasp, so it is helpful to be clear about the framework in which the theory is developed. First, one must be clear about the nature of the decision that is being analyzed. The decision with which the theory is concerned is a decision about the form in which a *given* amount of wealth is held. The individual's *volume* of wealth is determined by one set of decisions (regarding saving, consumption, and income), but the Keynesian theory of the demand for money is concerned with an entirely separate decision: What *proportion* of this wealth should be held in the form of money? Second, one must be clear about the alternative forms of wealth that are available to the individual. In a formal Keynesian model, individuals may hold their wealth (their individual portfolios) in the form of *either* money or bonds (or both); no other asset (such as equities or Treasury bills) is considered to be available. To be more exact, equities and Treasury bills are considered to be perfect substitutes for bonds, and so they need not be considered separately. "Money" is defined as an asset that is generally acceptable as a medium of exchange and that bears no monetary rate of interest. "Bonds" are defined to be irredeemable government debts (such as the Consols issued by the British government) whose "coupon rate" is fixed but whose price per unit can, and does, vary, so that their market rate of interest varies. Thus, the theory of the demand for money in the Keynesian model is concerned with explaining which variables determine the proportion of a portfolio held in the form of money (rather than bonds) over the decision period.

Closely related to this problem is that of explaining why people should hold money in their portfolios at all. After all, if an individual has decided to hold a certain volume of wealth on average over a given period, why should this wealth not be held entirely in the form of bonds (which earn interest) rather than money (which does not)? Keynes answered this question by pointing to the existence of uncertainty in the profitability of bonds and postulating that wealth owners dislike risk. As shown in the following chapters, later theorists have agreed on the importance of this consideration. But one of the explanations put forward by Keynes—and the one to which Keynesians give most emphasis, the speculative motive—is interpreted within the Keynesian model in such a way that it does not logically depend on the existence of uncertainty in order to be operative. Although Keynes implied that the speculative motive *does* depend on the existence of uncertainty, the Keynesian model's analysis of the speculative motive treated in isolation does *not* require postulating risk aversion. It merely requires individuals to aim to maximize the returns from their portfolios irrespective of their riskiness.

The Keynesian theory of the demand for money can be seen by considering this demand in three separate categories: the transactions motive; the precautionary motive; and the speculative motive for holding money. In Chapter 8 the Keynesian demand for money was presented as consisting of two parts $[M^D = M_1^D + M_2^D = kp\bar{y} + L_2(r) = L_1(\bar{Y}) + L_2(r)]$. The first part is usually considered to reflect the transactions motive (and sometimes the precautionary motive), and the second to reflect the speculative motive. The following three sections of this chapter outline the Keynesian understanding of these motives.

9.1 THE KEYNESIAN TRANSACTIONS MOTIVE

The demand function for money that arises from the transactions motive is essentially the same as the demand function postulated by the Cambridge Quantity Theorists. It appears that Keynes was very much the pupil of Marshall. This transactions demand for money is defined by Keynes (1936) in the following way:

> One reason for holding cash is to bridge the interval between the receipt of income and its disbursement. The strength of this motive . . . will chiefly depend upon the amount of income and the normal length of the interval between its receipt and its disbursement.

It is argued from this (together with an assumption that the interval between receipts and payments is stable and does not vary with the level of income or the rate of interest[1]) that the nominal money balances that the individual desires to satisfy the transactions motive is a constant proportion of money income; it equals $kp\bar{y}$ where k is a constant.

To be sure of the argument, consider this example. A certain man receives income of $20 at the beginning of each week, and he spends it at an even rate, so that it is completely spent at the time he receives his next income. His cash balance, therefore, is $20 at the beginning of the week, zero at the end of the week, and at declining intermediate levels as the week progresses. His *average* cash balance, therefore, over the week is approximately $10.[2] This average value is the cash desired to satisfy the transactions motive—the individual's transactions balance, held in order to finance expenditures. If the man's income doubles, his transactions balance will also double (to approximately $20), *ceteris paribus*. His transactions balance is then a constant proportion (1/2) of his weekly income (or 1/104 of his annual income). But note that this proportion will change if the interval between receipts and payments changes. Suppose, for example, that the man continues to receive $20 weekly income but that he now receives it in the form of $10 at the beginning of the week and $10 half way through the week. If we continue to assume that he reduces his balance to zero by the time he receives his next sum of income, his average balance will now be $5. It is a constant, but lower proportion (approximately 1/4) of his weekly income (and 1/208 of his annual income).

The conclusion follows that as long as the interval between receipts and payments is constant, the individual's transactions balance is a constant proportion of his money income, ($M_1^D = kp\bar{y}$), or $k = (p\bar{y}/M_1^D)$. The effects of a change in the interval between receipts and payments is shown in Figure 9.1, where the relationship between cash balances and time is shown by the dotted line when income is received weekly and by the solid line when income is received half-weekly.

The man's transactions balances, determined in this way, might be thought of as his desired transactions balances, in which case the transactions *demand* for money becomes meaningful. We might then aggregate over all individuals to obtain the aggregate demand for transactions balances. Alternatively, we might conceive of these transactions balances as the mechanistic result of the objectively given pattern of payments and receipts. This latter interpretation makes it difficult to think of the transactions *demand* for money, or *desired* transactions balances, since that concept would involve choice. Desired

[1]Keynes did not ignore the influence of interest rates on the demand for transactions balances, but he did relegate it to a second order of importance.

[2]This result clearly follows from the assumptions made. His cash at the beginning of day 1 is $20, at the end of day 1 is $(20 – (20/7)), at the end of day 2, it is $(20 – (40/7)), and so on until, at the end of day 7, it is $(20 – (140/7)) = 0. The average cash balance at these eight instants is therefore $10.

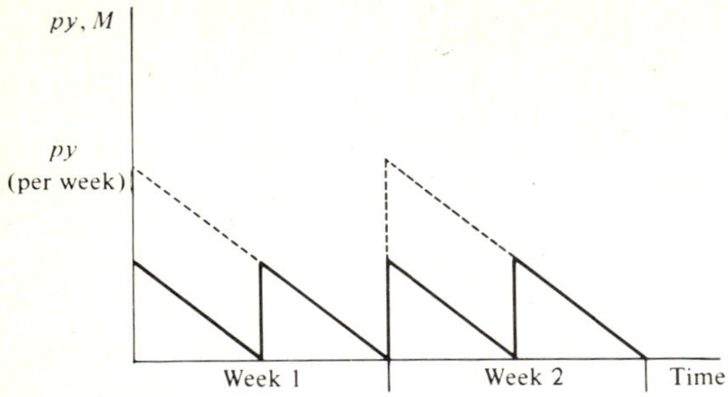

Figure 9-1

balances imply that the individual can choose the optimum payments pattern and therefore k.

We saw in Chapter 6 that the pre-Keynesian Quantity Theory tended to treat k as the result of individual choice in the short run, but to concentrate on the mechanistic interpretation of k for long-run analysis. But we should note that the Keynesian k is not the same as the Quantity Theorists' k. For the Quantity Theorists, k was the inverse of the velocity of *total* money balances; for Keynesians, it relates only to the velocity of *transactions* balances. The velocity of total money balances in the Keynesian system is affected also by the demand for speculative (and precautionary) balances, so that even if we interpret the Keynesian k as not being the result of individual choice, the velocity of total money balances is. Thus, for Keynesians the velocity of total money balances is a function of the interest rate. This is, of course, a result similar to the Quantity Theorists' views on the determinants of velocity in the short run, although Keynesians emphasize its significance to a much greater extent.

9.2 THE KEYNESIAN SPECULATIVE MOTIVE

Unlike the transactions demand for money, Keynes's theory of the speculative demand was different from earlier monetary theories. Although, as we saw in Chapter 6, several Quantity Theorists did analyze the relationship between the demand for money and the rate of interest on bonds, none, as Patinkin (1974) argues, gave it the rationale or the significance that Keynesianism does. The speculative demand has a key role in Keynesian monetary theory, for Keynes consistently used this element of the demand for money as a basis for his theory that the volume of desired money balances, and therefore the velocity of total money balances, depends upon the bond rate of interest. Keynes's analysis of the speculative motive is summarized by his well-known statement that it is based on the desire "of securing profit from knowing better than the market what the future will bring forth." More explicitly: "The individual, who believes that future rates of interest will be above the rates assumed by the market, has a reason for keeping actual liquid cash . . . ," rather than holding bonds, and vice versa (Keynes [1936]).

In other words, consider a woman who has a given amount of wealth which she can invest in either money or bonds, or both. At the time she makes the decision about which assets to buy, there is a current rate of interest on bonds. She may believe with certainty that the rate of interest will rise, fall, or stay the same over the period for which she will hold any bonds that she decides to buy. If she expects that the rate of interest will fall, then she expects to make a capital gain, since a fall in the interest rate involves a rise in the price of the bond. Adding this capital gain to the interest payments she receives, she will make a net profit by holding bonds. Since the financial profit she can make by holding money is, by definition, zero,[3] she will in this world of certainty decide to invest all her wealth in bonds. But suppose that, at the time she makes her decision, the rate of interest is lower. Then she may expect it to rise, and hence expect a capital loss on bond holdings. The capital loss expected may outweigh the interest earnings on any bonds held, and so the woman will expect to take a net loss on any bonds she buys. If this is so, the individual will decide to hold her wealth all in the form of money (on which she cannot have a loss). Hence, given the rate of interest she expects, she will desire to hold only money when the current rate of interest is low, and only bonds when the rate is high.

This demand for speculative balances can be analyzed more rigorously. Let the total volume of nominal wealth available for speculative purposes (that is, not used for transactions or precautionary purposes) be W. This can be held in the form of money, (M), and bonds whose nominal value is (B/r). The current rate of interest on bonds at the time the decision is being made is r_1. Once the decision to hold a certain proportion of bonds and money has been taken, it will not be revised for a certain period (a "year"). The rate of interest that is now expected (with certainty) to exist at the end of the year is $r^e_{1.2}$, and, for simplicity, assume that this expectation does not depend on the current rate, r_1. The speculative demand for money depends on the relationship between r_1 and $r^e_{1.2}$: for every dollar invested in bonds, the individual expects, with certainty, to earn r_1 in interest over the year, *plus* a capital gain, CG (or loss, if $CG < 0$), whose size depends on the relationship between r_1 and $r^e_{1.2}$. Specifically, the capital gain on a bond is measured by:

$$CG = \text{expected bond price} - \text{current bond price}$$

Expressed as a rate of capital gain per \$1 invested, this is:[4]

[3]It is always zero in nominal terms if we assume that interest is not received on money balances. It is zero in real terms if we assume that the price level is constant and expected to remain so.

[4]This follows from the fact that the bond price is the inverse of the rate of interest (for Consols). Therefore $CG = (1/r^e_{1.2}) - (1/r_1)$. Multiplying both sides by the current rate, r_1, we obtain $r_1.CG = (r_1/r^e_{1.2}) - 1$. Since r_1 is the inverse of the current price of the bond, we can rewrite the left-hand side of this equation as in the text (Eq. 9.1).

$$g = \frac{CG}{\text{current bond price}} = \frac{r_1}{r_{1.2}^e} - 1 \tag{9.1}$$

By buying one dollar's worth of bonds and holding them, then, the individual expects with certainty to earn $\$(r_1 + g)$ by the end of the year. Since the amount a man, say, expects to earn by holding cash is, by assumption, zero, this profit-maximizing individual will hold his entire portfolio in the form of bonds if he expects to make a net profit on bond holdings [that is, if $(r_1 + g) > 0$], and will hold it wholly in the form of money if he expects to take a net loss on bonds [that is, if $(r_1 + g) < 0$]. Since the expected rate is assumed to be unaffected by the current rate ($r_{1.2}^e$ is fixed), there is some critical value of r_1 at which the expected net gain on bonds is zero ($r_1 + g = 0$). Let this critical rate be r^{**}; then the man will expect a capital gain [for $(r_1 + g) > 0$ if $r_1 > r^{**}$] and will hold only bonds; if it is below, he will hold only money. Note that r^{**} is below the expected rate $r_{1.2}^e$. This may be seen intuitively from the fact that if the current rate is just a little below the expected rate, a small capital loss is expected. But this is offset by the positive current return on bonds, r_1. Only when the current rate is significantly below the expected rate will the expected capital loss be so large that it outweighs r_1 and produces a negative return in total. The dividing point, where r_1 is exactly offset by expected capital loss, is r^{**}. To be more precise, since r^{**} is defined as that current rate where $r_1 + g = 0$, we have $r^{**} + g = 0$. Since the capital gain on one dollar's worth of bonds is $(r_1/r_{1.2}^e) - 1 = g$, we can write the definition as $r^{**} + (r^{**}/r_{1.2}^e) - 1 = 0$. This can be simplified to $r^{**}(1 + (1/r_{1.2}^e)) = 1$ or $r^{**} = (r_{1.2}^e/1 + r_{1.2}^e)$. Therefore the critical rate, r^{**}, is below the expected future rate, $r_{1.2}^e$.

From this analysis it follows that the *individual's* speculative demand for money can be represented by the step function *ABCD* in Figure 9.2. When $r_1 > r^{**}$, the proportion of wealth held in the form of money is zero; when $r_1 < r^{**}$, the proportion is unity; and when $r_1 = r^{**}$, the individual is willing to hold any proportion of the portfolio in cash, since at that interest rate bonds, like money, yield a zero net return.

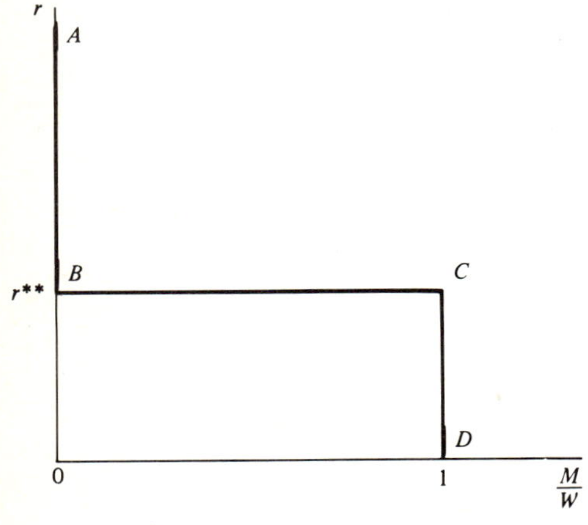

Figure 9-2

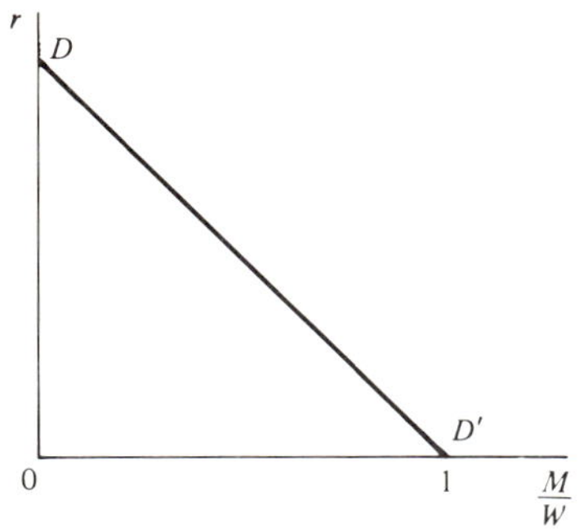

Figure 9-3

Although the analysis just outlined is a legitimate, although not the only, interpretation of Keynes's theory of the speculative demand for money, the step function of Figure 9.2 is not the usual representation of Keynes's theory. More familiar is the smooth, continuous function *DD′* shown in Figure 9.3. But *DD′* can be derived from *ABCD* if we consider *DD′* to be an *aggregate* demand function for speculative balances. For, if we assume that there are many individuals in the market and that each of them has a different expectation (that is, a different r^{**}), then for every rate of interest there will be some individual who is indifferent toward holding all bonds or all money (that is, whose demand curve is horizontal at that rate). Adding these individuals' demand curves horizontally, the market demand curve will approximate *DD′*. To gain an intuitive idea of the effect of aggregation, consider the demand curves in Figure 9.4. Individual α's expectations are such that the critical rate is $r^{**}(\alpha)$ and the demand curve is $A_\alpha B_\alpha C_\alpha D_\alpha$. For individual β the critical rate is $r^{**}(\beta)$ and the demand curve is $A_\beta B_\beta C_\beta D_\beta$. Summing these two curves, we derive the aggregate demand curve, *DEFGHD′* (the exact shape depending on the distribution of wealth between α and β). Clearly, the aggregate curve for a large number of individuals with differing critical rates will have a large number of steps and, in the limit, may be approximated by a curve like *DD′* of Figure 9.3.

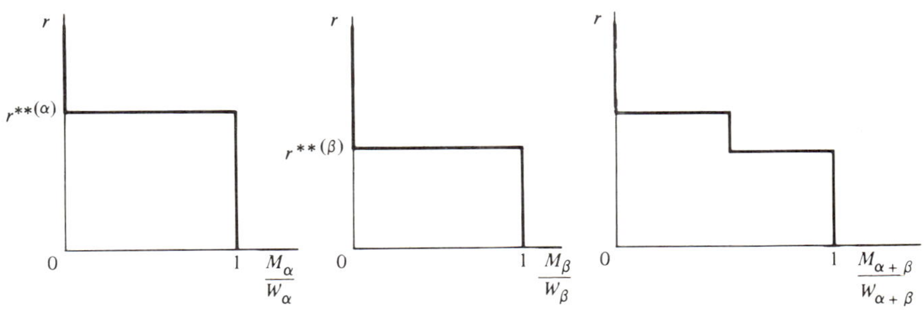

Figure 9-4

In Keynes's model, then, *differences* in individuals' expectations are crucial to the analysis of the money market. It is on the basis of this analysis that Keynes asserted (1936): "It is interesting that (the system's) sensitiveness to changes in the quantity of money should be so dependent on the existence of a *variety* of opinion...." For this variety of opinion is the basis of Keynes's analysis of the speculative demand, and the speculative demand is the basis for his hypothesis that the demand for money is interest-elastic: the theory of liquidity preference.

9.3 THE KEYNESIAN PRECAUTIONARY MOTIVE

The transactions and speculative motives are generally considered to be the basis of Keynes's demand function for money. The transactions motive explains the part that depends on money income, while the speculative motive explains the part that depends on the rate of interest. But Keynes also discussed a precautionary motive (or a security motive). The interesting point about this precautionary motive is that, in some passages, he used it as the basis for an element in the demand for money which depends mainly on the rate of interest (like the speculative demand), but in other passages he considers the demand for precautionary balances to depend mainly on the level of money income (like transactions demand).

A rigorous exposition and discussion of the precautionary demand for money (or, at least, one interpretation of it) are left for the next chapter. Here, we merely point out Keynes's two interpretations of it. The essence of the precautionary demand for money is *uncertainty* about the future. Return to the context of the example used earlier to illustrate the speculative demand for money, but now suppose that expectations concerning the future rate of interest ($r^e_{1.2}$) are not held with certainty. The individual believes that the interest rate *may* fall over the year, in which case there will be a net profit on bond holdings [$\$(r_1+g)>0$ for one dollar's worth of bond holdings], but the rate *may* rise sufficiently to cause a net loss on bond holdings [$\$(r_1+g)<0$]. Since the individual does not know with certainty (although perhaps with varying degrees of confidence, or probability) which event will occur, the return on bonds is risky. Thus the individual has some incentive to hold money, for, although money holdings do not earn a profit, no risk is involved. This incentive to hold money will depend on the current rate of interest, since the greater is this rate, the greater is the return on bonds, which will partially compensate for their riskiness. This is the basis of Keynes's argument (1936):

> Thus if a need for liquid cash may conceivably arise before the expiry of n years, there is a risk of a loss being incurred in purchasing a long-term debt and subsequently turning it into cash, as compared with holding cash. The actuarial profit or mathematical expectation of gain calculated in accordance with the existing probabilities ... must be sufficient to compensate for the risk of disappointment.

This, in Keynes's words, is termed "the precautionary-motive, i.e., the desire for security as to the future cash equivalent of a certain proportion of total resources," and it would appear that this precautionary demand for money depends on the rate of interest.

But, in discussing the precautionary motive at a later point in the *General Theory*, Keynes asserted "It may be . . . that this (cost of holding cash) is likely to be a minor factor except where large changes in the cost of holding cash (e.g., the profitability of bonds) are in question." Following on from this, he argued that the demand for precautionary balances can be treated as depending on the level of income rather than the rate of interest.

Keynes, then, had two different interpretations of the precautionary motive and did not clearly distinguish between them. As a result, some later writers have tended to neglect the precautionary motive and have concentrated on the transactions and speculative demands for money. Nevertheless, in the next chapter we shall follow the interpretation that treats the precautionary demand as being dependent on the rate of interest, as Keynes first presented it, and as being an important element in the demand for money.

9.4 DEMAND FOR MONEY AND THE LIQUIDITY TRAP

This chapter has outlined the three motives behind the demand for money in Keynes's *General Theory*. But a warning is in order. In any exposition such as this, much that was alive and interesting in Keynes's original analysis (for it was based on broad observation of actual financial behavior) has been brushed aside by the need for clarity and the desire to highlight the main arguments. For example, here the speculative demand for money has been described as dependent merely on the divergence of individuals' expectations and existing, unrealistically, in a world of certainty. The speculative motive was presented in this form in order to highlight the *essence* of Keynes's analysis of it, but in the *General Theory* itself, the speculative motive was less well defined and was analyzed in a more realistic world where expectations are uncertainly held. Indeed, in its final form, Keynes's description of the speculative motive is as a combination of speculative behavior proper and behavior of the kind that had earlier been classified under the precautionary motive. The relevance of this is easily seen, for the diversity of individuals' expectations is most plausible if uncertainty exists. Moreover, not only is our presentation of Keynes's *General Theory* version of the demand for money highly simplified; it is also true that, as Davidson (1972) notes, Keynes considered his presentation in the *General Theory* as a relatively superficial version of his own view.

Having noted this warning, and having read the foregoing outline of the Keynesian theory of the demand for money, we now have a more detailed understanding of the Keynesian money market than could be gained from

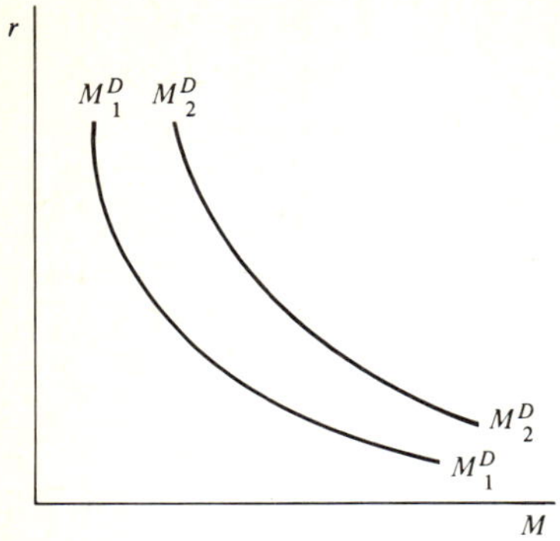

Figure 9-5

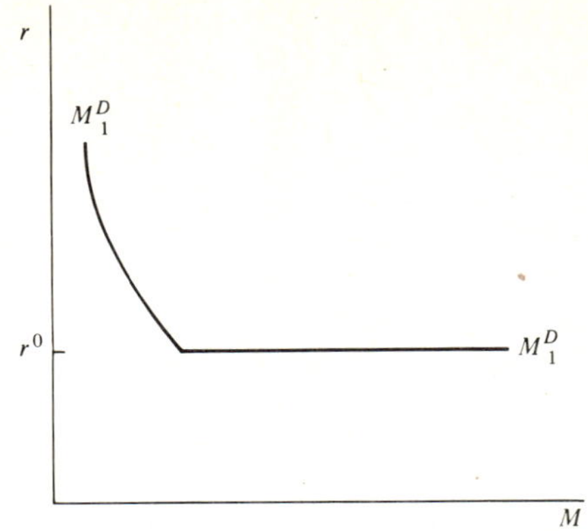

Figure 9-6

Chapter 8. In addition, we can now analyze more fully Keynes's hypothesis of a liquidity trap, the implications of which were outlined in Chapter 8.

Figure 9.5 correctly represents the Keynesian theory of the demand function for money. This demand for money is composed of two parts, one being related to the level of money income and completely inelastic with respect to the rate of interest, the other being dependent on the rate of interest: $M^D = kp\bar{y} + L_2(r)$. However ambiguous may be the interpretation of the precautionary and speculative motives, Keynes himself identified the first part of this demand function as being the work of the transactions and precautionary motives (or, at least, a "safe first approximation" of these motives, in Keynes's eyes), and the second part as being a manifestation of the speculative motive. By combining the two parts, the smooth, continuous liquidity preference curve ($M_1^D M_1^D$ or $M_2^D M_2^D$) of Figure 9.5 is derived, showing the demand for money as depending upon the rate of interest at given levels of income. If money income falls (because of reduced real income, $\bar{y}$, or prices, p), less money will be required for transactions purposes, although the speculative demand at any rate of interest will be unchanged. And so the demand curve for total balances with respect to the rate of interest will shift leftward.

But now suppose that there is a liquidity trap at r^0. That is, imagine that the liquidity preference curve is $M_1^{D'} M_1^{D'}$ of Figure 9.6. What is the explanation and the implication of such a demand curve? First, consider some explanations. One explanation is based on pure speculative behavior. When the rate of interest falls as low as r^0, it is postulated that individuals unanimously expect the rate to rise. Hence, there will be a widespread desire to hold all wealth in the form of money rather than bonds at r^0. An increase in the money supply will not lower the rate of interest since, r^0 being widely considered "too low" already, the increased stock of money will be willingly held at that interest rate in expectation of a rise in the rate. This idea that *unanimity* of speculators' expectations can cause the liquidity trap and a rigid interest rate throws further light on Keynes's remark (quoted earlier) that the system's sensitivity to monetary factors depends "on the existence of a *variety* of opinion."

An alternative explanation of the liquidity trap is based on precautionary behavior. That is, when the rate of interest is as low as r^0, the yield on bonds is inadequate to offset their riskiness, and so individuals prefer to hold their entire portfolios in money rather than bonds. Keynes considered both these explanations to be plausible. Some writers believe an explanation of the liquidity trap in terms of the precautionary motive to be preferable to one in terms of the speculative motive. They do so because it is unreasonable to assume that, as we assumed in our presentation of the speculative demand, the expected interest rate is independent of the current rate. At least in the long term, we may expect a relationship between the two: If the current rate of interest remains at r^0 for a long period, this may cause a downward revision of expectations concerning the future rate, the critical rate will fall, and the shape of the aggregate demand curve will change, thereby eliminating the liquidity trap if we confine our analysis to a world of certainty.

The main *implication* of the liquidity trap hypothesis is that, if it were correct, a reduction in money income would, by reducing transactions demand, shift the demand function for money leftward. But, with a fixed supply of money, this would not lower the equilibrium rate of interest, for the money that is released from transactions balances is willingly held as speculative balances at r^0 without any attempt to switch into bonds (that is, without any tendency for the rate of interest to fall). As the *IS-LM* analysis of Chapter 8 demonstrated, this has serious implications for the equilibrium level of employment. For the fall in money income associated with unemployment is prevented (by the liquidity trap) from lowering the rate of interest; as a result, investment is not stimulated and there is no force to move the economy out of its position of underemployment. Similarly, if a liquidity trap exists, an increase in the money supply is an ineffective reason for raising the level of money income.[5]

The analysis of Keynes's liquidity preference theory in this chapter, however, is useful not only for an understanding of Keynes's own theory. It is an essential basis for understanding the origin and significance of modern Keynesian contributions to the theory of the demand for money. At the beginning of this chapter, it was asserted that closely related to the theory of the demand for money is the problem of "why people should desire to hold money at all when they can hold interest-earning assets (for example, bonds) instead." Keynes answered this question asserting (1936, page 168) that there is "a necessary condition failing which the existence of a liquidity-preference for money as a means of holding wealth could not exist.... This necessary

[5]Keynes himself was skeptical as to whether a liquidity trap exists, but Friedman (1972) interprets Keynes's work as implying a strong belief in its significance.

condition is the existence of *uncertainty*." That is, individuals are assumed to dislike risk on their assets and, since bonds are assumed to be risky, whereas money is not, they have some reason for holding money rather than bonds in some circumstances. This risk aversion is the basis of Keynes's precautionary demand. An additional, or alternative, explanation of a desire to hold money is that individuals seek to maximize the profitability of their portfolios. Such a desire to maximize returns is the basis of Keynes's pure speculative motive, as described in Section 9.2. Generally, the theory of the individual's demand for money can be (and is) based upon the assumption that people aim both to maximize the return *and* minimize the riskiness of their portfolios.

This assumption about behavior is the basis of what has come to be known as the portfolio approach to the theory of the demand for money. Using this portfolio approach, several writers have refined and elaborated on Keynes's analysis of the demand for money. In particular, the speculative motive and one version of the precautionary motive have been rigorously analyzed by Tobin (1958); and Baumol (1952) and Tobin (1956) have explored the transactions demand and demonstrated that, under plausible assumptions, it too will depend on the rate of interest.

In fact, it appears to be empirically true that the demand for money *is* a function of a rate of interest (see Chapter 20). Keynesians can explain this observation by either the theory of the speculative demand, or the theory of the precautionary demand, or the modern theory of transactions demand. The next chapter rigorously examines the Keynesian development of each of these theories. It is shown that each of them is a different variant of the same basic portfolio approach—the basic theory that, in allocating a given amount of wealth between bonds and money, individuals aim to maximize returns and minimize risk.

CHAPTER

TEN

THE PORTFOLIO APPROACH AND THE DEVELOPMENT OF TRANSACTIONS AND PRECAUTIONARY MOTIVES

In Chapter 9, it was explained that Keynes's speculative demand for money is based on the assumption that individuals aim to maximize the profit on their portfolios and that his precautionary demand is based upon the assumption that individuals aim to maximize profit and minimize risk. Later writers, retaining the assumption of a return-maximizing, risk-minimizing portfolio owner, have rigorously analyzed these elements of the demand for money. They have demonstrated that under certain assumptions, desired precautionary balances and desired transactions balances will both depend on the rate of interest. This chapter presents an exposition of these arguments mainly in diagrammatic form.

10.1 PROBABILITY: RETURNS AND RISK

As an introduction to the exposition, the concepts of the profitability and the risk of a portfolio are explained. To do this, we make use of the statistical notion of a probability distribution. In Chapter 9, the return on $1 invested in bonds over a period was defined as:

$$R = r_1 + g$$

where r_1 is the rate of interest on bonds and g is the capital gain on the bond over that period. For money, on the other hand:

$$R \equiv 0$$

That is, money is defined as having no rate of interest and not yielding any capital gains or losses. Concentrate attention on the return on bonds. When contemplating a decision to buy a bond, the investor knows with certainty what r_1 is, for it is the current rate of interest which the bond will earn for as long as it is held. But in general, g can be estimated only with uncertainty. Suppose that the investor's decision is binding for one year; then g depends on the price of the bond (and, hence, on the rate of interest) that is expected to exist at the end of the year. In the Keynesian pure speculative demand as analyzed in Chapter 8, g is expected with certainty since expectations as to the future interest rate are held with certainty. But more generally, investors expect g to take one of a range of values. They may consider each of these values to be equally likely, but more often they will think some value of capital gains is more apt to occur than other values. The confidence they place in their expectations of capital gains of different values may be expressed in terms of probabilities. We may describe any given state of such expectations by a probability distribution.

Figure 10.1 shows one type of probability distribution. The investor expects that the profitability of bonds could be any value from R^1 to R^5. The degree of confidence that is placed in any estimate of profitability (R^i, where $i = 1 \ldots 5$) can be formalized by a probability number, $P(R^i)$.[1]

The heights of the vertical lines of Figure 10.1 indicate the value of $P(R^i)$

[1]Probability theory is a complete discipline in itself. Within it, the question of how to interpret the meaning of probabilities is contentious. In particular, are our probability numbers to be interpreted as objective probabilities given to the individual as facts, or subjective probabilities? If the latter, what are the rules individuals must obey in calculating these subjective probabilities? In this book we shall sidestep such issues, for they are not our main concern.

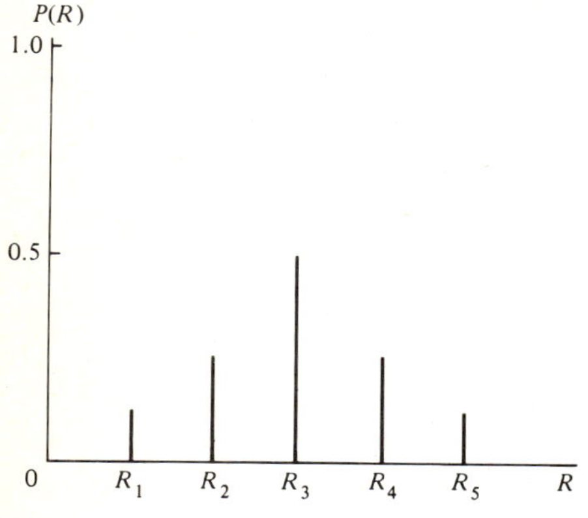

Figure 10-1

for each R^i. It can be seen that the probability of R^3 is greater than any other probability in this example and that the more extreme values of profitability have lower probabilities.

The example can be generalized to n possible outcomes (these outcomes being R^i where $i = 1, \ldots, n$). The definition of these probability numbers obeys certain rules. First, any probability number must be between zero and unity, or equal to either value [that is, $0 \leq P(R^i) \leq 1$]. Within this range, the nearer is a probability number to unity, the stronger is the expectation that the associated outcome (level of profitability) will actually occur. The nearer is the probability number to zero, the less is the confidence that is placed in the actual occurrence of the associated outcome. The limiting cases are where an outcome is expected with certainty to occur and so has a probability of unity, and also where an outcome is expected with certainty not to occur (that is, to be impossible) and so has a probability of zero. Second, if there are no more than n possible outcomes (R_i, where $i = 1, \ldots, n$), then the sum of the probabilities of these outcomes must equal unity [or $\Sigma^n P(R^1) = 1$]. If certain assumptions and rules hold, this follows from the rule that an outcome expected with certainty has a probability of unity, for (by assumption) it is certain that either one value of R^i or another within the range ($i = 1, \ldots, n$) must occur.

There are two features of a probability distribution, such as that of Figure 10.1, that are of special significance in a wide range of problems and are particularly important in the portfolio approach to monetary theory: These features are, first, a measure of the *average*, or the central tendency of the probability distribution, and second, a measure of the *dispersion* of the probability distribution. These measures are especially important in monetary theory because, for every portfolio, there is a probability distribution of returns; the central tendency of this distribution indicates (roughly speaking) the expected value of returns, whereas the dispersion of the distribution indicates the riskiness of these returns. The importance of this will be seen in Section 10.5, and we shall discuss its meaning more rigorously in Chapter 11, Section 11.3.

One measure of the central tendency of the distribution is the *mean* of the distribution. For any probability distribution:

$$P(R^1),\ P(R^2), \ldots, P(R^n)$$

The mean is defined as:

$$[R^1 \times P(R^1)] + [R^2 \times P(R^2)] + \cdots [R^n \times P(R^n)] = \sum_{i=1}^{n} R^i P(R^i)$$

To take a numerical example, Figure 10.2 presents in graphical form a probability distribution for the outcomes $R^1, \ldots, R^5$. Let these represent profits of value 1, 2, 3, 4, and 5 respectively. The graph shows the probability distribution as being:

$$P(1) = \tfrac{3}{36}; \qquad P(2) = \tfrac{6}{36}; \qquad P(3) = \tfrac{18}{36}; \qquad P(4) = \tfrac{6}{36}; \qquad P(5) = \tfrac{3}{36}$$

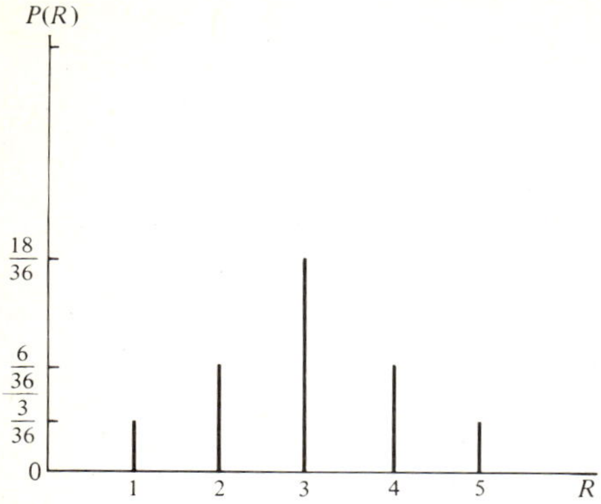

Figure 10-2

The *mean* of this probability distribution is then given by the summation:

$$(1 \times \tfrac{3}{36}) + (2 \times \tfrac{6}{36}) + (3 \times \tfrac{18}{36}) + (4 \times \tfrac{6}{36}) + (5 \times \tfrac{3}{36}) = 3$$

This mean of the probability distribution is frequently known as the *mathematical expectation* of the outcome (the mathematical expectation of returns, or profits, on assets in the case of monetary theory). This interpretation of the mean of the probability distribution is based on the Classical theory of probability, which implies that this mean value is the average return that will be achieved in the long run (or, more strictly, the limit as the number of experiments-predictions and observations of profitability approaches infinity). The mean is usually denoted by the Greek letter μ.

One measure of the dispersion of the distribution is its *standard deviation.* The standard deviation measures the extent to which the values of R in the probability distribution differ from the mean value. The standard deviation of the distribution is defined by the formula:

$$\sqrt{\sum_{i=1}^{n} (R^i - \mu)^2 P(R^i)}$$

To take a numerical example, the standard deviation of the probability distribution shown in Figure 10.2 is 1. This indicates, roughly speaking, that there is a probability of about .83 that the actual value of R will be within 1 (that is, one standard deviation) either side of μ in any particular outcome. Thus, the mean return on the portfolio is 3, but the actual return will not necessarily be the same as the mean return. Therefore we are interested in the likelihood with which the actual return will be within a certain range of the mean return. In this example, the standard deviation of 1 indicates a .83 probability that the return will be between 2 and 4.

The important point to note is that the greater is the standard deviation of the probability distribution, the lower is the probability that the actual value of R will be within a given distance from the mean value. The easiest way to illustrate this point is, instead of considering Figure 10.2's discrete probability

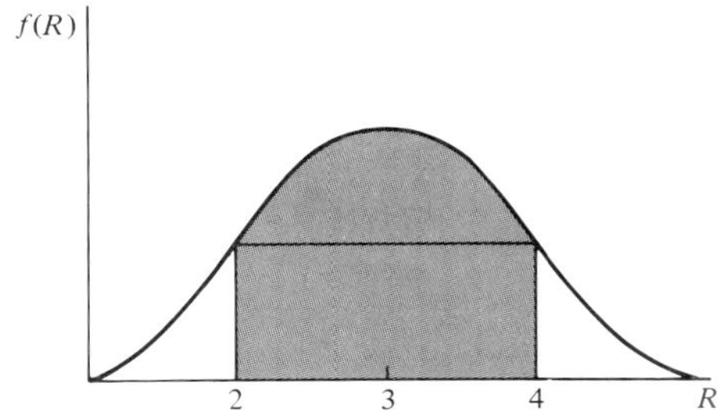

Figure 10-3

distribution used so far, to consider a continuous probability distribution described by a normal curve (as drawn in Figure 10.3). Just as there is a probability of approximately .83 that R will be within one standard deviation of the mean if the distribution is that of Figure 10.2, it can be shown that if the probability distribution is described by a normal curve, there is a probability of about .68 that the actual outcome of R will be within one standard deviation of the mean. In the instance of the normal curve, it can also be shown that there is a probability of .95 that R will be within two standard deviations on either side of the mean. Suppose that the normal curve has a mean of 3 and a standard deviation of 1. Then there is a .68 probability that R will be between 2 and 4 (this figure of .68 is the size of the heavily shaded area between $R = 2$ and $R = 4$ in Figure 10.3). But consider a second example: Suppose that, while we still assume the mean to be 3, we now postulate a normal curve with a greater spread, so that the standard deviation is greater than 1, say 1.5. In that case, there is a .68 probability that R will be between 1.5 and 4.5, and a .95 probability that it will be between 0 and 6. Here, the probability that R will be within 2 and 4 is less than .68 (for the area underneath any normal curve with a mean of 3 is smaller between $R = 2$ and $R = 4$ than between $R = 1.5$ and $R = 4.5$). Thus, by comparing the two examples, it can be seen that the greater is the standard deviation, the smaller is the probability that R will be within a given distance of the mean: the smaller is the probability, for example, that R will be within the distance of unity either side of the mean. In other words, the greater is the standard deviation of the probability distribution of returns, the less is the likelihood that the mean or expected value of returns will be achieved and the more risky is the portfolio. The standard deviation is usually denoted by the Greek letter σ.

For any given portfolio with a particular probability distribution of returns, the mean and the standard deviation are not the only possible measures of profitability and risk. But Tobin has shown (1958, 1965c) that several assumptions about the nature of the probability distribution or the nature of the individual's behavior and tastes would (if the assumptions were valid) justify the individual in treating μ as a measure of profitability and σ as a measure of risk. This demonstration is explained in Chapter 11 (Section 11.3).

The idea of a probability distribution is basic in the portfolio approach to liquidity preference theory. The use that has been made of this approach to develop the theory of the transactions and precautionary motives involves assuming that the individual has the opportunity to buy two types of assets: bonds and money. Each of these assets has a probability distribution of returns: that on money being described by $(\mu_M \sigma_M)$ and that on bonds by $(\mu_B \sigma_B)$. By choosing different combinations of money and bonds, the individual is said to be choosing different portfolios. Each of these portfolios has a probability distribution of returns $(\mu_W \sigma_W)$ whose mean and standard deviation depend on (1) the probability distribution of returns on money and on bonds, and (2) the proportion of money and bonds in the portfolio. Given the probability distribution of returns on each of these assets, the task of the optimizing individual is to select that combination of money and bonds that gives the optimum $(\mu_W \sigma_W)$—that is, to select the portfolio that is an optimum from the point of view of the desire for high returns (μ_W) and low risk (σ_W).

Having completed this summary of one of the basic tools of probability analysis, we shall outline a general model of the elements of portfolio analysis in the next section.

10.2 THE BASIC PORTFOLIO APPROACH MODEL

As in the general theory of consumer demand, there are two main elements in the portfolio approach to the theory of the demand for money. One element is the *opportunities* that are available to the individual; the other element is the *objectives* and the *preferences* of the individual. Both of these elements are represented in Part A of Figure 10.4, while Parts B and C represent the relationships between holdings of money and bonds and the levels of return and risk on the portfolio.

Consider, firstly, Part A of Figure 10.4. The axes measure the return and the risk of the portfolio in terms of the mathematical expectation (μ_W) and the standard deviation (σ_W) of the probability distribution of returns on the portfolio. The curves, $u_1, u_2, u_3, \ldots, u_n$, are indifference loci between risk and returns (the higher the subscript number, the greater is the utility represented by that indifference locus). The indifference curves reflect the *preferences* of the individual; as drawn in Figure 10.4, they indicate that the individual dislikes risk (for, given a certain level of μ_W, the individual's utility is lower the higher is σ_W) and likes returns. The individual's *objective* is assumed to be to reach the highest possible indifference curve—utility maximization. The *opportunities* available to the individual are represented by the line *OF*. This opportunity locus represents the combinations of risk and return the individual can obtain by holding the portfolio in differing combinations of money and bonds. As drawn here, *OF* represents a situation where the individual can obtain a greater return on the portfolio only by taking more

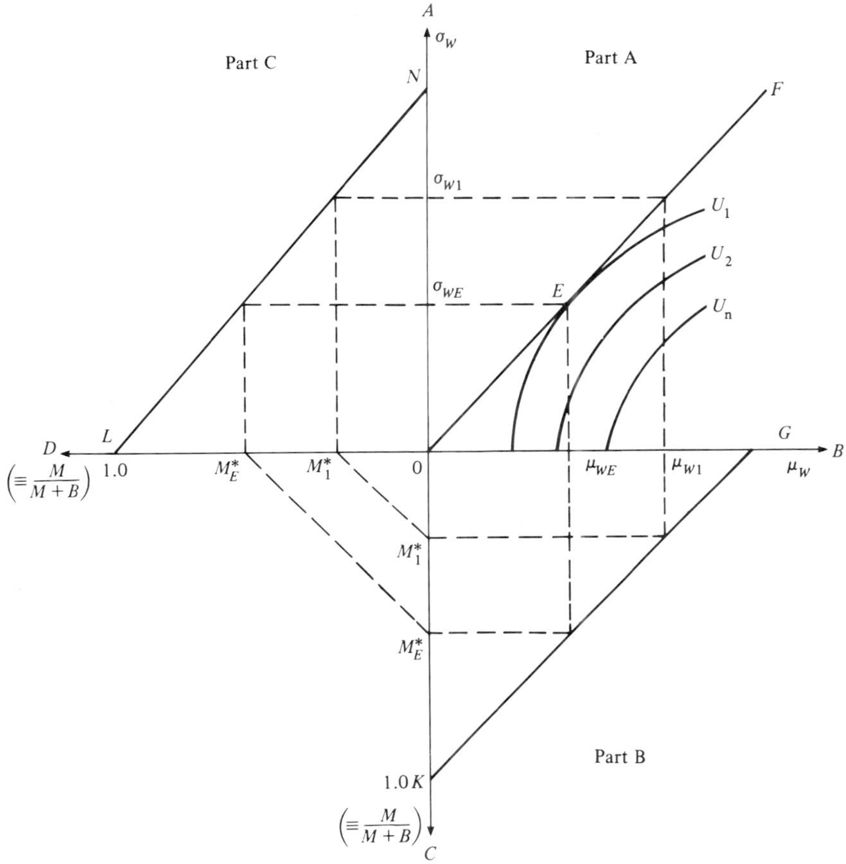

Figure 10-4

risk. That is, as the portfolio is changed by holding relatively more bonds and less money, its probability distribution has a higher μ_W and also a higher σ_W. The individual will be in equilibrium, will have an optimum combination, $(\mu_W \sigma_W)^*$, at the point of tangency between OF and an indifference curve. Any combination of risk and return is derived from a particular combination of money and bonds, so the equilibrium combination $(\mu_W \sigma_W)^*$ implies an equilibrium combination of money and bonds.

The relationship between particular combinations of money and bonds and particular combinations of return and risk on the portfolio is represented in Parts B and C of Figure 10.4. The vertical axis in Part B measures the proportion of money in the portfolio $[M/W = M/(M + B)]$. When the portfolio is held completely in the form of money, $M/W = 1$, and when it is wholly composed of bonds, $M/W = 0$. The locus KG represents the relationship between the proportion of money in the portfolio and the return on the portfolio (that is, the relationship between the mean of the probability distribution of returns on a portfolio, μ_W, and the proportion of money in that portfolio, M^*/W). As it is drawn in this figure, it reflects a situation where the profitability of the portfolio increases as the proportion of bonds in the portfolio increases (that is, as M/W decreases). In Part C, the horizontal axis measures M/W, the proportion of money in the portfolio. The locus LN represents the relationship between the proportion of money in the portfolio and the risk on the portfolio. As drawn, it indicates that the risk on the portfolio increases as the proportion of bonds increases.

Parts B and C of Figure 10.4 are the basis of the opportunity locus OF in Part A. For any given proportion of money in the portfolio [say, $(M/W)^1$], there is a probability distribution of returns on the portfolio that has a particular mean (μ'_w) and a particular standard deviation (σ'_w). These values, μ'_w and σ'_w, are then the coordinates of a point on OF (F'). Similarly, for any point on OF, there is a particular portfolio. For example, if equilibrium is established at E, the equilibrium proportion of money in the portfolio is $(M/W)^*$.

Figure 10.4 is the basis of a graphic exposition of the portfolio approach to liquidity preference theory. But the particular shapes of the loci as drawn there are not those that are implied by all types of liquidity preference theory. This is the most *general* form of the diagram, but, as will be seen in the following sections, this most general form is applicable only for analyzing the precautionary demand. In the analysis of the speculative and transactions demands, special assumptions are made and the opportunity loci are drawn in a different manner.

10.3 INTEREST ELASTICITY OF THE SPECULATIVE DEMAND

This exposition of the speculative demand is essentially the same as the hypothesis outlined in Section 9.2; it is merely presented differently. Consider Part C of Figure 10.5. The relationship between the risk on the portfolio and the proportion of money in the portfolio is represented by the segment LN of the horizontal axis. This reflects the assumption made in the analysis of the pure speculative demand that the future rate of interest (and, hence, the capital gain, CG, and the total return on a \$1 bond, $R = r + CG$) is forecast by the individual with certainty. Thus, whatever the proportion of bonds in the portfolio, the risk of the portfolio, the standard deviation σ_W, is zero.

Now consider Part B of Figure 10.5, which, for the pure theory of speculative demand, is the key part of the model. The individual has some expectation of what the rate of interest on bonds will be ($r^e_{1.2}$). Hence, there is some critical value for the rate of interest $-r^{**}$ as defined above (page 180). If the actual rate r_1 is above r^{**}, the individual expects to make a net gain on bond holdings ($R > 0$) and to take a loss ($R < 0$) if r_1 is less than r^{**}. As a result, there are two loci in Part B of the figure. K_1G_1 will exist if $r_1 > r^{**}$, for then the individual expects to make a net gain on any bond holdings, and μ_w will be larger, the greater is the proportion of bonds in the portfolio [the lower

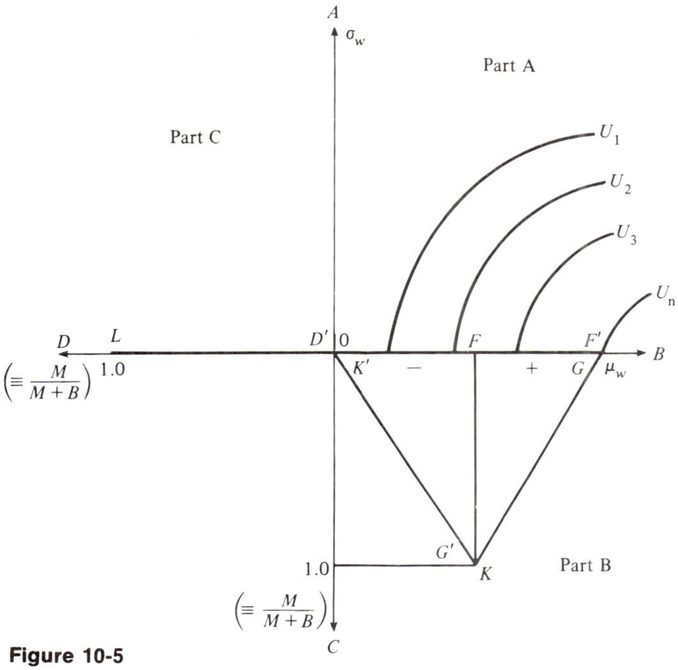

Figure 10-5

is $(M/W)]^*$. On the other hand, if $r_1 < r^{**}$, bond holdings are expected to involve losses. The greater the proportion of bonds in the portfolio, the greater will be losses on the portfolio, and the existing locus will be K_2G_2 (losses being described by negative values of μ_w).

Combining the loci of Parts B and C of Figure 10.5 in order to obtain the opportunity locus of Part A, it is clear that there will be two such opportunity loci: *OF* and *FF′*. Which one exists depends upon whether K_1G_1 or K_2G_2 exists and, hence, on the level of r_1 in relation to r^{**}. If *KG* exists, the expected profitability of bonds is positive ($r_1 > r^{**}$) and the expected profitability of the portfolio (μ_W) can take any value on the segment *FF′*, being greater the greater is the proportion of bonds in the portfolio [that is, the smaller is (M/W)]. Similarly, if K_2G_2 exists, the expected profitability of bonds is negative ($r_1 < r^{**}$) and μ_W can take any value on the segment *OF*. Since the gain or loss on bonds is expected with certainty, $\sigma_W = 0$ whatever the proportion of money and bonds in the portfolio. So the opportunity locus in Part A of the figure is either *FF′* or *OF* depending upon whether K_1G_1 or K_2G_2 exists.

We are now in a position to examine the effects on the pure speculative demand of a change in the rate of interest. Inspection of the figure makes it clear that these effects are limited and abrupt. They are *limited* because changes in the rate of interest affect *only* the individual's equilibrium position [and equilibrium demand for money as a proportion of wealth $(M/W)^*$]. When the change makes r_1 greater than r^{**}, from a position where r_1 was initially anywhere below r^{**}, the individual's utility-maximizing position will be where OF touches its highest indifference curve (that is, at F). This utility-maximizing position will remain unchanged as long as r_1 remains below (or equal to) r^{**}, but will change to F' (that is, the individual will be able to reach a higher level of utility) if r_1 rises above r^{**}. The effects are *abrupt* because a change from equilibrium at point F to F' involves a switch from holding the whole portfolio in money $[(M/W)^* = 1]$ to holding the whole portfolio in bonds $[(M/W)^* = 0]$. This may be seen by comparing the points on the vertical axis of Part B corresponding to the points F and F' on the horizontal axis (via the returns locus K_1G_1 or K_2G_2).

For the individual, then, the pure speculative motive implies a liquidity preference curve of the discontinuous shape represented in Figure 9.2. This theory of the interest elasticity of the demand for money is based on the individual's assessment of the available opportunities: at different rates of interest, the individual maximizes utility subject to different opportunity loci. It has, however, been criticized as too fragile a theoretical basis for liquidity preference. Its main weakness is its implication that the individual—not being a diversifier—will hold *either* money *or* bonds, never both. The theory of the interest elasticity of the transactions and precautionary demands is not open to this objection.

10.4 INTEREST ELASTICITY OF THE TRANSACTIONS DEMAND

As was pointed out in Chapter 3, Section 3.2, Keynes considered the transactions demand for cash to be proportional to income. The proportion (k) depended on "the character of banking and industrial organization, on social habits . . . ," etc., but was "nearly enough constant" in the short run. According to Keynes, it did not as a first approximation depend on the rate of interest. But, if one thinks carefully about Keynes's analysis presented in Chapter 9, Section 9.1, one can see that Keynes has not really given any reason why people should desire to hold transactions cash balances at all. Why should not individuals immediately invest all their receipts in bonds (which, unlike money, earn a rate of interest) and sell off bonds whenever they must make a payment? This would seem to be what profit-maximizing (or, in our model, utility-maximizing) individuals would do. The size of payments and receipts and the interval between them would then determine merely the size of average *bond* holdings over a period. Optimal *money* holdings would then be zero since, as soon as money is received as income, it is exchanged for bonds, and whenever money is obtained during the period by selling bonds, it is exchanged for goods.

However, the utility-maximizing individual will have a positive desire to hold *some* transactions balances in the form of money if we postulate that some kind of cost is involved in investing in bonds immediately after a receipt and disinvesting immediately before a payment. This cost could, for example, be a broker's fee, which is not a simple proportion of the amounts invested or disinvested by the broker. It could be, more generally, the cost of the time and trouble of investment. If there is such a cost of investing and disinvesting, it would provide a rationale for holding some money as transactions balances. But it would not give rise to Keynes's *interest-inelastic* demand for transactions balances. Instead, Baumol (1952) and Tobin (1956) have shown that if we rely on this assumption to explain the transactions demand for cash, this transactions demand will depend on the rate of interest if individuals are profit minimizers. This interest-elastic transactions demand for cash is analyzed in Figure 10.6.[2]

As in the speculative demand, we are here considering a world of certainty. So the locus relating σ_w to (M/W) in Part C is, again, the segment LN of the horizontal axis. However, many bonds are held in the portfolio, and the riskiness of the portfolio is zero, since the return on each bond is known with certainty.

The key part of the analysis is the loci KSG and $K'S'G'$ of Part B. Let us assume that the timing and the size of payments and receipts are given, and concentrate on the effects of changes in the interest rate on the proportions of

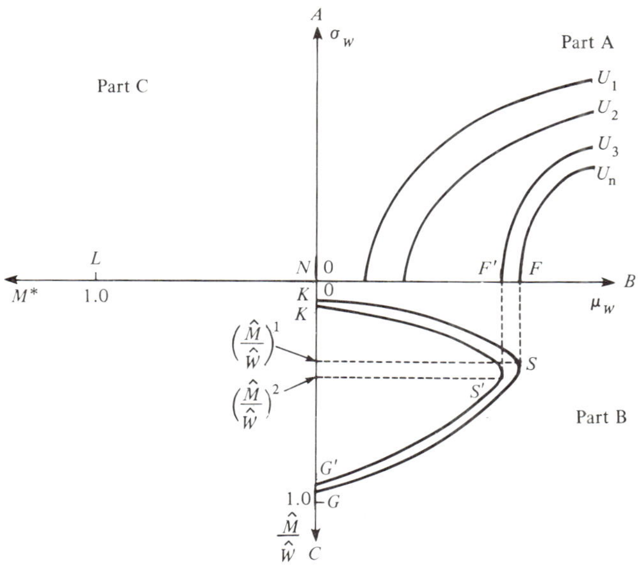

Figure 10-6

[2]Note that the size of the portfolio itself varies over the period. We assume that the portfolio decreases to zero by the end of the week—all receipts are spent. Thus, even if the proportion of money in the portfolio, (M/W), is constant over the week, the absolute amount, $M = (M/W) \times (M + B)$, varies. In this model, $[(M/W) \times (M + B)]$ should be treated as the average over the week, and we shall write $\hat{M}$, $\hat{B}$, $\hat{W}$, to denote these averages. In the case of the speculative demand, the size of the portfolio is constant over the period.

transactions reserves ($\hat{W}$) that are held in the form of money and bonds. The higher the average proportion of bonds in the portfolio, the greater will be the interest earnings on the portfolio at any given rate of interest. But, the higher is the average proportion of bonds in the portfolio, the more frequently will bonds have to be sold in order to make payments (and the more frequently will they have to be bought following receipts). If part of the broker's fee consists of a fixed charge per transaction (that is, if it does not depend on the amount of bonds involved in the transaction), the costs incurred by the individual will increase as the number of transactions in bonds increases. It follows that a high average proportion of bonds in the portfolio ensures high interest earnings but (because it involves frequent purchases and sales of bonds) also brings high costs. There will be some level of average bond holdings at which the difference between interest earnings and costs on the portfolio (net profitability) is maximized.

Suppose the individual is initially at such a position—the average bond holding (determined as a proportion of average wealth by the frequency of sales and purchases of bonds) is such that net profitability is maximized. Such a position is defined as the point where the marginal return on bond holdings (the rate of interest) equals the marginal cost (the change in costs incurred by changing the size of average bond holdings). Now suppose that there is a rise in the interest rate. As a result, the marginal return on the portfolio is now greater than its marginal cost, and so this portfolio no longer maximizes net profitability. The maximizing individual will change the portfolio until marginal return once again equals marginal cost. That is, as a result of the rise in interest rate, the average holding of bonds will be increased to the point where marginal cost has risen as much as the interest rate has risen. Thus, the rise in interest rate leads to a greater average holding of bonds in the portfolio. Conversely, when the rate of interest falls, there is an incentive to hold higher average money balances.

These implications are represented by the loci *KSG* and *K'S'G'*. When the interest rate is relatively high, *K'S'G'* exists; when it is relatively low, *K'S'G'* exists. *KSG* is outside *K'S'G'* at all points because, *ceteris paribus*, the higher is the interest rate, the greater is the net profitability of a given portfolio (since a given portfolio involves a given volume of bond transactions and, hence, given costs). If the rate of interest is, say, r_1, the locus *KSG* relating the portfolio's expected profitability to the average proportion of money balances will exist. This indicates that there will be some proportion of money, $(\hat{M}/\hat{W})$, in the portfolio (or of bonds, $[1-(\hat{M}/\hat{W})]$) where μ_W is maximized. If average money balances are greater than $(\hat{M}/\hat{W})^1$, the brokers' fees incurred in maintaining the lower average bond holdings will decline, but by less than the decline in interest earnings. If average money balances are lower than $(\hat{M}/\hat{W})^1$, the increase in brokers' fees will increase by more than the increase in interest earnings.[3] The result of this (and of the locus *LN* of

[3]The individual who wants to increase average bond holdings must increase the frequency of bond sales and purchases more than proportionately. Hence, because of the brokers' fees on such transactions, the cost of the portfolio is raised. This is shown in the ensuing paragraphs.

Part C) is that the opportunity locus in Part A of Figure 10.6 is the segment *OF* of the horizontal axis. The individual will be maximizing utility at point *F* and will there be holding average money balances, $(\hat{M}/\hat{W})^1$. If, however, the rate of interest were to fall to r_1^2, the locus $K_2S_2G_2$ would exist instead of $K_1S_1G_1$. For any given proportion of money in the portfolio, the return on the portfolio would be lower. The opportunity locus in Part A would be OF' and utility-maximizing average cash balances would rise to $(\hat{M}/\hat{W})^2$.

Profit Maximization

We have demonstrated that the transactions demand may therefore be interest-elastic if it is analyzed within the framework of the portfolio approach. But the apparatus of Figure 10.6 is more elaborate than we need to demonstrate the theory of the interest-elastic transactions demand; since the theory assumes certainty, we can ignore the risk axis of the figure. The important part of the diagram is Part B, and even here the diagram tends to hide the underlying factors at work: It is not immediately obvious why the curve *KSG* should have the shape drawn or why it should shift in the particular way that it does in response to a change in r_1. To overcome this difficulty, we shall now show how the same result as we derived above can be derived using a more conventional model (and, in the process, show what lies behind *KSG*). The model is similar to that of Baumol (1952), but it is not exactly the same. The result obtained is therefore formulated somewhat differently from Baumol's but has the same implications.

The individual, as a result of selling goods or labor services, receives an income at the beginning of each week. This income is held in the form of a stock of financial assets. In order to make payments during the week for goods or services, the individual, say a man, gradually depletes his stock of financial assets until, at the end of the week, his portfolio is zero. This stock of financial assets or wealth is represented in Figure 10.7 by the line FF'. This

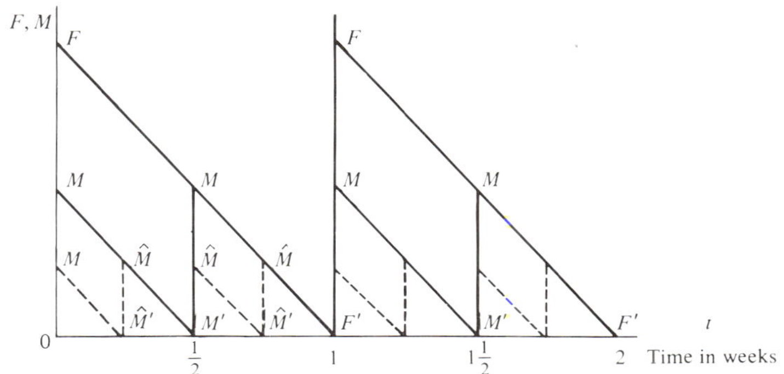

Figure 10-7

stock can be held in the form of either money or bonds (note that, to simplify the analysis, we assume that the initial receipt of income is in the form of bonds). Of course, all payments for purchases during the week must be made with money rather than bonds, but nevertheless, the individual need never hold money and can hold his financial asset stock solely in the form of bonds. For, whenever the individual has to make a purchase, he could, in principle, sell bonds at the instant when he has to hand over the money thereby never, in effect, holding a stock of money. More generally, however, the individual will sell bonds less frequently than he makes purchases.

For example, at the beginning of the week the man may hold half his financial assets in bonds and half in money, thereby holding a large enough stock of money to meet his first half-week's purchases; and half way through the week when his initial money stock is exhausted, he will sell the remaining bonds (half his original financial stock) for money and thereby have a stock of money to meet his second half-week's purchases. In that case, by making only two transactions in the bond market (the initial and the half-weekly sale of bonds), the individual holds a positive average stock of money, whereas in the extreme case (in which bonds are sold as frequently as there are payments to be met and at the same instant), the individual's money stock is always, in effect, zero. This case of two transactions is illustrated in Figure 10.7 as giving rise to a stock of cash represented by the MM' line. It can be seen that, given the FF' line representing financial stocks, the greater the number of sales of bonds per week (that is, the lower the amount of bonds sold at each time), the greater will be the number of steps in the MM' line and the lower will be the amount of money held at any time. (The case for four bond transactions is illustrated by the broken line $\hat{M}\hat{M}'$.)

The basic problem whose solution gives rise to the proposition that in this transactions model, average money holdings vary with the rate of interest, is this: How (given FF', the pattern of receipts) does a profit-maximizing individual decide on the optimal number of transactions between bonds and money? In other words, how does one decide on the optimal average holdings of money and bonds? According to the Keynesian theory of transactions demand (Chapter 9, Section 9.1), one will hold the whole of one's financial stock in the form of money balances, which, in terms of Figure 10.7, will be represented by the line FF'. But, because holding no bonds, the individual forgoes the possibility of earning interest on assets; from the point of view of earning interest, it is to the individual's benefit to hold as little money as possible (to sell bonds relatively frequently). On the other hand, frequent sales of bonds incur brokers' fees and, to minimize this cost, the individual should hold as high average money balances as possible. It is in reconciling these two aims—the maximization of interest earnings and the minimization of brokers' fees—that the individual arrives at an optimal average money stock.

We may represent the solution of this problem as the maximization of net profit. Let μ be the net profit on the portfolio of financial assets (interest earnings minus brokers' fees). Let r be the interest earned per bond per week;

c, the (fixed) cost per bond market transaction (brokers' fee); and n, the number of bond market transactions per period. $\hat{W}$ is the average holdings of financial assets per period ($OF/2$ in Figure 10.7); $\hat{M}$ is the average holdings of money, ($M/2$), and $\hat{B}$ ($= \hat{W} - \hat{M}$) is the average bond holdings.

Net profits are given by the function:

$$\begin{aligned} \mu &= r\hat{B} - cn \\ &= \text{total interest receipts} - \text{total brokers' fees} \end{aligned} \tag{10.1}$$

The problem is to maximize μ with respect to $\hat{M}$. Substituting into Equation 10.1 in the following way, we can express μ as a function of $\hat{M}$. In order to make payments for purchases during the week (total OF or $2\hat{W}$), the individual may sell bonds in lots of amount Q, so that $nQ = OF$ (or $n = 2\hat{W}/Q$). Each time a bond sale takes place, cash balances become $M = Q$ and, since M declines to zero before the next bond sale, average cash balances, $\hat{M}$, equal $Q/2$. Hence:

$$\begin{aligned} Q &= 2\hat{M} \text{ and} \\ n &= \frac{2\hat{W}}{2\hat{M}} \end{aligned} \tag{10.2}$$

Using Equation 10.2 and the fact that $\hat{B} = \hat{W} - \hat{M}$, we may rewrite Equation 10.1 as:

$$\mu = r\hat{W} - r\hat{M} - c\,\frac{2\hat{W}}{2\hat{M}} \tag{10.3}$$

Differentiating Equation 10.3 with respect to $\hat{M}$, we find the first-order condition for maximum μ to be:

$$\frac{\partial \mu}{\partial \hat{M}} = -r + \frac{c2\hat{W}}{2\hat{M}^2} = 0 \tag{10.4}$$

Rearranging terms, we find that the value of $\hat{M}$ that satisfies this first-order condition (the profit-maximizing value of average money balances) is:

$$\hat{M} = \sqrt{\frac{c2\hat{W}}{2r}} \tag{10.5}$$

From Equation 10.5 it can be seen, therefore, that optimal average money balances held for the purpose of making transactions in goods and services are an inverse function of the rate of interest. This result is the same as that obtained above by using Figure 10.6—a coincidence that is not surprising, since Equation 10.3 (with $\hat{M}$ replaced by $\hat{M}/\hat{W}$) is the equation of the loci KSG and $K'S'G'$ in that figure.

We can also derive the same result diagrammatically if we define the marginal revenue and marginal cost of the portfolio with respect to money balances. As can be seen from Equation 10.1, the individual's portfolio involves costs (cn) as well as returns ($r\hat{B}$). From Equation 10.3, it can be seen that these costs and returns can be expressed as functions of average money balances: $(c2\hat{W}/2\hat{M})$ and $(r\hat{W} - r\hat{M})$ respectively. The rate of change of these costs and returns as $\hat{M}$ changes is the marginal cost and marginal return from money balances, and by equating marginal cost with marginal return, we can find the profit-maximizing level of $\hat{M}$. This technique gives the same result as the technique used in the last paragraph.

Since $C = \dfrac{c2\bar{W}}{2\bar{M}}$ and $R = (r\hat{W} + r\hat{M})$, *marginal cost is*:

$$MC = \frac{\partial C}{\partial \hat{M}} = \frac{-c2\hat{M}}{2\hat{M}^2}$$

and marginal revenue is:

$$MR = \frac{\partial R}{\partial \hat{M}} = -r$$

From the curves described by these equations we may represent the argument diagrammatically, as in Figure 10.8. The marginal cost curve is CC'. If the rate of interest is r^1, then the marginal revenue curve is R_1R_1 and the optimal level of average money balances is that $(\hat{M}^1)$ at which marginal revenue equals marginal cost. If the rate of interest were greater than r^1 (say, r^2), the marginal revenue of money balances would be a greater negative number (the line R_2R_2) and the optimal level of average money balances would be lower than $\hat{M}_1$ at $\hat{M}_2$.

The conclusion is that as the rate of interest falls, a greater proportion of the individual's wealth that is held in order to meet discrepancies between payments and receipts will be held in the form of money balances (and vice versa). The theory indicates that the transactions demand is, therefore, interest-elastic as long as some kinds of costs are involved in the very act of buying and selling bonds. But remember that this is only a theory. It is an accurate model only if, as assumed, risk is ignored for the periods of time for

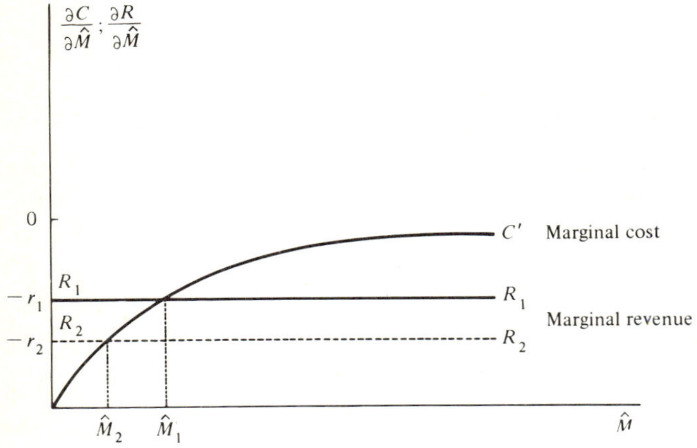

Figure 10-8

which decisions about transactions balances are made, if the nature of the costs of financial transactions is as specified, and, of course, if portfolio owners are utility maximizers in the manner postulated. The theory of an interest-elastic precautionary demand, on the other hand, has been developed on the assumption that the costs of financial transactions are zero but that risk is an important factor.

10.5 INTEREST ELASTICITY OF THE PRECAUTIONARY DEMAND

The theory of an interest-elastic transactions demand overcomes the major objection to the theory of a pure speculative demand, for the utility-maximizing individual will hold both money and bonds: a diversified portfolio. The model that Tobin develops (1958, 1965c), the risk-aversion demand for money, has the same advantage over the theory of pure speculative demand and, since it is based on the individual's response to portfolio riskiness, it can be considered as an elaboration of the first version of Keynes's theory of precautionary demand outlined above (pages 182–183). Figure 10.9 represents the elements of Tobin's model.

Unlike the pure speculative and transactions models, in this model the

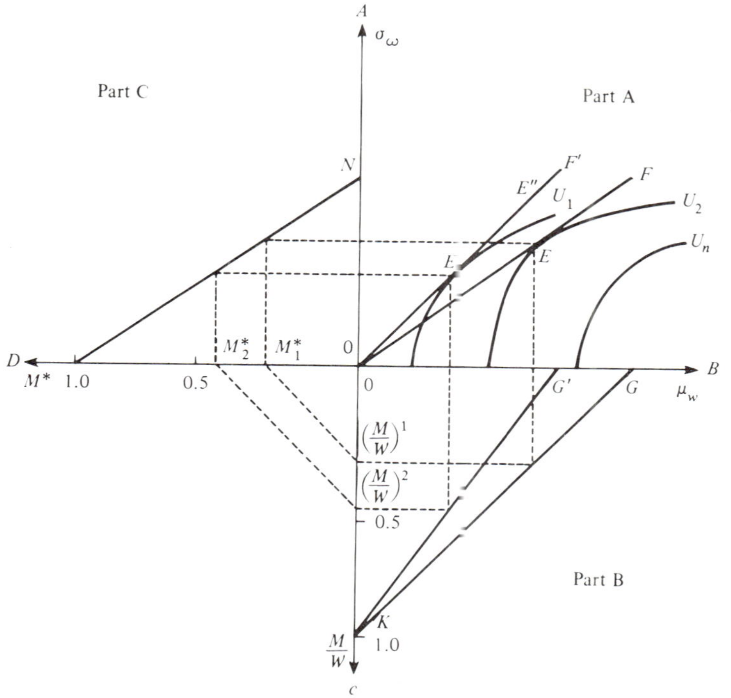

Figure 10-9

riskiness of the portfolio is positive and varies as the proportion of money varies. The return on money is expected, with certainty, to be zero. But the return per dollar on bonds ($R_B = r_1 + g$) is forecast only in the sense that there is a probability distribution of returns on the bonds. In Tobin's model, it is assumed that the mean of this probability distribution equals the current rate of interest ($\mu_B = r_1$). In other words, it is assumed that the mathematical expectation of capital gain or loss is zero. Although the individual thinks that the rate of interest may change and a capital gain or loss may be made, the probability of gain is as great as the probability of loss.[4] The risk attached to bond holdings is measured by the standard deviation of the probability distribution of returns on bonds, σ_B, which is assumed not to be zero. Because the returns on bonds are risky, whereas the return on money is not, the riskiness of the return on the whole portfolio, σ_W, will be greater, the smaller is the proportion of money in the portfolio, (M/W). This assumption is reflected by the shape of *LN* in Part C of Figure 10.9. The locus K_1G_1 in Part B indicates that, like its riskiness, the expected value of the return on the portfolio, μ_W, also increases as the proportion of money decreases.

From Parts B and C we may construct the opportunity locus OF_1 of Part A. This opportunity locus indicates that the individual can obtain a higher expected value of return on the portfolio only by incurring higher risk. The individual will be in equilibrium at point *E* and will there be holding the proportion $(M/W)^1$ of the portfolio in the form of money.

A change in the rate of interest will shift *KG*. A fall in this rate, for example, will cause the new locus to be *KG'*. That is, since the mathematical expectation of return on bonds equals the current rate of interest, a fall in r_1 leads to a fall in μ_B and so causes a fall in the expected value of the return on the portfolio. The absolute size of the fall depends on the proportion of bonds in the portfolio. The change in the rate of interest is, however, assumed not to affect *LN*. That is, however high or low the rate of interest may be, the individual attaches the same probabilities to the possibilities of falls or rises. For example, when the rate of interest is high, the individual does not consider it any less likely to remain constant than when the rate was low.[5] It follows from these assumptions about *KG* and *LN* that the opportunity locus in Part A will be shifted to *OF'* by a fall in the rate of interest and that equilibrium will be established at *E'*. At this new equilibrium, less risk is involved than at *E*, and the proportion of money is greater $(M/W)^2$.

[4]Thus, $\mu_B = \mu_{r_1} + \mu_g = \mu_{r_1} + 0 = r_1$. This is different from the assumption made in the model of speculative demand, where the essential fact is that the interest rate is expected to change: the mean of the probability distribution of capital gains, μ_g, is *non*-zero. Therefore, the model of this section, Tobin's model, is not the same as either the pure version or Keynes's final formulation of the speculative demand (which takes account of uncertainty) because here, $\mu_g = 0$. It also differs from Keynes's in other respects, such as the concept of uncertainty employed.

[5]This is another example of an assumption that differs from the one used by Keynes when he developed the speculative demand in a world of uncertainty. For Keynes, the more that r_1 differed from r^{**}, the greater was the probability that r would change.

This model, therefore, gives the result that the precautionary demand for money is interest-elastic, more money being desired when interest rates are low than when they are high. The model is appealing, but it has several weaknesses. One of the major faults is that there is no a priori reason why equilibrium should be established at E' after the fall in the rate of interest. If the indifference curves had been drawn slightly differently (and there is no theoretical reason to prevent this), the new equilibrium might be established at E''. If that happened, the demand for precautionary balances would be positively, rather than inversely, related to the rate of interest. Such a phenomenon could be described by saying that, although the fall in the rate of interest causes a "substitution effect" in the direction of less risk, it is fully offset by an "income effect" in the opposite direction: individuals, finding their real income reduced, are willing to take more risk to try to restore the expected value of the return on their portfolios. Other weaknesses of the model are discussed in Chapter 11.

10.6 SOME IMPLICATIONS OF KEYNESIAN LIQUIDITY PREFERENCE THEORY

It is clear that the interest elasticity of the speculative, transactions, and precautionary demands can be derived as implications of a basic model of portfolio analysis. The differences between the three theories arise from different special assumptions about the model. Two major conclusions may be drawn from this.

First, the speculative, transactions, and precautionary motives for holding money and for altering desired money balances in response to changes in the rate of interest are not really different. Instead, they are based on the same *motives* (minimization of risk and maximization of return) and differ only insofar as the *opportunities* for satisfying these motives differ (as a result of the existence or absence of transactions costs and differences in the nature and certainty of expectations).

Second, the portfolio approach to post-Keynesian liquidity preference theory brings us nearer to answering the question: "Why hold money at all when interest-bearing bonds can be held instead?" We can now see that Keynes's answer ("This necessary condition is the existence of uncertainty") is not adequate. For one thing, the pure speculative and transactions models outlined in Sections 10.3 and 10.4 demonstrate that uncertainty is not a *necessary* condition. The existence of transactions costs or of divergencies between the current and the expected rates of interest explain money holdings equally well. For another thing, the existence of uncertainty is not a sufficient condition for a desire to hold money, for the particular effects of uncertainty, analyzed in Section 10.5, depend upon the particular shape of the indifference curves. Consider, for example, what would happen if the individual were a risk lover rather than a risk averter. Then the indifference curves in Part A of

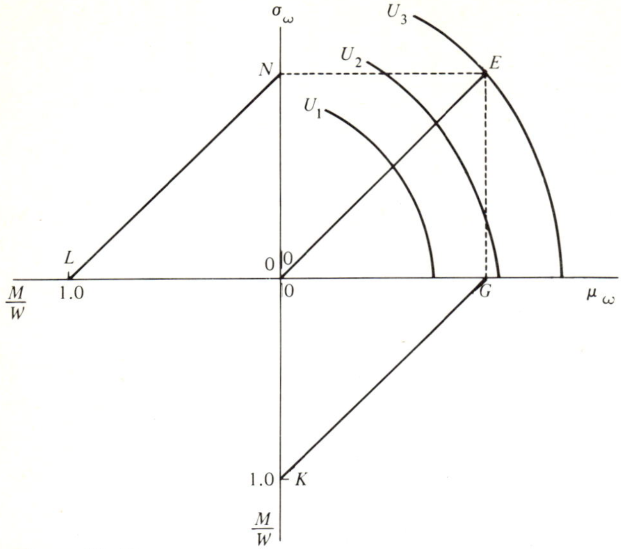

Figure 10-10

Figure 10.9 would be of the shape drawn in Figure 10.10. If that were the case, the individual would always be in equilibrium at a point like *E*, where the portfolio has maximum risk and maximum expected value of return. So, whatever the rate of interest, the individual who is a risk lover will always hold all the portfolio in the form of bonds despite the existence of uncertainty. Uncertainty, therefore, is not a sufficient condition for holding money balances when bonds are available as alternative assets. Moreover, casual empiricism indicates that today money balances are held even though individuals have the opportunity of holding as alternatives bonds to which no uncertainty attaches. If one holds a nonmarketable deposit in a financial institution other than a (checking-account) bank, one earns a certain interest rate and there is no possibility of capital loss (other than the bankruptcy of the institution). Such assets do, however, involve transactions costs. All these considerations indicate that the medium-of-exchange function of money is of primary relevance.

Apart from these two conclusions, the Keynesians' application of the portfolio approach has clarified some issues left untouched in Keynes's *General Theory*. For example, the approach sheds light on the question of whether an increase in the supply of money is most effective when it results from open-market operations or when it results from printing money. In answering such questions, Chapter 11 appraises some aspects of the *General Theory's* monetary theory in the light of the portfolio approach. However, the portfolio approach itself has many weaknesses and limitations. At least, the simple applications of the approach outlined in this chapter have such limitations, and the next chapter also explains some of the criticisms and extensions that have been made.

CHAPTER

ELEVEN

ADVANCED ASPECTS OF THE KEYNESIAN PORTFOLIO APPROACH

The Keynesian portfolio approach to the theory of the demand for money has been the dominant framework of monetary analysis in modern times. Although, as we saw in Chapter 10, it has been particularly fruitful in the development of Keynes's concept of the demand for money, its modern source can be traced to Hicks (1935). He, much more clearly than Keynes, treated the problem of the demand for money as one of allocating a given net wealth among alternative assets so as to maximize returns while taking account of risk. Since the time of Keynes, the fundamental theoretical work has been pursued most vigorously at Yale University. The distinctive feature of this work is the development of models based on utility theory of a special kind: the utility theory developed by von Neumann and Morgenstern (1944) for analyzing choices in situations of risk. It is within this school that the work of Tobin (1958), Markowitz (1959), Sharpe (1964), and others has developed.

One conclusion of the portfolio approach is immediately apparent. That is, the demand for money is not only a function of the relative returns on alternative assets—"the" rate of interest—but it also depends on the total level of wealth. The rate of interest determines, in a simple money-bonds portfolio, the utility-maximizing proportions of money and bonds in the portfolio. The size of the portfolio, the value of wealth, then determines the desired *amount* of money (and bonds). This is equivalent to a real balance effect in the real demands for money and bonds, the only difference being that now it should be called a wealth effect, since real wealth in this model consists of bonds as well as money. We shall see in Chapter 12 that the demand functions for money and bonds used in the Neoclassical/Keynesian synthesis models include this wealth effect.

A further aspect of the portfolio approach has yet to be demonstrated. In the most general formulations of this approach, money is not divided into separate balances, such as the "active" and "idle" balances or "transactions" and "speculative" balances of Keynes's *General Theory*. In Chapter 10 we have applied the portfolio approach to different "balances" in this sense. Now, in Section 11.1, we demonstrate that a model of the demand for undifferentiated money balances can be developed by integrating the models of Chapter 10. We also show the relevance of such a model to the idea of the liquidity trap.

The precautionary demand model of Chapter 10 is built on a certain concept of risk, the risk of taking a capital loss (or gain). In Section 11.2 we consider whether this is a satisfactory basis for analyzing the demand for money.

In Sections 11.1 and 11.2, therefore, we consider some aspects of the opportunity locus that is central to the portfolio analysis we have used. In Section 11.3, we consider the utility function employed in portfolio analysis. We show how the indifference curves we have used are based on von Neumann and Morgenstern's utility theory and consider some weaknesses that stem from this. Finally, in Section 11.4, we extend the portfolio approach to market analysis. Up to this point, we have been concerned with an individual's behavior in choosing between money and one type of bond with an interest rate given by the market. In Section 11.4, we consider the formation of market equilibrium interest rates in a world where individuals can choose between money and an assortment of many types of bonds.

11.1 PORTFOLIO ANALYSIS, THE LIQUIDITY TRAP, AND THE RELATIONSHIP BETWEEN DIFFERENT MOTIVES

A special hypothesis in Keynesian models is the theory of the liquidity trap. In the Neoclassical/Keynesian Synthesis it has played an important role in the analysis of involuntary unemployment at equilibrium. In this section we consider whether the post-Keynesian portfolio approach to liquidity preference theory includes the implication that a liquidity trap may exist. In essence, the liquidity trap is a situation in which all investors are in equilibrium when holding undiversified portfolios—portfolios entirely in the form of money. Our problem, then, is to discover whether the portfolio approach admits equilibria where portfolios consist solely of money.

Keynes's theory of a liquidity trap is based upon his theory of the speculative demand for money. Clearly, then, that version of the portfolio model which describes the pure speculative theory (Section 10.3) does admit the possibility of a liquidity trap. This can be seen from Section 10.3's discussion. There it was shown that if the current interest rate is less than the critical rate, individuals will hold all their wealth in the form of money. But the liquidity trap hypothesis requires that *all* individuals hold undiversified money balances. This will occur when all individuals have the same expectations regarding the future rates of interest and, hence, have the same values of r^{**} (for an individual's critical rate r^{**} depends upon her or his evaluation of the expected future rate, $r^e_{1.2}$). If that situation occurs—if the actual rate of interest is $r_1 < r^{**}$ for any one individual and thus $r_1 < r^{**}$ for all individuals—everyone will hold undiversified money balances. The speculative model, then, does include the possibility of a liquidity trap.

However, the main conclusions of Sections 10.4 and 10.5 regarding the post-Keynesian theories of transactions demand and precautionary demand were that these models were superior to the speculative model because, in general, they predicted that the individual will hold a diversified portfolio—all its wealth will not be in the form of money. In general, therefore, these models preclude the existence of a liquidity trap. But suppose we were to combine these three portfolio models of liquidity preference into one generalized Keynesian model of the demand for money. Would this integrated model allow for the existence of undiversified money holdings, the existence of a liquidity trap? In this section we construct such an integrated model and conclude that it would allow for nondiversification.

In so doing, we also solve a problem arising out of the fact that, as in Chapter 10, the models of the demand for money are treated separately. This problem is: Can an individual have all three (or any two) types of demand for money simultaneously? To answer this, note that each of the three types of interest elasticity is different from the others because each arises out of the existence of different "opportunities." The opportunities evoking the interest-elastic precautionary demand are inconsistent with those eliciting the pure speculative and the transactions demand. The first develops out of uncertainty, whereas the last two have been analyzed in a situation where expectations are held with certainty. Hence, a consistent individual cannot exhibit both precautionary and speculative (or transactions) behavior. Similarly, whereas the speculative and precautionary models are based on expectations concerning changes in the interest rate, the transactions model analyzes the demand for money over a period where the rate of interest is expected, with certainty, not to change. Hence, in general, a consistent individual cannot simultaneously exhibit the behavior analyzed in the transactions model and precautionary or speculative behavior.

So far we have, then, three different post-Keynesian explanations of interest elasticity in the demand for money, no two of which can both apply to a consistent individual. In this section we take the major elements from each model and combine them, using the three-quadrant diagram of portfolio analysis to explore the results. In combining these elements, a unified Keynesian theory of the interest elasticity of the demand for money is achieved that takes account of divergences between the present and the expected rate

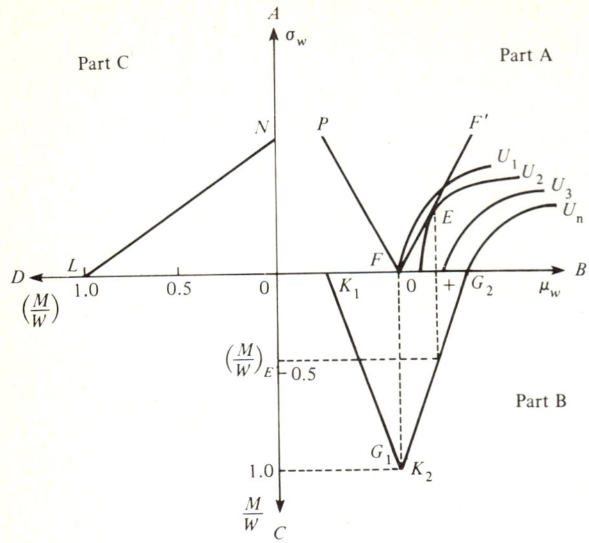

Figure 11-1

of interest (from the speculative model); of a probability distribution of the expected rate of interest (from the precautionary model); and of the existence of costs of financial transactions (from the transactions model).

The first step is to combine the elements of the speculative and the precautionary models. In this speculative-precautionary model, it is assumed that expectations concerning the rate of interest that will exist at the end of the decision period are described by a probability distribution (as in the precautionary model), but that the mean of this probability distribution (the expected value of the rate of interest) differs from the current rate of interest (as in the speculative model). This situation is represented in Figure 11.1. The $(\sigma_W, M/(M+B))$ locus LN of Part C shows that bonds are risky (since the standard deviation of the probability distribution of the future rate of interest is non-zero) and the standard deviation of returns on the portfolio increases linearly as the proportion of bonds increases. The $(\mu_W, M/(M+B))$ locus of Part B is the same as that of the speculative model (Figure 10.5). Given the expected value of the future rate of interest, the expected value of the return on the portfolio depends on the current rate of interest. If $r_1 > r^{**}$, net gains are expected and K_1G_1 will exist; if $r > r^{**}$, losses are expected and K_2G_2 will exist. The only difference in Part B from the speculative model is that here r^{**} is defined as a function of the mean of the probability distribution of the future rate of interest, whereas in the speculative model it is defined as a function of the expected future rate, which, being expected with certainty, was assigned a probability of unity.

In Part A, the loci of Parts B and C are combined. If K_2G_2 exists, the opportunity locus in Part A will be PF; if K_1G_1 exists, it will be FF'. It follows that as long as $r_1 < r^{**}$, the utility-maximizing individual will be in equilibrium at F and will hold the entire portfolio in money: if $r_1 > r^{**}$, equilibrium will be reached at some position like E and a diversified portfolio may be held $(0 < (M/W))_E < 1)$.

The conclusions are interesting. By combining the speculative model's assumption of independence between the current rate and the expected value of the future rate of interest with the precautionary model's assumption of a probability distribution of the future rate of interest, we find the following: First, changes in the current rate of interest do not affect the demand for money unless that rate is within the range $r_1 > r^{**}$ before and after the change, or unless $r_1 > r^{**}$ either before or after the change. Second, if the expected value of the rate implies an expected loss on bonds ($r_1 > r^{**}$), the individual will hold a nondiversified portfolio. These results demonstrate a limitation of Section 9.3's analysis of risk aversion and the precautionary model (in Chapter 9). That section's conclusion that, in general, risk averters will hold diversified portfolios depends on the assumption that the expected value of the rate of interest is the same as the current rate (that is, expected capital gains are zero). Here, different results have been obtained by assuming that the expected rate of interest is independent of the current rate. Even if we were to relax this assumption and assume, instead, that the expected rate does vary with (but does not identically equal) the current rate, it would again be found that a nondiversified portfolio is held when $r_1 < r^{**}$.

This result is intuitively dissatisfying. It implies that as long as there is an *expected* capital loss on bonds (greater than interest earnings), no bonds will be held, even though this expected value is only the mean of a probability distribution and although the probability distribution may be such that capital *gains* have a high probability. If such behavior is considered implausible, the conclusion reflects a weakness in describing risk and returns by the two parameters (σ and μ). Finally, note that this behavior is analogous to the Keynesian liquidity trap.

In order to integrate the transactions model with this speculative-precautionary model, it is now necessary to introduce the assumption that financial transactions involve costs. This integration involves some complications, since in the transactions model the portfolio is reduced to meet payments at times within the decision period (whereas in the speculative and precautionary models, assets are not sold until the end of the decision period). Hence, the effect on the model of introducing the assumption of an expected change in the rate of interest (from the speculative model) differs according to which point within the decision period this change is expected to occur. An expected change of interest rate at the very beginning of the decision period (before the portfolio is reduced to meet net payments) will affect the returns on the portfolio to a much greater extent (since more bonds will be affected than an expected change of interest rate at the end of the decision period. In

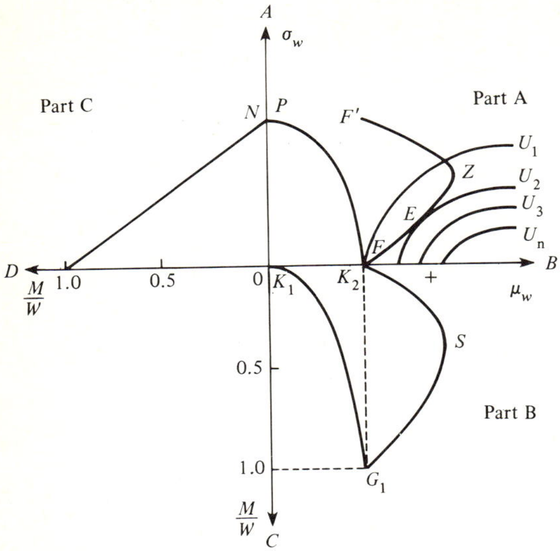

Figure 11-2

this section it is assumed that, given the probability distribution of a change in interest rates, the timing of any change is not known with certainty. As a result, the portfolio's probability distribution of returns [on which are based the (σ_W, $M/(M+B)$) and (μ_W, $M/(M+B)$) loci] is a function of the joint probability distribution of the two random variables: the future rate of interest and the number of bonds remaining in the portfolio at the time within the decision period when the rate of interest changes. (This last variable is expressed as a percentage of the average number of bonds in the portfolio.)

This integrated model, which combines three assumptions, each of which alone would give rise to an interest-elastic demand for money (an expected change in interest rates, uncertainty about future interest rates, and transaction costs), is represented in Figure 11.2. In Part C, the locus *LN* describes the assumption that the riskiness of the portfolio increases as a linear function of the proportion of bonds in the portfolio. In Part B, there are again two loci. Locus K_1G_1 will exist if the expected value of the future rate of interest is such that $r_1 < r^{**}$. Locus K_2SG_1 will exist if expectations are such that $r_1 > r^{**}$. Combining the loci of Parts B and C, the opportunity locus of Part A is derived. If $r_1 < r^{**}$, this locus is *PF* and the individual will maximize utility by *holding a nondiversified portfolio* ($M/(M+B) = 1$) *and a liquidity trap may exist.* If $r_1 > r^{**}$, this locus is *FZF'* and equilibrium will be reached at a point like *E*. Only the segment *FZ* of the locus *FZF'* is relevant to the individual's portfolio decision. (The segment *ZF'* can be disregarded by a risk averter since, for any portfolio on *ZF'*, there is a portfolio on *FZ* that offers the same μ_W and a lower σ_W.) Regarding the interest elasticity of the demand for money, it is again the case that only if $r_1 > r^{**}$ does the optimum portfolio mix depend on r_1. A rise in r_1 will cause *PF* to rotate clockwise around *F* if

$r_1 < r^{**}$ before and after the change, but equilibrium will be unchanged at F. A rise in r where $r_1 > r^{**}$ before and after the change will cause FZ to rotate clockwise around F, and this change in the slope of the opportunity locus will lead to a new equilibrium portfolio.

The model represented in Figure 11.2 demonstrates, therefore, that the speculative, precautionary, and transactions models can be combined into one model that implies an interest-elastic demand for money. It shows that it is possible to determine an optimal level of cash balances that simultaneously satisfies the wish to hold cash to speculate against bond prices, to hedge against risk, and to bridge the interval between payments and receipts. It answers the problem left unanswered by the separate post-Keynesian developments of the transactions and precautionary models: How much wealth should a rational individual allocate to transactions balances, precautionary balances, and speculative balances? For we may note that given their pure forms, no individual would simultaneously hold balances for all three purposes (since that would involve inconsistency in the perception of opportunities), but that if the major elements of each model are combined, the individual will hold one optimal cash balance that satisfies all three purposes. Moreover, it demonstrates that post-Keynesian liquidity preference theory does not preclude the existence of undiversified money holdings and a liquidity trap. But it should be noted that such behavior is, in general, only consistent with the post-Keynesian models where, as in this section, these models are combined with elements of pure speculative behavior. Keynes's hypothesis of a liquidity trap, therefore, depends heavily upon the existence of speculative behavior.

11.2 PROBLEMS IN THE CONCEPT OF RISK AND CERTAINTY

The precautionary demand of Section 10.5 and Section 11.1's model of an integrated precautionary, speculative, and transactions demand employ a particular concept of risk. The individual there is assumed to be concerned solely with the risk of a capital gain or loss on bond holdings. This concern gives rise to a positive but interest-elastic demand for money. The realism of this assumption may be questioned on two grounds.

The first is that in reality there are many interest-earning assets that carry no more risk of capital gain or loss than do non–interest-bearing bank deposits (money). The theory of the precautionary demand, therefore, is not a satisfactory explanation of the existence of a positive demand for money, although it may be satisfactory as an explanation of the demand for riskless bonds in a portfolio where the alternative assets are risky bonds. This leads us back to the point, made in Chapter 10, that the existence of uncertainty and risk cannot explain the existence of money and that therefore the distinguishing characteristic of money is, as Clower (1969) argues, its function as a Medium of Exchange rather than its characteristic of being a Store of Value without risk of capital gain or loss.

The second problem is that there are no a priori grounds for assuming that the choice between money and bonds is affected by risk of capital gain or loss—*capital risk.* It may as well be affected by *income risk*—the risk of a change in interest earnings. Matthews (1963) demonstrates that the relative importance of the two types of risk depends on the individual's *encashment period,* the length of time for which he or she intends to hold the bonds.

Consider this problem first within the context of the type of portfolio we have so far assumed to exist. Here the individual has a choice between either money or irredeemable bonds (British Consols, for example, whose maturity date is infinity). We have been able to assume a preoccupation with capital risk because the individual is assumed to plan to sell the bonds within a finite time period—that is, before their maturity date. If the rate of interest has risen before selling the bonds, the individual will make a capital loss. The investor may, however, have an infinite time horizon, planning never to sell the bonds but to live on interest receipts. Such investors are often characterized as belonging to the group of "widows and orphans" and may be thought of as the trustees of a charitable trust.[1] If an investor has an infinite time horizon, then there is neither a capital risk nor an income risk in buying a Consol. If the individual plans never to sell and adheres to this plan, a capital loss is not possible. Since the interest rate is known at the time of buying the bond, there is no risk of a change in income receipts. Even if the market rate of interest changes after purchase of the bond, this does not affect the interest yield, since the purchase price of the bond and the coupon rate are unaffected.

The problem becomes more interesting if we consider an individual who does not necessarily have an infinite time horizon and who has the opportunity to choose not only between money and Consols but also between money and a whole range of bonds with different maturities. Suppose that the individual is planning to invest for two years, but to encash half the investment after one year. Both capital risk and income risk could be completely avoided if half the individual's resources are invested in a one-year bond and half in a two-year bond. Each is bought at a given rate of interest and therefore carries no income risk. Each is redeemed at its known par value exactly at the time when the individual requires money. The investor therefore does not have to sell either bond at market prices and is free of capital risk. The investment could be planned, however, in such a way that it involves either capital risk or income risk, and either action may be taken in the search for profit.

Suppose again that the individual plans to encash half the investment after one year and half after two. The individual who expects the rate of interest on one-year bonds to be higher in one year's time than it is now, may adopt the following plan. The full amount will be invested now in one-year bonds and, after one year, half the capital sum (and interest receipts) will be

[1]Although such investors may be rare today, they were far from uncommon among the English middle classes in the first half of the twentieth century.

invested in a new one-year bond so as to take advantage of the expected higher interest rate. This plan would involve no capital risk but it would involve an income risk since expectations may not be realized. The individual may find that the rate of interest has fallen instead of risen by the end of the first year so that income in the second year is reduced. Alternatively, the individual who expects the rate of interest to fall by the end of the first year may plan to make a capital gain. This can be done by investing the whole sum in two-year bonds and planning to sell half at the end of the first year. The individual who adopts this plan will incur no income risk but will incur a capital risk, for the interest rate may rise instead of fall, and a capital loss must be taken on the bonds sold at the end of the first year.

These examples are enough to show that the precautionary demand models employed in Chapter 10 and in this chapter are highly simplified. There is no a priori reason why risk should be defined simply as capital risk. Moreover, the riskiness of a portfolio depends not only on the proportions of money and bonds in the portfolio, but also on the synchronization between the maturity dates of the bonds and the individual's planned encashment dates.

A completely separate problem is the assumption of certainty in the transactions demand model of Chapter 10. Not only is the interest rate assumed with certainty to be fixed, but income receipts and expenditures are assumed to be known with certainty. This last assumption has been modified by Miller and Orr (1966) and Orr (1971), and a more complicated model of the transactions demand has been obtained.

This model has been developed in the context of a firm's demand for transactions balances. Its receipts and expenditures at any point in time are not known with certainty and do not, in fact, follow a linear path. Therefore the time path of financial resources is as illustrated by the solid line in Figure 11.3 rather than as shown in Figure 10.7. If the firm did not invest its money receipts in bonds and disinvest in order to make expenditures, this line would also represent the time path of the firm's money balances. But since bonds

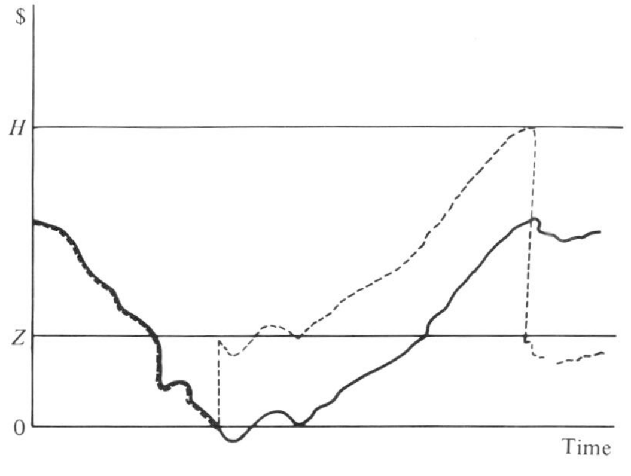

Figure 11-3

offer a positive interest rate, whereas money does not, the firm has an incentive to invest part of its transactions resources in the form of bonds. The existence of brokers' fees or other costs ensures, as in Baumol's model that we analyzed in Chapter 10, that not all these resources are held in the form of bonds. However, the existence of uncertainty prevents our arriving at a simple expression for optimal money balances. Instead, Miller and Orr show that the firm will maximize profits by choosing a maximum level of money balances and a minimum level. These are represented by the points H and 0 respectively in Figure 11.3. If cash balances reach H, the firm will buy bonds and thereby reduce its cash balances to Z. If they reach zero, the firm will sell bonds and raise its cash balances to Z. Therefore, the optimal pattern of money balances is as represented by the dashed line in Figure 11.3. The theoretical problem is to determine the variables on which H and Z depend. The results obtained are similar to those of Baumol; the optimum levels of H and Z depend on the rate of interest and the brokers' fee (among other things). The higher is the rate of interest, the lower will be H and Z, and consequently the lower will be average cash balances.

The transactions demand model based on certainty of linear receipts and expenditure is therefore highly simplified. But its extension to a world where receipts and expenditures give rise to random changes in financial resources is possible.

11.3 UTILITY THEORY AND PORTFOLIO ANALYSIS

The portfolio analysis of Chapter 10 is based on the assumption that the individual's indifference curves between risk and return slope away from the origin and represent higher utility the further to the right they are (and are concave from below). This assumption rests on the theory of utility developed by von Neumann and Morgenstern (1947) to analyze choices in situations where the benefits from each choice are uncertain. In order to appreciate some of the criticisms that have been raised against the indifference curves of the portfolio analysis, it is important to have some understanding of the relationship between the indifference curves and Neumann–Morgenstern (N–M) utility theory. In this section we do two things: first, we explore the relationship between the indifference curves and N–M utility theory; second, we outline two criticisms of Chapter 10's portfolio approach that center on this relationship.

To understand the relationship between utility theory and portfolio analysis, recall from Chapter 10 that each portfolio (a combination of money and bonds) is viewed by the investor as offering a yield and, though not certain of the yield from any portfolio, the owner attaches a probability to each possible yield. For the moment, we can simplify our analysis by considering portfolios where only two possible yields are expected: a gain, G, and a loss, L, each assigned a probability P_G, P_L. The N–M utility theory states that we can construct a utility function so that a utility number is

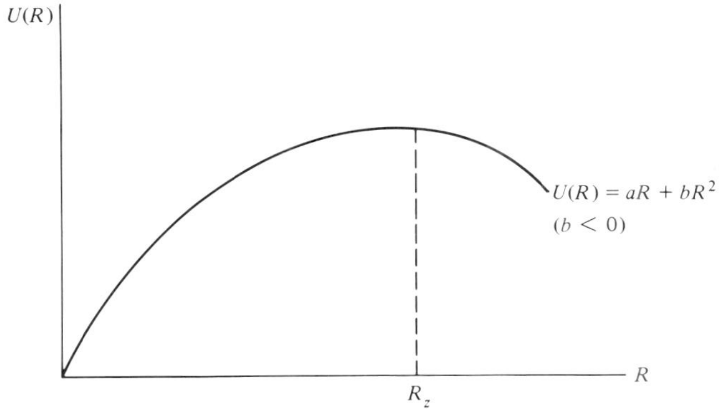

Figure 11-4

assigned to each income prospect like G and L. Let us denote as R all increases (or decreases) in wealth like G and L; then the general N–M utility function is:

$$U(R) = f(R)$$

It is important to note that $U(R) = f(R)$ can be of any form, but that in order to be able to derive the indifference curves of Figure 11.1 from this utility function, we must postulate that it has a particular form. That is, it is assumed that the utility function is described by the following quadratic equation:

$$U(R) = f(R) = aR + bR^2 \ (b < 0)$$

This utility function is illustrated in Figure 11.4.

To show the relationship between the utility function and the indifference curves we must state a theorem of von Neumann and Morgenstern. *If the utility function is constructed in a manner defined by von Neumann and Morgenstern, and if individuals behave "consistently" (as defined by N–M's axioms of consistency), an individual will behave so as to maximize the expected value of utility.* Specifically, suppose that an individual is confronted with a set of portfolios from which one must be chosen:

$$(G_1L_1), (G_2L_2), \ldots, (G_jL_j), \ldots, (G_nL_n)$$

The theorem states that the individual will choose that portfolio with the greatest expected value of utility of the payoff. The expected value of utility of a portfolio's payoff is:

$$E[U(G_jL_j)] = P_{G_j}U(G_j) + P_{L_j}U(L_j)$$

In order not to confuse concepts, note that this is clearly different from the *expected value* of the payoff:

$$E[(G_j, L_j)] = P_{G_j}(G_j) + P_{L_j}(L_j)$$

and from the *utility of the expected value* of the payoff:

$$U(E[(G_j, L_j)]) = U[P_{G_j}(G_j) + P_{L_j}(L_j)].$$

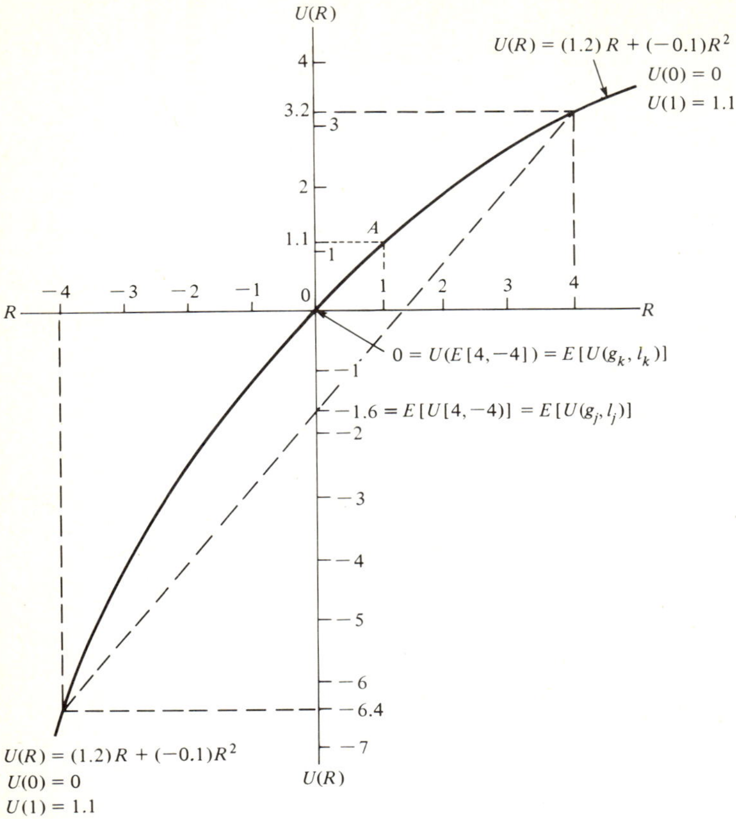

Figure 11-5

The difference between the expected value of utility (the N–M criterion) and the utility of expected value is important. Only the former measure is relevant to the indifference curve analysis of Chapter 10. The difference between the two concepts is illustrated in Figure 11.5. Suppose the individual's expectations regarding the jth portfolio are such that it is assigned probabilities $P_{G_j} = P_{L_j} = 0.5$ and gains and losses of $G = 4$ and $L = -G = -4$ are expected. Consider the utility of expected value of the payoff from this portfolio. The expected value of the payoff is:

$$E[R] = E[(G_j, L_j)] = (0.5)(4) + (0.5)(-4) = 0$$

The utility of this expected value (if the true utility function is as drawn in Figure 11.5) is:[2]

$$U(E[R]) = U(E[(G_j, L_j)]) = U(0) = 0$$

[2]Just to increase your familiarity with the figure, suppose that the expected value was non-zero: e.g., $E[R] = 1$. Then, from the coordinates of the point A in Fig. 11.5, we see that $U(E[R]) = 1.1$. But we will continue with the assumption that $E[R] = 0$.

Now consider the other concept, the expected value of the utility of the payoff. The utility of the payoff is:

$$U(G_j) = U(4); \qquad \text{and } U(L_j) = U(-4)$$

or $\qquad = 3.2 \qquad\qquad = -6.4$ from the diagram

The expected value of the utility of the payoff is:

$$E[U(G_j, L_j)] = (0.5)(3.2) + (0.5)(-6.4)$$
$$= -1.6$$

From this example it can be seen that the utility of expected value and the expected value of utility of a portfolio's payoff are different concepts and have different values on the utility function. The latter is the relevant concept in N–M utility analysis and our portfolio analysis; the optimal criterion for an investor is "choose that portfolio with the highest expected value of utility of payoff."

Derivation of Indifference Curves from N–M Utility

Having stated N–M's theorem that the individual chooses the portfolio with the highest expected value of utility, we must now establish the connection between N–M's theorem and the indifference curves of portfolio analysis. We begin with a nonrigorous explanation. If the indifference curves *are* related to N–M utility analysis in such a way that either approach leads to the choice of the same portfolio, then the maximization of the portfolio approach's utility function (that is, the attainment of the highest possible indifference curve) must be the same thing as the fulfillment of the N–M criterion (the achievement of the highest possible expected value of N–M utility). In other words, if $U^*(\mu, \sigma)$ is the utility function described by the indifference map and if $U(R)$ is the N–M utility function, these two functions must be uniquely related to each other: $U^*(\mu, \sigma) = f[U(R)]$. To show that they *are* so related, consider the following problem: Choose between two alternative portfolios, both having the same expected value of payoff, but the first portfolio has no risk (the expected return is expected with certainty), whereas the second portfolio does involve risk. It will be seen that the conclusion reached using the N–M utility function is the same as that reached using the indifference map's utility function (as long as the N–M utility function is as drawn in Figure 11.5 and the indifference curves are as drawn in Figure 11.1).

Consider the portfolios (G_j, L_j), (G_k, L_k). Suppose that the first is a risky portfolio with payoffs $G_j = 4$, $L_j = -4$ expected, with probabilities $P_{G_j} = P_{L_j} = 0.5$, while the second portfolio involves no risk ($P_{G_k} = P_{L_k} = 1$) but also offers no payoffs ($G_k = L_k = 0$); that is, the second portfolio contains only money. From Figure 11.5 it is clear that, although the expected values of the *payoffs* from these portfolios are equal, the expected value of *utility* of the second

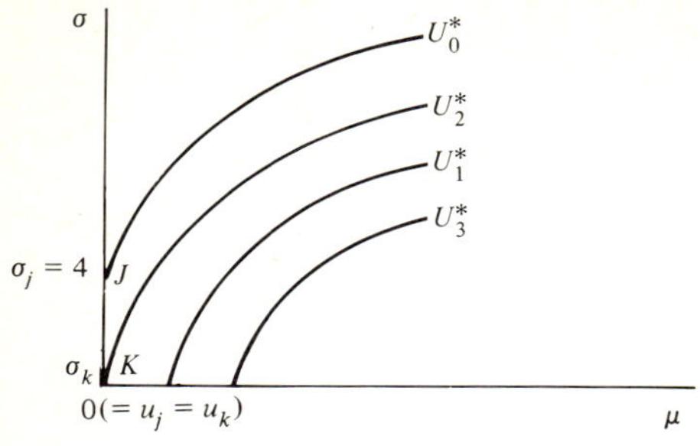

Figure 11-6

portfolio (G_k, L_k) is greater $(= 0)$ than the expected value of utility of the first portfolio $(= -1.6)$. Thus, by the N–M criterion, the portfolio (G_k, L_k) would be preferred. But it can be seen from Figure 11.6 that the same conclusion is reached by using the indifference curve analysis. Both portfolios offer the same expected value of payoff $(\mu_j = \mu_k = 0)$, but the standard deviation of the distribution of payoffs on portfolio (G_j, L_j) is greater than that on (G_k, L_k); $(\sigma_j = 4, \sigma_k = 0)$. The combinations of expected value and standard deviation of returns on portfolios, (G_j, L_j) and (G_k, L_k), are represented in Figure 11.6 by the points J and K respectively. As can be seen, K lies on an indifference curve further to the right than the curve on which J is located [that is, a higher value of $U^*(\mu, \sigma)$], and so the portfolio (G_k, L_k) would be chosen rather than the risky portfolio.

Thus, maximizing the expected value of the N–M utility function $U(R)$ gives the same result as maximizing the indifference map's utility function $U^*(\mu, \sigma)$. It can be shown that the two models give the same result when we consider choices between any two (or within any set of) portfolios, and so it can be seen that the two utility functions are uniquely related to each other. In fact, this relationship $U^*(\mu, \sigma) = f[U(R)]$ is clearly of the specific form, $U^*(\mu, \sigma) = E[U(R)]$. In other words, the indifference curves used in Chapter 10 can be considered as loci either of constant utility where utility equals $U^*(\mu, \sigma)$ or of constant expected value of N–M utility.

The proof that the indifference curves employed in Figure 11.1 are derived from a von Neumann–Morgenstern utility function such as that illustrated in Figure 11.5 can be shown more rigorously. The von Neumann–Morgenstern utility function that we postulate is a quadratic:

$$U = aR + bR^2 \qquad (b < 0) \tag{11.1}$$

where U is von Neumann–Morgenstern utility and the individual's decision rule is to maximize its expected value, $E(U)$.

First we can show that the individual who follows this decision rule is concerned only with the mean, μ, and the standard deviation, σ, of the probability distribution of returns on the portfolio. With a and b as parameters, the expected value of utility from Equation 11.1 is:

$$E(U) = aE(R) + bE(R^2) \tag{11.2}$$

Now $E(R)$ is the mean of the distribution of R—it is μ. Moreover, $E(R^2)$ can be expanded by adding and subtracting μ. Therefore Equation 11.2 can be rewritten as:

$$E(U) = a\mu + bE\{[(R - \mu) + \mu]^2\} \tag{11.3}$$

Carrying out the squaring of the term within the square brackets, we obtain:

$$E(U) = a\mu + bE\{(R - \mu)^2 + 2\mu(R - \mu) + \mu^2)\} \tag{11.4}$$

Now recollect that the expected value of a variable, x, is the mean of its probability distribution, or, in other words:

$$E(x) = \sum P^i x^i$$

where the P^i are probability numbers. Employing this definition, we can simplify Equation 11.4 to:

$$E(U) = a\mu + b \sum P^i(R^i - \mu)^2 + b2\mu \sum P^i(R^i - \mu) + b\mu^2 \tag{11.5}$$

And this allows us to simplify further. The term $\Sigma\, P^i(R^i - \mu)^2$ is the same as the variance of the probability distribution or its standard deviation squared: σ^2. The term $\Sigma\, P^i(R^i - \mu)$ equals zero since $\Sigma\, P^iR^i = \mu$ and $\Sigma\, P^i\mu = \mu$. Therefore Equation 11.5 can finally be written as:

$$E(U) = a\mu + b\sigma^2 + b\mu^2 \tag{11.6}$$

We have shown, therefore, that if the von Neumann–Morgenstern utility function is a quadratic, then any given expected value of utility is a function solely of the mean, μ, and standard deviation. If, therefore, the indifference curves we have employed represent constant levels of expected von Neumann–Morgenstern utility, their equation is:

$$\text{constant} = a\mu + b\sigma^2 + b\mu^2 \tag{11.7}$$

We can now show that such indifference curves do have the shape illustrated in Figure 11.5 if they are derived from a quadratic von Neumann–Morgenstern utility function. The slope of the indifference curves as drawn is positive, and so are the indifference curves represented by Equation 11.7. Differentiate that equation totally to obtain:

$$0 = ad\mu + 2b\sigma d\sigma + 2b\mu d\mu \tag{11.8}$$

and rearrange terms to:

$$\frac{d\mu}{d\sigma} = \frac{-2b\sigma}{a + 2b\mu} \tag{11.9}$$

The numerator on the right-hand side is positive, since b is assumed to be negative.[3] The denominator is positive since $a + 2b\mu$ is the marginal utility of returns, which we assume is positive; an individual whose total utility decreased as a result of a marginal increase in returns would be a strange individual.[4] Therefore, the slope $d\mu/d\sigma$ is positive—the indifference curves slope upward to the right, as in Figure 11.1.

Moreover, the indifference curves represented by Equation 11.7 are concave from below, as are those illustrated in Figure 11.6. In other words, if we differentiate Equation 11.9 with respect to σ, the resulting second derivative $d^2\mu/d\sigma^2$ is positive by the same reasoning as was used to demonstrate that the first derivative is positive.

Criticisms of the Model

Having seen that the indifference curves we have used in portfolio analysis are derivable as loci of constant expected von Neumann–Morgenstern utility, we are now in a position to examine two criticisms of the utility analysis employed in the portfolio approach. The first criticism concerns the shape of the von Neumann–Morgenstern utility function employed here. The second concerns its uniqueness.

We have seen that the risk averter's indifference curves employed in Chapter 10 and in this chapter can be derived from a quadratic von Neumann–Morgenstern utility function such as $U(R) = aR + bR^2$ $(b < 0)$. But this utility function has a shape that is open to criticism, for it implies that after some point (Z in Figure 11.4), an *increase* in R leads to a *decrease* in utility. That is, the marginal utility of R is a declining function of R and is negative for sufficiently large values of R. Introspection tells us that the idea of negative utility being derived from an increase in payoff does not correspond to actual evaluations of payoffs; thus it indicates that $U(R)$ is not an accurate representation of mental processes. It is on this basis that criticisms have been made of $U(R)$ and the portfolio approach's indifference curves derived therefrom.

It may appear that one way to overcome this criticism is to derive the indifference curves from an N–M utility function of a different (that is, nonquadratic) shape. However, as we have seen, the use of μ and σ as measures of return and risk is justified because it is an implication of the quadratic N–M function. If the N–M function were not quadratic, portfolio choices would be based upon other parameters of the probability distribution,

[3]See Eq. 11.1. The negativity of b is the characteristic of a risk averter's von Neumann–Morgenstern quadratic utility function.

[4]To be precise, the marginal utility of returns is the first derivative of the von Neumann–Morgenstern utility function $U = aR + bR^2$. That is, $MU = \partial U/\partial R = a + 2bR$. Therefore $a + 2b\mu$ is the marginal utility of returns when they are at their mean, or expected, value μ. In assuming that this is necessarily positive, we are restricting ourselves to that part of the utility function where they are positive. A necessary implication of a risk averter's quadratic utility function is that over some range, marginal utility is negative.

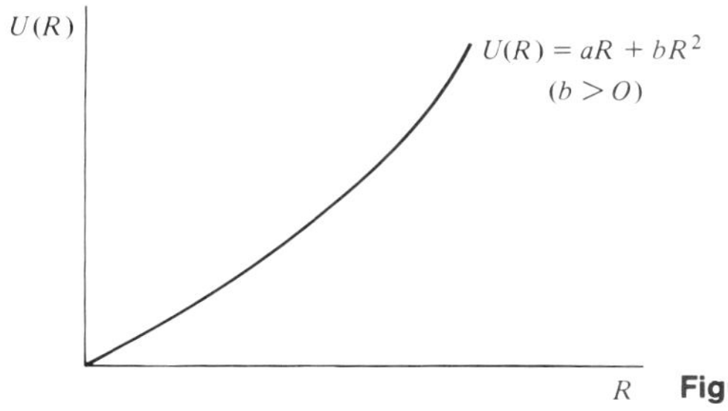

Figure 11-7

and these other parameters cannot be so easily interpreted as representing return and risk. So we are limited to a function whose shape is described by a quadratic equation. Why, then, do we not base our indifference curve analysis on the quadratic described by the equation $U(R) = aR + bR^2$ ($b > 0$) and the curve in Figure 11.7? Since this is a quadratic, it predicts that behavior is determined by μ and σ, and since it is convex from below (that is, $b > 0$), marginal utility is nowhere negative. Such a basis for the portfolio approach's indifference map would, however, be inappropriate. For the function represented in Figure 11.7 is the utility function of a risk lover rather than a risk averter (as can be seen by using it to compare the expected values of the utility of a risky and a riskless portfolio). The implied indifference curves would be of the shape drawn in Figure 10.10, leading to the erroneous conclusion that the individual holds no wealth in the form of money.

It seems, then, that if we wish to base simple portfolio analysis on von Neumann and Morgenstern's model of rational behavior, we are restricted to a model employing a quadratic N–M utility function with diminishing marginal utility ($b < 0$). Since we are so restricted, there is only one way in which we can overcome the implausibility of marginal utility being negative after some level of R: That is by restricting our analysis so that it is applicable only to individuals whose expectations and N–M utility function are such that they never consider portfolios with the possibility of a return R greater than the critical level (R_z in Figure 11.4).

We now turn to the second criticism of the N–M utility function and the portfolio analysis's indifference curves based thereon. The matter is raised by Hirshleifer (1965) in suggesting that the N–M utility function may not be unique. The indifference map is based upon a particular N–M utility function. If a different N–M utility function existed, then a different indifference map would exist. Hirshleifer postulates that individuals in fact have more than one N–M utility function and so have more than one indifference map. If that is so, the portfolio approach to the theory of money should be more complicated than that presented in Chapter 10, where it was assumed that the individual behaves in accordance with a unique indifference map.

The argument runs as follows: According to the N–M theory, the individual derives utility from payoffs. The utility derived from a particular payoff is determined by the individual's unique utility function; that is, the recipient of a particular payoff derives a particular utility *irrespective* of the state of the world—whether there is war or peace, rain or shine, the utility from a particular payoff is not affected. In other words, in N–M utility theory the utility function is invariant with respect to all variables except the individual's preferences for such things as income and safety (return and absence of risk), and these preferences themselves are generally considered to be unchanging with respect to external factors ("states of nature"). The criticism of the analysis is based on the idea that this invariance is intuitively implausible—external factors *do* influence preferences and the position and shape of the utility function.

As an example, consider the behavior of a bachelor man who does not buy life insurance. Life insurance is like holding a portfolio with negative risk, for it reduces other risks, in particular the risk for a household head that, owing to the possibility of the breadwinner's death, family income will become zero. Hence, one would assume that a risk averter—an individual with a utility function concave from below—would buy life insurance. If a certain bachelor does not do so, are we to infer that he is not a risk averter? That is the only inference we can make if we insist that he has a unique N–M utility function. But, since it is probably not true to infer that unmarried persons are risk lovers, Hirshleifer proposes an alternative conclusion based on the idea that we should not confine ourselves to postulating a single utility function. He suggests that the bachelor probably *is* a risk averter when faced with the prospect of gains and losses as long as the gains, if they occur, come in a world where all other factors, all "states of nature," are the same as they would be if losses should occur. In such a case, the prospects can be evaluated on a single, risk averter's utility function. But in the case of the bachelor considering life insurance, these conditions do not hold. For the prospect of a gain from life insurance is the prospect of a gain after death. The payoff from life insurance can be received only when the "state of nature" is "bachelor deceased." Since the bachelor, having no family, is likely to attach a lower utility to a gain received after death than to a gain received while still alive, a life insurance policy with the prospect of a posthumous gain, G, will be evaluated on a lower utility function than, say, a portfolio of bonds with the prospect of a lifetime gain, G. In other words, this bachelor man would have at least two utility functions [$U_1(R)$, $U_2(R)$ in Figure 11.8]. The higher curve evaluates prospects receivable in his lifetime, the lower one evaluates prospects receivable posthumously (assuming he does attach some utility to posthumous gains because they may be bequeathed to his favorite charity), but both are concave from below, indicating that he is a risk averter, given the "state of nature."

This idea that the utility function is not unique clearly has implications for portfolio analysis. Consider the portfolio model of Chapter 10. That model compares the proportion of money in the portfolio when the rate of interest is low with the proportion when the rate is high. The proportion is determined by tangency between the appropriate opportunity locus and an indifference

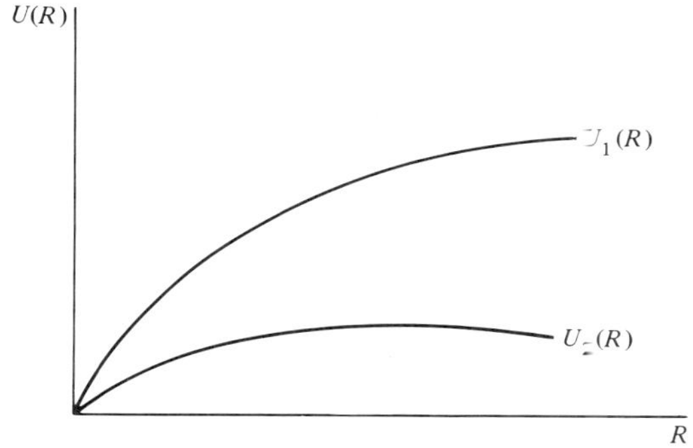

Figure 11-8

curve. But now suppose that the investor attaches different utilities to a gain according to whether there is a slump or a boom. Then the investor will have two different N–M utility functions. Moreover, since the indifference map is derived from the N–M utility function, the investor will have two different indifference maps for evaluating risk and return. To compare the effects of two different interest rates is now more difficult, for it may be that when interest rates are high there is a boom (which is expected to last the duration of the decision period) and that there is a slump when interest rates are low. If so, the model must be extended so that it uses one indifference map to determine money holdings when interest rates are low (that is, there is a slump) and another to determine money holdings at high interest rates (that is, during a boom). These complications reduce the elegant simplicity of the portfolio approach.

11.4 THE PORTFOLIO APPROACH, AGGREGATE ANALYSIS, EQUILIBRIUM PRICES, AND A VARIETY OF ASSETS

Section 11.3 explained some aspects of the *utility* theory employed in portfolio analysis; the present section explores some aspects of the *opportunity locus* employed in portfolio analysis. In particular, we are concerned with two aspects of Chapter 10's portfolio analysis: first, the fact that it assumed the rate of interest, and hence the price of bonds, to be exogenously determined (as is proper in the analysis of individual behavior in the absence of monopolistic or monopsonistic elements) and did not explore the determination of market equilibrium rates of interest; second, the fact that the analysis applied only to choices between money and one type of bond (Consols) and did not consider the theory of the demand for money in a world where many types of assets may be held.

This section extends the portfolio approach to overcome both these limitations. First, the formation of rates of interest (equilibrium asset prices) is discussed within the limited context of the two-asset (money-Consol) model of the *market* (rather than the individual). Second, using the portfolio ap-

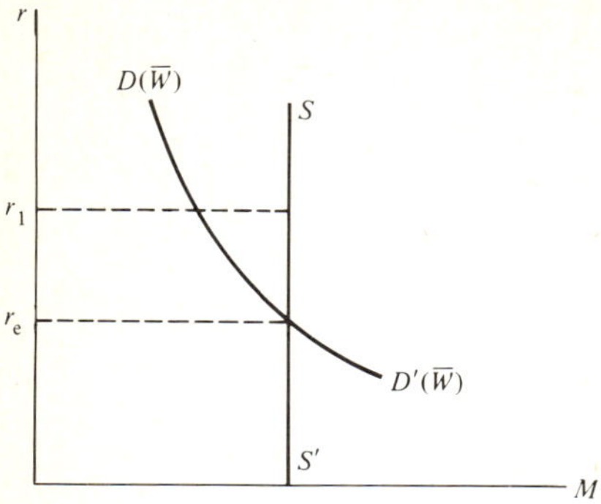

Figure 11-9

proach analysis of individual behavior, we examine the implications for the opportunity locus of introducing a variety of different assets. Finally, we use these results to examine the determination of equilibrium asset prices in a model of the market with this variety of assets.

First, then, let us remain in a two-asset world and consider the formation of market prices. We will concentrate on the portfolio approach to the precautionary motive as presented in Chapter 10. Suppose that the application of the precautionary motive portfolio analysis to every individual led to the derivation of an aggregate demand curve for money like M^DM^D in Figure 11.9. The supply of money is assumed to be fixed and is represented by M^SM^S. If the interest rate on British Consols is initially r^1, then clearly there will be an excess supply of money and, on the assumptions used in Keynes's analysis of the money market, an excess demand for these bonds. This is assumed to cause a rise in the price of Consols, that is, a fall in r. If we continue with Section 10.5's assumption that $\mu = r$ and σ is unrelated to r, then, using the portfolio analysis model, we see that this leads to an anticlockwise rotation of each individual's opportunity locus and an increase in each individual's demand for money. In terms of Figure 11.9, the fall in r continues until r^*, where the aggregate demand for money has increased sufficiently to clear the market.

Economizing on Risk by Diversification

Thus, as long as we remain in the two-asset world, the aggregation of individual demand curves for money is straightforward. Complications are introduced when more than two assets enter into the portfolio decision. As a preliminary, in this second part of this section, we consider a multiasset portfolio analysis of *individual* behavior. Let one of the assets be money (still assumed to be riskless and offering no return), and let the other assets be various types of bonds with different probability distributions of returns but all of them having a non-zero σ and μ. Whereas, in Chapter 10, the problem was to select an optimum combination of money and Consols, the problem now is to construct a model that analyzes the selection of an optimum combination of money and a range of bonds.

The analysis is based on the proposition that, under certain conditions, the optimum money-bonds portfolio can be identified by a two-stage process. Stage 1 involves identifying, from the large total of different risky assets (bonds) and combinations of risky assets (the *opportunity set*), that subset of bonds and combinations of bonds that are superior to all other bonds and combinations—superior in the sense that for any combination *not* in the subset there is at least one combination within the subset that offers higher (or as high) μ and as low (or lower) σ. Such a subset of the opportunity set is called an *efficient set* (and may be represented by an efficiency locus). Stage 1 is finalized by selecting from within the efficient set a single optimum bond or combination of bonds. Stage 2 is then relatively simple and involves choosing an optimum allocation of wealth between money (the riskless asset) and this optimum bond combination. Tobin (1958) demonstrates the legitimacy of such a two-stage procedure, and the matter is further discussed by Hicks (1962, 1967), Tobin (1965c), and Sharpe (1964).

Stage 1 can be analyzed as follows. In Figure 11.10 the points A, B, C, etc., represent the μ and σ obtainable by holding the individual bonds A, B, C, etc. Bond C, for example, has a probability distribution of returns with a greater mean and greater risk than bond B. If we were to consider a *combination* of B and C (and call this portfolio a composite asset), the mean and risk of this composite asset may be represented by the point X_1. That is, the mean of the composite asset's return is simply an average of the means of the individual assets' returns; the risk of the composite asset, however, is lower than the average of the two assets' risk. This reduction of risk by combining assets (portfolio diversification) is a common effect in portfolio holding and is a principle analogous to the maxim, "Don't put all your eggs in one basket!" It arises because, as long as the returns on two assets are not perfectly positively correlated, there is less probability that a high deviation from mean in one asset's returns will be *simultaneous* with an equally high deviation in the other asset's return (that is, the joint probability of high deviations in the same direction) than there is the probability of a high deviation on just one of

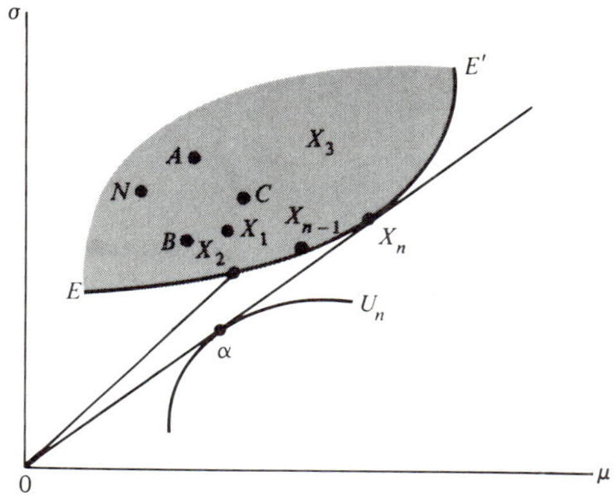

Figure 11-10

the assets. Analogously, dividing your eggs between two baskets reduces the probability that they will all get broken, since the probability that both baskets will be dropped is less than the probability that one alone will be dropped.

This principle of economizing on risk by diversification can be demonstrated more formally. First, it is easy to show that the mean (expected) return on the composite asset X_1 is simply an average of the expected returns on its component assets A and B. The return on X_1 is $R_X = aR_A + bR_B$ where R_X, R_A, and R_B represent the returns on the respective assets and a and b represent the proportions of A and B in the composite asset. We have probability distributions for R_X, R_A, and R_B, and, taking expected values, we obtain:

$$E[R_X] = aE[R_A] + bE[R_B] \qquad \text{or} \qquad \mu_X = a\mu_A + b\mu_B \tag{11.10}$$

Second, we can show that, in general, the risk on a composite asset can be reduced below that of its component assets. The variance (standard deviation squared) on an asset A is:

$$\begin{aligned}\sigma_A^2 &= \sum P^i(R_A^i - \mu_A)^2 \\ &= E(R_A - \mu_A)^2\end{aligned} \tag{11.11}$$

Now consider the composite asset X, which consists of assets A and B in the proportions a and b. Its variance is:

$$\sigma_X^2 = E[a(R_A - \mu_A) + b(R_B - \mu_B)]^2 \tag{11.12}$$

This can be expanded to:

$$\sigma_X^2 = a^2E(R_A - \mu_A)^2 + b^2E(R_B - \mu_B)^2 + 2abE[(R_A - \mu_A)(R_B - \mu_B)] \tag{11.13}$$

The first two expected values are the variances of assets A and B respectively, so we can write:

$$\sigma_X^2 = a^2\sigma_A^2 + b^2\sigma_B^2 + 2abE[(R_A - \mu_A)(R_B - \mu_B)] \tag{11.14}$$

Most significantly, the last term can be rewritten in terms of the standard deviations of assets A and B, σ_A and σ_B, and the correlation coefficient between the returns on the two assets, ρ_{AB}.[5] Thus, the equation can be rewritten as:

$$\sigma_X^2 = a^2\sigma_A^2 + b^2\sigma_B^2 + 2ab\rho_{AB}\sigma_A\sigma_B \tag{11.15}$$

It can be seen from Equation 11.15 that, given the proportions a and b of assets A and B in the composite asset, and given the variances of A and $B(\sigma_A^2, \sigma_B^2)$, the variance on the composite asset, σ_X^2, is a direct function of the correlation between the returns of the two assets. Since the standard deviation, our measure of risk, is simply the square root of the variance, the lower is the correlation between the two assets' returns, the lower will be the risk on the composite asset.

[5]This is possible because the correlation coefficient is defined as $\rho_{AB} = E[(R_A - \mu_A)(R_B - \mu_B)]/\sigma_A\sigma_B$. Therefore $E[(R_A - \mu_A)(R_B - \mu_B)] = \rho_{AB}\sigma_A\sigma_B$.

Moreover, given the correlation coefficient, the individual can adjust the proportions of A and B in the composite asset so as to minimize the risk on it. To illustrate this, let us take an extreme example and assume that $\rho_{AB} = -1$. In other words, the returns on A and B are perfectly negatively correlated; whenever one is high, the other is low. If $\rho_{AB} = -1$, then Equation 11.15 becomes:

$$\sigma_X^2 = a^2\sigma_A^2 + b^2\sigma_B^2 - 2ab\sigma_A\sigma_B \tag{11.16}$$

and this can be factorized as:

$$\sigma_X^2 = (a\sigma_A - b\sigma_B)^2 \tag{11.17}$$

Now, if the composite asset were composed of A and B in the proportions:

$$a = \frac{\sigma B}{\sigma_A + \sigma_B} \qquad b = \frac{\sigma A}{\sigma_A + \sigma_B}$$

then, substituting these into Equation 11.17, we can see that σ_X^2 can be reduced to zero. In less extreme cases, as long as the returns on A and B are not perfectly positively correlated—as long as we do not have $\rho_{AB} = 1$—then σ_X^2 (and σ_X) can always be reduced below both σ_A and σ_B by choosing a and b appropriately.

Having seen that the individual can hold composite assets with lower risk than, and the same average return as, the individual assets, we can proceed to consider stage 1 of the decision process. The individual now has to choose an optimum asset out of the set ($A, B, C, \ldots, N, X_1, X_2, X_3, \ldots, X_n$) of individual and composite assets. This set is illustrated in Figure 11.10 by the shaded area. From the diagram it is clear that the optimum point must be a point on the efficiency locus *EE*, because, for any attainable point *not* on *EE* (that is, to the left of *EE*), there is a point *on EE* that has at least as high a μ and a lower σ. (In general, the points on *EE* represent composite assets, for, as a result of diversification, combinations generally have a lower σ for a given μ than do individual assets.) Because of the superiority (or "dominance") of points on the efficiency locus over the other points in the opportunity set, our choice of an optimum combination of risky assets must be made from those combinations represented by points on the efficiency locus. The optimum combination is that which enables the investor to reach the highest level of utility.

To find the optimum composite asset (combination of risky assets), we assume that any asset combination (composite asset from the set X_1 to X_n) may be treated as a single asset, for we assume that however large an amount of resources is invested in, say, X_3, the proportions of individual assets within X_3 are unchanged [and hence the location of X_3 in the (μ, σ) plane is also unchanged]. Treating composite assets like X_1 to X_n as single assets is convenient, for we can then consider the opportunity locus generated by combining different proportions of the composite, risky asset and money. (This is similar to the way that in Figure 10.4, the opportunity locus is generated by combinations of different proportions of money and the *single* asset, Consols). The μ, σ combination denoted by X_n is obtained by holding all the portfolio in the risky composite asset X_n. But let us now introduce the possibility of holding money in Figure 11.10. If all the portfolio were held in money, the μ, σ combination would be 0, 0 (that is, the origin of the diagram). Any mixture of money and X_n gives rise to a μ, σ combination on the straight line $0X_n$, for, as the proportion of the portfolio in the composite asset X_n increases, the μ and σ of the portfolio increase proportionately. Similarly, the lines $0X_1$, $0X_2$, $0X_3$, and so on, can be constructed representing combinations of money with the composite assets X_1, X_2, X_3, etc., respectively. Which of these composite assets should be combined with money in the investor's portfolio? Clearly, the individual's highest indifference curve can be reached by holding the composite asset X_n with money, for the line $0X_n$ offers a higher μ with any given σ than do the lines $0X_1$, $0X_2$, $0X_3$, and so forth.

Thus stage 1 is completed. We have found the optimum combination of risky assets (the composite asset, X_n) and the only remaining problem is (stage 2) to determine the optimum proportions of the composite risky asset, X_n, with the riskless asset money. Since any combination on the line $0X_n$ is attainable, the optimum combination is denoted by the μ, σ attainable at the point where $0X_n$ is tangent with an indifference curve (α in Figure 11.10).

Aggregation and Market Prices

We see, then, that in a model where the individual is faced with a large variety of assets, the choice of an optimum portfolio of money and risky assets is a simple matter (for the individual). Now, however, we come to the third part of this section—the problem, dealt with by Sharpe (1964), of aggregating such individual behavior in order to analyze the determination of equilibrium market interest rates (asset prices). This problem, like the previous one, is most easily considered in two steps: step 1 is the analysis of the equilibrium prices of composite assets; step 2 is the analysis of the prices of individual assets. The analysis is considerably more complicated than usual price analysis, which involves merely the equating of a supply function with a demand function (indeed, in the present problem we do not even employ demand and supply curves). But, fundamentally, the customary theory of supply and demand underlies the present analysis.

In order to proceed with step 1 of the analysis, consider Figure 11.11. This diagram is based upon, and is similar to, Figure 11.10. But there is an important difference. In Figure 11.10, the opportunity set and the opportunity locus are constructed from the μ and σ of the individual assets, and these μ and σ relate to the *individual's* estimate of future prospects; in Figure 11.11, however, the opportunity set (shaded) and the opportunity locus $0E$ are meant to describe the (μ, σ) opportunities that confront *every* investor, for this diagram is concerned with aggregate behavior. Of course, if each individual held different expectations (different probability distributions), each

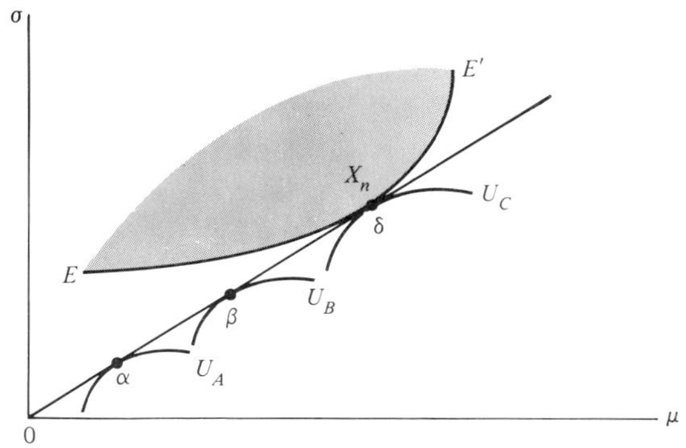

Figure 11-11

would be faced with a different opportunity locus. In order to use Figure 11.11 and to say that $0E$ describes the opportunity locus faced by all individuals, we arbitrarily assume that each individual's estimate of the future behavior of bond prices is the same as every other individual's. Thus, we assume that each individual's expectations are described by the same opportunity set, but note that we assume that each individual has different *preferences* described by different indifference maps. As a result, each individual reaches equilibrium at a different point on the opportunity locus. Assume that there are three individuals. Individual A's indifference map is such that a utility-maximizing equilibrium is reached at α on $0E$; individual B maximizes utility at β; and individual C maximizes utility at δ.

Figure 11.11 shows the individuals' points of equilibrium (α, β, and δ), given market conditions (the asset prices and the means and standard deviations of future returns summarized by the shape and position of the opportunity set). But it does not represent a situation of market equilibrium, for it will be seen that in the process of individuals reaching their equilibrium positions, market conditions will change. This can be noted when we consider the implications of the individuals desiring to be at α, β, or δ. Each portfolio represented by these points is a combination of money and the composite asset X_n. Equilibrium at δ involves holding all one's portfolio (W) in the composite asset; β involves holding 80 percent of the portfolio in the composite asset and 20 percent in money; and α involves holding 20 percent of the portfolio in the composite asset and 80 percent in money. In other words, all the individuals desire to hold some bonds, but the only types of bonds they desire to hold will be those that, in combination, form the composite asset X_n. In general, X_n does not include all the $A, \ldots, N$ types of individual bonds. Let us say it includes only bonds of types $A, \ldots, E$; then we have found that the individuals desire to hold only those types $(A, \ldots, E)$ of bonds in equilibrium. Clearly, then, if the individuals are in equilibrium at α, β, and δ, the market as described in Figure 11.11 (that is, by the shaded area of feasible μ, σ combinations) cannot be in equilibrium. For there are no willing holders of the bond of type $F, \ldots, N$ (no one is willing to hold any of the composite assets $X_1, \ldots, X_{n-1}$, which are combinations of $F, \ldots, N$), and we postulate that this excess supply of these bond types leads to falls in their prices—a phenomenon of market disequilibrium. Similarly, the points α, β, and δ may, in sum, involve an excess demand for the assets included in X_n, in which case the prices of these assets will rise.

As a result of these disequilibrium adjustments of asset prices, new market conditions are established. The fall in the prices of assets $F, \ldots, N$ (that is, the rise in their interest rates) is the same as a rise in the mean of their probability distributions, μ (if we retain Section 4.5's assumption that $\mu = r$). Since, for such assets, μ is rising, the points $F, \ldots, N$ move to the right of their positions in Figure 11.11. Similarly, the points representing those composite assets $X, \ldots, X_{n-1}$, which include $F, \ldots, N$, move rightward, and the efficiency locus EE', which is made up of such points, moves rightward. At the same time, because r and μ are falling for the assets $A, \ldots, E$, the point representing the composite asset X_n moves leftward. The disequilibrium adjustment process will continue until asset prices, rates of interest, and means are such that every asset enters at least one composite asset that lies on the opportunity locus. When that condition is satisfied, market equilibrium exists and there will be no tendency for asset prices to change. Such a situation is shown in Figure 11.12. It can be seen from this diagram that more than one composite asset lies on the opportunity locus and so, incidentally, equilibrium at any point on the opportunity locus (such as α) could be reached in more than one way. For example, α could involve holding the composite asset X_1 and the amount $(0X_1 - 0\alpha)$ of money, or it could involve holding the composite asset X_2 and the larger amount of money $(0X_2 - 0\alpha)$, or any similar arrangement.

Step 1 of the problem is now completed. It tells us that for the market to be in equilibrium, the prices of assets must be such that composite assets on the efficiency locus have a linear, or proportional, relationship between risk and return. (That is, for any composite asset on the efficiency locus, $\sigma = \epsilon\mu$ where ϵ is the slope of the opportunity locus.) While that conclusion gives us fairly rigorous conditions for the equilibrium prices of *composite* assets, it reveals little about the conditions for equilibrium in the prices of *individual*

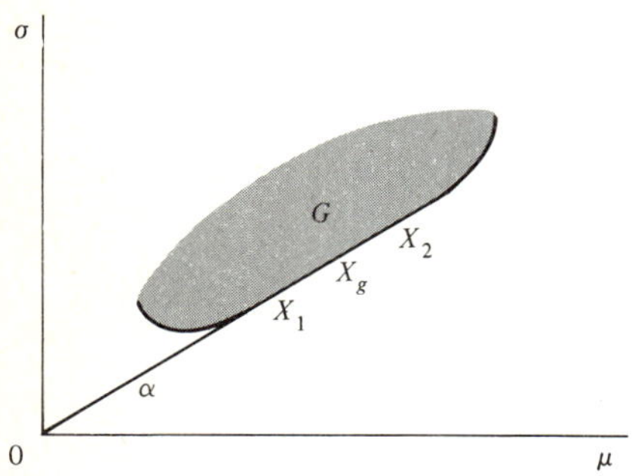

Figure 11-12

assets unless we know the relationship between the (μ, σ) of individual assets and the (μ, σ) of composite assets. Step 2 of the problem—the determination of equilibrium prices on individual assets—thus involves merely an analysis of the relations between individual assets and composite assets.

This step 2 analysis is complicated and need not occupy us here. Instead, we give merely an indication of the conclusion. Consider (in Figure 11.12) the individual asset G and the composite asset X_g, which includes G. Now X_g involves less risk than G because, once included in the combination X_g, the risk on G is partially offset by diversification. However, there is a limit to the extent to which risk can be reduced by diversification. Even though X_g reduces risk as much as possible by exploiting to a maximum the benefits of portfolio diversification, there is still some risk involved in holding the X_g combination of assets. It is plausible to suppose that this unavoidable (undiversifiable) risk arises because of general economic factors, such as the risk of booms and slumps, that affect the returns on all assets simultaneously (that cause an element of the returns on all assets to be perfectly correlated and hence an element of risk that is undiversifiable). The proposition we can state regarding the market equilibrium prices of individual assets is as follows: In equilibrium, those individual assets whose returns fluctuate to a large extent in response to general conditions (that is, whose risk is largely undiversifiable) have, *ceteris paribus*, lower prices (higher r and μ) than assets whose risk is diversifiable. This conclusion is intuitively plausible, for equilibrium implies that assets must be willingly held, and an asset with a high level of risk that is inevitable (that is not diversified away by the equilibrium portfolios containing this asset in combination with others) must have a high mean return, μ, to compensate for this fact. In other words, it must have a relatively low price.

We have now completed the material of this section. We have extended the portfolio analysis in the following ways: first, from the portfolio model of individual behavior in a money-Consols world, we have drawn implications concerning market equilibrium prices; second, in a two-stage analysis, we have extended the portfolio model so that it analyzes an individual's choices in a world with a wide variety of assets (this extension involved deriving an efficiency locus based upon the principle of reducing risk by portfolio diversification); last, in another two-step analysis, we extended this model to derive implications for market equilibrium prices in a many-asset world.

CHAPTER

TWELVE

THE NEOCLASSICAL/KEYNESIAN SYNTHESIS

In Chapter 8 we outlined the Keynesian model that dominated macroeconomic theory after the Second World War. In Chapters 9, 10, and 11 we examined the developments in the theory of the demand for money which took Keynes's *General Theory* as their starting point. These developments have been one of the most important aspects of Keynesian monetary theory, but they have been accompanied by developments both in the theory of the goods market and in the structure of the model as a whole. All these developments together have caused this Keynesian tradition to become known as the Neoclassical/Keynesian Synthesis, for its interpretation of Keynes's work has made his model appear to be essentially similar to that of Neoclassical price theory (microeconomics) and to the Neoclassical Quantity Theory.

In this chapter we summarize this Synthesis by looking at some of its specific features and then seeing how they all fit together. We begin by examining, in Sections 12.1 and 12.2, one particular development in the theory of the goods market: the inclusion of the Pigou Effect (or wealth effect) in the theory of the consumption function. We do not examine other specifically Neoclassical developments in the theory of the goods market and, in particular, we neglect the theory of the consumption function developed by Friedman (1957) and the theory of investment developed by Jorgenson (1963). We then, in Sections 12.3 and 12.4, examine the issue of whether money is neutral in the Neoclassical/Keynesian Synthesis model. This is significant because the debate over this issue highlights the essential features of this model, and, indeed, the very question of neutrality is itself a question typical of the Neoclassical school. In Section 12.5, we conclude by summarizing the main features of the synthesis interpretation of Keynes.

12.1 THE PIGOU EFFECT IN THE GOODS MARKET

The impact of Keynes's *General Theory* on the economics profession, at least in Britain, was remarkable.[1] Keynes's contemporaries within the Cambridge Quantity Theory tradition were forced to come to terms with his work and this necessity, for some, involved an attack on his conclusions. In Chapter 15, we shall refer to the consequent debate between Keynes and Robertson over interest rate theory. Here, we shall concentrate on the views of Pigou concerning the possibility of equilibrium with unemployment. To argue that Keynes's conclusion about the likelihood of unemployment equilibrium was a limited one, Pigou developed the theory of the consumption function so that, in his model, consumption was treated as a function of real wealth (as well as depending on income). The theory that a change in real wealth has an effect on consumption has become known as the theory of the Pigou Effect. It was developed by Pigou (1941, 1943, 1947), but it is also found in the work of Haberler (1941), and its implications were examined by Patinkin (1948, 1965). We are concerned with three questions: What is the Pigou Effect? What are its implications for the equilibrium level of employment? And what impact has it had on the development of Keynesian models?

As to the first question, the Pigou Effect may be defined as the theory that:

> Aggregate planned consumption is a function of the real value of the private sector's net wealth (and other variables).

In this form it is merely another statement of the goods market real balance effect considered in Chapter 5. There is, however, one difference. The real balance effect in its simplest form is developed within a model where the only form of wealth is money, and, therefore, in that model it refers to the effect on consumption of real money balances alone. The Pigou Effect is the application of this simple version of the real balance effect to an economy where other forms of wealth are available. These other types include financial assets other than money (bonds, for example) and physical assets, such as machinery and houses.

Microeconomics of Pigou Effect

The theory that underlies the Pigou Effect is the same as that underlying the real balance effect, which we examined in Chapter 5. That is, we can derive the proposition that consumption is a function of wealth from the utility-maximizing behavior of individuals who are choosing how to divide their consumption between present and future periods. It is worth examining that derivation again, since it will enable us to examine the relationship between Pigou's and Keynes's theories.

[1] See Friedman (1972) for his view that it had a less significant impact on the Chicago economists.

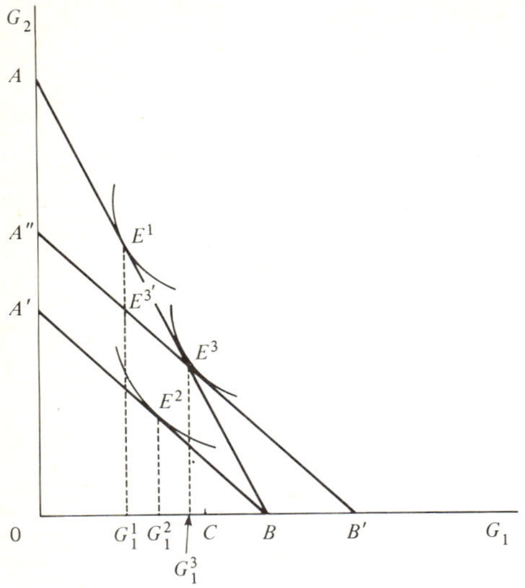

Figure 12-1

Figure 12.1 illustrates the behavior of an individual faced with a choice between present consumption of this period's goods, G_1, and future consumption of next period's goods, G_2. (This figure is analogous to Figure 5.3.) The slope of the budget line is determined by the rate of return on the assets that the individual carries from this period to the next. If we assume that next period's absolute price level is expected to be the same as this period's, this rate of return is the nominal yield on the financial assets (the rate of interest, r, if we assume that no capital gains are expected) and the rate of return on the physical assets (which is assumed to be equal to r).[2]

The slope of the budget line is $-(1+r)$, indicating that if one unit of G_1 is saved, it will enable $(1+r)G_1$ to be consumed in the next period. If the rate of interest is zero, the budget line is less steep than if it were positive; if $r = 0$, the budget line has a slope of -1. Given the slope, the intercept of the budget line is determined by the real income the individual receives in the first period and the real value of the assets held when entering the first period, for we shall make the simplifying assumption that the only income expected in the second period is the interest earned on assets carried forward. Thus, real income in the first period is represented by $0C$, and the real value of the assets at the start of the first period is CB. The maximum amount of goods that the individual can consume in the first period is therefore $0B$.

With the budget line AB, which exists when the rate of interest is positive, the individual will consume G_1^1 in this period and save $(0C - 0G_1^1)$. For, with the indifference curves as we have drawn them, the individual's

[2]Following the procedure adopted in Friedman's "Restatement" (1956a) of the Quantity Theory, we could also assume that these yields equal the implicit yield of money balances at the margin. See Chapter 7. This procedure is now widely adopted in monetary theory. See, for example, Johnson (1969) and Gurley and Shaw (1960).

utility-maximizing equilibrium is at E^1, where the positive rate of interest is equated to the individual's marginal rate of time preference (determined from the slope of the indifference curve at that point). If the rate of interest were zero, the budget line would be $A'B$ with a slope of -1. Equilibrium would then be established at E^2, and at that equilibrium, the individual would *still save a positive amount*. In this period, G_1^2 would be consumed and $(0C - 0G_1^2)$ would be saved.

This last point was used by Pigou (1947) to argue that Keynes should have included the Pigou Effect in his *General Theory*. For Keynes recognized that saving may be positive at a zero rate of interest. As we saw in Chapter 8, the Keynesian model implies that the *IS* curve may cut the horizontal axis at a zero interest rate. That means that, since positive investment is assumed, there is a positive level of saving at a zero interest rate. Thus, Pigou argued, Keynes assumed that equilibrium positions like E^2 are possible. But if such equilibrium positions are possible, then, according to Pigou, the Pigou Effect must operate. To see the reasoning behind this, we must explore the effect of a change in wealth.

Assume that the interest rate is zero and the budget line is initially $A'B$. Now assume a fall in this period's absolute price level so that the real value of the individual's assets when entering this period is increased from CB to CB'. It is increased because the fall in p involves an increase in $(M/p + B/rp)$, the real value of financial assets, bonds and money. The effect will be to shift the budget line rightward to $A''B'$, since the increase in the real value of financial assets means that there is an increase in the maximum possible amount of consumption (although this period's income is unchanged at $0C$). The consequence is that a new equilibrium is established at E^3 where consumption at G_1^3 is higher than it was previously (at G_1^2). Similarly, saving, $(0C - 0G_1^3)$, is lower than it was previously. This result is itself an example of the Pigou Effect; it is a demonstration that real consumption depends on the real value of wealth.

But the result is not an unambiguous one. Why is the new equilibrium established at E^3? Why are the indifference curves not of such a shape that the new equilibrium is established at $E^{3'}$, where consumption would be lower than in the initial equilibrium E^2? We saw in Chapter 5 that Patinkin answered this question by making the assumption that consumption goods are not inferior goods with respect to wealth; an increase in real wealth always increases real consumption, *ceteris paribus*. Pigou, however, presented an argument in support of this assumption that brings us back to Keynes's theory of positive saving at zero interest rates. Pigou asked why people should save at a zero interest rate. If there is a positive interest rate, we can explain saving by the fact that the interest received compensates for the sacrifice involved in postponing consumption. If there is a zero interest rate, there is no such financial compensation; therefore, individuals must accumulate savings for their own sake. In other words, they must receive some satisfaction merely from the ownership of assets—satisfaction derived, perhaps, from the status conferred by a given level of real wealth. Pigou argued that the ownership of wealth as such yields utility[3] (for such reasons as status) and that this is the explanation of Keynes's hypothesis that saving is positive even when the rate of interest is zero, that the *IS* curve crosses the horizontal axis. Moreover, Pigou assumed that the satisfaction derived from wealth as such involves diminishing marginal utility, so that the greater is the existing real value of an individual's wealth, the less is the utility from an increment to wealth. In other words, the less will be the utility of saving. It follows, therefore, that an increase in real wealth, *ceteris paribus*, causes the individual to consume more and save less; thus, consumption is not an inferior good in respect to wealth.

Macroeconomic Adjustment and Pigou Effect

Pigou, therefore, argued not only that planned consumption is a function of real wealth, but also that this was implicit in Keynes's own model even though Keynes, in discussing the consumption function, apparently failed to realize it.[4] But for Pigou, the wealth effect was not a mere debating point or demonstration of Keynes's inconsistency. Its implications appeared to be destructive of Keynes's general conclusion that unemployment equilibrium can exist even if wages and prices are flexible. The Pigou Effect implies that as long as there is this flexibility, the Keynesian model will contain an automatic tendency toward equilibrium at full employment.

In order to examine this implication, we must first rewrite the consumption function so that it explicitly includes the Pigou Effect. In Chapter 8 we employed Keynes's theory that planned real consumption is a function of real income alone:

$$c = f(\bar{y}) = a + b\bar{y} \tag{12.1}$$

If we now include the Pigou Effect, we must include actual real wealth, $\bar{w}$, as a variable:

$$c = f(\bar{y}, \bar{w}) = a + b\bar{y} + g\bar{w} \tag{12.2}$$

The implications of the Pigou Effect for full-employment equilibrium, however, hinge upon the effect of changes in the absolute price level upon the real value of financial assets. We may therefore simplify by assuming that

[3]The utility derived from wealth as such is not to be confused with the utility represented by the indifference curves of Fig. 12.1, for they refer to the utility derived from consumption in this period and the next. If someone wants to incorporate Pigou's own method of reasoning into Fig. 12.1, it can be done as follows: Pigou's argument involves the idea that all equilibria like E^2 and E^3—equilibria reached with a budget line where the financial interest rate is zero and the slope is (-1)—involve no saving or dissaving. Consumption of G_1 equals $0C$, current income, for all such equilibria. But the utility of wealth as such (the utility of status and similar conditions) is assumed to be equivalent to a positive implicit interest rate; therefore the budget lines are steeper than (-1) and consumption is less than income even though the financial rate of interest is zero.

[4]Nevertheless, Patinkin (1948), Leijonhufvud (1968), and others have shown that Keynes did explicitly consider the wealth effect in other contexts.

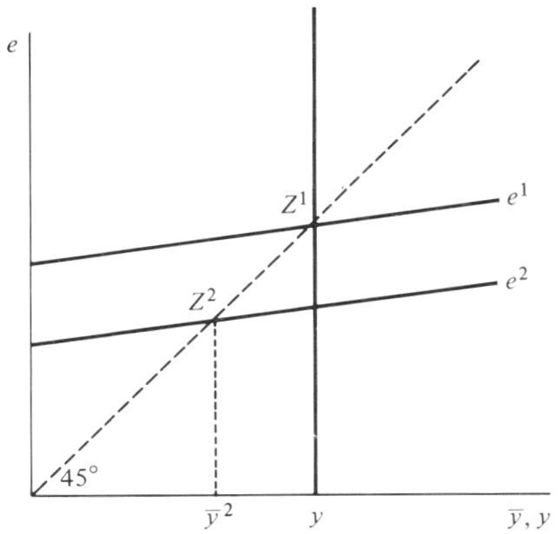

Figure 12-2

wealth consists only of bonds and money, so that:

$$\bar{w} = \frac{\bar{M}^S}{p} + \frac{\bar{B}^S}{rp} \tag{12.3}$$

where $\bar{B}^S$ is the nominal par value of bonds, so that $\bar{B}^S/r$ is their nominal market value. Then we can write the consumption function with the Pigou Effect as:

$$c = a + b\bar{y} + h\left(\frac{\bar{M}^S}{p} + \frac{\bar{B}^S}{rp}\right) \tag{12.4}$$

Following the method employed in Chapter 8, we may first examine the behavior of the goods market with this Pigou Effect. In Figure 12.2, let the planned expenditure function be initially e^1. This expenditure is composed of planned consumption, c^1, planned investment, i^1, and government expenditure, g^1. Bearing in mind the assumptions made in Chapter 8 concerning the linearity of the consumption and investment functions and the assumption that government expenditure is determined exogenously, the planned expenditure function can be written as:

$$e = a + b\bar{y} + h\left(\frac{\bar{M}^S}{p} + \frac{\bar{B}^S}{rp}\right) + d - fr + \bar{g} \tag{12.5}$$

Therefore e^1 exists because the variables on the right-hand side are at the particular levels $\bar{M}^{S1}$, $\bar{B}^{S1}$, p^1, r^1, and $\bar{g}^1$. With this planned expenditure function, equilibrium is possible at Z^1 with full-employment output y. Now assume that capitalists' expectations become more pessimistic so that the investment function shifts downward. That is, d falls. The expenditure function shifts downward to e^2 and the economy reaches the position of Z^2 with income at $\bar{y}^2$, which is less than the full-employment level.

Now, as long as wages and prices are not inflexible, the excess supply in the goods and labor markets will push money wages, W, and the absolute price level, p, downward. The consequence of the fall in p is that the real value of financial wealth, $(\bar{M}^S/p + \bar{B}^S/rp)$, rises, since the nominal stock of money and bonds, determined exogenously, is unchanged. Equation 12.5 indicates that this will cause an increase in planned consumption, which raises the whole expenditure function. That is, of course, the Pigou Effect. Because of it, the planned expenditure function rises again and continues to do so until it has returned to e^1, and equilibrium at Z^1 with full-employment income is restored. With flexible wages and prices, there is an *automatic* tendency to full employment in this model. It results from the effect of price changes on the real value of wealth.

Of course, this effect may be accompanied by changes in the rate of interest. The fall in prices releases money from transactions balances and into speculative balances. At the old rate of interest, this change involves an excess supply of money and an excess demand for bonds, and these excesses tend to push up the price of bonds or, equivalently, push down the rate of interest. The fall in the interest rate has an effect on planned expenditure, as can be seen from Equation 12.5; it causes an increase in planned investment and pushes the expenditure function upward just as the Pigou Effect does.[5] The former is an indirect mechanism, the latter a direct mechanism (just as we saw in Chapter 6, there are two similar mechanisms in the old Quantity Theory tradition). However, as seen in Chapter 8, the Keynesian model assumes that the indirect mechanism may not operate. The liquidity trap may prevent the rate of interest from falling; it may, in other words, prevent the appearance of excess supply in the money market and of excess demand in the bond market, or investment may be inelastic with respect to the interest rate. The point of the Pigou Effect is that it provides the model with a direct mechanism, so the failure of the Keynesian indirect mechanism does not prevent the model from having an automatic tendency toward full employment.

This can best be illustrated by the *IS*/*LM* analysis of Figure 12.3, for such

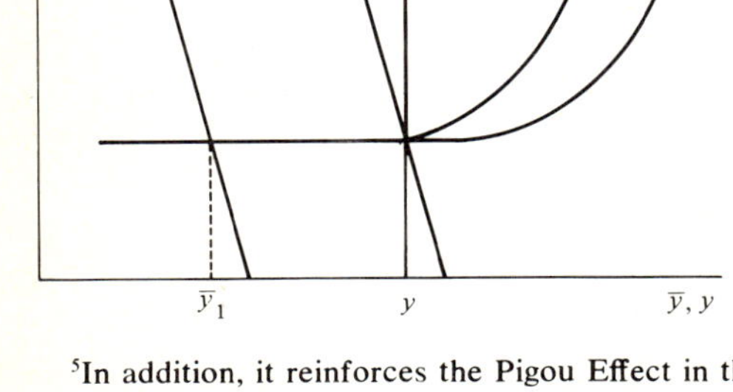

Figure 12-3

[5]In addition, it reinforces the Pigou Effect in the consumption function, since the fall in the interest rate raises the value of bonds, B^S/rp.

analysis explicitly introduces the money market. Let us start from the level of income $\bar{y}_1$, which has been brought about by the collapse of expectations assumed above. The steepness of the *IS* curve, IS_1, and the shape of the *LM* curve, LM_1, indicate that the indirect mechanism is inoperative. These shapes illustrate the existence of both a liquidity trap and an inelastic investment function. Despite this, as long as the excess planned supply of goods, which exists at $\bar{y}_1$, causes the absolute price level to fall, the Pigou Effect will cause the *IS* curve to shift rightward. It will shift until it reaches IS_2, at which point equilibrium is reached with full-employment income and output.

How a change in the real value of assets causes a shift in the *IS* curve can be seen from the algebraic expression of the *IS* curve. Recall that equilibrium in the goods market requires that $\bar{y} = e$, so that, by substituting from Equation 12.5 for e, we obtain:

$$\bar{y} = \frac{a + d + \bar{g} + h\left(\dfrac{\bar{M}^S}{p} + \dfrac{\bar{B}^S}{rp}\right)}{1 - b} - \frac{fr}{1 - b} \tag{12.6}$$

This is the equation of the *IS* curve for the model that includes the Pigou Effect. Inspection shows that the first term now includes the real value of financial wealth as a component, so an increase in the real value of financial assets shifts the *IS* curve rightward: at any given interest rate, the value of $\bar{y}$ that satisfies Equation 12.6 is higher.

The implication of Pigou's theory, therefore, is that if the wealth effect is included in a Keynesian model, the only cause of unemployment equilibrium can be rigid wages and prices, for such rigidity is the only condition that will prevent both the direct mechanism (Pigou Effect) and the indirect mechanism (via the Keynesian money market) from operating. This is a very Neoclassical conclusion, even though it is reached within the framework of the Keynesian model. For Keynes's Neoclassical predecessors concluded, through different reasoning, that rigidities in wages and prices are the fundamental explanation of unemployment.[6] In the next section, however, we examine some factors that limit the significance of this conclusion.

12.2 QUALIFICATIONS TO THE PIGOU EFFECT

The first set of qualifications to the Pigou Effect concerns the question of whether the assumptions implicit in the positive relationship between wealth and consumption are valid. We need rehearse the problems only briefly, for

[6]It should not be assumed that Pigou thought government policy (such as an increase in government expenditure to shift the *IS* curve) unnecessary as a cure for unemployment. He emphasized that although, on a priori reasoning, the Pigou Effect exists, its operation may be weak and slow and therefore the automatic tendency to full employment is consistent with long periods of unemployment, which can be shortened by government action.

we have already encountered them in our consideration of the real balance effect (Chapter 5).

First, there is the question of whether financial assets are components of net wealth—a question to which Pigou (1947) devoted some attention. It will be recalled from Chapter 3 that there are three views on the question of whether money is net wealth. In one view, outside money is, but inside money is not; therefore, the significance of the Pigou Effect partially depends on the relative proportions of inside and outside money as though most of it were not part of net wealth; if it is backed by government bonds held by the banking system, those bonds are not really outside assets, since their interest yield is offset by future tax payments. On this second view, then, inside money is not net wealth, outside money is not net wealth (except for the part backed by gold, foreign bonds, or the state's equity in nationalized industries), and outside bonds are not net wealth. That view implies that the Pigou Effect is so weak as to be irrelevant. The third view treats all money as net wealth and therefore argues that the assets relevant to the Pigou Effect are, in fact, large in quantity.

The second question concerns the role of expectations. We saw in Chapter 5 that if the fall in the price level induces expectations of further declines, they can lead to a decrease, rather than an increase, in present consumption, although the result is ambiguous.

Even if the Pigou Effect in the consumption function does cause a fall in the price level and shift the *IS* curve rightward, however, the Pigou Effect's implication of an automatic tendency toward full employment is not without qualification. One theoretical curiosity has been noted by Bailey (1971). That is, not only may planned demand for goods be affected by real financial wealth, but so may planned supply. In other words, an increase in real balances may cause y, the full-employment level of output and income, to

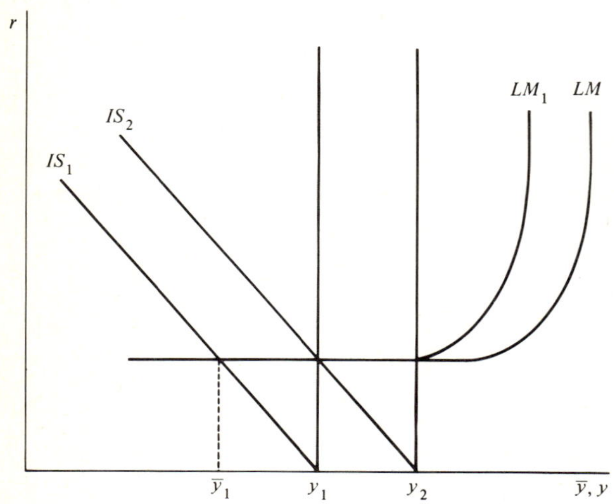

Figure 12-4

increase. The difficulty of reaching full employment if that were the case is illustrated in Figure 12.4. If initially the curves are IS_1 and LM_1, actual income is $\bar{y}_1$, and planned (full-employment) income is y_1, excess supply push down prices. This will have the usual effect of pushing the LM curve rightward to LM_2, for example, and, via the Pigou Effect, pushing the IS curve to IS_2. But in this model, the rise in the real value of nominal money balances also causes the planned supply of goods, the full-employment level of national income, to rise to y_2. It is impossible to say a priori whether the shift in full-employment income as a result of the fall in the price level is as great as the increase in actual income $\bar{y}$. If it is at least as great, the fall in the price level does not reduce the excess supply of goods despite the Pigou Effect; if it is less, then the Pigou Effect does reduce the excess supply but by less than it would otherwise do.

The question is, Why should we expect an increase in real balances to increase full-employment income? Two arguments may be adduced. The first is the idea that real balances are directly related to consumption. Holders of money balances receive some implicit services from them—services that are difficult to specify but that may be treated in principle as a component of national income. An increase in real balances therefore causes an increase in national income and, given the full-employment supply of goods, causes an increase in the full-employment supply of "goods and (money) services" or in national income defined this way. In terms of this formulation, it is possible that although the operation of the Pigou Effect may increase planned consumption, this increased demand is wholly satisfied by the consumption of the increased services of money leaving the excess supply of goods unchanged. The second argument is that money is a factor of production. Real balances enter the production function, so that an increase in them increases the planned supply of goods, just as would an increase in the supply of labor.

These views of money as, in a vague sense, providing consumption services or as being a factor of production have been used in several areas of monetary theory.[7] Their validity and theoretical basis is, however, not well established, but if one does accept them, they can, as we have seen, seriously qualify the Pigou Effect's implications.

Despite these qualifications to the theory of the Pigou Effect (or wealth, or real balance, effect) it has become an accepted component of Keynesian models. The models of the Neoclassical Keynesian Synthesis include the Pigou Effect as a distinctive feature. In the next two sections we shall examine how these models, with the Pigou Effect, are employed to analyze the neutrality of money.

12.3 NEUTRALITY OF MONEY IN OUTSIDE MODELS

We saw in Chapter 6 that the pre-Keynesian Quantity Theory tradition included the long-run proposition that changes in the money supply cause

[7]See Chapter 18 for an example from monetary growth models.

equiproportionate changes in the absolute price level. In the short run, changes in the money supply may have effects on real income and interest rates, but as a long-run proposition the secular rate of change in the price level is a function of the secular rate of change in the money supply, whereas interest rates and real income are not. In Chapters 19 and 21 we shall see that the modern Quantity Theory of the Chicago school contains similar propositions. Such propositions imply that *money is neutral* in the long run. The long-run effect of a change in nominal money supply is to leave unchanged all real variables: real balances are unchanged (since M^S and p change by the same proportion), real income is unchanged, and the mix of consumption goods and investment goods is unchanged (because the interest rate, and all relative prices, are unaffected).

The question of whether money is or is not neutral in this sense has been a source of contention throughout the history of monetary theory. Unfortunately, several confusions have bedeviled the debate. One is the idea that if money is neutral in the sense that a change in the nominal money supply has no effect on real variables in a monetary economy, then a monetary economy is no different from a barter economy and money is a veil or a mere lubricant for the workings of an essentially barter economy. This idea involves invalid reasoning, for it is illegitimate to examine a comparison of two equilibrium positions of a monetary model and conclude that our findings are the same as they would be if we compared equilibrium in a monetary model with equilibrium in a barter model. The two models may be qualitatively different because of the presence of money in the former, and in Chapter 14 we shall examine arguments suggesting that they are so. If money is a lubricant, the adjective "mere" is inappropriate to it: an automobile engine without oil is qualitatively different from one with oil.

Another confusion involves the distinction between long-run neutrality and short-run neutrality. Keynesians have attacked the Quantity Theory tradition for its emphasis on neutrality and compared it with a Keynesian model where money is not neutral because the demand and supply of money have an important role in determining whether real income is at a full-employment or an unemployment level. But this Keynesian model is explicitly a short-run model, whereas the Quantity Theory's neutrality proposition is a long-run proposition.[8]

In order to avoid that particular confusion, we shall confine ourselves,

[8]Related to this is the confusion we examined in Chapter 4. That is, if some pre-Keynesian Quantity Theorists of the Neoclassical school built models with an internal inconsistency, this inconsistency existed because they included the Homogeneity Postulate (or Say's Identity) in the goods market. The reason for this appears to have been a desire, in some places, to demonstrate that money is neutral, but what their models involved was neutrality at every instant, so that disequilibrium could never arise. As we saw in Chapter 4, the neutrality of the model in the sense of neutrality at equilibrium positions alone can be assumed even if we abandon the Homogeneity Postulate in favor of the real balance effect, so that the money supply does have an effect on real variables in disequilibrium positions.

here and in Section 12.4, to models that are at full employment. This is, indeed, the method adopted by Keynesian writers on the question of neutrality, for they have employed models typical of the Neoclassical/Keynesian Synthesis. These models assume both a high degree of flexibility of prices and interest rates (that is, no rigid money wages or goods prices and no liquidity trap) and the existence of a wealth effect. They thereby ensure that equilibrium is always reached at full employment, and the most common experiment involves starting at full employment, increasing the money supply, and examining the real variables in the new full-employment equilibrium. It should be noted, however, that this type of comparative statics exercise differs from the Quantity Theorists' proposition of long-run neutrality. In that tradition, it was usually (although not always) assumed that the economy was growing, whereas in the comparative statics exercises that we examine here, it is assumed that full employment involves a given level of real income. Thus, we are examining a nongrowing stationary economy, or, since investment is assumed to be positive and therefore the capital stock is growing, we are examining a growing economy at a point in time. In Chapter 18 we shall examine the different question of the effect of money on the growth path of a growing economy.

Money Illusion in Liquidity Preference

Consider first, a Keynesian model that regards money and bonds as outside assets but does *not* include a wealth effect. This would be the Synthesis school's interpretation of Keynes's *General Theory*. If we adopt Keynes's own formulation and write the demand function for money as:

$$M^D = kpy + L_2(r) \tag{12.7}$$

with money market equilibrium being given by:

$$\bar{M}^S = kpy + L_2(r) \tag{12.8}$$

then money is not neutral in this model.

Suppose that the model is initially at full-employment equilibrium (a condition assumed by writing y, rather than $\bar{y}$, in the above equations) and imagine an exogenous rise in the money supply: It is doubled, for example, by the government's printing new dollar bills and distributing them as gifts. The money and goods markets will reach a new equilibrium at full employment, but it will be one where the absolute price level has more than doubled. This can be seen from Figure 12.5. The IS and LM curves are initially IS^1 and LM^1. The doubling of the nominal money supply causes the LM curve to shift to LM^2. If the absolute price level were to double, then the LM curve would shift to LM^3. The reason for this can be seen from Equation 12.8. If $\bar{M}^S$ and p are both doubled and nothing else changes, then total demand will not have increased to maintain equality with supply, for, although the nominal transactions demand has doubled, desired speculative balances are unchanged.

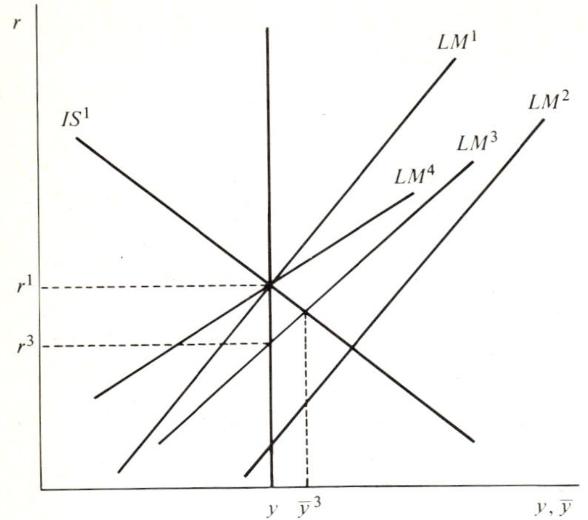

Figure 12-5

Therefore a fall in the rate of interest from r^1 to r^3 is required in order to maintain money market equilibrium with full-employment income if $\bar{M}^s$ and p double: the LM curve is LM^3. But with LM^3, there is an excess demand for goods. The level of real output that is demanded is $\bar{y}^3$, but this is greater than full-employment maximum production, y. Consequently, the absolute price level rises further and continues to do so until the LM curve reaches LM^4.

Our new equilibrium is therefore the same as our initial equilibrium in that the rate of interest is at r^1 and real income at y. But a real variable has changed. The doubling of the money supply has caused the price level to more than double; therefore, in the new equilibrium, the real value of money balances, $\bar{M}^S/p$, is changed. Money is not neutral in this model.

It is instructive to examine why it is not neutral. The result stems from the fact that there is *money illusion* in Equation 12.7's demand function for money. Money illusion can be defined as follows:

> An individual's behavior reflects money illusion if his or her demand or supply in real terms changes in response to a change in nominal variables alone.

A change in the absolute price level, a nominal variable, leaves all the real variables, y and r, that affect the individual's demand for money in Equation 12.7 unchanged, so the change is in a nominal variable alone. But it causes a change in the real value of an individual's demand for money, for it leaves real transactions demand unchanged (at $kpy/p = ky$) but causes a change in the real value of speculative demand [$(1/p)L_2(r)$ with r unchanged]. This money illusion is the source of nonneutrality in this model. It can be argued that, in a sense, money illusion is the source of nonneutrality whenever we find that money is not neutral. (See, for example, Johnson [1962].)

Money illusion in the demand function for money is a minor example of nonneutrality in the Keynesian model. It is easily overcome by writing the Keynesian demand function for money as:

$$M^D = kpy + pL_2(r) \tag{12.9}$$

so that the demand for real balances, M^D/p, is a function only of the real variables y and r (a conclusion first demonstrated by Patinkin [1954]). This procedure is adopted by the Keynesian models of the Synthesis school. But those models, unlike the one just considered, also include a wealth effect which then gives rise to nonneutrality in an outside asset economy.

Fixed Nominal Bond Supply

Let us examine a model where the demand function for money contains no money illusion, but where all demand functions contain a wealth effect. The real demand for goods is a function of real wealth (again, ignoring physical assets, for simplicity):

$$e = f\left(\bar{y}, r, \frac{\bar{M}^S}{p} + \frac{\bar{B}^S}{rp}\right) \tag{12.10}$$

The demand for real balances is a function of real wealth:

$$\frac{M^D}{p} = f\left(\bar{y}, r, \frac{\bar{M}^S}{p} + \frac{\bar{B}^S}{rp}\right) \tag{12.11}$$

and the real demand for bonds is a function of real wealth:[9]

$$\frac{B^D}{rp} = f\left(\bar{y}, r, \frac{\bar{M}^S}{p} + \frac{\bar{B}^S}{rp}\right) \tag{12.12}$$

The nominal supply of bonds, $\bar{B}^S$, and money, $\bar{M}^S$, is determined by the government. Equilibrium in the goods market requires equality between actual income, $\bar{y}$, and planned expenditure, e, and since we assume price flexibility and a wealth effect, this automatically implies that equilibrium is reached at full-employment income $\bar{y}$. Equilibrium in the money and bond markets requires equality between planned demand for money and bonds and the exogenously determined supplies. Both bonds and money are outside assets and are treated as net wealth by the private sector.[10]

[9]The introduction of a wealth effect in the demand functions for money and bonds may strike the reader as a startling innovation since we did not discuss it in connection with the Pigou Effect. In fact, it is not. Its rationale can be found in the model we used in Chapter 5 to derive the real balance (wealth) effect in the demand function for goods. Indeed, we saw there (in a model without bonds) that an increase in real balances increases the demand for real balances. Similarly, in the portfolio analysis of Chaps. 10 and 11, we saw that utility analysis determines the *proportion* of wealth held in the forms of money and bonds, so that the amount of wealth determines the *level* of the demands for money and bonds.

[10]For example, money consists of government-issued notes, and bonds are the liabilities of the government, with the interest on them being paid out of the profits from nationalized industries.

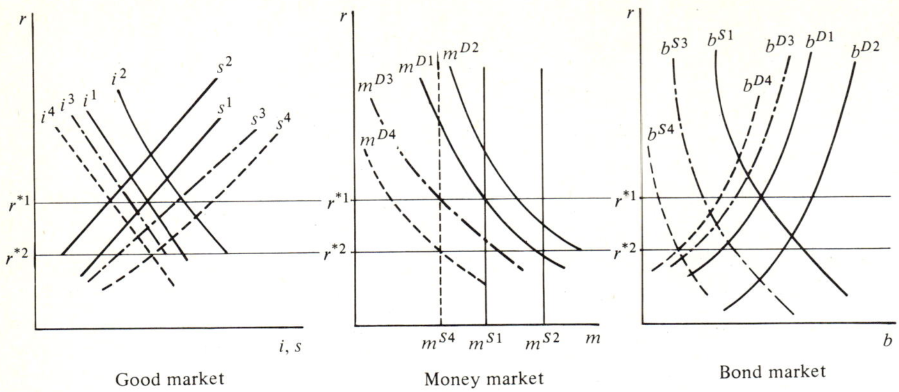

Figure 12-6

The effect of an increase in the money supply in this model is illustrated in Figure 12.6. The three parts of the diagram show the goods market, money market, and bond market respectively, and all the variables are measured in real terms, so the demand curves correspond to those in Equations 12.10 to 12.12. The goods market is represented by the curves of planned saving and planned investment instead of by the planned expenditure and supply of goods curves.[11]

These saving and investment curves are derived from the equations that lie behind Equation 12.10. To make them explicit, we are assuming that saving is a function of income, the rate of interest, and the real value of wealth:

$$s = f\left(\bar{y}, r, \frac{\bar{M}^S}{p} + \frac{B^S}{rp}\right) \qquad (12.13)$$

so that, *ceteris paribus*, if *r* increases, saving increases, and if the real value of wealth increases, saving decreases.[12]

Investment is a function of the rate of interest and the real value of wealth:

$$i = f\left(r, \frac{\bar{M}^S}{p} + \frac{B^S}{rp}\right) \qquad (12.14)$$

[11]It will be recalled from Chap. 8 that equilibrium in the goods market can be represented either by equality of planned expenditure and actual income, $\bar{y} = e$, or, equivalently, by equality between planned saving and planned investment $s = i$. If investment were greater than saving, there would be excess demand in the goods market (in a model without a government sector or foreign sector).

[12]This saving function differs from the standard Keynesian one in that *r* is explicitly assumed to have a direct effect on saving and in that it includes a wealth effect. If we were to omit *r*, the second variable within the parentheses in Eq. 12.13, it would not materially affect the shape of the saving function since *r* has an indirect effect in the same direction through its effect on the real value of wealth.

so that if r increases, planned investment decreases, and if wealth increases, planned investment increases.[13]

Suppose that the model is initially in equilibrium with the demand and supply curves and the saving and investment curves labeled with superscript 1. There the equilibrium rate of interest r^{*1} equilibrates all three markets. Now let there be an increase in the nominal money supply through the distribution of new money as a gift by the government; $\bar{M}^S$ doubles, for example.[14] The immediate consequence, before prices or any other variables change, will be a rightward shift of the real money supply line to m^{S2} in Part B of Figure 12.6, but there will also be shifts of other curves. The real saving curve will shift leftward to s^2 because the increased real money supply involves an increase in real wealth and this, via the wealth effect, causes planned saving to be lower at any rate of interest. For a similar reason, the planned investment curve shifts rightward to i^2. At the same time, the wealth effect in the demand function for real balances causes the demand function in the money market to shift to m^{D2}, since the higher is real wealth, the greater is the demand for real balances. Note, however, that (measuring at the initial interest rate, r^{*1}) the demand function for money does not shift as far to the right as the supply function. The reason is that, although the supply of money has doubled, the stock of financial wealth, $(M^S/p + B^S/rp)$, in real terms has less than doubled because the number of bonds, B^S, is unchanged. Since we assume that, given the rate of interest and real income, there is a desire to hold a constant proportion of real wealth in the form of real money balances, the demand for real balances less than doubles. Finally, because of the wealth effect in the bond market, the demand curve for bonds shifts rightward to b^{D2}.

As a result of these shifts in the curves, there is excess demand for goods, excess supply of money, and excess demand for bonds at the initial interest rate (and these excess demands and supplies sum to zero as a result of Walras' Law if we ignore the labor market). In order to proceed further with the analysis, we must make some assumption about which variables respond directly to the excess demand (or supply) in each market. We assume that excess demand in the goods market has a direct effect on the absolute price level, pushing it upward; and excess demand in the bond market has a direct effect on the rate of interest, pushing it downward (and the bond price upward).

[13]It is difficult to rationalize this effect of wealth on investment in the way that we have explained the wealth (Pigou) effect on consumption. It is most easily rationalized as an allocation effect. Recall that the wealth that enters these equations consists of financial assets. If their real value rises, firms find that the proportion of financial assets to physical assets (the stock of investment goods) has risen and, since nothing else has changed, they seek to restore the initial equilibrium allocation by increasing their stock of physical assets, and this increase affects their flow demand for investment goods.

[14]It would be more realistic to assume that the increased money supply is distributed through a government budget deficit, but that assumption would complicate the exposition.

The rise in the absolute price level has an effect in shifting the curves to new positions. It shifts the supply curves of money and bonds leftward from m^{S2} and b^{S2}, since these curves refer to real values and the rise in p reduces the real value of the nominal supply. It shifts the demand curves for money and bonds leftward as a result of the wealth effect, for the rise in p reduces the real value of wealth. For the same reason, the saving curve shifts rightward from s^2 and the investment curve shifts leftward from i^2. Consideration now must be given to the question of how far the curves shift and the level of the new equilibrium interest rate.

Suppose that the absolute price level doubles as a result of excess demand for goods. If that happens, then, at the old interest rate r^{*1}, the real value of wealth will have fallen below its initial level. The initial real value of wealth is:

$$\frac{\bar{M}^{S1}}{p^1} + \frac{\bar{B}^{S1}}{rp^1}$$

If, after the money supply is doubled, the price level doubles, the real value of wealth will be:

$$\frac{2\bar{M}^{S1}}{2p^1} + \frac{\bar{B}^{S1}}{2rp^1}$$

This value is lower because the nominal supply of bonds is unchanged. Therefore, if the price level doubles, the investment and saving curves will be i^3 and s^3, showing that, as a result of the wealth effect, lower investment and higher saving occur at the initial interest rate. Similarly, because of the operation of the wealth effect, the demand curves for money and bonds will shift to the left of their initial positions, to m^{D3} and b^{D3}. The supply curve of bonds will shift to b^{S3} because the rise in the absolute price level halves the real value of the stock of bonds at any interest rate; and the supply curve of money returns to m^{S1} because the doubling of $\bar{M}^S$ has been offset by the doubling of p. Consequently, a doubling of the price level moves the economy to a position where there is excess supply of goods, excess supply of money, and excess demand for bonds at the initial interest rate. Therefore, the new equilibrium rate of interest cannot be at its initial level if the price level doubles. It could not be at its initial level even if the price level should less than double, for although that might restore the investment and saving curves to their initial positions, it would not eradicate the excess demands and supplies in the money and bond markets. The final equilibrium position will therefore be with the rate of interest r^{*2} and the curves labeled with superscript 4.[15]

[15]This is reached by prices more than doubling. The reader may wonder how this occurs since, with the curves labeled 3 (a doubling of prices), there is excess supply in the goods market and, hence, downward pressure on the price level, at the initial interest rate r^{*1}. The explanation is that the rate of interest does not remain at r^{*1} once the initial equilibrium is disturbed but, simultaneously with the changes in the price level, the interest rate falls, thereby ensuring excess demand for goods.

In this model of outside bonds and outside money, therefore, money is not neutral. An increase in the money supply causes the economy to reach a new equilibrium where the rate of interest (and real balances and the real stock of bonds) is lower than it was initially.

The source of this conclusion is the existence of a wealth effect in the demand functions for money, bonds, and goods, plus the fact that one component of the private sector's (financial) net wealth is the stock of bonds whose nominal value at any given interest rate is fixed. This ensures that a rise in the absolute price level, by reducing the real value of bonds, affects excess demand in each market in such a way that equilibrium cannot be reached at the initial interest rate.

Indexed Bonds

This fact implies that if we were to alter our assumption about the nature of outside bonds, the conclusion would be different. We could, for example, assume that with any given interest rate, the real value of the stock of bonds is invariant with respect to prices. This would be the case if bonds were indexed so that their price automatically kept pace with the absolute price level. Then the real value of wealth would be:

$$\frac{\bar{M}^S}{p} + \frac{p\bar{B}^S}{rp}$$

and a doubling of the money supply accompanied by a doubling of the absolute price level would leave the real value of wealth unchanged, *ceteris paribus*, and a new equilibrium would be established with the curves at their initial position. This, essentially, is the assumption made by Metzler (1951),[16] and it yields the result that a change in the nominal money supply, all things being equal, is neutral. However, even in this model a change in the money supply is not neutral if it is accompanied by a change in the stock of bonds, $\bar{B}^S$. This is precisely what happens if the money supply is changed by open-market operations, one of the most common techniques of monetary policy in actual use. For open-market operations to increase the money supply involves the government in buying government bonds from private sector owners in exchange for money; the money stock in the hands of the private sector, $\bar{M}^S$, goes up thereby, and the stock of bonds held, $\bar{B}^S$, goes down. In the case we have considered in the preceding paragraphs, this fall in $\bar{B}^S$ reinforces the nonneutrality that results from the wealth effect. In the new case where a change in the price level does not affect the real value of bonds, open-market operations would again cause money to be nonneutral. Suppose

[16]In fact, Metzler assumed that the financial assets that are an alternative to money are equities rather than government bonds. Formally, however, the assumption is similar to ours for the essential property that equities are assumed to have is that changes in the absolute price level do not change the real value of an equity.

that, initially, real wealth is:

$$\frac{\bar{M}^{S1}}{p^1}+\frac{p^1\bar{B}^{S1}}{p^1}$$

(where, for simplicity, the initial equilibrium rate of interest is assumed to be 1). The money supply is then doubled by an open-market purchase of bonds so that the immediate effect on real wealth is:

$$\frac{2\bar{M}^{S1}}{p^1}+p^1\frac{(\bar{B}^{S1}-\bar{M}^{S1})}{p^1}$$

If the price level were then to double, real wealth at the initial rate of interest would be:

$$\frac{2\bar{M}^{S1}}{2p^1}+2p^1\frac{(\bar{B}^{S1}-\bar{M}^{S1})}{2p^1}$$

Since this is clearly lower than the initial level of real wealth, the wealth effect ensures that the new equilibrium cannot be established at the same interest rate and at a doubled absolute price level. The reasoning is similar to that used in the analysis of Figure 12.6.

We have seen, therefore, that money is not neutral in an economy with outside money and outside bonds that take the form of British Consols. In addition, in an economy where money is outside money and bonds are indexed outside bonds, money is neutral only if the money supply is changed by some method other than open-market operations. In these cases, monetary policy has a significant effect. It can change the equilibrium rate of interest and therefore, if investment is a function of the interest rate, the rate of investment. Money is more than a veil. But these examples are unrealistic. In a modern economy, much of the money supply is inside money, many bonds are issued by firms rather than the government and are therefore inside bonds, and even government bonds may be considered to be inside bonds if future tax liabilities are discounted at the same rate as future interest receipts.

12.4 NEUTRALITY OF MONEY IN INSIDE MODELS

A model that does not include some "inside" money and "inside" bonds is very unrealistic. For, inside money includes bank deposits where the corresponding assets of the banks are loans to the private sector, and inside bonds are bonds issued by firms. We must therefore examine whether money is neutral in models with these types of assets.

Consider an economy where the only form of money is inside money and the only form of bond is that which is the liability of firms. The government (or banking system) supplies inside money but, by the definition of inside money, it can increase the supply only by purchasing inside bonds. Money is held as an asset by private sector investors (firms) and savers (households).

Bonds are an asset to savers (households) but a liability to investors (firms). The behavior functions of households and firms, separately, include the wealth effect (as do Eqs. 12.11 to 12.14, although in modified form). However, and this is the important factor, the assumption that all financial assets are inside assets and thus are simultaneously the liability of one part of the private sector to another, plus the assumption that there are no distribution effects within the private sector, ensures that the *aggregate* behavior functions for the private sector as a whole contain no wealth effects. As a result, as we shall see, money is neutral in this extreme model.

First let us be sure that in a pure inside model all financial assets owned within the private sector are simultaneously private sector liabilities, so that the aggregate net financial assets of the private sector are zero. Households hold money issued by the government, $M^S(H)$, and bonds issued by firms, $B^S(H)$. They do not borrow. Thus, the net financial wealth of households is:

$$NW(H) = M^S(H) + B^S(H) \tag{12.15}$$

Firms hold money balances as assets, $M^S(F)$, and bonds as liabilities, B^S. Therefore their net financial wealth is:

$$NW(F) = M^S(F) - B^S \tag{12.16}$$

The government (banking system) issues money as liabilities, M^S, and these liabilities are exactly matched by its holding of bonds, $B^S(G)$, issued by firms. Its net financial wealth is therefore zero:

$$NW(G) = B^S(G) - M^S = 0$$

Since the money liabilities of the government are held only by firms or households $[M^S = M^S(H) + M^S(F)]$, and since bonds issued by firms are held only by government or households $[B^S = B^S(G) + B^S(H)]$, the net wealth of the government can be rewritten as:

$$B^S - B^S(H) - M^S(H) - M^S(F) = 0 \tag{12.17}$$

or

$$0 = M^S - B^S(H) - B^S \tag{12.18}$$

It follows from this that the aggregate net financial wealth of the private sector equals zero. This can be seen if we add Equations 12.15 and 12.16 to obtain the net wealth of the private sector:

$$\begin{aligned} NW(H + F) &= M^S(H) + M^S(F) + B^S(H) - B^S \\ &= M^S - B^S(H) - B^S \end{aligned} \tag{12.19}$$

Comparison between Equations 12.19 and 12.18 indicates that the private sector's net financial wealth equals zero.

This implies that the net wealth of one part of the private sector (households) is exactly offset by the net liabilities of the other part (firms).[17] A rise in the real value of households' net financial wealth involves an equal decline in that of firms. This, by itself, is of no particular significance for the model. What makes it important is the Neoclassical/Keynesian Synthesis assumption that there are *no distribution effects.* Absence of distribution effects may be defined as implying:

> A rise in the real value of wealth for one part of the private sector, accompanied by an equal decline (or increase in real liabilities) for another part, causes the demand of the first in the goods, money, and other markets to rise by an amount that is exactly offset by the fall in demand from the other part of the private sector.

Thus, for example, a rise in the real wealth of households, exactly offset by a rise in firms' real liabilities, causes an increase in households' consumption, exactly offset, *ceteris paribus*, by a decline in firms' investment, so that private sector expenditure remains unchanged. The assumption of no distribution effects, together with the equality of firms' net liabilities and households' net assets, means that the aggregate excess demand functions for the private sector contain no wealth effects.

The demand function for goods, unlike Equation 12.10, contains no net wealth term since, as we have seen, the wealth effects on consumption and investment are assumed offsetting:

$$e = f(\bar{y}, r) \tag{12.20}$$

Similarly, the private sector's demand for real balances has no wealth term, unlike Equation 12.11:

$$\frac{M^D}{p} = g(\bar{y}, r) \tag{12.21}$$

Equilibrium in the goods and money markets with output at full employment, y, implies zero excess demand or:

$$f(y, r) - y = 0 \tag{12.22}$$

and

$$g(y, r) - \frac{M^S}{p} = 0 \tag{12.23}$$

respectively. These equations alone are sufficient to indicate that money is neutral in this model, for we do not need to consider explicitly the labor or bond markets. Assuming that output is at full employment $\bar{y} = y$ is, by the

[17]From Eq. 12.17 we know that $B^S = B^S(H) + M^S(H) + M^S(F)$. Substituting this into Eq. 12.16's expression for firms' net wealth, we obtain $NW(F) = M^S(F) - B^S(H) - M^S(H) - M^S(F)$; this simplifies to $NW(F) = (-1)[B^S(H) + M^S(H)]$. In other words, the net financial wealth of firms is the negative of the net wealth of households.

definition of full employment used in Chapter 8, the same as assuming that the excess demand (or supply) of labor is zero. And Walras' Law tells us that if the goods and money markets, as well as the labor market, are in equilibrium (Eqs. 12.22 and 12.23), then the bond market must be in equilibrium. Concentrating on the goods and money markets, therefore, suppose that, starting from an initial equilibrium in which Equations 12.22 and 12.23 hold, there is a doubling of the money supply.[18] Now consider whether there exists a new full-employment equilibrium in which no real variable has changed. If the price level were to double, then, clearly, real balances would be unchanged and, as can be seen from Equations 12.22 and 12.23, this is consistent with a new equilibrium (excess demands equal zero) without any change in the rate of interest or real output. In this model, therefore, money is neutral.

Two points concerning this conclusion are worthy of note. First, it was developed by Gurley and Shaw (1960), Modigliani (1963), and Patinkin (1965), when it remained widely accepted that inside money is not net wealth to the private sector. As we saw in Chapter 3, the view was subsequently put forward by Pesek and Saving (1967) and Johnson (1969) that even inside money is net wealth to the private sector. This, however, would not change the conclusion that money is neutral in an economy where money and bonds are both of the inside variety. This fact can most easily be seen by considering the net wealth produced by inside money to be incorporated in the capitalized value of the banking system's profits. That is, replace the word "government" in the present section with the work "banking system." The doubling of the price level ensures that the real value of these capitalized profits remains unchanged, so that there is no wealth effect from this source to cause the new equilibrium to differ from the initial equilibrium.

The second point is that in this model the price level is determinate. In the initial equilibrium with its particular money supply, there is one price level when the money supply doubles, the price level doubles, and no other value of p can exist in the new equilibrium. In order to say this, we must be able to describe the forces that exist in disequilibrium and that ensure that the price level moves toward its unique equilibrium value when equilibrium is disturbed. The significant feature is that these disequilibrium forces *do not include the wealth effect, or real balance effect.* For, as we have seen, in the inside model, the net wealth of the private sector does not enter the aggregate behavior functions of the private sector. In the absence of the wealth effect, what is it in this model that ensures a tendency toward equilibrium? What, in the example we have considered, causes the price level to double as a result of the doubling of the money supply? It is a *portfolio allocation effect.* This increase in the money supply causes an excess supply of real balances at the initial interest rate, as can be seen by imagining that the equilibrium in Equation 12.23 is disturbed by a rise in M^S. However, it causes no dis-

[18]Being an inside money model, this can occur only when the government (banking system) buys firms' bonds for money.

equilibrium in the goods market at the initial interest rate since, in the absence of the real balance effect, no variables change in Equation 12.22. Instead, the excess supply of money is matched by an excess demand for bonds. This can be seen not only by the mechanical application of Walras' Law, but, more significantly, by noting that some bonds previously held by households are now held by the government, which has bought them in exchange for money in order to increase the money supply. Thus, at the initial interest rate, households' demand for bonds is unchanged, but the available supply is reduced. There is therefore a disequilibrium in portfolios, in the allocation of private sector wealth between different assets: an excess supply of money and excess demand for bonds. This disequilibrium causes the interest rate to fall (the price of bonds to rise), resulting in an effect on the goods market. The fall in the interest rate causes an increase in investment (and decrease in saving), thereby inducing an excess demand for goods and causing the price level to rise. The rise in p continues until the new equilibrium is reached, with p doubled and the interest rate at its initial equilibrium level.

In the inside model, therefore, determinacy of the price level is ensured by interaction between the money and bond markets and the goods market. But here this interaction occurs not through the wealth effect but through changes in the interest rate induced by portfolio disequilibrium. The conclusion resurrects the question we discussed in Chapter 5: Is the real balance effect the sine qua non of monetary theory in that, without it, we can have no consistent model with a determinate price level? Here we have seen that determinacy can be guaranteed even without the real balance effect or the wealth effect.

The pure inside money and inside bonds economy is no more realistic than a pure outside economy. It would be more realistic to assume a mixture of inside and outside bonds and money. If that mixture were the case, money would, in general, be nonneutral. Indeed, this was one of the main points made by Gurley and Shaw (1960). A monetary economy is different from a barter economy and monetary policy can affect the interest rate, thereby affecting the rate of investment.

12.5 ESSENTIAL FEATURES OF THE NEOCLASSICAL/KEYNESIAN SYNTHESIS

We can now draw together the elements of the Neoclassical/Keynesian Synthesis and attempt to reach a view on what this tradition amounts to. Such a task is highly relevant to modern monetary theory, since recent years have seen the development of a New Keynesian tradition that is founded on a critique of the Old Keynesianism's Synthesis. This New Keynesianism is founded on the work of Clower (1965, 1967) and Leijonhufvud (1968). We shall examine it in Chapter 13.

The first element of the Synthesis is the emphasis in this tradition on the derivation of macroeconomic behavior relations from a basis of individuals' utility-maximizing decisions. We have seen in Chapters 10 and 11 that in this tradition the aggregate demand function for money—Keynes' liquidity preference function—is derived from models of individual utility maximization. Similarly, the consumption function theory of Pigou (1947), Friedman (1957), and Modigliani and Brumberg (1954) is an attempt to derive the aggregate consumption function from individuals' utility-maximizing behavior. And the theory of aggregate investment developed in the years since the *General Theory* is firmly rooted in the profit-maximizing behavior of the individual firm, as in Jorgenson (1963). These tendencies themselves ensure a strong link between the macroeconomic models of the Synthesis and Neoclassical price theory, but the tendency to base theories of aggregate behavior on theories of individual behavior is not in itself a rejection of Keynes's own method. In the *General Theory*, Keynes did not develop in detail the microeconomic foundations of all his macroeconomic theories, but he certainly made forays in that direction. He stated, for example, the principles of profit maximization that lie behind the demand function for labor. Moreover, even where Keynes did not specify the underlying microeconomic model, he clearly thought in terms of aggregate behavior being derived from theories of individual behavior. His consumption function, for example, was stated as a "fundamental psychological law" and was therefore conceived as being a derivation from theories of individual behavior.

The emphasis of the Neoclassical/Keynesian Synthesis on the utility-maximization basis of macroeconomics stems, therefore, from Keynes's own view of the world and is unobjectionable, in general terms, if our criterion is its being a development of Keynes's work. However, it has a specific feature that, as we shall see in Chapter 13, gives rise to criticisms from the New Keynesians. That is, by employing the utility-maximization models of Neoclassical price theory, the old Keynesians tend to ignore the nature of the constraints on individual behavior that derive from the operation of the macroeconomic system as a whole. The Synthesis starts with individuals' behavior and from this builds macroeconomic theories of aggregate behavior by simply summing the behavior functions of individuals. It therefore starts and finishes without considering how the end point affects the starting point (although the idea, developed in Chapter 8, of being off the demand curve for labor is an exception to this general method). It can be argued that this is contrary to Keynes's own method.

Consider, for example, the theory of consumption and the labor market. In microeconomic theory we assume that the individual faces a given wage rate, set of goods prices, and interest rate. These, we may assume, are at those levels which equilibrate the relevant markets. Individuals then decide on the amount of labor they wish to supply and, simultaneously, the amount of goods they wish to consume, and these decisions are such as to maximize utility. In this way we obtain the supply function of labor in the labor market of the Neoclassical/Keynesian Synthesis and the consumption function in the goods market. But what is the constraint on this utility maximization? Consumption cannot be treated as constrained by current income for, since individuals themselves choose how much to work, they each choose their own income.[19] The only constraints facing the individual in the system are the relative prices of goods, labor, and future goods, and those variables which are given from previous periods (such as accumulated wealth). Current income, determined by the macroeconomic system, has no real significance as a constraint on consumption in this utility-maximizing model. It did, however, play an important role in Keynes's own work.

The second feature of the Neoclassical/Keynesian Synthesis is closely related to the first. It is that in analyzing macroeconomic equilibrium the Old Keynesians employ a basic assumption that prices are flexible. More specifically, prices react to disequilibrium faster than do quantities. If there is aggregate excess supply in the goods market, the absolute price level falls and equilibrium is reestablished. This effect of the fall in the price level is achieved through the Pigou Effect in the goods market and through the increase in the real value of the money supply (or decrease in the demand for nominal balances) in the money market that pushes down the rate of interest. Both these conditions increase aggregate demand. The fall in the price level works, that is, through shifting the *IS* and *LM* curves rightward to the point where planned demand has risen to again equal planned supply. Since full-employment output is defined to be planned supply, this speed of adjustment of prices generally ensures an automatic tendency toward full employment, and the Pigou Effect is, as we saw in Section 12.1, crucial to this. The alternative to assuming great flexibility of prices is to assume relatively inflexible prices and flexible quantities. If we were to do that, we could argue that excess supply in the goods market is eliminated by decreases in the quantity of output and, therefore, in national income. Excess supply would cause us to move away from equilibrium at full employment and thereby place an income constraint on individuals' utility-maximizing decisions. The New Keynesians argue that implicit in Keynes's own work is an emphasis on the relative inflexibility of all prices, so that quantities bear the full burden of adjustment, and that the Old Keynesians are at fault in adopting the Neoclassical assumption that prices are highly flexible.

The third feature of the Neoclassical/Keynesian Synthesis is seen in its treatment of the neutrality of money, examined in Sections 12.3 and 12.4. It will be recalled from Chapter 3, Section 3.4, that the question of whether money is neutral really concerns the question of whether there is a fundamental difference between a barter economy and a monetary economy. But the Old Keynesian tradition analyzes the neutrality of money by assuming that the economy's stable equilibrium is at full employment and examining the

[19]Friedman (1957), for example, argues on the basis of utility maximization that (permanent) consumption is a function of permanent income, and he states that one possible way to think of permanent income is as planned (that is, chosen) income.

equilibrium price level and interest rate at full employment before and after a change in the money supply. It thereby ignores the central question in the distinction between a barter and a monetary economy, the question of whether a monetary economy does have a tendency to full employment. This, clearly, is related to the features discussed in the preceding paragraphs, for the essence of these analyses of neutrality is an assumption of price flexibility. In the case of Keynes's own work, money was in general considered not neutral; the existence of money was an important factor in explaining the existence of unemployment and, since Keynes concentrated attention on positions of unemployment, a change in the money supply was not neutral because it could in general (although not always) change the equilibrium level of real income and output.

Finally, the writers of the Neoclassical/Keynesian Synthesis build their macroeconomic models by implicitly or explicitly employing Walras' Law as the basic principle linking together the money market, bonds market, goods market, and labor market. It is difficult to do this and at the same time retain, within the framework of the Synthesis, a meaningful concept of unemployment. If unemployment is defined as an excess supply of labor, as it is within the Synthesis tradition, then by Walras' Law there must be an excess of planned demand over planned supply in some other market, or markets. Since the Synthesis, in the form represented in Chapter 8 (which draws heavily on the formulation of Patinkin [1965]), treats full-employment income as planned supply in the goods market, excess supply in the labor market is accompanied by excess supply in the goods market. Moreover, since this unemployment occurs at a rate of interest which allows the economy to be on the *LM* curve, there is no excess demand in the money (or bonds) market. Thus, there is excess supply in two markets of this model when unemployment exists, but no excess demands. Walras' Law is difficult to fit in.

Nevertheless, Keynesian models in the tradition of the Synthesis are built around the assumption of Walras' Law. This is achieved in several ways. One is to concentrate on positions of full-employment equilibrium, for there the difficulty we have noted does not arise. This is the procedure adopted in discussions of the neutrality of money, as we saw in Sections 12.3 and 12.4. Another way is to argue that if there is an excess supply of labor, there is an excess demand for money since unemployed workers who offer labor for hire are simultaneously asking for (have a demand for) money in return. This is the approach of Kuenne (1963), but it is hard to reconcile it with the concept of the demand for money that is employed in the standard *IS*/*LM* analysis. Finally, the Synthesis writers' use of models based on Walras' Law for analyzing both full-employment and unemployment positions may be achieved by reinterpreting the meaning of excess supply and excess demand, so that in situations of unemployment they no longer refer to the difference between planned demand and supply. This is the approach adopted by Patinkin (1965, Chapter 13, and our Chapter 8) for analyzing the labor market, but in doing this he is a forerunner of the New Keynesians. For the essence of their argument is that the concept of planned demand and planned supply, which we used in Chapter 8 and the present chapter, is inappropriate in a monetary economy: Keynes's work can be understood only if we abandon it. For planned demand and supply are concepts derived from Neoclassical price theory's model of utility-maximizing behavior in a world where prices are highly flexible. Moreover, as we have seen above, although the assumptions of this model do lie behind the Neoclassical/Keynesian Synthesis, they are not necessarily appropriate for the interpretation of Keynes's work. The difficulty the Synthesis has in employing Walras' Law is a manifestation of this unsuitability according to the New Keynesians whose work is presented in the next chapter.

CHAPTER
THIRTEEN

KEYNESIAN REAPPRAISAL AND GENERAL DISEQUILIBRIUM ANALYSIS

The Keynesian model which we examined earlier, especially in Chapters 8 and 12, is the one that evolved between the publication of Keynes's *General Theory* (1936) and the mid-1960s. Its distinguishing feature is an attempt to frame Keynes's theories in terms of Walrasian general equilibrium analysis. Walrasian analysis is a method developed primarily to deal with the equilibrium of a full-employment economy, whereas Keynes's objective was to show that unemployment is the more general case. Therefore, the attempt to integrate the two methods involves certain difficulties and is completely successful only when considering full-employment equilibria in the Keynesian model. The problem of the neutrality of money at full employment, considered in Chapter 12, is therefore the most suitable problem for this Neoclassical/Keynesian Synthesis. But even then, the Walrasian method is not well suited for analyzing how the economy moves from one full-employment equilibrium to another; it cannot, as we shall see, handle the forces of disequilibrium with ease. The theory of the wealth effect or Pigou Effect is central to this synthesis, for it is this effect that ensures that the equilibrium of the system is at full employment as long as prices are flexible. Indeed, as we saw in Chapter 4, flexibility of prices is central to the Walrasian method: an excess of planned supply over planned demand in any market is instantaneously cured by a fall in the relative price of the item traded in that market.

All these characteristics can be seen most clearly in the work of Patinkin (1965). His model is explicitly a Walrasian general equilibrium model with instantaneous adjustment of prices. It works well as long as positions of full-employment equilibrium are examined in the context of, for example, the neutrality of money. In such a situation Walras' Law holds, for the sum of excess demands in all markets (including the excess demand for money) equals zero, and excess demand is defined as *planned* demand minus *planned* supply. It works less well when unemployment is considered. For one thing, unemployment equilibrium can exist only if the absolute price level is rigid (or if there are no components of private sector net wealth whose real value increases with a fall in p), since otherwise the wealth effect fails to ensure that full employment is reached.

Moreover, the meaning of Walras' Law is unclear when there is unemployment, since there is then an excess of planned supply over planned demand in the labor and goods markets, but the fact that r and $\bar{y}$ are the coordinates of a point on the *LM* curve even when there is unemployment implies that there is no corresponding excess demand for money or bonds. This problem with Walras' Law can be overcome if we redefine the excess demand for money and bonds. After all, the excess supply of goods is defined as the difference between planned supply, y, and planned demand, e (where, with unemployment, e equals actual income, $\bar{y}$). Similarly, we could say that the planned demand for money is the demand that would exist if income were at the full-employment level $M^D = pf[y, r, (\bar{M}^S/p) + (\bar{B}^S/rp)]$ instead of the demand that exists when income is at its actual level, $\bar{M}^D = pf[\bar{y}, r, (\bar{M}^S/p) + (\bar{B}^S/rp)]$. In that case, excess planned supply in the goods and labor markets would be accompanied by excess planned demand in the money market (and, by similar reasoning, in the bond market). Such an amendment, however, is unsatisfactory unless the Walrasian model has a sound concept of the difference between actual income and full employment.

Finally, since the Walrasian model is based on the concepts of planned demand and planned supply, the meaning of Keynes's *involuntary* unemployment is unclear. If it is represented by the distance between the planned demand and planned supply curves in the labor market, unemployment is in a sense voluntary: it can arise only because real wages are too high or, in other words, because workers choose to offer too much labor at the going wage rate; if money wages are rigid, it is because workers choose not to work at lower money wages. For this reason, in Section 8.3 we considered unemployment as involving positions off the demand curve, but, strictly speaking, this assumption involves a break with Walrasian methods.

Because the Walrasian method involves these difficulties for the analysis of unemployment, Patinkin (1965, chapter 13), begins to depart from it. This, together with the work of Clower (1965) and Leijonhufvud (1968), has given an impetus to the search for a method that is more suitable for the analysis of unemployment; the building of models where general disequilibrium, rather than general equilibrium, is at the center. These attempts may be called the New Keynesianism or the Keynesian Reappraisal. Fundamental to them all is the clarification of the concepts of demand, supply, and excess demand, so we can distinguish between the concepts of planned demand and supply that are used in Walrasian models and the concepts of planned demand (and supply) that were central to Keynes's analysis. We shall call Walrasian planned demand *notional* demand and Keynesian planned demand *effective* demand. In Section 13.1 we examine these different concepts and show their relationship to the concept of involuntary unemployment. In Section 13.2 we examine the New Keynesians' view of the non-Walrasian nature of the price system in an economy with general disequilibrium. In Sections 13.3 and 13.4 we give a preliminary summary of the distinction between the New Keynesianism and the Neoclassical/Keynesian Synthesis. In Chapter 14 we proceed to discuss some specifically monetary aspects of the New Keynesianism.

The emphasis in the present chapter is on the methods developed by the New Keynesians for analyzing general disequilibrium. We shall not consider the entirely separate question of whether these new methods accurately represent Keynes's own method. Whereas Clower (1965) and, particularly, Leijonhufvud (1968) claim to be faithful interpreters of Keynes's work, other writers, such as Yeager (1973) and Jackman (1974), have correctly emphasized the similarities between Keynes's own formulations and those of the Neoclassical Synthesis.

13.1 EFFECTIVE DEMAND, NOTIONAL DEMAND, AND INVOLUNTARY UNEMPLOYMENT

In Chapter 8 and the subsequent chapters we have treated consumption as a function of *actual* income, $\bar{y}$. This is the same as Keynes's own treatment and that of the Neoclassical/Keynesian Synthesis. It corresponds to Keynes's concept of *effective demand.* The consumption that people desire may be at some level, but their effective consumption demand may be much lower, since, to be effective, demand must be backed by money. If we assume that borrowing is impossible, this money is limited by actual income (and wealth, if we take account of the wealth effect). Thus, Keynes's consumption function is based on the idea that individuals are constrained by their actual income. In Walrasian general equilibrium theory, they are also constrained in their consumption decisions, but the constraint is of a different nature. Here individual workers are constrained by the given real wage rate (and the given price of their assets) in deciding upon their own optimum consumption. Given these prices, individuals choose both how much work they wish to perform (that is, how much labor income they wish to receive) and how much consumption they each desire. Since this real wage and other prices are at their equilibrium level, each individual is actually able to perform the chosen amount of labor and receive the chosen amount of income. In the Keynesian system, there is an additional constraint. Not only is the individual constrained by the real wage rate in the choice of the amount of work; she or he is also constrained by the possibility of not being able to achieve the amount of employment desired. The demand for labor by capitalists may be too low.

Thus, actual income may be lower than desired income, and it is actual income that determines the individual's consumption plans.

Clearly, to understand the Keynesian idea of effective demand for consumption goods, we must simultaneously understand the Keynesian idea of constraints in the labor market. These two aspects have been developed separately; Patinkin (1965) developed the New Keynesian concept of the labor market, Clower (1965) developed the New Keynesian concept of the consumption function. The two were integrated in a simplified model by Barro and Grossman (1971), and the integration has been generalized by writers such as Benassy (1975b) and Grandmont and Laroque (1974).

Constraints on Utility Maximization

Two concepts important to this work were introduced by Clower in his theory of the consumption function. As noted earlier, the concept of *notional demand* is the Walrasian idea of planned demand; the concept of *effective demand* is the Keynesian idea. Clower explained the distinction between the two by postulating that individuals follow a *dual-decision*, or two-stage decision, process. We can illustrate it with Figure 13.1. The left-hand quadrant shows the relationship between the supply of labor and income. The minimum level of income, measured on the vertical axis, is the return on the individual's nonhuman wealth, R_1. This is exogenously determined since the market yield per asset is given to the individual, the volume of whose assets is predetermined by choices made in the previous period. It is what the individual receives when supplying no labor. Total real income, y, is R_1 plus income

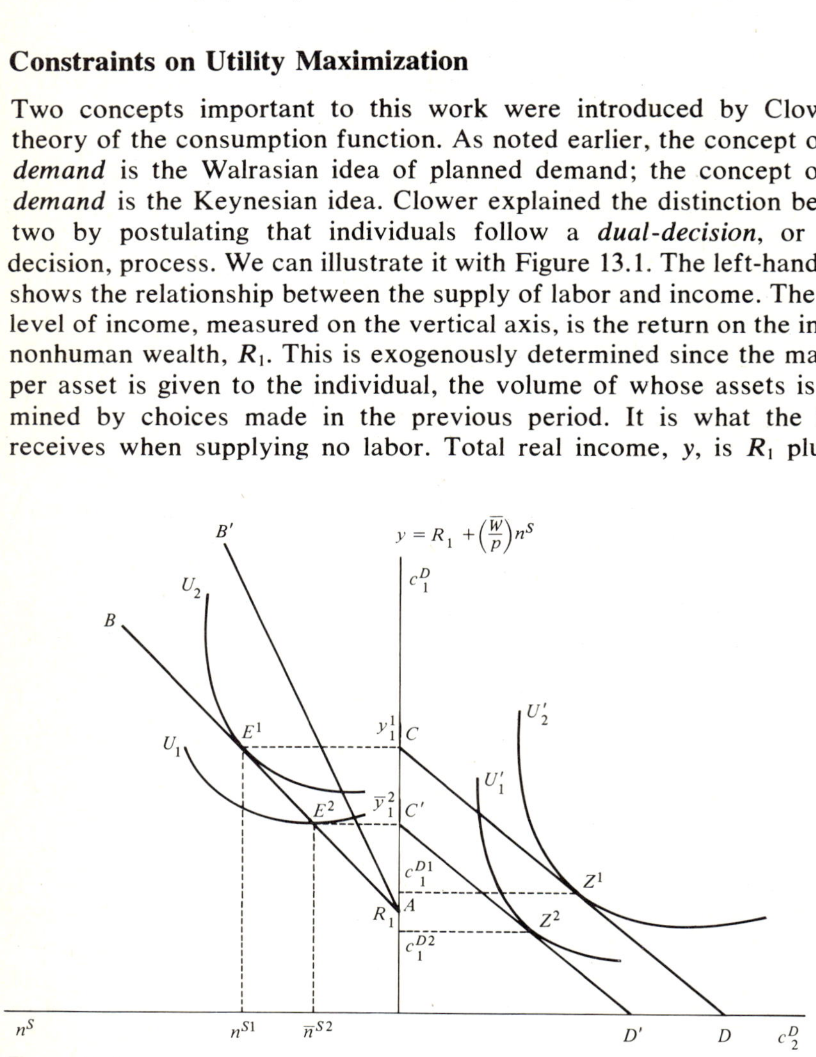

Figure 13-1

from work: $y = R_1 + (\bar{W}/p)n^s$. Income from work equals the amount of labor supplied times the given real wage. The budget line which individuals each face when choosing the amount of labor they plan to supply and the amount of income they plan to obtain is a line such as *AB* or *AB'*. *AB* would exist if the real wage equals 1, *AB'* if it is 2. The individual's utility map is represented by the indifference curves, with higher indifference curves representing higher levels of utility. They take the particular form shown because work is assumed to be a disgood, whereas income is a good; they show that with a given level of income, an increase in work reduces utility. The right-hand quadrant shows the relationship between this period's real income and planned consumption, y_1 and c_1^D on the vertical axis, and next period's consumption, c_2^D, on the horizontal axis. For simplicity, we assume that income in period 2 consists solely of the return on assets carried forward from period 1.[1] The budget line is a line such as *CD* or *C'D'*. Its intercept on the vertical axis is determined by the level of income that results from the utility maximization conducted in the left-hand quadrant, since this determines the maximum feasible consumption demand in the present period, c_1^D. Its slope is determined by the yield on assets carried forward from period 1 to period 2; the higher is the return on assets, the further to the right will be the intercept on the horizontal axis. The indifference curves have the usual shape and are drawn on the assumption that a rightward parallel shift of the budget line will increase the demand for both present and future consumption goods.

The individual makes decisions relevant to each quadrant simultaneously: At one instant, the individual chooses desired supply of labor, desired current income, current consumption, and future consumption. The two indifference maps are different aspects of the same utility function. Suppose that the real wage is 1, so that the budget line in the left-hand quadrant is *AB*. The individual will reach equilibrium at E^1 where the choice is made to supply n^{s1} amount of labor and obtain y^1, real income this period. Because the person has chosen y_1^1 real income, the budget line in the right-hand quadrant is *CD*. Given this budget line, equilibrium is reached at Z^1 in that quadrant. That is, the choice is made to consume c_1^{D1} in the present period and save $s_1^{D1} = y_1^1 - c_1^{D1}$.

The individual's planned consumption, saving, and supply of labor in the current period reached at points E^1 and Z^1 are what Clower names his *notional* demands (and supplies). They are the concepts of planned demand and supply that are employed in Walrasian general equilibrium analysis.

If general equilibrium is actually attained, then we need concern ourselves only with these notional demands and supplies. The nature of Walrasian general equilibrium is that all these plans of the individual and all other individuals are realized and mutually consistent. Since each individual is able to supply the amount of labor each plans to supply, Walrasian general

[1]This quadrant is obviously similar to the figures used in Chaps. 5 and 12 to analyze the wealth effect or Pigou Effect.

equilibrium implies full employment. Keynes, however, was concerned with involuntary unemployment, and Clower argues that this concern implies that notional demands and supplies are unrealized.

Refer to Figure 13.1 again. Suppose that the individual is able to work only $\bar{n}^{s2}$ hours of labor. The notional supply of labor is n^{s1}, but employers will not hire anyone for that number of hours. In consequence, the worker's actual income in this period is $\bar{y}_1^2$, less than the desired income of y_1^1. In other words, equilibrium in the left-hand quadrant is reached at E^2 rather than E^1, for here is the maximum level of utility attainable when the constraint is no longer determined solely by $\bar{w}/p$ and R_1, but also by the maximum amount of labor that can actually be supplied, $\bar{n}^{s2}$. This fact has an effect in the right-hand quadrant. It means that the appropriate budget line is now $C'D'$, rather than CD. Its intercept is determined by the individual's actual income, $\bar{y}_1^2$, rather than the desired income, y_1^1. In the light of the constraint represented by this budget line, the individual will now maximize utility in the consumption (and saving) decision at Z^2, rather than Z^1. Planned consumption in this period will be c_1^{D2}, rather than c_1^{D1}. Planned saving will be $s_1^{D2} = \bar{y}_1^2 - c_1^{D2}$ instead of $s_1^{D1} = y_1^1 - c_1^{D1}$.[2] *This* concept of planned consumption is a concept of *effective demand* for consumption goods.

Thus, Clower's distinction between notional and effective demands hinges on the distinction between the constraints on utility maximization appropriate to each concept. In the case of effective demand for goods, the individual's utility maximization is subject to the quantity constraint of the amount of labor that is actually supplied (and, hence, the amount of actual current income), whereas, in the event of notional demand, this element is absent from the constraint. Clower graphically presents his *dual-decision hypothesis* thus: The individual *first* makes utility-maximizing decisions on the assumption that the only constraint is the real wage and the return on nonhuman assets. That is, workers each calculate their own notional supply of labor and demand for goods. They *then* find that their actual supply of labor is less than their notional supply, and they recalculate their demand for goods to decide on their own effective demands subject to this new constraint.

Clearly, effective demand rather than notional demand is the concept of planned demand relevant to Keynes's short-run consumption function. Keynes expressed consumption as a function of *actual* income. Moreover, this practice was adopted by almost all the writers in the Neoclassical/Keynesian Synthesis school and it is the practice adopted in Chapter 8. Why, then, is Clower's elucidation of the nature of the underlying utility-maximization process so significant? The reason is that it has led to an exploration of the conditions in the labor, money, and goods markets that underlie the existence of the extra constraint upon which Keynesian effective

[2]The shape of the Keynesian short-run consumption function with a marginal propensity to consume less than 1 implies that the shape of the indifference curves is such that saving falls by a smaller proportion than income.

demand is founded. And this research has shown that these conditions are inconsistent with the assumptions underlying Walrasian general equilibrium analysis.

Involuntary Unemployment

In order to examine this conclusion in Sections 13.2 and 13.3, we must first move from consideration of individual behavior to look at aggregate market behavior. Aggregation of individuals' effective demand for consumption goods need not concern us here. We shall assume that all consumers encounter a constraint on their supply of labor that affects their demand for consumption goods, as in Figure 13.1. On certain assumptions, we may then aggregate over all individuals to obtain a consumption function with actual, rather than planned, income as the determining variable. The question now is the nature of the labor market constraint. What position in the labor market prevents individuals from supplying the amount of labor that is their notional supply? Patinkin (1965) has argued that the labor market position can be understood only if we distinguish between capitalists' *notional demand* for labor and their *effective demand* for labor (although he does not employ these terms).

Consider Figure 13.2. The planned supply curve of labor, $n^s n^s$, is the sum of individuals' notional supplies. The planned demand curve, $n^D n^D$, is the sum of capitalists' notional demands. These are the curves we have employed in Chapter 8's representation of the labor market, and there we argued that for consistency in the Keynesian model, we must consider firms to be off the notional demand curve for labor when there is unemployment. We did so because that curve is based on the Neoclassical postulate that firms maximize profits subject only to the constraints of their production function and the prices of inputs and outputs. Subject to this constraint, the firm employs labor up to the point where its marginal product equals the real wage, (W/p). This

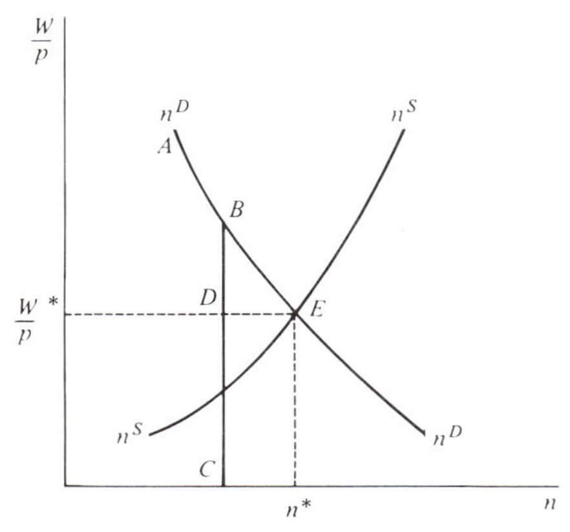

Figure 13-2

statement, however, assumes that the firm can actually sell the output produced at this profit-maximizing level of employment. If firms find that they cannot, in fact, sell this desired output, then their demand for labor will be subject to a constraint with an additional element, their actual sales (actual supply), and they will be forced off their notional demand curve.

In other words, to use reasoning similar to that employed in elaborating Clower's model of the consumption function, we can present Patinkin's labor market model as follows: The notional demand function for labor, $n^D n^D$, is that which exists when firms calculate their notional supply of goods according to a profit-maximization process with Neoclassical constraints. If firms find that their actual supply of goods is less than their notional supply, their effective demand for labor will be different from their notional demand. It will be reached subject to the constraint of actual sales in addition to the constraints of the production function and prices. The aggregate effective demand for labor will be represented by *ABC*, while notional demand is represented by $n^D n^D$.[3]

The concept of effective demand in the labor market enables us to define the concept of involuntary unemployment more precisely. Let n^* with real wage $(W/p)^*$ be the full-employment level of labor demand and supply. At that point, the amount of labor workers choose to supply (the notional supply) is the same as capitalists choose to demand when they can sell all their profit-maximizing output (the notional demand for labor). But how is involuntary unemployment defined? In the predominant version of the Neoclassical Synthesis as represented, for example, by W. L. Smith (1956), unemployment is defined as the difference between firms' *notional* demand for labor and the full-employment amount of labor. Thus, firms are always on their notional demand curve and unemployment can occur only when the real wage is above its equilibrium level, $(W/p)^*$. Such a concept is illustrated in Figure 13.3. Here, if the real wage is $(W/p)^1$, there is unemployment of $(n^* - n^{D1})$; if the real wage is $(W/p)^*$, there is necessarily full employment, for in this conception firms cannot be off their notional demand curves for labor. Because of its adherence to notional demand curves, this method is Walrasian through and through. Its implication is that unemployment can occur only if real wages are above their equilibrium level $(W/p)^*$. The implication[4] would remain, and the concept would continue to be essentially Walrasian if we were to modify it slightly and define unemployment as the distance between the notional demand curve and the notional supply curve (rather than n^*) at a given real wage. Again, unemployment would exist only when the real wage

[3]This figure is attributable to Barro and Grossman (1971), rather than Patinkin (1965). The latter does not draw an effective demand curve such as *ABC*, but refers to individual points off the notional demand curve, as we have done in Sec. 8.3.

[4]Barro and Grossman (1971) argue that this implication is not only theoretically invalid because of its failure to account for sales constraints, but that it is also empirically implausible. For the model of Fig. 13.3 suggests that real wages rise in slumps (and fall in booms), whereas the opposite is in fact observed.

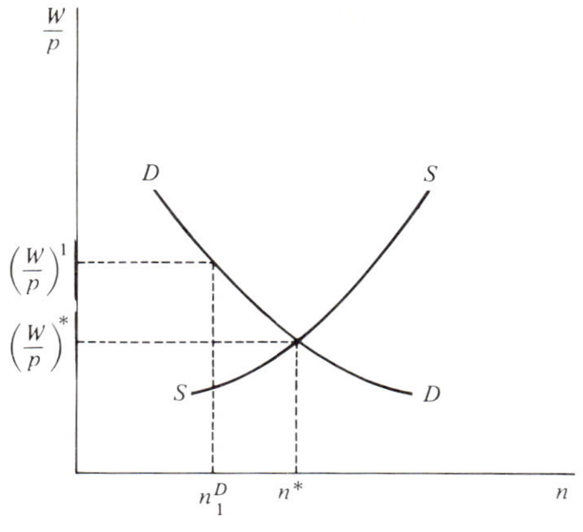

Figure 13-3

was above $(W/p)^*$. In this Walrasian framework, it is difficult to avoid the conclusion that unemployment is, in a sense, entirely voluntary. For, when one considers what causes the real wage to be too high, the answer is in general that, as in Keynes's hypothesis, workers' resistance to a lower money wage is what keeps it raised. In this model, unemployment therefore occurs only because workers, however unwittingly, choose it instead of suffering it involuntarily.

In the Keynesian model elaborated by the New Keynesians and employed in Chapter 8's analysis of the labor market, however, we may define involuntary unemployment as existing even if the real wage is at its equilibrium level. In Figure 13.2, involuntary unemployment may be defined as an excess of notional supply over *effective* demand. Suppose that initially there is full employment at the real wage, $(W/p)^*$, and that firms' notional demand curve for labor, $n^D n^D$, is relevant. Then, as a result of a decline in effective demand for goods, firms find themselves constrained by their sales so that the effective demand curve *ABC* becomes relevant. Even if the real wage remains unchanged, involuntary unemployment of *DE* will exist. It is this involuntary unemployment, excess supply of labor, that prevents individuals from selling their desired amount of labor. Their income is therefore constrained and their consumption demand is a function of actual income, as in Figure 13.1. This concept of involuntary unemployment clearly captures an essential element of Keynesian thought: That unemployment is determined by demand for goods and is not merely the effect of real wages being too high. It is a concept that requires the New Keynesians' distinction between effective and notional demand.[5]

[5]Although we have distinguished notional from effective demand in the labor market, we have employed the notional supply curve of labor and have not distinguished it from effective supply. In more sophisticated models of general disequilibrium, such a distinction is made. It is particularly relevant in models of inflationary disequilibrium with excess demand for goods and labor.

We have seen, therefore, that the distinction between effective and notional demands allows us to characterize the notions of excess supply of goods and excess supply of labor (involuntary unemployment). Effective and notional demands coincide if there is no excess supply anywhere in the system; in that case, we may confine attention to the Walrasian concept of notional demand. If there is excess supply, then the two differ and effective demand is the relevant concept. Effective demand is derived from individual utility maximization of firms' profit maximization when there is disequilibrium—a quantity constraint in the labor or goods market respectively. Since Keynes was primarily concerned with such situations, effective demand, rather than notional demand, is a central concept in Keynesian analysis.

The problem remains, however, as to the source of this disequilibrium. We have analyzed the effective demand for goods on the assumption that the actual supply of labor is constrained by the effective demand for labor to be less than the notional supply. We have analyzed the labor market by assuming that firms' actual supply of goods is constrained by the effective demand for goods to be less than the notional supply. The question is why these constraints exist. We turn to consider it in the following section.

13.2 PRICE AND QUANTITY FLEXIBILITY

Leijonhufvud (1968) and others argue that the significance of effective demand functions in Keynesian analysis and their insignificance—their equivalence to notional demands—in Walrasian analysis stems from differences in assumptions concerning price flexibility. In the analysis of market equilibrium, we may assume either that disequilibrium causes prices to react instantaneously to eradicate it or that quantities react more quickly than prices. The former, it is argued, is the Walrasian assumption and the latter is the Keynesian assumption. Moreover, the Keynesian assumption is thought to be more realistic.

To see the distinction in general terms, let us begin by considering Figure 13.4. It represents the market for any good, x. The vertical axis measures the money price of that good; the horizontal axis measures quantity. The demand and supply curves represent notional demand and supply, given the money prices of all other goods. Suppose that initially the demand and supply curves are those labeled superscript 1 and the price is at its equilibrium level, p^1. Now, for some reason, demand declines so that the demand curve is $x^{D2}x^{D2}$. In consequence, excess supply of AB exists at the initial price. Pure Walrasian analysis assumes that this excess supply causes a fall in price so that it "instantaneously" reaches its new equilibrium level, p^2. At that price, excess supply no longer exists. We could, alternatively, make the extreme assumption that the price is rigid at p^1. The shift of the notional demand curve to $x^{D2}x^{D2}$ then gives rise to a notional excess supply that is not eradicated by a

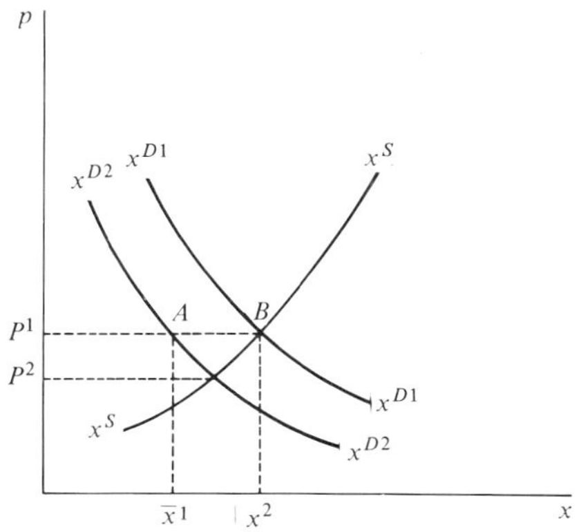

Figure 13-4

price fall. Instead of price changing, quantities change. The amount sold, *actual* supply, falls short of the notional planned supply. It equals $\bar{x}^1$ instead of x^2. (All this reasoning is based on the simplifying assumption—not employed in a full Walrasian general equilibrium model—that prices in other markets are constant.)

Thus, we can make a sharp distinction between models where prices adjust most quickly in response to equilibrium and those where quantities adjust most quickly. In the Walrasian model, prices are assumed to adjust instantaneously, but it is worth elaborating this concept. In Chapter 4 (Section 4.2) we introduced the idea, developed by Walras (1954), of an auctioneer who oversees a process of *tatonnement* or groping toward a set of equilibrium prices. In its pure form this involves the auctioneer's calling out a set of prices and traders' giving notice of how much of each good they would like to buy and sell at these prices. If these demands and supplies do not match each other, the prices were disequilibrium prices and no trades take place, and in calling out the next set of prices the auctioneer adjusts them upward and downward (for goods in excess demand and excess supply respectively). The process is repeated until an equilibrium price set is found. In a modified form the same results can be achieved by supposing that the traders negotiate conditional contracts between themselves but abide by them only if the prices at which they were negotiated turn out to be equilibrium prices.

Such a *tatonnement* or recontracting process appears to take time, so at first sight it seems that equilibrium prices are not reached *instantaneously* in the Walrasian model. But the important point is that in the Walrasian market model, no actual purchases or sales take place during this process. Goods are bought and sold only when the equilibrium price is found, and none occurs at disequilibrium prices. Thus, the time that elapses during the *tatonnement* process is not real economic time: the Walrasian assumption is formally the same as the assumption that prices adjust instantaneously. If, on the other hand, we assume that trade occurs at the disequilibrium price, p^1, then we are assuming that prices do in a meaningful sense take time to adjust. The distinct

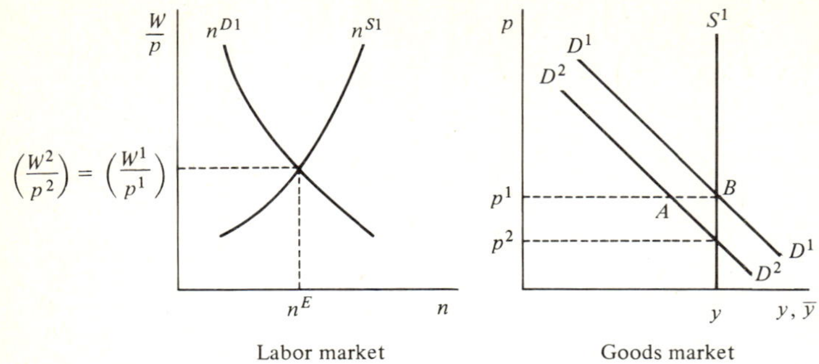

Figure 13-5

and important aspect of the assumption that trade occurs at p^1 is not that the price is absolutely rigid—that condition is assumed for simplicity alone—but that trades are made at disequilibrium prices. Even if the price does decline toward p^2, in a non-Walrasian model trade occurs before it reaches p^2. Thus in Walrasian models prices adjust quickly (effectively instantaneously), while in non-Walrasian models trade occurs at disequilibrium prices, and that implies that changes in quantities are significant sources of adjustment.

Now consider the significance of the distinction between instantaneous price adjustment and disequilibrium trading in a two-market model that has a direct relevance to macroeconomics. Figure 13.5 shows notional demands and supplies in the labor and goods markets.[6] The notional demand for and notional supply of labor are functions of the real wage. The equilibrium amount of labor, n^*, determines the notional supply of goods, y, in the goods market (via the production function, as in Chapter 8). The notional demand for goods is a function of the absolute price level among other things. The fact that the demand curve for goods slopes downward with respect to the price level reflects the operation of the real balance effect or Pigou Effect: a fall in the price level increases the aggregate demand for goods. We shall make the Walrasian assumption that prices adjust instantaneously to excess demands and supplies, and we shall assume for simplicity that disequilibrium in either market affects only one price variable. Excess supply in the goods market causes a fall in the absolute price level, the money price of goods; excess supply in the labor market causes a fall in nominal wages, W, the money price of labor.

Suppose that initially the curves are those with superscript 1. Equilibrium exists at the price level p^1 and money wage W^1 (real wage W^1/p^1). Now suppose that the demand for goods declines because of a change in con-

[6]In the goods market we shall assume that there is no distinction between consumption goods and capital goods. We shall assume investment demand to be constant and analyze only changes in consumption demand.

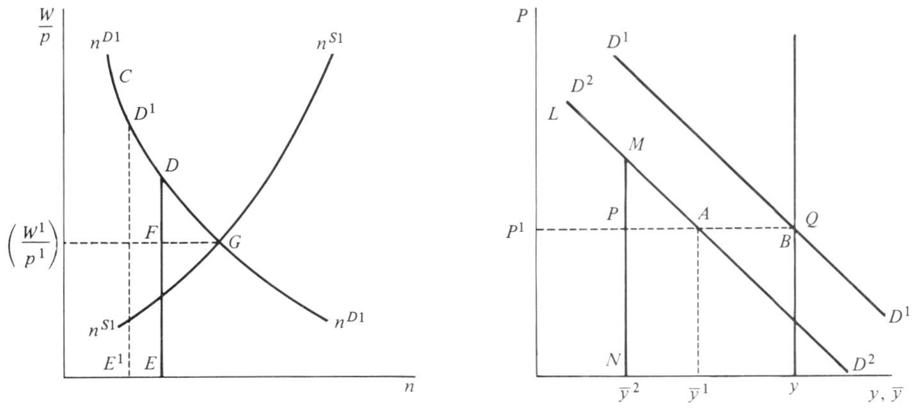

Figure 13-6

sumers' tastes. That is, the notional demand curve in the goods market shifts to D^2D^2. At the price level, p^1, excess supply of AB then exists in the goods market. Our Walrasian assumptions, however, imply that the price level instantaneously declines, so that goods market equilibrium is reestablished at the full-employment level of income, y, and with the lower price level, p^2. This change in the price level, of course, requires some adjustment in the labor market, for if money wages remained at W^1, real wages at W^1/p^2 would be higher than the equilibrium level, W^1/p^1, and there would be excess supply of labor. The Walrasian assumptions imply that this excess supply of labor instantaneously causes a fall in the money wage rate to W^2, so that W^2/p^2 equals W^1/p^1 and equilibrium in the labor market is maintained. Thus, assuming instantaneous price flexibility, excess supplies of goods and labor do not exist, and full employment is maintained. Effective demands, therefore, are the same as notional demands since no one is constrained by inability to realize her or his notional supplies.

Figure 13.6, however, illustrates the process that would occur if there were not instantaneous price adjustment and as a result trade takes place at disequilibrium prices. Specifically, it is constructed on the extreme assumption that prices are rigid. With the notional supply curve of y and the notional demand curve of D^1D^1, equilibrium in the goods market is established with the absolute price level, p^1. With the notional demand and supply curves, $n^{D1}n^{D1}$, $n^{S1}n^{S1}$, in the labor market equilibrium is established with the money wage, W^1 (real wage W^1/p^1). Again assume that a shift in consumer tastes causes the notional demand curve for goods to shift to D^2D^2, so that excess supply of AB exists in the goods market. Since this is not instantaneously eradicated by a fall in the price level that causes, through the Pigou Effect, a rise in the demand for goods, the excess supply in the goods market has an effect on the labor market. Firms find that they cannot sell their notional planned supply of goods with the price level stuck at p^1. Therefore, their effective demand for labor becomes *CDE* in the labor market figure. In the labor market there is, then, an excess of (notional) supply over (effective) demand of *FG*. Unemployment exists to this extent. Moreover, if money wages are rigid, this unemployment will continue to exist, since real wages will not decline to eradicate the excess supply of labor. Indeed, as we shall see, unemployment will, in fact, worsen.

There is, therefore, a substantial difference between Walrasian models where instantaneous price flexibility is assumed and models where price rigidity is assumed. Two important tasks remain. First, we must examine the relevance of the rigid-price model to the concept of the multiplier. Second, we must show explicitly that the conclusions of the rigid-price model do not arise from the assumption of complete price rigidity but from the assumption that trade occurs at disequilibrium prices (that is, at prices that may be moving toward equilibrium but are not at it).

The initial fall in the notional demand curve gives rise in the rigid-price model to a Keynesian multiplier. We have left Figure 13.6 at the point where actual sales are $\bar{y}^1$ and less than the full-employment supply of goods y. This, as we have seen, leads to an excess supply of labor, but that is not the end of the matter. The excess supply of labor means that workers cannot in fact sell their notional planned supply of labor. In consequence, their effective demand for goods falls below their notional demand. In Figure 13.6 the resulting effective demand in the goods market is represented by *LMN*, and the excess of (notional) supply over (effective) demand for goods at the price level p^1 increases to *PQ*. As a result, firms can now sell only $\bar{y}^2$ of goods instead of $\bar{y}^1$, and this decrease has an effect on the labor market, decreasing the effective demand curve for labor from *CDE* to CD^1E^1. Mutual interaction between the goods and labor markets ensures that this process continues still further, an event that is exactly implied by the Keynesian multiplier process.[7]

This multiplier process in the rigid-price model illustrates the view of Leijonhufvud and Clower that in such a model there is a "deviation-amplifying feedback-loop." A disturbance such as the initial fall in notional demands for goods sets up a process that magnifies the deviation from full employment. In the Walrasian flexible-price model of Figure 13.5, by contrast, instantaneous price changes act as a "deviation-counteracting feedback-mechanism" and ensure that disturbances from full-employment equilibrium are corrected.

We now turn to the important qualification to the above analysis. The differences in results between the flexible- and rigid-price models occur not

[7]One may ask whether the model will finally settle down with given effective demand curves and a particular level of output and employment. As in the usual multiplier analysis, it will do so if the marginal propensity to consume is less than 1. For then each decline in the effective demand for labor causes a less-than-proportionate decline in the effective demand for goods, so that the leftward shifts of the effective demand curves in the labor and goods markets become successively smaller.

because of complete price rigidity in the latter model.[8] They appear because prices are not so flexible as to adjust instantaneously to their equilibrium levels. In other words, trading does occur at disequilibrium prices, so that capitalists selling goods and workers selling labor find that they cannot sell all they desire to sell. This limitation affects the constraint on their decisions so that their effective demands are less than their notional demands. As an interpretation of reality, this gives the non-Walrasian model great appeal, since trading does, in reality, occur at disequilibrium prices. As an interpretation of Keynes's work, it implies that his conclusion that unemployment may exist is not founded on an assumption of price rigidity (rigidity of money wages, for example), but on an assumption that prices do not *instantaneously* adjust to their equilibrium levels. In the following section we consider the specifically Keynesian hypotheses and others that have been invoked as explanations of relative price inflexibility.

13.3 SOURCE OF NONINSTANTANEOUS PRICE ADJUSTMENT

The relevance to the concepts of effective demand and involuntary unemployment of noninstantaneous price adjustment was demonstrated in Section 13.2 in the context of a two-market model. More generally, it could be demonstrated in an n market model that if the $(n - 1)$ relative prices do not instantaneously adjust to their equilibrium levels, effective demands (and supplies) will differ from notional demands (and supplies), and excess supply in any market (such as unemployment in the labor market) has a Keynesian interpretation.

A Keynesian model, for example, can be built with four markets, those for labor, goods, money, and bonds. Such a model has three relative prices: those in terms of money or labor (money wages), goods (the absolute price level), and bonds (the reciprocal of the interest rate). Leijonhufvud (1968) argues that Keynes's own model, in fact, had *five* markets, since the market for goods was dichotomized into the market for consumption goods and the market for capital goods. It therefore has *four* relative prices, since the absolute price level is replaced by the two price levels, that of consumption goods and that of capital goods. In a Keynesian model of either type, the problem to be considered now is why any of the four or five prices fail to adjust instantaneously to equilibrium.

Labor Market Search Behavior

We may begin with the problem of price adjustment in the market for labor and the market for consumption goods. First consider the essential implication of the fact that Walras's auctioneer does not really exist. The

[8] Although in much New Keynesian work complete rigidity is assumed for simplicity.

auctioneer's role in the Walrasian model is essentially to provide all individuals with *information* that is instantaneously updated and is *costless*. That is, the auctioneer provides information on the set of prices that would permit equilibrium and the realization of all individuals' (notional) plans. The auctioneer's absence from reality implies that real individuals can obtain information about equilibrium prices only through a costly and time-consuming process. They will therefore not adjust prices instantaneously to their equilibrium levels if there is a deviation from equilibrium.

The nature of the market behavior of individuals in situations where information is not costlessly and instantaneously available has been analyzed by Alchian (1969) and others. Alchian argues with reference to the labor market, for example, that if workers lose their jobs they will not immediately take new ones at a lower wage even though this lower wage may be one permitting the equilibrium of the labor market. The reason is that workers do not know what the best wages that they can get are, and they will therefore not immediately accept any new job; they will spend time searching for information about wages available. Search has benefits, since the greater is the time spent searching, the greater is the probability of obtaining accurate knowledge of the highest available wage. It also has costs, since the greater the time spent searching, the greater the amount of earnings forgone. Balancing these benefits and costs at the margin, a utility-maximizing individual will, if becoming unemployed because of a too-high wage rate, choose an optimal search period before accepting a job at a lower wage rate. In other words, for a certain period, money wages are inflexible—not absolutely rigid but inflexible for a given period. This is so because, for this period, the supply of labor is highly elastic at the old money wage rate; workers choose to withdraw their labor temporarily and to engage in search, rather than immediately accept a lower wage rate.

This model of the labor market is illustrated in Figure 13.7. The notional demand and supply for labor are functions of the real wage, but we have drawn the figure with the money wage rate on the vertical axis. Therefore, $n^D n^D$, $n^{S1} n^{S1}$, and $n^{S2} n^{S2}$ are notional demand and supply curves whose posi-

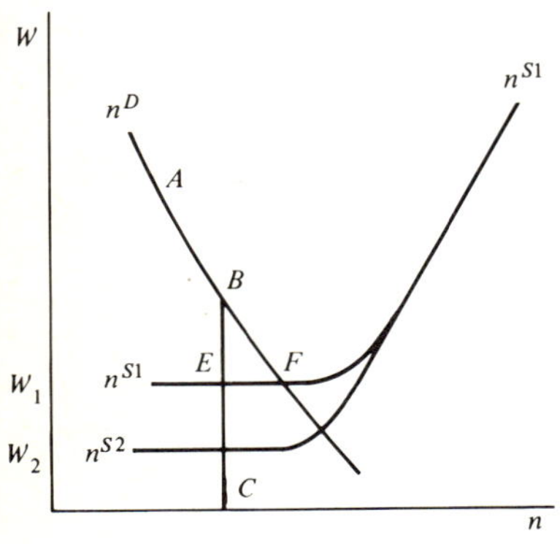

Figure 13-7

tions depend on the price level; if the price level were higher, the demand curve would be higher and further to the right; also, the supply curve would be higher and further to the left, since a given level of money wages would then involve lower real wages. In our use of the figure we shall assume the price level to be constant. We have drawn the diagram with money rather than real wages on the axis to highlight the assumption that wage negotiations take place with money wages as their direct object. Money wages are to be initially at W_1 and equilibrium is established at F, the intersection of the notional demand and supply curves, $n^D n^D$ and $n^{S1} n^{S1}$. A disturbance in the goods market then causes firms to find that they cannot sell their optimum output; so the effective demand for labor falls, as represented by the effective demand curve ABC. Jobs (or working hours), to the extent EF, are lost, but this loss does not cause money wages or, therefore, real wages to fall. Money wages remain at W_1 as workers spend time searching for information rather than accept jobs at lower wages. Thus money wages are sticky. They are not absolutely rigid, as is postulated by the Neoclassical/Keynesian Synthesis explanation of unemployment. (See Chapter 8.) Instead, they tend to move in a downward direction. As workers conclude their search periods, the horizontal part of the labor supply curve shifts downward so that the supply curve shifts to one like $n^{S2} n^{S2}$ and the nominal wage rate falls to W_2. The point is, however, that money and real wages do not adjust instantaneously in response to a fall in demand. The reason for this relative inflexibility is that information is costly and obtaining it is time-consuming in the absence of a Walrasian auctioneer.

An analysis of the stickiness of goods prices could be developed along similar lines for a world where information is not perfect. But the stickiness of goods prices is particularly interesting in the New Keynesian models when we consider the price of *capital* goods. For these, more than consumer goods, are influenced not only by imperfect information about the present but also by imperfect information about the *future*, since the yield of capital goods is a future yield. This imperfect information about the future is compounded by, and inextricably bound up with, the money and bond markets in the New Keynesian models. In other words, Keynes's theory of speculative demand or liquidity preference is seen as being crucial to the relative stickiness of capital goods prices. Indeed, Leijonhufvud (1968) argues that liquidity preference, rather than stickiness of money wage rates, is central to Keynes's analysis of unemployment.

Liquidity Preference

To consider the stickiness of capital goods prices, it is necessary to understand the theory of price determination in the capital goods market. Figure 13.8 illustrates one such model based on the concepts of stocks and flows used by Witte (1963). The left-hand figure illustrates the demand and supply curves for a stock of capital at a point of time. The supply curve is

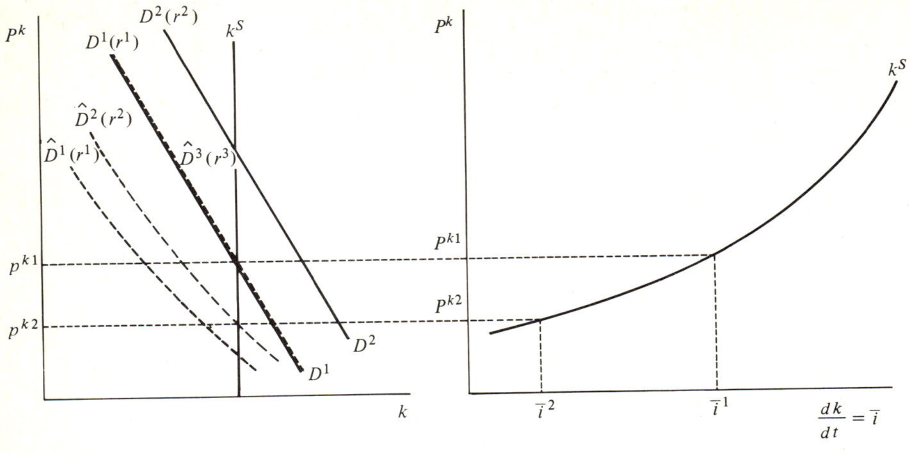

Figure 13-8

vertical, k^S, since it is assumed that at any instant the stock of capital goods is given. The demand curve is downward-sloping, indicating that firms' desired holdings of stocks of physical capital at any instant are higher, the lower is the price of capital goods, p^k. There are several demand curves. Restricting attention to those drawn as solid lines, the lower is the rate of interest, the higher is the demand curve; the demand curve D^1D^1 exists at the interest rate r^1, and the curve D^2D^2 exists at the lower rate r^2. The rationale for this relationship is that the interest rate determines the discount rate applied to expected future income streams. Given expectations of the income derived from capital goods, the demand for capital goods at a given price will be greater, the lower is the interest (and discount) rate.

Given the demand and supply curves in the left-hand figure, the (stock) equilibrium price of capital goods is determined. If the rate of interest is r^1 the demand curve is D^1D^1, and the equilibrium price is p^{k1}. The right-hand diagram illustrates the flow supply curve of capital goods; the higher is the price of capital goods, the greater will be the rate of production of capital goods per period. Since the rate of increase of capital goods is the same thing as aggregate actual investment, the figure implies that investment is a function of the price of capital goods. But as the left-hand diagram shows, the price of capital goods is itself a function of the interest rate, since the latter determines the demand curve *ceteris paribus*. It follows that the rate of investment is a function of the interest rate.

The model represented by Figure 13.8 implies that there is one rate of interest and price of capital goods that ensures that investment is at the level required for full-employment general equilibrium. Suppose that the amount of planned investment that would equal planned saving at full employment is i^1. This would imply that the full-employment equilibrium price of capital goods is p^{k1}, and (ignoring the dashed-line demand curves) the full-employment equilibrium interest rate is r^1. Suppose that these levels of i, k^D, and r are the existing ones and that prices in other markets are "right"—the economy is at full-employment equilibrium. Then capitalists' expectations become more pessimistic for some reason. In consequence, the demand curves for capital goods at any given interest rate shift downward to those drawn with dashed lines. If the rate of investment is to be maintained at i^1, the price of capital goods must be maintained at p^{k1}, and this requires that the interest rate should fall to r^3. At r^3 the new demand curve reflecting pessimism is $\hat{D}^3$, which coincides with the D^1D^1 curve that existed previously at the higher interest rate, r^1. If it falls only to r^2, the price of capital goods will fall from p^{k1} to p^{k2}, and consequently, the rate of increase in the capital stock, the rate of investment, will decline from i^1 to i^2. It will fall below the full-employment level.

The New Keynesians argue that the operation of liquidity preference does, in fact, prevent the interest rate from falling instantaneously to the level r^3 that would ensure general full-employment equilibrium. The price of capital goods does fall to p^{k2}, at least temporarily. The reason lies in the theory of the speculative demand for money. As the interest rate falls, individuals expect that it will in the future rise again toward its "normal" level. They therefore increase their holdings of money balances and decrease their holdings of bonds. In this way, a cushion is provided to the fall in the interest rate, since the sales of bonds exert a downward pressure on bond prices. In the extreme case of a liquidity trap, this cushion becomes absolute: the interest rate and price of capital goods get stuck at r^2 and p^{k2}. But the New Keynesians are not concerned with extreme cases, such as the liquidity trap, alone. As long as the rate of interest does not fall instantaneously to r^3, as long as p^k does not instantaneously readjust to p^{k1}, the buying and selling of capital goods occur at disequilibrium prices, such as p^{k2}. Among other things, the existence of a speculative demand for money ensures that in fact the interest rate does not fully and instantaneously adjust to r^3.

The analysis of the behavior of the price of capital goods—its failure to adjust instantaneously to the full-employment equilibrium level—is central to Leijonhufvud's New Keynesian analysis. As long as investment occurs with the price of capital goods at p^{k2}, there will be excess supply in the markets for goods. Investment at $\bar{i}^2$ is lower than the notional planned saving that consumers wish to do at full employment (lower, that is, than $\bar{i}^1$). Saving, in some theories, represents a demand for future goods while investment determines the future supply of goods. Therefore, a disequilibrium price of capital goods, such as p^{k2}, can be thought of as causing an excess demand for future goods concomitant with the excess supply of present goods. Leijonhufvud (1968) and Davidson (1972) argue that it occurs because individuals do not have perfect knowledge of future demands and supplies but base their actions on imperfect knowledge of the future. Capitalists' expectations are uncertain and volatile; therefore, demand curves for capital goods shift leftward initially. Individuals have particular expectations of what the interest rate should be, and these views on the normal rate are based on past experience rather than on accurate knowledge of the future. These views then cause the demand for money and bonds to be such as to prevent the interest rate from falling sufficiently.

The relative inflexibility of the price of capital goods can, therefore, be attributed to the role of imperfect knowledge. The analysis, discussed earlier, of the failure of money wages to adjust instantaneously can also be interpreted in terms of expectations and imperfect information; given imperfect information about the labor market, workers do not instantaneously adjust their expectations of the obtainable money wage.

We can therefore state the essence of the new Keynesian analysis as follows: As long as prices do not adjust instantaneously to their equilibrium levels, effective demand will differ from notional demand and will reinforce the deviation of output, employment, and other quantities from their full-employment equilibrium level. The reason why, in reality, prices do not adjust instantaneously to equilibrium levels lies in the existence of imperfect information and imperfect expectations. Indeed, expectations can at times cause complete rigidity of prices (as in the hypothesis of the liquidity trap), but such complete rigidity is not a necessary assumption for the analysis of disequilibrium.

13.4 NEW KEYNESIANISM AND THE THEORY OF UNEMPLOYMENT

It will be recalled from Chapters 8 and 12 that the models of the Neoclassical/Keynesian Synthesis treat Keynesian unemployment as existing at equilibrium positions. Unemployment equilibrium is then explained as the result of one of three rigidities—complete downward rigidity of money wages, complete downward rigidity of the interest rate (the liquidity trap), or inelasticity of the investment function.[9] The New Keynesians, and particularly Leijonhufvud, treat unemployment as a disequiilibrium problem. It stems not from complete rigidity of money wage rates or the interest rate, but from the fact that they and other prices do not adjust instantaneously to their equilibrium levels. Quantities—effective demands and supplies—adjust more quickly than prices. This absence of instantaneous price adjustment is seen as the fundamental characteristic of Keynes's work. In particular, it is argued that Keynes emphasized the role of expectations and imperfect information in preventing prices from instantaneously adjusting to their equilibrium levels. In Leijonhufvud's interpretation, expectations in the markets for bonds and capital goods are seen as being of particular importance as the source of general disequilibrium.

[9]The inelasticity of the investment function can also be seen as a problem of complete rigidity of the interest rate. As we saw in Chap. 8, the problem of an inelastic investment function stems from the fact that the interest rate is assumed to be downwardly rigid at zero—that it cannot be negative.

The question to be considered now is whether this New Keynesianism is fundamentally distinct from the Neoclassical/Keynesian Synthesis model. One interpretation is that there is only a marginal difference between the two models. The New Keynesianism, like the Synthesis or even more so, emphasizes the importance of deriving macroeconomic theories from theories of individual utility maximization and profit maximization. Unlike the Synthesis model, it makes clear the nature of the constraints that individuals and firms face and thereby elucidates the basis of the theory that consumption is a function of actual income and the demand for labor is determined by conditions in the goods market. But this can be seen as merely filling a hole in the theories of the Synthesis school, for its writers have always accepted the fact that consumption is a function of actual income and the demand for labor is a derived demand. What they failed to do was merely to elaborate the underlying model of constrained utility maximization behind these macroeconomic theories.

Another interpretation is that the absence of a theory of constrained utility maximization from the Synthesis model renders the model fundamentally inconsistent and prevents the development of Keynesian theory. The absence of a theoretical basis for constrained utility maximization causes the Synthesis model to overlook the significance of expectations, imperfect information, and therefore of noninstantaneous price adjustment. A work such as Patinkin (1965) is based upon Walrasian assumptions of price flexibility without seeing that they are inconsistent with the Keynesian consumption function and Keynesian ideas of the demand for labor. Since unemployment equilibrium can be explained in such models only by the special assumptions of wage or interest rigidity, the Keynesian theory of unemployment appears as a special case of the Neoclassical theory of full employment. The New Keynesians reverse the ordering; the fact that, in reality, prices do not in general adjust instantaneously without being absolutely rigid implies that the New Keynesians' unemployment disequilibrium (or disequilibrium with excess demand for labor) is the general case and that Walrasian full-employment equilibrium is the special case.

If one accepts the view that the New Keynesians have established a fundamentally more satisfactory basis for macroeconomic theory, it remains true that several problems in its analysis have yet to be settled. For one thing, the theory of search behavior in the labor market developed by Alchian (1969) presents problems for the concept of involuntary unemployment and constrained utility maximization. It implies that the temporary rigidity of money wages results from workers' own decision to temporarily withdraw their labor in order to search. Therefore, the fact that their income is thereby reduced cannot be seen as an exogenous constraint on their consumption demand, as it is in Clower's dual-decision hypothesis. Another problem is that since the New Keynesianism rests so heavily on the fact that prices do not adjust instantaneously in the absence of a Walrasian auctioneer, it requires a theory of how prices in all markets are determined. As Arrow (1959), Grandmont and

Laroque (1974), and others have argued, if there is not general equilibrium, individuals and firms cannot be regarded as facing given market-determined prices. Individuals and firms have the power to affect prices, but the exact process of price adjustment in complex markets still requires analysis. Finally, there is the problem of whether the New Keynesianism involves a fundamental revision of the theory of money and of money's role in the economy. This is the question to which we turn in Chapter 14.

CHAPTER

FOURTEEN

MONEY AND NON-WALRASIAN ECONOMIES

The New Keynesians' development of the theory of general disequilibrium in a non-Walrasian model is paralleled by developments in the theory of money. One question that arises is whether, in a monetary economy, Walras' Law is valid when the effective demands for goods and labor are less than notional demands. In other words, if there is an excess of supply over effective demand in those markets, is there necessarily an excess demand for money? Related to this is the question of whether the existence of money as a Medium of Exchange is at the root of general disequilibrium and involuntary unemployment.

These questions concerning the role of money in the operation of a monetary economy are examined in Section 14.1. In Section 14.2 we explore a more fundamental question: that of why money exists. What is the reason for a monetary, rather than a barter, economy existing? We shall see that this question can be considered only when we abandon the assumption that the economy has a Walrasian structure.

14.1 MONEY AND GENERAL DISEQUILIBRIUM IN A MONETARY ECONOMY

In the Neoclassical/Keynesian Synthesis, the most general models analyze money as being essentially the same as any other commodity. There are n goods in the economy, each with its own market (or excess demand equation). In addition, there is a market, the $(n + 1)$st, that is the market for money. The excess demand for money is related to the excess demands for the n goods through Walras' Law and therefore has the same properties as the excess demand for any good. The question to which we now turn is whether Walras' Law is valid in a model with general disequilibrium. We shall find that a model of general disequilibrium can be built where a form of Walras' Law holds. We shall then turn to consider whether, despite this, money does in some sense have a special role to play in general disequilibrium.

Recall from Chapter 4 that Walras' Law is defined as a relationship between the planned excess demands, the excess of planned demand over planned supply, in the $(n + 1)$ markets of the economy, including the market for money:

$$\sum_{i=1}^{n+1} p_i x_i^{XD} \equiv \sum_{i=1}^{n+1} p_i(x_i^D - x_i^S) \equiv 0 \tag{14.1}$$

The demands and supplies to which Walras' Law relates are planned, *ex ante* demand and supply rather than actual sales and purchases. The problem raised by the New Keynesians' elaboration of demand concepts in conditions of disequilibrium is the following: Should the planned demand and supply in Walras' Law be *effective* demand and supply or *notional* variables? Is Walras' Law valid under all conditions irrespective of whether planned demand is defined as effective or notional?

The discussion of this question was initiated by Clower (1965), who argued that Walras' Law does not hold in disequilibrium. With excess supply in the labor market (unemployment), the sum of *effective* excess demands will be less than zero. The effective demand by firms for labor will be less than supply, and the effective demand by workers for goods will be less than supply. Leijonhufvud (1968) points out that Clower reached this conclusion because of the particular view that is taken of the demand for money. If, instead, we note that workers offer to supply labor in return for money and that firms' supply of goods is an offer of goods in return for money, excess supply in the goods and labor markets is matched by excess demand for money. A formulation in these terms is derived by Tucker (1971). In a model with four markets—for labor, goods, bonds, and money—Tucker argues that Walras' Law is obeyed if we formulate the money market and the three other markets in terms of effective excess demand. That is, if there is excess supply in all markets except that for money, we should interpret the x_i^D variables in Equation 14.1, planned demand, as *effective* demand rather than notional demand. If, in the markets for goods, labor, and bonds, there is an excess of notional supply over effective demand, then there will be an excess effective demand for money.

By this device Walras' Law is satisfied, but it appears at first sight that money has been robbed of any special significance. The excess demand for money is merely a reflection of the excess demands for other goods in the same way that excess demand on any of the $(n + 1)$ markets is a reflection of excess demands on the remaining n markets. This is always the case when Walras' Law holds, but it does not in fact imply that money is the same as any other commodity. In particular, it does not prevent our making the assumption that money has the special property of being exchangeable for all goods, whereas goods do not exchange for goods—the assumption that, as we saw in Chapter 1, is fundamental to Clower's description of a monetary economy. Indeed, this assumption can be thought of as the rationale for the validity of Walras' Law formulated in terms of effective demands. As Tucker (1971) argues, the fact that money is the Medium of Exchange means that no special market institution exists for trading in money. There are shops and other institutions for trading in goods, employment offices for trading in labor, and stock exchanges for trading in bonds. But there is no special institution for trading in money. Instead, an effective demand for money can be expressed only by offering to supply goods, labor, or bonds on their markets. Therefore, an effective excess supply in those markets must involve directly an effective excess demand for money—Walras' Law is satisfied.

The fact that money has this special property of being the Medium of Exchange leads some New Keynesians to argue that its existence is fundamental to the existence of involuntary unemployment and general disequilibrium. We saw in Chapter 13 that the source of general disequilibrium may be perceived as a lack of perfect information that prevents instantaneous price adjustment. Leijonhufvud (1968) and Benassy (1975a) argue that this lack of information arises from the fact that goods do not exchange for goods—that money acts as the Medium of Exchange. A graphic example is the case of unemployed workers offering to work for employers who are themselves constrained by actual sales lower than their planned supply of goods. An omniscient planner may know that the workers' extra income, if employed, would increase their effective demand sufficiently to enable an employer to sell all the extra output produced by them and thereby to increase profits. In the absence of such a planner, how can the employer gain this information? The workers do not offer to work in return for the employers' production of goods; they offer to work for money and employers have no way of knowing whether, by increasing their labor force and wage bill—their payments of money—their sales will increase sufficiently to compensate them for their increased wage bill. The workers employed by one firm may spend the money on other firms' goods—and probably will. In consequence, firms will not hire the unemployed workers for although the truth is that an increase in employment would by assumption, improve firms' profits and workers' utility, there is no way in which this information is conveyed. The fact that exchange takes place through money prevents this information from being conveyed and ensures that the exchange of labor for money will not occur.

Conditions for Exchange

The demonstration of this fact by Benassy (1975a) formally establishes the point. Assume that there are three markets, a market for labor, a market for the single (consumption) good, and a market for money.[1] Workers supply labor for money and demand goods for money, firms supply goods and demand labor for money. Benassy establishes the conditions under which workers and firms will be willing to engage in exchange. Workers will be willing to sell labor for money if, for them

$$\frac{\alpha_m}{p_m} - \frac{\alpha_n}{p_n} > 0 \tag{14.2}$$

and firms will be willing to buy labor for money if, for them

$$\frac{\alpha_n}{p_n} - \frac{\alpha_m}{p_m} > 0 \tag{14.3}$$

To use these conditions, we must explain the notation. The subscript n refers to labor, the subscript m refers to money, and we shall employ subscript c for the consumption good. The variable p_m is the price of money (defined as 1), and p_n is the price of labor, which is assumed to be positive.

The variables α are unusual. They are measures of excess (effective) demand or supply. If, for example, a worker's actual sales of labor are less than that person's planned (effective) supply, α_n is defined as negative for that worker. Similarly, if a firm's actual sales of goods are less than its (effective) supply, α_c will be negative for it. If a worker's (effective) demand for goods is equal to the amount actually purchased, this α_c will be zero. Similarly, if a firm's (effective) demand for labor is equal to the amount it actually purchases, its α_n will be zero. As we saw in Chapter 13, the New Keynesians' analysis of unemployment implies that for workers:

$\alpha_n < 0$ (they sell less labor than they wish)

$\alpha_c = 0$ (they can buy all the goods they demand, so that their effective demand is satisfied)

We may therefore assume that, for workers:

$$\alpha_m > 0$$

In other words, they obtain less money than they demand, since their offer of labor in return for money is not fully realized. For firms:

$\alpha_n = 0$ (they can buy all the goods they demand, so that their effective demand is satisfied)

$\alpha_c < 0$ (they sell less goods than they wish)

and:

$$\alpha_m > 0$$

[1]The market for money need not be conceived as a specific institution but merely as the existence of a demand for, and supply of, money. We shall assume that an individual's excess demand for money is the negative of the sum of his or her excess demands on the other markets, although Benassy does not make this assumption.

since they obtain less money than they desire to obtain in return for their goods.

If we insert these values for workers' and firms' α's into Equations 14.2 and 14.3, we find that the conditions expressed by Equation 14.3 are not satisfied. In other words, the conditions for firms to be willing to hire labor are not satisfied. Thus, the expression in Equation 14.2 for workers has the following signs:

$$\frac{\alpha_m}{p_m} - \frac{\alpha_n}{p_n} = (+) - (-) = +$$

so that workers are willing to sell labor for money. The expression in Equation 14.3 for firms has the signs:

$$\frac{\alpha_n}{p_n} - \frac{\alpha_m}{p_m} = (0) - (+) = -$$

so that firms are not willing to buy labor for money, since the expression is not positive, as required by equation 14.3.

This type of analysis lies behind the assertion that the existence of money, the fact that exchanges can take place only through the Medium of Exchange, is a condition for the existence of unemployment. If workers could engage in barter and sell labor to firms directly for the consumption good produced by them, then both workers and firms would be willing to engage in trade. For workers, the condition for them to be willing to sell labor for goods is:

$$\frac{\alpha_c}{p_c} - \frac{\alpha_n}{p_n} > 0 \qquad (14.4)$$

and this is satisfied if there is unemployment, since α_c then is zero and α_n is negative for them. For firms, the condition for them to be willing to buy labor for goods is:

$$\frac{\alpha_n}{p_n} - \frac{\alpha_c}{p_c} > 0 \qquad (14.5)$$

this condition is satisfied if there is unemployment, since for them α_n is zero and α_c is negative. Thus, with unemployment, firms would in this simple example of barter be willing to take on extra labor and unemployment would be eliminated.

It can be seen, then, that the existence of money can be thought to lie at the root of unemployment. The fact that exchange takes place through money prevents firms from obtaining the information that if they employed more labor, their sales of the consumption good would increase.

Role of Decentralized Decisions

However, this does not imply that a nonmonetary, barter economy necessarily ensures that the unemployed workers are hired. The argument of the last paragraph indicates that barter will ensure this, but the concept of barter which is used, the direct trade of labor for the single consumption good, defines a much simplified form of barter that would not occur in a complex economy. In an economy where there is more than one good and individual firms specialize in production, workers cannot merely exchange their labor for the good produced by the firm employing them. If they were to do this, they could do so only with the idea that they would then exchange some of their receipts of the good for the other goods they desire. But in the absence of perfect information, the workers do not, at the time of selling their labor for the one good, know whether they will be able to carry out these secondary exchanges at a given set of prices. They may find that the good with which they have been paid is in excess supply so that they cannot exchange it to the desired extent for other goods. Given that risk, the workers will not be willing to exchange labor for the good produced by a potential employer. Abolition of money and reversion to indirect barter will not increase the amount of labor employed.[2]

It is not the case, therefore, that employment bargains that are concluded in terms of money are the source of unemployment. The existence of money, the Medium of Exchange, entails a failure of information, but similar failures are not excluded in a complex barter system. This raises the question of whether the New Keynesians have demonstrated that Keynesian involuntary unemployment is a monetary phenomenon. One argument supporting this interpretation of their work is that Leijonhufvud, as we saw in Chapter 13, makes the demand function for money central to his explanation of why prices do not instantaneously adjust to their equilibrium levels. In his view, the interest elasticity of the demand for money prevents the instantaneous adjustment of the price of capital goods to its full-employment equilibrium level, and this, rather than the relative inflexibility of other prices, is the most fundamental example of noninstantaneous adjustment.[3] A second argument that could be propounded is that the concept of effective demand and its divergence from notional demand, matters that are central to the analysis of unemployment, cannot be fully developed without taking into account the role of money and credit.

The reason for this is as follows: In Chapter 13 we saw that the New Keynesians' concept of effective demand in a market involves constraints that arise from inability to realize notional supply on another market. For example, the workers' effective demands for consumption goods are lower than their notional demands if they cannot sell their desired supply of labor on the

[2]The same conclusion would be reached if we were to assume the employing firm promises to pay its workers with a varied bundle of consumption goods. The firm would have to hire workers at a given wage on the assumption that it could then exchange the good produced by the workers for goods produced by other firms. This assumption would have to be based on imperfect information and therefore might turn out to be wrong. Firms would be no more willing to buy extra labor than in a monetary economy.

[3]It should be noted, however, that the interest elasticity of the demand for money is significant for the price of capital goods only if the prices of labor and consumption goods fail to instantaneously adjust.

labor markets. Their failure to sell the desired amount of labor affects their budget constraint in the goods market. But that analysis ignores the fact that an individual may be able to borrow money in order to maintain purchasing power at the level it would have been if that individual had been able to sell all the desired supply of labor. If the workers are able to borrow, then their effective demands for goods may be the same as their notional demand. Alternatively, instead of borrowing, an individual may draw upon accumulated money balances. If effective demand for goods is lower than notional demand when income is less than desired income, either there is some constraint on borrowing and on the drawing down of money balances, or the individual's utility function leads to the choice of not borrowing or drawing upon money balances to the full extent necessary to maintain her or his notional demand for goods. Similarly, firms' effective demand for labor is not directly constrained by the proceeds of sales but must also take account of monetary and credit factors. Monetary factors are, therefore, crucial to the concept of effective demand that is at the base of the New Keynesian analysis. This, however, has not always received sufficient prominence in their analysis of effective demand. Leijonhufvud, for example, considers effective damand to be demand subject to an income constraint rather than a constraint of income and money or income and credit.

14.2 THE EXISTENCE OF MONEY

In Chapter 1 we briefly considered the question of why money exists. We are now in a position to investigate it further, for the problem is indirectly related to the work of the New Keynesians. This relationship exists because, as Hahn (1973) argues, the existence of money can be explained only in a model where the Walrasian assumptions do not hold—precisely the type of model with which the New Keynesians are concerned.[4]

We can begin by enumerating the essential features of a simple Walrasian model of a market day. We may then examine how, by dropping one or another of these features, the existence of money can be explained. The first feature of such a model is that real time does not exist. This is so in two senses: Within the market day, all transactions occur at a single instant; and in a simple Walrasian model, we are concerned only with a single market day with trading of existing goods and with no consideration of goods that will exist in the future. The second feature of a simple Walrasian model is that no uncertainty exists; all individuals have certain knowledge of the prices and qualities of goods and of all factors relevant to their tastes. The third feature

[4]However, the New Keynesians are concerned with general *disequilibrium* in a non-Walrasian monetary economy, whereas the modern writers on the existence of money are involved with explaining the existence of a monetary economy and, while they use a non-Walrasian model, they are concerned with general *equilibrium*.

is that there are no transaction costs; in particular, information is costless, so the individual's certain knowledge is obtained for nothing.

The dropping of any one of these Walrasian assumptions does not necessarily enable us to explain the existence of money. In particular, the work of Debreu (1959) demonstrates that we can assume that future goods *are* taken into account by traders and that a type of uncertainty *does* exist, and yet still provide no role for money. The demonstration of this fact involves an elaboration of the concept of a good.

In a simple Walrasian model, goods are differentiated only by their intrinsic characteristics, so that we have x_i, x_j, and so on. All exist at the instant of trade. If we wish to take account of future goods, we must further differentiate goods according to their date. Thus, x_i (say, apples) existing now is $x_{i,t}$, and x_i (apples) existing in the future is $x_{i,\,t+n}$. There are markets in each of these commodities. The market for presently existing perishable goods, $x_{i,t}$, is a spot market; that for future goods, $x_{i,\,t+n}$, is a futures market in which contracts are made for future delivery.

If we wish to take account of uncertainty, we must differentiate commodities still further. Assume that we are uncertain about what the state of the world will be at time $(t + n)$. We do not know, for example, whether the climate will be wet or dry, and let us assume that the good x_i is a raincoat. A raincoat in wet weather is a different good from a raincoat in dry weather, and we may therefore differentiate the future raincoat, $x_{i,\,t+n}$, into two goods: $x_{i,\,t+n,w}$ and $x_{i,\,t+n,\,d}$. The first is the future raincoat when the weather at time $(t + n)$ is wet, the second is the raincoat when it is dry. There are assumed to be markets in each of these contingent goods. An individual who purchases $x_{i,\,t+n,\,w}$, for example, is entering into a future conditional contract. The price, $p_{x_{i,\,t+n,\,w}}$, is paid in return for an offer to deliver a raincoat at time $(t + n)$ if and only if it rains at that time. If it does not rain at time $(t + n)$, the individual will have paid the price but will not receive the raincoat.

Debreu demonstrates than an equilibrium price set for an economy consisting of goods thus differentiated exists. But there is nothing in Debreu's model to prevent all trade from occurring at the first instant of time. All purchases and sales of present goods (spot markets) and future contingent goods (conditional future markets) may take place in one instant. There is, therefore, no reason for money to be held, since transactions are perfectly synchronized although uncertainty is assumed to exist and traders recognize the existence of the future. Money is not required as a Medium of Exchange *within* the market day, since all transactions are synchronized, and it is not required as a Store of Value *from* one market day to a future market day, since decisions about the future are all made on the first day and subsequent markets are unnecessary. Even if we were to postulate that subsequent market days do exist and that money is required as a Store of Value from one to another, this does not, as Hahn (1973) points out, give a rationale for the existence of money, for a sequence of market days is inessential to the model; the assumption that later market days exist is arbitrary.

One way out of this difficulty is to postulate that individuals learn new information over time. This suggestion by Radnor (1968) would give some reason for the existence of a sequence of market days and of money as a Store of Value linking these days. Similarly, if one postulates that on any one market day some conditional futures markets do not exist, so that one cannot at any one instant make all transactions relating to the present and the future, there would be a reason for a sequence of market days and a Store of Value to exist. Hahn (1973) suggests that such incompleteness in the set of markets may result from the existence of setup costs. However, by concentrating on the necessity of replacing the Debreu model with a sequence of market days, such methods merely account for the existence of a Store of Value. There is no reason why that Store of Value should be money rather than bonds or physical capital.

Emergence of Medium of Exchange

As we saw in Chapter 1, the essential feature of money is that it is the Medium of Exchange, whereas other Stores of Value are not. To explain the existence of a Medium of Exchange, we must concentrate on what occurs *within* the market day rather than on the sequence of market days. One line of reasoning that follows this method abandons the third feature of Walrasian models and assumes that exchange is not costless—that transaction costs do exist. Niehans (1971) and others have shown that if there are transactions costs and if these differ from one good to another (or from one pair of goods to another), the existence of money, the Medium of Exchange within the market day, can be explained by postulating that exchanges involving money have the lowest (zero) transactions costs.

Niehans's argument is in terms of analyzing the emergence of a monetary economy out of a barter economy. Suppose that there exists a barter economy with $(n+1)$ goods and that there are $\frac{1}{2}n(n+1)$ trading posts for effecting pairwise exchanges of goods.[5] As Clower (1967, 1969) and others point out, if barter exchange were replaced by monetary exchange so that goods would not exchange for goods but only for money, then there would need only be n trading posts [if one of the $(n+1)$ goods becomes money] and society would have saved resources—the costs of exchange—by using money as a Medium of Exchange. But this does not explain how the monetary economy emerges in the absence of a benevolent dictator who decrees it in order to benefit society. Niehans is concerned with that question. Recognizing that trade takes place between individuals, he explains the emergence of a Medium of Exchange by considering individuals' utility-maximizing behavior when transaction costs exist.

Consider the individual's demand for two of the $(n+1)$ goods, x_i, x_j, in the barter economy. Figure 14.1 shows this person's budget constraint with

[5]See Chap. 1, Sec. 1.1. The expression in the text here differs from that used there only because an economy of $(n+1)$ goods is assumed here, whereas n goods are assumed there.

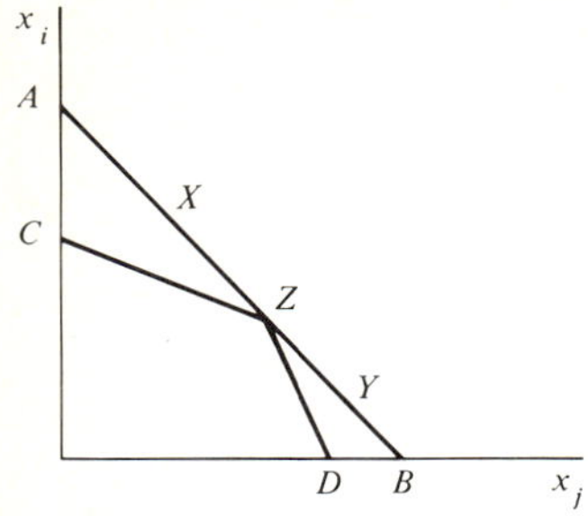

Figure 14-1

respect to the two goods. Their price ratio determines the slope of the line *AB*, and we shall assume that the initial endowment of the two goods is represented by the point *Z*. Although the line *AB* through *Z* indicates the price ratio of the two goods, it does not represent the budget constraint. For we assume that the individual faces transactions costs; when trying to sell x_j for x_j or vice versa, the individual has to forgo some of the initial endowment in order to pay these costs. These may either be direct costs, such as a tax or the cost of physically transporting the goods to the buyer and from the seller, or indirect costs, such as the cost of obtaining information about exchange possibilities. Suppose that these costs are proportional to the amounts of the goods exchanged. Then the individual's budget constraint will be a line such as *CZD*. It is kinked at *Z* because the individual subject to this budget constraint, if maximizing utility at the point *X*, will be choosing to buy good x_i and sell x_j. That is, the individual will exchange some x_j from the endowment *Z* for some x_i. This involves transactions costs, and the same would be true if the individual were to attempt to reach *Y*. Away from *Z*, therefore, the budget line must be below the price line, since transactions costs prevent the individual's consuming the whole endowment. Points such as *X* and *Y* are unattainable. If, however, *Z* were the point on *CZD* that touched the highest attainable indifference curve, the individual would wish to retain the initial endowment and not trade x_i for x_j or vice versa. Therefore, at *Z* the individual would face no transactions costs and could consume the entire endowment.

The fact that the budget line is kinked when transactions costs exist has implications for the possibilities of trading. The exact implications depend on the shape of the indifference map, and Figure 14.2 illustrates the argument for one indifference map. If there were no transactions costs, the budget line would be a straight line, such as *AB*, going through the point *Z* of the initial endowment. The individual would seek to trade x_i for x_j to reach *X*. With a certain level of proportional transactions costs, the budget line *CZD* would exist and the individual would seek to remain at *Z* choosing not to trade and being satisfied with the endowment of x_i and x_j. Thus, if transactions costs exist, the greater is the likelihood that the individual will not wish to exchange the two goods. Moreover, the greater are transactions costs, the lower is the

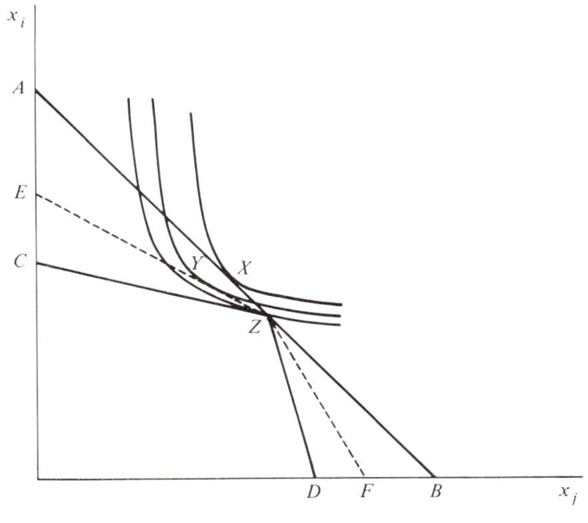

Figure 14-2

desirability of trade. If, for example, transactions costs were lower than those giving rise to *CZD*, the budget line *EZF* would exist and the individual would choose to trade x_i and x_j for each other to reach *Y*.

Niehans assumes that exchanges between some pairs of goods involve higher transactions costs than others. Pairs with higher transactions costs will, *ceteris paribus*, be traded less frequently than other pairs, as we have seen. If we then make some dynamic assumptions concerning the manner in which the frequency of trade affects transactions costs, we can analyze the emergence of one commodity as money or Medium of Exchange. Suppose, for example, that the more frequently a good is involved in exchange, the lower become the transactions costs associated with exchanging it. Now let us assume an initial situation in which one good, x_m, is such that exchanges involving it all have lower transactions costs than exchanges between other pairs of goods. That is, assume that there is an economy with three goods, x_i, x_j, and x_m, so that, for pairwise exchanges, three trading posts are required $(x_m x_i)$, $(x_m x_j)$ and $(x_i x_j)$. The transactions costs on the first two trading posts are assumed to be lower than those on $(x_i x_j)$, and therefore more trade occurs on those trading posts than on $(x_i x_j)$. In consequence, transactions costs on $(x_m x_i)$ and $(x_m x_j)$ fall still further, thereby further encouraging the concentration of trade at those posts. At some point, the transactions costs at the trading posts involving x_m will decline to zero. Then, if not before, all trade at $(x_i x_j)$ will cease and that trading post will become inactive. For then, even if individuals wished to exchange x_i for x_j, it would be more profitable to exchange them indirectly through x_m. An individual, who wished to sell x_i and buy x_j would incur transactions costs if doing so directly, but would incur none by first selling x_i for x_m and then buying x_j for x_m. If the individual attempted direct exchange, the budget line would be *CZD* in Figure 14.2; if indirect exchange were used, the budget line would be AB, thereby enabling the individual to reach a higher indifference curve.

In a process such as this, one good, x_m, emerges as the Medium of Exchange, and nonmoney goods x_i and x_j do not exchange for each other but do exchange, for money. The number of active trading posts in this economy with $(n + 1) = 3$ goods declines from $\frac{1}{2}n(n + 1) = 3$ to $n = 2$.

Time and Information

Analyses such as those of Niehans demonstrate that the existence of transactions costs within a single market period can explain the existence of money as a Medium of Exchange *within the market day*. Moreover, the theory of the interest-elastic transactions demand, which we considered in Chapter 10, suggests that transactions costs can explain why money, rather than bonds, is held as a Store of Value *from one market day to another*. Thus, it appears that transactions costs are sufficient to explain the existence of money. But there are several weaknesses with analyses such as this one.

The first weakness is that there is no reason why money, x_m, should not be merely a fictitious Medium of Exchange. In other words, the model is timeless and there is nothing to prevent all individuals from making simultaneous transactions at any one instant. An individual wishing to sell x_i for x_j may simultaneously sell x_i for x_m and buy x_j for x_m, so x_m, money, is not actually held for any time period. The problem is that the analysis gives no reason why purchases and sales are separated in time so that money as a Medium of Exchange is actually held. This problem is common to many of the analyses of the existence of money. Some writers, such as Ostroy (1973), overcome the problem by assuming that the economy is so decentralized that any individual can trade with only *one* other individual at any moment, with the result that the individual's two exchanges (x_i, x_m) and (x_j, x_m) cannot take place at the same instant. This is one way of assuming that the Walrasian auctioneer is absent. Ostroy then utilizes this assumption to demonstrate that the use of money permits the individuals to obtain information about market conditions and trading possibilities more efficiently than barter does. But Ostroy only removes one step further back the question of why purchases and sales are separated in time. His model leaves open the question of why the economy is decentralized in the particular way that is assumed.

The second weakness in the model of transactions costs that we have examined is that the existence of transactions costs themselves is not explained. One explanation of such costs is implicit in the work of Brunner and Meltzer (1971).[6] They assume that individuals have imperfect knowledge of market opportunities. In particular, they have imperfect knowledge of the prices and qualities of different goods, the degree of their information varies

[6]Their work, however, does not directly explain the existence of costs which are related to the quantity of goods exchanged in each transaction.

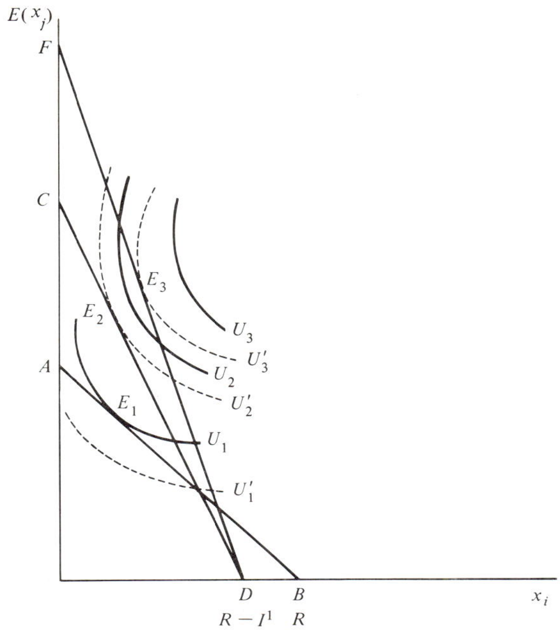

Figure 14-3

from one good to another, and obtaining information is costly. Individuals may invest in information and thereby maximize the attainable level of utility. They can also choose indirect exchanges so that they exchange x_i for x_m and then x_m for x_j, rather than exchanging x_i for x_j. Imagine a barter economy with $(n + 1)$ goods where an individual has chosen a particular transactions chain, a particular chain of indirect exchanges, in order to sell x_i from the endowment and ultimately purchase x_j. For this particular transactions chain, the individuals can invest in information. That is, they can spend time and resources on obtaining information about market conditions, the qualities of the different goods in the transactions chain, and the relative prices of goods. This investment in information yields a net return that is a function of the amount of time and resources devoted to investment. The effect of investment in information is illustrated in Figure 14.3.

In Figure 14.3 we assume a simple transactions chain, that of direct barter. The individual is endowed with x_i and has the possibility of exchanging it for x_j. Let us assume that a certain woman's initial endowment of x_i is R on the horizontal axis. On the vertical axis, we do not measure x_j but the expected value of x_j, $E(x_j)$. We do so because the woman does not know with certainty the price at which she can exchange x_i for x_j, her knowledge can be represented only as a probability distribution of such prices. The expected value of this probability distribution of prices, $E(p_j/p_i)$, determines the expected value of the maximum amount of x_j that could be consumed by exchanging all of x_i for x_j. Thus, it determines the slope of the budget line through R.

Let the budget line initially be AB so that the woman maximizes utility at E_1. Now, she may invest in information so as to gain better knowledge of the relative price of x_i and x_j. This has three effects. First, it reduces the amount of her endowment available for consumption from R to $R-I^1$ if she has devoted I^1 resources to investment in information. Therefore, the intercept of the budget line shifts leftward. Second, the budget line changes its slope. The information obtained is such that the woman learns of better relative prices than she initially knew. Therefore the expected value of the probability distribution of the relative price increases and the expected value of the amount of x_j that can be obtained in exchange for x_i rises. As a result of these two effects, the budget line shifts from AB to CD. The third effect is that the increase in information reduces the standard deviation of the probability distribution of relative price. In terms similar to those of the portfolio analysis considered in Chapter 10, the riskiness of trade declines. Assuming that the woman is a risk averter, this increases her utility and thereby shifts the indifference curves downward. The indifference map becomes the one represented by dotted indifference curves so that a given combination of x_i and x_j in consumption is associated with a higher level of utility.

The consequence of investment in information up to I^1 is, therefore, that the individual is able to reach E_2 rather than E_1 and thereby reach a higher level of utility.

Now suppose that a third good, x_m, is introduced. This good is such that relatively few resources need to be invested in order to obtain information about its price and qualities. The individual may then choose to exchange x_i for x_j indirectly. A man, say, may sell x_i for x_m and buy x_j with x_m. Because information about the exchanges $(x_i x_m)$ and $(x_m x_j)$ is less costly to obtain than information about $(x_i x_j)$, when there is indirect exchange involving x_m, a given investment in information will have a greater effect on the slope of the budget line, the expected value of the indirect exchange ratio between x_i and x_j. The budget line will increase its slope. If I^1 is invested in information, then the budget line will become FD rather than CD and utility will be increased by moving from E^2 to E^3. Moreover, the use of x_m may reduce risk, thereby shifting the indifference curves further downward and reinforcing the increase in utility that results from the use of x_m.

The analysis demonstrates that on the assumptions made, the use of indirect exchange involving x_m is more profitable than direct exchange. It can be argued from this analysis that indirect exchange will become the rule and x_m will become the Medium of Exchange, money. This development is given further impetus if the very use of x_m increases knowledge of its qualities—its portability, storage costs, consistency, and so on. The source of the development of indirect exchange and the use of x_m as money is, in this model, the existence of uncertainty and the difference in the costliness of obtaining information about the qualities and exchange possibilities of different goods. This finding, however, does not render uncertainty either a necessary or a sufficient condition for the existence of money in a one-period model. It is not a necessary condition, since transactions costs arising from sources other than the costliness of uncertainty-reducing information can account for the existence of a Medium of Exchange. It is not a sufficient condition since uncertainty in this model would not account for the existence of money if it were not for the assumption that information is costly. Basically, therefore, Brunner and Meltzer's model is an analysis of the effect of transactions costs on the emergence of money, and the existence of uncertainty is introduced as a rationalization of why individuals are willing to pay a particular type of transactions cost: the cost of information.

In this section, we have seen that the existence of money cannot be explained in a Walrasian economy even if that model is extended in the manner of Debreu to include uncertainty and the fact that a future exists. If we follow the method of dividing time into market days, we have two problems. We must explain why money, rather than bonds, exists as a Store of Value to link a sequence of market days (and why a sequence of market days exists in the first place). We must also explain why a Medium of Exchange exists to facilitate transactions within any one market day. The latter task is the most fundamental, and the assumption that transaction costs exist is one method of approaching it. However, such a method must be complemented by an explanation of why transactions are not synchronized, since, as we saw in Chapter 1, nonsynchronization is a necessary condition for the Medium of Exchange to exist. Moreover, it is not clear that the historical emergence of money can be explained by models that examine its emergence from a barter economy, for economies employing generalized barter have certainly never existed.

PART FOUR

MONEY AND THE THEORY OF INTEREST RATES

CHAPTER

FIFTEEN

REAL AND MONETARY THEORIES OF THE RATE OF INTEREST

The rate of interest on bonds is a central matter of concern in monetary theory. As long as investment, and possibly saving, is thought to be related to it, the interest rate is a variable that links a financial market to a real market. It is a link between financial conditions and the economy's rate of accumulation of physical capital and is therefore central to the problem of how money affects the real economy. In this chapter we shall briefly outline three summary models of the determination of the rate of interest.

In Section 15.1, we shall consider a simple model of a "real" theory of interest: the theory that the interest rate is determined by the real forces of investment and saving, productivity and thrift. We shall frame the model in terms of the market for loanable funds, the demand for and supply of new bonds, and we shall assume that these demands and supplies are functions of planned saving and planned investment alone. In Section 15.2 we shall consider a monetary loanable-funds model where the demand for and supply of new bonds (loanable funds) depend on the demand and supply functions for money as well as on planned saving and investment. In Section 15.3 we shall consider a different monetary theory of the interest rate, the Keynesian liquidity preference theory. In all these sections we shall be concerned with partial equilibrium models, but in Section 15.4 we shall consider the general equilibrium nature of the problem of the theory of interest.

15.1 A REAL MODEL OF THE INTEREST RATE

We have seen in Chapters 6 and 12 that an important proposition in the pre-Keynesian Quantity Theory tradition was the idea that, in the long run at least, changes in the supply of money have only one effect—an equiproportionate change in the price level. That is, changes in the money supply do not affect the rate of interest, which is determined solely by the real forces of productivity and thrift. In some cases, this was stated as a general equilibrium proposition: In the short run during which the economy adjusts to long-run equilibrium, a change in the money supply may affect the interest rate, but in long-run equilibrium, it is independent of the money supply. In other cases, the proposition concerned partial equilibrium; the only variables that affect the interest rate even in the short run are saving and investment, and their effect is *independent* of changes in the money supply. We are concerned here with the latter interpretation.

Since the interest rate on bonds is inversely related to their price, the forces determining it must be analyzed in the bond market. It is a trivial exercise to draw a demand curve and supply curve for bonds, as in Figure 15.1, and establish that the equilibrium interest rate is r^*. The specific features of our simple real theory of interest are, however, two. First, the supply of bonds arises solely from firms' desire to invest and to issue bonds to finance investment; the planned supply of bonds equals the planned level of investment. The demand for bonds develops solely from consumers' desire to save and to buy bonds with the saved portion of income; planned demand for bonds equals planned saving. That is, it is assumed that a fall in the interest rate increases desired investment and therefore the planned supply of bonds, so that the supply curve is downward-sloping; it also decreases planned saving and therefore the planned demand for bonds, so that the demand curve is upward-sloping. The second feature is that, since investment and saving are flow concepts, the demand and supply curves in Figure 15.1 must relate to the

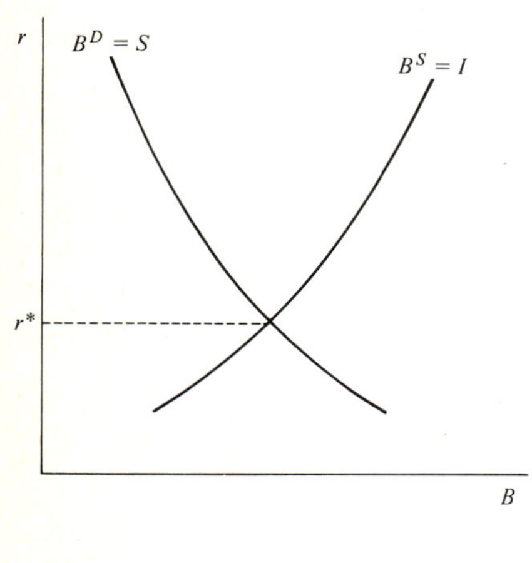

Figure 15-1

flow demand for and supply of bonds. The supply curve, for example, refers to the desire of firms to increase the stock of bonds outstanding or, in other words, to issue new bonds. Thus, in this model we are concerned with the demand for and supply of new bonds rather than with the existing stock of bonds, and, since we are dealing with flows, we must specify the time period to which the model refers. In this chapter we shall assume that time is divided into discrete weeks, so that the demand and supply curves in the figure refer to the flow of new bonds per week.

In this simple real model of the bond market, we have a demand and supply function and the equilibrium interest rate is determined by their equality. The equilibrium condition is:

$$B^D = B^S \tag{15.1}$$

Since we have assumed that demand and supply of bonds equal saving and investment, we may write the equilibrium condition as:

$$S = I \tag{15.2}$$

In this model, then, the interest rate is determined solely by equality of planned saving and planned investment.

This partial equilibrium result clearly ignores several factors that one might consider important. First, because it is a partial equilibrium result, it ignores the effects of other markets on the saving and investment curves and therefore on the demand and supply curves for bonds. In particular, it may be thought that in reality an increase in the supply of money or a change in the absolute price level will shift the saving and investment curves through the operation of the Pigou Effect (as we assumed in Chapter 12, where we considered general equilibrium). Second, it is based on the assumption that the only assets that consumers can hold are bonds; they cannot put their savings into money holdings. Similarly, the only assets that firms can hold are physical capital; they do not hold money, so they do not issue bonds to increase their money holdings and they cannot finance purchases of capital goods by running down money balances. In the next section we shall see that a monetary loanable-funds model can be built by including money as an asset.

15.2 A MONETARY LOANABLE-FUNDS MODEL

The simple real model of the interest rate discussed in Section 15.1 was not always advanced by writers in the pre-Keynesian Quantity Theory tradition. As we saw in Chapter 6, writers as early as Thornton (1802) explicitly considered the role of monetary factors in the short run and Thornton was not alone in this. But the introduction of the demand for and the supply of money into the theory of interest has received greatest attention in Keynesian work in the form of liquidity preference theory and in the writings of those contemporaries of Keynes who introduced money by extending the loanable-funds model instead of using liquidity preference theory. Such loanable-funds writers worked either within the Swedish school, whose starting point was the ideas of Wicksell (1936) and whose most representative work is that of Ohlin (1937), or within the English school, whose best representative is Robertson (1937). In this section we examine a loanable-funds model that summarizes the manner in which writers such as these incorporated the demand for and supply of money into the theory.

The model is again formulated in terms of the flow demand for and supply of loanable funds, new bonds. Now, however, we take account of two sources of demand and two sources of supply. The sources of loanable funds, or, in other words, the flow demand for bonds, are assumed to consist of planned saving *plus* any increase in the stock of money over the week:

$$B^D = S + \Delta M^S \tag{15.3}$$

The demand for loanable funds, or flow supply of bonds, is assumed to arise from the demand for finance in order to invest in capital goods *plus* the demand for loans from those who wish to build up their stock of money balances:

$$B^S = I + \Delta M^D \tag{15.4}$$

The condition for equilibrium in the bond market, therefore, is:

$$S + \Delta M^S = I + \Delta M^D \tag{15.5}$$

This equation contains all the elements in the demand for and supply of new bonds, but some points need clarification. First, it may be asked why the whole of a rise in the stock of money goes into the purchase of bonds even if we assume that lenders are those who initially receive the increased money supply. Surely some of it may be used for the purchase of goods that are consumed. The answer is, of course, that such doubts have a correct basis because unwanted money may indeed be used to purchase things other than bonds; but this fact does not render our equation invalid, for such purchases of commodities are taken into account by the saving term, S. If part of ΔM^S goes into buying goods, this increase in consumption involves an equal fall in S; hence, it would be double-counting to reduce ΔM^S by that amount to measure the amount of new money that goes into buying bonds. Second, we may wonder why only two components go, respectively, into the demand for and supply of bonds; surely people borrow (issue bonds) for reasons other than to finance investment, for example. The answer is that, yes, borrowing includes activities such as consumer borrowing and other actions, but that when we enter all such additional factors on the sides of demand and supply, they cancel each other out.[1] Thus our demand and supply equations for new bonds are so highly aggregated that they omit explicit use of some important components of supply and demand, but this type of equation was widely used by loanable-funds theorists.

[1]For a disaggregated exposition, see Conard (1959, Chap. 13).

Having specified the components of the demand for and supply of new bonds, we must consider their determinants. S and I are assumed to be functions of the rate of interest on bonds. In addition, we can assume ΔM^D to be a function of the interest rate on grounds similar to those proposed by Keynes in his liquidity preference theory,[2] and we assume ΔM^S is exogenously determined. The equilibrium condition, Equation 15.5, may therefore be written as:

$$I(r) + \Delta M^D(r) = S(r) + \Delta M^S \qquad (15.6)$$

and the interest rate is in equilibrium at the level that causes this equation to be satisfied. This is represented diagrammatically by Figure 15.2: the B^S curve is the horizontal sum of II and ΔM^D ΔM^D, and the B^D curve is the sum of SS and ΔM_1^S ΔM_1^S. The equilibrium interest rate is r_1, and at the rate of interest, investment and saving are, in our example, equal to each other, as are the increase in money supply and desired increase in money balances. It will be seen in the next paragraphs, however, that equilibrium in this market could be reached with $B^S = B^D$ but with an excess of S over I and of ΔM^D over ΔM^S (or vice versa), and that this is an important possibility.

Consider the sense in which this is a monetary theory of the interest rate employing a partial equilibrium approach. Suppose, using Figure 15.2, that the

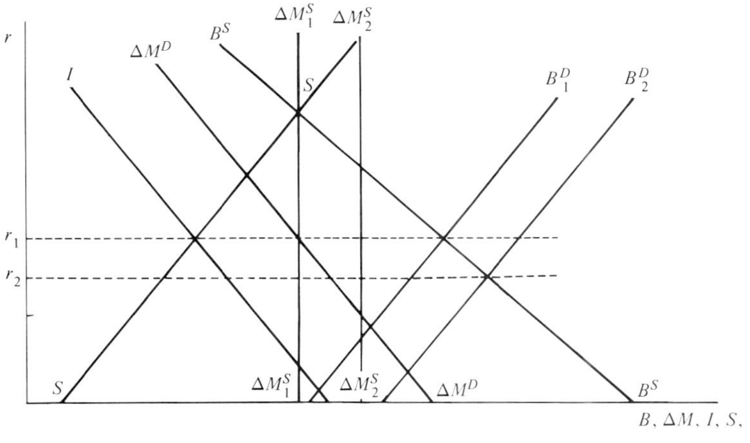

Figure 15-2

[2]Of course, liquidity preference theory does not propose that ΔM^D, the *change* in the stock demand for money, is a function of the rate of interest. Instead, it proposes that the *level* of the demand for a stock of money M^D is a function of the interest rate. But this second proposition can, at one level, be taken to imply the first because the demand for a change in money balances over a period, $(t+1)-t$, is $\Delta M^D(t+1)-t = M_{t+1}^D - M_t$, and since M_{t+1}^D is a function of the interest rate according to our second proposition, ΔM^D is also a function of the interest rate. We shall see in Chap. 16, however, that there are difficulties in deriving a theory of flows from a theory of stocks, and we have ignored these difficulties in this footnote.

money supply, instead of increasing at the rate ΔM_1^S, were increased at the rate ΔM_2^S. As a result, the demand curve for new bonds would shift to B_2^D and the equilibrium rate of interest would fall to r_2 from r_1. In this sense, the rate of interest is clearly partially a monetary phenomenon—it is determined by the real forces of saving and investment *and* the monetary forces of the demand for and supply of money, and its level can be changed by a change in the monetary forces. We shall see in Section 15.4, however, that when we adopt a general equilibrium view, the monetary loanable-funds model may be considered to be a "real" theory of the interest rate.

15.3 LIQUIDITY PREFERENCE THEORY

Keynes (1936) proposed a theory of interest which, like the monetary loanable-funds theorists, took account of monetary factors. Indeed, he argued that the interest rate is *primarily* a monetary phenomenon and this contention led to several controversies between himself and writers such as Ohlin and Robertson. We shall not investigate those controversies here, but in Section 15.4 we shall note that they essentially concerned questions of general equilibrium. There are, however, two substantial differences between Keynes's liquidity preference theory and the monetary loanable-funds theory, which can be seen even in a partial equilibrium model.

The first is that Keynes analyzes the determinants of the interest rate in the money market. He deals with the demand for and supply of money and assumes that the interest rate's equilibrium level is where these are equated. This is in contrast with the loanable-funds model's concentration on the demand for and supply of bonds. Keynes's procedure is strange when one considers that the interest rate is an expression of the price of bonds, but we shall see in Chapter 16 that the use of Walras' Law in a general equilibrium model can, on certain assumptions, show that concentration on the money market is equivalent to concentration on the bond market. Even within a partial equilibrium approach, we can rationalize Keynes's procedure by assuming that a modified version of Walras' Law holds in the financial markets. We could assume, that is, that the excess demand for money always equals the excess demand for bonds, so that equilibrium in the money market necessarily implies equilibrium in the bond market. Figure 15.3 illustrates the Keynesian money market and bond market employing that assumption and the assumptions that the supplies of money and of bonds are exogenous.[3]

The second substantial difference between Keynes's liquidity preference theory and loanable-funds theories is that the former is expressed in terms of

[3]This modified version of Walras' Law is implied in the simplified Keynesian theories of the demand for money where, as we have done in Chaps. 10 and 11, it is assumed that the individual has a given level of wealth and can choose between only money and bonds as the assets in which to hold it.

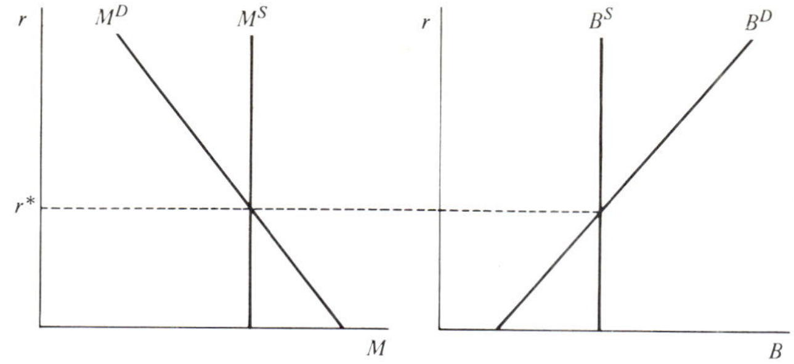

Figure 15-3

stocks and the latter in terms of flows. The demand curves for money and bonds in Figure 15.3 refer to the demand for a stock of money and a stock of bonds at an instant of time, rather than a flow or a change in the stock over time. The supply curves refer to the outstanding stocks of these assets, rather than to increases in the stock. We shall see in Chapter 16 that this difference in the structure of the models, the flow dimension of loanable funds and the stock dimension of liquidity preference, is the source of much controversy. There are many difficulties in assessing whether this is a fundamental difference between the two models or whether they are essentially identical models.

15.4 A GENERAL EQUILIBRIUM VIEW OF REAL AND MONETARY THEORIES

In the last three sections we have considered real and monetary theories of the interest rate from a partial equilibrium point of view. But this is not a very meaningful way to discuss the question of whether the interest rate is a real phenomenon determined by the forces of productivity and thrift, rather than a monetary phenomenon that can be altered by the money supply so that monetary policy can have an influence on accumulation. In order to answer this question, we must introduce the connections between the money and bond markets on the one hand and at least the goods markets on the other. The Neoclassical method for studying these connections is to build a general equilibrium model and examine whether a change in the money supply causes a change in the interest rate between the initial general equilibrium and the new one. If the interest rate does change, then we may characterize interest as a monetary phenomenon; if it does not, we may characterize it as real.

This, of course, is the question with which we were concerned in Chapter 12. It is the question of whether or not money is neutral. The models considered there were framed in terms of liquidity preference theory although they also explicitly included the stock demand for and supply of bonds. We saw there that even though liquidity preference theory was employed, money may be neutral on certain assumptions and the interest rate may be a real phenomenon, although on other assumptions it will not be. Keynes himself argued that money is not neutral, and we may rationalize his argument on several grounds. Within the Neoclassical/Keynesian Synthesis model, we could contend that Keynes thought that absolute rigidity of money wages or of the interest rate prevented the interest rate from adjusting to equate saving and investment at full-employment real income. Or within that framework, we could argue that Keynes's formulation of the speculative demand in nominal, rather than real, terms prevented the neutrality of money even if full employment were maintained. (See Chapter 12.) More plausible as an explanation of Keynes's assertion is the New Keynesian argument that because the demand for money is interest-elastic, the interest rate will not adjust instantaneously to equate saving with investment and therefore real income will change. However, that argument is not concerned with the general equilibrium rate of interest—the traditional framework for the neutrality question—but with the phenomena of disequilibrium.

Whatever the rationale for Keynes's assertion concerning the monetary nature of the interest rate, it was disputed by loanable-funds theorists such as Robertson. He maintained that even in a monetary loanable-funds model, the interest rate is fundamentally determined by the forces of productivity and thrift. We may therefore examine the loanable-funds model in a general equilibrium framework to see whether money can on certain assumptions be neutral in such a model.

Consider Figure 15.4. Suppose that the curves are initially those labeled

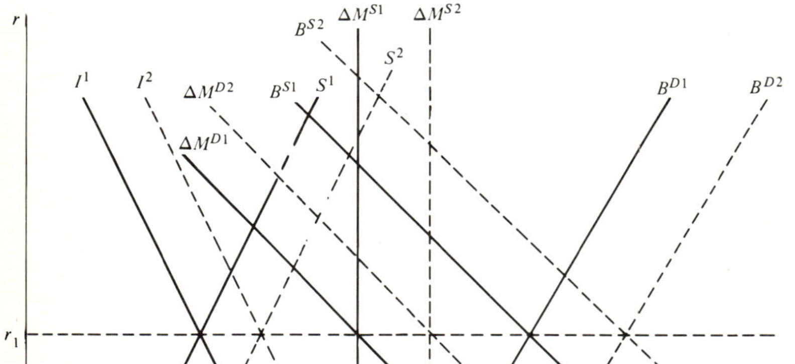

Figure 15-4

superscript 1 and the equilibrium interest rate is r_1. Bear in mind that the curves represent nominal, rather than real, variables and that we are assuming the Pigou Effect or real balance effect to be inoperative. Now let there be an increase in the rate of change in the money supply, so that the increase in money supply per week is ΔM_2^S. Then the demand curve for bonds will be $B^{D2}\ B^{D2}$ and the interest rate will fall toward r_2, at which level equilibrium in the loanable-funds market will be restored. But when the interest rate falls below r_1, an excess demand for goods develops, since, at any level below r_1, there is an excess of planned investment over planned saving. This disequilibrium in the goods market has the effect of causing an increase in the absolute price level. The rise in the price level causes the nominal savings and investment curves and the nominal demand curve for increased money balances to shift rightward to those labeled superscript 2, since we assume that individuals plan their real saving, real investment, and real demand for money as functions of the interest rate. In consequence, the new equilibrium will be reached at the same interest rate, r_1, as before the increase in the rate of change of the money supply. In this case, therefore, money is neutral in the monetary loanable-funds model. The rate of interest is unaffected by changes in the rate of growth of the money supply and, because of the requirement that the goods market must be in equilibrium, it is determined solely by the positions of the planned saving and investment functions.

The same result can equally well be obtained in a Keynesian general equilibrium model, as we saw in Chapter 12. The question of whether interest is a real or monetary phenomenon is therefore quite separate from the question of whether we use a liquidity preference or a loanable-funds model, as long as the question is posed within a general equilibrium framework. This brings us to the more general question, discussed in the following chapter, of whether the two models are in any sense different.

CHAPTER

SIXTEEN

THE NONEQUIVALENCE OF LIQUIDITY PREFERENCE AND LOANABLE-FUNDS THEORIES OF INTEREST

In the previous chapter we discussed two different monetary theories of interest: a liquidity preference and a monetary loanable-funds model. They appear to be very similar, but there are some differences of approach. There is a considerable body of literature concerned with the problem of whether these differences are substantial or whether the theories are fundamentally identical. In this chapter we review the debate and, as a preliminary, we must specify the features upon which most attention has been concentrated.

The first feature is the stock or flow nature of the theory. The liquidity preference theory is formulated in terms of the demand for money as a desired *stock* of money and the supply of money being the existing stock of money. The loanable-funds theory, on the other hand, is concerned with the demand for and supply of a *flow* of loanable funds or bonds over a period of time; it is a flow theory, so even that part of it which is concerned with demand for and supply of money is concerned with flows—the *change* in the desired and actual stock of money over a period. The question is whether a flow theory can be converted into a stock theory (or vice versa) without any change in its implications. If it can, that difference between loanable funds and liquidity preference is seen to be unimportant.

Section 16.1 offers a preliminary discussion of this question and explains the conclusion of Patinkin (1958) that a flow theory is equivalent to a stock theory.

Second, though, even if a theory in terms of flow concepts can be expressed equivalently in terms of stock concepts, the liquidity preference and loanable-funds theories would still differ because the former considers the rate of interest to be determined by the demand for and supply of money, whereas the latter analyzes the demand for and supply of bonds. The question is whether this is a fundamental difference or whether, on the other hand, the models can be formulated so that the rate of interest which equilibrates the money market also equilibrates the bond market. This question is discussed in Section 16.2.

In Section 16.3 we return to the question of whether a flow theory is equivalent to a stock theory. We show that the conclusion, reached in Section 16.1, that they are equivalent is based on special assumptions and crucially depends on the definitions of stock equilibrium and flow equilibrium.

16.1 THE POSSIBILITY OF EQUIVALENCE BETWEEN STOCK AND FLOW THEORIES

In discussing whether stock and flow theories can be expressed in equivalent form, we shall take as our specific example the problem of whether the loanable-funds flow theory can be expressed as a stock theory of the bond market. Recall that in Chapter 15 we summarized the flow loanable-funds theory in the equilibrium condition:

$$S(r) + \Delta M^S = I(r) + \Delta M^D(r) \tag{16.1}$$

We now need to introduce subscript notation to clarify the distinction between different measurements of time. We assume that time can be divided into discrete periods (weeks), and the flows in Equation 16.1 refer to amounts per week. We shall denote the week with which we are concerned as week (period) T and shall therefore write the flow equilibrium condition as:

$$S(r)_T + \Delta M^S_T = I(r)_T + \Delta M^D(r)_T \tag{16.2}$$

We also assume that each week contains a large number of instants. The instant at the beginning of week T will be denoted as t, so, for example, the stock of money at that instant will be written as M^S_t. The last instant of week T, which is also the beginning of the next week, will be written as $t+1$, so, for example, the stock of money at the end of week T and beginning of the next week is M^S_{t+1}.

Throughout this chapter we shall assume that individuals are situated at instant t and are making decisions. These decisions are concerned with objectives for either stocks at instant t, stocks at the future instant $t+1$, or flows over the intervening week T. We shall see in Section 16.3 that our model is fundamentally affected by whether we assume one or another of these objectives to be relevant. In the present section we shall assume that the individual makes decisions with respect to flows over week T, as in the loanable-funds model, and we shall then demonstrate that this is equivalent to a model where the individual is, instead, concerned with the stock at the end of the period, instant $t+1$. This is the type of comparison with which Patinkin (1958) was concerned.

Equation 16.2 represents the equilibrium condition for a loanable-funds model where the variables are *measured* in terms of flows and which we may rationalize by saying that individuals' objectives or *behavior* are concerned with flows. Consumers' and investors' desires with respect to money balances concern the rate of increase of their money balances; similarly, their desired acquisition of physical capital (in the case of investors) and of savings assets (in the case of savers) is influenced by the rate of change of physical capital and savings assets, rather than by a desired stock at instant $t+1$.

However, Equation 16.2, although written in terms of flow measures, may equally well be rationalized by assuming that consumers and investors formulate their objectives in terms of desired stocks—the stocks of money, physical capital, and bonds that at instant t they wish to hold at instant $t+1$. To illustrate this, let us deal with a summary version of Equation 16.2, where the components on each side are aggregated into a flow demand for bonds and a flow supply of bonds respectively:

$$\Delta B_T^D = \Delta B_T^S \tag{16.3}$$

Now suppose that lenders, demanders of bonds, have in mind a desired stock of bonds to be held at $t+1$. Similarly, borrowers have a desired stock of bonds that they wish to be outstanding at $t+1$. Let these desired stocks be B_{t+1}^D and B_{t+1}^S respectively. If, at the start of week T, the existing stock is B_t, this implies that over week T lenders plan to accumulate $(B_{t+1}^D - B_t)$ bonds, and borrowers plan to supply $(B_{t+1}^S - B_t)$ bonds. These plans are expressed in terms of flows even though the individuals' objective is an end-of-period stock. As we saw in Chapter 3, a change in a stock variable over a nonzero time period is a flow. We may therefore write these plans of lenders and borrowers in terms of flows:

$$\Delta B_T^D = (B_{t+1}^D - B_t) \tag{16.4}$$

and

$$\Delta B_T^S = (B_{t+1}^S - B_t) \tag{16.5}$$

In consequence, the flow equilibrium condition, Equation 16.3, can be written in terms of stocks:

$$B_{t+1}^D - B_t = B_{t+1}^S - B_t \tag{16.6}$$

or, by adding B_t to both sides:

$$B_{t+1}^D = B_{t+1}^S \tag{16.7}$$

In this example, whenever there is flow equilibrium, Equation 16.3, there is stock equilibrium, Equation 16.7.

Thus, we have seen that a model formulated in terms of flows can be rewritten in terms of stocks (and vice versa). The idea that individuals are concerned with flows over a defined period can be made formally equivalent to the idea that individuals are concerned with end-of-period stocks, and either model can be written equivalently in terms of flow or stock variables. On these grounds, it can be argued that the fact that liquidity preference theory is formulated in terms of stocks and loanable funds in terms of flows does not constitute a significant difference between the models. However, as we shall see in Section 16.3, this conclusion would not hold if we were to interpret liquidity preference theory as referring to stocks at instant t instead of at instant $t+1$.

16.2 THE POSSIBILITY OF EQUIVALENCE BETWEEN MONEY MARKET AND BOND MARKET THEORIES

Let us assume for the present that the conclusion reached in Section 16.1 is valid; it is a matter of indifference whether the demand and supply functions in a market are expressed in stock or flow terms. We now have to consider the second distinction between liquidity preference and loanable-funds models; the former is concerned with the market for money, whereas the latter is concerned with the bond market.

Hicks (1939) demonstrated that this distinction is insignificant in a general equilibrium model where Walras' Law holds. Let us assume that there are n goods in the economy and there also exist bonds and money, Thus, there are $(n+2)$ markets. For simplicity, we shall assume that this is an exchange economy so that supply in each market is fixed. We shall also assume for simplicity that time is divided into weeks and that the demand for money, bonds, and goods is concerned with end-of-period stocks[1] (although we shall omit the time subscripts). Our model is similar to that employed in Chapter 4, and general equilibrium can be represented by the equation system:

$$x_i^{XD} = f_i\left(\frac{p_1}{p}, \ldots, \frac{p_i}{p}, \ldots, \frac{p_n}{p}, r, \sum \frac{p_i}{p}\bar{x}_i^S + \frac{\bar{M}^S}{p} + \frac{\bar{B}^S}{rp}\right) - \bar{x}_i^S = 0 \tag{16.8}$$

$$(i = 1, \ldots, n)$$

$$\frac{M^{XD}}{p} = f_{n+1}\left(\frac{p_1}{p}, \ldots, \frac{p_i}{p}, \ldots, \frac{p_n}{p}, r, \sum^n \frac{p_i}{p}\bar{x}_i^S + \frac{\bar{M}^S}{p} + \frac{\bar{B}^S}{rp}\right) - \frac{\bar{M}^S}{p} = 0 \tag{16.9}$$

$$\frac{B^{XD}}{rp} = f_{n+2}\left(\frac{p_1}{p}, \ldots, \frac{p_i}{p}, \ldots, \frac{p_n}{p}, r, \sum^n \frac{p_i}{p}\bar{x}_i^S + \frac{\bar{M}^S}{p} + \frac{\bar{B}^S}{rp}\right) - \frac{\bar{B}^S}{rp} = 0 \tag{16.10}$$

$$p = \sum \theta_i p_i \tag{16.11}$$

[1]If we think of goods as consumption goods, we may assume that they are perishable at instant $t+1$. Therefore, individuals at instant t desire a particular stock of them at instant $t+1$ and plan to consume them at the next instant

We therefore have $(n+3)$ equations (including the definition of the absolute price level) to determine the $(n+2)$ prices. These consist of the n relative prices of goods, the absolute price level, and the rate of interest. As in Chapter 4's model, Walras' Law ensures that any one of the $(n+3)$ equations is derivable from (linearly dependent on) the remaining $(n+2)$, so we have only $(n+2)$ linearly independent equations to determine the $(n+2)$ prices. Thus, the model is able to determine these equilibrium prices, including, of course, the equilibrium interest rate.

The use of Walras' Law in this manner implies that the model represented by Equations 16.8 to 16.11 could equally well be represented if we omitted any one of the equations. We could omit Equation 16.9 and represent the model in terms of the goods and bond markets. Alternatively, we could omit Equation 16.10 and represent the model in terms of the goods and money markets. We could then interpret the goods and bond markets model as a loanable-funds model and the goods and money markets model as a liquidity preference model. But, since both are simply different formulations of Equations 16.8 to 16.11 with Walras' Law, both yield the same equilibrium interest rate. Which one we employ is a matter of indifference.

This interpretation has achieved wide currency, but it does not completely settle the issue. The first problem is that loanable-funds and liquidity preference theorists did not usually design their models in a general equilibrium framework and therefore tended to argue that the interest rate is determined by either the bond market or the money market. As Patinkin (1958) pointed out, in a general equilibrium model the interest rate, like other prices, is determined by the simultaneous equilibrium of *all* markets. Even if we drop the money market equation from the model, the interest rate is determined by equilibrium in the markets for goods, bonds, and money, and the same is true if we omit the bond market. We are merely ignoring one market, but its influence is not abolished thereby. Thus, the general equilibrium model makes it difficult to see in what sense the operation of either the bond market or the money market has a distinctive role to play in the determination of the interest rate. This problem is summarized by considering what type of theory of interest would exist if we dropped the equation for the peanut market.

The second problem is that the general equilibrium model does not facilitate consideration of disequilibrium. Writers such as Klein (1950) and Johnson (1961) have argued that the essential difference between loanable-funds and liquidity preference theories lies in their different assumptions concerning the excess demands that result in changes in the interest rate. Liquidity preference theory postulates that the interest rate changes if there is excess demand or supply in the money market irrespective of the situation in the bond market; loanable-funds theory postulates the opposite. This formulation overcomes the problem stated in the last paragraph, for it gives some meaning to the idea that the interest rate is tied to the operation of one market rather than another, but it does so without violating Walras' Law and without violating the principle that in general equilibrium all prices are simultaneously determined.

Klein's argument is most easily considered if we aggregate all goods markets into one so that the model is formulated in the customary macroeconomic framework of the Neoclassical/Keynesian Synthesis. We then have three markets, those for goods, bonds, and money. Excess demand in the goods market is measured by the excess of planned investment over planned saving. Walras' Law then takes the form:

$$(I - S) + (B^D - \bar{B}^S) + (M^D - \bar{M}^S) = 0 \tag{16.12}$$

If we examine general equilibrium, we may, for example, ignore the bond market. That rate of interest which equilibrates the money and goods markets must also equilibrate the bond market if Walras' Law, Equation 16.12, holds. Figure 16.1 illustrates this proposition. If the curves are initially those with superscript 1, the equilibrium interest rate is r_1, and it is meaningless to ask which market determines the interest rate since it equilibrates all three markets. Now suppose that for some reason the supply of money increases to $\bar{M}^{S2}$ and the planned investment schedule shifts rightward to I^2 I^2, but nothing else changes. Thus, an excess supply of money and an excess demand for goods exist, but there is equilibrium in the bond market. A loanable-funds model would predict that this type of disequilibrium in the goods and money markets would not induce any change in the interest rate, since the bond market is not in disequilibrium. A liquidity preference model would predict that the interest rate would fall toward r_2 in order to eradicate disequilibrium in the money market. Thus, the two models differ in their interpretations of the behavior of the interest rate in disequilibrium.[2]

Klein's interpretation as summarized in the last paragraph is not very

Figure 16-1

[2]However, if we examine a disequilibrium situation where the goods market is in equilibrium, the money market in excess supply, and the bond market in excess demand in accordance with Walras' Law, the movement of the interest rate will accord with both the loanable-funds and liquidity preference predictions.

useful if we view it from the standpoint of a Walrasian model. In such a model, differences in the speed of adjustment of prices (and interest rate) are irrelevant, since time does not enter in a meaningful sense. We may as well assume, as in the pure Walrasian model, that all prices and the interest rate instantaneously adjust so that disequilibrium does not exist. Patinkin (1958) does not suggest this extreme assumption, but he makes the formally equivalent assumption that the speed of adjustment of different prices is the same. He therefore argues that Klein's interpretation is not significant because at the same time as the interest rate falls toward r_2, the price level rises, causing shifts in the curves in all markets. The interest rate finally settles at some level that does equilibrate all markets.[3] Therefore it is meaningless for Klein to adopt the liquidity preference theory and interpret it as arguing that the disequilibrium movements of the interest rate are tied to disequilibrium in the money market. They are affected by the simultaneous disequilibrium in the money and other markets and the simultaneous changes in the price level.

However, if we abandon the Walrasian framework and adopt the framework of the New Keynesians, Klein's argument becomes more significant. For we saw in Chapter 13 that writers such as Leijonhufvud (1968) argue that, once we abandon the Walrasian assumption that transactions do not occur in real time, we may consider the fact that prices adjust at different speeds in response to disequilibrium. Thus, the disequilibrium situation illustrated in Figure 16.1 becomes interesting. For, if we were to assume that the interest rate adjusts to disequilibrium in the money market (in liquidity preference theory) more quickly than the price level adjusts to goods market disequilibrium, it is meaningful to make an extreme assumption of constancy in the price level and consider movements in the interest rate in isolation from movements in the price level. We may then pose the question of whether these movements in the interest rate result from money market disequilibrium or bond market disequilibrium and take the differing answers to this query as a significant difference between loanable-funds and liquidity preference theories.

16.3 FURTHER CONSIDERATION OF STOCK AND FLOW MODELS

We saw in Section 16.1 that a flow model of behavior can be considered as equivalent to a model of behavior where individuals are concerned with end-of-period stocks. Each model can be written using either stock or flow variables and each has the same equilibrium condition. Foley (1975), however,

[3]The fact that the interest rate does not actually reach r_2 (unless, for some reason, the curves in all markets shift appropriately) can be seen from the fact that, in Fig. 16.1, r_2 would not equilibrate the goods market. The analysis of exactly where the interest rate would be in the new equilibrium, if we take account of changes in the price level and of the resultant shifts in the curves, is the same as the analysis of the neutrality of money in Chap. 12.

shows that there is in general no similar equivalence between equilibrium in a flow model and equilibrium in a model concerned with *beginning-of-period* stocks. That is, if we assume that lenders, for example, desire at instant t a particular flow of bond purchases, ΔB_T^D, over week T and that the equilibrium condition is $\Delta B_T^D = \Delta B_T^S$, the model will be entirely different from one where lenders at instant t desire an equivalent increase, ΔB_t^D, in the bonds they hold at instant t, and the equilibrium condition is $B_t^D = B_t^S$.

Consider three markets, those for goods, bonds, and money, in a production economy. Look, first, at the supply side of each market. The goods market is in fact two markets—one for the consumption good that must be consumed during the week, the other for the capital good that can be held from one week to the next. Because it is a production economy, there is a flow supply of new goods produced during the week. In the money and bonds markets, we shall assume that both are of the outside variety and that the government runs a deficit during the week, so there is a positive flow supply of each. Now turn to the demand side of each market. Let us assume initially that the demand for capital goods, bonds, and money is a demand for end-of-period stocks and the demand for consumption goods is for a flow of consumption goods during the week. As we saw in Section 16.1, this is equivalent to a model where all markets are flow markets, since we showed there that plans for end-of-period stocks are equivalent to plans for flows over the period. Thus, even though plans concern stocks, the equilibrium conditions for the model may be written as flow equations:

$$C_T^D = C_T^S \tag{16.13}$$

$$K_T^D = K_T^S \text{ or } K_{t+1}^D - K_t^S = K_{t+1}^S - K_t^S \tag{16.14}$$

$$B_T^D = B_T^S \text{ or } B_{t+1}^D - B_t^S = B_{t+1}^S - B_t^S \tag{16.15}$$

$$M_T^D = B_T^S \text{ or } M_{t+1}^D - M_t^S = M_{t+1}^S - M_t^S \tag{16.16}$$

Equation 16.13 defines equilibrium in the market for consumption goods and Equations 16.14 to 16.16 define equilibrium in the three markets for assets—physical capital, bonds, and money respectively.

Now let us make a different assumption about demand. Assume that in the consumption goods market, demand at instant t again refers to a demand for a flow over week T. But in the asset markets, individuals do not plan at instant t for the assets they desire to hold at instant $t + 1$. Instead, they choose the amounts of the three assets they wish to hold immediately, at instant t, and they attempt to attain these holdings instantaneously. Then the four equilibrium conditions of the markets for week T must be written:

$$C_T^D = C_T^S \tag{16.17}$$

$$K_t^D = K_t^S \tag{16.18}$$

$$B_t^D = B_t^S \tag{16.19}$$

$$M_t^D = M_t^S \tag{16.20}$$

Inspection of Equations 16.18 to 16.20 indicates that the equilibrium conditions for those markets are not written in terms of flow variables or, in other words, they do not use flow *measurements*. This is appropriate, since the stock *behavior* assumed in the model gives rise to an equilibrium that is, in general, different from the equilibrium yielded by behavior with respect to flows (or end-of-period stocks). The reason for this difference is as follows: In the flow (or end-of-period stock) equilibrium model of Equations 16.13 to 16.16 or of Section 16.1, individuals are each choosing stocks for instant $t+1$. They must therefore be assumed to base their choices on their own expectations at instant t of what the price in each market will be in week $T+1$, for at instant t they are choosing assets to be carried forward into that week. Market equilibrium (flow equilibrium) over week T as expressed by Equations 16.13 to 16.16 will therefore reflect those expectations concerning week $T+1$. In Equations 16.17 to 16.20, however, individuals at instant t are choosing assets to be held during week T, and therefore the relevant expectations concern only the prices in week T. In consequence, there is no reason to expect that the equilibrium attained in the beginning-of-period stock model of Equations 16.17 to 16.20 is the same as that attained in the end-of-period stock (or within-period flow) model. The equilibrium set of prices on the three asset markets, including the interest rate, will, in general, be different in the two models.

If, therefore, we interpret the loanable-funds model as a flow model and liquidity preference as a theory of *beginning-of-period* stock asset market equilibrium (instead of adopting Patinkin's [1958] interpretation that it concerns end-of-period stocks), then the stock-flow distinction constitutes a significant difference between the models. It is not an ineradicable difference, for we could make the special assumption that individuals have perfect foresight. Let us assume that they have, that their expectations of future prices are always correct. Then consider a man who attempts to achieve a desired level of stocks in each week. First, consider a beginning-of-period plan. In weeks T and $T+1$ he chooses, say, B_t^{D*} and B_{t+1}^{D*} respectively as the stocks of bonds to be held at the first instant of each week. These separate choices are made on the basis of the prices he expects, in each week respectively (such as $p_{t,T}^e$ and $p_{t+1,T+1}^e$), to exist in weeks T and $T+1$. Now assume, instead, that he attempts to achieve end-of-period desired stocks. At the beginning of week $T-1$, he has chosen to hold B_t^{D+} at the end of that week or the beginning of week T. The choice is made on the basis of the prices that, at instant $t-1$, he expects to exist during week T (such as $p_{t-1,T}^e$). Similarly, at the beginning of week T, he chooses to hold B_{t+1}^{D+} at the end of that week, and this choice is made on the basis of his expectations at instant t, of prices in week $T+1$ (such as $p_{t,T+1}^e$). If the man has perfect foresight so that his expectations are always correct, then $p_{t,T}^e = p_T$ and so does $p_{t-1,T}^e = p_T$. Therefore, in the case of perfect foresight, an end-of-period stock equilibrium model (or flow model) is the same as a beginning-of-period stock equilibrium model. Perfect foresight, however, is a very restrictive special assumption, and although it may enable us to show the equivalence of loanable-funds and liquidity preference theories, it is not clear that it strengthens the validity of either theory.

Walras' Law Again

The distinction between end-of-period, beginning-of-period, and flow equilibrium models forces us to return to the questions considered in Section 16.2. There we showed that Walras' Law enables us to consider a general equilibrium theory of interest where either the bond market or the money market is "suppressed." However, the concept of Walras' Law employed there is the one that, in Chapter 4, we derived from the individuals' budget constraint and this derivation was implicitly based on end-of-period behavior. Recall that the budget constraint considered there (in Section 4.2) stated that individuals cannot plan to consume more goods *during* the period (flow) and hold more assets *at the end of* the period (end-of-period stock) than they hold at the beginning of the period in an exchange economy. Extending this statement to a production economy, aggregating over all individuals, and assuming the existence of bonds, money, and physical capital as assets, such a budget constraint yields the Walras' Law equation:

$$B_{t+1}^D - B_t^S = (-1)[(M_{t+1}^D - M_t^S) + (K_{t+1}^D - K_t^S) + (C_T^D - Y_T)] \qquad (16.21)$$

In such a model there is one Walras' Law equation and it concerns only flows (and changes in stocks which, as we saw in Chapter 2, are also flows).

But this budget constraint is not a full description of the constraints on individuals' demands if the economy is described by the equilibrium conditions of Equations 16.17 to 16.20. For there the asset markets concern *beginning-of-period* stocks (Eqs. 16.18 to 16.20), whereas the consumption goods market concerns flows. In such circumstances, the individual is subject to two budget constraints. First, the decisions the individual makes at instant t concerning holdings of assets at that instant are constrained by total holdings of assets at t:

$$K_t^D + B_t^D + M_t^D = K_t^S + B_t^S + M_t^S \qquad (16.22)$$

Aggregating over all individuals, the excess demand for a stock of any one of these assets at instant t is the negative of the sum of the excess demands for the other two:

$$B_t^D - B_t^S = (-1)[(M_t^D - M_t^S) + (K_t^D - K_t^S)] \qquad (16.23)$$

Second, the individual has to make flow decisions concerning consumption over period T, and these decisions imply a budget constraint similar to the one considered in Chapter 4 and a Walras' Law relation like Equation 16.21. Specifically, the flow budget constraint is that:

$$C_T^D + B_{t+1}^D + M_{t+1}^D + K_{t+1}^D = Y_T + B_t^S + M_t^S + K_t^S \qquad (16.24)$$

or, in other words, consumption over the period, plus assets held at the end of the period, is constrained by income and initial assets. Rearranging terms and considering the variables as aggregated over individuals, this implies:[4]

$$B_{t+1}^{D} - B_{t}^{S} = (-1)[(C_{T}^{D} - Y_{T}) + (M_{t+1}^{D} - M_{t}^{S}) + K_{t+1}^{D} - K_{t}^{S})] \qquad (16.21)$$

Thus, even in a model where the asset markets concern beginning-of-period stocks, we cannot dispense with the flow budget constraint since flow production (Y) and consumption (C) decisions are necessarily subject to flow constraints. Instead, in such a model the individual is subject to two constraints on any asset decisions, a beginning-of-period stock constraint or wealth allocation constraint, and a flow (or end-of-period) constraint. Aggregating over individuals, we have one Walras' Law equation applicable to flow markets (Eq. 16.21) and another applicable to beginning-of-period stock markets (Eq. 16.23). If, like Foley (1975), we think of liquidity preference theory as referring to beginning-of-period asset equilibrium (Eqs. 16.17 to 16.20), this conception enables us to understand the validity of the portfolio analysis discussed in Chapters 9, 10, and 11. For that analysis considers decisions about the allocation of wealth independently of decisions about the amount of wealth (saving). In the light of the present discussion, it is clear that that procedure is valid only if we have a stock wealth constraint separate from a flow constraint; as we have seen, these two separate constraints exist only if we have a beginning-of-period model of asset markets[5]. The loanable-funds model, by contrast, can have only one constraint, a flow constraint.

In conclusion, we have seen in this chapter that the formal equivalence of liquidity preference and monetary loanable-funds theories depends on the model builder's vision of the world. If the vision is that of general equilibrium, then the interest rate is determined by simultaneous equilibrium in all markets. It is then of no consequence whether we ignore the bond market or the money market even if both money and bonds are traded on stock and flow markets. If the appropriate vision is that of disequilibrium, then the disequilibrium of the money market does not necessarily imply bond market disequilibrium if the model is built in terms of flows or end-of-period stocks,

[4]Since $(K_{t+1}^{D} - K_{t}^{S})$ is equivalent to the planned flow of investment, we have:

$$\begin{aligned} B_{t+1}^{D} - B_{t}^{S} &= (-1)[(I_{T}^{D} + C_{T}^{D} - Y_{T}) + (M_{t+1}^{D} - M_{t}^{S})] \\ &= (-1)[(I_{T} - S_{T}) + (M_{t+1}^{D} - M_{t}^{S})] \end{aligned}$$

This is the same as Eq. 16.21's version of Walras' Law with the goods market written explicitly in flow terms.

[5]These considerations also enable us to reject the argument of Lloyd (1960). Starting from the idea that asset markets, such as that for bonds, have two conditions for equilibrium, one a stock condition, $B_{t}^{D} = B_{t}^{S}$, and the other a flow condition, $B_{t+1}^{D} - B_{t}^{S} = B_{t+1}^{S} - B_{t}^{S}$, he argues that Walras' Law does not permit us to "suppress" the bond market (or money market) in the manner discussed in Section 16.2. For Walras' Law enables us to "suppress" only one equation, whereas each market is now characterized by two excess demand or equilibrium equations. Here we have seen, however, that in the beginning-of-period asset market model with flow production and consumption, there are two Walras' Law equations. One enables us to "suppress" the flow equilibrium condition of the bond (or money) market, the other, its stock equilibrium condition.

and the question of which market influences the disequilibrium behavior of the interest rate is relevant. The fact that one model is framed in terms of stocks and the other in terms of flows is an insignificant distinction if we assume that the stock model refers to end-of-period stocks when time is divided into discrete periods. If, however, the stock model refers to beginning-of-period stocks in discrete time, stock and flow models are not equivalent unless we assume perfect foresight. In this case, therefore, the distinction between loanable funds and liquidity preference hinges on the theoretician's vision concerning the best way in which to periodize economic decisions and equilibrium conditions.

CHAPTER

SEVENTEEN

THE TERM STRUCTURE OF INTEREST RATES

In Chapters 15 and 16, and at various earlier points, we have examined theories that attempt to explain what determines the level of the interest rate. We have treated the problem as if there were just one interest rate in the economy—the yield on one particular kind of bond that is known to give its owner a rate of interest payments per period in perpetuity and that therefore represents a loan that is expected, with certainty, to be never repaid (irredeemable). As a result, our theories have little direct applicability to the world, for there exists, in fact, a wide variety of bonds and other securities. Some, but very few, have the characteristics we have assumed, while most are expected to be redeemed at some future date (the futurity of repayment varying from one bond to another), and many differ according to the certainty with which interest payments and redemption can be expected. Further differences among bonds arise because of differences in the tax structure applicable to the income from them, differences in the minimum value of amounts tradable, and other features. The fundamental question of this chapter is whether it is possible to develop a theory explaining the relationship between the interest rates on bonds with different characteristics.

We are not, however, attempting to explain interest rate differentials related to all types of differences between bonds. Instead, we shall assume that for all bonds there is certainty that the promised interest rate will be paid and the principal will be redeemed; that is, there is no default risk, although other risks, such as that of capital loss if the bond is sold before its redemption date, are not excluded throughout this chapter. In fact, we shall assume that between bonds all except one feature is the same. The feature that we allow to vary among bonds is their *term to maturity*, the length of time between now and the time when a purchaser of a bond may expect it to be redeemed. In other words, we are concerned with the *term structure* or *maturity structure* of interest rates—the difference between the interest rate on a bond whose owner is to be repaid by the issuer, say, at the end of one year and that on one that is to be repaid at the end of 20 years but is otherwise identical. We are interested here in theories that explain why such differences occur and what their size and direction may be.

The significance of theories of the term structure is twofold. The first aspect, and the one of most relevance for the issues with which this book is generally concerned, is purely theoretical. It relates to the assumptions on which we can build models that have only one bond rate of interest. In other words, on what assumptions can we assume that the maturity structure or term structure of interest rates can be summarized by one interest rate? The second aspect is of greater relevance for those concerned with framing monetary policy. That is, different theories of the term structure have different implications for whether monetary policy can or cannot directly influence any particular interest rate—the rate, for example, on a bond with 20 years to maturity.

In Section 17.1 we explain some of the concepts used in the analyis. In Sections 17.2 and 17.3 we examine two extreme theories, the pure expectations hypothesis and the pure segmentation hypothesis, which produce some directly opposite conclusions. In Section 17.4 we consider the relationship between these theories and liquidity preference theory and the alternative models that overcome some of the deficiencies of the two pure models.

17.1 AN EXPLANATION OF CONCEPTS

We are concerned with the interest rate on a bond, but we must be careful in defining this concept, for there are several possible interpretations. One meaning of the interest rate is the *coupon rate* on the bond, $\hat{r}$. The coupon is simply the amount of money, $\$C$, received in interest on the bond each period, which we shall define as a year. The par value of the bond is the amount of money, $\$A$, that will be repaid by the issuer of the bond when redeeming it. The coupon *rate* is the annual coupon expressed as a percentage of the par value. It is $\hat{r} = C/A$ per annum, but this is not a useful concept, for the bond owner will not actually receive this rate (although, of course receiving the coupon, C) unless the amount paid for the bond—the principal, P—equals the par value of the bond, A.

We could define the rate the bond owner receives as the *interest yield*, r. This is the annual coupon expressed as a ratio over the principal actually invested in the bond (the price actually paid), $r = C/P$ per annum. Clearly, this will be higher than the coupon rate if the price of the bond is below its par value and vice versa. Even this, however, is not a complete measure, for C does not include all items of income received from the bond. In particular, it does not include the redemption value, A, that will be received on maturity and it takes no account of the fact that interest is compounded—that the coupon itself receives interest if it is reinvested.

Maturity Yield

To take account of these sources of revenue from the bond, we do not use the interest yield, but define the interest rate as the *maturity yield*, R, instead. The maturity yield, $R_{t,n}$, is how we shall write the maturity yield now (at time t, which is the beginning of year T) on an N-year bond that is to be redeemed at the end of the Nth year from now—that is, after N years have elapsed or, in other words, at instant $t+n+1$. For an N-year bond with positive redemption value A, it is defined as being equal to the interest yield on an N-year bond with redemption value of zero. This equality is defined as equality of the maximum amount of wealth that can be accumulated on each bond by the end of year N. The concept is clearer when presented algebraically. The maximum amount of wealth, V_n, that can be accumulated by the end of year N on an N-year bond with a positive redemption value A is:

$$V_n = C_1 + C_2 + C_3 + \cdots + C_n + A \qquad (17.1)$$

We shall assume that $C_1 < C_2 < C_3 < \cdots < C_n$ because interest is not actually paid each year but is, we shall assume, automatically reinvested at the original interest yield, so the amount of coupons paid each year, C, rises. The maximum amount of wealth, V'_n, that can be accumulated by holding an N-year bond with a zero redemption value is:[1]

$$V'_n = P(1 + r_{t,n})^n \qquad (17.2)$$

Our definition of the maturity yield, $R_{t,n}$, is that it equals that value of $r_{t,n}$ that gives equality between V_n and V'_n. Thus, for Equations 17.1 and 17.2, the definition implies:

$$P(1 + R_{t,n})^n = C_1 + C_2 + C_3 + \cdots + C_n + A \qquad (17.3)$$

or

$$R_{t,n} = n\sqrt{\frac{1}{P}(C_1 + C_2 + C_3 + \cdots + C_n + A - 1)} \qquad (17.4)$$

In other words, the maturity yield on a bond is inversely related to the price of the bond at the time of purchase, P, and positively related to its par value

[1]This follows from the fact that at the end of the first year the bond owner's wealth equals principal, P, plus the amount of interest $[C = (C/P)^P = r_{t,n}P]$, earned during the year: $V'_1 = P + r_{t,n}P = P(1 + r_{t,n})$. At the end of the second year, it equals this, plus the extra year's interest earned on it, if the interest receipts are reinvested at $r_{t,n}: P(1 + r_{t,n}) + rP(1 + r_{t,n}) = P(1 + r_{t,n})^2$. Thus, at the end of the Nth year, the maximum amount accumulated is $V'_n = P(1 + r_{t,n})^n$.

(redemption value A) and coupon. It should be noted that the derivation of the maturity yield assumes that annual interest payments are automatically reinvested in the bond at the same yield.

This maturity yield is what we shall call the interest rate on an N-year bond. It has the advantage of taking account of all the receipts earned by the bond owner who holds the bond to maturity. It also has the advantage of taking the compounding of interest into account.

Even though we shall define the interest rate on a bond as the maturity yield, this definition does have some weaknesses. The main weakness can be seen by rearranging the terms in our definition of $R_{t,n}$ to:

$$P = \frac{1}{(1+R_{t,n})} n(C_1 + C_2 + C_3 + \cdots + C_n + A) \tag{17.5}$$

This shows that $R_{t,n}$ is by definition that rate of interest which, if used for discounting, makes the present value of the bond's income equal to the price that must be paid for the bond. This is a desirable feature of a measure of yield, but, in this case, it holds only if the sum that is being discounted is the total income that has been accumulated by the redemption date in N year's time $(C_1 + \cdots + C_n + A)$, and it is discounted *from that date back* [the discount factor being $1/(1+R_{t,n})^n$]. In other words, it is assumed that the bond owner cannot touch the coupons when they accrue, but must leave them invested at the same coupon rate and interest yield until the end of the N years; if that were not so, the owner could consume the interest when it is received each year and would be interested in the present value of the coupons when discounted from the date that they are received rather than from the end of the N years [the owner would, that is, apply discount factors as $C_1/(1+R_{t,n})$, $C_2/(1+R_{t,n})^2$, etc]. This, clearly, is something of a weakness in our definition of the interest rate, for, in general, the owners will be able, and will wish, to receive the coupons at the date they accrue so that they may use them as they please instead of being forced to leave them invested, earning the same yield as is the initial principal, until the end of the N years. If individuals do receive the coupons at the date of accrual, they will estimate their present value by discounting them from that date instead of from the end of the life of the bond, and our maturity yield is not the appropriate rate when discounting is conducted on that basis. Nevertheless, we shall continue to work with the maturity yield, rather than any other definition of the interest rate, for it has been used in several studies of the term structure and, apart from anything else, it involves simpler arithmetic than is involved in other measures of interest rate.[2]

[2]The concept of the interest rate used in previous chapters differs from the concept of the maturity yield. First, the interest rate employed elsewhere in this book is the rate on an irredeemable bond. Second, it is based on the assumption that interest receipts are withdrawn and consumed at the time of receipt, rather than reinvested. Given this second assumption, we can see that the interest rate we have used elsewhere (the interest yield, $r = C/P$) is the rate of

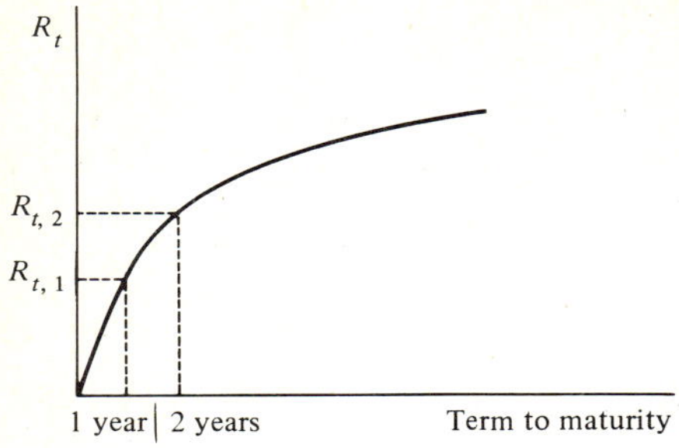

Figure 17-1

Yield Curve

Another concept we shall employ is that of a *yield curve.* This is simply a diagram or chart showing the actual interest rate on a bond (maturity yield, in our case) as a function of the bond's term to maturity. Such curves are illustrated in Figure 17.1, where the interest rate, R, is measured on the vertical axis and the term to maturity of the bond, N years, is measured on the horizontal axis. For example, in Figure 17.1 the present interest rate on a one-year bond (a bond that will be redeemed one year from now) is $R_{t,1}$, that on a two-year bond is $R_{t,2}$, and so on. It is important to note that the curve may in reality have any of the shapes drawn in Figure 17.2. Indeed, it may have any shape—long rates may be higher or lower than, or the same as, any particular shorter rate. Moreover, from the point of view of the empirical relevance of theories of the term structure, all of which attempt to explain yield curves like those in Figures 17.1 and 17.2, it should be noted that such yield curves are not directly observable in bond markets. One reason is that a

---

discount that is applicable to the interest receipts on an irredeemable bond. This justifies the assumption made, for example, in Chap. 10, that the interest rate divided by the amount of the coupon, C, is the inverse of the price of a British Consol, for the interest yield, $r = C/P$, has this property. Assume that the price of the irredeemable bond is equal to the discounted value of future receipts when a discount rate, d, is used whose value does not vary with the futurity of the receipt:

$$P = \frac{C}{(1+d)} + \frac{C}{(1+d)^2} + \frac{C}{(1+d)^3} + \cdots + \frac{C}{(1+d)^n} + \frac{A}{(1+d)^n}$$

This sum of a geometric progression reduces to:

$$P = \frac{C}{d}\left[1 - \frac{1}{(1+d)^n}\right] + \frac{A}{(1+d)^n}$$

Since it is an irredeemable bond, n is infinity. As n approaches infinity, the last expression approaches $P = C/d$, since $1/(1+d)^n$ and $A/(1+d)^n$ approach zero. Therefore $d = C/P$, and the discount rate is the same as the interest yield.

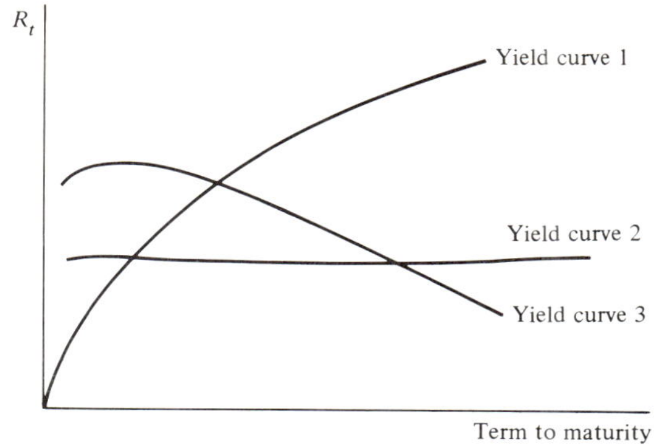

Figure 17-2

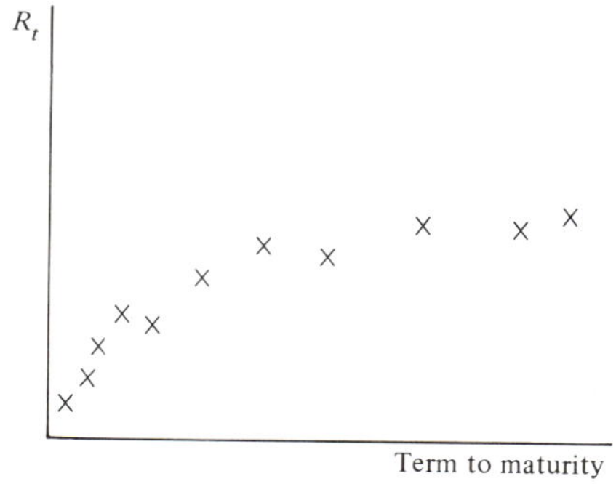

Figure 17-3

continuum of bonds of different maturities does not exist. Instead, there are gaps in the maturity structure, so what may be observed are only discrete points such as those illustrated in Figure 17.3. To obtain a continuous yield curve, it is necessary to construct it theoretically by interpolating between the discrete observations. There is, however, a further difficulty. The discrete observations in Figure 17.3 refer to real bonds, which differ in many respects other than their term to maturity alone. Thus, the observed interest rate on each is not only a function of its term to maturity but is also affected by each bond's tax features, default risk, and other characteristics. The theoretical yield curves of Figures 17.1 and 17.2, on the other hand, are based on the assumption that such characteristics are absent.

We must also define the concept of expected interest rates, for this concept is crucial to the theory of the term structure. By the expected rate one year from now, on a two-year bond we do not mean the rate that we now expect to exist in a year's time on a bond that now has two years to maturity (and will then have one year). Instead, we mean the rate we now expect to exist one year from now on a bond which, if bought at that time, has a term of two years from that date. We shall denote all expected rates by the lowercase letters r^e, and we shall use subscripts such as ${}_tr^e_{t+1,1}$ to indicate that the rate is that which, now at time t, is expected on a bond that has a term of one year when bought and that is to be bought at the beginning of the second year from now (instant $t+1$).

17.2 "PURE" EXPECTATIONAL THEORY OF THE TERM STRUCTURE

In this section we are concerned with a theory of the term structure that has received much discussion in the literature. We may call it a "pure" theory in the sense that it is based on highly simplifying assumptions, and an "expectational" theory in the sense that it relates the rate of interest on any bond to expected future rates on bonds of shorter maturity.

We must begin by enumerating the assumptions that are employed. It is assumed that there are no taxes or other costs involved in holding or trading bonds, so that the income from a bond consists simply of interest receipts, capital gains, and the repayment of par value when the bond is redeemed. We assume certainty in the sense of absence of default risk. We shall also make the assumption that individuals' expectations, in particular their expectations concerning the interest rates that will exist in the future, such as ${}_tr^e_{t+j,n}$, are held with certainty. This assumption is crucial for the analysis. We shall see in Sections 17.3 and 17.4 that the removal of this assumption would invalidate the pure expectational theory unless individuals are assumed to be risk-neutral rather than risk averters or risk lovers. People hold expectations regarding the future levels of interest rates on bonds that, at those future dates, have particular maturities (for example, they have expectations concerning the rate on one-year bonds in future years), and people are profit maximizers. Using these assumptions, the theory tackles the problem of explaining the shape of the yield curve; that is, what is the relationship between the current interest rate on a particular long-term bond and the current interest rates on shorter-term bonds? It comes to the following conclusion: A long-term interest rate is a function (specifically, some average) of the *expected* future rates on short-term bonds, and, therefore, its relationship to current short-term rates depends on the relationship between present short rates and expected future short rates.

The reasoning by which the conclusion is reached is intuitively plausible. Consider first the behavior of an individual. Suppose that someone (say a man) is planning to invest in bonds and not to sell his investment before the end of year N. He has two options: either he can buy a long bond which matures at the end of year N and hold it until maturity, or he can invest in a short bond, say a one-year bond, and when it matures reinvest the proceeds in another one-year bond and so on until the end of year N. The individual is assumed to be a profit maximizer in the special sense that he will choose whichever of these options gives him the greatest level of wealth at the end of the year N. So we must examine what the value of each of these options will be at that time. In the case of the first option, if the interest rate (maturity yield) on the long bond is $R_{t,n}$ [recall this assumes that this man reinvests at the same yield any interest (coupon) which he receives on the bond before its redemption], the value at the end of year N will be the price paid plus the total receipts from the bond. That is, it follows from Equation 17.3 that at the end of N years, the value of the investment in the N-year bond is:

$$V_n(\text{Option 1}) = P(1 + R_{t,n})^n \tag{17.6}$$

In the case of the second option, the value at the end of N years depends on rates of interest that can be earned on one-year bonds in each of the N years. If the rate on a one-year bond in the first year is $R_{t,1}$, the rate on a one-year bond bought at the beginning of the second year is $R_{t+1,1}$, and so on, the value of this series of investments at the end of n years is:

$$V_n(\text{Option 2}) = P(1 + R_{t,1})(1 + R_{t+1,1})(1 + R_{t+2,1}) \cdots (1 + R_{t+n,1}) \tag{17.7}$$

This holds because the value of the man's wealth at the end of the first period is the principal invested (P) plus the receipts from the first year's bond ($PR_{t,1}$)—the product of the first two terms in Equation 17.7; its value at the end of the second year (assuming that all proceeds are reinvested at the same yield) is the same $[P(1 + R_{t,1})]$ plus the net receipts from the second year's bond, which depends on the one-year interest rate in the second year and which equals $R_{t+1,1}$ $[P(1 + R_{t,1})]$. The value at the end of the second year is, therefore, the product of the first three terms on the right-hand side of Equation 17.7. Proceeding in this manner, we find that the value at the end of N years is the product of all the terms on the right-hand side. Now it is important to note that investors do not know what the rates of interest on one-year bonds will be in future periods ($R_{t+1,1}, R_{t+2,1}, \ldots, R_{t+n,1}$), but they do have ***expectations*** regarding their values. If we denote these expected values by ${}_tr^e_{t+1,1}, {}_tr^e_{t+2,1}, \ldots, {}_tr^e_{t+n-1,1}$, we can reformulate Equation 17.7 in terms of the expected value of Option 2 N years from now:

$$V_n(\text{Option 2}) = P(1 + R_{t,1})(1 + {}_tr^e_{t+1,1})(1 + {}_tr^e_{t+2,1}) \cdots (1 + {}_tr^e_{t+n-1,1}) \tag{17.8}$$

Now clearly the profit-maximizing individual will invest in the N-year bond if the Nth year value of Option 1 (Equation 17.6) is greater than the expected Nth year value of Option 2 (Equation 17.8) and will invest in the sequence of one-year bonds if the value of Option 2 is greater. If the two are equal, the investor will be indifferent.

We must now move to the aggregate level and, to do so, we assume for simplicity that all individuals have the same expectations of future one-year rates, so that V_n(Option 2) is the same for every individual. By considering aggregate behavior we find that equilibrium is reached only when V_n(Option 1) = V_n(Option 2). Suppose that the Nth year value of Option 1 was greater than that of Option 2; then all individuals would wish to buy N-year bonds rather than a sequence of one-year bonds. Similarly, since it involves them in smaller outgoings over the N years, ***borrowers*** would prefer to borrow over N years by issuing a sequence of one-year bonds and no N-year bonds. As a result, there would be an excess demand for N-year bonds and an excess supply of one-year bonds. The price of N-year bonds, therefore, would rise and that of one-year bonds fall. This is the same as a fall in the interest rate on N-year bonds ($R_{t,n}$) and a rise in that on one-year bonds ($R_{t,1}$), as shown by Equation 17.5. These changes cause V_n(Option 1) to fall and V_n (Option 2) to rise, and they will, clearly, continue until these Nth-year values of the two options are equal.

In other words, the condition for equilibrium in the market for bonds is:

$$V_n(\text{Option 1}) = V_n(\text{Option 2})$$

Or, from Equations 17.6 and 17.8:

$$P(1 + R_{t,n})^n = P(1 + R_{t,1})(1 + {}_t r^e_{t+1,1})(1 + {}_t r^e_{t+2,1}) \cdots (1 + {}_t r^e_{t+n-1,1}) \qquad (17.9)$$

By rearranging terms in Equation 17.9, we find that in equilibrium there is a particular relationship between the long-term (N-year) rate and the values of short-term (one-year) rates that are expected over the period (N years) of the long-term bond:

$$R_{t,n} = n\sqrt{(1 + R_{t,1})(1 + {}_t r^e_{t+1,1}) \cdots (1 + {}_r r^e_{t+n-1,1})} - 1 \qquad (17.10)$$

The long rate, plus unity, equals the geometric average of each year's expected short rate, plus unity, over the period of the long bond.

From this we can derive the predictions of the theory, and, clearly, they depend on what assumptions we make regarding expected future short rates. If, for example, future short rates are expected to be the same in every year as the present short rate, $R_{t,1}$, the present long-term rate will equal the present short rate and the yield curve will be horizontal, as in Figure 17.4.[3] If, on the other hand, short rates are expected to rise so that expected short rates are greater than $R_{t,1}$, the long-term rate, $R_{t,n}$, will be greater than the current short-term rate, $R_{t,1}$, and the yield curve will be upward-sloping, as in Figure 17.5. Conversely, if short-term rates are expected to fall, the yield curve will be downward-sloping. Thus, whatever the shape of the yield curve, the pure expectational theory can explain it by assuming that short rates are expected to change in a particular direction.[4]

[3]This can be seen from the following: If future one-year rates are expected to be the same as the present one-year rate, then all the variables, ${}_r r^e_{t+j,1}$, equal $R_{t,1}$. Therefore we may rewrite Eq. 17.10 as:

$$\begin{aligned} R_{t,n} &= n\sqrt{(1 + R_{t,1})_1 \cdot (1 + R_{t,1})_2 \cdots (1 + R_{t,1})_n} - 1 \\ &= n\sqrt{(1 + R_{t,1})^n} - 1 \\ &= R_{t,1} \end{aligned}$$

so that the long rate equals the short rate.

[4]The theory can even account for humped curves. A yield curve that for example, rises for maturities up to j years and falls for maturities of between j and n years can be explained by assuming that individuals expect short rates to rise over the next j years but to fall in subsequent years.

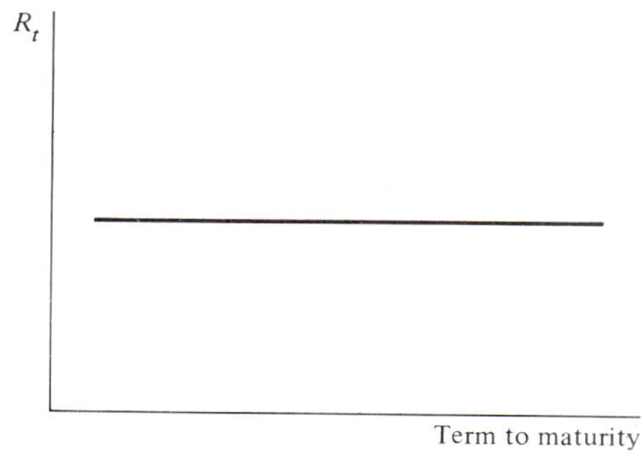

Figure 17-4

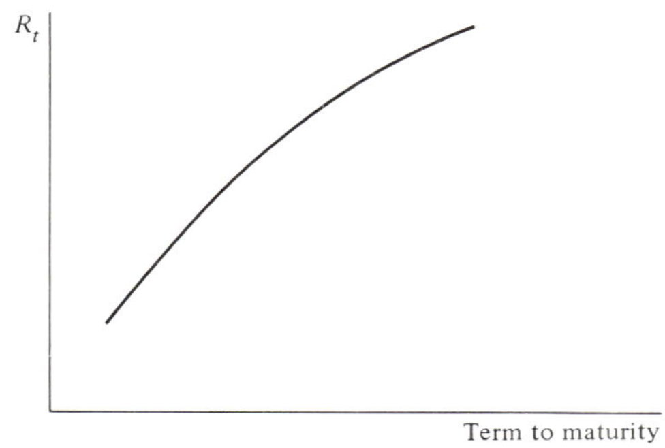

Figure 17-5

This pure expectational theory was stated, in the same form as our presentation, by Hicks (1939), although he himself advocated the liquidity preference theory which we consider in Section 17.4. It was also stated in a slightly different form by Lutz (1940) and Conard (1959). In this pure form, the theory has several weaknesses. The first is that it assumes individuals' expectations of future short rates to be held with certainty, or else that individuals are not concerned with the risk that arises from uncertain expectations. The second is that it assumes that individuals hold expectations of what future short rates will be until year N. If the long bond is, for example, a 20-year bond, individuals are assumed to have expectations concerning what one-year rates will be in 20 years' time.[5] In Sections 17.3 and 17.4 we consider the implications of dropping these assumptions.

The third weakness of the expectational theory is that it is based on the assumption that all lenders and borrowers have the same expectations. This assumption of uniformity ensures that if Option 1 gives a better return than

[5]As Joan Robinson (1951) puts it, to explain the rate on an irredeemable bond (where n equals infinity), the model must assume that individuals predict what short rates will be in all periods until Kingdom Come.

Option 2 for one lender, it gives a better return for all lenders and there is unambiguously an aggregate excess demand for the bond involved in Option 1. If this assumption is incorrect,[6] the analysis of the relationship between the equilibrium price of long and short rates would have to take into account the distribution of expectations between lenders and borrowers with different weights in the market.

The fourth weakness of the model is its implication that an individual lender, for example, will invest only in one type of bond whenever bond prices are not in equilibrium or whenever the individual's expectations change from what they are when equilibrium exists. For example, an individual lender who thinks that Option 1 offers a better return than Option 2 will switch all his or her wealth into the long bond and hold no short bonds. This objection, however, is not important if we make the Walrasian assumption that bond prices adjust instantaneously in response to disequilibrium. In that case, although some individuals may attempt to switch all their wealth into the long bond, the similar attempts by other individuals will ensure that the price of the long bond relative to that of the short bond instantaneously adjusts, so that the value of Option 1 equals that of Option 2 and individuals are indifferent between long and short bonds.

The final weakness of the model is that it gives no account of how expectations of future short rates are formed. This omission presents particular difficulties for empirical work, since it is impossible to test an equation, such as Equation 17.10, unless we have observations of the expected short rates, or know by what observable variables they are determined, or at least can hypothesize some model of their determination. The great significance of Meiselman's work (1962) is that, apart from attempting to overcome several other weaknesses in the pure expectational theory, he extended it to incorporate a theory of how individuals form expectations of future short rates.

We now turn to consider this development of the pure expectations hypothesis. To understand Meiselman's model, it is necessary to note that *if* the expectational theory is correct, data on actual long rates on the yield curve will give a measure of implicit expectations concerning future short rates. The interest rate on a one-year bond that is now expected to obtain in the Nth year from now is, if the expectational hypothesis is correct:[7]

$$ {}_t\hat{r}^e_{t+n-1,1} = \frac{(1+R_{t,n})^n}{(1+R_{t,n-1})^{n-1}} - 1 \tag{17.11}$$

[6]This possibility is suggested by surveys of expectations conducted by White (1971) and Malkiel and Kane (1967), although there is no a priori reason why it should be wrong.

[7]Equation 17.11 is derived in the following way from Equation 17.10. To take a specific example, consider the short rate that is expected now to exist on a one-year bond at the beginning of the third year from now, so that $N = 3$. Equation 17.10 implies that:

$$(1+R_{t,2})^2 = (1+R_{t,1})(1+{}_tr^e_{t+1,1})$$

and

$$(1+R_{t,3})^3 = (1+R_{t,1})(1+{}_tr^e_{t+1,1})(1+{}_tr^e_{t+2,1})$$

We have written this expected short rate as ${}_t\hat{r}^e_{t+n-1,1}$, rather than ${}_tr^e_{t+n-1,1}$, to indicate that it is the actual expected rate only if the pure expectational hypothesis is correct. Equation 17.1 states that if the expectational theory is correct, we may calculate the one-year rate expected now to exist in the nth year from our knowledge of the present rates on bonds which have, respectively, n years and $(n-1)$ years to maturity. Meiselman postulates that the expected future short rates so calculated, ${}_t\hat{r}^e_{t+n-1,1}$ are in fact the short rates that are expected, ${}_tr^e_{t+n-1,1}$. He then formulates the hypothesis that these expectations are formed by an error-adjustment process. This is similar to Friedman's hypothesis concerning expectations of future income, which we considered in Chapter 7. In terms of expected short rates, it is the hypothesis that:

$${}_t\hat{r}^e_{t+j,1} = {}_{t-1}\hat{r}^e_{t+j,1} + \gamma(R_{t,1} - {}_{t-1}\hat{r}^e_{t,1}) \tag{17.12}$$

In terms of the subscripts we have chosen, this equation says that present expectations of the rate on a one-year bond in j years' time, ${}_t\hat{r}^e_{t+j,1}$, is the same as what last year the individual expected the rate to be j years from now, ${}_{t-1}\hat{r}_{t+j,1}$, plus some proportion γ of the error that was made last year in forecasting this year's one-year rate $(R_{t,1} - {}_{t-1}\hat{r}^e_{t,1})$.

The essence of Meiselman's hypothesis, therefore, is that any long rate is a function of expected short rates—the basic proposition of the pure expectational theory—and that present experience leads people to adjust their expectations of future short rates. This adjustment of expectations in the light of present experience is assumed to affect expectations of what short rates will be one year from now, or over the second year $(j = 1)$, the year after $(j = 2)$, and for several more years, although Meiselman concludes that γ, and therefore the effect of the present on future expectations, declines as j increases. An error in forecasting this year's short rate has a large effect on expectations of next year's short rate but a much smaller effect on expectations of what the short rate will be in, say, 20 years' time.

To conclude our consideration of the pure expectations hypothesis, consider its relevance for the construction of theoretical macroeconomic models and its policy implications. The implication for theory is that it is legitimate to use just one interest rate to represent the market for bonds; it is legitimate to consider, for example, the interest rate on a long-term bond, as

---

Dividing the second equation by the first and rearranging terms, we obtain:

$${}_tr^e_{t+2,1} = \frac{(1 + R_{t,3})^3}{(1 + R_{t,2})^2} - 1$$

or, more generally,

$${}_tr^e_{t+n-1,1} = \frac{(1 + R_{t,n})^n}{(1 + R_{t,n-1})^{n-1}} - 1 \equiv {}_t\hat{r}_{t+n-1,1}$$

Keynesian models do, and ignore the interest rates on short-term bonds. This is legitimate because, as Equation 17.10 shows, given expectations, there is a unique relationship between the rate on any long-term bond and the rate on any bond of shorter term. More fundamentally, this arises because the assumption underlying the model is that bonds of different maturities are perfect substitutes for one another. Individual lenders and borrowers are indifferent about holding a short bond and a long bond as long as the expected return from holding a sequence of short bonds is the same as the return on holding a long bond. If these returns differ, lenders will instantaneously attempt to switch all their assets into the more profitable option, and the same applies, *mutatis mutandis*, for borrowers. It is this arbitrage that lies behind Equation 17.10 and that implies that all bonds are perfect substitutes.

The implications for policy result from the same assumptions. The pure expectational theory of Equation 17.10 implies that the central bank or government cannot affect the term structure of rates unless it affects expectations. Specifically, it cannot, for example, succeed in pushing up the long rate, $R_{t,n}$, relative to the short rate, $R_{t,1}$, by selling long bonds. Doing so would initially create an excess supply of long bonds, but as soon as their price fell and $R_{t,n}$ rose, lenders would attempt to switch out of any short bonds they held, thereby creating an excess supply of short bonds that would push up $R_{t,1}$. Given expectations, equilibrium would be restored only when the initial term structure is reached again, although in the new equilibrium all interest rates would be higher than initially. The only way in which the central bank could change the term structure, according to this theory, is if it could affect expectations. Moreover, the theory implies that if the central bank is not attempting to change the term structure but is attempting to change the level of the long rate without worrying about the level of short rates, it does not need to change the supply of long bonds in order to change the long rate. It could, for example, increase the supply of short bonds. This would create an excess supply of short bonds, which would tend to push up their interest rate, but through the process of arbitrage, an excess supply of long bonds would thereby result, and this would have the desired effect of pushing up the long rate. This effect is reinforced if Meiselman's theory of the formation of expectations is correct, for then the rise in the present short rate causes an upward revision of expectations so that long rates rise further.[8]

[8]Two episodes of United States monetary history illustrate the significance of these policy implications. In the 1950s the Federal Reserve adopted a policy known as "Bills Only" in which it attempted to influence all interest rates by sales and purchases of only short bonds (bills). The feasibility of this policy depended on the validity of the expectation theory's assumption of arbitrage between short and long bonds. In the 1960s the Federal Reserve adopted "Operation Twist," which was an attempt to push down long rates by selling long bonds and to push up short rates by reducing the supply of short bonds. Such a policy could be successful in changing the term structure only if the pure expectational theory is invalid (or if the policy itself affects expectations).

17.3 "PURE" SEGMENTATION THEORY

We have seen that one assumption underlying the pure expectational theory is that expectations concerning future rates are held with certainty. If we assume that individuals are risk averters (as in Chapters 10 and 11 where we considered the portfolio theory of the demand for money), then the introduction of uncertainty can provide a rationale for the absence of the perfect arbitrage that was assumed in the pure expectational theory. Bonds of different maturities in such a situation are no longer perfect substitutes for one another, since different maturities involve different risks of capital gain or loss. This line of reasoning has been followed by Culbertson (1957, 1965) and Conard (1959) in arguing that bond markets are segmented into more or less separate markets for bonds of different maturities. If it were carried to the extreme, such an argument would imply that lenders (and borrowers) are interested in bonds of only one maturity, and that even if the return on a sequence of shorter bonds were considerably higher than the return on those bonds, they would not attempt to switch into shorter bonds. Therefore, expectations concerning short rates would have no role in determining long rates. Employing such an extreme form of the segmentation model, let us examine its rationale.

Suppose that a given man is uncertain as to the future rate of interest on any bond; his expectations of future short rates, that is, take the form of a probability distribution. Assume, moreover, that he is a risk averter of an extreme kind: he maximizes utility by reducing the risk on his portfolio to zero irrespective of the expected return on the portfolio.[9] Also, departing from the demand-for-money model of Tobin (1958), we shall assume that the individual dislikes both income risk and capital risk.[10] In these circumstances, as we saw in Chapter 11, the lender can maximize utility, or reduce risk to zero, by holding bonds whose term to maturity equals his encashment period. If he plans to realize his loans for cash at the end of year N, he will be subject to a capital risk if he holds a bond whose term to maturity is greater than N years. If, for example, he holds a bond whose term to maturity is now $(N+1)$ years, he is uncertain as to its interest rate in N years' time; he is uncertain, that is, concerning $R_{t+n,1}$, the one-year rate that will exist at the end of N years. Therefore, he is uncertain of what the price of the bond will be when he wishes to sell it and he risks making a capital loss or gain. If, on the other hand, he buys a one-year bond now, he is uncertain of the rate of interest on one-year bonds over the years that will remain before he wishes to realize his investment; he is uncertain of $R_{t+1,1}, R_{t+2,1}, \ldots, R_{t+n,1}$. In that case, therefore,

[9]In terms of the argument of Chaps. 10 and 11, this assumption could be based on the idea that the utility function is of a special kind that includes σ but not μ as an argument.

[10]For the definition of these terms, see Chap. 11. Tobin's model does not explicitly introduce income risk, since the only bond is an irredeemable bond and it is assumed that the individual's encashment period is of finite length.

there is a risk that the income derived from a sequence of one-year bonds will not be at its expected value. The only way in which the man can reduce both income and capital risk to zero is by now buying an N-year bond and, given his extreme risk aversion, this is what he will do. However high the relative returns on a sequence of short bonds or on a bond of more than N years to maturity, he will hold only an N-year bond.

A similar argument would apply in the case of the maturity of bonds that borrowers wish to supply. More generally, if we assume that individuals have both liabilities and assets, we may argue that they will eliminate risk by matching the maturity of their assets (bond holdings) to the maturity of their liabilities; on such an argument, the maturity of, for example, a lender's liabilities determines the encashment period for his assets. A financial institution, for example, which we shall assume borrows only by issuing one-year bonds, will invest only in one-year bonds, since by assumption it wishes to eliminate risk.[11]

A model such as this is based, then, on the absolute dominance of hedging behavior. Borrowers and lenders hedge their risks by matching either the maturity of bonds to encashment periods, or the maturity of assets to liabilities. In such a model, the term structure of rates, the yield curve, is determined by the demand and supply of each maturity, which are not affected by the expected values of rates of interest. If lenders with short encashment periods (such as financial institutions with short liabilities) and borrowers with long assets (such as firms that wish to finance long-term investment projects) are more numerous than those with the opposite characteristics, we will find that when the present rate on short bonds equals the rate on long bonds, there will be excess demand for short bonds and excess supply of long bonds. This condition will cause the price of short bonds to rise relative to that of long bonds, or, in other words, the short interest rate to fall relative to the long rate. This will restore equilibrium with an upward-sloping yield curve, not because short lenders are thereby tempted toward long bonds—such arbitrage is excluded in this extreme model by extreme risk aversion—but because the fall in the short rate will cause some short lenders to withdraw from the bond market and some short borrowers to enter the market, and similar effects will occur at the long end until demand equals supply in each sector.

The model's implication for the building of theoretical macroeconomic models is that we may again build models with just one interest rate in them. The rationale for this is different, however, from its rationale in the pure expectational model, for it is no longer true that, given expectations, there is a

[11]The construction of an example such as this is difficult in a pure model, since we may ask how the institution makes a profit if both its liabilities and its assets are one-year bonds. One assumption that can rationalize such an example is that bond markets are imperfect, so that those who lend to the institution are not able to lend to those borrowers whose bonds are held by the institution.

unique relationship between short and long rates. Here the rationale derives from consideration of what we want the macroeconomic model to highlight. Suppose that, following the practice of Keynesian economics, we wish to emphasize the significance of the relationship between the money market, the bond market, and the market for fixed capital.[12] Then we may build our model with one interest rate, the rate on long bonds, in it. For the long rate determines the supply of long bonds, and this long borrowing may be assumed to be done by those whose assets are long or, in other words, by those who borrow in order to invest in fixed capital. A fall in the long rate, therefore, will increase the amount of long borrowing and of fixed investment by extremely risk-averse firms. Moreover, the long rate will provide a link with the money market in such a model (as would short rates), since extremely risk-averse lenders may hold either (riskless) money or long bonds that are riskless for them if their encashment periods match the maturity of the long bonds.[13]

The model's implications for policy are that the central bank can alter the term structure of interest rates by altering the relative supplies of long and short bonds. Moreover, the central bank cannot influence the long rate by altering the supply of short bonds alone. That is in direct contrast to the policy implications of the pure expectational theory.

17.4 LIQUIDITY PREFERENCE AND INTERMEDIATE MODELS OF THE TERM STRUCTURE

Both the pure expectational theory and the pure segmentation theory are extreme models. The major aspect of their extreme nature is their respective assumptions concerning attitudes to risk. The pure expectational theory assumes that either uncertainty is absent or that individuals are risk-neutral, so that uncertainty does not concern them; they are interested in profit maximization alone. The pure segmentation or hedging theory assumes that uncertainty concerning future interest rates is present and that individuals are pure risk averters; in their choice of bonds they are interested only in reducing risk to zero.

Because these assumptions are extreme, modifications are frequently introduced into the theories. Culbertson (1957), for example, does not adopt a pure segmentation theory. He assumes that there is some substitutability between bonds of different maturities but that risk aversion prevents the perfect arbitrage between short and long bonds that is assumed by the pure expectational theory. In the case of the expectational theory, Hicks (1939)

[12]See Leijonhufvud (1968), who emphasizes the importance of the long rate in Keynes's work.

[13]But if such opportunities for riskless bond holding were available, we could not explain the lenders' demand for money by Tobin's model of risk aversion. We would have to posit the existence of transactions costs of some form.

introduces the idea that there is a liquidity or risk premium in each rate of interest to reflect the riskiness of bonds of different maturities. In other words, the expectational theory may be represented by the modified form of Equation 17.10:

$$R_{t,n} = n\sqrt{(1+R_{t,1})(1+{}_tr^e_{t+1})\cdots(1+{}_tr_{t+n-1,1})} - 1 + (L_n - L_1) \qquad (17.13)$$

where L_j is a liquidity or risk premium that is zero on a bond or asset, such as money, that is free of capital risk. It causes the rate on a J-year bond to diverge from what it would be if the return from a J-year bond were equated with the return on a sequence of shorter bonds. The liquidity premium reflects the fact that the risk of an N-year bond $(j = n)$ differs from the risk on a sequence of short bonds, a sequence, say, of one-year bonds $(j = 1)$. The extent and nature of the risk differ from one lender (and borrower) to another because of differences in encashment periods. The equilibrium value of L_j (L_n and L_1 in Eq. 17.13) therefore depends on the relative market weights of borrowers and lenders with various encashment periods.

Hicks's idea of a liquidity or risk premium has attracted much attention from writers such as Meiselman (1962) and Leijonhufvud (1968) because he made particular assumptions concerning the nature of encashment periods. With Hicks's assumptions, Equation 17.13's model of liquidity premiums can be interpreted as a version of liquidity preference theory. He assumed that, in general, L_j increases with the length to maturity of the bond. In other words, long bonds have a higher liquidity premium than short bonds: $L_1 < L_2 < \cdots < L_n$. Hicks argued that this characteristic arises because lenders in general have short encashment periods and are concerned with capital risk; they therefore prefer to buy short bonds in order to reduce this risk. Borrowers, on the other hand, are assumed to issue bonds in order to finance investment in fixed capital and therefore prefer to supply long bonds in order to reduce their risk of capital loss. In other words, there is a "constitutional weakness" in the bond market that will ensure that, given expectations of future short rates, there will be an excess demand for short bonds (pushing their price down and their rate up) and an excess supply of long bonds unless their relative interest rates reflect liquidity premiums of the form $L_1 < L_2 < \cdots < L_n$. This hypothesis implies that the slope of the yield curve has an upward bias.[14]

Hicks considered his theory, with its particular assumptions concerning

[14]This can be seen by considering Eq. 17.13 and comparing it with Eq. 17.10. Equation 17.10 indicates, as shown in footnote 3, that if the short rate is expected to remain constant, $R_{t,n} = R_{t,1}$, so that the yield curve would be horizontal. Hicks's argument implies that if all liquidity premiums, such as L_n and L_1 in Eq. 17.13, were zero, then $R_{t,n} = R_{t,1}$ would involve excess supply of the N-year bond, so its price would fall and its rate rise. In other words, $(L_n - L_1)$ would become positive, so that $R_{t,n} = R_{t,1} + (L_n - L_1)$. This implies that in equilibrium, $L_1 < L_2 < \cdots < L_n$. It also implies that there is a bias in the yield curve that causes it to be upward-sloping (the long rate is above the short rate by $(L_n - L_1)$) when expectations are such that, in the absence of liquidity premiums, it would be horizontal.

encashment periods and attitudes to capital risk, to be an important element in Keynes's theory of interest. He interpreted the idea that there is a constitutional weakness and hence positive and increasing liquidity premiums on bonds as the essence of Keynes's explanation (in Chapter 13 of his *General Theory*) of why interest exists on bonds but not on money. For money is assumed to be free of capital risk and therefore to have a liquidity premium of zero. Hicks saw this preference for capital certainty, this risk aversion, as the basis of Keynes's theory of the demand for money, liquidity preference theory, and it can therefore be seen as a precursor of Tobin (1958).[15] Hicks's model of the term structure with positive liquidity premiums can be seen, therefore, as a version of the theory of the demand for money and equilibrium interest rates in a world where bonds of varying maturities (rather than only irredeemable bonds) exist. This can be represented by assuming that money is a riskless asset and for that reason is at the origin of the yield curve with a zero term to maturity and an interest rate of zero.

Hicks's model, however, has several weaknesses. If it is interpreted as the basis of the theory of the demand for money, its weakness is the implication that if short-term bonds exist that are as riskless as money, they should also bear zero interest. This implication leaves the model unable to explain why interest is paid on time deposits at banks but not on demand deposits or, in the terms in which the matter was discussed in Chapter 11, why the demand for non–interest-bearing demand deposits and cash is positive when the interest rate on other riskless assets, such as time deposits, is positive. More generally, Hicks's theory has been criticized by writers such as Meiselman (1962) on the grounds that there is no a priori reason to expect that individuals are primarily concerned with capital risk rather than income risk or, even if they are concerned solely with capital risk, to assume that lenders primarily have short encashment periods and borrowers issue bonds to finance the holding of long assets. Meiselman's criticism is, correctly, that liquidity premiums may take the form $L_1 > L_2 > \cdots > L_n$.

Short-Term Expectations of the Long Rate

Hicks's model represents an early attempt to overcome the limitations of the pure expectational model in a world where there is uncertainty and risk aversion, but if we abandon his particular assumptions concerning the preferences of borrowers and lenders for long and short bonds, the model is constructed at a high level of generality. At that level, it still retains the weakness of the pure expectational model that, to explain the rate on an N-year bond, individuals must have expectations concerning the rates on

[15]Hicks (1939) also thought that default risk on bonds was a component of Keynes's theory of interest, and he argued that this concept of default risk should be expanded along the lines subsequently pursued by Ostroy (1971) to develop a theory of liquidity preference more satisfactory than that of Keynes.

short bonds N years hence. Later models, such as those of Malkiel (1966), Luckett (1967), Modigliani and Sutch (1967), Masera (1972) and White and Burman (1974), follow a different approach. They have in common the idea that individuals hold expectations concerning the behavior of long-term (and generally short-term) rates over the near future or, in other words, over a period shorter than the long rate's term to maturity. This belief differs from the pure expectational theory's view that individuals hold expectations concerning short rates over the far future, or up to the redemption date of the long bond. It, rather than Hicks's modification of the pure expectational theory, may be considered as based on Keynes's liquidity preference theory in the sense that it is based on the assumption underlying Keynes's theory of the speculative demand—that asset holders hold expectations concerning what the rate of interest on irredeemable bonds will be in the near future.

The theoretical basis of this implication varies in its details among the writers named, but, as in the case of Modigliani and Sutch (1967), we may assume that the lender's encashment period is the same as the term to maturity of the short bond and therefore less than that of the long bond. In their model, the individual lender, therefore, has to take into account the uncertain possibility of a capital gain or loss on the long bond. This does not lead to a pure segmentation theory since the individual is not assumed to be a pure risk averter. Indeed, by contrast, the lender is assumed to be willing to choose to hold either the short bond or the long bond over the encashment period according to which one offers the highest expected value of return. If the present interest rate on the short bond (say, a one-year bond) is $R_{t,1}$, and the interest rate on the long bond is $R_{t,n}$, this implies that in equilibrium the relationship between the short rate and the long rate is:

$$R_{t,1} = R_{t,n} + g^e_{t,t+1} \tag{17.14}$$

where $g^e_{t,t+1}$ is the expected value of the percentage gain on the long bond at the end of the one-year period.[16] We saw in Chapter 10 that the expected capital gain on a bond that is not held until redemption is a function of its current rate and the rate that is expected to hold on it at the end of the encashment period. Therefore we may rewrite Equation 17.14 as:

$$R_{t,1} = R_{t,n} + f(R_{t,n}, {}_tr^e_{t+1,n-1}) \tag{17.15}$$

It is apparent that expectations of the future long rate (the long rate that will hold in the near future) are relevant to the relationship between the current short rate, $R_{t,1}$, and the current long rate, $R_{t,n}$.

[16]Bearing in mind that $R_{t,n}$ denotes the maturity yield of the long bond throughout this chapter, its use in Eq. 17.16 is strictly valid only if we assume that the price at which an individual buys the long bond equals its par value. For, in Eq. 17.14, $R_{t,n}$ represents the amount of the interest earned over the short period, whereas the definition of the maturity yield, as in Eq. 17.4, causes it to reflect also the par value that is received upon redemption. Since in the present model the long bond is not held until redemption, the maturity yield is not appropriate unless we make the above assumption.

An alternative model is one suggested by White and Burman (1974). In their model, they take explicit account of risk aversion along the lines suggested by Sharpe (1964) which, as we saw in Chapter 11, is based on the von Neuman-Morgenstern utility theory. They also follow a suggestion by Malkiel (1966) and build their model on the assumption that individuals have a definite horizon for expectations. That is, individuals do not attempt to predict the course of (short or long) interest rates beyond some future date, $t + j$, except by assuming that interest rates will be constant thereafter. These two specific features allow White and Burman to rewrite the terms of Equation 17.15. The return on the long bond over the short (say, one-year) period must include a liquidity premium, L_n, to account for the risk averter's preference for absence of capital risk. Since we are assuming in Equation 17.15 that the period is the same as the term to maturity of the short bond, the short bond is riskless and has a liquidity premium of zero. Therefore, instead of Equation 17.15, White and Burman's model implies an equation like:

$$R_{t,1} = R_{t,n} + f\ R_{t,n}, {}_t r^e_{t+1,n-1}) - L_n \tag{17.16}$$

Or, if we wish to consider the relationship between the rates on two bonds of different maturity (n and m), each of which is longer than the period under consideration, we would have to take account of the risk premiums and capital gain on each:

$$R_{t,m} + f(R_{t,m}, {}_t r_{t+1,m-1}) - L_m = R_{t,n} + f(R_{t,n}, {}_t r_{r+1,n-1}) - L_n \tag{17.17}$$

The value of Sharpe's work (1974) is that it allows us to calculate the factors upon which the L_j terms depend.[17] The value of the assumption that interest rates are expected to be constant after some future date j is that, in empirical work, it enables us to simplify the relationship between ${}_t r^e_{t+j,m-j}$ and ${}_t \hat{r}_{r+j,m-j}$.

We may conclude this chapter by noting that the pure expectational theory of the term structure and the pure segmentation theory are based on extreme assumptions concerning uncertainty and expectations. More sophisticated models are able to overcome the limitations of each. Moreover, although many writers on the theory of the term structure have been primarily concerned with its policy implications, we have seen in this chapter that the theory also has important connections with the theory of money and the building of macroeconomic models.

[17]As indicated in Chap. 11, the determining factor of the relative risk premiums on different assets (or bonds of different maturity in this case) is the covariance of their prices.

PART FIVE

MONEY IN DYNAMIC MODELS

CHAPTER

EIGHTEEN

NEUTRALITY AND GROWTH MODELS

In Chapter 12 we considered the neutrality of money in comparative static Walrasian models. Here we consider neutrality in the context of a growing economy. In this context, the criterion for whether or not money is neutral is usually stated more directly than is customary in the comparative static model. Instead of judging the neutrality of a *once-and-for-all increase* in the money supply according to the constancy of the equilibrium interest rate, in growth models we consider a *change in the rate of growth* of the money supply and examine its effect on the capital/labor ratio that exists on the equilibrium growth path. If the government were to double the rate of growth of the money supply (rather than its level), would the capital/labor ratio in an economy growing along an equilibrium path increase or decrease and therefore imply nonneutrality? Or would it remain unchanged, in which case money would be neutral?[1]

We shall see here that money is *in general* nonneutral in growth models, but this is not true for all models; whether an increase in the rate of growth of the money supply increases, decreases, or leaves unchanged the equilibrium growth path's capital/labor ratio varies from one model to another. In the comparative static analysis of Chapter 12, the source of the differences between the conclusions of various models was the disparity in their assumptions concerning the existence of different mixtures of inside and outside assets. For example, we saw that if the only financial asset is outside money, then money is neutral. In the context of growth models, however, the distinction between inside and outside assets does not play a significant role. Indeed, money is, in general, found to be nonneutral in growth models even

[1]To distinguish this concept of neutrality in growth models from the concept of comparative static neutrality, growth neutrality is sometimes designated as superneutrality.

when the only financial asset is outside money, and monetary growth models differ from one another quite apart from their dissimilar assumptions concerning the mix of inside and outside money.

If the comparative static analysis of neutrality has focused attention on the distinction between outside and inside assets, what has been the focus of the analysis of neutrality in growth models? Monetary growth models are distinguished by two particular types of assumptions. The first concerns the dynamics of price-level adjustment. The Neoclassical models considered in Sections 18.1 to 18.3 differ from the Keynes-Wicksell model of Section 18.4 primarily because the former assume that the absolute price level adjusts instantaneously to maintain equilibrium in the money market at every instant, whereas the latter assumes that it changes in response to goods market disequilibrium and that the goods and money markets may be in disequilibrium. The second type of assumption is one that distinguishes one Neoclassical model from another. It concerns the theories of saving that are employed in the different Neoclassical models and, associated with this, the role that money is assumed to play in the economy—whether, for example, money is treated as a factor of production. The problems of modeling the price adjustment mechanism, of formulating the saving function, and of defining money and its contribution to national income are problems that can be considered in a comparative static framework. But they have been given most attention in the context of growth models and, since different assumptions have different implications for the growth neutrality of money, we shall consider them here.

In Section 18.1 we set out the basic Neoclassical growth model constructed for a one-good world without money, and we compare the stability of its equilibrium growth path with the stability of the Harrod-Domar model's equilibrium. In Section 18.2 we examine the price adjustment assumption of the Neoclassical monetary growth model and derive the basic result of Neoclassical growth models: that an increase in the rate of growth of the money supply causes an increase in the equilibrium capital/labor ratio. In Section 18.3 we show how this result can be altered by altering the saving hypothesis and by defining money as a factor of production, although the model in general yields nonneutrality even with these alterations. In Section 18.3 we examine the Keynes-Wicksell model which, although different from the Neoclassical model in that it drops the assumption of equilibrium at every instant in the goods and money markets, also reaches the conclusion that money may be either neutral or nonneutral.

18.1 THE BASIC NEOCLASSICAL GROWTH MODEL WITHOUT MONEY

The question of the neutrality of money in growth models is concerned with the capital/labor ratio or capital/output ratio on the equilibrium growth path and the possibility or impossibility of monetary policy changing these ratios. In this it differs from the comparative static analysis of neutrality in the short-run Neoclassical/Keynesian Synthesis model. In that model it is assumed that the capital/labor and capital/output ratios at full-employment output are given; the forces that may change them are not examined. Although in Chapter 12 we discussed the effect of monetary policy on the equilibrium interest rate, we did not study the effects of changes in the interest rate on the equilibrium capital/labor or capital/output ratio.

In the Neoclassical growth model (either with or without money), variations in the capital/labor and capital/output ratios are fundamental to the stability of the equilibrium growth path. In this section we shall examine the essential features of the Neoclassical growth model, illustrating the argument with a one-sector model without money, and we shall see how variations in the capital/labor and capital/output ratios ensure stability. We shall begin by setting out, as a contrast, a version of the Harrod-Domar model where the capital/output ratio is assumed fixed and where, in consequence, the equilibrium growth path is highly unstable.

The growth model based on the work of Harrod (1939) and Domar (1946) is based on some restrictive simplifying assumptions, but it nevertheless enables us to derive a fundamental equation, the equation of the equilibrium growth path.[2] Let n' be the rate of growth of society's productive capacity. Since we shall assume that there is no technical progress, we may define n' as the rate of growth of the labor force. If, therefore, the economy is now at full employment and if the output/labor ratio is fixed at $(y/n)_0$, then aggregate output must grow at the rate n' if full employment is to be maintained. The conventional name given to n' is *natural rate of growth.*

The Harrod-Domar model is primarily concerned not with the natural rate of growth but with the *warranted rate of growth.* This is the rate of growth of y that can be achieved if the goods market is in equilibrium in each period[3] in the sense of equality between planned expenditure and actual income, or, in other words, equality between planned saving and planned investment.[4] The warranted rate of growth, then, requires

$$s_T = i_T \tag{18.1}$$

[2]It should be emphasized that the model discussed here is a very crude version of the Harrod-Domar model and that it ignores many of the subtleties that concerned Harrod and Domar.

[3]Or at every instant if we work with a continuous, instead of a discrete, time model. If we employ a discrete time model, it is most convenient to use the word "equilibrium" to mean flow equilibrium or end-of-period stock equilibrium.

[4]This is the same meaning of goods market equilibrium as was employed in Chap. 8. It ignores planned supply (full-employment income), and planned demand is to be interpreted as effective demand, as in Chap. 13.

The simplest Harrod-Domar model assumes that planned saving is a constant proportion $\hat{s}$ of income:

$$s_T = \hat{s}\bar{y}_T \tag{18.2}$$

where $\hat{s}$ is the average and marginal propensity to save. It is also assumed that planned investment is a constant proportion of the change in income, so that planned investment is represented by a crude accelerator relation:

$$i_T = v(\bar{y}_T - \bar{y}_{T-1}) \tag{18.3}$$

Substituting from Equations 18.2 and 18.3 into Equation 18.1, the goods market equilibrium condition is expressed as:

$$\hat{s}\bar{y}_T = v(\bar{y}_T - \bar{y}_{T-1})$$

or, rearranging terms:

$$\frac{\hat{s}}{v} = \frac{(\bar{y}_T - \bar{y}_{T-1})}{\bar{y}_T} \tag{18.4}$$

The expression on the right-hand side is the rate of growth of actual income—the change in income expressed as a proportion of its current level. The expression on the left is the ratio of the average (and constant) propensity to save to the accelerator coefficient v. Since Equation 18.4 is derived from the goods market equilibrium condition, it implies that $\hat{s}/v$ is the rate of growth that will be achieved if the goods market is in equilibrium. It is the warranted rate of growth.

Suppose that the economy is initially at full employment and that the warranted growth rate $\hat{s}/v$ equals the natural growth rate n':

$$\frac{\hat{s}}{v} = n' \tag{18.5}$$

Then the economy can grow at the rate that maintains full employment, n', and that maintains goods market equilibrium, $\hat{s}/v$. In other words, the equilibrium growth path is the full-employment path if the values of $\hat{s}$, v, and n' happen to be those that satisfy Equation 18.5. This (or any other) equilibrium growth path is, however, an unstable equilibrium path. If Equation 18.5 is satisfied but then, say, the average propensity to save declines for some reason, we will have:

$$\frac{\hat{s}}{v} < n'$$

so that goods market equilibrium causes $\bar{y}$ to grow at less than the rate required to maintain full employment. Given the exogenous nature of $\hat{s}$, v, and n', the fall in $\hat{s}$ sets up no endogenous forces to restore the equality of Equation 18.5. Therefore the warranted growth rate represented by that equation is an unstable equilibrium growth rate.[5]

[5]In other words, any warranted growth rate is an unstable equilibrium rate.

If a change in one of the three variables were to produce an endogenous and offsetting change in $\hat{s}$, v, or r', then the full-employment equilibrium growth rate of Equation 18.5 would be a stable equilibrium rate. We shall see that the Neoclassical growth model, in contrast with the Harrod-Domar model, assumes that v varies endogenously so as to ensure that Equation 18.5 is satisfied. In that model, therefore, if we start from full employment, the equilibrium growth path is that which provides full employment, and it is a stable equilibrium growth path.

As a preliminary to studying the Neoclassical model, it should be noted at this stage that v can be interpreted as the capital/output ratio $k/\bar{y}$. This can be seen from a simple rationalization of the crude accelerator of Equation 18.3. Suppose that the fixed capital/output ratio is v, so that production of y_T output requires a capital stock of:

$$k_T = vy_T \tag{18.6}$$

in period T. If we define planned investment in period T as the difference between the required capital stock in period T and that in period $T - 1$:[6]

$$i_T = k_T - k_{T-1} \tag{18.7}$$

From our definition of v in Equation 18.6, this implies that:

$$\begin{aligned} i_T &= vy_T - vy_{T-1} \\ &= v(y_T - y_{T-1}) \end{aligned}$$

This is the crude accelerator postulated in Equation 18.3, so that v, the accelerator coefficient, may be interpreted as v, the capital/output ratio $(v = k/y)$.

Neoclassical Growth

Now we may examine the Neoclassical growth model without money and consider the difference between it and the simple Harrod-Domar model. Figure 18.1 illustrates our assumptions concerning the behavior functions and technical relations of the model and illustrates our analysis. It relates to an economy where there is no supply or demand for money or any other financial asset—all transactions being conducted through barter. The only asset in the economy, therefore, is physical capital which, in real terms, we denote as k. The employed labor force (n) is assumed, for simplicity, to comprise the whole population. The horizontal axis in Figure 18.1 measures

[6]This definition creates a difficulty in measuring the time dimension of the flow of investment, for, if a higher capital stock is demanded at the beginning of period T, the planned rate of investment is greater than if a gradual increase of the capital stock over period T, to reach k_T by the end of the period, is planned. We shall ignore these difficulties and assume that the capital stock k_T, is installed at the beginning of period T, but the change in capital stock is measured as though spread over period T.

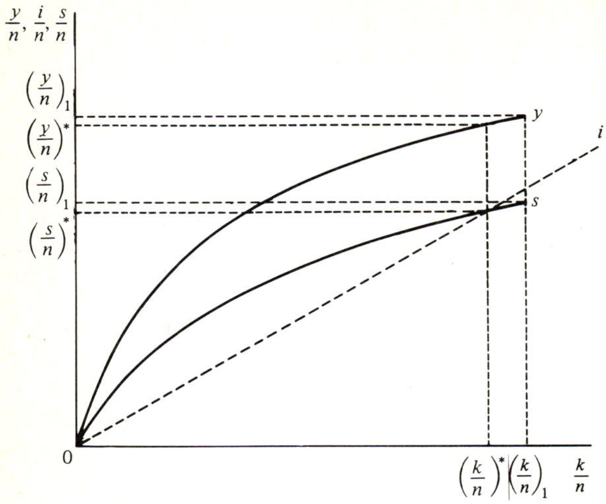

Figure 18-1

the ratio of capital to labor (k/n) or, in other words, the economy's per capita stock of capital. The vertical axis measures output per worker (y/n) in real terms (that is, per capita earned income), and along the same axis we measure the real value of investment and saving per capita (i/n, s/n).

Now let us consider the figure's curves. $0y$ represents per capita output, (y/n), as a function of the per capita capital stock (k/n):

$$\frac{y}{n} = f\left(\frac{k}{n}\right) \tag{18.8}$$

In other words, it represents the production function:

$$y = y(n, k)$$

if we assume that this production function gives constant returns to scale and diminishing marginal returns to inputs. Its convexity from below follows from the assumption that there are diminishing marginal returns to (diminishing marginal productivity of) capital. The curve $0s$ represents planned saving per capita, s/n. On the assumption that each individual has a fixed average propensity to consume ($\hat{c}$), saving per worker is a fixed proportion (s) of actual per capita earned income, ($\bar{y}/n$), and the line represents the equation:

$$\frac{s}{n} = \hat{s}\left(\frac{\bar{y}}{n}\right) = (1 - \hat{c})\left(\frac{\bar{y}}{n}\right) \tag{18.9}$$

Saving per worker is higher the higher is k/n, because earned income is higher the higher is k/n: that is, from Equations 18.8 and 18.9:

$$\frac{s}{n} = \hat{s}\left[f\left(\frac{k}{n}\right)\right] \tag{18.10}$$

It is assumed that at every point of time the goods market is in equilibrium in the sense that planned saving equals planned investment:

$$\frac{s}{n} = \frac{i}{n} \tag{18.11}$$

so that the $0s$ curve represents investment as well as planned saving. This must be the case since, in the absence of any financial assets, all saving must take the form of an accumulation of physical assets, but it is nevertheless an assumption worth noting. Finally, consider the curve $0i^*$. This is not a behavioral function showing people's plans, but instead measures $(i/n)^*$, the level of per capita investment that would be necessary to maintain the capital/labor ratio (k/n) constant. It slopes upward for the following reason: Assuming that the labor force is growing at the constant rate, n', which is determined exogenously by birth and death rates, the capital stock must grow at the rate n' if the capital/labor ratio is to remain constant. Since the amount of investment is the amount by which the capital stock grows, the required amount of investment per worker is:

$$\left(\frac{i}{n}\right)^* = \frac{kn'}{n} \tag{18.12}$$

which, clearly, is higher the higher is k/n.

We can now analyze the equilibrium growth path of this economy. The conclusion we shall reach is that the economy is on an equilibrium growth path when *aggregate* output (earned income), y, saving, s, and capital stock, k, are growing at the same rate as the labor force, n, is growing. That is, all these aggregate variables are growing at the rate n' on the equilibrium growth path. Since these variables are growing at the rate n' and since the labor force is growing at the same rate, the per capita values of these variables must be constant on the equilibrium path. In Figure 18.1 this equilibrium is reached with per capita values of output, saving, and capital equal to $(y/n)^*$, $(s/n)^*$, and $(k/n)^*$; that is, the equilibrium rate of growth is reached when planned per capita saving equals the level of per capita investment that is required to keep the capital/labor ratio constant:

$$\frac{s}{n} = \left(\frac{i}{n'}\right)^* = \frac{kn'}{n} \tag{18.13}$$

If the economy is at the point where this equilibrium growth condition, Equation 18.13, is satisfied, it will show no tendency to move away, whereas, if the economy is not at such a point, there is a tendency to move toward it. This can be seen by imagining that, instead of being at $(y/n)^*$, $(s/n)^*$, and $(k/n)^*$, these variables were at $(y/n)_1$, $(s/n)_1$, and $(k/n)_1$ in Figure 18.1. If they were, s/n would be less than $(i/n)^*$—saving (investment) per worker would be less than the amount necessary to maintain the capital/labor ratio constant. As a result, the capital/labor ratio would fall and would continue to do so until it reached $(k/n)^*$, at which point the other variables would have the values $(y/n)^*$ and $(s/n)^*$ and saving would just equal the amount of investment required to keep the ratio constant. The argument holds, *mutatis mutandis*, if we imagine that (k/n) is initially to the left of $(k/n)^*$. Thus, the economy tends toward an equilibrium where y/n, s/n, and k/n take the constant values $(y/n)^*$, $(s/n)^*$, and $(k/n)^*$, so that aggregate output, saving, and capital stock are growing at the same rate, n', as the population. The equilibrium rate of growth of the economy is therefore n'.

The Neoclassical growth model, therefore, does not differ from the Harrod-Domar model in its description of the full-employment equilibrium growth path. In the Harrod-Domar model, the path is described by:

$$\frac{\hat{s}}{v} = n' \tag{18.5}$$

whereas, in the Neoclassical model it is described by:

$$\frac{s}{n} = \frac{k}{n}n' \tag{18.13}$$

The latter can be rewritten, however, in the same form as the Harrod-Domar condition. From Equation 18.9 we can rewrite Equation 18.13 as:

$$\frac{\hat{s}\bar{y}}{n} = \frac{k}{n}n'$$

or, by rearranging terms:

$$\frac{\hat{s}\bar{y}}{k} = n'$$

Since $v = k/y$, this can be rewritten as:

$$\frac{\hat{s}}{v} = n'$$

This is the same as the Harrod-Domar condition. The Neoclassical model does, however, differ from the Harrod-Domar model insofar as the equilibrium growth path is stable. Using Figure 18.2, suppose, for example, that the economy is initially on the full-employment equilibrium path with $(k/n)_1$ capital per head; then, for some reason, $\hat{s}$, the average propensity to save, falls. In Figure 18.2 the savings curve swings downward from $0s_1$ to $0s_2$ and, as we have seen, the capital stock per head automatically falls to the level $(k/n)_2$, at which the new $0s$ curve intersects the $0i^*$ curve. In terms of Equation 18.13, when s/n falls because of the fall in $\hat{s}$, the level of k/n automatically falls, so maintaining the equality of the two sides of the equation. Alternatively, to interpret the Neoclassical model in terms of the Harrod-Domar equation, Equation 18.5, the fall in $\hat{s}$ leads to a fall in v, so that the growth rate remains at n' and full employment is maintained with a lower capital output ratio. In Harrod-Domar terms, that is, the fall in the average propensity to save in the Neoclassical model causes a fall in the capital/output ratio. The capital/output ratio is represented diagrammatically by the inverse of the slope of a ray from the origin to the $0y$ curve, the production function.

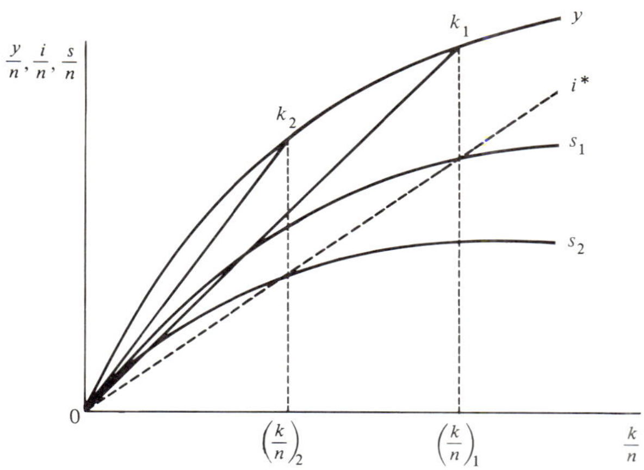

Figure 18-2

In Figure 18.2 the capital/output ratio, v, is initially the inverse of the slope of $0k_1$; in the new equilibrium, it is lower, being the inverse of the slope of $0k_2$.

Thus, in the Neoclassical growth model, in contrast with the Harrod-Domar model, the existence and stability of the full-employment equilibrium growth path are ensured by endogenous adjustments of v or, equivalently, k/n.[7] There exists an equilibrium capital/labor ratio $(k/n)^*$ that is constant over time as the economy grows along its equilibrium path. The equilibrium path and the equilibrium capital/labor ratio will change if $\hat{s}$, the average propensity to save out of real income, or n', the rate of growth of population, changes.

The models presented in this section have not permitted us to consider the role of money. In the following two sections we introduce money into the Neoclassical model and find that, in general, changes in the rate of growth of the money supply change the equilibrium capital/output and capital/labor ratios. This occurs via the effects of monetary policy upon the average propensity to save.

18.2 A NEOCLASSICAL GROWTH MODEL WITH MONEY

The basic Neoclassical model developed in Section 18.1 may now be extended to a monetary economy. There are several different approaches to building such a model, and in the present section, we shall follow an approach similar to that of Tobin (1965b) and Sidrauski (1967a). In the nonmonetary model, individuals could only save by acquiring physical capital; we now assume that

[7]In the Neoclassical model, a fall in the capital/labor ratio, k/n, implies a fall in the capital/output ratio v because the production function is concave from below. If it were, instead, a straight line through the origin, the capital/output ratio, which is itself a ray through the origin, would be constant whatever the level of k/n.

they can also save by acquiring outside money (although we continue to assume that bonds do not exist). This new asset affects behavior. Consequently, we must reformulate and add to the behavior functions and technical relations employed in the previous section.

Money Market

In particular, we must now include a money market in the model. The per capita demand for real balances is assumed to be a function of per capita real output, y/n (reflecting the transactions demand for money), and the relative return on money compared with the alternative asset, physical capital, reflecting the asset demand for money. This relative return is a function of the expected rate of inflation, π^e, and the marginal productivity of physical capital, r^k. We can therefore write the demand function for real balances *per capita* as:

$$\frac{M^D}{pn} = f\left(\frac{y}{n}, \pi^e, r^k\right) \tag{18.14}$$

But this form requires some explanation. The Keynesian demand function for money considered in earlier chapters may be simplified to (in per capita terms):

$$\frac{M^D}{pn} = f\left(\frac{y}{n}, r^B\right) \tag{18.15}$$

where r^B represents the rate of interest on bonds and is included as a result of speculative or precautionary behavior. Equation 18.14 differs from this by replacing r^B with r^K to reflect the fact that the asset that is an alternative to money in this simple growth model is physical capital. It also differs by including π^e. This variable is generally excluded from the short-run Keynesian model's demand functions for money, such as Equation 18.15, because those models are usually built on the assumption that expected rates of inflation and deflation are zero. In the Neoclassical growth model, however, the expected rate of change of the absolute price level plays a central role and cannot be assumed to be zero. We therefore have to include it explicitly in Equation 18.14's demand function for money, for, if π^e is positive, the expected rate of return on real balances is negative, since a rising absolute price level reduces the real value of money balances; that is, an individual who holds $(M/p)_t$ real balances at time t expects that these real balances will be reduced by time $t+1$ if π^e is positive.

Figure 18.3 illustrates Equation 18.14's demand function for money in terms of the expected rate of inflation. Given r^K and y/n, the per capita demand for real balances is negatively related to π^e; the higher is the expected rate of inflation, the lower will be the demand for real balances, M^D/pn, as shown by the demand curve *MM*. If the marginal products of physical capital r^K were higher, the demand curve *MM* would be further to the left; if per capita output were higher, the demand curve would be further to the right.

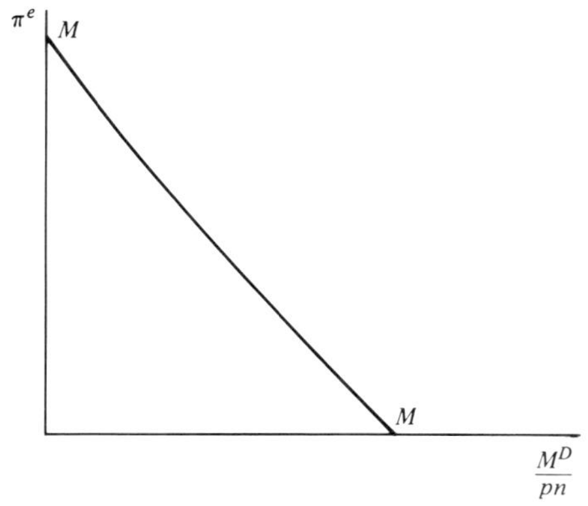

Figure 18-3

The total supply of money is assumed to be exogenously determined in nominal terms, M^S, by the government. We shall assume that nominal balances consist only of outside money and that the aggregate stock of nominal balances is increasing over time. This increase may be assumed to arise from the government's paying subsidies that are financed by the printing of new money. If the change in the stock of money per period is $\dot{M}^S$, the percentage rate of change is $\dot{M}^S/M$. We shall denote this as μ. If π is the rate of inflation $(\dot{p}/p)$, we can write the rate of change of real balances as:

$$\frac{\dfrac{\dot{M}^S}{\dot{p}}}{\dfrac{M^S}{p}} = \mu - \pi \tag{18.16}$$

Equilibrium in the money market requires that the per capita demand for real balances at any instant equals the supply of real balances per person:

$$\frac{M^D}{pn} = \frac{M^S}{pn} \tag{18.17}$$

It is a basic assumption of the Neoclassical model that the money market is always in equilibrium because the price level adjusts instantaneously to ensure the equality of the two sides of Equation 18.17. Therefore the equations of the money market provide us with the Neoclassical model's theory of price-level adjustment. If the nominal money supply is growing at the rate μ and the demand for real balances per person is constant, then Equation 18.17 implies that:

$$0 = \mu - \pi - n' \tag{18.18}$$

or

$$\pi = \mu - n' \tag{18.19}$$

In other words, equilibrium in the money market is ensured by the fact that the rate of inflation adjusts to equal the rate of increase of per capita nominal money supply (the rate of increase of total nominal money supply, μ, minus the rate of increase of population, n').

Before leaving the money market, we must return to the demand function for real balances and ask what determines the variables y/n, r^K, and π^e, which themselves determine the demand for money. As can be seen from Figure 18.2, if the production function is represented by the curve $0y$, output per head, y/n, is uniquely determined by the capital/labor ratio k/n. At the same time, r^K, the marginal product of capital, is the slope of $0y$ itself (or a tangent to $0y$) at the point above k/n. Thus, y/n and r^K are uniquely related to the capital/labor ratio k/n, and in the demand function for money we can substitute k/n for these variables. A more interesting problem is what determines the expected rate of inflation π^e. We shall follow Stein (1970) and assume that the expected rate of inflation equals the rate of growth of the per capital nominal money supply:[8]

$$\pi^e = \mu - n' \tag{18.20}$$

These considerations enable us to rewrite the demand function for real balances, replacing Equation 18.14 with:

$$\frac{M^D}{pn} = f\left(\frac{k}{n}, \mu - n'\right) \tag{18.21}$$

This implies that, given k/n (and therefore r^K and y/n), the demand for real balances is constant if the rate of growth of the nominal money supply per capita $(\mu - n')$ is constant. If $(\mu - n')$ is constant, then, from Equation 18.19's money market equilibrium condition, we see that the constancy of the demand for real balances implies that the actual rate of inflation equals $(\mu - n')$ and (from Eq. 18.20) that it equals the expected rate of inflation.

Savings Function

Having considered the nature of the money market in the Neoclassical model, we must now note that the savings function is different in the Neoclassical monetary model from the function employed in Section 18.1's nonmonetary model. For the present, we shall adopt a simple savings function, although we shall see in Section 18.3 that the model is sensitive to the type of savings function adopted. We shall assume that planned consumption per person is a constant proportion, $\hat{c}$, of "disposable" income per person.

[8]In other words, as can be seen from a comparison between Eqs. 18.20 and 18.19, individuals expect the rate of inflation to be that which would actually occur if the per capita demand for real balances were constant and the money market were in equilibrium. Other writers use different assumptions concerning expectations. Sidrauski (1967b), for example, assumes that π^e is a function of past rates of inflation. One assumption that is rejected in the Neoclassical growth model is that π^e *always* equals π—expected inflation always equals current inflation—for that would lead to instability of the equilibrium growth path. However, on the ***equilibrium growth path***, $\pi^e = \pi$ even when Eq. 18.20 is our theory of expectations.

Total disposable income in a period is defined as the earned income or output, y, plus the change in the stock of real balances, $\dot{M}^S/\dot{p}$, per period. This income is so defined because the change in the stock of real balances in this outside money economy is an increase in wealth and may therefore be considered as a component of income. In per capita real terms, the consumption function is, therefore:

$$\frac{c}{n} = \hat{c}\left(y + \frac{\dot{M}^S}{\dot{p}}\right)\frac{1}{n} \tag{18.22}$$

From the definition set out in Equation 18.16, we can substitute for $\dot{M}^S/\dot{p}$ and rewrite the consumption function as

$$\frac{c}{n} = \hat{c} = \left[\frac{y}{n} + (\mu - \pi)\frac{M^S}{pn}\right] \tag{18.23}$$

Planned saving, in the usual national-income accounting sense of the amount of output which people do not consume, is therefore:

$$\frac{s}{n} = \frac{y}{n} - \hat{c}\left[\frac{y}{n} + (\mu - \pi)\frac{M^S}{pn}\right]$$

or, simplifying:

$$\frac{s}{n} = \hat{s}\frac{y}{n} - \hat{c}(\mu - \pi)\frac{M^S}{pn} \tag{18.24}$$

where $\hat{s}$, equals $(1 - \hat{c})$. An important alternative form of Equation 18.24 follows from the fact that since the money market is assumed to be always in equilibrium, the demand for real balances equals the supply of real balances (Eq. 18.17). Therefore we shall employ the savings function in the form:

$$\frac{s}{n} = \hat{s}\frac{y}{n} - \hat{c}(\mu - \pi)\frac{M^D}{pn} \tag{18.25}$$

This is the same as the savings function that was employed in the non-monetary model of Section 18.1 (Eq. 18.9) except for the fact that saving now depends on the rate of change of real balances $(\mu - \pi)$ and the desired and actual level of real balances per person, M^D/pn, as well as the level of output.

We shall maintain the assumption employed in Section 18.1 that planned saving always equals planned and actual investment:

$$\frac{s}{n} = \frac{i}{n} \tag{18.26}$$

This, like the assumption that the rate of inflation always adjusts to equilibrate the money market, is a crucial assumption for the Neoclassical model. It implies that the goods market is never in disequilibrium.

Nonneutrality

We may now employ Figure 18.4 to analyze the effect of monetary policy upon the equilibrium capital/labor and capital/output ratios. The curve $0y$ measures output per capita as a function of the capital/labor ratio, k/n. It is

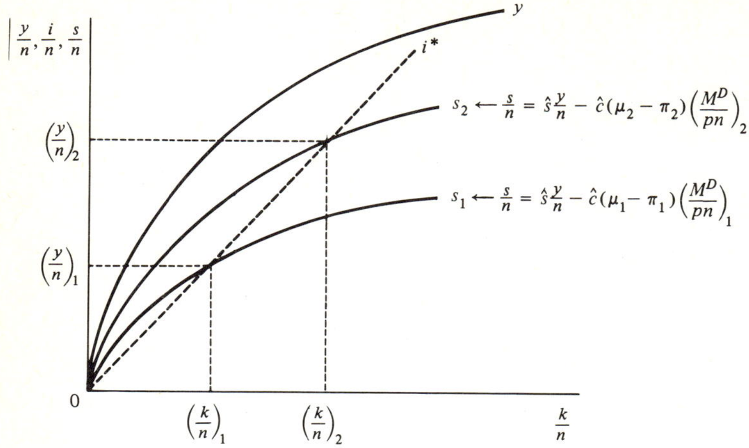

Figure 18-4

based upon the same production function as was assumed in Section 18.1 (Eq. 18.8). The curve $0i^*$ again represents the amount of investment per capita, $(k/n)n'$, which is required to maintain the capital/labor ratio constant when population is growing at the rate n'. The curve $0s$ represents saving per capita according to the saving function of Equation 18.25. Whereas, in Section 18.1, constancy of $\hat{s}$ (or $\hat{c}$) ensured stability of the saving curve in relation to $0y$, now the saving curve will shift if the amount of the increase in the real per capita money supply per period, $(\mu - \pi)M^D/pn$, changes.

Suppose that, initially, $0s_1$ exists as the saving curve. That is, the rate of increase in the nominal money supply is μ_1 and the rate of inflation is π_1. By the same reasoning as employed in Section 18.1, equilibrium will be reached at the point where $0s_1$ intersects $0i^*$. The equilibrium capital/labor ratio is $(k/n)_1$ and the equilibrium level of output per person is $(y/n)_1$, so that the capital stock and total output are growing at the same rate, n', as the population. Now assume that the government increases the rate of growth of the total nominal money supply from μ_1 to μ_2. We must examine the effect of this on the savings function and, in particular, on the term $(\mu - \pi)M^D/pn$. Equilibrium in the money market ensures that the rise in μ to μ_2 causes the rate of inflation to rise the same extent from π_1 to π_2 so that $(\mu_2 - \pi_2)$ equals $(\mu_1 - \pi_1)$. This follows from Equations 18.18 and 18.19 since, as we saw above, for any given μ, $\pi = \mu - n'$, and since n', the rate of population growth, is constant, $\mu - \pi$ is constant. However, the demand function for real balances, Equation 18.21, implies that the demand for real balances per person falls. The fall in M^D/pn results from the fact that the rise in the rate of increase of the nominal money supply from μ_1 to μ_2 increases the expected rate of inflation, π^e, by Equation 18.20. It therefore causes a decline in the demand for real balances, since the increase in π^e is equivalent to a reduction in the yield on real balances. The significance of the fall in M^D/pn is that it causes the savings curve to rise to $0s_2$. In consequence, the equilibrium capital/labor ratio becomes $(k/n)_2$ rather than $(k/n)_1$, and the level of output per person changes to $(y/n)_2$.

It follows from this analysis that in the Neoclassical growth model, money is not neutral. A change in the rate of growth of the nominal money supply causes a change in the capital/labor ratio on the equilibrium growth path. In particular, this result, formulated by Tobin (1965b) and Sidrauski (1967a), suggests that a higher rate of growth of the nominal money supply and, consequently, a higher rate of inflation induce a higher level of capital per person.

It is worth recapitulating how this result occurs. The central part of the mechanism is that the ratio of saving to output increases when the rate of growth of the nominal money supply increases, or, in other words, when the ratio of consumption to output decreases. This occurs because, paradoxically, an increase in the rate of growth of the nominal money supply, μ, causes a decline in the non-output component of disposable income—a decline, that is, in the amounts by which real balances per person increase in each period, $(\mu - \pi)M^S/pn$—and since consumption is related to this component of disposable income, it causes a decline in consumption at any given level of output. The reason why $(\mu - \pi)M^S/pn$ declines is that, for money market equilibrium, the real money supply per person, M^S/pn, equals the demand for real balances and the latter declines because an increase in the rate of growth of the money supply raises inflationary expectations and thereby lowers the rate of return on real balances.

18.3 ELABORATION OF THE NEOCLASSICAL MONETARY GROWTH MODEL

The result obtained in Section 18.2, that money is not neutral in a growing economy, is a fundamental conclusion of the Neoclassical growth model. We have seen that central to the mechanism behind it are the assumptions concerning the savings function and the determination of the expected rate of inflation. However, a wide range of assumptions concerning these will produce the same result.

Consider the saving function. Following Stein (1970), Johnson (1967), or Tobin (1955), we may assume that saving is a function of wealth rather than (or as well as) income. If saving were a negative function of wealth and r^k (proxied by k/n), the consumption and savings functions described by Equations 18.22 to 18.25 would be replaced by:

$$\frac{s}{n} = \hat{s}\left(\frac{k}{n}, \frac{M^S}{pn}\right) \tag{18.27}$$

with the implication that saving at any given capital/labor ratio (the height of the $0s$ curve) is higher, the lower are real balances. If the rate of growth of the nominal money supply increased, thus causing an increase in expected inflation, the demand for real balances would fall and, since permanent money market equilibrium is assumed, the price level would rise to ensure a fall in M^S/pn. In consequence, the $0s$ curve would swing upward (from a position like $0s_1$ to $0s_2$ in Figure 18.4) and the same result would be obtained as when we assumed that saving is a function of income.

Nonneutrality in this case (and in Section 18.2) stems from the fact that saving is assumed to be a stable function either of disposable income (including the amount of increases in real balances) or of wealth (including the level of real balances). Sidrauski (1967a) provides one example where money is neutral in the Neoclassical growth model. In his model, saving, and therefore investment in physical capital, is assumed to be a function of the rate of return on physical capital and the (constant) rate of time preference. The equilibrium capital stock is that which equates the marginal product of capital to the given rate of time preference,[9] and changes in the rate of growth of the money supply do not affect these parameters in his model. Therefore money is neutral.

Another example where money would be neutral is a model where money is only inside money, so that increments to the money stock are not increments to net wealth and cannot be counted as a component of disposable income. Changes in real balances, in such a case, do not affect the savings curve even if saving is assumed to be a function of disposable income, as in Section 18.2.

Money as Factor of Production

The Neoclassical model may be elaborated in several ways. One important elaboration suggested by Marty (1962), Levhari and Patinkin (1968), and Stein (1970) involves defining money as a factor of production which enters the production function. This has a significant effect on the model just as it did on the comparative static model examined in Chapter 12. Here it ensures that money is nonneutral even if the savings function is of the type adopted by Sidrauski. The reason is that, if the production function takes the form:

$$\frac{y}{n} = f\left(\frac{k}{n}, \frac{M^S}{pn}\right) \tag{18.28}$$

instead of the form of Equation 18.8, a change in real balances per person, resulting from a change in the expected rate of inflation, alters the marginal product of capital. This production function also ensures the nonneutrality of money even if money is entirely inside money. But the nonneutrality of

[9]Given the rate of population growth and the rate of depreciation of physical capital. In this chapter we assume the latter to be zero.

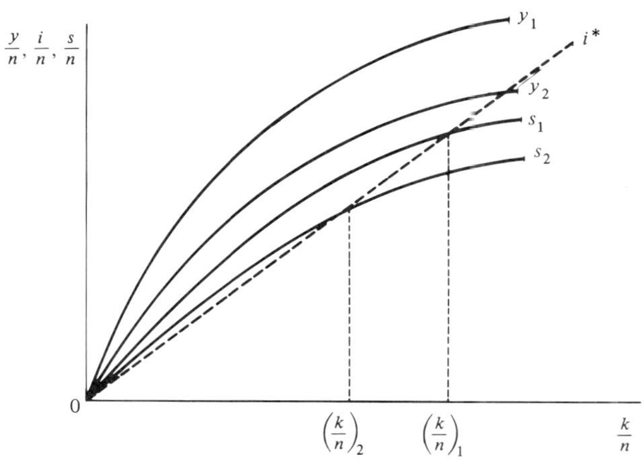

Figure 18-5

money with this production function is of a different nature from that found in Section 18.2. There, an increase in the rate of growth of the money supply increases the equilibrium capital/labor ratio, whereas here it may decrease it. This result is illustrated in Figure 18.5.

Figure 18.5 is constructed on the assumption that money is inside money which, contrary to the arguments of Pesek and Saving (1967),[10] we shall assume is not counted as a component of net wealth. Although inside money is assumed not to be net wealth, it is assumed to facilitate production, so that the production function takes the form of Equation 18.28 and the marginal product of real balances is positive. Therefore, the position of the $0y$ curve in Figure 18.5 depends on the level of real balances. The ratio of saving to output, s/y, however, is not affected by the level of real balances, since an increase in real inside balances is not itself a component of disposable income, and we are again using Section 18.2's assumption that saving is a simple proportion of disposable income. Consequently, the position of the $0s$ curve is determined solely by the position of the $0y$ curve. Assume that initially these curves are $0y_1$ and $0s_1$. The equilibrium capital/labor ratio will therefore be $(k/n)_1$ and the economy will grow at the equilibrium rate of n', the rate of growth of population. Now suppose that the rate of growth of the nominal money supply is increased. By the argument of Section 18.2, this increases the expected rate of inflation and decreases the demand for real balances per person. Since money market equilibrium requires the demand for real balances to equal the supply, the supply of real balances declines. According to the production function of Equation 18.28, this decrease in

[10]See Chap. 3. The argument of Pesek and Saving is developed by Stein (1970) to show that on certain assumptions, we can obtain the same result as is obtained in Fig. 18.5 even if we assume that inside money does affect net wealth.

supply causes a decline in the level of income at any given level of the capital/labor ratio and, in consequence, the $0y$ curve shifts to $0y_2$. As a result, the saving curve shifts to $0s_2$ and the equilibrium capital/labor ratio declines to $(k/n)_2$.

In this model, therefore, money is not neutral. An increase in the rate of growth of nominal balances causes a decline in the equilibrium capital/labor ratio. This result follows because a rise in the rate of growth of the money supply, by raising inflationary expectations, reduces both the demand for real balances and (because the money market is in equilibrium) the real value of the money supply. This reduction in real balances affects the production function, since real balances are assumed to be a factor of production and thereby causes the $0y$ curve to swing downward. The change in real balances does not affect the ratio of saving to output since, being inside money, it is assumed not to affect net wealth or disposable income. Therefore the $0s$ curve also swings downward and the capital/labor ratio on the equilibrium path declines.

A more ambiguous result would be obtained if we assumed that money consists, in part at least, of outside money. For then, as in the models of Section 18.2, a decline in real balances would exert an upward influence on the ratio of saving to output. Although this decline would cause the $0y$ curve to fall, the saving curve $0s$ might either fall, rise, or remain in its initial position.[11]

As we noted in Chapter 6, the concept of money as a factor of production is not well defined. It is not clear why a decline in real balances, *ceteris paribus*, should be thought to change the marginal product of capital. The justification for such an assumption requires the development of the work considered in Chapter 14 on why money exists and what its role in a monetary economy is. As an alternative, writers such as Levhari and Patinkin (1968) and Johnson (1967) have proposed treating money as a consumers' good rather than a producers' good. Instead of entering the production function, real balances are assumed to directly yield utility to consumers. With this approach, the problem arises of how to measure the utility yield of real balances, but whatever measure is chosen, the model is similar to those examined in Section 18.2 in that the $0y$ curve is not affected by monetary policy. An increase in the rate of growth of the nominal money supply again causes a reduction in real balances held at any instant. In consequence, disposable income is lower than it would otherwise be, but now this is so not only because the amount by which real balances increase is reduced, but also because the lower real balances give a lower total utility yield.[12] The result of this is ambiguous. Since the utility yield of real balances must be consumed,

[11]If the $0s$ curve remained in its initial position, the equilibrium capital/labor ratio would remain unchanged. But even then, money would be nonneutral in the sense that the equilibrium capital/output ratio would have changed as a result of the $0y$ curve having swung downward.

[12]Particularly in Levhari and Patinkin's method of measuring this yield, however, this depends on the elasticity of demand for real balances.

the saving curve $0s$ may swing upward or downward, thereby increasing or reducing the capital/labor ratio on the equilibrium growth path. It does so because there are now two influences on the ratio of saving to output and, hence, on the position of the $0s$ curve. First, the smaller amount of increases in real balances per period reduces disposable income and therefore, as in Section 18.2, reduces consumption and raises saving. Second, the smaller amount of utility from real balances reduces the proportion of consumption accounted for by the consumption of the utility of real balances and raises the proportion of consumption that takes the form of consumption of goods. This shift exerts a downward influence on the amount of output that is saved.

18.4 KEYNES-WICKSELL MONETARY GROWTH MODEL

The Neoclassical growth model is a highly simplified one. It is simplified in the sense that saving is assumed always to equal investment and that the demand for real balances always equals the supply. At any instant, equilibrium exists in all markets. Since actual and planned investment always equals saving, we therefore do not examine the determinants of investment in the Neoclassical model; the capital stock changes by the amount of planned saving. Moreover, equality of planned saving and investment implies that there is never an excess demand for goods, but nevertheless the price level changes; π is generally positive.

The Framework

The Keynes-Wicksell model developed by Stein (1966, 1969) and Rose (1966) involves a modification of the Neoclassical model to allow for the fact that goods and money markets may be in disequilibrium at any instant. This modification involves two substantial innovations. First, a bond market is introduced, whereas, in the Neoclassical model, the only assets are money and physical capital. The bond market is introduced, although this is not absolutely necessary, because if there is disequilibrium in the goods market, planned investment diverges from planned saving and we must analyze the determinants of both (whereas, in the Neoclassical model, we need only consider the determinants of saving). The bond market allows us to do this by relating planned investment to the bond rate of interest. Second, a different assumption about changes in the absolute price level is introduced. It is assumed that prices only rise, inflation is only positive, if there is excess demand for goods or, in other words if planned investment exceeds planned saving. Employing Walras' Law and assuming that the rate of interest instantaneously equilibrates the bond market, this excess implies that inflation occurs only if there is too low an interest rate to equilibrate the goods market and therefore an excess supply of real balances on the money market. Unlike the Neoclassical model, inflation is zero when all markets are in equilibrium.

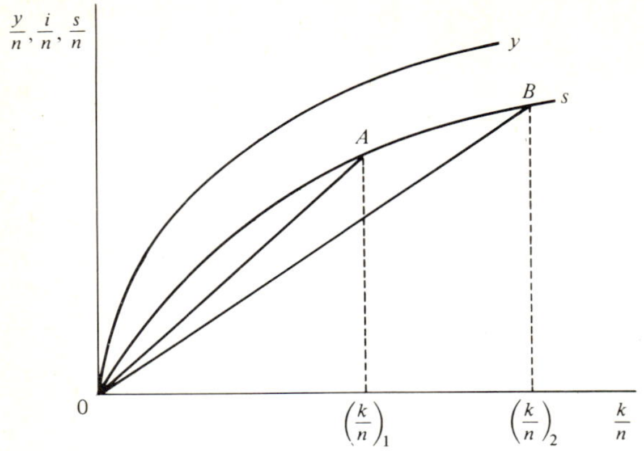

Figure 18-6

We shall find that the Keynes-Wicksell model, like the Neoclassical model, implies that money is nonneutral in that it affects the capital/labor ratio on the equilibrium growth path. Unlike the latter model, however, it allows us to analyze the processes through which this effect occurs without assuming that all markets are always in equilibrium. As a result, the source of nonneutrality in the Keynes-Wicksell model is, as we shall see, different from its source in the Neoclassical model; it does not necessarily arise from the effect of real balances on the saving function or the production function.

In order to analyze the Keynes-Wicksell model and compare it with the Neoclassical model, it is necessary to employ a diagram different from those used in the previous sections. We shall develop it, however, by initially deriving the figure for the case of the Neoclassical model and showing how it is related to the figures employed in Sections 18.2 and 18.3. Consider Figure 18.6, which is the same as that employed in the previous sections. We are interested now in the ratio of *actual* saving to the capital/labor ratio. Since, in the Neoclassical model, actual saving equals planned saving, we are therefore concerned with the relationship between planned saving per person, s/n, and the capital/labor ratio, k/n; that is, with the ratio s/k. This ratio is measured by the slope of a ray from the origin to the $0s$ curve. When the capital/labor ratio is $(k/n)_1$, the saving/capital ratio, s/k, is the slope of $0A$. If the capital/labor ratio is higher at, say, $(k/n)_2$, the saving/capital ratio is lower, being the slope of $0B$.

This relationship may be represented in Figure 18.7. The horizontal axis measures the capital/labor ratio and the vertical axis measures the ratio of actual saving to capital, $\bar{s}/k$ (which in the Neoclassical case equals the ratio of planned saving to capital, s/k). The curve S_1S_1 illustrates the relationship that we examined in the last paragraph; as k/n rises, $\bar{s}/k$ falls. As we have seen in the previous sections, the equilibrium growth path requires a capital/labor ratio, k/n, such that $\bar{s}/k$ equals the rate of growth of population, n'. The reason is that actual saving, $\bar{s}$, is the same as actual investment, $\bar{\imath}$, and is therefore equal to the growth of the capital stock, so that $\bar{s}/k$ equals the rate

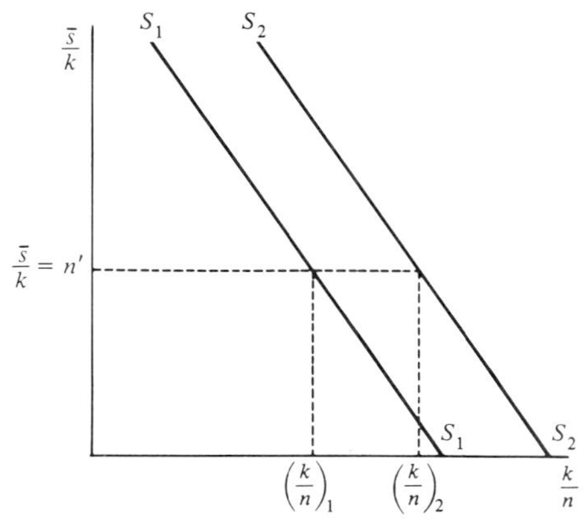

Figure 18-7

of growth of the capital stock, k. (Henceforth in this section we shall use actual saving and actual investment $\bar{s}$ and $\bar{\imath}$ interchangeably; planned saving and investment are not identically equal, but their *ex post* values are.) If the capital/labor ratio is to remain constant, as it must on the equilibrium growth path, the rate of growth of k must equal the rate of growth of population, so we must have $\bar{s}/k = n'$.[13] If we measure n' on the vertical axis of Figure 18.7, we can therefore find the equilibrium capital/labor ratio. With the saving curve S_1S_1, the equilibrium ratio is $(k/n)_1$, since that ensures that $\bar{s}/k = n'$.

In the Neoclassical model of Section 18.2, a rise in the rate of growth of the money supply causes a change in the equilibrium capital/labor ratio by causing (via a decline in real balances) an upward swing of the $0s$ curve in Figure 18.6. In consequence, the curve relating s/k and $\bar{s}/k$ to the capital/labor ratio—the SS curve in Figure 18.7—shifts rightward to, say, S_2S_2. A new equilibrium capital/labor ratio is established at $(k/n)_2$.

We shall use Figure 18.7 to illustrate the Keynes-Wicksell model. First, however, several preliminary points concerning the details of the model are necessary. We must begin by examining the relationship between planned saving and actual saving in this model, since we no longer assume that the two are equal. We shall assume that planned saving per person is a function of output per person:

$$\frac{s}{n} = \hat{s}\,\frac{y}{n} \qquad \text{or} \qquad \frac{s}{k} = \hat{s}\,\frac{y}{k} \tag{18.29}$$

where $\hat{s}$ is the marginal and average propensity to save. Note that this equation says that planned saving is a function of output and not of disposable income (which includes increases in real balances) or of real wealth

[13]As we saw in Sec. 18.1, this is the same as the condition that $\hat{s}/v = n'$; it is met at that capital/labor ratio where the $0s$ curve intersects the $0i^*$ curve.

(which includes the level of real balances). We write it in this way to highlight the fact that the effect of real balances on planned saving is not a necessary component of the Keynes-Wicksell model and is not the source of non-neutrality, whereas it is in the basic Neoclassical model of Section 18.2. Planned investment is assumed to be a function of the rate of interest on bonds, but we must be more explicit than this. Since we wish to consider a model with a positive rate of inflation, the relevant interest rate is the real rate of interest, approximated by:

$$\rho = r - \pi \tag{18.30}$$

where ρ is the real rate, r is the nominal interest rate, and π is the rate of inflation. (See Chapter 2.) We assume that firms wish to maintain a constant capital/labor ratio if the real rate of interest equals the marginal product of capital, $\partial y/(\partial(k/n))$, so, in that case, planned investment would have to be such that it would increase the capital stock at the same rate as the population was growing:

$$\frac{i}{k} = n' \qquad \text{or} \qquad i = kn' \tag{18.31}$$

(In other words, i would equal the variable i^* that we employed in Section 18.1.) If the real rate of interest is lower than the marginal product of capital, investment would be higher than kn', so that firms would be planning to increase the capital/labor ratio over time and would plan to decrease that ratio if the real rate of interest were higher than capital's marginal product. Thus,

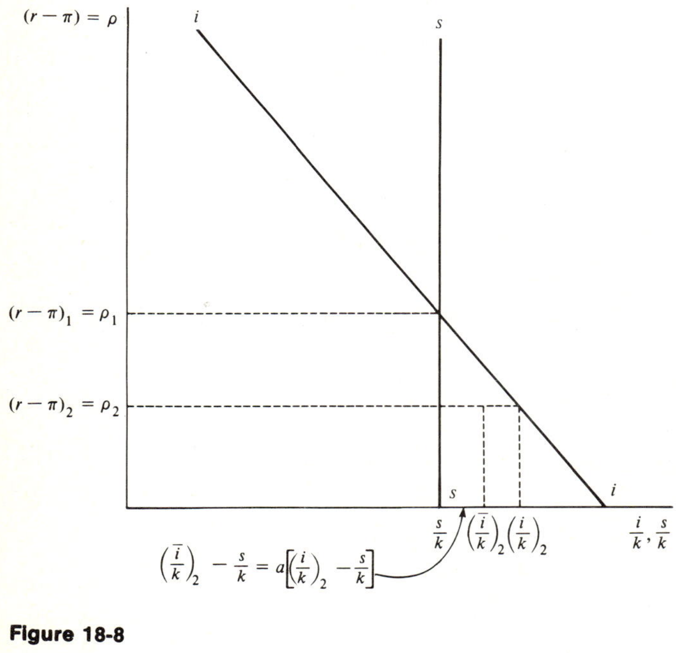

Figure 18-8

we can write the planned investment function as:

$$\frac{i}{k} = n' - f\left[\frac{\partial y}{\partial\left(\frac{k}{n}\right)} - (r - \pi)\right] \qquad f' > 0 \tag{18.32}$$

The saving function of Equation 18.29 and the investment function of Equation 18.32 are represented in Figure 18.8 (which, it should be noted, is not the same as the analogue of Figure 18.7).

In Figure 18.8 the investment function *ii* measures the ratio of planned investment to the capital stock i/k. It is drawn for a given rate of population growth, n', and a given marginal product of capital. If either were higher, *ii* would be further to the right. The saving function *ss* represents desired saving as a proportion of the capital stock and is drawn for a given output/capital ratio. If the latter were higher, the *ss* curve would be further to the right. The real rate of interest that equilibrates the goods market is $(r - \pi)_1$, for there saving and investment plans are equated. If the real rate of interest were below $(r - \pi)_1$, there would be excess demand in the goods market which, as we shall see, is assumed to be accompanied by a positive rate of inflation.

Disequilibrium and Inflation

For the present, however, we are concerned with a different aspect of excess demand. When there is excess demand for goods, it is impossible for the planned investment demand of firms and the planned consumption demand of households all to be satisfied. In other words, actual saving will be above planned saving, actual investment will be below planned investment, or both situations will occur (with actual saving necessarily equaling actual investment). We shall assume that actual saving and investment are above planned saving and below planned investment when there is excess demand. This assumption can be formalized as:

$$\frac{\bar{\imath}}{k} = \frac{s}{k} + a\left(\frac{i - s}{k}\right) \tag{18.33}$$

where $\bar{\imath}$ is actual investment (saving) and a is a parameter whose value is between zero and 1. Equation 18.33 says that when planned investment exceeds planned saving, actual investment is equal to planned saving plus a times the difference between planned saving and planned investment. In Figure 18.8, this is illustrated by the value $(\bar{\imath}/k)_2$ for the ratio of actual investment to capital when the real rate of interest is at $(r - \pi)_2$. At that real interest rate, planned saving is given by (s/k) and is less than planned investment given by $(i/k)_2$. Equation 18.33 implies that actual saving or investment, $(\bar{\imath}/k)_2$, is then $(s/k) + a[(i/k)_2 - (s/k)]$.

The assumption represented by Equation 18.33 allows us to overcome one problem presented by the existence of goods market disequilibrium: the problem of the relationship between planned saving and actual investment.

Our assumption implies that they diverge, whereas, in the Neoclassical model, such a possibility cannot arise. We must now turn to another problem related to goods market disequilibrium: the problem of inflation. An essential feature of the Keynes-Wicksell model is the assumption that the absolute price level rises, that π is positive, only if there is excess demand in the goods market. When that occurs, the rate of inflation is proportional to the excess demand for goods, being:

$$\pi = b\left(\frac{i}{k} - \frac{s}{k}\right) \tag{18.34}$$

Thus, in Figure 18.8 when the real rate of interest is $(r-\pi)_2$, excess demand of $(i/k)_2 - (s/k)$ implies that the rate of inflation is $\pi_2 = b[(i/k)_2 - (s/k)]$. If the real rate of interest were lower, the consequently greater excess demand would involve a higher rate of inflation.

One point to note about the inflation hypothesis of Equation 18.34 is that although it is framed in terms of the excess demand for goods, it could equally well be formulated in terms of excess supply of money and bonds. This formulation is permissible through the application of Walras' Law to the goods and money markets. Another point to note is that this hypothesis enables us to simplify the exposition of the model, since we can rearrange Equation 18.34 to define planned investment in terms of the rate of inflation and planned saving:

$$\frac{i}{k} = \frac{\pi}{b} + \frac{s}{k} \tag{18.35}$$

This definition of planned investment can then be substituted into Equation 18.33's definition of actual investment so that actual investment is defined in terms of planned saving and the rate of investment:

$$\frac{\bar{i}}{k} = \frac{a\pi}{b} + \frac{s}{k} \tag{18.36}$$

Therefore actual investment (and saving) is equal to planned saving plus a proportion of the rate of inflation.

Nonneutrality

We are now able to return to Figure 18.7, reproduced here as Figure 18.9, and apply it to the Keynes-Wicksell model. The curve s_1s_1 illustrates the relationship between planned saving per unit of capital, s/k, and the capital/labor ratio. It slopes downward to the right for the same reason as the planned (and actual) saving curve in Figure 18.7 slopes in that direction. The curve $\bar{s}_1\bar{s}_1$ represents the relationship between actual saving (and investment) per unit of capital, $\bar{s}/k$, and the capital/labor ratio, k/n. From Equation 18.36 we know that $\bar{s}/k$ (or $\bar{i}/k$) is greater than planned saving s/k by $a\pi/b$, so the curve $\bar{s}_1\bar{s}_1$ is above s_1s_1 by that amount. We have seen that the rate of inflation

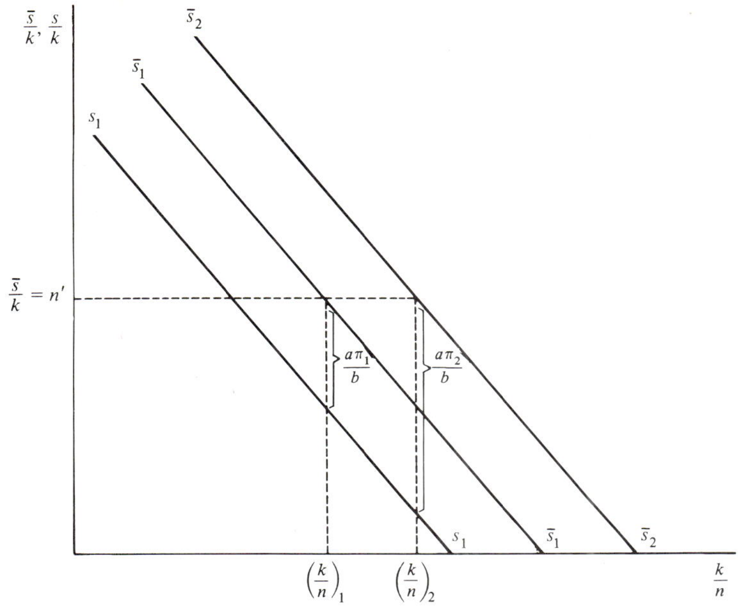

Figure 18-9

is assumed to be greater, the greater is the difference between planned investment and planned saving. Therefore, anything that increases this difference or excess demand for goods will cause the difference between actual and planned saving to increase. Given the planned saving curve s_1s_1, the curve $\bar{s}_1\bar{s}_1$ will be higher, the higher is excess demand in the goods market. As in Figure 18.7, the equilibrium capital/labor ratio is that which causes the ratio of actual saving to capital to be equal to the rate of growth of population, n'. In Figure 18.9, this equilibrium capital/labor ratio is $(k/n)_1$ when the curve of actual saving is $\bar{s}_1\bar{s}_1$.

Now let us examine the effects of a change in the rate of growth of the nominal money supply—a change in $\dot{M}^S/M$ or μ. In order to do this, let us suppose, for simplicity, that the bond market is always in equilibrium but that the money market and goods market may be in disequilibrium. By Walras' Law, excess supply in the money market in this case involves excess demand in the goods market and therefore involves a positive rate of inflation.

Referring to Figure 18.9, suppose that, initially, the rate of growth of nominal money supply in aggregate terms μ_1 is such as to maintain an excess supply of money and an excess demand for goods at each period and thereby to create inflation of π_1. This gives rise to the curve $\bar{s}_1\bar{s}_1$ for actual savings per unit of capital, and the equilibrium capital/labor ratio is $(k/n)_1$. Now suppose that the rate of growth of the money supply is increased to μ_2. This increase will cause a greater excess supply of money, since the demand for money at each instant will fall. It will do so since we shall assume that the demand function for money is, as in the Neoclassical model (Eq. 18.14):

$$M^D = f\left(\frac{y}{n}, \pi^e, r^k\right) \tag{18.37}$$

so that a higher expected rate of inflation reduces the demand for money and, as in that model (Eq. 18.20), the expected rate of inflation is positively related to the rate of growth of the money supply:

$$\pi^e = \mu - n' \tag{18.38}$$

The increase in the excess supply of money implies, by Walras' Law, an increase in the excess demand for goods. This increase, in turn, by Equation 18.34, implies a rise in the rate of inflation from π_1 to π_2.[14] The rise in π implies an increase in the difference, $a\pi/b$, between the planned saving curve and the actual saving curve in Figure 18.9. The curve of actual saving and investment becomes $\bar{s}_2\bar{s}_2$ instead of $\bar{s}_1\bar{s}_1$, and the equilibrium capital/labor ratio is established at $(k/n)_2$.

Thus, we can see in the Keynes-Wicksell model that a change in the rate of growth of the nominal money supply changes the capital/labor ratio on the equilibrium growth path so that money is not neutral. In the form of the model that we have presented, in particular, a rise in the rate of growth of the money supply causes a rise in the capital/labor ratio on the equilibrium growth path.

While retaining the basic framework of the Keynes-Wicksell model, we could make small amendments and demonstrate that money is neutral, or that an increase in the rate of growth of the money supply is nonneutral but causes a *decline* in the capital/labor ratio on the equilibrium growth path. Suppose, for example, that in Equation 18.33, $a = 0$. Thus, even when planned investment exceeds planned saving, actual saving and investment equal planned saving; it is assumed in this case that savers cannot be forced to save more than they desire to, so that their consumption plans are always fully realized. In that instance, the curve of actual saving in Figure 18.9 always equals the planned saving curve. What happens to the equilibrium capital/labor ratio then depends on what happens to planned saving. If we replace the planned saving function of Equation 18.29 with one where saving depends inversely on real balances:

$$\frac{s}{n} = f\left(\frac{y}{n}, \frac{M^S}{pn}\right) \tag{18.39}$$

then a rise in the rate of growth of the money supply can reduce planned saving per person. This occurs because, as in the Neoclassical model, our

[14]In terms of the goods market diagram, Figure 18.8, the situation is that the real interest rate will have fallen from a level, such as $(r - \pi)_1$, to a lower level. It should be borne in mind, however, that the planned saving and investment curves in that figure do not remain constant.

money market hypothesis (Eqs. 18.37 and 18.38) implies that the demand for real balances falls in response to a rise in the rate of growth of the money supply. Since the money market is not in equilibrium, however, this hypothesis, unlike the Neoclassical model, does not necessarily imply that the supply of real balances falls. If the supply of real balances at any instant is raised by the increase in the rate of growth of the money supply, the savings function of Equation 18.39 implies that the *ss* curve in Figure 18.9 shifts leftward. Since this represents actual as well as planned saving on the present assumptions, its leftward shift would imply that the capital/labor ratio on the equilibrium growth path where $\bar{s}/k = n'$ is decreased.

18.5 COMPARISON OF NEOCLASSICAL AND KEYNES-WICKSELL MONETARY GROWTH MODELS

Both Neoclassical and Keynes-Wicksell growth models give the result that the capital/labor ratio on the equilibrium growth path may be altered by a change in the rate of growth of the money supply. Money will in general be nonneutral in both models (although, with special assumptions, it may be neutral), and, if nonneutral, either model can imply that an increase in the rate of monetary expansion may either increase or decrease the equilibrium capital/labor ratio. Moreover, there is no fundamental difference between the basic functions employed in the model. The production function in each is the basic neoclassical production function with diminishing marginal productivity of capital. It is this that gives rise to the shape of the s/k curve of Figures 18.6 and 18.8, and that is common to both models. The saving function in each model is essentially the same, for, as we have seen, saving may be assumed to depend, or not to depend, on real balances in either model. The demand function for real balances is the same in each model. The only difference between the models' behavior functions is that in the Keynes-Wicksell model, the planned investment function must be specified and this necessity stems from the more basic difference between the models.

The basic difference between the models is that the Neoclassical model assumes that all markets are permanently in equilibrium, whereas the Keynes-Wicksell model assumes that they may be in disequilibrium. In fact, since the latter model assumes that inflation occurs only if the goods market is in disequilibrium, it implies that on the equilibrium growth path with inflation, the goods market is permanently in disequilibrium; the equilibrium growth path, therefore, is followed even though, in each period, there is excess supply of goods.

Although the Keynes-Wicksell model is built on the assumption that the goods and money markets can be permanently in disequilibrium, it is different from the short-run Neo-Keynesian (Keynesian Reappraisal) models reviewed in Chapter 13, even though those models, too, focus on disequilibrium states. One difference is that the growth model reviewed in Section 18.4 concentrates on disequilibrium in the sense of excess demand for goods, whereas the Neo-Keynesian models are, in essence, concerned with excess supply in the goods market, but this difference is not a fundamental one, since the Neo-Keynesian models have been extended, for example, by Barro and Grossman (1971) to situations of excess demand and inflation. The basic difference is that the Neo-Keynesian short-run models focus on the links between the labor and goods markets. In unemployment, they are concerned with the relationship both between an excess supply of labor and the effective demand for goods and between an excess supply of goods and the effective demand for labor. In inflation, they are concerned, among other things, with the relationship between the excess demand for goods and the effective supply of labor (with frustrated consumers, for example, reducing their supply of labor). The Keynes-Wicksell growth model examined here, by contrast, does not examine the labor market. It is built on the assumption that unemployment does not exist.

In this respect the Keynes-Wicksell growth model is, again, similar to the Neoclassical model (although, when the Keynes-Wicksell model is extended to allow the possibility of cycles, unemployment is introduced). It differs only to the extent that there is excess demand rather than equilibrium in the goods market so that, if we make the Keynesian assumption that the excess demand for labor is positively related to the excess demand for goods, there is over-full employment in some sense rather than full employment in the Keynes-Wicksell model. Since this model does not explicitly allow for unemployment, we may ask in what sense it is in the tradition of Keynes and Wicksell. As far as Wicksell is concerned, one similarity is in the role of interest rates in the inflationary process. As can be seen from Equation 18.32, planned investment, and therefore the excess of planned investment over planned saving and thus the rate of inflation, are all functions of the discrepancy between the marginal productivity of capital and the (real) rate of interest on bonds. If the bond interest rate is below the marginal productivity of capital, there is an increase in inflationary pressure. As will be recalled from Chapter 6, this is reminiscent of Wicksell's theory of the indirect mechanism through which money affects the economy. The other similarities between the model and Wicksell and its relationship to Keynesian theory cannot be considered here in the context of a pure growth model; they appear in the Keynes-Wicksell model's theory of the trade cycle.

As long as we confine our attention to pure growth models, neither the Neoclassical model nor the Keynes-Wicksell model is as close to Keynes as the Harrod-Domar model. The latter emphasizes that on the equilibrium growth path, $\hat{s}/v$, being the warranted rate or the rate that equilibrates the goods market, $\hat{s}/v$ may or may not equal the rate of growth of the population, n'. If it is lower than n' and we start with unemployment or full employment, unemployment will grow over time. Even if $\hat{s}/v = n'$ and we start at, and continue with, full employment, this equilibrium growth path is unstable, and any disturbance, such as a decline in the average (marginal) propensity to save, will cause permanent unemployment to develop. This problem is clearly a Keynesian one and is essentially concerned with the thesis of some Keynesian writers that capitalist economies have a long-run tendency toward stagnation and unemployment. By contrast, both the Neoclassical and Keynes-Wicksell growth models argue that the equilibrium growth path (where $\hat{s}/v = n'$) exists and is a stable equilibrium path in the sense that divergences from it will set up forces that return the economy's rate of growth to n'. In such models, there are no difficulties in attaining permanent full employment.

CHAPTER

NINETEEN

MONEY AND INFLATION

The models considered in preceding chapters are not specifically concerned with inflation, continuous increases in the price level. In some of them price rises are treated as central, but (excepting Chapter 18) in a comparative static sense. The study of the neutrality of money in Chapter 12, for example, was focused on the effect on the equilibrium price level of an increase in the money supply. We were not concerned with the speed at which the new level was reached. The problem of inflation, however, is a dynamic one; it concerns the rate of change of the price level, rather than its equilibrium level.

That there is a relationship between money and the price level of goods, (including its rate of change) may appear self-evident. After all, the price level is the price of goods as a whole in exchange for money; it is thus the inverse of the price of money in terms of goods. However, it is not self-evident that the relationship is such that changes in the supply of money *cause* changes in the price level or determine its rate of change.

In discussing whether this causality does exist, there are two points to bear in mind. First, in a general equilibrium framework, conditions in all markets are supposed, a priori, to affect conditions and prices in others. If we model the economy as three interrelated markets—those for money, goods, and labor—the relative price of goods in terms of money, the price level, is determined as much by conditions in the goods and labor markets as by those in the goods and money markets. Thus, we find that much modern writing on inflation theory concerns the working of the labor market and its relation to the goods market. The disputes over the operation of the labor market and, in particular, the role of expectations in the inflationary process have dominated the field, as can be seen from Friedman (1968), Phelps (1970), and Tobin (1972). Second, once we recognize that in a general equilibrium framework there is no a priori reason for thinking that only changes in the money supply determine changes in the price level, we must break the problem of money's role in causing inflation down into consideration of several propositions. The idea that increases in the money supply cause inflation may be interpreted in several ways. It may be a statement of a necessary condition: Whatever initiates and drives inflation, it cannot continue unless the money supply increases. It may be a statement of a sufficient condition that is as good as any other: Increases in the money supply can, like other factors, cause inflation and determine its rate. Or, it may be a statement of a unique sufficient condition: The rate of increase in the money supply, and it alone, determines the rate of inflation. In the models of money and inflation that we shall consider, we identify which of these propositions is at issue.

19.1 MONEY IN ELEMENTARY QUANTITY THEORY AND KEYNESIAN THEORY APPROACHES

The pre-Keynesian Quantity Theory approach held as its central tenet the proposition that in the long-run, increases in the money supply are a necessary condition for increases in the price level and that the rate of growth of the money supply uniquely determines the rate of inflation. Illustrating this proposition in terms of the crude Quantity Theory's Cambridge Equation:

$$M^S = kpy \tag{19.1}$$

the propositions follow directly. Writing Equation 19.1 in logarithmic terms, differentiating with respect to time and assuming that k and y are constant, we obtain:

$$\frac{d \ln M^S}{dt} = \frac{d \ln p}{dt}$$

This can be more conveniently written as:

$$\dot{M}^S = \dot{p} \tag{19.2}$$

In other words, the rate of change of the price level equals the rate of change of the money supply. This formal result hides the processes that lie behind the equations. They are worth spelling out. Equation 19.1 is an equilibrium condition written with the exogenous supply of money on the left-hand side and the demand for money on the right. The only variable that is supposed to move so as to equilibrate the money market is the price level, and it has an unambiguous positive effect on the demand for money (kpy). If we treat Equation 19.2 as the actual time path of the money supply and price level, then we are assuming that the money market is in fact in equilibrium at every instant.

These last two points have been revised in the modern Chicago Quantity Theory tradition. The work of Cagan (1956) and his successors has emphasized that not only does the price *level* affect the demand for nominal balances, but also that its *rate of change*, the rate of inflation, influences the demand for real money balances. And Goldman (1972) has modified Cagan's model so that the money market is not assumed to be always in equilibrium. We shall examine these developments in Sections 19.2 and 19.3.

Inflationary Gap

In contrast with the Quantity Theory approach, whether pre-Keynesian or modern, is the "inflationary gap" approach based on the Keynesian model (Keynes [1940]). The contrast lies, at one level, in the fact that this approach is rooted in conditions in the goods market, whereas the Quantity Theory approaches are based upon the demand for, and supply of, money. Thus, the inflationary gap model is best illustrated by the simple goods market of Figure 19.1. With full-employment output being y, there will be no excess demand if the expenditure function is e_1. If, however, the expenditure function is e_2, excess demand of AB will exist, and this inflationary gap is assumed to give rise to price increases.

The simplest model of the inflationary gap implies that money has no significant relationship with inflation. For one thing, it does not suggest that an increase in money supply is a uniquely important *cause* of the inflationary gap. An upward shift in the expenditure function to e_2 may result from many sources. Capitalists' expectations may become more optimistic, thereby shifting the investment function rightward; a tax cut or a rise in transfer payments may shift the consumption function upward; or, among other causes, a rise in the money supply may (via the real balance effect or the effect on interest rates) cause shifts in the investment or consumption functions. Moreover, the simple model does not suggest that an *accommodating* rise in the money supply is a necessary condition for inflation. It does not do so because it says nothing at all about the demand for money and therefore does not preclude the assumption that velocity rises as p rises. A model based on Figure 19.1

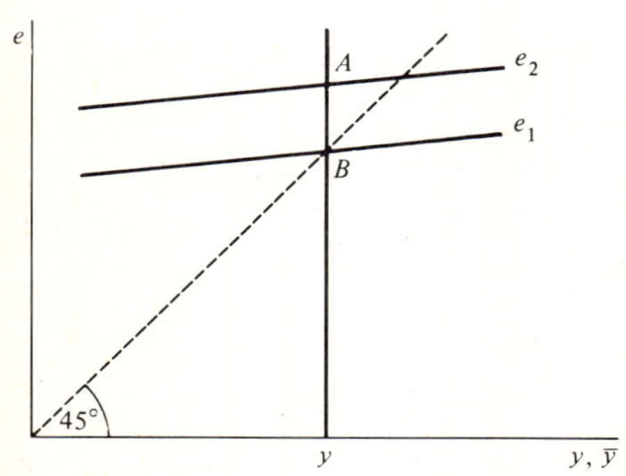

Figure 19-1

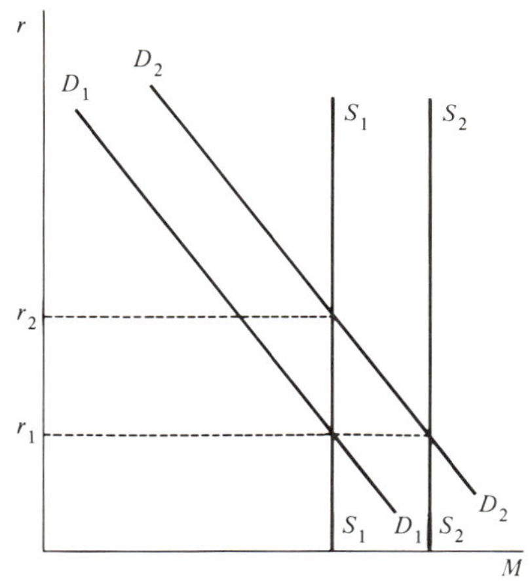

Figure 19-2

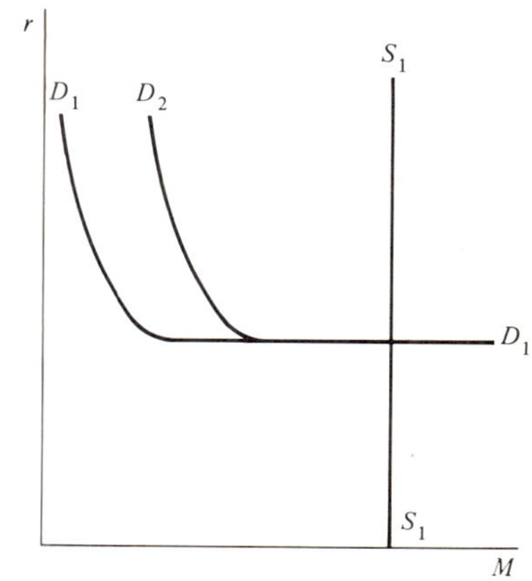

Figure 19-3

alone forces us to make some assumption about the money market but leaves open the choice of assumption. A continuing inflationary gap of AB is consistent with any one of the Keynesian money market models illustrated in Figures 19.3 and 19.4. Before considering them, note that if we exclude the real balance effect from consideration, the only connection between the money market and the goods market in the Keynesian model is through the rate of interest. If an accommodating rise in the money supply is necessary in order to sustain inflation in this model, it must be because, without it, money market conditions push up the interest rate which, by reducing investment, brings the expenditure function down from e_2 and closes the inflationary gap. This is the situation if the money market is as illustrated in Figure 19.2 but not if it is as in Figures 19.3 and 19.4.

In Figure 19.2, suppose that in a preinflationary equilibrium, the interest rate is r_1 and the demand and supply curves for nominal balances are those

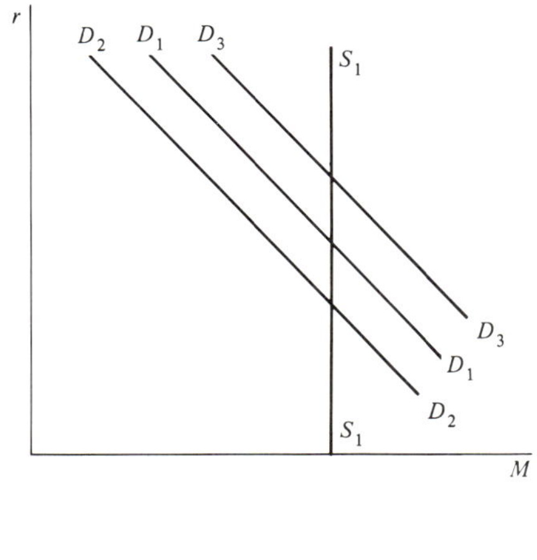

Figure 19-4

labeled subscript 1. Now an exogenous change causes the expenditure function in the goods market to shift upward and therefore causes prices to rise. This increase shifts the demand curve for nominal balances to D_2D_2. If the supply remains unchanged, the interest rate will be forced upward, having the effect of closing the inflationary gap in the goods market. The rise in price level will therefore not be continuous and, assuming that the process is completed quickly, will be so short-lived as not to warrant the name "inflation". In this model of the money market, inflation could be sustained only if the money supply were to be increased to match the increase in demand for nominal balances. If, for example, the money supply were increased to S_2S_2 when the demand curve for nominal balances was D_2D_2, the inflationary gap in the goods market could be sustained. In this Keynesian model, therefore, one of the conclusions of the pre-Keynesian Quantity Theory is maintained: An accommodating increase in the money supply is a necessary condition for inflation.

However, alternative Keynesian assumptions about the demand function for money would not permit that conclusion. In Figure 19.3, for example, it is assumed that the demand function for nominal balances is perfectly interest-elastic in the relevant range. In that case, a rise in the price level with a given money supply would not necessarily cause an increase in the interest rate. If the price rise causes the demand curve to shift from D_1D_1 to D_2D_2, it will not cause an increase in interest rate (although a sufficiently large increase in price level will). More significant is the case illustrated in Figure 19.4.

This figure represents the extreme Keynesian argument put forward by the Radcliffe Committee (1959). The idea is that, instead of the demand for nominal balances being a stable function of the price level and nominal interest rate, as in Figures 19.2 and 19.3, it is a highly volatile function. In consequence, if the demand curve in a preinflationary situation is initially D_1D_1, we cannot predict that a rise in price level will shift it rightward. This volatility is supposed to be due to the private sector's unstable propensity to replace money by credit as a Medium of Exchange, so that the velocity of money at any interest rate is unstable (or, looked at in another way, to reduce the demand for money as an asset and replace it by intermediary deposits in portfolios). If there is inflation and the money supply does not keep pace with it, the private sector will finance its high level of expenditure, the inflationary gap, by extending credit within the sector (such as trade credit) or through financial intermediaries. Thus, a price rise may cause the demand for transactions balances in real terms to fall as credit replaces money in transactions, thereby causing the demand curve for nominal balances to remain at D_1D_1. Or it may even precipitate a more than compensating fall in demand for real balances if there is a particularly sharp development of credit, so that the demand curve for nominal balances may even shift leftward to D_2D_2. Finally, the demand curve for nominal balances may shift to, say, D_3D_3 if the demand for real balances falls but by less than in proportion to the increase in price level.

The point about the Radcliffe argument is the unpredictability as to which of these outcomes will occur. And even if the demand curve for nominal balances were to shift to the right to a moderate extent, the shift would not, in the Radcliffe Committee's view, close the inflationary gap, since it was thought that only large changes in interest rates would affect the level of investment.

The modern Quantity Theory approach to inflation is in strong opposition to the Radcliffe version of the Keynesian model, for it emphasizes the stability of the demand function for money. Like the pre-Keynesian Quantity Theory, it focuses on the money market rather than the goods market but, unlike either the simplest versions of pre-Keynesian Quantity Theory or the Keynesian model,[1] it is founded on the proposition that the rate of inflation itself is an argument in the demand function for money. This approach is considered in the following section.

19.2 MODERN QUANTITY THEORY AND HYPERINFLATION

The demand function for money upon which the modern Quantity Theory is based has as its arguments the relative rates of returns on money and alternative assets, and wealth or a proxy for it as the scale variable or budget constraint. As seen in Chapter 7, these rates include the rate of inflation or, strictly speaking, the *expected* rate of change of the price level, as well as the nominal rate of interest on bonds, nominal yield on equities, and other yields. Chicago Quantity Theorists have attempted to derive empirical support for the proposition that such a demand function is stable from data drawn from economies undergoing severe hyperinflationary experiences. Such studies include the fundamental work of Cagan (1956).[2] As was seen in Chapter 7 and will be noted in Chapter 22, the stability of the demand function for money is a basic tenet of the modern Quantity Theory. The importance for this school of work, such as Cagan's contributions, is that if the demand function for money is found to be stable during hyperinflations, periods when the monetary system is under severe strain, then the assumption has passed a demanding test. The other significant aspect of Cagan's work, and the reason why it is the foundation for much subsequent work on hyperinflations, is his formulation of the theoretical model to be tested.

The model is based upon a demand function for real money balances of the form:

$$\ln\left(\frac{M}{p}\right)_t^D = -\alpha\dot{p}_t^{\text{exp}} - \gamma \tag{19.3}$$

[1]It is an exaggeration to say that the pre-Keynesian Quantity Theorists ignored the rate of inflation as a determinant of the demand for money. See Chap. 6, Sec. 6.2. But the rate did not play a significant role in their analysis of inflation.

[2]The reliability of Cagan's empirical tests is, however, questioned by the work of Jacobs (1975).

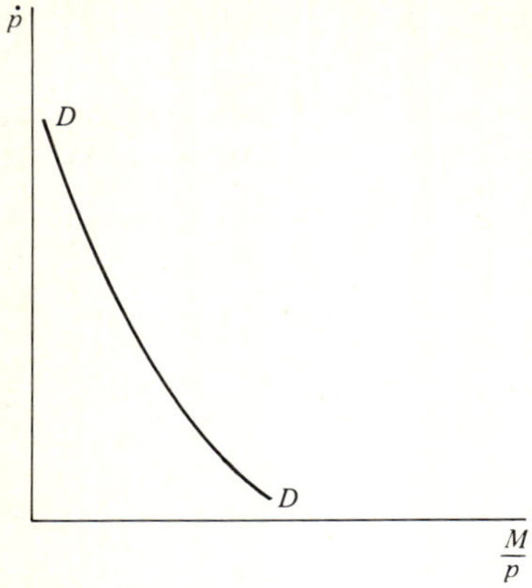

Figure 19-5

That is, the demand for real balances at time t (in logarithmic terms) is a function of the expected rate of change of the price level, $\dot{p}_t^{\exp}$ (α and γ are parameters). This demand function can be thought of as an abbreviation of Friedman's general demand function (Eq. 7.1), since it relates the demand for real balances to the expected rate of inflation alone and omits the other rate of return and scale variables that are specified in Chapter 7. The rationale offered for this abbreviation is that during hyperinflations, changes in the rate of inflation are so great that their effect completely dominates the effect of changes in the other variables. This demand function is illustrated in Figure 19.5.

In this demand function for money, the parameter α is crucial. It determines the elasticity of demand for real balances with respect to the expected rate of inflation. The higher is α, then, for any particular value of the expected rate of inflation, the greater will be the percentage decline in demand for real balances induced by a 1 percent increase in the expected inflation rate.[3] It will be seen below that the effect of changes in the expected inflation rate on the demand for real balances is central to the question of whether inflation can proceed without proportional increases in the nominal money supply.

The second component of the model is a theory of expectations. Cagan employs the adaptive expectations or error adjustment model, which in Chapter 7 we examined in the context of anticipated income (Eq. 7.13). That is, the rate of inflation which in period T is expected to hold in future is the same as what in the previous period was expected for the future plus a proportion, β, of the difference between T's actual inflation rate and the rate which in period $(T-1)$ was expected to hold in the future:

$$\dot{p}_T^{\exp} = \dot{p}_{T-1}^{\exp} + \beta(\dot{p}_T - \dot{p}_{T-1}^{\exp}) \tag{19.4}$$

[3]From Eq. 19.3, which is equivalent to $(M/p)^D = e^{-\alpha\dot{p}^{\exp}-\gamma}$, the elasticity of demand for real balances with respect to the expected rate of inflation is $(d(M/p)^D/d\dot{p}^{\exp})(\dot{p}^{\exp}/(M/p)^D) = -\alpha\dot{p}^{\exp}$.

In the Cagan model the equivalent expression is in terms of continuous time, and the relevant error (the term within square brackets) is measured instantaneously (that is, with the same time subscript on current and expected inflation). Thus, the rate of change of the expected rate of inflation is written:

$$\frac{d\dot{p}_t^{\exp}}{dt} = \beta(\dot{p}_t - \dot{p}_t^{\exp}) \tag{19.5}$$

which is the equivalent form of Equation 19.4's adaptive expectations model.

The third component of Cagan's model is the assumption that the demand for real balances, $(M/p)^D$, always equals the supply of real balances, (M/p). In consequence, the demand function of Equation 19.3 can be written in terms of the stock of money:[4]

$$\ln\left(\frac{M}{p}\right)_t = -\alpha\dot{p}_t^{\exp} - \gamma \tag{19.6}$$

The most interesting implication of Cagan's model is the possibility that hyperinflations proceed without an accommodating proportional increase in nominal balances. Thus, although the model is derived from the modern Quantity Theory tradition, it contains within it the possibility that increases in the money supply are not a necessary condition for hyperinflation. Whether or not this is a real possibility depends on the true values of the parameters α and β. Cagan and other writers conclude that, empirically, these values have always been such that hyperinflations cannot be self-sustaining but do, instead, ultimately require proportional increases in the money supply.

The significance of the values of α and β can be understood intuitively in terms of the identity underlying the pre-Keynesian Quantity Theory. Defining k as $k \equiv (M^D/py)$ and assuming the demand for money always equals supply $M^D \equiv M$, we obtain as an identity:

$$M \equiv kpy$$

Employing this identity, the crude version of the pre-Keynesian Quantity Theory assumes k and y constant so that p can rise only if M rises at the

[4]In fact, Cagan introduces this as a simplifying assumption. He argues more generally that there can at any instant be a discrepancy between the actual and desired stock of real balances $[(M^D/p) - (M/p) \gtrless 0]$ and that the stock of real balances adjusts, through changes in the price level, in the direction of eradicating any discrepancy. The speed of adjustment is, in general, assumed to be proportional to the size of the discrepancy:

$$\frac{d\ln\left(\frac{M}{p}\right)}{dt} = \pi\left[\ln\left(\frac{M}{p}\right)^D - \ln\left(\frac{M}{p}\right)\right] \tag{19.7}$$

where π is the factor of proportionality. However, he then assumes, for simplicity, that π is large, and he considers this to imply that discrepancies are eradicated instantaneously and that $M^D/p = M/p$. It will be seen in Sec. 19.3 that this simplifying assumption considerably affects Cagan's conclusions.

same rate. The essence of Cagan's model, however, is that k is not constant. Instead, it is an inverse function of the rate of inflation itself. This is so because the rate of inflation has a direct effect on the expected rate of inflation (Eqs. 19.4 and 19.5), and the expected rate has an inverse effect on the demand for real balances (Eq. 19.3) which, for a given y, is what determines k. The rate at which k falls in response to a given rate of inflation depends on the sensitivity of expectations to the current rate of inflation (the parameter β) and on the sensitivity of the demand for real balances to the expected inflation rate (proportional to α as noted in footnote 3). To the extent that, given real income y, inflation occurs with a decline in k rather than a rise in M, it can be said that the rise in prices is financed by an increase in velocity (since k is the inverse of velocity).

Long-Run Equilibrium

The dynamic behavior of the model represented by the demand function for money (Eq. 19.3), the expectations function (Eq. 19.5), and the money market equilibrium identity (Eq. 19.7) can be analyzed algebraically; in this way, the significance of the value of $\alpha\beta$ can be demonstrated more rigorously. The question of whether an equal rate of monetary expansion is a necessary condition for a given rate of inflation is the same as that of whether the long-run equilibrium rate of inflation is a stable equilibrium. For, by definition, this long-run equilibrium rate is itself equal to the rate of monetary expansion. When actual inflation is greater than this equilibrium rate, only if it shows no tendency to return to it can we say that the inflation rate is partially financed by increases in velocity rather than in money supply. As a result, we should be clear at the beginning on what is meant by the long-run equilibrium rate of inflation, p^*.

This equilibrium rate is that which is equal to the rate of increase of the money supply and to the expected inflation rate. This fact can be understood intuitively by consideration of Figure 19.6. The demand curve for real

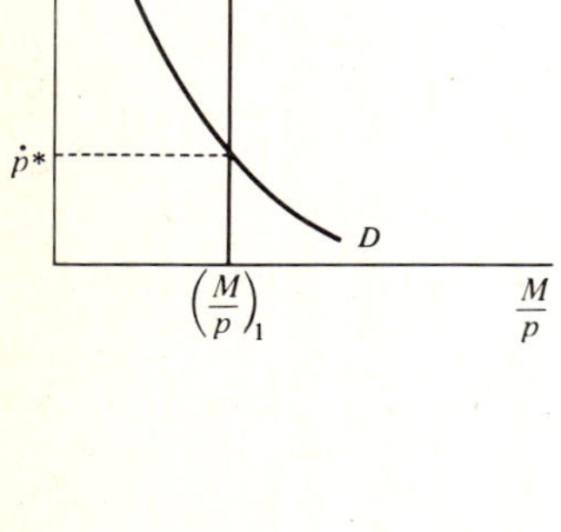

Figure 19-6

balances is drawn on the assumption that the expected inflation rate equals the current rate. With this demand curve and with the constant supply of real balances (M/p), the equilibrium inflation rate is $\dot{p}^*$. The fact that the supply of real balances is constant at $(M/p)_1$ implies that the rate of increase of the nominal money supply $\dot{M}^S$ equals the rate of inflation. Thus, the equilibrium inflation rate is that which equals the rate of growth of M and the expected rate of inflation.

Algebraically, the conditions for the long-run equilibrium inflation rate can be derived as follows. Differentiate the demand function for real balances Equation 19.6 with respect to time to obtain:

$$\frac{d \ln \left(\frac{M}{p}\right)}{dt} = -\alpha \frac{d\dot{p}^{\text{exp}}}{dt} \tag{19.8}$$

The left-hand expression for the rate of change of real balances equals the rate of change of M minus the rate of change of p. Therefore we can write:

$$\dot{M}^S - \dot{p} = -\alpha \frac{d\dot{p}^{\text{exp}}}{dt} \tag{19.9}$$

where $\dot{M}^S$ is the rate of change of the nominal money supply. Substituting for $d\dot{p}^{\text{exp}}/dt$ from the adaptive expectations hypothesis (Eq. 19.5) and rearranging terms, we obtain:

$$\alpha\beta\dot{p} - \alpha\beta\dot{p}^{\text{exp}} + \dot{M}^S = \dot{p} \tag{19.10}$$

or

$$\frac{\dot{M}^S - \alpha\beta\dot{p}^{\text{exp}}}{1 - \alpha\beta} = \dot{p} \tag{19.11}$$

This is an expression for the inflation rate as defined by Cagan's theory of the demand for money, expectations formation, and identity of equilibrium in the money market. It is not itself a definition of the *equilibrium* rate of inflation. The equilibrium rate, $\dot{p}^*$, is that which is unchanging:

$$\frac{d\dot{p}^*}{dt} = \frac{d\left(\frac{\dot{M}^S - \alpha\beta\dot{p}^{\text{exp}}}{1 - \alpha\beta}\right)}{dt} = 0 \tag{19.12}$$

It requires, in other words:

$$\left[\frac{1}{1 - \alpha\beta}\right]\frac{d\dot{M}^S}{dt} - \left[\frac{\alpha\beta}{1 - \alpha\beta}\right]\frac{d\dot{p}^{\text{exp}}}{dt} = 0 \tag{19.13}$$

Since $(d\dot{M}^S/dt) \equiv 0$ (the rate of change of the money supply is assumed constant) and $\alpha\beta \neq 0$, it follows that long-run equilibrium requires $(d\dot{p}^{\text{exp}}/dt) = 0$, constancy in the expected rate of inflation. From Equation 19.5 we know that this constancy is achieved only when the expected rate equals the current rate $\dot{p}^{\text{exp}} = \dot{p}$. And, from Equation 19.9, it is clear that when we do have long-run equilibrium with $(d\dot{p}^{\text{exp}}/dt) = 0$, we must have $\dot{p} = \dot{M}^S$. Thus, for the inflation rate to be the long-run equilibrium rate, we must have:

$$\dot{M}^S = \dot{p}^{\exp} = \dot{p}^* \tag{19.14}$$

The current rate of inflation equals the expected rate and the rate of growth of money supply.

Stability of Equilibrium

That completes our discussion of what is meant by the long-run equilibrium rate of inflation $\dot{p}^*$. Now we may consider its stability, bearing in mind that this is crucial to the question of whether an acceleration of inflation requires an acceleration of the rate of growth of the money supply. Suppose that for some arbitrary reason the rate of inflation rose above the rate of growth of money supply. Would forces exist that would return it to its equilibrium value, or would it remain higher than $\dot{M}^S$? The key to the answer is in Equation 19.11. This equation shows that the stability of the equilibrium inflation rate $\dot{p}^*$ depends upon the value of $\alpha\beta$.

Let us show algebraically why stability depends upon $\alpha\beta$. Suppose we are initially in long-run equilibrium $\dot{p}^* = \dot{p}^{\exp} = \dot{M}^S$, the rate of growth of the money supply is, and continues to be, constant, but then some exogenous shock causes a rise in the inflation rate to $\dot{p}_1 > \dot{p}^*$. Since we now have $\dot{p} > \dot{p}^{\exp}$, it follows from Equation 19.5 that $(dp^{\exp}/dt) > 0$. Now, we know from differentiating Equation 19.11 that changes in the rate of inflation are related to changes in the rate of growth of the money supply and changes in expectations:

$$\frac{d\dot{p}}{dt} = \frac{1}{1-\alpha\beta}\frac{d\dot{M}^S}{dt} - \left[\frac{\alpha\beta}{1-\alpha\beta}\right]\frac{d\dot{p}^{\exp}}{dt} \tag{19.15}$$

Since, as we have found, $(d\dot{p}^{\exp}/dt) > 0$, and since we assume the rate of growth of the money supply is constant $((d\dot{M}^S/dt) = 0)$, it follows that the sign of $d\dot{p}/dt$ depends upon $\alpha\beta$. If $0 < \alpha\beta < 1$, then the term within square brackets is positive and it follows that $(d\dot{p}/dt) < 0$; the rate of inflation declines when it is greater than $\dot{M}^S$ (and increases when $\dot{p} < \dot{M}^S$ and $d\dot{p}^{\exp}/dt$ is negative), so that with $\alpha\beta < 0$, $\dot{p}^*(=\dot{M}^S)$ is a stable equilibrium rate of inflation. If, however, $\alpha\beta > 1$, it follows that the term within square brackets is negative, so that $(d\dot{p}/dt) > 0$; the rate of inflation rises when it is greater than $\dot{M}^S$ (and declines when it is below $\dot{M}^S$ and $d\dot{p}^{\exp}/dt$ is negative) so that the inflation rate $\dot{p}^* = \dot{M}^S$ is an unstable equilibrium rate.

In the second case, where $\alpha\beta > 1$, it is clear that any exogenous increase of the inflation rate above the rate of growth of the money supply can give rise to an ever-increasing rate of inflation, even though the rate of growth of the money supply is kept constant. If, however, $\alpha\beta$ is less than 1, a rate of inflation higher than the rate of monetary expansion can only be temporary. In the latter instance, a rate of monetary expansion equal to the inflation rate is (except for temporary disturbances) a necessary condition for inflation,

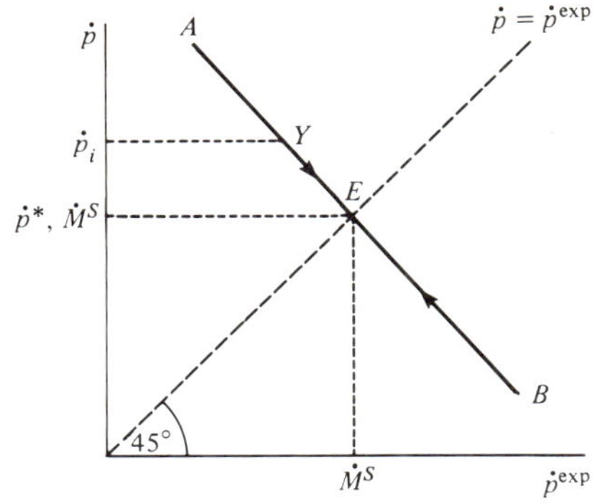

Figure 19-7

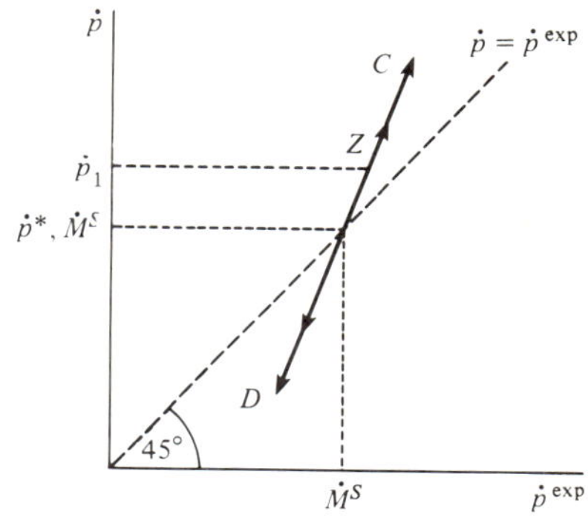

Figure 19-8

whereas in the former case disturbances are self-reinforcing rather than temporary, so this necessary condition does not hold.

Following Goldman (1972), this conclusion can be illustrated using Figures 19.7 and 19.8. In the former, the line AB represents Equation 19.11 when $0 < \alpha\beta < 1$; in the latter, CD, represents the same equation when $\alpha\beta > 1$. Thus, in each case the slope of the line is $[-\alpha\beta/(1-\alpha\beta)]$ and its intercept depends upon $\dot{M}^S$. The long-run equilibrium rate of inflation is $\dot{M}^S$ in each case, for only when this equality holds is the economy at E, where $\dot{M}^S = \dot{p}^{exp} = \dot{p}^*$. Now suppose that with the same $\dot{M}^S$, the rate of inflation is above the expected level at $\dot{p}_1$, for some reason. In Figure 19.7, the relation between $\dot{p}$ and $\dot{p}^{exp}$ means that the economy is at point Y. As we have seen, that causes $\dot{p}^{exp}$ to rise and $\dot{p}$ to decline; so the economy moves along AB from Y toward E and the inflation rate $\dot{p} = \dot{M}^S$ is reached. However, in Figure 19.8, $\dot{p}_1$ exists when the economy is at Z. In this case the divergence of $\dot{p}$ from $\dot{p}^{exp}$ again causes $\dot{p}^{exp}$ to be above its long-run equilibrium value, but this now induces further increases in $\dot{p}$. Consequently, the economy moves further and further away from X and the inflation rate increases even though the rate of monetary expansion is constant. Similar conclusions hold with respect to decreases in the inflation rate.

19.3 MONEY MARKET EQUILIBRIUM AND THE POLICY PARADOX

Cagan's empirical work suggests that $\alpha\beta < 1$ in hyperinflations, a proposal supported by the results of other studies.[5] This implies that a rate of inflation equal to the rate of increase of the money supply is a stable equilibrium rate, and the possibility of a self-accelerating rate of inflation ever greater than the monetary expansion is not relevant to real-world hyperinflations. Neverthe-

[5]See Laidler and Parkin (1975) for a summary of related studies. Note, however, the criticism by Jacobs (1975) of the empirical methods used in such studies.

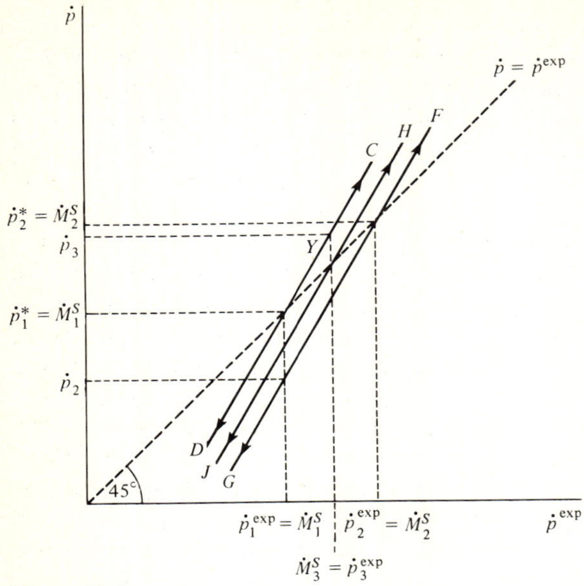

Figure 19-9

less, Cagan's *theoretical* model does not preclude the possibility of $\alpha\beta > 1$ in principle, and Goldman (1972) has demonstrated that this model is constructed in such a way that its policy implications in such a case are distinctly nonmonetarist.

Goldman's principal results can be summarized before being demonstrated. He points out that if $\alpha\beta > 1$ in Cagan's model, then an *increase* in the rate of growth of the money supply causes a *decrease* in the rate of inflation. This results from Cagan's simplifying assumption that the demand and supply of real balances are always equal (Eq. 19.6).[6]

If $\alpha\beta > 1$, an increase in the rate of growth of the money supply *decreases* the rate of inflation. This fact can be seen by differentiating Equation 19.11 to obtain (if we assume $(d\dot{p}^{exp}/d\dot{M}^S) = 0$):

$$\frac{d\dot{p}}{d\dot{M}^S} = \frac{1}{1-\alpha\beta} \tag{19.16}$$

which is negative if $\alpha\beta > 1$. The result should, however, be interpreted carefully. It says that the actual rate of inflation is inversely related to the rate of monetary expansion; it does not say that the long-run equilibrium rate of inflation, $\dot{p}^*$, is inversely related to $\dot{M}^S$. The distinction is illustrated[7] in Figure

[6]In addition, Goldman demonstrates that when equilibrium is unstable, Cagan's simplifying assumption $M^D \equiv M$ is not derivable, as Cagan claims, from the assumption that the adjustment factor π in $(d \ln (M/p)/dt) = \pi[\ln (M/p)^D - \ln (M/p)]$ is sufficiently large. See footnote 4.

[7]Algebraically, $d\dot{p}/d\dot{M}^S = 1/(1-\alpha\beta)$ only when $\dot{M}^S$ and $\dot{p}^{exp}$ are independent. In long-run equilibrium, however, $\dot{M}^S = \dot{p}^{exp}$ so that $(d\dot{p}/d\dot{M}^S) = 1$, since Eq. 19.11 then becomes $\dot{M}^S(1 - \alpha\beta/(1-\alpha\beta)) = \dot{p}$.

19.9. Here *CD* represents the relationship between $\dot{p}$, $\dot{M}^S$, and $\dot{p}^{\text{exp}}$ when the rate of monetary expansion is $\dot{M}_1^S$, while *FG* represents it when this rate is at the higher value, $\dot{M}_2^S$. Suppose the economy is initially at *X*, with the money supply growing at $\dot{M}_1^S$ and inflation at its equilibrium rate, $\dot{p}_1^*$. If the money supply growth rate is raised to $\dot{M}_2^S$ and somehow the economy is forced onto its new equilibrium inflation rate, then inflation will be at its new, higher equilibrium inflation rate, $\dot{p}_2^*$. However, the point of the result we have demonstrated, $(d\dot{p}/d\dot{M}^S) < 0$ if $\alpha\beta > 1$, is that the model contains nothing to enable it to reach this new equilibrium rate. Instead, with the new rate of monetary expansion at $\dot{M}_2^S$, the curve *FG* exists and the only inflation rate consistent with $\dot{M}_2^S$ and the existing level of expectations, $(\dot{p}_1^{\text{exp}})$, is $\dot{p}_2$. (And after moving to this lower rate of inflation, the economy moves in a southwesterly direction along *FG*.)

To illustrate Goldman's point from another perspective, suppose that with monetary expansion at $\dot{M}_1^S$, we observe the economy at a point on *CD* where it is off its equilibrium path; it is at *Y* so that inflation is at $\dot{p}_3$, the expected inflation rate is $\dot{p}_3^{\text{exp}}(<\dot{p}_3)$, and inflation is accelerating. By *raising* the rate of growth of the money supply to $\dot{M}_3^S = \dot{p}_3^{\text{exp}}$, the curve *HJ* is established and the only rate of inflation consistent with $\dot{M}_3$ and $\dot{p}_3^{\text{exp}}$ is $\dot{p}_3$. In this way, by raising the rate of monetary expansion, the rate of inflation is reduced and, since it is brought to its equilibrium level, its self-acceleration is ended.[8]

Now, the important point about Goldman's argument is that this paradoxical implication of Cagan's model, that inflation can be inversely related to the rate of monetary expansion, results from Cagan's arbitrary simplifying assumption that the money market is always in equilibrium:

$$\left(\frac{M}{p}\right)^D \equiv \frac{M}{p} \tag{19.17}$$

for it is this assumption that is crucial in the derivation of Equations 19.11 and 19.16. Suppose that, instead, the actual stock of real balances may at any instant differ from the desired stock, and that when it does so, it adjusts over time (noninstantaneously) toward the desired stock at a rate proportional to the discrepancy. This hypothesis can be written:

$$\frac{d \ln\left(\frac{M}{p}\right)}{dt} = \pi\left[\ln\left(\frac{M}{p}\right)^D - \ln\left(\frac{M}{p}\right)\right] \tag{19.7}$$

$$(\pi > 0)$$

Or, in other words:

$$\dot{p} = \dot{M}^S + \pi\left[\ln\left(\frac{M}{p}\right) - \ln\left(\frac{M}{p}\right)^D\right] \tag{19.18}$$

$$(\pi > 0)$$

[8] This is once again the algebraic result that by setting $\dot{M}^S = \dot{p}^{\text{exp}}$, we obtain $\dot{p} = \dot{M}^S = \dot{p}^{\text{exp}}$ from Eq. 19.11.

Differentiating Equation 19.18, it is clear that with this hypothesis, $d\dot{p}/d\dot{M}^S$ is always positive. Thus, generalizing Cagan's model to allow for disequilibrium in the money market overcomes the paradox that an increase in the rate of growth of M may reduce the inflation rate.[9]

Goldman's result is reminiscent of those obtained in other areas of monetary theory. For example, as we saw in Chapter 18, the properties of monetary growth models are altered when we abandon the Neoclassical hypothesis that inflation can occur even if the goods and money markets are always in equilibrium and replace it with the Keynes-Wicksell hypothesis that inflation occurs only when there is an excess supply of goods (or, by Walras' Law, an excess demand for money in a two-market model). Analogously (but not identically), in Cagan's model the properties change when we replace the Neoclassical assumption that the goods and money markets are always in equilibrium with one to the effect that, given the rate of monetary expansion, the rate of inflation depends upon disequilibrium in the money market (Eq. 19.18) and, by Walras' Law, the goods market.

19.4 FRIEDMAN'S THEORY OF NOMINAL INCOME

The model considered above was developed as a theory of hyperinflation. It was precisely on the grounds that in hyperinflations the rate of inflation swamps the effects of interest rates and real income on the demand for money that Cagan justified the specification of the inflation rate as the only argument in the demand function. This, however, restricts the applicability of his model. For analyzing the role of money in less severe inflations, we should, in principle, use a demand function for money whose arguments include a scale variable and also rate-of-return variables other than the inflation rate. Friedman (1970, 1971) does appear to provide us with precisely such a model, although its applicability is severely limited by its simplifying assumptions. It is presented as a model of the determination of national income, but, as will be seen, it has implications for the long-run equilibrium inflation rate.

Friedman's model, like Cagan's, is based upon the demand function for money, rather than on the equations of the goods market. But his demand function takes account of the idea that desired money balances depend upon a scale variable (nominal income in this case) and the nominal rate of interest on alternative financial assets (bonds):

$$M^D = f(Y, r) \tag{19.19}$$

This function is Keynesian in inspiration but, whereas comparative static Keynesian models ignore the rate of price change, this is hardly permissible in

[9]It also leads to a change in the conditions under which the equilibrium inflation rate is unstable. Whereas in Cagan's simplified model the system is unstable, and self-accelerating inflation can occur if $\alpha\beta > 1$, here it is unstable if $(\pi + \beta) < \alpha\pi\beta$.

a model that is designed to permit the analysis of inflationary situations. To introduce the rate of inflation, Friedman postulates that the nominal interest rate is always equal to the real rate, ρ, plus the rate of inflation:[10]

$$r = \rho + \dot{p} \tag{19.20}$$

so that

$$M^D = f[Y, (\rho + \dot{p})] \tag{19.21}$$

Also, he postulates that the income elasticity of this demand function is unity, so it can be expressed as a velocity function.[11]

$$\frac{M^D}{Y} = f(\rho + \dot{p}) = f(r) \tag{19.22}$$

Friedman makes several further simplifying assumptions. In particular, it is assumed that the current nominal rate of interest always equals its expected value, which is assumed to equal the expected real rate and inflation rate:

$$r = r^e = \rho^e + \dot{p}^e \tag{19.23}$$

Then, noting that the expected rate of inflation can be defined as the difference between the expected growth rates of real and nominal income:

$$\dot{p}^e = \dot{Y}^e - \dot{y}^e \tag{19.24}$$

Assuming (rather arbitrarily) that the difference between the expected real rate of return on capital and the expected rate of growth of real income is a constant, q:

$$\rho^e - \dot{y}^e = q \tag{19.25}$$

we may substitute from Equations 19.23, 19.24, and 19.25 to replace r in Equation 19.22. We obtain thereby:

$$M^D = Yf(q + \dot{Y}^e) \tag{19.26}$$

This demand function has the implication that desired velocity M^D/Y is constant in long-run equilibrium. Although desired velocity is a function of q and $\dot{Y}^E$, the first term is, as we have seen, assumed constant and the second term is constant on the long-run equilibrium growth path by the definition of that concept (constancy of the rate of growth and, hence, of the expected growth rate).

[10]This postulate, $r = \rho + \dot{p}$, can be treated as a mere definition. When it is, the real interest rate is defined merely as the nominal rate minus the inflation rate and, given the latter, it varies whenever the nominal rate varies. Alternatively, it can be treated as a hypothesis which suggests that ρ is determined by other factors and that there is some equilibrating mechanism that ensures that the equation always holds. The second interpretation seems to accord with Friedman's. He can be thought to identify ρ with the marginal productivity of physical capital, so that it is not defined simply as a "residual" from the nominal rate and inflation rate.

[11]See Chap. 20, Sec. 20.1, for the explanation of the relationship between the velocity function and the assumption of unit income elasticity.

The implication that desired velocity is constant in long-run equilibrium also implies that the long-run equilibrium rate of growth of nominal income equals the rate of growth of the money supply. This follows from the Quantity Theory identity:

$$MV \equiv Y \text{ or } MV \equiv p\bar{y}$$

If V is constant, then the rate of change of M must equal the rate of change of $\bar{Y}$ (or $p\bar{y}$).[12]

Nominal Income or Price Level

Thus, according to Friedman's model of nominal income, in the long run the rate of change of nominal income equals the rate of change of the nominal money supply. Several points about this conclusion are noteworthy. First, the demand function for money with which the analysis begins is radically transformed in the course of it, and the transformation is based on assumptions that may be disputed. Second, it is of significance only if the long-run equilibrium rate of growth is stable, for otherwise the rate of change of nominal income would, if disturbed, not converge on the rate of change of the money supply. Stability depends upon what happens to $\dot{Y}^e$ when $\dot{Y}$ diverges from equilibrium. Third, it is a theory of nominal income, $p\bar{y}$, rather than the price level, p, or its rate of change, $\dot{p}$. The rate of change of nominal income may be decomposed into three parts:

$$\frac{d \log (p\bar{y})}{dt} = \dot{p} + \dot{y} + \dot{z} \tag{19.27}$$

where $z = (\bar{y}/y)$, y equals planned or "full-employment" output, and $\bar{y}$ is actual output. That is, the rate of change of nominal income equals the rate of inflation, plus the rate of change of full-employment output, plus the rate of change of the ratio of actual output to full-employment output.[13] Thus, the conclusion that in long-run equilibrium, the rate of growth of nominal income equals that of the money supply does not by itself tell us anything about the rate of inflation; in principle, it is possible that a positive rate of monetary growth is accompanied by zero inflation and positive rates of growth of full-employment output ($\dot{y} > 0$) or of the rate of capacity utilization ($\dot{z} > 0$). To obtain from it a theory of the relation between monetary expansion and *inflation* ($\dot{p}$), it is necessary to consider these variables further.

The rate of growth of capacity output, $\dot{y}$, may be assumed positive and yet not prevent us from concluding that the rate of monetary expansion determines the rate of inflation. The crucial thing is to assume that $\dot{y}$ is itself

[12]Writing the identity in logarithms, we have $\log M - \log V \equiv \log \bar{Y}$. Differentiating with respect to time and assuming that $(d \log V/dt) = 0$, we have $d \log M/dt = d \log \bar{Y}/dt$ or $\dot{M} = \dot{\bar{Y}}$.

[13]Equation 19.27 is derived as follows: $d \ln p\bar{y}/dt = d \ln p/dt + d \ln \bar{y}/dt$. But $\bar{y} \equiv y(\bar{y}/y)$, so that $\ln \bar{y} = \ln y + \ln (\bar{y}/y)$, and $d \ln \bar{y}/dt = d \ln y/dt + d \ln (\bar{y}/y)/dt = d \ln y/dt + d \ln z/dt$.

unaffected by the rate of monetary expansion, so $\dot{y}$ itself can be treated as a constant for the present purpose. Then, combining Equation 19.27 with the conclusion that $d \log(p\bar{y})/dt$ equals the rate of growth of the money supply and writing $\dot{y}^*$ for the constant rate of capacity growth, we have:

$$\dot{M}^S - \dot{y}^* = \dot{p} + \dot{z} \tag{19.28}$$

Or, in other words, in long-run equilibrium, the *excess* of the rate of growth of the money supply over the rate of growth of capacity equals $\dot{p} + \dot{z}$.

The rate of growth of z, however, does appear to present something of a problem. For it may be that with $(\dot{M}^S - \dot{y}^*)$ positive, inflation is zero ($\dot{p} = 0$) and the excess rate of growth of money simply causes output $\bar{y}$ to rise relative to full-employment output y (it causes, that is, $\dot{z} > 0$). In order to consider this possibility, it is necessary to consider the concept of the Phillips Curve. We shall do this in Chapter 21, Section 21.3, and it will be seen there[14] that the monetarist theory of the Phillips Curve developed by Friedman (1968) and Phelps (1968) has an implication that is highly relevant to the present problem. For the conclusion of the Friedman/Phelps model of the Phillips Curve is that in long-run equilibrium, $\bar{y}/y = 1$ if full-employment output is appropriately defined (as, in their terminology, the level of output produced when unemployment is at its "natural rate"). If, in long-run equilibrium, z equals unity, it follows that in that state its rate of change is zero $\dot{z} = 0$. From Equation 19.28, therefore, it follows that according to the present section's model of the demand for money and the Friedman/Phelps model of the Phillips Curve, the excess of the rate of monetary expansion over the rate of growth of capacity equals the rate of inflation in long-run equilibrium.

19.5 INFLATION AND THE INTEREST RATE

In this chapter we have introduced the interest rate into our arguments at several points. But different aspects of interest rate behavior under inflation have been emphasized at each point, and it is now necessary to consider this behavior within a general framework. The necessity for such a perspective derives from the fact that the theoretical models considered in this chapter ascribe quite different, and in some ways inconsistent, roles to the interest rate. The Keynesian inflation gap model forced us to make some specific assumptions about the shapes of the curves in the money market because, with general Keynesian assumptions, inflation would cause the nominal interest rate to rise in response to money market disequilibrium. There, the nominal rate was affected by the change in the price *level* rather than *rate* of inflation, and it affected the demand for real and nominal balances. In Cagan's

[14]The reader may wish to read Section 21.3 before leaving this chapter. It is equally relevant here and in Chap. 21, and it is comprehensible irrespective of whether the intervening chapters have been read.

model, by contrast, the nominal or real interest rate has no effect on the demand for money. And in Friedman's model, the nominal rate is assumed to affect the demand for nominal balances but, being concerned essentially with long-run equilibrium, the model treats that nominal rate as a constant.

The theoretical framework that permits us to consider the behavior of the interest rate under inflationary conditions is derived from the work of Irving Fisher (1896, 1930). He was concerned to investigate, among other things, the effects of inflation upon the nominal interest rate. In this he defined the nominal rate as a function of the real rate of interest and expected rate of inflation as:

$$r = \rho + \dot{p}^e \tag{19.29}$$

Fisher treated this relationship between the nominal and real rates of interest as an equilibrium one reached because both borrower and lender allow for the expectation of inflation-induced decreases in the real value of the principal. Fisher put forward the same long-run equilibrium analyses that we have encountered in the models of Cagan and Friedman: In long-run equilibrium, a rise in the rate of growth of the money supply will generate an equal rise in the rate of inflation, and hence, an equal rise in the expected rate of inflation ($\dot{p}^e$) and in r, the nominal rate.

In all this discussion, it is assumed that the real rate of interest is invariant to changes in the rate of growth of the money supply, the assumption of the neutrality of money. We have seen in Chapter 18 that the Neoclassical growth model does not lend support to this assumption, for there the rate of growth of the money supply does, under a wide variety of assumptions, have an effect upon the marginal product of capital. Nevertheless, we shall maintain the assumption in order to simplify our discussion of the Fisher Equation.

Fisher's approach to the determination of nominal interest rates is believed by some writers to capture the dominant or sole determinant of nominal interest rates in inflationary circumstances. Such is the theory of Yohe and Karnovsky (1969), for their empirical study is based upon an equation where the only explanatory variable for the nominal rate is expected inflation:

$$r = a + b\dot{p}^e \tag{19.30}$$

(ignoring error terms). Such a concept of the determination of the nominal rate may also be said to underlie the work of Cagan (1956).

However, Equation 19.30 is a very restrictive model of the determination of nominal rates. It concentrates on price expectations alone; it therefore precludes Keynesian analysis of the effects of real income, the price *level*, and the nominal money supply upon r. The Keynesian analysis is derived from the liquidity preference theory of the money market. In equilibrium the Keynesian model has

$$M = pf(\bar{y}, r) \tag{19.31}$$

which may be solved for r:

$$r = g\left(\frac{M}{p}, \bar{y}\right) \tag{19.32}$$

As can be seen, the Keynesian approach explains the nominal rate by variables different from those used in Equation 19.30.

Writers such as Darby (1975) and Feldstein and Eckstein (1970) have attempted to combine both the Keynesian effects on r (real balances and real income) and the Fisher effect (of inflation expectations). In empirical work, therefore, this model is formulated as:

$$r = f\left(\dot{p}^e, \frac{M}{p}, \bar{y}\right) \tag{19.33}$$

With several modifications, it has been subject to empirical estimation. The estimates of writers such as Carr, Pesando, and Smith (1976) are sensitive to the assumptions made concerning how expectations are formed, but they do produce some results to suggest that the price expectations effect dominates the others. Such a result conforms to the standard theoretical model based on Equation 19.33, for, since Friedman (1968), it is customary to postulate that with $\bar{y}$ predetermined on its long-run growth path, a change in money supply M has an initial but temporary depressing effect on r. The fall in r pushes up the price level, thereby tending to reduce M/p toward its initial level. However, the rise in p alters inflationary expectations $\dot{p}^e$, which has its own (positive) effect on r. If, instead of a once-for-all rise in M, we consider a permanent increase in the rate of growth of M, the price level will come to rise at the same new rate as M, leaving (M/p) unchanged, but, in long-run equilibrium, raising $\dot{p}^e$ to the same level as the new rate of growth of M. In consequence, the dominant determinant of the nominal rate is, in such models, considered to be the expected rate of inflation (itself determined by the rate of growth of M).

PART SIX

EMPIRICAL STUDIES AND POLICY ISSUES

CHAPTER

TWENTY

EMPIRICAL STUDIES OF MONETARY RELATIONSHIPS

With rare exceptions, such as in Chapter 7, we have studiously avoided all mention of empirical studies throughout this book. We have concentrated on the problems of building theoretical macroeconomic models that include monetary factors and on the conclusions yielded by different models. The emphasis has been on questions of pure theory. In this chapter we correct the emphasis and survey some of the research that tests the fundamental theoretical propositions against empirical data. Although recent decades have witnessed a profusion of econometric studies of monetary relationships, these studies have concentrated on relatively few such relationships. Much of the work has focused on two areas. The first is concerned with the relationship between the theory of the demand for money and empirical data. The second is involved with estimating directly the effect of monetary policy on the level of nominal income.

These two types of research are related to each other in that each yields information that is, to a greater or lesser degree, relevant to assessing the impact of monetary policy. However, different techniques and technical problems are involved in each area of research. In studying the demand function for money, we use the technique of estimating a *structural equation.* In explicitly studying the effect of monetary policy on nominal income, we may either estimate a set of structural equations or a *reduced form equation.* The distinction between them may be illustrated with a simple model of the goods and money markets.

Let nominal planned consumption be a function of nominal income and money balances:

$$C = k_1 + a\bar{Y} + bM + \varepsilon_1 \quad (0 < a < 1, 0 < b < 1) \tag{20.1}$$

The term k_1 is a constant and ε_1 is a random error term. Let nominal planned investment be a linear function of the bond interest rate:

$$I = k_2 + cr + \varepsilon_2 \qquad (c < 0) \tag{20.2}$$

Equilibrium in the goods market, $\bar{Y} = C + I + G$, therefore implies:

$$\bar{Y} = k_3 + a\bar{Y} + bM + cr + \bar{G} + \varepsilon_3 \tag{20.3}$$

where $k_3 = k_1 + k_2$, $\varepsilon_3 = \varepsilon_1 + \varepsilon_2$, and $\bar{G}$ is exogenously determined government expenditure. The demand for money may be represented by a Keynesian liquidity preference function, which in simple linear form is:

$$M^D = k_4 + d\bar{Y} + er + \varepsilon_4 \qquad (e < 0) \tag{20.4}$$

The supply of money is a function of nominal income (because this influences the private sector's desired ratio of cash to money and therefore the proportion of high-powered money that remains with the banks), the interest rate on government bonds, and the stock of high-powered money, H, which we shall assume to be exogenously determined by government policy:

$$M^s = f\bar{Y} + gr + hH + \varepsilon_5 \tag{20.5}$$

Money market equilibrium requires:

$$M^D = M^S = M \tag{20.6}$$

The system comprising Equations 20.1 to 20.6 represents our model of the economy. These equations are the structural equations of the model. We may also derive from them a reduced form equation—one that relates one of the endogenous variables to the exogenous variables of the model. A reduced form in which monetary theory is particularly interested is the one expressing nominal income as a function of the exogenous variables. The only exogenous variables in this model are high-powered money and government expenditure, so the relevant reduced form is:

$$Y = l + mH + q\bar{G} + \theta \tag{20.7}$$

where l, m, and q are parameters and θ is a random error term. Equation 20.7 is derived by solving Equations 20.1 to 20.6, so the parameters and the error term l, m, q, and θ are functions of the parameters and error terms of those equations.[1]

[1]Specifically:

$$m = \frac{h(be + c)}{z}; \quad q = \frac{e - g}{z};$$

and

$$\theta = [(e - g)\varepsilon_3 - (bg + c)\varepsilon_4 + (be + c)\varepsilon_5]1/z$$

where

$$z = (1 - a)(e - g) + d(bg + c) - f(be + c).$$

Empirical studies vary according to whether they confront structural equations or reduced form equations with empirical data. There are advantages and disadvantages with each approach, but either of them may be used to answer two types of questions. The first is whether the model represented by Equations 20.1 to 20.6 or by Equation 20.7 is a valid model. Validity is judged in a special sense. The model is evaluated according to whether the data suggest that there is a systematic relationship between the variables on the right-hand side of the equations and those on the left,[2] and that the relationship would not be improved by omitting a variable or adding a new variable. The criteria for making this judgment vary from one study to another but commonly include the coefficient of determination (R^2), the standard error of the parameter estimates, and measures of autocorrelation, multicollinearity, and heteroscedasticity.[3] The second question relates to the values of the parameters, assuming the model to be valid or true in the above sense. In Equation 20.7, for example, we may be concerned with whether m is large or small and, therefore, whether government-induced changes in the stock of high-powered money will have a large or a small effect on nominal income.

In the rest of this chapter, we shall proceed as follows: Sections 20.1 to 20.3 consider empirical studies on the structural equation representing the demand function for money. In Section 20.1 we shall be concerned with studies that yield conclusions on whether current income, permanent income, or nonhuman wealth is the appropriate budget constraint or scale variable in the demand function for money. In Section 20.2 we shall discuss the question of whether the theory that the demand for money is a function of interest rates is supported by the data. In Section 20.3 we shall appraise the results surveyed in the previous two sections. In Sections 20.4 and 20.5 we shall consider empirical work on reduced forms, such as Equation 20.7.

Throughout the chapter we shall see that much of the controversy surrounding this empirical work concerns the validity of the propositions advanced by the New Quantity Theorists, or the monetarists. In the next chapter we shall survey this controversy more generally, taking into account both theoretical and empirical arguments.

20.1 WEALTH, INCOME, AND THE DEMAND FOR MONEY

In our earlier discussions of the demand function for money, we have encountered three major propositions. In Chapter 9 we considered a simple Keynesian demand function, the type that lies behind the standard *LM* curve

[2]In general, the equilibrium conditions, such as Eq. 20.6, are assumed to hold a priori. We shall be concerned only with work of this nature. More recent empirical work does not make this assumption.

[3]For an introduction to these concepts, see Johnston (1972).

of macroeconomics textbooks. It represents the demand for real money balances as a function of an interest rate (to represent the speculative demand) and of real income (to represent transactions demand):

$$M^D = pf(\bar{y}, r) \tag{20.8}$$

In Chapters 10 and 11 we considered the post-Keynesian studies of the demand for money, such as those of Tobin (1958), which suggest that it is a function of an interest rate and nonhuman wealth:

$$M^D = pf(w_N, r) \tag{20.9}$$

In Chapter 7 we discussed the New Quantity Theory's analysis of the demand for money. We saw there that, in its pure form, it could be represented by an equation, such as Equation 20.9, modified so that the wealth variable includes human as well as nonhuman wealth. In its modified form, as in Friedman (1959), however, it represents the demand for money as a function of permanent income without an interest rate variable:

$$M^D = f(Y^P) \tag{20.10}$$

Equations 20.8 to 20.10 represent the basic formulations of three hypotheses that have been subjected to empirical test. Each differs from the others in its choice of scale variable: current income, nonhuman wealth, and permanent income. In this section we consider what judgments may be made concerning the merits of each.

The earliest of the modern empirical studies, such as those of Kisselgoff (1945) and Tobin (1947), were concerned with Keynesian formulations that were much more faithful to Keynes's own equation than is Equation 20.8. They accepted Keynes's distinction between active and idle balances, or transactions and speculative balances:

$$M^D = M^{\text{active}} + M^{\text{idle}} = kp\bar{y} + L_2(r) \tag{20.11}$$

and attempted to test the proposition that the demand for idle balances is a function of the bond rate of interest. Their findings appear to support the proposition, but the work is based on such dubious assumptions that we need not consider it here. The basic problem with those studies is that arbitrary assumptions must be made in order to divide total, observable money balances into active and idle components.[4] Later Keynesian studies, such as those of Latané (1954, 1960) and Christ (1963), are more firmly based in that they estimate the demand for *total* money balances as a function of an

[4]The method used to make this division is to calculate historical data on velocity $\bar{Y}/M$. It is then assumed that in the year when $\bar{Y}/M$ is at its maximum, all money is employed as active balances, so that no idle balances are held. Thus, it is assumed that $(\bar{Y}/M)_{\max} = 1/k$, the velocity of transactions balances, and it is then assumed that k is the same in all other years. In order to measure idle balances in each year, this value of k is used to measure $kp\bar{y}$ and, subtracting this measure from M, to derive an estimate of idle balances.

interest rate. However, these studies estimate versions of Equation 22.8 in the special form:

$$\frac{M}{\bar{Y}} = a\frac{1}{r^L} + b \tag{20.12}$$

where a and b are parameters and r is the interest rate on long bonds, and this form itself is based on arbitrary a priori assumptions. Here the assumption implicit in the equation is that the demand for money has an income elasticity of unity.[5] It is not necessary to make this assumption in order to carry out empirical work, and the assumption is not supported by economic theory. Indeed, the Baumol (1952) theory of the transactions demand for money implies that its income elasticity is less than unity—there are economies of scale in money holdings. If we wish to test such a theory, we cannot employ a function such as Equation 20.12, since it constrains the empirical regression equation to be of a form other than that implied by the theory. Nevertheless, the studies of Latané and Christ found that Equation 20.12 could account for 76 percent of the variation in $M/\bar{Y}$, and that there consequently appeared to be a systematic relationship between the interest rate and the ratio of money to income. Throughout this chapter it must be borne in mind that the money market is assumed to be in equilibrium, so that a relationship involving the stock of money is to be interpreted as one involving the demand for money, since $M^D = M^S = M$ in equilibrium.

The first relevant work on the validity of a simple Keynesian equation, such as Equation 20.8, was that of Meltzer (1963) and Brunner and Meltzer (1963). For, these writers explicitly formulate their work so as to give a comparative test of the validity of a simple Keynesian equation as against other equations. In Meltzer's classic article, equations similar to Equations 20.8, 20.9, and 20.10, expressed in linear logarithmic form, were fitted to annual United States data for the period 1900–1958. The results thus enable us to judge between the alternative theories represented by these equations. Meltzer concludes from his estimates that a Keynesian equation (like Eq. 20.8) is inferior to a nonhuman wealth equation (like Eq. 20.9). He argues that the Keynesian equation should be rejected on two grounds.

First, fitting the Keynesian equation in the following form:

$$\ln\left(\frac{M}{p}\right) = c + b\ln r + c\ln y \tag{20.13}$$

to data for 1900–1958, the coefficient of determination is high and the estimates of b and c are statistically significant. However, when the data are separated into the subperiods 1900–1929 and 1930–1958, it is found that the estimate of b is not statistically significant for the first period. In other words,

[5]Rewrite the equation as $M^D = \bar{Y}[a(1/r^L + b]$. The definition of income elasticity of demand is $(\partial M^D/\partial \bar{Y})\bar{Y}/M^D$. Differentiating the demand function, we have $\partial M^D/\partial \bar{Y} = a(1/r^L) + b$. Rearranging the terms of the demand function, we have $\bar{Y}/M^D = [1/a(1/r^L) + b]$. Therefore $(\partial M^D/\partial \bar{Y})\bar{Y}/M^D = [a(1/r^L) + b/a(1/r^L) + b] = 1$.

the data suggest that when real income, $\bar{y}$, is included in the demand function for money, the demand for money appears to be unaffected by the interest rate in 1900–1929. This contradicts the Keynesian hypothesis of liquidity preference.

Second, Meltzer tests a modified Keynesian equation of the following form:

$$\ln\left(\frac{M}{p}\right) = a + b \ln r + c \ln \bar{y} + d \ln\left(\frac{W_N}{p}\right) \tag{20.14}$$

This differs from the textbook Keynesian liquidity preference function because real nonhuman wealth is included as a variable. It might be thought of as a representation of Keynesian portfolio theories of the demand for money such as Tobin's (1958), where wealth acts as the budget constraint and income reflects the implicit yield on money balances derived from their services as a Medium of Exchange (transactions demand). Meltzer finds, however, that when wealth is included in the equation, as here, the estimate of c is not statistically significant, whereas d is. It appears, therefore, that changes in income have no significant effect on the demand for money when the effect of nonhuman wealth is taken into account.[6]

By contrast, Meltzer finds that an equation, such as Equation 20.9, expressing a relationship between the demand for money, an interest rate, and nonhuman wealth fits the data well. The regression equation:

$$\ln\left(\frac{M}{p}\right) = a + b \ln r + d \ln\left(\frac{W_N}{p}\right) \tag{20.15}$$

is found to have a high coefficient of determination and statistically significant estimates of b and d. He concludes, therefore, that this is a more valid structural equation for the demand for money than is the Keynesian equation. This conclusion is supported by Brunner and Meltzer (1963), who use a different procedure to test the relative merits of the equations.[7]

Nonhuman Wealth or Permanent Income

Meltzer (1963) and Brunner and Meltzer (1963) found not only that an equation with nonhuman wealth fits the data better than one with current

[6]There is, however, a technical difficulty in stating this conclusion confidently. That is, the time series of income and wealth move together, so that these two variables are highly correlated. In other words, the interpretation of the regression result is made difficult by multicollinearity.

[7]The procedure used by Brunner and Meltzer is to express the demand function for money in the form of an equation with the desired velocity of money on the left-hand side. The equation is estimated using data for a 10-year period. The estimates of the parameters obtained in this way are then used, together with knowledge of the independent variables in the eleventh year, to predict the value of the dependent variable, velocity, in the eleventh year. This procedure is repeated for a succession of periods and the predictions are compared with the actual values of the dependent variable. It was found that a velocity equation based upon Equation 20.15 gave more successful predictions than one based upon the Keynesian demand function for money.

income; they also found that it performs better than equations that have permanent income as an explanatory variable. This is the question on which much modern empirical research concentrates: Do explanations of the demand for money or desired velocity in terms of permanent income fit the data better than equations in terms of nonhuman wealth?

In Chapter 7 we saw that Friedman (1959) found that a demand function for money similar to Equation 20.10 appeared to fit United States data for the period 1870–1954. The method Friedman uses is to express the function in the form of an equation for desired velocity:

$$V = \frac{Y}{M} = a(y^P)^b \frac{Y}{(Y^P)} \tag{20.16}$$

or, in logarithmic form,

$$\ln V = \ln a + b \ln y^P + \ln\left(\frac{Y}{Y^P}\right) \tag{20.17}$$

where a and b are parameters, y^P is permanent real income (measured in per capita terms), Y^P is permanent nominal income, and Y is current nominal income. Friedman estimates the values of a and b from data that have a special form. The data consist of annual values of the variables averaged over each trade cycle so that, instead of using annual values of, say, y^P, he used cycle averages of these annual values. Thus, the parameters are estimated from secular or trend data. Another point to note about Friedman's data is that, as explained in Chapter 7, no data exist on permanent income. Instead, the proxy variable (called anticipated income in Chapter 7) is used, and it is measured as a geometrically weighted sum of past and present levels of current income:

$$y_t^P \simeq y_t^A = \beta \sum_{i=0}^{n} (1-\beta)^i \bar{y}_{t-i} \qquad (0 < \beta < 1)$$

Therefore, to estimate a and b, in Equation 20.17 Friedman uses data such as the cycle average of the values of *anticipated* income.

Using such data, Friedman estimated the value of a to be 1/0.003 and the value of b to be −0.81. For the moment, however, we are not concerned with the values of a and b, but with how well the theory fits the data. In other words, by normal criteria we are concerned with statistics such as the coefficient of determination and the standard errors of the estimates of a and b. But in the article by Friedman (1959), these criteria are not used. His method for judging the validity of the equation is to take the values of a and b estimated from cycle-average data and then, for each year, to insert into Equation 20.16 the measured values of y^P, Y^P (or y^A and Y^A), and Y. These then give a measure of "computed" velocity; the value of velocity V^* that would exist in each year—even years within cycles—if the estimates of a and b were exactly true estimates of an annual velocity equation. The resulting estimate of velocity V^* is then compared with the actual level of velocity. Friedman's result is

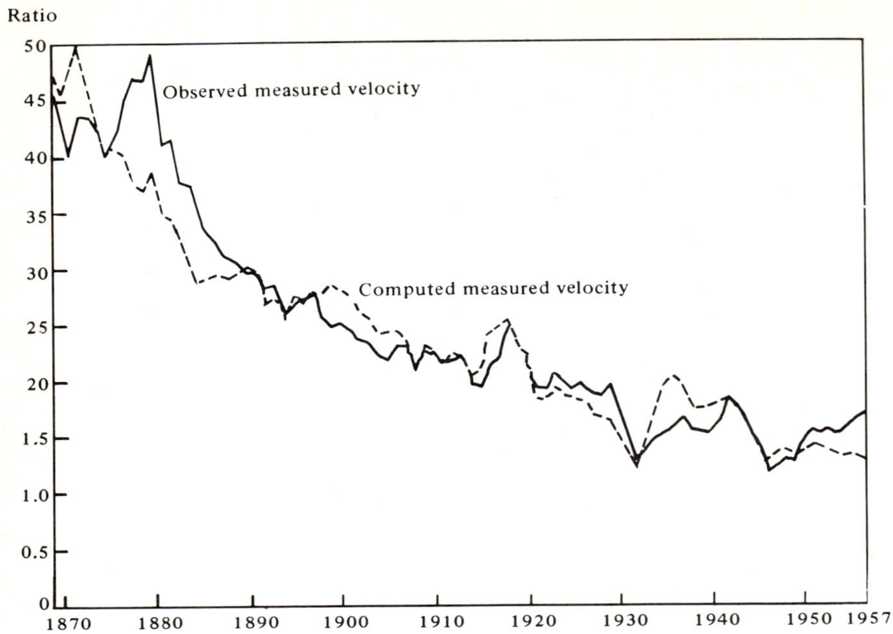

Figure 20-1. Reprinted from: M. Friedman, "The Demand for Money: Some Theoretical and Empirical Results," *Journal of Political Economy*, vol. 67 (August 1959), 340, by permission of The University of Chicago Press. Copyright 1959 by The University of Chicago Press.

reproduced in Figure 20.1 and, as can be seen, although the estimate of velocity (named computed measured velocity) does not exactly coincide with observed velocity, it does have the same secular downward trend and the same tendency to rise in booms and fall in slumps.[8]

Although the results of Friedman (1959) suggest that the data support the theory that the demand for money is a function of permanent income alone (for this is the theory from which the velocity equation, Equation 20.16, is derived), the result is controversial. One aspect of the controversy concerns the role of interest rates, for Friedman's equation suggests that they have no

[8]With Friedman's estimates of a and b, computed velocity V^* has a secular downward trend, owing to his estimate of b as -0.81. This estimate implies that the elasticity of velocity with respect to permanent income is negative; as permanent income rises, desired velocity falls. Since the secular trend of current income is related to permanent income (or its proxy, anticipated income), this implies that as current income grows on its trend, the trend of velocity is downward. The same thing can be said in terms of the demand for money. The estimate of velocity's elasticity as -0.81 implies that the elasticity of the demand for money with respect to permanent income is $+1.81$. As permanent income rises, the demand for money rises more than proportionately. Friedman's estimates, however, do not fit the data well for more recent years. His data stop in 1954 but in the 1960s and 1970s there appears to have been a reversal in the trend of actual velocity.

separate influence on velocity or the demand for money except insofar as their effect is captured by the influence of permanent income. Friedman's equations represent a hypothesis like that of Equation 20.10. The significance of interest rates is a separate issue to which we return in the following section, but it does have a bearing on the question of whether permanent income or nonhuman wealth is a better independent variable in the demand function for money. If, in fact, an interest rate does affect the demand for money, then an equation which excludes it does not enable us to accurately judge the significance of the variables that are included in the equation (such as permanent income or nonhuman wealth). Another aspect of the controversy is that other writers, notably Meltzer (1963), Brunner and Meltzer (1963), and Laidler (1966a), have tested the validity of the permanent income hypothesis in comparison with equations representing the nonhuman wealth hypothesis. We turn to their results now.

Meltzer (1963) finds that an equation in terms of nonhuman wealth (our Eq. 20.15) fits the data better than the permanent income equation for the demand for money considered in Chapter 7:

$$\ln \frac{M}{p^P} = a + by^P \tag{20.18}$$

where p^P is permanent prices and y^P is permanent real income and these are measured as anticipated prices and income.[9] Using annual United States data for 1900 to 1958, Meltzer finds that the nonhuman wealth equation fits the data better than the permanent income equation in two senses. First, the coefficient of determination is higher, implying that a greater proportion of the variance in the dependent variables is related to an interest rate and nonhuman wealth than to permanent income. Second, when the data are divided into subperiods, it appears that the permanent income equation is slightly less stable than the nonhuman wealth equation from one period to another.

Laidler (1966a) comes to the opposite conclusion on the relative merits of nonhuman wealth and permanent income as independent variables. He finds that a permanent income equation performs significantly better than an equation in terms of nonhuman wealth. One difficulty in comparing Laidler's results with those of Meltzer is that they formulate the hypotheses in terms of different types of equations. Particularly notable is the fact that Laidler expresses the nonhuman wealth hypothesis in an unusual form. Instead of using an equation like Equation 20.15, Laidler's formulation of the hypothesis is:

$$\left(\frac{M}{p}\right)_t = a + b \sum (1-k) y^P_{t-i} + g \sum (y^T - c^T)_{t-i} + dr_t \tag{20.19}$$

[9]Equation 20.18 is the same as Equation 7.17 expressed in linear logarithmic form. It should be noted that the stock of money and permanent income are expressed in per capita terms in Friedman's formulation and in one of the formulations tested by Meltzer.

where y^T and c^T are transitory income and consumption[10] and all variables except the interest rate are measured in per capita terms. In simple national income accounting terms, saving may be defined as income less consumption, $s = \bar{y} - c$. With Friedman's distinctions, this may be rewritten as $s = y^P + y^T - c^P - c^T = (y^P - c^P) + (y^T - c^T)$. Friedman (1957) proposes that c^P is a proportion k of y^P; $c^P = ky^P$, so that the savings expression can be rewritten $s = (1-k)y^P + (y^T - c^T)$. It follows that the terms $\Sigma(1-k)y^P$ and $\Sigma(y^T - c^T)$ in Equation 20.19 together represent the sum of past savings and therefore equal current wealth. In fitting Equation 20.19 to the data, Laidler simplifies it by expressing it in terms of first differences:[11]

$$\left(\frac{M}{p}\right)_t - \left(\frac{M}{p}\right)_{t-1} = b(1-k)y^P + g(y^T - c^T) + d(r_t - r_{t-1}) \qquad (20.20)$$

It is then simplified further by dropping the term c^T on the ground that transitory consumption is small and uncorrelated with transitory income.

Thus, Laidler's equation representing the nonhuman wealth hypothesis finally takes the form of:

$$\left(\frac{M}{p}\right)_t - \left(\frac{M}{p}\right)_{t-1} = b(1-k)y_T^P + gy_T^T + d(r_t - r_{t-1}) \qquad (20.21)$$

He compares it with an equation representing the permanent income hypothesis, which is also expressed in the form of first differences:

$$\left(\frac{M}{p}\right)_t - \left(\frac{M}{p}\right)_{t-1} = b(y_T^P - y_{T-1}^P) + d(r_t - r_{t-1}) \qquad (20.22)$$

Using annual United States data for the period 1892–1960 (excluding war years), Laidler finds that Equation 20.22 fits the data better than Equation 20.21. The permanent income hypothesis is better supported than the nonhuman wealth hypothesis.[12]

Difficulties in Interpretation

Laidler's results on the relative merits of permanent income and nonhuman wealth as explanatory variables are not conclusive. In particular, they

[10]Transitory income is defined as the difference between current income and permanent income $y^T = \bar{y} - y^P$. Similarly, if we have a concept of permanent consumption analogous to the concept of permanent income, we can define transitory consumption as $c^T = c - c^P$, as does Friedman (1957). Thus, in Friedman's definitions there are two components—transitory and permanent—to both income and consumption.

[11]The terms y^P and $(y^T - c^T)$ are the first difference of Σy^P and $\Sigma(y^T - c^T)$, since the flow of income or consumption in any one period is the increase in the stock represented by the sum of previous periods' flows. If $t-1$ is the first instant of period T, the flow over period T represents the increase in the sum between $(t-1)$ and t. Laidler, in fact, uses a half-year lag.

[12]This result is obtained when M is defined as private sector holdings of currency and demand deposits (M_1) and also when it is defined to include time deposits as well (M_2): However, when money is defined as time deposits alone ($M_2 - M_1$), the nonhuman wealth hypothesis is better supported by the data.

are weakened by the unusual form in which he expresses the nonhuman wealth hypothesis (Eqs. 20.20 and 20.21). The advantage of this formulation is that it avoids the use of a variable measuring nonhuman wealth directly, for existing data on nonhuman wealth cannot confidently be accepted as accurate. The disadvantage, however, is that the equation is based on two sets of theories. One set is that permanent consumption is a stable proportion k of permanent income, that transitory consumption is small and not systematically related to transitory income, and that we can use as a proxy for permanent income the variable described in Chapter 7 as anticipated income. The second set is that the demand for money is a function of nonhuman wealth. If Equation 20.21 performs poorly, we do not know whether this reflects badly on the first set of theories or the second.

This problem of formulating equations so that they unambiguously represent one theory alone is a common problem throughout econometrics. It is particularly intractable when we test theories that include permanent income as a variable, and this difficulty makes it hard to test unambiguously Friedman's permanent income hypothesis of the demand for money. The reason for this difficulty is that since we cannot measure permanent income, we use anticipated income as a proxy and the construction of data on anticipated income is itself based on a theory of how anticipations are formed.

The problem arising from this procedure can be illustrated by a simple example. Suppose we wish to test a simple formulation of the permanent income hypothesis of the demand for money:

$$M_t^D = \alpha Y_t^P \tag{20.23}$$

and we use anticipated income as our measure of permanent income. We saw in Chapter 7 that Friedman's theory of how anticipations are determined can be approximated by:

$$Y_t^A = \beta\,[\bar{Y}_t + (1-\beta)\bar{Y}_{t-1} + (1-\beta)^2\bar{Y}_{t-2} + \cdots + (1-\beta)^n\bar{Y}_{t-n}] \tag{20.24}$$

so that, substituting this into Equation 20.23 for Y^P, the regression equation (omitting the error term) is:

$$M_t^D = \alpha\beta[\bar{Y}_t + (1-\beta)\bar{Y}_{t-1} + (1-\beta)^2\bar{Y}_{t-2} + \cdots + (1-\beta)^n\bar{Y}_{t-n}] \tag{20.25}$$

The first problem with using this type of regression equation to test the validity of the permanent income hypothesis (represented by Eq. 20.23) is that it comprises two hypotheses. One is that the demand for money is a function of permanent income; the other is that permanent income can be proxied by anticipated income, which is itself a weighted sum of past and present actual incomes (as in Eq. 20.24). Therefore, if Equation 20.25 does not fit the data well, we do not know whether it is because the theory of the demand for money is incorrect or because the hypothesis concerning anticipated income is wrong. The second problem is that even if the data do support Equation 20.25, we cannot unambiguously conclude that the permanent income hypothesis and the theory of anticipated income are supported by the data. This is because Equation 20.25 could equally well have been derived from a totally different theory of the demand for money.

The derivation of Equation 20.25 from a different theory of the demand for money can be seen from the following simple example. Suppose that desired money balances are a simple function of current income, as is implied by the Crude pre-Keynesian Quantity Theory:

$$M_t^D = \alpha \bar{Y}_t \tag{20.26}$$

In addition, suppose that at any point in time there is disequilibrium in the money market, so that the actual demand for money differs from the desired stock. In other words, assume that if, at the beginning of a period, actual money balances $\bar{M}_{t-1}^D$ are less than the money balances individuals desire to hold at the end of the period M_t^D, then individuals only build up their money balances by some proportion, π, of the discrepancy:

$$\bar{M}_t^D = \bar{M}_{t-1}^D + \pi(M_t^D - \bar{M}_{t-1}^D) \tag{20.27}$$

Equation 20.27, representing this partial adjustment hypothesis, can be expanded and written as:

$$\bar{M}_t^D = \pi(M_t^D + (1-\pi)M_{t-1}^D + (1-\pi)^2 M_{t-2}^D + \cdots + (1-\pi)^n M_{t-n}^D) \tag{20.28}$$

so that the actual stock of money held at any time is a function of the present and past desired stock of money. Our simple theory of the desired stock of money, M_t^D, is that it is a proportion, α, of current income as expressed in Equation 20.26. So we may substitute from this into Equation 20.28 to obtain:

$$\bar{M}_t^D = \alpha\pi(\bar{Y}_t + (1-\pi)\bar{Y}_{t-1} + (1-\pi)^2\bar{Y}_{t-2} + \cdots + (1-\pi)^n\bar{Y}_{t-n}) \tag{20.29}$$

The point to note is that Equation 20.29 is formally identical to 20.25.[13] This is the case even though the latter is derived from the theory that the demand for money is a function of *permanent* income and that the actual money stock always equals the desired money stock, whereas the former is based on the theory that the demand for money is a function of *current* income and that the actual money stock only partially adjusts to the desired stock in one period. If it is found that Equation 20.25 (or, equivalently, Eq. 20.29) is supported by the data, one cannot know whether it is a relationship with permanent or with current income that has generated the data.

In order to test the validity of the permanent income hypothesis, more sophisticated formulations than Equation 20.25 or Friedman (1959) are required. In particular, one must explicitly test for the presence or absence of lags in adjusting actual to desired balances.

[13]Although Eq. 20.25 has the desired stock of money, M^D, as the dependent variable rather than the actual money stock held, $\bar{M}^D$, as in Eq. 20.29, it is equivalent to the latter since estimation of it is based on the assumption that the actual stock equals the desired stock.

20.2 INTEREST RATES AND THE DEMAND FOR MONEY

All modern theories of the demand for money consider that interest rates on alternative assets are determinants of this demand. Whether nonhuman wealth or total wealth proxied by permanent income is the appropriate measure of the size of the portfolio, the desired allocation of the portfolio between money and other assets is treated as a function of the assets' relative rates of return. This is the proposition put forward even in the New Quantity Theory of Friedman (1956a) and certainly in Keynesian theories such as those of Baumol (1952) and Tobin (1956). Moreover, it is a proposition generally supported by empirical studies where demand functions for money that include at least one interest rate as an independent variable are usually found to fit the data well.

Nevertheless, there has been controversy over whether or not empirical data do support the idea that the demand for money is a function of an interest rate. This argument stems from the findings of Friedman (1959). His study leads him to an agnostic but generally negative view on whether interest rates do affect velocity (or the demand for money). He reports an inability to "find any close connection between changes in velocity from cycle to cycle and any of a number of interest rates" and finds that, within cycles, the residual changes in velocity that remain unexplained by the permanent income hypothesis are "much too small to reflect any very sensitive adjustment of cash balances to interest rates." But Friedman acknowledges that his findings are tentative and argues for further research on the empirical significance of interest rates. The further research that has been conducted by, for example, Meltzer (1963) and Laidler (1966b) suggests that interest rates do affect the demand for money even when it is postulated that permanent income is also an explanatory variable. That is, whereas the implication of Friedman's finding that:

$$M^D = f(Y^P) \tag{20.30}$$

appears to be a valid theory of the demand for money, other writers find that equations such as:

$$M^D = f(r, Y^P) \tag{20.31}$$

fit the data better.[14]

Since all empirical research other than that of Friedman (1959), Friedman and Schwartz (1963b), and related studies finds that the demand for money or velocity in the United States is systematically related to interest rates even when permanent income is employed as an explanatory variable, it is interesting to consider why Friedman is led to doubt the validity of this relationship.

[14]Some, such as Meltzer (1963), find that an equation such as $M^D = f(r, W_N)$ gives a still better fit, however.

One possible explanation is that the definition of money employed by Friedman in the dependent variable includes currency, demand deposits, *and* time deposits. It is defined as M_2, and the results may be contrasted with those found where money is defined as M_1 (currency and demand deposits alone). Since time deposits bear interest at a rate that is related to the market rate on bonds, we would expect on theoretical grounds that a rise in the bond rate will lead to a desire to switch wealth out of M_1 balances into time deposits but a lesser movement out of time deposits and therefore out of M_2, which includes them. Thus, we may expect that M_1 will fluctuate more sensitively than M_2 in response to changes in the bond rate. Johnson (1962) suggests that Friedman's use of M_2 is responsible for his finding that interest rates have little effect. And Christ (1963) and Meltzer (1963) find empirical support for the idea that the demand for M_1 shows greater interest sensitivity than the demand for Friedman's M_2.

The resolution of this issue, however, requires a decision on whether the theory of the demand for money should be concerned with money defined to include time deposits or money defined to exclude them. If we should be concerned with M_2 rather than M_1, then Friedman's use of this variable in empirical work is not objectionable, and if this is the source of his findings on interest sensitivity, then those findings are highly relevant.[15]

However, his definition of money is not, in fact, the explanation for Friedman's unusual findings on the role of interest rates. For writers such as Meltzer (1963), Brunner and Meltzer (1963), and Laidler (1966a, 1966b) find that an interest rate is significant even when money is defined as M_2. Instead, the explanation for Friedman's results is that he uses an erroneous technique for estimation. This is suggested by Meltzer (1963) and Teigen (1964), and by Laidler (1966b), who corrects Friedman's technique and finds that an interest rate is a significant determinant of the demand for money.

As noted in Section 20.1, Friedman estimates an equation like 20.17 by using secular data—the average over cycles of annual data. Having estimated the coefficients a and b, Friedman then computes the annual levels of velocity implied by the equation. Within each cycle, the variation of velocity that is not accounted for by the equation—the divergence between actual velocity and that computed from the equation— is then correlated with interest rates and no significant relationship is found. Laidler (1966b) argues that this finding

[15]There are two approaches to the question of the appropriate definition of money. One is to consider from the point of view of pure theory what the distinguishing features of money are as compared with other financial assets. If, for example, it is thought that the crucial feature of money is that it bears no financial interest rate, then time deposits should be excluded from the definition. The second is to treat the appropriate definition as an empirical matter. If it is found empirically that M_2 is more stably related to other economic variables than are M_1 and time deposits, it may be argued according to some criteria that M_2 is the most appropriate definition of money balances. The question of the appropriate definition of money is at least as old as the nineteenth-century debate between the banking and currency schools, surveyed by Viner (1937). Surveys of recent discussions of the issue are provided by Friedman and Schwartz (1969) and Laidler (1969).

arises because Friedman calculates the secular relationship between velocity and permanent income incorrectly. Instead of relating velocity to permanent income alone, as does Equation 20.17, velocity should be related to both permanent income and an interest rate even when using secular data. Thus, according to Laidler, Friedman is examining the relationship between interest rates and the within-cycle residuals from an incorrect secular relationship.

Laidler supports this argument by noting that secular (cycle-average) data give support to a demand function for money of the form:

$$\log\left(\frac{M}{p}\right) = a + b\log\left(\frac{Y^P}{p}\right) + c\log r \tag{20.32}$$

and the estimated value of the coefficients is different when the equation is:

$$\log\left(\frac{M}{p}\right) = a + b\log\frac{Y^P}{p} \tag{20.33}$$

The latter is similar to the demand function implied by Friedman's velocity equation, so that Laidler's result implies that Friedman's estimates of a and b are based on an incorrect specification. In other words, Laidler finds that both permanent income and an interest rate influence the demand for money when using secular data and that Friedman's equation without an interest rate explicitly includes leads to the effect of the interest rate's being picked up by the coefficient on permanent income in Equation 20.33. Laidler then applies Equation 20.32 with the coefficients estimated from secular data to compute annual, within-cycle levels of the demand for money, and it is found that the computed demand for money is much closer to the actual demand for money than when a similar exercise is conducted using Equation 20.33. It follows that the reason why Friedman is unable to find a significant role for an interest rate in annual data is that the equation which he estimates from secular data is incorrectly specified to exclude interest rates.

Liquidity Trap

Apart from the question of whether the demand for money is a function of an interest rate—which appears to be settled in favor of an affirmative answer—there are several questions concerning the exact nature of this relationship that empirical studies have attempted to answer. One of the most important from the point of view of the Neoclassical/Keynesian synthesis is whether the demand for money does exhibit a liquidity trap. The existence of a liquidity trap implies that when the interest rate is at some sufficiently low level, the interest elasticity of the demand for money approaches infinity. A corollary of this—that interest elasticity is higher at low interest rates than at high rates—has been investigated by Bronfenbrenner and Mayer (1960) and Laidler (1966b). The results obtained are not conclusive but do suggest that a liquidity trap has not existed in the United States in this century. Pifer (1969) and Eisner (1971), however, test the hypothesis more directly.

Pifer estimates an equation that, in logarithmic form, can be written as:

$$\ln M_t = \ln a + b \ln (r_t - r^{\min}) + c \ln W_{N_t} + d \ln \bar{Y}_t + e \ln M_{t-1} \qquad (20.34)$$

where W_N represents nonhuman wealth and $r^{\min}$ is the hypothetical interest rate at which the demand for money approaches infinity. That is, assuming b is negative, M_t approaches infinity as r_t approaches $r^{\min}$.[16] The method by which the validity of Equation 20.34 is judged involves calculating the statistical significance of the estimates of the parameters[17] with various values of $r^{\min}$. Pifer's results cast doubt on the hypothesis that $r^{\min}$ is significantly different from zero and suggest, therefore, that there is no liquidity trap at a positive rate of interest. Eisner, however, argues that Pifer follows an incorrect statistical test, and using other criteria, he finds that $r^{\min}$ is approximately 2 percent. In other words, when the interest rate r_t approaches a level of approximately 2 percent, the demand for money approaches infinity.[18]

Eisner's results, therefore, suggest that the hypothesis of a liquidity trap at a positive interest rate is supported by the data. However, as with all estimates of the parameters of the demand function for money, the validity of the estimated values depends upon the validity of the specification of the function. The estimate of a liquidity trap at 2 percent in Equation 20.34 can be accepted only if the demand for money is a logarithmic function with nonhuman wealth and current income as independent variables. Moreover, the reliability of the estimate depends on the validity of the estimation technique. In this connection the points discussed in the following section are especially relevant.

20.3 EMPIRICAL KNOWLEDGE OF THE DEMAND FUNCTION FOR MONEY

The studies surveyed in Sections 20.1 and 20.2 suggest that the demand for money in the United States is a stable function of the returns on alternative

[16]This can be seen by rewriting Eq. 20.34 in nonlogarithmic form: $M_t = a(r_t - r^{\min})^b W_{Nt}^c Y_t^d M_{t-1}^e$. Or, assuming b is negative, this can be written as $M_t = [a/(r_t - r^{\min})^{-b}] W_{Nt}^c Y_t^d M_{t-1}^e$. As r_t approaches $r^{\min}$, the denominator of the first term approaches zero; therefore the value of the solution approaches infinity. It should be noted that the idea of the liquidity trap embodied in Eq. 20.34 is different from that tested by Laidler (1966b). Here, the proposition to be tested is that the *demand for money* approaches infinity when the rate of interest approaches $r^{\min}$. In Laidler's work, the proposition tested is that the *interest elasticity* of the demand for money approaches infinity. For a discussion of the difference between these propositions, see Eisner (1963).

[17]The maximum likelihood estimation method is used.

[18]The interest rate used for these estimates is the yield on corporate bonds with 20 years to maturity. The data with which the test is conducted do not, of course, include any observation of money holdings near to infinity. But the shape of the curve estimated from real data on money and interest rates suggests that if the interest rate were to approach 2 percent, demand for money would approach infinity.

assets and that this function is stable over long periods even when the interest rate on one asset is used to represent the structure of returns.[19] They do not suggest conclusively whether nonhuman wealth or permanent income (as a proxy for total wealth) is the scale variable most stably related to the demand for money. On this question, different studies produce different conclusions, and these studies cannot be directly compared, for each varies according to the data used, the time period covered, the method of estimation, or the precise formulation of the theories.

Moreover, on general grounds, those theories in terms of nonhuman wealth and those in terms of permanent income are both difficult to test. Measures of nonhuman wealth are unreliable on theoretical grounds since it is, in principle, unclear which financial assets are or are not part of the private sector's net wealth; the choice depends on the resolution of the dispute surveyed in Chapter 3 concerning the relevance of the distinction between inside and outside money (and other assets). But even those items which are unambiguously part of private sector wealth are in some cases extremely difficult to measure. The stock of physical capital (or its net increase) is notoriously difficult to measure and data on nonhuman wealth used in empirical studies, such as that of Goldsmith (1962), may be questioned on these grounds at least. In the case of permanent income equations, other general problems arise. Since data on permanent income do not exist, anticipated income, measured as a function of present and past incomes with the weights declining geometrically, is used as a proxy. (See Chapter 7.) This, as we saw in Section 20.1, creates the problem that empirical tests of the permanent income theory are, in fact, tests of at least two theories. One theory is that the demand for money is a function of permanent income, the other is that permanent income is closely related to the data on anticipated income. Empirical tests of equations based on these two sets of theories cannot yield conclusions on the permanent income theory of the demand for money unless we know that permanent income *is* related to the anticipated income data. Doubts in this connection are reinforced by the finding of Tobin and Swan (1969) that the weights usually employed in constructing the anticipated income data give less accurate predictions than other weights.[20]

We must remain undecided, therefore, on the question of whether the demand for money is a stable function of nonhuman wealth or permanent income.

[19]There does, however, remain the question of which interest rate is the most representative. Different empirical studies use different interest rates in their estimates. One explicit attempt to choose the most appropriate interest rate is that of Laidler (1966b).

[20]One of their results suggests that the weight of present income in anticipated income equals unity. In other words, $Y_T^A = \bar{Y}_T$. This would imply that a relationship between the demand for money and a correct measure of anticipated income is indistinguishable from a relationship with current income. However, Feige (1967), in a study of the demand for money, estimates that the weight of current income in anticipated income is significantly different from unity.

In addition, there are technical grounds for caution in judging all the results surveyed in Sections 20.1 and 20.2. The most important of these reasons is that the studies surveyed use methods, such as ordinary least squares regression, that take no account of the fact that the demand function for money is one structural equation within a system of several simultaneous equations. This gives rise to several problems. One is the problem of *identification.* Unless we specify the supply function for money and other equations of the system, we cannot know whether the demand function is identifiable. Only if the other equations have certain properties can we know whether the estimated parameters of the demand function result from data generated by the intersection of a stable true demand function and a shifting supply function, or whether the demand function is itself shifting. Only if the former is known to be so can we be sure that an empirical relationship between the money stock and a set of independent variables is an empirical demand function. Another is the problem of *simultaneous equation bias.* To solve the identification problem, it is sufficient to specify the other structural equations, to ensure that the structural equations are identified, and to examine the resulting properties of the model. But even if the model is such that the demand function is properly identified as such, a true estimate of the parameters of this function will not be obtained with a technique such as ordinary least squares regression. The estimates will be biased unless a technique such as two-stage least squares is used to estimate the demand and supply functions for money simultaneously.

Problems such as these[21] need not lead us to jettison the results obtained by the single-equation studies of the previous two sections. For now a considerable body of work exists that is concerned with estimating the demand function for money within models where the supply function and, sometimes, other structural equations are estimated simultaneously. These include Brunner and Meltzer (1964) and Teigen (1964), and estimations of the demand function in large econometric models, such as the estimates reported by De Leeuw (1965). The results of none of the simultaneous equation studies lead one to conclude that single-equation estimates of the demand for money are seriously erroneous despite the theoretical differences in the estimation methods.

20.4 ESTIMATES OF REDUCED FORMS

In the 1960s and 1970s much controversy between monetary economists centered on the estimation and interpretation of reduced forms such as Equation 20.7. The debate was begun by Friedman and Meiselman (1963), who estimated the reduced forms of models to be much simpler than the model set out at the beginning of this chapter. They then interpreted their

[21]For further study, see, for example, Johnston (1972).

estimates as having implications for the relative virtues of Keynesian and modern Quantity Theory models and for the importance of money in the economy.

Friedman and Meiselman derived one reduced form from a simple Keynesian model of the goods market alone. This model can be represented by an equilibrium condition:

$$\bar{Y} = C + I + G + (X - Z) \tag{20.35}$$

Or, subtracting total taxes, T, from both sides, this can be written in terms of disposable income:

$$\bar{Y} - T = C + I + (G - T) + (X - Z) \tag{20.36}$$

where X represents exports and Z imports, all variables are in nominal terms, and all those on the right-hand side are *ex ante* values. Consumption is a linear function of disposable national income:

$$C = a + b(\bar{Y} - T) \tag{20.37}$$

and all other variables on the right-hand side of Equation 20.36 are assumed to be exogenous and can be named autonomous expenditure, A;

$$I + (G - I) + (X - Z) \equiv A \tag{20.38}$$

One reduced form of this model is in terms of the endogenous variable disposable income:

$$(\bar{Y} - T) = \frac{a}{1-b} + \frac{1}{1-b} A \tag{20.39}$$

Another is in terms of the endogenous variable consumption:[22]

$$C = \frac{a}{1-b} + \left(\frac{1}{1-b} - 1\right) A = e + fA \tag{20.40}$$

Friedman and Meiselman choose to work with an equation like Equation 20.40 as the reduced form of the simple goods market model. They estimate the values of e and f from United States data for the period 1897–1958 and consider the empirical validity of the equation and the stability of e and f.

They also estimate an equation that can be considered as a reduced form of a Crude Quantity Theory model. Such a model may consist of a demand function for money:

$$M^D = d + k(\bar{Y} - T) \tag{20.41}$$

[22]Equation 20.39 is obtained by substituting Equation 20.37 into Equation 20.36 and solving for $(\bar{Y} - T)$. Equation 20.40 can be obtained either by writing Equation 20.37 with $(\bar{Y} - T)$ on the left-hand side, substituting this for $(\bar{Y} - T)$ in Equation 20.36, and solving for C; or by noting that $\bar{Y} - T = C + A$ so that $C = (\bar{Y} - T) - A$ and, on the basis of this, subtracting A from both sides of Equation 20.39.

plus the assumption that the money supply is exogenous and the equilibrium condition that the supply of money equals the demand:

$$M^S = M^D \tag{20.42}$$

Then the appropriate reduced form expressing disposable income as a function of the exogenous variable is:

$$(\bar{Y} - T) = -\frac{d}{k} + \frac{1}{k} M \tag{20.43}$$

In order to estimate an equation where the dependent variable is comparable to that of Equation 20.40's crude Keynesian reduced form, Friedman and Meiselman argue that Equation 20.43 should not be the only reduced form of the Crude Quantity Theory to be estimated, and, in addition, they estimate:[23]

$$C = g + hM^S \tag{20.44}$$

The results obtained by Friedman and Meiselman are remarkable. Using annual data for the period 1897–1958 as a whole, the correlation coefficient between money and consumption (Eq. 20.44) is 0.985, whereas that between autonomous expenditure and consumption (Eq. 20.40) is only 0.756. Writing the equations in terms of annual first differences so that the dependent variable is $\Delta C = (C_T - C_{T-1})$, the results are even more striking. The correlation coefficient between ΔC and ΔA is only 0.095. Moreover, when the data for any subperiod are examined, the correlation coefficient relating to M^S is always higher than that relating to A (with the one exception of the great depression years of 1929–1939). Similar results—much higher correlation coefficients on equations with M^S as the independent variable than on equations with A—were obtained with several variants of the basic equations.

Friedman and Meiselman interpret the correlation coefficient on an equation as indicating the empirical stability of the relationship represented by that equation. A low correlation coefficient on Equation 20.39, for example, is taken to indicate that the value of the parameters e and f, $(a/(1-b)$ and $1/(1-b)-1)$ is relatively unstable over time. In other words, b, the marginal propensity to consume, and $1/(1-b)$, the simple Keynesian multiplier, are

[23]The theoretical basis of Eq. 20.44 as a version of the Quantity Theory raises some problems. Friedman and Meiselman can derive Eq. 20.43 from a Crude Quantity Theory model, and Eq. 20.44 can be considered to derive from the same model. It can, for example, be given a rationale by arguing that, as well as there being a systematic relationship between $(\bar{Y} - T)$ and M^S (the direction of causation running from M^S) as in Eq. 20.43, consumption is a function of disposable income: $C = a + b(\bar{Y} - T)$ or, in other words, $(\bar{Y} - T) = (C - a)1/b$. Substituting this into Eq. 20.43 would yield Eq. 20.44 where $g = a - db/k$ and $h = b/k$. This, however, would cause difficulties in comparing the estimates of Eq. 20.44 with those of Eq. 20.40, for the stability of the parameters of each depend on the stability of b. An alternative would be to derive Eq. 20.44 from the hypothesis that the demand for money is a function of planned consumption (instead of disposable income) together with the money market equilibrium condition $M^S = M^D$. But the hypothesis $M^D = f(C)$ would be an unusual form for the Crude Quantity Theory.

unstable (as well, possibly, as the intercept of the consumption function). From a comparison of the low correlation coefficients on autonomous expenditure and the high ones on the money supply equations, Friedman and Meiselman draw two distinct but related conclusions. The first is that the relative instability of the multiplier and stability of the relationship between consumption and the money supply mean that "control over the stock of money is a far more useful tool for affecting the level of aggregate money demand than control of autonomous expenditures." Bearing in mind that A includes $(G - T)$, we find that this implies that government deficits do not have a reliable effect on national expenditure, output, and income. The second conclusion is that "the quantity theory approach to income change is likely to be more fruitful than the income-expenditure theory [Keynesian] approach; that the first corresponds to empirical relations that are far more stable over the course of business cycles than the second" (Friedman and Meiselman, 1963). In other words, the Keynesian model consists of behavior relations that are empirically less stable than those of the Crude Quantity Theory.

A Test of Keynes?

These conclusions have, of course, proved to be highly contentious and have been challenged in several ways. One criticism is that an equation like Equation 20.40 is not a reduced form of the Keynesian model even if we accept that G, T, X, and Z are truly exogenous variables. Therefore, its empirical performance does not reflect on the validity of the Keynesian model. This is so because Equation 20.40 is drawn from a model of the goods market alone, whereas the Keynesian model includes a theory of the money market and the links between it and the goods market. In terms of equations, a simple linear Keynesian model would include a goods market equilibrium condition:

$$\bar{Y} = C + I + G + (X - Z) \tag{20.45}$$

a theory of endogenous consumption:

$$C = a + b(\bar{Y} - T) \tag{20.46}$$

a theory of investment:

$$I = d - er \tag{20.47}$$

a demand function for money:

$$M^D = k\bar{Y} + g - hr. \tag{20.48}$$

and a money market equilibrium condition:

$$M^S = M^D \tag{20.49}$$

where the money supply is assumed exogenous. Solving these five equations for any one of the five endogenous variables, we can obtain a reduced form with the exogenous variables as arguments. Solving for consumption, for example, the reduced form would be:

$$C = f[(G - T), (X - Z), M^S] \tag{20.50}$$

In other words, in this Keynesian model the money supply would affect consumption as well as some of the variables that Friedman and Meiselman include in their definition of autonomous expenditures. The money supply affects consumption because, as a result of liquidity preference, it affects the interest rate which, in turn, affects investment, income, and therefore consumption. Only if the money supply did not affect the interest rate, if, for example, a liquidity trap existed (or if investment were completely interest-inelastic), would it be appropriate to omit it from the reduced form of the Keynesian model. Friedman and Meiselman's reduced form, therefore, can be thought of as a version of a Keynesian model with a liquidity trap.[24]

The point can be illustrated by the *IS/LM* curves of Figures 20.2 and 20.3. If the curves have the shapes as drawn in Figure 20.2, then real income (and nominal income and consumption) can be increased either by a rightward shift in the *IS* curve from IS_1 to IS_2 or by a rightward shift in the *LM* curve from LM_1 to LM_2. The former could result, for example, from an increase in one item of autonomous expenditure such as government expenditure; the latter could result from an increase in the money supply. If, however, the curves have the shapes drawn in Figure 20.3 indicating that there is a liquidity trap, an increase in the money supply that shifts the *LM* curve from LM_1 to LM_2 will have no effect on the level of income, but a shift in the *IS* curve from IS_1 to IS_2 will.

Thus Friedman and Meiselman's use of a reduced form such as Equation 20.40 does not allow them to draw conclusions about the validity of the Keynesian model. At best, it yields conclusions about a special case of the

[24]We shall see in Chap. 21 that Friedman has argued that the liquidity trap is a central feature of the Keynesian model.

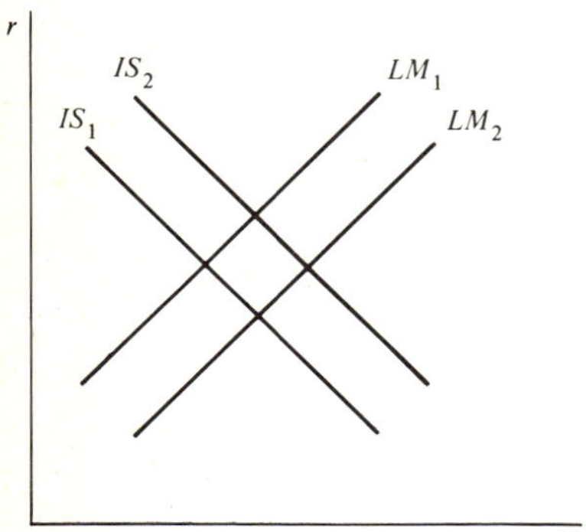

Figure 20-2

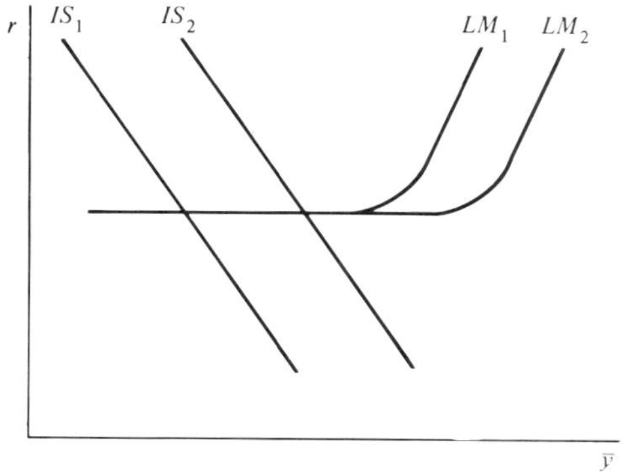

Figure 20-3

model—that where a liquidity trap exists. In order to overcome this problem, Friedman and Meiselman also estimate an equation of the form:

$$C = e + gA + hM^S \tag{20.51}$$

which includes both autonomous expenditures and the money supply as exogenous variables. This is closer to (but, primarily because of the definition of the variables, not the same as) the reduced form appropriate to the general Keynesian model. They examine the partial correlation coefficients between consumption and A, and consumption and M^S, respectively, and again conclude that the relationship between the money supply and the endogenous variable (with A held constant) is more stable than that relating to autonomous expenditure (with M^S held constant). This result, like the previous ones, casts doubt on the validity of the Keynesian model.

Exogenous or Endogenous

The next criticism of Friedman and Meiselman's results can also be interpreted as saying that they misrepresent the Keynesian model. In a more general view, this criticism states that Friedman and Meiselman define their variables incorrectly and that therefore the results obtained and the implied insignificance of fiscal policy are incorrect (whether or not their tests are truly tests of the Keynesian and Quantity Theory models). This criticism has been made by Ando and Modigliani (1965), De Prano and Mayer (1965), and Hester (1964). The most important aspect of it is the argument that the variables included in autonomous expenditures, A, are not all truly autonomous; some are themselves functions of national income or consumption. The variable A is not, therefore, a pure exogenous variable but, instead, includes some endogenous components.

If this argument is correct, it implies that Equation 20.40 (or Eq. 20.51) is not a true reduced form equation of the Keynesian (or any other) model, since in a reduced form equation an endogenous variable such as C is expressed as a function only of the exogenous variables of the model. The problem concerns not only the appropriateness of a name—the description of Equation 20.40 as a reduced form; the difficulty is that the estimates of such an equation are invalid estimates of the effect of autonomous expenditures on consumption. Recall that by Friedman and Meiselman's definition of A (Eq. 20.38), the reduced forms of disposable income and consumption (Eqs. 20.39 and 20.40) can be written as:

$$(\bar{Y} - T) = \frac{a}{1-b} + \frac{1}{1-b}[I + (G - T) + (X - Z)] \tag{20.52}$$

and

$$C = \frac{a}{1-b} + \left(\frac{1}{1-b} - 1\right)[I + (G - T) + (X - Z)] \tag{20.53}$$

respectively. Assume, for example, that Z, planned imports, are a function of disposable income so that as disposable income rises, planned imports rise. In other words:

$$Z = z(\bar{Y} - T) \tag{20.54}$$

where z $(0 < z < 1)$ is the marginal and average propensity to import. Now suppose that the goods market is in equilibrium and this equilibrium is then disturbed by an exogenous rise in investment, I. One effect of this will be to raise equilibrium disposable income and consumption; if none of the other variables in A changes, the change in equilibrium disposable income will be $\Delta(\bar{Y} - T) = (1[1-b])\Delta I$ and the change in consumption will be $\Delta C = [(1/[1-b]) - 1]\Delta I$. But according to Equation 20.54, one of the other variables in A will change; the increase in disposable income will itself cause a rise in imports Z and will therefore cause a fall in the balance of payments component $(X - Z)$ of A. Thus, one of the components of A may be negatively correlated with consumption. This will cause Friedman and Meiselman's definition of autonomous expenditure, $A = I + (G - T) + (X - Z)$, to tend to have a lower correlation with consumption than a truly exogenous definition of autonomous expenditure. This criticism is reinforced by the argument that not only is Z in fact endogenous, but so are other components of A. For example, total tax receipts T are endogenous, so that if we assume that investment, government expenditure, and exports are truly exogenous, the true definition of autonomous expenditure is $A' = I + G + X$, and we should expect this to be more highly correlated with C than is A.[25]

[25]Strictly speaking, as noted by Ando and Modigliani (1965), the explanation of the effect of the endogeneity of Z and T is not correct. In terms of the deterministic model of Eqs. 20.36 to 20.40, and 20.54 it is instructive, but econometric models are not deterministic.

The equations of an econometric model must include an error term, as do the equations of the model at the beginning of this chapter. The effect of the endogeneity of Z, for example, is then to be explained by the fact that Z, and therefore A, is correlated with the error term in the reduced form Eq. 20.40. Since the correlation between Z and the error term in Eq. 20.40 is negative if the marginal propensity to import is positive, the correlation coefficient between A and C will be biased downward in comparison with the true correlation between A' and C.

Ando and Modigliani, DePrano and Mayer, and Hester find that if the definition of autonomous expenditure is changed so that it includes only exogenous variables, the correlation between autonomous expenditure and consumption (and other measures of the goodness of fit of the reduced form) is significantly increased. Indeed, when this and other amendments[26] are made, these writers find that a reduced form relating consumption to autonomous expenditure performs approximately as well as one relating consumption to the money supply (although it should be noted that each critic uses one or several "truly exogenous" definitions of autonomous expenditure different from those used by the others).

Related to the criticism that Friedman and Meiselman's "autonomous expenditure" is not really exogenous and, because of its negative endogenous components, biases their results downward, is the argument that the money supply is not truly exogenous, and its endogeneity biases *upward* the results on the reduced form relating consumption to money supply. Ando and Modigliani (1965), for example, consider that an increase in national income and consumption may cause an increase in the money supply. It could, for example, cause an increase in interest rates, which causes banks to raise the proportion of their long-term loans, thereby reducing their liquidity ratio or cash ratio. If that were the case, then any correlation between M^S and C would be greater than that which is due solely to a causal effect running from money supply to consumption. Even if changes in money supply were to have no effect on consumption, we would observe a positive correlation between the two if a rise in national income were to cause an increase in both consumption and money supply. Ando and Modigliani, however, do not support this criticism with an adequate empirical test, for they, too, fail to use a money supply variable that can confidently be considered as exogenous.

Predictive Power

There is further evidence that, contrary to the conclusions of Friedman and Meiselman, empirical tests do not give strong grounds for preferring a reduced form with money supply over one with autonomous expenditures. This evidence comes from Poole and Kornblith (1973). They provide new evidence on the relative merits of reduced forms in terms of autonomous expenditure and those in terms of money supply. The evidence is different from that previously considered in that, first, it draws on data more recent than those used by Friedman and Meiselman and those critics we have

[26] In particular, the critics of Friedman and Meiselman argue that the years in which the United States was engaged in a major world war were extraordinary years when, on a priori and empirical grounds, one would expect to find unusual behavior relations—a shift in the consumption function, for example. Therefore, they contend that the relevant data for testing the reduced forms consist of time series that exclude those years and conduct tests using such data (as well as, in some tests, using inclusive data).

discussed.[27] Second, a method of testing is used that is different from the methods previously used. In particular, this method differs from the Friedman and Meiselman technique of fitting equations to time series and comparing the correlation coefficients.

Poole and Kornblith use data drawn from the 1929–1958 period to estimate[28] the parameters of a number of alternative reduced forms in terms of either autonomous expenditures or money supply. A total of 13 reduced forms is estimated in order to compare the relative performance of different definitions of autonomous expenditure and money supply. With these estimates of the parameters, observed actual values of the independent variables in the years 1959–1970 are inserted and the equations' predictions of the values of the dependent variable (consumption) in the years 1959–1970 are thereby calculated. These predictions are then evaluated against actual data for consumption in 1958–1970 and the predictive performance of the various reduced forms is compared.[29]

The results obtained are quite different from those of Friedman and Meiselman. Several of the definitions of autonomous expenditure give better predictions of C than when the money supply is used as the only independent variable in the reduced form. In particular, the definitions used by Hester (1964) that exclude items which may be thought to be endogenous give better predictions than money supply. Moreover, multiple regression equations of the same form as our Equation 22.51 but with a "more exogenous" measure of A give better predictions than money supply alone. The indication thus is that, on most definitions of autonomous expenditure, the Keynesian hypothesis that both autonomous expenditure and money supply systematically influence income and consumption may be more reliable than a simple Quantity Theory hypothesis.

It should be noted, however, that Poole and Kornblith found that reduced forms including *either* money supply *or* autonomous expenditures alone *or* both tended to systematically underpredict consumption. It was found that there was serious bias in the predictions of the equations. This suggests that the reduced forms used may be misspecified and drawn from hypotheses about behavior relations that are too simple to be accurate. Although there

[27]The data are more recent in that they come from time series ending in 1970, whereas the other writers use time series ending in 1958. It is also more recent in that the data for the period to 1958 were partially revised and therefore different at the time that Poole and Kornblith wrote from what they were when used by the other writers.

[28]They use the period of 1929–1958 rather than 1897–1958 because, although Friedman and Meiselman used the latter period, Ando and Modigliani, De Prano and Mayer, and Hester draw many of their most significant results from the former period. Poole and Kornblith were concerned to evaluate the results not only of Friedman and Meiselman but also of their critics.

[29]The predictions are evaluated against actual values by examining the mean square error of prediction and its components.

may be some advantages in working with reduced forms—in particular, the simplicity of the work involved in estimating them and reestimating them against new data—the alternative method of testing structural equations and large models consisting of many simultaneous structural equations is advantageous in that it enables tests of the underlying behavioral hypotheses to be made. Several such models do exist and, in all cases, predict that exogenous changes in both autonomous expenditures (such as some components of government expenditure) and money supply will cause systematic changes in national income, consumption, and other endogenous variables. A comparative assessment by Christ (1975) of the predictive ability of nine such big econometric models concludes that they are all able to predict gross national product for one quarter in the future with a root mean square error of 1 percent or less. However, the reliability of their predictions and the underlying structural equations is controversial.

20.5 FURTHER EXPERIMENTS WITH REDUCED FORM EQUATIONS

The general conclusions reached by Friedman and Meiselman have been supported by work conducted at the Federal Reserve Bank of St. Louis. From that source Andersen and Jordan (1968) report the comparative results of estimating reduced forms with variables measuring monetary and fiscal policy respectively as the independent variables.

The basic similarity between the work of Andersen and Jordan and that of Friedman and Meiselman arises from the fact that the former's fiscal policy variables are related to one component of the latter's autonomous expenditure, and monetary policy variables are related to the money supply. Therefore, Andersen and Jordan's finding that monetary policy has a more systematic influence on the economy than fiscal policy is related to Friedman and Meiselman's findings concerning the money supply and autonomous expenditure. Their work is, however, different from that of Friedman and Meiselman. The type of reduced form equation used is of the following form:

$$\Delta \bar{Y} = a - b\Delta L + c\Delta F \qquad (20.55)$$

where all variables are in nominal terms and are measured as quarterly values. First differences are used so that $\Delta \bar{Y}$, for example, measures the change in nominal gross national product from one quarter to the next.[30] Fiscal policy is represented by F and three separate measures of F were used. One was a measure of high-employment government expenditure, E; another was a measure of high-employment government receipts, R; a third was a mea-

[30]Another measure of changes, known as central differences, is also used.

sure of the high-employment[31] government deficit or surplus, $E-R$. Monetary policy is represented by L and two separate measures were used. One was the money stock, M^S; the other was the stock of high-powered money, H, held by the banking system or directly by the private sector. Thus, the Andersen and Jordan study differs from that of Friedman and Meiselman in that it is directly concerned with the effects of *policy* variables upon gross national product and exclusively concerned with the effects of *changes* in policy variables; also, the variables employed as measures of policy include some that can be more confidently identified as exogenous than those employed by Friedman and Meiselman.

A further difference is that Andersen and Jordan estimate a more sophisticated lag structure. Whereas in some of their tests Friedman and Meiselman use a simple lag so that consumption is found to be related to the level of the money supply in a previous period, Andersen and Jordan use a model where GNP is related to the independent variables' values in several previous periods. Their technique for estimating the lag in the effect of a change in policy is that developed by Almon (1965). It involves assuming a particular general form for the lag structure and a particular length of time for the effects of policy to work themselves out, and then testing the validity of these assumptions. The general form of the lag structure is a polynomial (Andersen and Jordan use a fourth-degree polynomial), and Andersen and Jordan estimate that the full effects of policy change are all felt within four quarters.

Despite the differences in their models, the results obtained by Andersen and Jordan reinforce the conclusion that Friedman and Meiselman draw from their study: that monetary policy is more effective than fiscal policy. They examine three different concepts of "effectiveness." The first concerns the size of the effect of a policy change. Examination of the regression coefficients[32] b and c in equations like Equation 20.55 leads to the conclusion that a \$1 change in money supply or high-powered money leads over several quarters to a much greater change in gross national product than does a \$1 change in taxes or government expenditure. The second concerns the "reliability" or "stability" of the relationship between the policy variables and gross national product. The statistic used to measure this quality is the t-ratio

[31]The concept of high-employment variables measures the value of what, for example, the government deficit would be in a particular quarter if the economy were at approximately full employment in that quarter. It is therefore more of an exogenous variable than the actual level of deficit in that quarter. For, with given tax rates, for example, actual tax receipts in any quarter depend on the level of gross national product, whereas the level of tax receipts that would be obtained if income were near to full employment is not dependent on what the actual level of income is (although this independence can be questioned, as will be seen, on the ground that the government adjusts tax rates in response to changes in income).

[32]Or, to be more precise, examination of the beta coefficients that are derived from the regression coefficients. If $\hat{b}$ is the regression coefficient estimate of b, σ_L is the standard deviation of the L variable and σ_Y the standard deviation of GNP, the beta coefficient measuring the response of GNP to changes in L is $\beta_{YL} = \hat{b}(\sigma_L/\sigma_Y)$.

that measures the statistical significance of the regression coefficient estimates of b and c. The t-ratios from their regressions indicate that the estimates of b are significantly different from zero, whereas the estimates of c are not. Finally, Andersen and Jordan estimate the speed with which the effects of a change in policy are felt. They find that, allowing four quarters for the effect to be felt, the proportion of the full effect of a change in money supply felt within two quarters is much greater than the proportion of the full effect of a change in government expenditure.

Endogeneity and Government Reaction Function

The results obtained by Andersen and Jordan, like those of Friedman and Meiselman, are striking in their apparent support of the proposition that monetary policy is much more significant than fiscal policy. However, they are open to several criticisms, as has been made clear by Davis (1969) and De Leeuw and Kalchbrenner (1969). One criticism is similar to that already considered in the context of the Friedman and Meiselman study. It is that when the money supply is used as the measure of monetary policy, this variable is not truly exogenous. Changes in money supply may themselves be induced by changes in gross national product, so that the relationship between the two does not necessarily reflect only the effect of money supply on expenditure and output. Andersen and Jordan's finding that changes in the money supply occur before the complete change in GNP to which they are related does not overcome this objection. For, a simple Keynesian model with an induced money supply and a lagged multiplier would suggest that if an increase in investment leads to an increase in the demand for bank loans and thereby to an increase in money supply, the full effects of the change in investment on total expenditure will not be felt for several quarters. The change in money supply and the change in GNP in such a model both result from the change in desired investment, but the change in GNP follows the change in money supply, as observed by Andersen and Jordan. This objection to their conclusion is partially overcome when they use high-powered money rather than the money supply as a measure of monetary policy. High-powered money may be considered to be more nearly exogenous than the money supply, but there are grounds for thinking that even the stock of high-powered money is at least partially endogenously determined.

Regarding the question of endogeneity, Ando and Modigliani (1976) and Gordon (1976a) explore the possibility of bias in Andersen and Jordan's results. They are concerned with whether bias exists because the reduced forms are incorrectly specified. In principle, such misspecification can result if the policy variables L and F are endogenously determined, as they will be, in fact, if the government systematically alters the policy variables in an attempt to stabilize the economy. In terms of levels rather than changes, the estimated Andersen-Jordan equation (Eq. 20.55) is:

$$Y = a_0 + b_0L + c_0F \tag{20.56}$$

For this reduced form to be accurately specified, no exogenous variables other than L and F can have a systematic effect on Y. In fact, there will be some other relevant exogenous variables; at the very least, exports will influence Y. Let us denote by A these exogenous variables that are omitted by Andersen and Jordan. Then the true reduced form of the economy is (ignoring random errors):

$$Y = a_1 + b_1 L + c_1 F + d_1 A \tag{20.57}$$

and Equation 20.56 is a truncated version of this. The question is whether Andersen and Jordan's results are biased by using the truncated form. The answer which Ando and Modigliani (1976) explore is that it depends on the correlation between L, F, A, and the error term.

Suppose that the government does what the voters expect it to do and tries to stabilize the economy. When there is a fall in A, the government changes either fiscal policy, monetary policy, or both. Then there will be a functional relation between A and the policy variables:

$$A = gL + hF \tag{20.58}$$

Substituting this into Equation 20.57, we see that the true relation between fiscal and monetary policy and nominal income (ignoring random errors) is:

$$Y = a_1 + (b_1 + d_1 g)L + (c_1 + d_1 h)F \tag{20.59}$$

Thus, Andersen and Jordan's estimates of b and c in Equation 20.55 would, in this case, be estimates of $(b_1 + d_1 g)$ and $(c_1 + d_1 h)$ respectively. These coefficients include both the direct effect of the policies on income (b_1 and c_1) and the total effect on income of exogenous changes in autonomous expenditures after taking account of the fact that policy responds ($d_1 g$ and $d_1 h$ respectively).

Let us be more specific about the nature of the policy response. If the government tries to stabilize nominal income, it will increase F in response to a fall in A (for example, it will increase the full-employment budget deficit by reducing tax rates in response to a fall in exports). In other words, h will be negative and since d_1 is positive, the consequence is that $(c_1 + d_1 h)$ is less than c_1 and the effect of fiscal policy on Y is underestimated by estimating $(c_1 + d_1 h)$. Alternatively, suppose that the government tries to stabilize interest rates. If A falls (the *IS* curve shifts leftward), the government will have to reduce the money supply to shift the *LM* curve leftward and thereby stabilize interest rates. In such a case, the parameter g in Equation 20.58 would be positive, since L is measured by the supply of money or high-powered money. With g positive, $(b_1 + d_1 g)$ is greater than b_1 and its estimate is higher than the true value of the coefficient measuring money's effect.

From this it follows that, depending on the policies of the government during the period covered by the data which Andersen and Jordan use, their estimates of the effect of monetary policy may have an upward bias while the estimated effect of fiscal policy may be lower than its true value. Gordon

(1976a) finds that such biases probably did exist during the period between 1953 and 1974 (or, rather, in its component subperiods). However, it is not clear whether the biases were sufficiently strong to make the Andersen-Jordan conclusions worthless.

Another criticism of Andersen and Jordan's conclusions concerns the speed with which the effects of fiscal and monetary policy are felt. If, instead of Andersen and Jordan's particular Almon lag techniques, different techniques are employed for estimating the lag, it can be shown that their conclusions on the relative immediacy of monetary policy's effects can no longer be put forward with confidence. Moreover, whereas Andersen and Jordan used quarterly data for the period 1952-I to 1968-II, the choice of a different period can upset the results obtained. In this connection, we should note the results obtained by Poole and Kornblith (1973). Using the version of the model where L is measured by the money supply and F by government expenditure, Poole and Kornblith estimated b and c using data from the same period as Andersen and Jordan; they then examined the ability of the equation to predict changes in gross national product, given the changes in L and F, in the period 1968-III to 1971-III. It was found that the model's ability to predict changes in GNP was no better than the ability of Friedman and Meiselman's model to predict the level of consumption from the money supply in 1959 to 1970 (and therefore worse than the ability of some definitions of autonomous expenditure to predict consumption).

Finally, in evaluating the Friedman/Meiselman or Andersen/Jordan results with reduced forms, it is interesting to compare them with the results obtained from large econometric models. Such models are based on the estimated coefficients of each of a large number of structural equations instead of a single reduced form which is in principle, but may not be in fact, the solution to a system of structural equations. Whereas the monetarist work on reduced forms indicates that fiscal policy is relatively ineffective, most large econometric models have coefficients that suggest that a change in real government expenditure *does* have a significant effect on real expenditure and output over the short run. Fromm and Klein (1973) indicate that fiscal policy is generally found to have its greatest effect on real income within two to three years, that this effect represents a multiplier significantly greater than unity, and that the money supply also has an effect.

The question, therefore, is whether the large econometric models with their structural estimates and their conclusion that both fiscal and monetary policy have important effects are closer to the truth than the monetarist reduced forms. Ando and Modigliani (1976) attempt to show that if "their" model (the MPS large econometric model) is a good representation of the economy, it is not necessarily contradicted by the Andersen and Jordan results because those results are biased in the manner we have seen. In addition, Modigliani (1977) reports the results of tests showing that if the coefficients of the MPS model are the true coefficients, the estimated coefficients of an Andersen and Jordan reduced form may turn out to be different, but that the difference may not be statistically significant. Finally, Modigliani (1977) carries out a similar test to that of Poole and Kornblith (1973), except here the comparison is between the predictive accuracy of an Andersen and Jordan equation on the one hand and, on the other, a forecasting equation where the coefficient on fiscal policy (government expenditure) is given the value that the MPS model estimates it to have. He finds that using the coefficient estimated from the large structural model enables significantly more accurate predictions to be made than are possible with the estimated Andersen and Jordan equation.

It appears, then, that estimates of reduced forms do at first sight support the proposition that changes in the money supply are a more significant instrument of policy than changes in fiscal policy (or autonomous expenditure). However, care is needed in interpreting these results, and the proposition that *both* fiscal policy and control of the money supply are important cannot be rejected.

CHAPTER

TWENTY ONE

MONETARISM AND KEYNESIANISM

In this book we have examined several different tendencies or schools within monetary theory. One way to think of them is as differing according to the theoretical assumptions that are employed in building macroeconomic models appropriate to a monetary economy. This is the approach that we have generally adopted. One model differs from another according to whether uncertainty is present or absent, whether a growing economy or a stationary state is assumed, whether instantaneous adjustment of prices to their equilibrium levels is assumed, and so on. Another way to view the differences among models concentrates on the differences between their implications for policy. This aspect is the most significant in the heated debate between those who subscribe to monetarist models and those who are advocates of Keynesian models: monetarists are in favor of one type of macroeconomic policy, Keynesians of another.

The division between the two schools over questions of policy is a twofold one. First, monetarists emphasize that if the authorities do attempt to influence aggregate demand and output, control of the money supply will be a much more significant instrument than fiscal policy. In other words, "Money matters," and, in some versions of monetarism, it is stated that "Only money matters." Keynesians, by contrast, argue that both changes in the money supply and fiscal policy have an effect. We examine this "crowding-out" debate in Sections 21.1 and 21.2. The second policy difference, however, is even more fundamental. It concerns the question of whether *any* stabilization policy, even that based upon control of the money supply, can affect real output and employment in either the short or the long run. Monetarists, employing a model of inflation that distinguishes between the long-run and the short-run relationships between inflation and unemployment, contend that in long-run equilibrium where the expected rate of inflation equals the actual rate, even monetary policy cannot influence real output or unemployment, although monetary policy may have a short-run influence (Section 21.3). In Section 21.4, however, we see that if expectations are "rational," then, according to monetarist models, monetary policy has no effect even on real variables even in the short run. In Section 21.5, we examine some criticisms of the conclusions drawn by monetarists from the rational expectations model and note that if prices or wages adjust relatively slowly, stabilization policy will succeed in affecting real output in the short run.

Before examining these debates, it is necessary to consider whether, leaving aside the disputes over how expectations are formed and whether there are rigidities (Sections 21.3, 21.4, and 21.5), there are significant differences in the underlying behavioral equations and transmission mechanisms of the Keynesian and monetarist models. This dissimilarity is explored in Sections 21.1 and 21.6.

21.1 MONETARIST AND KEYNESIAN THEORETICAL MODELS: THE PORTFOLIO APPROACH

One way to examine the theoretical similarities and differences between Keynesian and monetarist models is to examine them at their highest level of generality. This can be done if we consider each in terms of portfolio equilibrium. Tobin (1961, 1969) presents the Keynesian model in such terms and Friedman (1972a) and Brunner and Meltzer (1972, 1973) offer portfolio models as the basis for monetarist views on the effect of money supply on national income.

One can think of an individual or firm, or the private sector, which is the sum of individuals and firms, holding a portfolio of assets at any one time. The range of assets considered will vary from one writer to another, as does the specification of which financial assets contribute to the net wealth of the private sector. But, in general, we may start by including money, government bonds, and physical capital (including consumer durables) in the portfolio. Thus, in nominal terms, the portfolio can be defined as:

$$W \equiv M + B + K \tag{21.1}$$

It should be borne in mind that each of these categories includes subcategories: B, for example, includes government bonds of different maturities. The proportion of total wealth that is held in the form of any one asset—money, for example—depends on the relative rates of return on all assets and, therefore, on their relative prices. Without concerning ourselves with the question of how to define these rates of return, we can assume that each asset yields a positive return consisting partly of financial yield and partly of an implicit yield of services (the service of acting as a medium of exchange, for example, in the case of money). The private sector's portfolio will be in equilibrium when, for each individual, the proportions in which assets are held are such as to equate the marginal rates of return on the various assets.[1] Thus, the proportions in which assets are held are, given wealth, determined by the relative rates of return, and the amount of each asset that is held depends upon these rates of return and the volume of wealth.

Portfolio Equilibrium and Transmission Mechanisms

Suppose that the portfolio is initially in equilibrium and that then the supply of money is increased without a decline in the stock of any other asset. The increase in the private sector's stock of money will have two effects. First, assuming that money is a component of net wealth, it will increase the stock of wealth, the size of the portfolio. Therefore, if the relative yields on assets remain unchanged, we can isolate a wealth effect on the demand for each asset, money, bonds, and physical capital. We generally assume that the wealth effect is positive, so that the demand for each asset increases. Second, however, there is a substitution, or portfolio allocation effect. The wealth effect will have increased the demand for money (and the other assets), but we assume that, in general, this increase in the demand for money is less than the increase in the supply. Indeed, according to our discussion in the last paragraph, we can assume that at the initial yields, the proportion in which assets are desired is unchanged: the demand for money as a proportion of wealth is unchanged, but the new supply of money means that the stock of money is now a greater proportion of (the larger amount of) wealth than previously. There is now, consequently, an excess supply of money at the initial set of relative yields. The private sector will therefore try to exchange its excess money holdings for other assets, reducing money toward the desired proportion and raising its holdings of bonds and physical capital so as to restore the initial proportions between these assets, the proportions desired at the initial set of yields. However, in trying to do so, the private sector will

[1]Defining portfolio equilibrium in terms of equality of marginal rates of return is to argue in a very general way. Strictly speaking, equality of marginal rates of return is only the equilibrium condition for assets that are perfect substitutes—the assets of differing maturity, for example, that were assumed to exist in Chap. 17's pure expectational theory of the term structure. In a world where the characteristics of assets vary from one to the other—where, for example, the yield on one is more certain than the yield on another—the marginal yield on one will be different from that on another to reflect these different characteristics. In the case of differences in uncertainty, for example, there will be risk premiums incorporated in the equilibrium marginal returns on the riskier assets. The formulation in the text will, however, suffice for our purposes since we can abstract from *changes* in the differences between assets and assume, for example, constant risk premiums. Under such assumptions, changes in the relative marginal returns on assets follow only from the same causes as would induce changes in their relative marginal returns when risk premiums are absent, as assumed in the text.

cause a change in the set of relative yields. The yields on bonds and physical capital will be driven down by the increased demand for them and the relative yield on money will rise. A new equilibrium will be established where the yields on bonds and physical capital are lower than previously relative to that on money, so that the private sector is willing to hold the increased stock of money in its portfolio. The new portfolio equilibrium, therefore, is one where the desired proportion of money is higher than formerly and the increased supply of money is matched by an increase in demand.

But macroeconomic monetary theory is not only concerned with behavior that relates to stocks of assets including money. It is fundamentally interested in the relationship between changes in asset portfolios and the *flow* of national income in real or nominal terms (or other flows, such as consumption and investment). How do the portfolio adjustments considered so far affect such flow variables?

One mechanism that would exist when the increase in the money supply is an increase in net wealth would be that of the *wealth effect* (or real balance or Pigou Effect). The increase in net wealth itself causes an increase in planned consumption, which in turn has an effect on national income. However, this mechanism would not operate in the same way where the increase in money supply is engineered through a purchase of bonds by the government, an exchange of bonds for money. Such an operation would not involve an increase in net wealth, but only a change in its composition.

A second mechanism that would operate (to different degrees) whatever the manner in which the money supply is increased comes through the effect of the monetary increase on the demand for the stock of physical capital. As we have seen, the *portfolio allocation effect* (and in some cases, the wealth effect) ensures that an increase in money supply will only be held in equilibrium portfolios if the relative return on physical capital (and other assets) is reduced. To use Tobin's terminology, portfolios are in equilibrium only when the yield on capital required to induce asset owners to hold the existing stock of physical capital—the "supply price of capital"—equals the actual yield. If the stock of money (or bonds) is increased, the supply price of capital falls and asset owners attempt to increase their holdings of physical capital. In other words, if the economy is stationary when portfolios are in equilibrium, the increase in money supply will induce a positive rate of planned investment. This will continue until the stock of capital (or its price) has increased to the point where its marginal yield equals the new, lower supply price of capital. The increase in desired investment will affect real or nominal national income. Even when portfolios reach their new equilibrium, the higher stock of physical capital may affect the growth of national income, although the demonstration of such an effect on growth depends on the growth model employed. Leaving to one side the question of long-run growth effects, the increased money supply will, through its effect on the demand for physical capital, affect investment and income.

The type of portfolio analysis outlined here is relatively noncontentious.

However, macroeconomic models can be characterized as differing according to the simplifying assumptions they introduce into this portfolio analysis. Tobin (1961) argues that the standard Keynesian model outlined in Chapter 8 involves the simplifying assumption that bonds and physical capital can be treated as if they were perfect substitutes, so that the two basic assets between which wealth owners choose are money and bonds/capital. This appears to be what is implied by the fact that the standard Keynesian model considers wealth owners' choices only in terms of a single relative return, the return on bonds relative to that on money (which is assumed to be zero). If bonds and physical capital are perfect substitutes, then it is legitimate to treat them as one asset with a common rate of return, the return on bonds. If this assumption were not made, so that three separate assets would be considered, portfolio choices would have to be analyzed in terms of two relative returns. This the standard Keynesian model does not do.

Tobin considers this simplifying assumption to be too restrictive. He advocates a more general portfolio model along the same lines as the one we have used here to analyze the effects of an increase in the money supply. But this model does not imply that only changes in the money supply will change the demand for the stock of physical capital. A change in the supply of bonds (which either does or does not increase net wealth) will also cause a change in the demand for physical capital through the portfolio allocation effect and, when net wealth is changed, through the wealth effect on the demand for assets. Thus, in Tobin's model, changes in the money supply are not the only forms of financial policy that affect investment and income flows.

This model is presented, for example, in Tobin (1972), as being in opposition to monetarist assumptions about portfolio behavior. Monetarism argues that the money supply is uniquely important. Within the context of the present portfolio model, that contention would imply that the wealth and portfolio allocation effects arising from an increase in the money supply are important, whereas those caused by changes in other assets are not. Whereas Tobin argues that changes in the supply of nonmoney assets, such as government bonds, will have significant wealth and substitution effects on expenditure and the supply price of capital (demand for physical capital), monetarism contends that the only significant effects we need examine are those that emanate from changes in the money supply.

This difference between monetarism and Tobin's type of Keynesianism gives rise to a highly significant policy difference. Monetarists maintain that the crucial instrument for monetary policy and the crucial indicator of financial tightness or ease is the relative size of the money stock. Tobin argues that since it is not only changes in the money supply that affect portfolio equilibrium and the equilibrium relationship between asset stocks and income flows, policy instruments should not be confined to the money supply, and the indicator of financial conditions should be the supply price of capital, since this is affected by all the relevant factors. For practical purposes, argue Tobin and Brainard (1968), this is represented by the yield on equities. Related to this is the fact that in Tobin's analysis, the effect of a change in the money supply varies according to the manner in which it is changed, whereas Friedman (1972) argues that this is of secondary importance compared with the fact of an increase itself. In Tobin's analysis, an increase in the money supply will have a greater effect if it is engineered by government deficit spending (so that government purchases of goods are financed by printing money that is initially received by the sellers of these goods), greater than if the money supply is increased by open-market purchases of bonds. This is for two reasons. The former method involves an increase in net wealth,[2] whereas the latter does not, so that in the former case the wealth effect as well as the portfolio allocation effect is felt. In addition, the government spending itself has a direct effect on the demand for goods and hence the level of output; this effect is the subject of elementary multiplier analysis in the goods market. Friedman (1972b) argues that concentration on such "first-round" effects is inadequate. He considers that the long-run effects of a change in the money supply are more significant and that they are independent of the manner in which the money supply is changed. In Friedman's view, the first-round effects are transient, whereas a change in the money supply, because it has a permanent effect on the stock of money, has an enduring effect however it is engineered. Friedman's contention on this has a central role in the "crowding-out" debate which we shall review in Section 21.2.

The portfolio approach is one way to examine the differences between Keynesian and monetarist models, and we have done so by taking Tobin as representative of the former and Friedman of the latter. The differences come down to two. First, there are differences concerning the degree of abstraction employed, with Friedman abstracting from first-round effects. And, second, there are differences concerning the degree of substitution between money, bonds, and physical capital, with Friedman's conclusions implying that substitutability between money and physical capital is very high (and that between money and bonds is relatively low). The latter argument can be interpreted in terms of *IS* and *LM* curves.

Degree of Substitution

An extreme form of monetarism could be based on the assumption that, empirically, money and bonds are not substitutes, so that the demand for

[2]Government deficit spending will increase private sector net wealth insofar as it increases the stock of financial assets held that are liabilities of the government (where the discounted value of interest receipts is not offset by discounted future taxes). To say that it increases total net wealth involves assumptions that other components of wealth are not reduced by the operation, and, in particular, that private sector holdings of physical capital are not reduced by the government's purchase of goods. We examine this assumption from the point of view of equilibrium private sector holdings of physical capital when we turn to the "crowding-out" debate in Sec. 21.2.

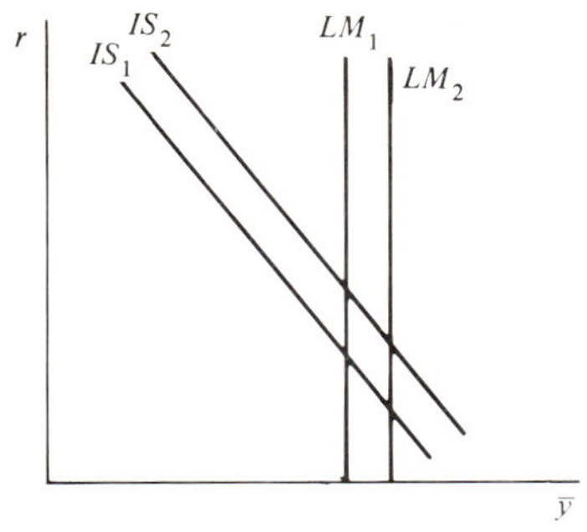

Figure 21-1

money is completely inelastic with respect to the interest rate on bonds. In that case, the *LM* curve would be vertical and, as a result, fiscal policy would have no effect on real income.[3] This can be seen from Figure 21.1. With a vertical *LM* curve, LM_1, an increase in government expenditure that shifts the *IS* curve from IS_1 to IS_2 will not alter equilibrium real income. It will merely cause a rise in the interest rate and a reduction in private demand for goods to offset the increased government demand. An increase in the money supply, however, will, by shifting the *LM* curve to LM_2, affect the level of real income (assuming that output is not restricted by the full-employment capacity constraint).

That the basis of monetarism is the assumption that, empirically, the *LM* curve is vertical is the conclusion one might draw from Friedman's finding (1959) that the demand for money is not a function of the interest rate. One might also draw this conclusion from the attempt in Friedman (1970, 1971) to construct a monetarist theory by modifying the *IS/LM* model with additional assumptions. We have already seen (Section 19.4) that, starting from the Keynesian theory where the demand for money is a function of the interest rate on bonds and nominal income:

$$M^D = f(\bar{Y}, r) \tag{21.2}$$

Friedman makes several simplifying assumptions and substitutions until he obtains the demand function in the form of

$$M^D = Yf(q + \dot{Y}^e) \tag{21.3}$$

where q is a constant. In other words, it might appear that the demand for money is not a function of the interest rate in Friedman's model.

However, Friedman (1966, 1972) denies that monetarist conclusions depend upon a vertical *LM* curve. Indeed, to interpret the demand function for money in Equation 21.3 as refuting Friedman's denial would be a mistake. One reason is that even in the final form, Equation 21.3, the interest rate does

[3]Friedman (1970, 1971, 1972) and Friedman and Meiselman (1963) have forcefully argued that monetarism provides a theory of nominal income and not of real income. Nevertheless, the particular argument examined here is not affected by being framed in terms of real income.

affect the demand for money and it is not even assumed to be constant. Variations in the expected rate of change of nominal income $\dot{Y}^e$ will affect the demand for money because, as is made clear by the way this variable is introduced into the function in Section 19.4, they involve variations in the nominal rate of interest. Even if we are concerned only with the equilibrium growth path of the economy and assume that expectations such as $\dot{Y}^e$ are constant in such a situation, the interest rate will affect the demand for money but will be treated as a constant in the long run. That would imply not that Friedman ignores the role of interest rates, but that he abstracts from them in abstracting from first-round effects and concentrating upon long-run equilibrium.

If an assumption that the *LM* curve is vertical is not the distinguishing mark of monetarism, what is? Friedman (1972) appears to suggest a weaker empirically testable difference in the portfolio approach of monetarists and Keynesians. The latter are defined as basing their models on the assumption that there is a liquidity trap, so that, in the Keynesian model against which monetarism is ranged, increases in the money supply have *no* effect on national income.[4] However, although this assumption is implicit in elementary textbook expositions of the crude multiplier, it is not employed in any developed Keynesian models. It cannot, therefore, be considered as an assumption distinguishing Keynesians from monetarists.

Immediate or Ultimate Effects

We are left, then, with the fact that monetarists and Keynesians adopt broadly similar portfolio models for analyzing the effects of monetary policy. Both agree that the first-round effects of an increase in the money supply may generally be expected to be expansionary through its effects on wealth and rates of return that cause an increase in demand for physical capital.[5] Friedman (1972) indicates that the main difference is that Keynesians emphasize these first-round effects, whereas monetarists emphasize "ultimate effects." Thus, according to Friedman, much Keynesian analysis of fiscal policy stresses the "once-for-all shift of the *IS* curve"—a change in expenditure *flows*—whereas monetarists emphasize the long-run effects of changes in *stocks* of assets.[6]

Blinder and Solow (1973) interpret this view in terms of Figures 21.2 and 21.3. The first-round effects of fiscal policy which Keynesians are thought to emphasize is the shift from $\bar{y}_1$ to $\bar{y}_2$ in Figure 21.2; this shift results simply

[4]We saw in Chap. 20 that this version of the Keynesian model is the basis of most of the reduced forms employed by Friedman and Meiselman (1963) in testing the effect of autonomous expenditure.

[5]However, Friedman appears to emphasize, to a greater extent than Tobin, the direct wealth effect on consumption that results from an increase in money supply.

[6]This assertion is, however, surprising in view of Tobin's concentration on the asset account, or portfolio equilibrium.

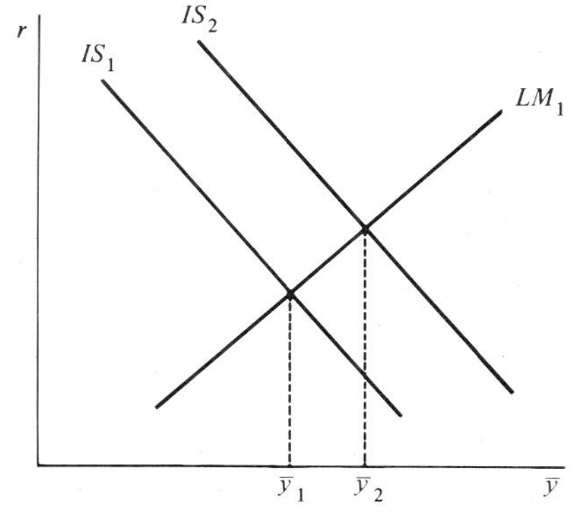

Figure 21-2

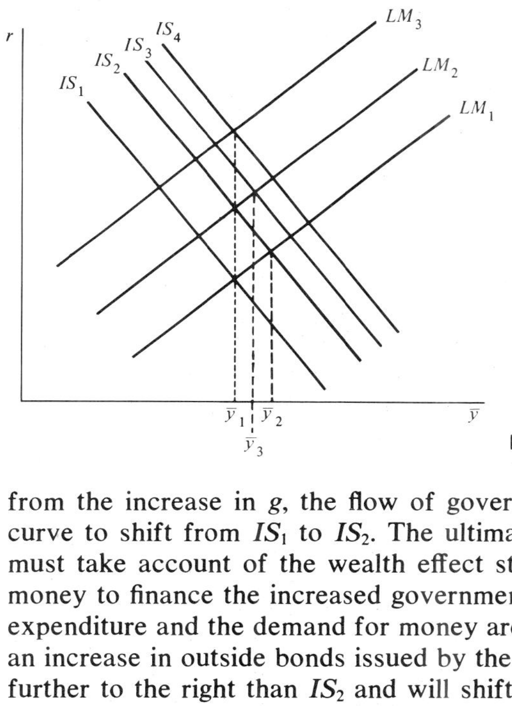

Figure 21-3

from the increase in *g*, the flow of government expenditure, causing the *IS* curve to shift from IS_1 to IS_2. The ultimate effect emphasized by Friedman must take account of the wealth effect stimulated by the issue of bonds or money to finance the increased government expenditure. Assuming that both expenditure and the demand for money are positive functions of real wealth,[7] an increase in outside bonds issued by the government will shift the *IS* curve further to the right than IS_2 and will shift the *LM* curve to the left of LM_1. The resulting ultimate equilibrium, in Figure 21.3, may be, according to Friedman's view, with IS_3 and LM_2 at y_3, or the wealth-induced shifts in the *IS* and *LM* curves may even be such as to cause ultimate equilibrium to be at $\bar{y}_1$ (with IS_4 and LM_3), so that fiscal policy has no expansionary effect—the multiplier is zero. It can be argued that monetarists believe this last possibility to be in fact the case.[8] Government expenditure financed by issuing outside money, on the other hand, will have a clearly expansionary effect, since the wealth effect

[7]Blinder and Solow assume the price level is fixed.

[8]A monetarist model in these terms is explicitly developed by Rasche (1973), but there prices are assumed to be flexible.

on the demand for money will, in general, be outweighed by the increase in the money supply. Thus the *LM* curve would shift rightward, reinforcing the rightward shift of the *IS* curve.

The idea that the ultimate effect of fiscal policy is zero, as in the example given, is one of the most recent points of dispute between monetarists and Keynesians. Although an old idea, it has been given prominence by Friedman's insistence on the importance of ultimate effects. It is known as the hypothesis of crowding out—the theory that bond-financed government expenditure merely crowds out private expenditure so that total expenditure remains unchanged. To put the most common version of the theory another way, in the context of an *IS*/*LM* model, if the *IS* (and, possibly, the *LM*) curve shifts, this shift leaves real income unchanged and must, therefore, cause a change in the interest rate. An increase in the government deficit, therefore, merely leads to a higher equilibrium interest rate that reduces private investment so that government expenditure crowds out private expenditure.

Our discussion of Figure 21.3 gives one possible cause of crowding out—the wealth effect on the demand for money which causes the *LM* curve to be shifted leftward by the financing of government expenditure. Several others have been offered by monetarists. However, Keynesians have argued that concentration on ultimate effects makes the crowding-out hypothesis difficult to sustain. We turn to these arguments in the following section.

21.2 CROWDING OUT AND THE GOVERNMENT BUDGET CONSTRAINT

The idea that fiscal policy is impotent because it crowds out private expenditure and merely diverts resources to the public sector (supposedly "distorting" the allocation of resources) has an ancient lineage. It was a direct corollary of the pre-Keynesian Quantity Theorists' emphasis on Say's Law as a long-run proposition. For, since this assumes that supply creates its own demand, the economy is assumed to be always at full employment. If resources are always fully employed, government expenditure on goods can be met only by diverting resources from goods produced for private demand; private sector expenditure is merely crowded out and government deficits leave real national income unchanged at the full-employment level.

The modern Quantity Theorists' crowding-out theory is not, however, restricted to full-employment equilibria. The argument of a vertical *LM* curve (Figure 21.1) or of offsetting wealth effects (Figure 21.3) does not depend on any assumption that national income is initially at the full-employment level. The theoretical monetarist argument for crowding out consists of demonstrating that on certain assumptions, crowding out will occur even if there initially is unemployment. Apart from the assumptions of a vertical *LM* curve and offsetting wealth effects that we have already reviewed, several alternative bases for the proposition are suggested by Carlson and Spencer (1975). One possibility is that government deficits themselves have a depressing effect on private sector expectations and thereby cause a reduction in private investment plans at all rates of interest. Thus, whereas an increase in the government deficit initially shifts the *IS* curve rightward, the consequent shift in the investment schedule may cause it to revert to its initial position. Or it may be that a similar dislike of deficits reduces "confidence" and thereby increases the (precautionary) demand for money. Here, following the increased deficit, the *LM* curve will shift leftward and the ultimate equilibrium level of real income may be at its initial level. The argument in these cases, however, is not very convincing, for, if crowding out is to occur in the sense of the multiplier being zero, one must make the arbitrary assumption that the expectation and confidence effects exactly offset the initial increase in deficit.

An alternative and more theoretically rigorous monetarist model of crowding out is based on the work of David and Scadding (1974). This argument is based on an assumption that the private sector is "ultrarational," meaning that individuals view the government as merely an extension of themselves. Thus, if the government increases its investment expenditure and finances it by issuing bonds, the future consumption yielded by the investment reduces by the same amount the demand for future consumption yielded by private investment. Private investment, accordingly, falls by exactly the amount that government investment has increased. The ultimate effect, therefore, is that the *IS* curve remains in its initial position and that real income is unchanged by the government deficit. Similarly, an increase in government expenditure on consumption goods and services would, if individuals are ultrarational, be exactly offset by a decline in private consumption (even if the expenditure is financed by taxes rather than bond issues). The assumption of ultrarationality is a very restrictive one and its realism may be doubted. However, David and Scadding argue that it is consistent with an observed long-run stability in the ratio of saving to national income.[9]

The theoretical models of crowding out are therefore simple models whose conclusions follow simply from particular, restrictive assumptions. In general, however, the Keynesian reply has not concentrated on criticizing these assumptions.[10] Instead, Blinder and Solow (1973), Tobin and Buiter (1974), and Brunner and Meltzer (1972)[11] argue that the ultimate effects we have

[9]This model of crowding out, like the model that relies on expectations and confidence, does not depend on a rise in the equilibrium interest rate to crowd out private expenditure.

[10]This is so although the empirical studies of the demand for money establish that, contrary to the apparent implication of Friedman (1959), it *is* a function of an interest rate. These studies constitute a criticism of the assumptions of the model that is based on a vertical *LM* curve.

[11]Brunner and Meltzer cannot be classified as Keynesians. While disagreeing with Friedman on several issues, they advance the main propositions of monetarism. However, in the article cited, they develop the Keynesian criticisms of crowding out.

considered so far are not in fact true long-run equilibrium solutions. As will be recalled from our discussion of long-run equilibrium in Chapter 5, the concept requires that asset stocks are unchanging. If asset stocks are changing and private expenditure and demand for money are subject to wealth effects, then the *IS* and *LM* curves will be shifting from period to period. In such a case, no period's short-run equilibrium would be a long-run equilibrium, for it would not be sustainable from period to period.

Budget Constraint Model

In order to consider a long-run equilibrium position where asset stocks are unchanging, the Keynesian writers introduce the *government budget constraint*. This concept has been implicit in the literature of monetary economics for a long time, but its explicit use for long-run equilibrium comparative static analysis stems from the work of Christ (1967, 1968). It is simply a statement that, in a closed economy without a banking system, government expenditure, G, must be financed either by taxes or by issuing new bonds or creating outside money:

$$G - T = \dot{B} + \dot{M} \tag{21.4}$$

where B is the number of bonds (issued at face value of \$1) and $\dot{B}$ and $\dot{M}$ represent the change (not the percentage rate of change) in outstanding bonds and money supply per period. With such a constraint, it is clear that long-run equilibrium in a model with wealth effects requires the budget deficit $G - T$, to be zero so that $\dot{B} = \dot{M} = 0$. Since we may assume that total tax receipts are a function of national income:

$$T = t(\bar{Y}) \qquad 0 < \frac{dT}{d\bar{Y}} < 1 \tag{21.5}$$

the implication is that, following an initial disturbance or policy change such as an increase in G, the economy reaches long-run equilibrium only when $\bar{Y}$ has reached a new level where $T = G$.

Blinder and Solow (1973) follow the now common practice of writing the government budget constraint in a form more sophisticated than Equation 21.4. They use it to criticize the model of crowding out developed in Figure 21.3. They begin by noting that governments have not only to finance $(G - T)$, the difference between expenditure on goods and services and tax receipts (net of subsidies), but *also* to finance the interest payments on outstanding debt. To represent this procedure, we may simplify by assuming that each bond has a par value of \$1 and is an irredeemable bond with a coupon of \$1 per period. Then total interest payments per period are B and the market value of the stock of bonds is B/r (where r is the interest rate). The government budget constraint then becomes:

$$G + B - T = \dot{B}\left(\frac{1}{r}\right) + \dot{M} \tag{21.6}$$

where $\dot{B}(1/r)$ is the change in the number of bonds evaluated at current market price. Explicitly recognizing that government interest payments are a component of private sector income leads Blinder and Solow to write the consumption function as:

$$C = c(\bar{Y} + B - T, W) \tag{21.7}$$

where $\bar{Y}$ is nominal income excluding government interest; B, the number of bonds, measures interest receipts; and T is subtracted to give *disposable* income.

W represents nominal private sector wealth:

$$W \equiv M + \frac{B}{r} + K \tag{21.8}$$

where K is the nominal value of physical capital. Similarly, the tax function becomes:

$$T = t(\bar{Y} + B) \tag{21.9}$$

These equations allow us to write the goods market equilibrium equation as:

$$\bar{Y} = c\left[(1-t)(\bar{Y} + B), M + \frac{B}{r} + K\right] + I(r) + G \tag{21.10}$$

The money market equilibrium equation, taking account of a wealth effect in the demand for money, is:

$$M^S = M^D = L\left(r, \bar{Y}, M + \frac{B}{r} + K\right) \tag{21.11}$$

These two equilibrium conditions together allow us to find the equilibrium level of nominal income, $\bar{Y}$—or, treating the price level as fixed, real income, $\bar{y}$—in any period. They allow us to determine short-run equilibrium. In other words, the *IS* and *LM* curves in any period are derived from Equations 21.10 and 21.11 respectively.

The introduction of the government budget constraint:

$$G + B - t(\bar{Y} + B) = \dot{B}\left(\frac{1}{r}\right) + \dot{M} \tag{21.12}$$

involves an extension of the basic two equation *IS*/*LM* type model of Equations 21.10 and 21.11. This equation is a differential one that determines changes in B and M. It therefore determines the movement of the *IS* and *LM* curves from one period to the next, since they contain B and M as arguments. To find the long-run equilibrium solution of the whole model, we need only examine Equation 21.12, for we know that, by definition, this stationary state occurs only when:[12]

$$G + B - t(\bar{Y} + B) = 0 \tag{21.13}$$

[12]In this, we are following the standard Keynesian practice of arbitrarily assuming that $\dot{K} = 0$ (even though $I > 0$). Thus, the only assets that we need explicitly to consider in defining long-run equilibrium are B and M ($\dot{B} = \dot{M} = 0$ being the equilibrium condition). Blinder and Solow (1973) do, however, also consider the case where K is not treated as a constant.

From Equation 21.13, it follows that the change in long-run equilibrium income that results from a change in government expenditure (treated as exogenous) is:

$$\frac{d\bar{Y}}{dG} = \left\{ \frac{1 + \left[1 - \dfrac{\partial T}{\partial(Y+B)}\right]\dfrac{dB}{dG}}{\dfrac{\partial T}{\partial(Y+B)}} \right\} \tag{21.14}$$

when tax rates, defined by the tax function $t(\bar{Y} + B)$, are held constant.[13] This result shows that, in considering long-run equilibrium, a rise in government expenditure which initially causes a deficit is expansionary. That is, $d\bar{Y}/dG$ is positive, since $dT/d(Y + B)$ is positive (and less than unity), and dB/dG is either positive or zero. The term dB/dG is zero if the whole deficit is financed by the creation of outside money; it is unity if the deficit is financed wholly by new bond issues. This, indeed, indicates that a deficit financed partly or wholly by bond issues is ultimately *more* expansionary than if financed wholly by creating money. For, in the former case, $0 < dB/dG \leq 1$, whereas, in the latter case, $dB/dG = 0$.

Analysis of Policies

This last result appears paradoxical, for, in analyzing short-run equilibrium, the opposite is the case—monetary financing is more expansionary. These short- and long-run results are presented in Figures 21.4 and 21.5. Figure 21.4 shows the short- and long-run equilibrium changes resulting from a bond-financed deficit. Initially the curves are IS_1 and LM_1, and income is $\bar{Y}_1$. As we saw in Figure 21.3, the short-run effect of a bond-financed rise in government expenditure is to shift the *IS* curve rightward to *IS*. This results both from the increase in G itself plus the wealth effect of increased bonds on private expenditure (Eq. 21.10). There is also a leftward shift of the *LM* curve to LM_2 because the wealth effect induces an increase in the demand for money (Eq. 21.11). Thus, the new short-run equilibrium level of income is $\bar{Y}_2$. Figure 21.5 shows the situation when the deficit is financed by creating money. Here the *IS* curve shifts by the same extent in the short run, from IS_1' to IS_3' but the *LM* curve shifts *rightward* to LM_2' because the increase in the supply of money is greater than the wealth-induced increase in demand. Thus, short-run equilibrium income is established at $\bar{Y}_2'$, which is greater than $\bar{Y}_2$, the result in the bond-financed case.

However, our analysis of Equation 21.14 suggests that $\bar{Y}_2'$ and $\bar{Y}_2$ cannot both be long-run equilibrium positions for, in the long run, bond financing is more expansionary. If they are both only short-run equilibrium positions, the reason is that income has not risen sufficiently to induce large enough

[13]Equation 12.14 is obtained by taking the total differential of Equation 21.13 and rearranging terms.

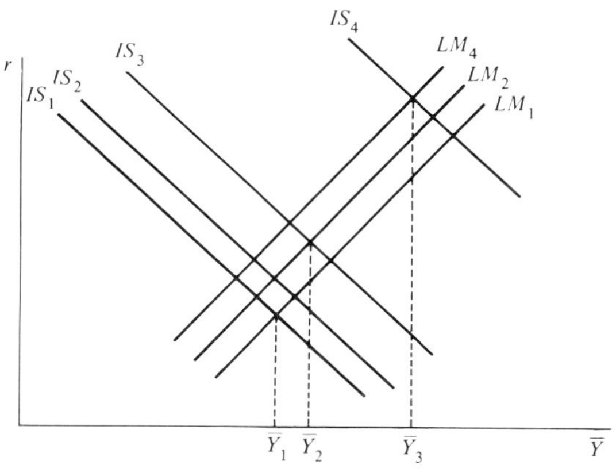

Figure 21-4

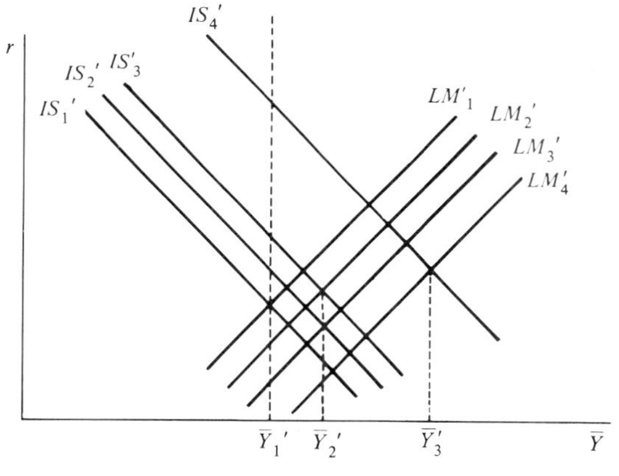

Figure 21-5

increases in tax revenue per period to match the increase in government expenditure. In other words, at such positions, $T < (G + B)$ and, therefore, by the government budget constraint, $\dot{M} + \dot{B}(1/r) > 0$. In subsequent periods, the *IS* and *LM* curves will continue to shift, in Figures 21.4 and 21.5, in the same directions as in the first period. Ultimately, with the curves labeled subscript 4, a position of long-run equilibrium will be established at $\bar{Y}_3$ in Figure 21.4 if deficits are bond-financed and at $\bar{Y}_3'$ in Figure 21.5 if deficits are financed by money. Equation 21.14 dictates that $\bar{Y}_3$ must be greater than $\bar{Y}_3'$.

The explanation for this paradoxical result is that if deficits are bond-financed, income must ultimately rise sufficiently to produce tax receipts T (at given tax rates) that not only match the increased government expenditure on goods and services, G, but also cover the interest payments on the increased government debt. If deficits are, on the other hand, financed by the creation of money, long-run equilibrium is established when income has merely risen sufficiently to produce tax revenues that match the increased expenditure on goods and services.

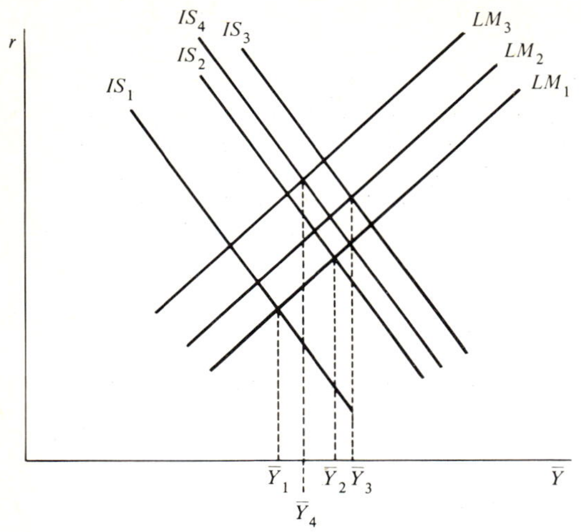

Figure 21-6

The result obtained by introducing the government budget constraint is, then, that whatever the short-run effect of fiscal policy, long-run equilibrium is established only if increased government deficits have an expansionary effect (and the required expansion is smaller in the case of deficits accompanied by increases in money supply). It follows that in the sense of long-run comparative statics, fiscal policy does not crowd out private expenditure through wealth effects (as suggested in discussing Figure 21.3).

There are several limitations of this result. The first is that the system may be unstable so that long-run equilibrium is never reached. Blinder and Solow (1973) explore this question and demonstrate that if deficits are wholly financed by issuing money, the stability condition $((\partial\dot{M}/\partial M)<0)$ is always satisfied. As deficits continue (as M expands), $\dot{M}$ approaches zero, or, in other words, the deficits become progressively smaller. If deficits are wholly financed by bond issues, the stability condition $((\partial\dot{B}/\partial B)<0)$ is satisfied only if the parameters of the goods and money market behavior functions have certain values. However, when the system is stable, then a bond-financed deficit must be expansionary not only in the long run but also in the short run. That is, referring to Figure 21.6, suppose that, ignoring the wealth effects, an increase in G shifts the IS curve from IS_1 to IS_2. If the system is stable in the sense of having a tendency toward long-run equilibrium, the wealth effects of bond issues then must induce a shift of the curves to IS_3 and LM_2 (with $\bar{Y}_3$ greater than $\bar{Y}_2$) rather than to IS_4 and LM_3 (with $\bar{Y}_4$ less than Y_2). If the system is not stable, it will never reach a long-run equilibrium. There is no possibility of a long-run equilibrium being reached with income merely the same as, or lower than, the level of income that existed before the rise in G. Thus, if the thesis that bond-financed fiscal policy crowds out private expenditure is treated as a proposition concerning long-run equilibrium, it is an impossibility in Blinder and Solow's model.[14]

[14]These results are derived as follows. Solve Eqs. 21.10 and 21.11 for $\bar{Y}$ and r in each period:

$$\bar{Y}_t = F(M^S, B, K; G) \tag{21.15}$$

$$r_t = H(M^s, B, K; G) \tag{21.16}$$

Define:

$$\sigma = \frac{\dfrac{\partial I}{\partial r} - \left(\dfrac{B}{r^2}\right)\dfrac{\partial C}{\partial w}}{\dfrac{\partial M^D}{\partial r} - \left(\dfrac{B}{r^2}\right)\dfrac{\partial M^D}{\partial W}} > 0$$

$$\mu = \frac{1}{1 - \dfrac{\partial C}{\partial Y} + \sigma\dfrac{\partial M^D}{\partial Y}} > 0$$

$$\alpha = \frac{\partial C}{\partial W} + \left(1 - \frac{\partial M^D}{\partial W}\right)\sigma > 0 \text{ (since } 0 < \frac{\partial M^D}{\partial W} < 1\text{)}$$

$$\beta = \frac{\partial C}{\partial W} - \frac{\partial M^D}{\partial W}\sigma$$

Then the short-run multiplier for increases in money supply is $\partial\bar{Y}/\partial M = F_M = \mu\alpha$. This is unambiguously positive, so the net wealth effect in this case (the shift in the *IS* and *LM* curves that occurs after we have already taken account of the pure effect of ΔG on the *IS* curve) is expansionary. The short-run multiplier for increases in bonds (their net wealth effect) is $\partial\bar{Y}/\partial B = F_B = \mu\beta$. However, the sign of β cannot be known without knowing the values of $\partial C/Y\partial W$, $\partial M^D/\partial W$ and the parameters of σ. Therefore we do not know on a priori grounds whether bond financing does produce a negative net wealth effect that offsets the pure expansionary effect of ΔG and that could restore the initial equilibrium position (crowding out). But the long-run stability conditions allow us to reach a conclusion on this as follows.

Substitute from Eqs. 21.15 and 21.16 (holding G constant) into Eq. 21.1. Then, if wholly money financing is employed ($\dot{B} = 0$), we obtain:

$$\dot{M} = G + B - t[F(M, B, K) + B]$$

and

$$\frac{\partial \dot{M}}{\partial M} = -\frac{\partial T}{\partial(Y+B)} \cdot F_M = -\frac{\partial T}{\partial(Y+B)}\mu\alpha$$

Therefore, from our earlier consideration of the derivatives which this expression comprises, $\partial\dot{M}/\partial M < 0$ and stability of long-run equilibrium is ensured.

If bond financing is exclusively employed ($\dot{M} = 0$), we obtain:

$$\dot{B} = H(M, B, K)\{G + B - t[F(M, B, K) + B]\}$$

and

$$\frac{\partial \dot{B}}{\partial B} = r\left(1 - \frac{\partial T}{\partial_{\bar{Y}} + B)} - \frac{\partial T}{\partial(\bar{Y}+B)} \cdot F_B\right) + H_B(G + B - T)$$

For stability, we require $(\partial\dot{B}/\partial B) < 0$; since $(G + B - T)$ is zero in the neighborhood of equilibrium, and since $r > 0$, this reduces to:

$$1 - \frac{\partial T}{\partial(\bar{Y}+B)} - \frac{\partial T}{\partial(\bar{Y}+B)} \cdot F_B < 0$$

The second limitation of Blinder and Solow's analysis, however, is that even if the model is stable around its long-run equilibrium position, this may be of little relevance: Government expenditure (or some other policy or exogenous variable) may change again before long-run equilibrium is ever reached. This criticism has been raised by Hansen (1973) and Carlson and Spencer (1975).

Finally, the Blinder and Solow model excludes the possibility of price changes. It therefore does not allow for the effects on behavior functions that may occur if an expansion of nominal income consists partly of a rise in prices. This inflation would itself have wealth effects and, as emphasized in monetarist models of the demand for money, would affect the rate of return on money and therefore the demand for money.

We may conclude that the debate over crowding out—in its strongest form, the proposition that bond-financed increases in government expenditure merely displace an equal amount of private expenditure and leave income unchanged—is in its infancy. Its theoretical formulation has been confined within the framework of the Neoclassical/Keynesian Synthesis and the *IS/LM* model. Within that model, its proponents merely argue for its plausibility as a proposition about short-run equilibrium positions (except for Friedman [1972], who formulates it as a long-run proposition) if any one of a set of alternative assumptions is made, although the realism of the assumptions is not explored. Its critics concentrate on the question of long-run equilibrium. They demonstrate the invalidity of crowding out as a proposition about long-run equilibrium and, also, as a short-run proposition if long-run equilibrium is stable. This argument of the critics is based on the assumption that bond and money financing of government deficits increases net wealth and that private expenditure and demand for money are subject to wealth effects. In this, it is a critique of Friedman's ideas on the ultimate effect of deficits, but it is not directly a critique of the model based on the assumption of ultrarationality. Nor is it a critique of the model that is based on the assumption concerning the depressing effect of deficits on expectations.

---

for local stability. In other words, only if:

$$F_B = \mu\beta > \frac{1 - \dfrac{\partial T}{\partial(\bar{Y} + B)}}{\dfrac{\partial T}{\partial(\bar{Y} + B)}}$$

is the system stable in the neighborhood of long-run equilibrium. For this to be the case, it is a necessary condition that $\beta > 0$ (since we know on a priori grounds that $\mu > 0$). Thus, the stability conditions guarantee that if the system has long-run stability under bond financing, β is positive and the net wealth multiplier of bond financing in the short run, $F_B = \mu\beta$ is positive and reinforces, rather than offsets, the effect of ΔG.

21.3 THE PHILLIPS CURVE AND THE LONG-RUN INEFFECTIVENESS OF STABILIZATION POLICY

The crowding-out debate concerns the relative effectiveness of monetary policy and fiscal policy in altering aggregate demand. As we have seen, monetarists argue that changes in the money supply alone are effective in this respect. The monetarist work to be considered in this section goes even further and contends that in the long run, even changes in the money supply or in its rate of growth will have no effect upon *real* output or employment but will influence only the rate of inflation. In the long run, even money is neutral. It will be seen in Section 21.4, moreover, that the introduction of rational expectations may render money neutral even in the short run. Before proceeding, it should be noted that here we are concerned with an aspect of neutrality that is different from the one considered in Chapter 12. There we examined models that were at full-employment equilibrium and asked whether a change in the money supply would affect any real variables (such as the interest rate, relative prices, or real wealth) *at full employment*. Here, by contrast, we are concerned with the question of whether a change in the money supply can affect the level of employment (and real output) itself.

The idea that monetary (or fiscal) policy has no long-run effect upon employment and real output stems from the fundamental work of Friedman (1968b) and Phelps (1968) on the concept of the Phillips Curve. In Chapter 19, Section 19.4, we noted that a theory of nominal income does not by itself tell us how a change in nominal income, Y, is divided between its components, the price level and real income ($p\bar{y}$). Until the work of Friedman and Phelps, the Phillips Curve was thought to give us a generally applicable technique for solving this problem. As formulated by Phillips (1958), Lipsey (1960), and Samuelson and Solow (1960), the Phillips Curve was essentially a relationship between the rate of change of nominal wage rates and the level of unemployment. The idea is illustrated in Figure 21.7.

Two things about it are important for our present purposes. The first is the theory behind the Phillips Curve. It was formulated by Phillips (and with less impact by Irving Fisher [1926]) simply as an observed statistical relation without much support advanced in the way of theoretical underpinning. Lipsey subsequently explained the curve as resulting from the behavior of the labor market in disequilibrium. His theory was that excess demand in that market causes nominal wages to rise toward an equilibrium level (and to fall in response to excess supply); that the *speed* of adjustment, the rate of change of nominal wages (measured on the vertical axis of Figure 21.7), is related to the *size* of the excess demand for labor; and that the size of excess demand is related to the rate of unemployment (U, which is measured on the horizontal axis of Figure 21.7). This theory has been attacked by Friedman and Phelps with devastating results. The second important point is that several writers on the Phillips Curve replace $\dot{W}$ on the vertical axis with $\dot{p}$, so

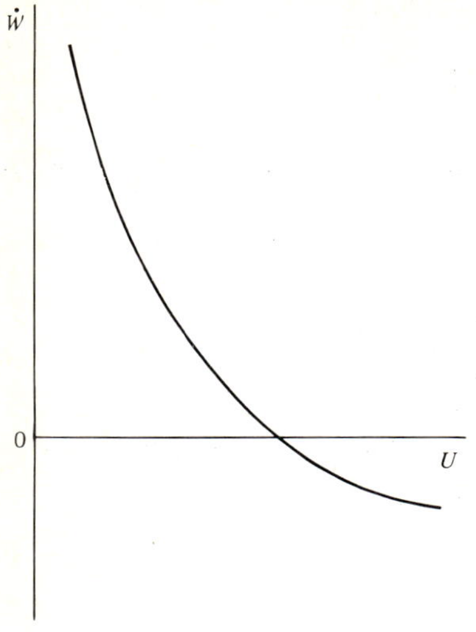

Figure 21-7

that the curve expresses the rate of *price* inflation as a function of unemployment. This version of the Phillips Curve is illustrated in Figure 21.8 and it is the one with which we shall work in this and the following sections. The substitution of $\dot{p}$ for $\dot{W}$ is a simplification that can be rationalized in several ways, the simplest of which is the assumption that prices are deter-

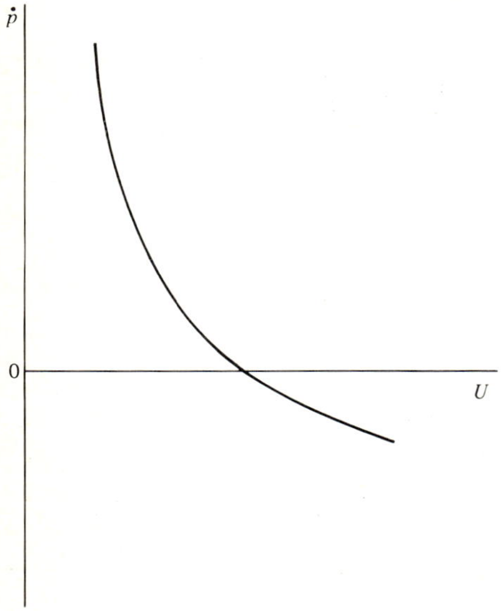

Figure 21-8

mined as a relatively constant proportional markup on wage costs per unit of output.[15]

Expectations

The Phillips Curves illustrated in Figures 21.7 and 21.8 can be written as:

$$\dot{W} = f(U) \tag{21.17}$$

and

$$\dot{p} = h(U) \tag{21.18}$$

respectively. The distinguishing feature of the curve was the assumption that it was relatively stable over time. The point of the Friedman/Phelps model, however, is that within it Equations 21.17 and 21.18 are shown to be unstable in general. This conclusion is reached on the basis of two assumptions. First, contrary to Lipsey's model, it is argued that dis equilibrium in the labor market does not lead to adjustments of nominal wages as such, but of real wages, (W/p). Second, it is assumed that wage bargaining involves the setting of W so as to reach a particular real wage given p, but since bargaining takes place at discrete intervals (once a year, say), the price level taken into account is the one that is expected to obtain during the life of the wage contract. Thus, at instant t, the nominal wage, W_t, is set to obtain a particular real wage, (W_t/p_t^e), where p_t^e is the price level which at t is expected to exist during the following period.

On the basis of these assumptions, we can rewrite Equations 21.17 and 21.18. Retaining temporarily the assumption that U is a measure of labor market disequilibrium (although Friedman and Phelps argue, as we shall see, that U is too crude a measure), the Friedman/Phelps hypothesis is that the "expected" real wage, (W_t/p_t^e), changes as a function of U. Algebraically, the rate of change of this "expected" real wage is $\dot{w}_t - \dot{p}_t^e$ where $\dot{p}^e$ is the expected rate of price inflation. We may therefore replace Equation 21.17 with:

$$\dot{w} - \dot{p}^e = f(U)$$

or

$$\dot{w} = \dot{p}^e + f(U) \tag{21.19}$$

Similarly, the price inflation form of the Phillips Curve may be written:

$$\dot{p} = \dot{p}^e + h(U) \tag{21.20}$$

[15]Let price per unit of output be always higher than wage costs per unit by a percentage, α. Then $p = (1 + \alpha)w(N/q)$ where w is the wage rate per hour, N is work hours employed, and q is output. Now $N/q = 1/z$, where z is average productivity, and the price equation can be written $p = (1 + \alpha)w/z$. Writing this in logarithmic form, differentiating with respect to time, and assuming $(1 + \alpha)$ is a constant, we obtain $\dot{p} = \dot{w} - \dot{z}$, where the dot indicates rate of change. In other words, the Phillips Curve in terms of $\dot{p}$ is, for a given rate of productivity increase $\dot{z}$, parallel to that in terms of $\dot{w}$ and below it by $\dot{z}$.

These equations indicate that $\dot{w}$ and $\dot{p}$ are unstable functions of U in the sense that their values for any particular rate of unemployment depend upon the expected rate of inflation. The idea is intuitively appealing. At any given rate of unemployment, workers will want, and employers will agree to, a higher rate of increase of nominal wages if they expect to experience a high rate of increase of prices than if they expect low price inflation.

One more step is needed before examining the implications of the Friedman/Phelps model. It has to be noted that they consider Equations 21.19 and 21.20 insufficiently precise, since the rate of unemployment alone does not measure disequilibrium in the labor market. For, it is argued, some unemployed are voluntarily not employed,[16] and the measure of this voluntary unemployment is a level of U, called the natural rate of unemployment, U^N. If the actual rate of unemployment U is equal to U^N, the labor market is in equilibrium in the Friedman/Phelps model. If U is higher than U^N, there is excess supply of labor, and if U is less than U^N, there is excess demand. This hypothesis is represented by replacing Equation 21.20 with:

$$\dot{p} = \dot{p}^e + h(U - U^N) \quad (h(0) = 0) \tag{21.21}$$

In other words, when unemployment equals its natural rate, the rate of inflation equals the expected rate of inflation, since the only force causing nominal wages and thence prices to rise is, in those circumstances, the expectation of inflation. Equation 21.21 gives us, therefore, another way to define the natural rate of employment. It is that rate at which $\dot{p} = \dot{p}^e$. And if we follow Friedman and Phelps's original work in assuming that the expected inflation rate is a function of the current rate,[17] the fact that $\dot{p} = \dot{p}^e$ at U^N means that it is that unemployment rate at which long-run equilibrium obtains.

Long-Run Equilibrium

The Friedman/Phelps hypothesis is illustrated in Figure 21.9. Its essence is that, first, instead of the stable Phillips Curve illustrated in Figure 21.8, there is a whole family of such curves, SR_0, SR_1, SR_2, and so on. Which one is relevant at any time depends on the expected rate of inflation. The higher is $\dot{p}^e$, the further to the right is the curve, indicating that for any given level of $(U - U^N)$, $\dot{p}$ is higher than it would otherwise be (Eq. 21.21). Second, these Phillips Curves are only short-run in the sense that no point on them, except for the one directly above U^N, is attainable in long-run equilibrium; for, as we

[16]The explanation of the determinants of this voluntary unemployment is considered in Phelps (1970) to reside in the fact that individuals rationally choose to be unemployed while searching for an optimum job.

[17]The concept of the long-run equilibrium rate of inflation was discussed in Chap. 19, Sec. 19.2. Here, as in Cagan's model, it can be assumed that the expected rate of inflation is a function of the current rate because expectations are formed according to the adaptive expectations model, $(d\dot{p}^e/dt) = \alpha(\dot{p} - \dot{p}^e)$. Thus it is only when $\dot{p}^e = \dot{p}$ that $\dot{p}^e$ is constant $(d\dot{p}^e/dt = 0)$ and, from Eq. 21.21, $\dot{p}$ is therefore constant when U equals the given U^N.

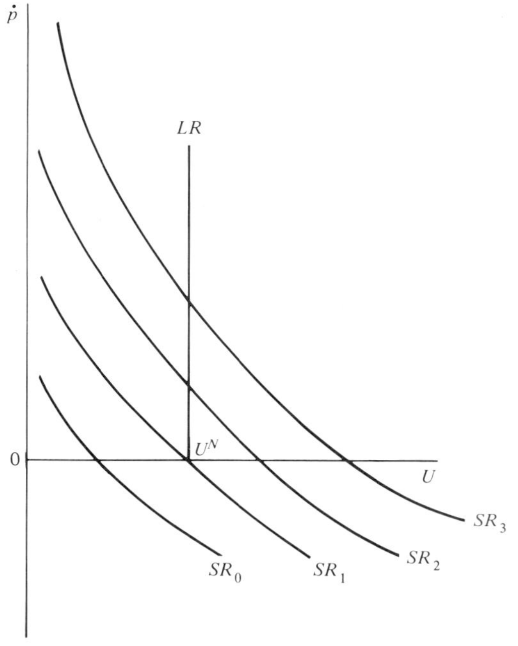

Figure 21-9

have seen in the last paragraph, the natural rate of unemployment is defined as that rate (the only one) at which long-run equilibrium exists. In long-run equilibrium, therefore, the Phillips Curve is *LR*, a vertical line above the natural rate of unemployment which indicates that in long-run equilibrium the rate of unemployment can only be U^N and the rate of inflation associated with it can be anything. (More precisely, there is no $\dot{p}$ uniquely related to U^N, but at U^N, $\dot{p}$ may be uniquely related to, and determined by, another variable, such as the rate of increase of the money supply.)

The Friedman/Phelps model suggests that long-run equilibrium is stable in the sense that any deviation of unemployment from the natural rate gives rise to forces that cause unemployment to return to the natural rate. This stems from the idea that the expected rate of inflation $\dot{p}^e$ adjusts toward the current rate;[18] if, starting from long-run equilibrium of zero current and expected inflation, inflation for some reason develops, individuals will eventually fully adjust their expectations of future inflation upward.[19] The stability of long-run equilibrium has a remarkable implication: the government cannot choose to reach, by monetary and fiscal policy, a particular unemployment rate and a particular inflation rate unless the desired unemployment rate is the natural rate U^N. The idea of stability and this implication of it is illustrated in Figure 21.10.

[18]As in the adaptive expectations hypothesis, see footnote 17.

[19]It will be shown in due course that the assumption of eventual, rather than instantaneous, adjustment is crucial for the distinction between short-run and long-run equilibrium positions.

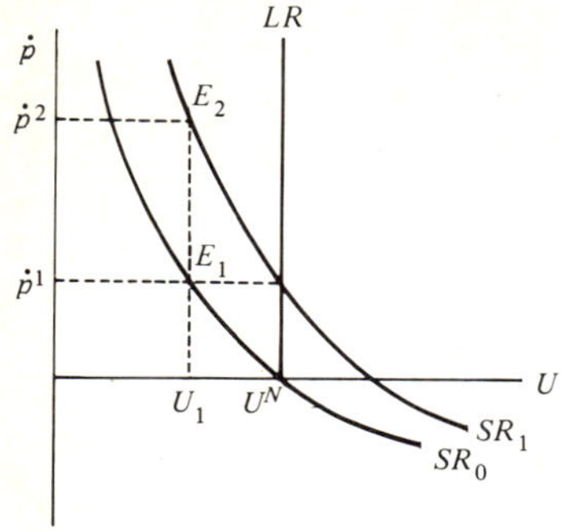

Figure 21-10

Suppose that the rate of unemployment is initially U^N, the expected inflation rate (equal to the current rate) being zero, with the associated short-run Phillips Curve being SR_0.

Now suppose that the government attempts to reduce unemployment to U_1 by increasing aggregate demand. Keynesians argue that it may increase demand either by increasing the money supply or by running a budget deficit (even if financed by bond issues), whereas monetarists contend that an increase in the money supply is the surest way to increase demand, but that distinction is not important for the present argument. What matters at the moment is the *effect* of an increase in demand rather than its source. If, initially, expectations remain unchanged, the economy can move along SR_0 to a position, such as E_1, where unemployment is reduced to U_1 and current inflation is raised to $\dot{p}_1$. As long as the expected rate of inflation remains unchanged at $\dot{p}^e = 0$, this particular position can be maintained and the government will have succeeded in reducing the rate of unemployment to U_1 and obtaining a given rate of inflation, $\dot{p}_1$. But, according to the Friedman/Phelps model, the expected rate will not remain unchanged. In subsequent periods, expectations will be revised in accordance with the first period's experience of inflation; $\dot{p}^e$ will rise above zero toward $\dot{p}_1$, and, in consequence, the short-run Phillips Curve will shift rightward. When expectations are fully adjusted, we will have $\dot{p}^e_2 = \dot{p}_1$, and the relevant Phillips Curve will be SR_1. With that short-run Phillips Curve, the government can only maintain inflation at $\dot{p}_1$ if it permits unemployment to return to the natural rate, U^N. If it fails to do so and maintains a level of aggregate demand that can only be met by unemployment being U_1, the rate of inflation will rise to $\dot{p}_2$ at E_2. Clearly, E_2 could not be a long-run equilibrium position, since there would be a divergence between the current rate of inflation and the expected rate which underlies SR_1 ($\dot{p}_2 > \dot{p}^e_2$). In fact, if the authorities try to maintain unemployment at U_1 and expectations adjust toward the current rate, there would be an explosive tendency, as the short-run Phillips Curve would continue to shift rightward and the $\dot{p}$ appropriate to U_1 would continue to increase.

It follows that the only level of unemployment attainable in long-run equilibrium is U^N. The government can affect the level of unemployment only in the short run, or, in other words, as long as the government forces the economy to remain out of long-run equilibrium. Preventing the attainment of long-run equilibrium means that the government maintains a high level of aggregate demand in order to keep unemployment at U_1, below the natural rate, and to cause the economy to be at points such as E_1 and E_2 on short-run Phillips Curves. Such points are, however, attainable only to the extent that the current rate of inflation diverges from the expected rate, $(\dot{p} - \dot{p}^e) \gtrless 0$. The choice of U_1 can be a successful policy, in other words, only if inflation is not fully anticipated. This follows from Equation 21.21, since if U_1 does not equal U_N, $g(U_1 - U_N)$ does not equal zero and $(\dot{p} - \dot{p}^e)$ cannot be zero. The government can therefore permanently maintain the economy at U_1, only if there is a permanent discrepancy between actual and expected inflation rates. Since it is assumed that when expected inflation lags behind the actual inflation, it nevertheless adjusts toward the actual rate, the only way in which a permanent discrepancy can be maintained at U_1 is if there is a never-ending acceleration of the actual rate. This acceleration would be secured by the phenomenon examined in the last paragraph, a continuous shift from one short-run curve to another if unemployment is maintained at U_1 (but not if it is allowed to return to its natural rate). The penalty the government must face if it tries to maintain unemployment below the natural rate is an ever-increasing rate of inflation.

Assumptions and Implications

The Friedman/Phelps model's implication that in long-run equilibrium, monetary policy cannot affect the level of unemployment means that it cannot affect the level of real output (if we assume a unique relationship between output and unemployment). The natural rate of unemployment characterizing that equilibrium is, as we have seen, a concept of full employment. The implication, therefore, is that in long-run equilibrium, output is at its capacity level, and that since this equilibrium is stable, the economy has an automatic tendency to this level.[20] This relates directly to the analysis of long-run equilibrium in Chapter 19, Section 19.4. We saw there that Friedman's theory of nominal income is a theory of long-run equilibrium inflation which is equivalent to the Crude (pre-Keynesian) Quantity Theory:

$$\dot{M}^s = \dot{p}$$

if the rate of growth of capacity is assumed to be zero and if actual real output equals capacity output $(\bar{y}/y = 1)$. The Friedman/Phelps model examined here is a theory of why, in long-run equilibrium, $\bar{y}/y = 1$.

[20]We have examined the stability of the model from the point of view of its reaction to excess demand or overfull employment, $U_1 < U^N$. The same considerations would have applied if we had started from a position of underemployment, $U_1 > U^N$.

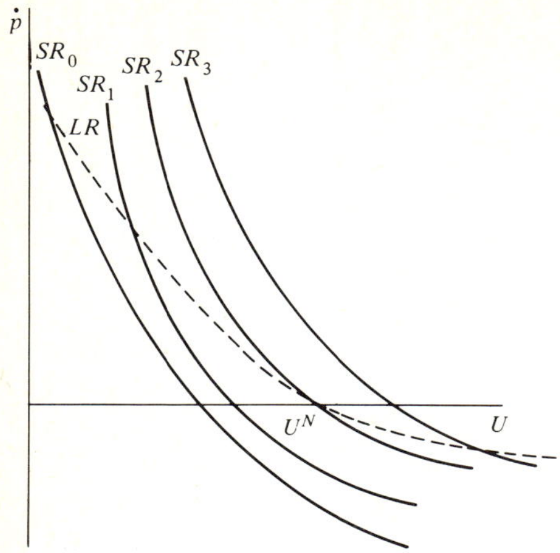

Figure 21-11

The Friedman/Phelps model considered here has been criticized on empirical, rather than theoretical, grounds. The crucial point is that Equation 21.21 is a special case of the more general equation:

$$\dot{p} = \alpha\dot{p}^e + h(U - U^N) \quad [h(0) = 0] \tag{21.22}$$

which is obtained by making the special assumption that $\alpha = 1$. This assumption is of central importance for the Friedman/Phelps hypothesis, for if it were not valid, then the long-run equilibrium Phillips Curve would not be the vertical line LR in Figure 21.10. Instead, it would be the downward-sloping curve LR in Figure 21.11. Suppose, for example, that $0 < \alpha < 1$. From Equation 21.22 we know that when $U = U^N$, we have:

$$\dot{p} = \alpha\dot{p}^e + h(0)$$
$$= \alpha\dot{p}^e$$

If $0 < \alpha < 1$, this means:

$$\dot{p} < \dot{p}^e$$

In other words, α less than unity implies that when the economy is at the natural rate of unemployment, $\dot{p}$ is not, in general, at the long-run equilibrium rate of inflation. It is generally below the expected rate when unemployment is U^N, and it therefore exerts a downward pressure on $\dot{p}^e$ and thereby a downward tendency in $\dot{p}$ itself. Thus, U^N is not generally a long-run equilibrium position if $\alpha < 1$. Instead, long-run equilibrium can be reached at rates of unemployment between zero and the natural rate, as is described by LR in Figure 21.11. The steepness of LR is greater, the closer to unity is α. The fundamental empirical question, therefore, is whether α is equal to, or less than unity. The empirical validity of the Friedman/Phelps hypothesis was thrown into doubt by the work of Perry (1970), Gordon (1971), and others who estimated α as significantly less than unity for the United States. However, later work on data which included figures drawn from the late 1960s and early 1970s when inflation was accelerating revealed that the difference between α and unity was not statistically significant. Gordon (1972) suggests that this can be explained by the idea that only when inflation develops a strong positive trend that is not expected to be reversed do firms and workers fully adjust current prices (and wages) in line with expected inflation.

21.4 RATIONAL EXPECTATIONS AND THE SHORT-RUN INEFFECTIVENESS OF STABILIZATION POLICY

Within the Friedman/Phelps model, monetary (and fiscal) policies have no effect on the long-run equilibrium level of unemployment or real output, but in the short run they may. If it exists, this short-run role for stabilization policy is not to be ignored, for it can be argued that long-run equilibrium is never attained in any real economy and that we always live in the short run. Monetarism in its most highly developed form, however, puts forward the proposition that if expectations are "rational," then even in the short run, stabilization policy is ineffective or, more accurately, the distinction between the short run and the long run is invalid if the former is defined merely in terms of errors in expectations. The proposition is developed by Lucas (1972) and Sargent and Wallace (1975). It hinges on the fact that within the Friedman/Phelps model, as has been seen, unemployment is under the control of the authorities to the extent that current inflation diverges from the expected rate, whereas, if expectations are rational, such divergences cannot occur unless the authorities somehow manage to adopt a completely unpredictable monetary (or, for Keynesians, fiscal) policy. If (in the Friedman/Phelps model) there can be no systematic divergence of $\dot{p}$ from $\dot{p}^e$, there can be no systematic divergence of U from U^N even in the short run and even if the government is attempting to reach an unemployment level different from the natural rate.

Despite its startling conclusions, the rational expectations model is simple, has an appealing elegance, and may at first sight appear to be intuitively plausible. It starts with the assumption that the expected rate of inflation within a period, $\dot{p}_t^e$, is an unbiased predictor of actual inflation, $\dot{p}_t$, given all the information available at the beginning of the period, z_{t-1}:

$$\dot{p}_t^e = E(\dot{p}_t|z_{t-1}) \tag{21.23}$$

In other words, if the actual rate, $\dot{p}_t$, is unaffected by random disturbances and determined only by a systematic relationship with variables which, at the beginning of the period are known (z_{t-1}), then the inflation rate is perfectly predictable and we can assume that it is perfectly predicted, $\dot{p}_t^e = \dot{p}_t$. In such circumstances, deviations of expectations from actual inflation are precluded and policy will be ineffective in the short run. But the assumption that random disturbances have no effect is unduly restrictive and the rational expectations hypothesis is not limited to such a simple case. More generally, Equation 21.23 implies that $\dot{p}_t^e$ may diverge from $\dot{p}_t$ to the extent that some random influences, by definition unknowable at the beginning of the period, affect $\dot{p}_t$. Let these random influences[21] be ϵ_t; then the assumption is that:

$$\dot{p}_t - \dot{p}_t^e = \epsilon_t \tag{21.24}$$

The assumption that the expected and actual inflation rates diverge only by a random factor is the essence of rational expectation. A corollary is that individuals have a knowledge of the true structural relations in the economy; at the beginning of any period, they can predict the behavior of economic variables as well as a true econometric model of the economy can, for they, like such an ideal model, know all there is to be known about the relations among economic variables (including those between past and future variables), and they also know all the past values of the variables.

Ineffectiveness of Policy

In a very general way, Equation 21.24, in combination with the Friedman/Phelps hypothesis, immediately indicates that monetary policy is unable to alter the difference between U and U^N in a systematic way, for it implies that the economy can only be off the long-run Phillips Curve, to the left or right of U^N, in a random manner. If monetary policy (or fiscal policy) follows any systematic rule, such as relating the rate of growth of the money supply to last period's unemployment, it and its structural effect on $\dot{p}_t$ become part of the information, z_{t-1}, upon which expectations, $\dot{p}_t^e$, are based, and they do not enable the monetary authorities to cause a systematic deviation between $\dot{p}_t$ and $\dot{p}_t^e$. But let us examine the working of the rational expectations model in more detail.

Let us start by writing the Friedman/Phelps equation of the Phillips Curve (Eq. 21.21) in a simplified linear form:

$$\dot{p}_t = \dot{p}_t^e - \beta(U_t - U_t^N) + \beta\gamma_t^s \tag{21.25}$$

This implies:

$$U_t = U_t^N - \frac{1}{\beta}(\dot{p}_t - \dot{p}_t^e) + \gamma_t^s \tag{21.26}$$

In these equations we assume that unemployment (and hence the rate of inflation) is influenced by γ^s, a random variable (with $E(\gamma^s) = 0$) reflecting

[21]Strictly speaking, ϵ_t may include other types of forecasting errors as long as it is uncorrelated with z_{t-1}. It may, for example, be due to the individuals' random errors in adding and therefore to a random influence on $\dot{p}_t^e$ rather than to the existence of random influences on $\dot{p}_t$. The concept of rational expectations was first formulated by Muth (1961), even though its significance for the theory of stabilization policy was not examined until a decade later.

changes in the supply of labor that are unpredictable and not amenable to control by the government.

Now let us suppose that the true relation between the rate of growth of the money supply and the rate of inflation is:

$$\dot{p}_t = \dot{M}_t + \gamma_t^d \tag{21.27}$$

where γ^d is a random variable with zero mean. Equation 21.27 assumes that the velocity of money is constant and that real income is constant except for random variations (represented by γ^d), but these assumptions are introduced for simplicity alone.[22] If the last equation represents the true structural relation between prices and money supply, the rational expectation of the inflation rate would be equal to the expected rate of growth of the money supply:

$$\dot{p}_t^e = \dot{M}_t^e \tag{21.28}$$

Now suppose that the government systematically attempts to change the money supply and its rate of growth in such a way as to attempt to keep unemployment below the natural rate. It attempts to achieve $U_1 (0 < U_1 < U^N)$ and does so by reacting to the previous period's unemployment according to the following rule:

$$\dot{M}_t = \lambda_0 + \lambda_1 (U_{t-1} - U_1) + \gamma_t^m \tag{21.29}$$

In other words, the authorities increase the money supply at the rate λ_0 plus some proportion $(0 < \lambda_1 < 1)$ of the excess of last period's unemployment over the target level of unemployment. In addition, there is a random element γ_t^m with zero mean, which influences the rate of growth of the money supply. The question posed and answered by the rational expectations hypothesis is whether this policy, while designed to achieve U_1, can be successful. The determination of the money supply in accordance with Equation 21.29 is a structural relation of the economy, a systematic element that is part of the information, z_{t-1}, upon which expectations are based. Accordingly, a rational expectation of the rate of growth of the money supply is:

$$\dot{M}^e = \lambda_0 + \lambda_1 (U_{t-1} - U_1) \tag{21.30}$$

Subtracting this from Equation 21.29, we see that the only error in predicting the rate of growth of money is the random influence on the money stock that occurs after the prediction is made:

$$\dot{M}_t - \dot{M}_t^e = \gamma_t^m \tag{21.31}$$

Subtracting Equation 21.28 from 21.27 and substituting from Equation 21.31, we see that the only sources of error in expectations of inflation are, in this model, the random influences on the price level and on the money supply:

$$\dot{p}_t - \dot{p}_t^e = \gamma_t^m + \gamma_t^d \tag{21.32}$$

[22]Sargent and Wallace (1975) employ an *IS/LM* framework in their rational expectations model instead of our simple Quantity Theory equation, but the results are unaffected.

If we substitute this into Equation 21.26, our simplified Friedman/Phelps model of the Phillips Curve, we obtain:

$$U_t = U_t^N - \frac{1}{\beta}(\gamma_t^m + \gamma_t^d) + \gamma_t^s \tag{21.33}$$

In other words, actual unemployment is not U_1 even though the government's monetary policy is aimed at achieving that level. Instead, it is some level that diverges from the natural rate in a random manner and whose expected value equals the natural rate (since the random disturbance terms are assumed to have mean values of zero). If we conceive of government policy as concerning the choice of λ_0 and λ_1, it is clear from Equation 21.33 that these do not enter into the determination of U_t and policy is powerless. If policy decisions concerning the money supply were made in an unpredictable manner, they would be encapsulated in γ_t^m, and only then would policy have an effect.[23]

[23]The simple model presented here is based upon that of Gordon (1976b). An equally simple model which concentrates upon the determination of real output rather than unemployment is that discussed by Fischer (1977). There we begin with the wage contract discussed in Sec. 21.2, where the nominal wage rate for period T, w_t is determined at the beginning of the period in accordance with expectations of the price level for period T. Normalizing to unity, we have:

$$\frac{W_t}{p_t^e} = 1 \quad \text{or} \quad W_t = p_t^e \tag{21.34}$$

The supply of output (real national income) is assumed to be a decreasing function of the real wage since diminishing marginal productivity implies that the demand for labor is such a function. Hence, by assumption, so is the actual amount of employment and, via the production function, so is output. This supply function is, in its simplest form:

$$y = \left(\frac{W_t}{p_t}\right)^{-1} \tag{21.35}$$

Substituting for the nominal wage rate from the previous equation and taking logarithms, we obtain:

$$\log y_t = (\log p_t - \log p_t^e) \tag{21.36}$$

Or, differentiating with respect to time, we obtain the rate of growth of the supply of output:

$$\dot{y}_t = \dot{p}_t - \dot{p}_t^e + \gamma_t^y \tag{21.37}$$

where γ_t^y is included to indicate the existence of random influences. The real demand for output, e_t, is, for simplicity, treated as determined by the real money supply with velocity a constant except for a random influence. In rates of growth we have:

$$\dot{e}_t = \dot{m}_t - \dot{p}_t - \gamma_t^d \tag{21.38}$$

Assuming $\dot{y}_t = \dot{e}_t$, the rates of growth of supply and demand for output are equated by adjustments in the (rate of growth of) prices, we can solve Eqs. 21.37 and 21.38 for $\dot{p}_t - \dot{p}_t^e$ in terms of $\dot{m}_t^e$, $\dot{p}_t^e$, and the random disturbance terms. The solution to the model is essentially the same as that developed in the text, since $\dot{m}_t^e$ and $\dot{p}_t^e$ can be eliminated from the $\dot{p}_t - \dot{p}_t^e$ equation and $\dot{p}_t - \dot{p}_t^e$ can be shown to depend only on the random disturbance terms in the supply and demand functions for goods. Since planned supply depends on $\dot{p}_t - \dot{p}_t^e$ (Eq. 21.37), this implies that it is unaffected by a systematic monetary policy. Note that Fischer, differing from the model in the text, does not include a random element in $\dot{m}_t$ (although its inclusion would not affect the conclusions drawn) and his own model is not in terms of rates of change.

The conclusion of the rational expectations model appears to be, therefore, that monetary (or fiscal) policies are unable to affect real output or unemployment even in the short run unless these policies are themselves unpredictable. Furthermore, since rational expectations are formed on the basis of (or, more exactly, are conditional upon) knowledge of all previous values of economic variables and their systematic interrelations, the only unpredictable elements in policy are those that are random and, with zero mean, uncorrelated with any events that occurred in previous periods. The clear implication is that stabilization policy is futile and should be abandoned, and this proposition is one having a long tradition in monetarist thought even though not until the 1970s was it theorized in terms of the rational expectations hypothesis. Modern contributions to the tradition begin with the argument of Simons (1936) and Friedman (1948) for a monetary rule such as, "Let the money supply grow x percent per year," instead of having a stabilization policy that alters the money supply in response to recently observed events. The argument is founded on the belief that the economic system would be stable if left alone (and if certain banking reforms were introduced). This was complemented by the demonstration by Friedman (1953) that, within a simple model, the conditions under which a stabilization policy will be successful may be highly restrictive.

21.5 CRITICISMS OF THE RATIONAL EXPECTATIONS HYPOTHESIS

The conclusions examined in Sections 21.4 and 21.5 are at the center of the monetarist criticism of Keynesianism, for they argue against any stabilization policy, either fiscal or monetary. But are they incontrovertible conclusions that must be accepted by Keynesians? In the present section we consider the acceptability of the rational expectations hypothesis and its conclusion that even short-run stabilization policy is ineffective.

One line of criticism is that although individuals do have rational expectations in the sense that their expectations make the most efficient use of all the information known to them (z_{t-1}), the information known to the government differs from that known to the individuals of the private sector. In consequence, individuals' expectations of the rate of growth of the money supply, $\dot{M}_t^e$, in the model of the last section need not necessarily diverge from $\dot{M}_t$ only by the random factor, γ_t^m; the government can engineer discrepancies between $\dot{p}_t^e$ and $\dot{p}_t$ even if it follows a policy systematically related to previous events, since its knowledge of these events (and of its own rules) differs from that of the private sector. The likelihood of there being such differential information is open to dispute. It is arguable that as an empirical matter, the availability of economic information and analytical techniques is so great that differential information is implausible. The agents, such as corporations and unions, that have the greatest effect on prices and wages, have the same information about the economy as does the government and are able to predict the government's own reaction to the information—that is why they employ economists and econometricians. It has also been asserted that on theoretical grounds, such a situation is bound to arise, since the costs of wrongly predicting government policy and the rate of inflation are so great that there is a considerable return on investing in information.

A second line of criticism, although one that we shall not consider, is that even if all information is shared equally, there is no reason to think that individuals do have rational expectations. They may form their expectations in the manner predicted by the adaptive expectations (error-adjustment) model examined in Chapters 7, 17, and elsewhere in this book. Why should one model of expectations be preferred, in principle, to another?

A third criticism, made by Modigliani (1977), is that since the rational expectations hypothesis implies that even temporary deviations from the natural rate of unemployment are impossible (except as random deviations), the theory finds it impossible to explain such major depressions as occurred in the 1930s. The existence of the Great Depression is, according to this argument, a crude but strong empirical demonstration that the rational expectations hypothesis is wrong. The monetarist response put forward by Sargent (1976) is that the experience of the 1930s can be explained by a rise in the natural rate of unemployment rather than by deviations from it. This view is complemented by that of Darby (1976), that, in any case, the usually accepted figures for unemployment in the late 1930s are higher than the true figures.

Finally, the assumption of wage or price rigidities leads to the conclusion that even if expectations are rational, policy can influence the level of output or unemployment in the short run. Two different models that demonstrate this finding are those of Phelps and Taylor (1977) and Fischer (1977); we shall consider the latter one. It is based upon the idea that wages are rigid but in the special sense that they are fixed for two periods ("years") at a time; the wage contract agreed at any instant is binding for the next two "years." This implies that at any one time a proportion of firms, θ, is operating with wage contracts entered into at the beginning of the period and a proportion $(1-\theta)$ is operating with contracts entered into at the beginning of the previous period. Those drawn up at the beginning of the period are designed to maintain real wages on the basis of the expectations existing then of prices during the period: $({}_{t-1}W_t/{}_{t-2}p_t^e) = 1$, where the leading subscript indicates that nominal wages are set at the end of $(t-1)$ and the expected price level is that which, at the end of $(t-1)$, is expected to hold during t. Those drawn up at the end of the period-before-last are based upon the expectations held then of prices in period t: in other words they set $({}_{t-2}W_t/{}_{t-2}p_t^e) = 1$. Following the same procedure for deriving a supply of output function as adopted in Equations 21.34 and 21.35, we can derive one for each of the groups of firms and, weighting each one by the relative size of the group, add them to obtain the aggregate supply function in logarithmic terms:

$$\log y_t = \theta[\log p_t - \log ({}_{t-1}p_t^e)] + (1-\theta)[\log p_t - \log ({}_{t-2}p_t^e)] + \gamma_t^s \tag{21.39}$$

This equation makes clear that the government can influence the supply of output in period t if it can influence the ratio of the present price level to what at $(t-1)$ it was expected to be *or* its ratio in terms of what at $(t-2)$ it was expected to be.

The question is whether an assumption that these expectations are formed rationally prevents a systematic, predictable government policy from having that influence. The answer is that in the present model, rational expectations do not cause policy to lack influence even if that policy is predictable and predicted. Suppose that, as with the monetary policy described by Equation 21.29, the government adjusts the money supply of period t in accordance with disturbances that occur up to and *including* period $(t-1)$ and that the money supply in period t determines p_t. The private sector therefore has at $(t-1)$ a rational expectation of p_t, and this is described by ${}_{t-1}p_t^e$. It is based upon this sector's knowledge of all the data up to the end of $(t-1)$ and of how the government systematically reacts to these data [how, for example, the government adjusts the money supply of period t in response to the level of unemployment or output in $(t-1)$ and earlier periods]. At $(t-2)$, also, a rational expectation of p_t is formed $({}_{t-2}p_t^e)$, but this is on the basis of more limited information. At that point in time, the private sector again knows how the government reacts to data (on experienced unemployment or output), but it does *not* know at $(t-2)$ what these data will be at $(t-1)$—at the time when the government will be deciding on the money supply, and hence p_t, for period t. At instant $(t-2)$ when this rational expectation is being formed, it is impossible to take into account the data that will occur at $(t-1)$ and upon which the government will base its decision for the money supply and prices in t (m_t^s, p_t), for these data, U_{t-1} or Y_{t-1}, will be affected during $(t-1)$ by random disturbances with zero mean, as in Equation 21.26 or 21.39. From this it follows that the price expectations formed two periods previously can deviate from the actual price level of period t by a factor that depends upon the government's systematic response to the events of period $(t-1)$. Thus the difference $(p_t - {}_{t-2}p_t^e)$ can be manipulated by a systematic government policy and, as implied by Equation 21.39, such a policy will affect a real variable, the supply of output.

It appears, then, that rigidity of nominal wage rates (or, more generally, of prices or wages) can permit monetary or fiscal policy to be effective in the short run even if expectations are formed rationally. This conclusion must be interpreted carefully, however, for otherwise it would be all too easy to claim that the assumption of rigid wages and prices is arbitrary and highly restrictive. First, rigidity here does not mean that wage rates are fixed and unresponsive to market forces. It merely signifies that they adjust to market forces relatively slowly, since some wage contracts have more than a period to run before they can be revised. Second, the assumption of relative slowness of wage adjustment is not necessarily arbitrary but can, at least in principle, be explained in terms of utility and profit maximization. If the price level changes in each period in a way that can most accurately be predicted on the basis of information available only at the beginning of the period, workers and firms are taking an avoidable risk (of miscalculating the real wage implied by the nominal wage) if they set the real wage before that information becomes available. Nevertheless, they may choose to do precisely that when this risk is more than offset by the saving in costs that workers and firms would suffer if they had more frequent wage bargaining (firms, for example, risking strikes every time the contract is up for negotiotion). Third, another way to look at the Fischer model is to say that although at any one time the private sector and the government have the same information, the nominal wage for period *t* is set (by workers and firms) on the basis of less information than is available to the government when, at a later date, it sets the money supply and hence the price level for period *t*. Ultimately, therefore, the model is a sophisticated case of differential information. It is an example of how differential information may be relevant as a result of possibly optimal choices of contract periods even though at any one instant the government and the private sector have no secrets from each other.

21.6 MONETARISM AND KEYNESIANISM

The heat generated by the debates between monetarists and Keynesians is considerable, but it is not always clear that the debate is over real differences. Let us conclude by trying to assess whether the differences are actual or imaginary.

The first area of debate is over the question of whether control of the money supply is a more reliable instrument for controlling aggregate demand than is fiscal policy alone. In terms of *theoretical* models, there is no real distinction between monetarists and Keynesians on this matter. Both employ what is essentially an *IS*/*LM* framework for developing their propositions, although monetarists such as Brunner and Meltzer (1973) do, while using the framework, argue that it is too simple to be able to incorporate monetarist ideas. They differ in that, in the context of the crowding-out debate, the monetarists make specific additional assumptions that affect the conclusions reached within the *IS*/*LM* framework (Section 21.2). This, however, is not a sufficient basis for arguing that there are major theoretical differences. Indeed, in a fundamental sense the theoretical models of the two schools are the same, for they both concentrate on government policy that affects aggregate *demand* to such an extent that both neglect problems of production and aggregate supply. The real difference between the schools insofar as they are concerned with the choice between monetary and fiscal policy is a difference that stems from empirical findings. These were considered in Chapter 20, where it was seen that the empirical findings are far from conclusive for either side.

The second area of debate concerns the effectiveness of stabilization policy even if it takes the form of control of the money supply. In Sections

21.3 and 21.4 we saw that monetarists conclude that stabilization policy cannot affect unemployment or real output in the long run or even in the short run. The conclusion reached there, and in the monetarist discussions of inflation and hyperinflation surveyed in Chapter 19, is that control of the rate of change of the money supply enables the authorities to control only the rate of inflation. This conclusion is essentially the same as that of the crude, or "long-run," version of the pre-Keynesian Quantity Theory (see Chapters 4 and 6) and appears to contradict the claim of Friedman (1956b) that the modern Quantity Theory is different from its predecessor in being essentially a theory of the demand for money (Chapters 7 and 20) rather than a theory of the price level. It is a conclusion that is contested by Keynesians. The Keynesian argument is, essentially, that wages and prices are not perfectly flexible. We saw in Section 21.3 that *long-run* equilibrium can be attained with unemployment less than the natural rate and that the long-run Phillips Curve is downward-sloping if current inflation adjusts less than fully to the expected rate ($\alpha < 1$). And we saw in Section 21.5 that short-run equilibrium more or less than the natural unemployment rate can be attained if wage rates (or prices) adjust at less frequent intervals than those at which monetary policy is adjusted. The Keynesian view that stabilization policy *can* affect real variables is based, therefore, on an assumption that wages and prices are not perfectly flexible. Indeed, this assumption of relative inflexibility is the essence of Keynesian economics. As we saw in Chapter 8, the textbook model of Keynesian theory argues that unemployment greater than zero (or, in the present context, greater than the natural rate) results from rigidity in the wage rate or interest rate, two specific examples of rigid relative prices. And in Chapter 13 we saw that while modern interpretations of the Keynesian model do not assume absolute rigidity, they do assume that relative prices, such as wage rates or interest rates, are relatively sluggish. This assumption is crucial to them.

At one level, therefore, the Keynesian/monetarist debate is a dispute over whether or not relative prices in real economies are perfectly flexible, although that, in itself, scarcely warrants the ardor with which the debate is pursued.

BIBLIOGRAPHY

Alchian, A. A.: "Information Costs, Pricing, and Resource Unemployment," *Western Economic Journal*, Vol. 7, pp. 109–128, June 1969.

Almon, S.: "The Distributed Lag between Capital Appropriations and Expenditures," *Econometrica*, Vol. 33, pp. 178–196, January 1965.

Andersen, L. C., and J. L. Jordan: "Monetary and Fiscal Actions: A Test of Their Relative Importance in Economic Stabilization," *Review—Federal Reserve Bank of St. Louis*, Vol. 50, November 1968.

Ando, A., and F. Modigliani: "The Relative Stability of Monetary Velocity and the Investment Multiplier," *American Economic Review*, Vol. 55, pp. 693–728, September 1965; "Rejoinder," Vol. 55, pp. 786–790, September 1965.

Ando, A., and F. Modigliani: "Impacts of Fiscal Actions on Aggregate Income and the Monetarist Controversy: Theory and Evidence," in J. L. Stein (ed.), *Monetarism* (New York: American Elsevier, 1976).

Archibald, G. C., and R. G. Lipsey: "Monetary and Value Theory: A Critique of Lange and Patinkin," *Review of Economic Studies*, Vol. 26, pp. 1–22, October 1958.

Arrow, K.: "Toward a Theory of Price Adjustment," in M. Abramovitz et al., *The Allocation of Economic Resources: Essays in Honour of Bernard Francis Haley* (Stanford, Calif.: Stanford, 1959).

Bailey, M. J.: *National Income and the Price Level: A Study in Macroeconomic Theory*, 2d ed. (New York: McGraw-Hill, 1971).

Barro, R. J., and H. I. Grossman: "A General Disequilibrium Model of Income and Employment," *American Economic Review*, Vol. 61, pp. 82–93, March 1971.

Baumol, W. J.: "The Transactions Demand for Cash: An Inventory Theoretic Approach," *Quarterly Journal of Economics*, Vol. 66, pp. 545–556, November 1952.

Baumol, W. J.: *Economic Dynamics*, 3d ed. (London: Collier and Macmillan, 1970).

Becker, G. S., and W. J. Baumol: "The Classical Monetary Theory: The Outcome of the Discussion," *Economica*, Vol. 19, pp. 355–375, November 1952.

Bell, G. L., and L. S. Berman: "Changes in the Money Supply in the United Kingdom, 1954–1964," *Economica*, Vol. 33 (new series), pp. 148–165, May 1966.

Benassy, J.-P.: "The Disequilibrium Approach to Monopolistic Price Setting and General Monopolistic Equilibrium," *CEPREMAP Discussion Paper* (Paris) March 1974.

Benassy, J.-P.: "Disequilibrium Exchange in Barter and Monetary Economies," *Economic Inquiry*, Vol. 13, pp. 131–156, June 1975a.

Benassy, J.-P.: "Neo-Keynesian Disequilibrium Theory in a Monetary Economy," *Review of Economic Studies*, Vol. 42, pp. 503–524, October 1975b.

Blinder, A. S., and R. M. Solow: "Does Fiscal Policy Matter?" *Journal of Public Economics*, Vol. 2, 319–337, November 1973.

Bronfenbrenner, M., and T. Mayer: "Liquidity Functions in the American Economy," *Econometrica*, Vol. 28, pp. 810–834, October 1960.

Bronfenbrenner, M., and T. Mayer: "Rejoinder to Professor Eisner," *Econometrica*, Vol. 31, pp. 539–544, July 1963.

Brunner, K.: "Stock and Flow Analysis: Discussion," *Econometrica*, Vol. 18, pp. 247–251, July 1950.

Brunner, K.: "A Schema for the Supply Theory of Money," *International Economic Review*, Vol. 2, pp. 79–109, January 1961a.

Brunner, K.: "Some Major Problems in Monetary Theory," *American Economic Association Papers and Proceedings*, Vol. 51, pp. 47–56, May 1961b.

Brunner, K., and A. H. Meltzer: "Predicting Velocity: Implications for Theory and Policy," *Journal of Finance*, Vol. 18, pp. 319–354, May 1963.

Brunner, K., and A. H. Meltzer: "Some Further Investigations of Demand and Supply Functions for Money," *Journal of Finance*, Vol. 19, pp. 240–283, May 1964.

Brunner, K., and A. H. Meltzer: "The Uses of Money: Money in the Theory of an Exchange Economy," *American Economic Review*, Vol. 61, pp. 784–805, December 1971.

Brunner, K., and A. H. Meltzer: "Money, Debt, and Economic Activity," *Journal of Political Economy*, Vol. 80, pp. 951–977, September/October 1972.

Brunner, K., and A. H. Meltzer: "Mr. Hicks and the 'Monetarists'," *Economica*, Vol. 40, pp. 44–59, February 1973.

Cagan, P.: "The Monetary Dynamics of Hyperinflation," in M. Friedman (ed.) *Studies in the Quantity Theory of Money* (Chicago: Chicago University Press, 1956).

Cagan, P.: *Determinants and Effects of Changes in the Stock of Money, 1875–1960*, National Bureau of Economic Research, Studies in Business Cycles, No. 13 (New York: National Bureau of Economic Research, 1965).

Carlson, K. M., and R. W. Spencer: "Crowding Out and Its Critics," *Review—Federal Reserve Bank of St. Louis*, Vol. 57, pp. 1–17, December 1975.

Carr, J., J. E. Pesando, and L. B. Smith.: "Tax Effects, Price Expectations and the Nominal Rate of Interest," *Economic Inquiry*, Vol. 14, pp. 259–269, June 1976.

Chiang, A. C.: *Fundamental Methods of Mathematical Economics*, 2d ed. (New York: McGraw-Hill, 1974).

Christ, C. F.: "Interest Rates and 'Portfolio Selection' among Liquid Assets in the U.S.," in *Measurement in Economics: Studies in Mathematical Economics and Econometrics in Memory of Yehuda Grunfeld* (Stanford, Calif.: Stanford, 1963), pp. 201–218.

Christ, C. F.: "A Short-Run Aggregate Demand Model of the Interdependence and Effects of Monetary and Fiscal Policies with Keynesian and Classical Interest Elasticities," *American Economic Review*, Vol. 57, pp. 434–443, May 1967.

Christ, C. F.: "A Simple Macroeconomic Model with a Government Budget Restraint," *Journal of Political Economy*, Vol. 76, pp. 53–67, January–February 1968.

Christ, C. F.: "Economic Forecasting and Forecasting Models," *International Economic Review*, Vol. 16, pp. 54–74, February 1975.

Clower, R.: "The Keynesian Counterrevolution: A Theoretical Appraisal," in F. H. Hahn and F. P. R. Brechling (eds.), *The Theory of Interest Rates*, Proceedings of the International Economic Association Conference, 1962 (New York: St. Martin's, 1965), pp. 103–125.

Clower, R. W.: "Introduction," in R. W. Clower (ed.): *Monetary Theory* (Harmondsworth, England: Penguin, 1969a).

Clower, R. W. (ed.): *Monetary Theory* (Harmondsworth, England: Penguin, 1969b).

Clower, R. W.: "A Reconsideration of the Microfoundations of Monetary Theory," *Western Economic Journal*, Vol. 6, pp. 1–9, December 1967. Reprinted in R. W. Clower (ed.): *Monetary Theory* (Harmondsworth, England: Penguin, 1969c).

Clower, R. W., and M. L. Burstein: "On the Invariance of Demand for Cash and Other Assets," *Review of Economic Studies*, Vol. 28, October 1960.

Clower, R. W., and D. W. Bushaw: "Price Determination in a Stock-Flow Economy," *Econometrica*, Vol. 22, pp. 328–343, July 1954.

Conard, J. W.: *An Introduction to the Theory of Interest* (Berkeley: University of California Press, 1959).

Crick, W. F.: "The Genesis of Bank Deposits," *Economica*, Vol. 7, pp. 191–202, June 1927.

Culbertson, J. M.: "The Term Structure of Interest Rates," *Quarterly Journal of Economics*, Vol. 71, pp. 485–517, November 1957.

Culbertson, J. M.: "Intermediaries and Monetary Theory: A Criticism of the Gurley–Shaw Theory," *American Economic Review*, Vol. 48, pp. 119–132, March 1958.

Culbertson, J. M.: "The Interest Rate Structure: Towards Completion of the Classical System," in F. H. Hahn and F. P. R. Brechling (eds.), *The Theory of Interest Rates* (London: Macmillan, 1965), pp. 173–205.

Currie, L. B.: *The Supply and Control of Money in the United States*, 2d ed., rev. (Cambridge, Mass.: Harvard University Press, 1935).

Darby, M. R.: "Postwar U.S. Consumption, Consumer Expenditures and Saving," *American Economic Review*, Vol. 65, pp. 217–222, May 1975.

Darby, M. R.: "Three and a Half Million U.S. Employees Have Been Mislaid: Or, An Explanation of Unemployment 1934–1941," *Journal of Political Economy*, Vol. 84, pp. 1–16, February 1976.

David, P. A., and J. L. Scadding: "Private Savings: Ultrarationality, Aggration and 'Denison's Law'," Part 1, *Journal of Political Economy*, Vol. 82, pp. 225–249, March–April 1974.

Davidson, P.: *Money and the Real World* (London: Macmillan, 1972).

Davis, R. G.: "How Much Does Money Matter? A Look at Some Recent Evidence." *Monthly Review of the Fed. Reserve Bank of New York*, Vol. 51, pp. 119–131, June 1969.

Debreu, G.: *Theory of Value: An Axiomatic Analysis of Economic Equilibrium*, Cowles Foundation for Research in Economics, Monograph No. 17 (New York: Wiley, 1959).

De Leeuw, F.: "The Demand for Money: Speed of Adjustment, Interest Rates and Wealth," *Staff Economic Studies*, Board of Governors of the Federal Reserve System, October 1965.

De Leeuw, F., and J. Kalchbrenner: "Monetary and Fiscal Actions: A Test of Their Relative Importance in Economic Stabilization—Comment," *Review—Federal Reserve Bank of St. Louis*, Vol. 51, pp. 6–11, April 1969.

De Prano, M., and T. Mayer: "Tests of the Relative Importance of Autonomous Expenditures and Money," *American Economic Review*, Vol. 55, pp. 791–792, September 1965.

Domar, E. D.: "Capital Expansion, Rate of Growth, and Employment," *Econometrica*, Vol. 14, pp. 137–147, April 1946.

Duesenberry, J. S.: *Income, Saving and the Theory of Consumer Behaviour* (Cambridge, Mass.: Harvard University Press, 1949).

Eisner, R.: "Another Look at Liquidity Preference," *Econometrica*, Vol. 31, pp. 531–538, July 1963.

Eisner, R.: "Non-Linear Estimates of the Liquidity Trap," *Econometrica*, Vol. 39, pp. 861–864, September 1971.

Eshag, E.: *From Marshall to Keynes: An Essay on the Monetary Theory of the Cambridge School* (Oxford, England: Blackwell, 1963).

Fair, R. C., and D. M. Jaffee: "Methods of Estimation for Markets in Disequilibrium," *Econometrica*, Vol. 40, pp. 497–514, May 1972.

Feige, E. L.: "Expectations and Adjustments in the Monetary Sector," *American Economic Association Papers and Proceedings*, Vol. 57, pp. 462–473, May 1967.

Feldstein, M., and O. Eckstein: "The Fundamental Determinants of the Interest Rate," *Review of Economics and Statistics*, Vol. 52, pp. 363–375, November 1970.

Fischer, S.: "Recent Developments in Monetary Theory," *American Economic Review*, Vol. 65, pp. 157–166, May 1975.

Fischer, S.: "Long Term Contracts, Rational Expectations, and the Optimal Money Supply Rule," *Journal of Political Economy*, Vol. 85, pp. 191–205, February 1977.

Fisher, Irving: *Appreciation and Interest* (New York: Macmillan, 1896).

Fisher, Irving: *The Rate of Interest: Its Nature, Determination and Relations to Economic Phenomena* (New York: Macmillan, 1907).

Fisher, Irving: *Elementary Principles of Economics* (New York: Macmillan, 1911a).

Fisher, Irving (assisted by Harry G. Brown): *The Purchasing Power of Money: Its Determination and Relation to Credit, Interest and Crises* (New York: Macmillan, 1911b).

Fisher, Irving: "A Statistical Relationship Between Unemployment and Price Changes," *International Labor Review*, pp. 496–502, 1926.

Fisher, Irving: *The Money Illusion* (New York: Adelphi, 1928).

Fisher, Irving: *The Theory of Interest* (New York: Macmillan, 1930).

Flemming, J. S.: "The Consumption Function When Capital Markets Are Imperfect: The Permanent Income Hypothesis Reconsidered," *Oxford Economic Papers*, Vol. 25 (new series), pp. 160–172, July 1973.

Foley, D. K.: "On Two Specifications of Asset Equilibrium in Macroeconomic Models," *Journal of Political Economy*, Vol. 83, pp. 303–324, April 1975.

Friedman, M.: "A Monetary and Fiscal Framework for Economic Stability, *American Economic Review*, Vol. 38, pp. 245–264, June 1948.

Friedman, M.: *Essays in Positive Economics* (Chicago: The University of Chicago Press, 1953).

Friedman, M.: "The Quantity Theory of Money: A Restatement," in M. Friedman (Ed.), *Studies in the Quantity Theory of Money* (Chicago: The University of Chicago Press, 1956a), pp. 3–21.

Friedman, M. (Ed.): *Studies in the Quantity Theory of Money* (Chicago: The University Chicago Press, 1956b).

Friedman, M.: *A Theory of the Consumption Function*, National Bureau of Economic Research, No. 63 (Princeton, N.J.: Princeton University Press, 1957).

Friedman, M.: "The Demand for Money: Some Theoretical and Empirical Results," *Journal of Political Economy*, Vol. 67, pp. 327–351, August 1959.

Friedman, M.: "Interest Rates and the Demand for Money," *Journal of Law and Economics*, Vol. 9, pp. 71–85, October 1966.

Friedman, M.: "The Role of Monetary Policy," *American Economic Review*, Vol. 58, pp. 1–17, March 1968.

Friedman, M.: "Quantity Theory," *International Encyclopaedia of the Social Services*, Vol. 10, pp. 432–447, 1968b.

Friedman, M.: "A Theoretical Framework for Monetary Analysis," *Journal of Political Economy*, Vol. 78, April/May 1970.

Friedman, M.: "A Monetary Theory of Nominal Income," *Journal of Political Economy*, Vol. 79, pp. 323–337, March/April 1971.

Friedman, M.: "Comments on the Critics," *Journal of Political Economy*, Vol. 80, pp. 906–950, September/October, 1972.

Friedman, M., and D. Meiselman: "The Relative Stability of Monetary Velocity and the Investment Multiplier in the United States, 1897–1958," in *Stabilization Policies*, papers prepared for the Commission on Money and Credit (Englewood Cliffs, N.J.: Prentice-Hall, 1963), pp. 165–268.

Friedman, M., and A. J. Schwartz: *A Monetary History of the United States, 1867–1960*, National Bureau of Economic Research, Studies in Business Cycles, No. 12 (Princeton, N.J.: Princeton University Press, 1963a).

Friedman, M., and A. J. Schwartz: "Money and Business Cycles," *Review of Economics and Statistics*, Vol. 45, pp. 32–64, February 1963b, Supplement.

Friedman, M., and A. J. Schwartz: "The Definition of Money: Net Wealth and Neutrality as Criteria," *Journal of Money, Credit, and Banking*, Vol. 1, pp. 1–14, February 1969.

Friedman, M., and A. J. Schwartz: *Monetary Statistics of the United States: Estimates, Sources, and Methods*. National Bureau of Economic Research, Studies—Business Cycles, No. 20 (New York: National Bureau of Economic Research, 1970).

Frisch, R.: "Propagation Problems and Impulse Problems in Dynamic Economics," in *Economic Essays in Honour of Gustav Cassel* (London: Allen & Unwin, 1933), pp. 177–205.

Fromm, G., and L. R. Klein: "A Comparison of Eleven Econometric Models of the United States," *American Economic Association Papers and Proceedings*, Vol. 63, pp. 385–393, May 1973.

Fullarton, John: *On the Regulation of Currencies* (London: J. Murray, 1844).

Giffen, R.: *Essays—Finances* (London: G. Bell, 1880).

Giffen, R.: *Growth of Capitals* (London: G. Bell, 1889).

Giffen, R.: *Economic Enquiries and Studies* (London: G. Bell, 1904).

Gilbert, J. C.: "The Demand for Money: The Development of an Economic Concept," *Journal of Political Economy*, Vol. 61, pp. 144–159, April 1953.

Goldman, S. M.: "Hyperinflation and the Rate of Growth in the Money Supply," *Journal of Economic Theory*, Vol. 5, pp. 250–257, October 1972.

Goldsmith, R. W.: *The National Wealth of the United States in the Post-War Period*, National Bureau of Economic Research, Studies—Capital Formation and Financing, No. 10 (Princeton, N.J.: Princeton University Press, 1962).

Goldsmith, R. W.: *The Flow of Capital Funds—the Post-War Economy*, National Bureau of Economic Research, Studies in Capital Formation and Financing, No. 12 (New York: National Bureau of Economic Research, 1965).

Goodhart, C.: "Analysis of the Determination of the Stock of Money," in M. Parkin and A. R. Nobay (eds.), *Essays in Modern Economics* (London: Longmans, 1973).

Gordon, R. J.: "Inflation in Recession and Recovery," *Brookings Papers on Economic Activity* (1), pp. 105–166, 1971.

Gordon, R. J.: "Wage–Price Controls and the Shifting Phillips Curve," *Brookings Papers on Economic Activity* (2), pp. 385–421, 1972.

Gordon, R. J.: "Comments on Modigliani and Ando," in J. L. Stein (ed.) *Monetarism*, pp. 52–66 (New York: American Elsevier, 1976a).

Gordon, R. J.: "Recent Developments in the Theory of Inflation and Unemployment," *Journal of Monetary Economics*, Vol. 2, pp. 185–219, April 1976b.

Grandmont, J.-M.: *Temporary General Equilibrium Theory*, CEPREMAP Discussion Paper, Paris, 1976.

Grandmont, J.-M., and G. Laroque: *On Temporary Keynesian Equilibria*, CEPREMAP, Paris, 1974.

Grandmont, J.-M., and Y. Younes: "On the Role of Money and the Existence of a Monetary Equilibrium," *Review of Economic Studies*, Vol. 39, pp. 355–372, July 1972.

Green, H. A. J.: *Aggregation in Economic Analysis: An Introductory Survey* (Princeton, N.J.: Princeton University Press, 1964).

Gurley, J. G.: "The Radcliffe Report and Evidence," *American Economic Review*, Vol. 50, pp. 672–700, September 1960.

Gurley, J. G., and E. S. Shaw: *Money in a Theory of Finance* (Washington, D.C.: The Brookings Institute, 1960).

Haberler, G.: *Prosperity and Depression*, 5th ed. (London: Allen & Unwin, 1964). Originally published, Geneva: League of Nations, 1937.

Hahn, F. H.: "Money and General Equilibrium," unpublished paper.

Hahn, F. H.: "On the Foundations of Monetary Theory," in M. Parkin and A. R. Nobay (eds.), *Essays in Modern Economics* (London: Longmans, 1973).

Hancock, K. J.: "Unemployment and the Economist in the 1920's," *Economica*, Vol. 27 (new series), pp. 305–321, November 1960.

Hansen, A. H.: *A Guide to Keynes* (New York: McGraw-Hill, 1953).

Hansen, B.: "On the Effects of Fiscal and Monetary Policy: A Taxonomic Discussion," *American Economic Review*, Vol. 63, pp. 546–571, September 1973.

Harris, L.: "Professor Hicks and the Foundations of Monetary Economics," *Economica*, Vol. 36, pp. 196–208, May 1969.

Harrod, R. F.: "An Essay in Dynamic Theory," *Economic Journal*, Vol. 49, pp. 14–33, March 1939; Errata, p. 377, June 1939.

Hart, A. G.: *Debts and Recovery* (New York: Twentieth Century Fund, 1938).

Hart, A. G.: "Connecting Links between Monetary Policy and Fixed Investment," in G. Pontecorvo et al. (eds.), *Issues in Banking and Monetary Analysis* (New York: Holt, Rinehart and Winston, 1967), pp. 120–142.

Hawtrey, R. G.: *Trade and Credit* (London: Longmans, 1928).

Hawtrey, R. G.: *The Art of Central Banking* (London: Longmans, 1932).

Hayek, F. A.: *Monetary Theory and the Trade Cycle.* Trans. by N. Kaldor and H. M. Croome (London: Jonathan Cape, 1933).

Hayek, F. A.: *Prices and Production*, 2d ed., enlgd. (London: G. Routledge, 1935).

Hester, D. D.: "Keynes and the Quantity Theory: A Comment on the Friedman–Meiselman CMC Paper," *Review of Economics and Statistics*, Vol. 46, pp. 364–368, November 1964.

Hicks, J. R.: "A Suggestion for Simplifying the Theory of Money," *Economica*, Vol. 2 (new series), pp. 1–19, February 1935.

Hicks, J. R.: "Mr. Keynes and the 'Classics': A Suggested Interpretation," *Econometrica*, Vol. 5, pp. 147–159, April 1937.

Hicks, J. R.: *Value and Capital* 1939 (Oxford, England: Oxford University Press, second edition published 1946.).

Hicks, J. R.: *A Contribution to the Theory of the Trade Cycle* (Oxford, England: Oxford University Press, 1950).

Hicks, J. R.: "Liquidity," *Economic Journal*, Vol. 72, pp. 787–802, December 1962.

Hicks, J. R.: *Critical Essays in Monetary Theory* (Oxford, England: Oxford University Press, 1967).

Hirshleifer, J.: "Investment Decision under Uncertainty: Choice-Theoretic Approaches," *Quarterly Journal of Economics*, Vol. 79, pp. 509–536, November 1965.

Hirshleifer, J.: "Investment Decision under Uncertainty: Applications of the State-Preference Approach," *Quarterly Journal of Economics*, Vol. 80, pp. 252–277, May 1966.

Hume, David: *Essays, Moral, Political and Literary*, ed. by T. H. Green and T. H. Grose (London: Longmans, Green, 1875). See, especially, "Of Money" and "Of the Balance of Trade."

Jackman, R.: "Keynes and Leijonhufvud," *Oxford Economic Papers*, Vol. 26, pp. 259–272, July 1974.

Jacobs, R. L.: "A Difficulty with Monetarist Models of Hyperinflation," *Economic Inquiry*, Vol. 13, pp. 337–361, September 1975.

Johnson, H. G.: "The General Theory after Twenty-five Years," *American Economic Association Papers and Proceedings*, Vol. 51, pp. 1–17, May 1961.

Johnson, H. G.: "Monetary Theory and Policy," *American Economic Review*, Vol. 52, pp. 335–384, June 1962.

Johnson, H. G.: "Money in a Neo-Classical One-Sector Growth Model," in H. G. Johnson (ed.), *Essays in Monetary Economics* (London: Allen & Unwin, 1967), pp. 143–178.

Johnson, H. G.: "Inside Money, Outside Money, Income, Wealth and Welfare in Monetary Theory," *Journal of Money, Credit and Banking*, pp. 30–46, February 1969a.

Johnson, H. G.: "Pesek and Saving's Theory of Money and Wealth: A Comment," *Journal of Money, Credit and Banking*, Vol. 1, pp. 535–537, August 1969b.

Johnston, J.: *Econometric Methods*, 2d ed. (New York: McGraw-Hill, 1972).

Joplin, T.: *Outlines of a System of Political Economy* (London: Baldwin, Cradock & Joy, 1823).

Joplin, T.: *An Analysis and History of the Currency Question* (London: J. Ridgway, 1832).

Jorgenson, D. W.: "Capital Theory and Investment Behaviour," *American Economic Association's Papers and Proceedings*, Vol. 53, pp. 247–259, May 1963.

Kaldor, N.: "A Model of the Trade Cycle," *Economic Journal*, Vol. 50. pp. 78–92, March 1940.

Keynes, J. M.: *A Treatise on Money* (London: Macmillan, 1930).

Keynes, J. M.: *The General Theory of Employment, Interest and Money* (London: Macmillan, 1936).

Keynes, J. M.: *How to Pay for the War* (London: Macmillan, 1940).

Kisselgoff, A.: "Liquidity Preference of Large Manufacturing Corporations (1921–1939)," *Econometrica*, Vol. 13. pp. 334–346, October 1945.

Klein, L. R.: *The Keynesian Revolution* (New York: Macmillan, 1947).

Klein, L. R.: "Stock and Flow Analysis in Economics," *Econometrica*, Vol. 18, pp. 236–241, July 1950.

Kuenne, R. E.: *The Theory of General Economic Equilibrium* (Princeton, N.J.: Princeton University Press, 1963).

Laidler, D.: "Some Evidence on the Demand for Money," *Journal of Political Economy*, Vol. 74, pp. 55–68, February 1966a.

Laidler, D.: "The Rate of Interest and the Demand for Money: Some Empirical Evidence," *Journal of Political Economy*, Vol. 74, pp. 543–555, December 1966b.

Laidler, D.: "The Definition of Money: Theoretical and Empirical Problems," *Journal of Money, Credit and Banking*, Vol. 1, pp. 508–525, August 1969.

Laidler, D. and J. M. Parkin: "Inflation: A Survey," *Economic Journal*, Vol. 85, pp. 741–809, December 1975.

Lange, O.: "Say's Law: A Restatement and Criticism," in O. Lange, F. McIntyre, and T. O. Yutema (eds.), *Mathematical Economics and Econometrics* (Chicago: The University of Chicago Press, 1942), pp. 49–68.

Latané, H. A.: "Cash Balances and the Interest Rate: A Pragmatic Approach," *Review of Economics and Statistics*, Vol. 36, pp. 456–460, November 1954.

Latané, H. A.: "Income Velocity and Interest Rates: A Pragmatic Approach," *Review of Economics and Statistics*, Vol. 42, pp. 445–449, November 1960.

Lavington, F.: *The English Capital Market* (London: Methuen, 1921).

Leijonhufvud, A.: *On Keynesian Economics and the Economics of Keynes: A Study in Monetary Theory* (New York: Oxford University Press, 1968).

Levhari, D., and D. Patinkin: "The Role of Money in a Simple Growth Model," *American Economic Review*, Vol. 58, pp. 713–753, September 1968.

Lipsey, R. G.: "The Relationship Between Unemployment and the Rate of Change of Money Wage Rates in the U.K. 1862–1957: A Further Analysis," *Economica*, Vol. 27, pp. 1–31, 1960.

Liviatan, N.: "On the Long-Run Theory of Consumption and Real Balances," *Oxford Economic Papers*, Vol. 17 (new series), pp. 205–218, July 1965.

Lloyd, C. L.: "The Equivalence of the Liquidity Preference and Loanable Funds Theories and the New Stock-Flow Analysis," *Review of Economic Studies*, Vol. 27, pp. 206–209, June 1960.

Lloyd, C. L.: "The Real Balance Effect: *Sine Qua* What?" *Oxford Economic Papers*, Vol. 14 (new series), pp. 267–274, October 1962.

Lucas, R. E.: "Expectations and the Neutrality of Money," *Journal of Economic Theory*, Vol. 4, pp. 103–124, April 1972.

Luckett, D. G.: "Multi-Period Expectations and the Term Structure of Interest Rates," *Quarterly Journal of Economics*, Vol. 81, pp. 321–329, May 1967.

Lutz, F. A.: "The Structure of Interest Rates," *Quarterly Journal of Economics*, Vol. 55, pp. 36–63, November 1940.

Malkiel, B. G.: *The Term Structure of Interest Rates: Expectations and Behaviour Patterns* (Princeton, N.J.: Princeton University Press, 1966).

Malkiel, B. G. and E. J. Kane: "The Term Structure of Interest Rates: An Analysis of a Survey of Interest-Rate Expectations," *Review of Economics and Statistics*, Vol. 49, pp. 343–355, August 1967.

Malthus, T. R.: *Definitions in Political Economy* (London: J. Murray, 1827).

Markowitz, H. M.: *Portfolio Selection: Efficient Diversification of Investments*, Cowles Foundation for Research in Economics, Monograph No. 16, (New York: Wiley, 1959).

Marshall, A.: *Principles of Economics* (New York: Macmillan, 1890).

Marshall, A.: *Money, Credit and Commerce* (London: Macmillan, 1923).

Marshall, A.: *Memorials of Alfred Marshall.* ed. by A. C. Pigou (London: Macmillan, 1925).

Marshall, A.: *Official Papers.* ed. by J. M. Keynes (London: Macmillan, 1926).

Marty, A. L.: "Notes on Money and Economic Growth," *Journal of Money, Credit and Banking*, Vol. 1, pp. 252–265, May 1969.

Masera, R. S.: "*The Term Structure of Interest Rates: An Expectations Model Tested on Post-War Italian Data* (Oxford, England: Oxford University Press, 1972).

Matthews, R. C. O.: "Expenditure Plans and the Uncertainty Motive for Holding Money," *Journal of Political Economy*, Vol. 71, pp. 201–218, June 1963.

McCulloch, J. R.: *The Principles of Political Economy* (Edinburgh: W. & C. Tait, 1825).

Meade, J. E.: "The Amount of Money and the Banking System," *Economic Journal*, Vol. 44, pp. 77–83, March 1934.

Meigs, A. J.: *Free Reserves and the Money Supply* (Chicago: The University of Chicago Press, 1962).

Meinich, P.: "Lloyd and the Real Balance Effect: A Comment," *Oxford Economic Papers*, Vol. 16 (new series), pp. 438–440, November 1964).

Meiselman, D.: *The Term Structure of Interest Rates* (Englewood Cliffs, N.J.: Prentice-Hall, 1962).

Meltzer, A. H.: "The Demand for Money: The Evidence from the Times Series," *Journal of Political Economy*: Vol. 71, pp. 219–246, June 1963.

Metzler, L. A.: "Wealth, Saving and the Rate of Interest," *Journal of Political Economy*, Vol. 59, pp. 93–116, April 1951.

Mill, J.: *Commerce Defended* (London: C. & R. Baldwin, 1808).

Mill, J.: *Elements of Political Economy* (London: Baldwin, Cradock and Joy, 1821).

Mill, J. S.: *Essays on Some Unsettled Questions of Political Economy* (London: J. W. Parker, 1844).

Mill, J. S.: *Principles of Political Economy* (London: J. W. Parker, 1848).

Miller, M. H., and D. Orr: "A Model of the Demand for Money by Firms," *Quarterly Journal of Economics*, Vol. 80, pp. 413–435, August 1966.

Minsky, H. P.: "Can 'It' Happen Again? (Collapse of the Financial System)," in D. Carson (ed.), *Banking and Monetary Studies* (Homewood, Ill.: Irwin, 1963), pp. 101–111.

Minsky, H. P.: "Financial Intermediation in the Money and Capital Markets," in G. Pontecorvo et al. (eds.), *Issues in Banking and Monetary Analysis* (New York: Holt, Rinehart and Winston, 1967), pp. 33–56.

Modigliani, F.: "Liquidity Preference and the Theory of Interest and Money," *Econometrica*, Vol. 12, pp. 45–88, January 1944.

Modigliani, F.: "The Monetary Mechanism and Its Interaction with Real Phenomena," *Review of Economics and Statistics*, Vol. 45, No. 1, pt. 2., pp. 79–107, February 1963.

Modigliani, F.: "The Monetarist Controversy or Should We Forsake Stabilization Policies?" *American Economic Review*, Vol. 67, pp. 1–19, March 1977.

Modigliani, F., and R. Brumberg: "Utility Analysis and the Consumption Function," in K. K. Kurihara (ed.), *Post Keynesian Economics* (New Brunswick, N.J.: Rutgers University Press, 1954).

Modigliani, F., and R. Sutch: "Debt Management and the Term Structure of Interest Rates: An Empirical Analysis of Recent Experience," *Journal of Political Economy*, Vol. 75, pp. 569–589, August 1967, Supplement.

Muth, J. F.: "Rational Expectations and the Theory of Price Movements," *Econometrica*, Vol. 29, pp. 315–335, July 1961.

Niehans, J.: "Money and Banking in General Equilibrium with Transactions Cost," *American Economic Review*, Vol. 61, pp. 773–783, December 1971.

Ohlin, B. G.: "Some Notes on the Stockholm Theory of Savings and Investment," Parts I and II, *Economic Journal*, Vol. 47, pp. 53–69, March 1937; Vol. 47, pp. 221–240, June 1937a.

Ohlin, B. G.: "Alternative Theories of the Rate of Interest," *Economic Journal*, Vol. 47, pp. 423–427, September 1937b.

Orr, D.: *Cash Management and the Demand for Money* (New York: Praeger, 1971).

Ostroy, J. M.: "The Informational Efficiency of Monetary Exchange," *American Economic Review*, Vol. 63, pp. 597–610, September 1973.

Patinkin, D.: "Price Flexibility and Full Employment," *American Economic Review*, Vol. 38, pp. 543–564, September 1948.

Patinkin, D.: "Price Flexibility and Full Employment: Reply," *American Economic Review*, Vol. 39, pp. 726–728, June 1949a.

Patinkin, D.: "Involuntary Unemployment and the Keynesian Supply Function," *Economic Journal*, Vol. 59, pp. 36–83, September 1949b.

Patinkin, D.: "Wicksell's 'Cumulative Process'," *Economic Journal*, Vol. 62. pp. 835–847, December 1952.

Patinkin, D.: "Keynesian Economics and the Quantity Theory," in K. K. Kurihara (ed.), *Post-Keynesian Economics* (New Brunswick, N.J.: Rutgers University Press, 1954).

Patinkin, D.: "Liquidity Preference and Loanable Funds: Stock and Flow Analysis," *Economica*, Vol. 25 (new series), pp. 300–318, November 1958.

Patinkin, D.: "Reply to R. W. Clower and H. Rose," *Economica*, Vol. 26 (new series), pp. 253–255, August 1959.

Patinkin, D.: "Financial Intermediaries and the Logical Structure of Monetary Theory," *American Economic Review*, Vol. 51, pp. 95–116, March 1961.

Patinkin, D.: *Money, Interest and Prices*, 2d ed. (New York: Harper & Row, 1965).

Patinkin, D.: "The Chicago Tradition, the Quantity Theory, and Friedman," *Journal of Money, Credit and Banking*, Vol. 1, pp. 46–70, February 1969.

Perry, G.: "Changing Labor Markets and Inflation," *Brookings Papers on Economic Activity* (3), pp. 411–441, 1970.

Pesek, B. P., and T. R. Saving: *Money, Wealth and Economic Theory* (New York: Macmillan, 1967).

Pifer, H. W.: "A Non-linear, Maximum Likelihood Estimate of the Liquidity Trap," *Econometrica*, Vol. 37, pp. 324–332, April 1969.

Phelps, E. S.: "Money Wage Dynamics and Labour Market Equilibrium," *Journal of Political Economy*, Vol. 76, pp. 678–711, 1968.

Phelps, E. S. et. al.: *The Microeconomic Foundations of Employment and Inflation Theory* (New York: Norton, 1970).

Phelps, E. S. and J. B. Taylor: "Stabilizing Powers of Monetary Policy Under Rational Expectations," *Journal of Political Economy*, Vol. 85, pp. 163–190, February 1977.

Phillips, A. W.: "The Relationship Between Unemployment and the Rate of Change of Money Wage Rates in the U.K. 1861–1957," *Economica*, Vol. 25, pp. 283–299, 1958.

Pigou, A. C.: "The Value of Money," *Quarterly Journal of Economics*, Vol. 32, pp. 38–65, November 1917.

Pigou, A. C.: *The Economics of Welfare* (London: Macmillan, 1920).

Pigou, A. C.: *Theory of Unemployment* (London: Macmillan, 1933).

Pigou, A. C.: *The Economics of Stationary States* (London: Macmillan, 1935).

Pigou, A. C.: *Employment and Equilibrium* (London: Macmillan, 1941).

Pigou, A. C.: "The Classical Stationary State," *Economic Journal*, Vol. 53, pp. 343–351, December 1943.

Pigou, A. C.: "Economic Progress in a Stable Environment," *Economica*, Vol. 14, 1947.

Pigou, A. C.: *The Veil of Money* (London: Macmillan, 1949).

Polak, J. J., and W. H. White: "The Effect of Income Expansion on the Quantity of Money," *International Monetary Fund Staff Papers*, Vol. 4., pp. 398–433, August 1955.

Poole, W., and E. B. F. Kornblith: "The Friedman-Meiselman C. M. C. Paper: New Evidence on an Old Controversy," *American Economic Review*, Vol. 63, pp. 908–917, December 1973.

Radcliffe Committee: *Committee on the Working of the Monetary System*: *Report* (London, Her Majesty's Stationery Office, Cmnd 827, 1959).

Radner, M.: "Competitive Equilibrium under Uncertainty," *Econometrica*, Vol. 36, pp. 31–58, January 1968.

Rasche, R. H.: "A Comparative Static Analysis of Some Monetarist Propositions," *Review—Federal Reserve Bank of St. Louis*, pp. 15–23, December 1973.

Ricardo, D.: *Principles of Political Economy and Taxation* (London: J. Murray, 1817).

Ricardo, D.: *Works and Correspondence*. ed. by P. Straffa and M. Dobb (Cambridge, England: Cambridge University Press, 1951–1973). 10 vols. and index.

Riefler, W. W.: *Money Rates and Money Markets in the United States* (New York: Harper, 1930).

Robertson, D. H.: *Money* (London: Nisbet, 1922).

Robertson, D. H.: *Banking Policy and the Price Level* (London: P. S. King, 1926).

Robertson, D. H.: "Alternative Theories of the Rate of Interest," *Economic Journal*, Vol. 47, pp. 428–436, September 1937.

Robertson, D. H.: *Essays in Monetary Theory* (London: P. S. King, 1940).

Robertson, D. H.: *Essays in Money and Interest*, selected by John Hicks (London: Collins, 1966). Reprint of essays originally published 1928–1955.

Robinson, J.: "The Rate of Interest," *Econometrica*, Vol. 19, pp. 92–111, April 1951.

Rose, H.: "Unemployment in a Theory of Growth," *International Economic Review*, Vol. 7, pp. 260–282, September 1966.

Samuelson, P. A.: "Interactions between the Multiplier Analysis and the Principle of Acceleration," *Review of Economics and Statistics*, Vol. 21, pp. 75–78, May 1939.

Samuelson, P. A.: "The Simple Mathematics of Income Determination," in L. A. Metzler et al., *Income, Employment and Public Policy: Essays in Honour of Alvin Hansen* (New York: Norton, 1948), pp. 133–155.

Samuelson, P. A. and R. M. Solow: "Analytical Aspects of Anti-Inflation Policy," *American Economic Review*, Vol. 50, pp. 177–194, May 1960.

Sargent, T. J.: "A Classical Macroeconomic Model for the United States," *Journal of Political Economy*, Vol. 84, pp. 207–237, April 1976.

Sargent, T. J., and N. Wallace: "Rational Expectations, the Optimal Monetary Instrument, and the Optimal Money Supply Rule," *Journal of Political Economy*, Vol. 83, pp. 241–257, April 1975.

Say, J.-B.: *A Treatise on Political Economy.* Translated by C. R. Prinsep from the 4th French ed. (London: Longmans, 1821). First ed., Paris: 1803.

Say, J.-B.: *Complete Course of Practical Political Economy* (Paris: 1828/29). This is the French edition. Reference to any English editions is unavailable.

Sayers, R. S.: "Monetary Thought and Monetary Policy in England," *Economic Journal*, Vol. 70, pp. 710–724, December 1960.

Schumpeter, J. A.: *Economic Doctrine and Method: An Historical Sketch.* Translated by R. Aris (London: Allen & Unwin, 1954).

Schumpeter, J. A.: *History of Economic Analysis.* ed. by E. B. Schumpeter (Oxford, England: Oxford University Press, 1959).

Sharpe, W. F.: "Capital Asset Prices: A Theory of Market Equilibrium under Conditions of Risk," *Journal of Finance*, Vol. 19, pp. 425–442, September 1964.

Sharpe, W. F.: *Portfolio Theory and Capital Markets* (New York: McGraw-Hill, 1970).

Sidrauski, M.: "Rational Choice and Patterns of Growth in a Monetary Economy," *American Economic Association Papers and Proceedings*, Vol. 57, pp. 534–544, May 1967a.

Sidrauski, M.: "Inflation and Economic Growth," *Journal of Political Economy*, Vol. 75, pp. 796–810, December 1967b.

Simons, H. C.: "Rules versus Authorities in Monetary Policy," *Journal of Political Economy*, Vol. 44, pp. 1–30, February 1936.

Simons, H. C.: *Economic Policy for a Free Society* (Chicago: The University of Chicago Press, 1948).

Smith, A.: *An Enquiry into the Nature and Causes of the Wealth of Nations* (London: 1776).

Smith, W. L.: "A Graphical Exposition of the Complete Keynesian System," *Southern Economic Journal*, Vol. 23, pp. 115–125, October 1956.

Smith, W. L.: "Time Deposits, Free Reserves, and Monetary Policy," in G. Pontecorvo et al. (eds.), *Issues in Banking and Monetary Analysis* (New York: Holt, Rinehart and Winston, 1967), pp. 79–113.

Sowell, T.: *Classical Economics Reconsidered* (Princeton, N.J.: Princeton University Press, 1974).

Stein, J. L.: "Money and Capacity Growth," *Journal of Political Economy*, Vol. 74, pp. 451–465, October 1966.

Stein, J. L.: " 'Neoclassical' and 'Keynes–Wicksell' Monetary Growth Models," *Journal of Money, Credit and Banking*, Vol. 1, pp. 153–171, May 1969.

Stein, J. L.: "Monetary Growth in Perspective," *American Economic Review*, Vol. 60, pp. 85–106, March 1970.

Teigen, R. L.: "Demand and Supply Functions for Money in the United States: Some Structural Estimates," *Econometrica*, Vol. 32, pp. 476–509, October 1964.

Thornton, H.: *An Enquiry into the Nature and Effects of the Paper Credit of Great Britain* (London: Hatchard, 1802). Reprinted by Farrar and Rinehart Inc., New York, 1939.

Tobin, J.: "Liquidity Preference and Monetary Policy," *Review of Economics and Statistics*, Vol. 29, pp. 124–131, May 1947.

Tobin, J.: "A Dynamic Aggregative Model," *Journal of Political Economy*, Vol. 63, pp. 103–115, April 1955.

Tobin, J.: "The Interest-Elasticity of Transactions Demand for Cash," *Review of Economics and Statistics*, Vol. 38, pp. 241–247, August 1956.

Tobin, J.: "Liquidity Preference as Behaviour Towards Risk," *Review of Economic Studies*, Vol. 25, pp. 65–86, February 1958.

Tobin, J.: "Money, Capital and Other Stores of Value," *American Economic Association Papers and Proceedings*, Vol. 51, pp. 26–37, May 1961.

Tobin, J.: "Commercial Banks as Creators of 'Money'," in D. Carson (ed.), *Banking and Monetary Studies, in Commemoration of the Centennial of the National Banking System* (Homewood, Ill.: Irwin, 1963), pp. 408–419.

Tobin, J.: "The Monetary Interpretation of History," *American Economic Review*, Vol. 55, pp. 464–485, June 1965a.

Tobin, J.: "Money and Economic Growth," *Econometrica*, Vol. 33, pp. 671–684, October 1965b.

Tobin, J.: "The Theory of Portfolio Selection," in F. H. Hahn and F. P. R. Brechling (eds.), *The Theory of Interest Rates* (London: Macmillan, 1965c), pp. 3–51.

Tobin, J.: "A General Equilibrium Approach to Monetary Theory," *Journal of Money, Credit and Banking*, Vol. 1, pp. 15–29, February 1969.

Tobin, J., and W. C. Brainard: "Financial Intermediaries and the Effectiveness of Monetary Controls," *American Economic Association Papers and Proceedings*, Vol. 53, pp. 383–400, May 1963.

Tobin, J., and W. C. Brainard: "Pitfalls in Financial Model Building," *American Economic Association Papers and Proceedings*, Vol. 58, pp. 99–122, May 1968.

Tobin, J., and W. Buiter: *Long Run Effects of Fiscal and Monetary Policy on Aggregate Demand*, Cowles Foundation Discussion Paper No. 384, Dec. 13, 1974.

Tobin, J., and C. Swan: "Money and Permanent Income," *American Economic Review*, Vol. 59, pp. 285–295, May 1969.

Tooke, T.: *Considerations on the State of the Currency* (London: J. Murray, 1826).

Tucker, D. P.: "Macroeconomic Models and the Demand for Money under Market Disequilibrium," *Journal of Money, Credit and Banking*, Vol. 3, pp. 57–83, February 1971.

Turner, R. C.: *Member Bank Borrowing* (Columbus: Ohio State University, 1938).

Turvey, R.: *Interest Rates and Asset Prices* (London: Allen & Unwin, 1960).

Valavanis-Vail, S.: "A Denial of Patinkin's Contradiction," *Kyklos*, Vol. 8, pp. 351–366, 1955.

Viner, J.: *Studies in the Theory of International Trade* (New York: Harper, 1937).

Von Neumann, J., and O. Morgenstern: *Theory of Games and Economic Behaviour*, 2d ed. (Princeton, N.J.: Princeton University Press, 1947).

Walras, L.: *Elements of Pure Economics*. Trans. and ed., W. Jaffé (Homewood, Ill.: Irwin, 1954). First ed., Lausanne, Switzerland: 1874–1877; definitive ed., Paris: Pichon, 1926.

White, W. R.: "Expectations, Investment and the U.K. Gilt-Edged Market—Some Evidence from Market Participants," *Manchester School of Economics and Social Studies*, Vol. 39, pp. 293–314, December 1971.

White, W. R., and J. P. Burman: "The Term Structure of Interest Rates—A Cross Section Test of a Mean-Variance Model," in H. G. Johnson and A. R. Nobay (Eds.), *Issues in Monetary Economics* (Oxford, England: Oxford University Press, 1974).

Wicksell, J. G. K.: *Interest and Prices*. Translated by R. F. Kahn (London: Macmillan, 1936). First ed., Jena, Germany: 1898.

Wicksell, J. G. K.: *Lectures on Political Economy.* ed. by Lord Robbins, trans., by E. Classen (London: Routledge, 1934/1935). First imprint: Lund, 1901.

Witte, J. G., Jr.: "The Microfoundations of the Social Investment Function," *Journal of Political Economy*, Vol. 71, pp. 441–456, October 1963.

Yeager, L. B.: "The Keynesian Diversion," *Western Economic Journal* (now *Economic Enquiry*), Vol. 11, pp. 150–163, June 1973.

Yohe, W. P. and D. S. Karnovsky: "Interest Rates and Price Level Changes 1952–1969," *Review—Federal Reserve Bank of St. Louis*, Vol. 51, pp. 18–38, December 1969.

INDEX